Juanita M. Hurd
2431 George St

PONDERING THE PROVERBS

BIBLE STUDY TEXTBOOK

PONDERING THE PROVERBS

by
Donald Hunt

Paraphrase By Kenneth Taylor

College Press, Joplin, Missouri

Second Printing - 1977
Third Printing - 1983
Fourth Printing - 1988

Printed and Bound in the
United States of America

International Standard Book Number: 0-89900-018-5

TABLE OF CONTENTS

INTRODUCTION

"Who wants to read an 'Introduction' to a book, especially to a commentary?" Nearly nobody. They are considered necessary for the studious but "too dry" for the average reader. May I ask, "Who, then, wants to write an 'Introduction' if nearly nobody is going to read it?" Well, maybe we can make this 'Introduction' different so it will be interesting both to write and to read. And shouldn't an 'Introduction' to such an interesting book as Proverbs be interestingly written?

As a book Proverbs is vastly different from the other books of the Bible. Nearly two-thirds of the 915 verses is devoted to short, pithy sayings (many great "memory verses") rather than extended, connected material. When Fred Smith was editing "The Plea", a magazine with small-size pages filled with sayings, poems, and short articles (a boon to those putting out "church bulletins"), in his readers' response column was one from O. L. Mankamyer: "You are putting out a good paper, but it is like reading the dictionary: it is always changing subjects." And Proverbs might be likened to a dictionary in that it (1) it is a very important book; and (2) it is always changing subjects. However, the first 9 chapters are extended material on wisdom, and there are also other sections especially devoted to subjects toward the end of the book.

As the first verse of Proverbs indicates, its authorship is attributed to Solomon. At just what stage of his life he compiled it, we cannot be sure, but we suppose that since he was a famous proverb collector and learner (I Kings 4:32), it was probably toward the latter part of his life. Yet since in his old age his idolatrous wives turned away his heart from worshipping Jehovah (I Kings 11:4), it seems that we should not place its composition too close to that period of declension, or that which he had just written did him no good. We would, therefore, think it was probably written when he was younger—possibly in the height of his health and vigor.

Chapters 25-29 contain proverbs that King Hezekiah's men were inspired to add to Solomon's writings. Chapter 30 is said to be the words of one "Agur". Chapter 31 contains some words of one "King Lemuel" which his mother taught him. Besides these clear notations, some think "the words of the wise" in 22:17 indicate that from there to the end of Chapter 24 is another section. The word "also" in 24:23 might so indicate.

Since Solomon is speaking to his son throughout the first 9 chapters, the material is in the "first person" grammatically (as is the material in 30:1-9, 18:20 and 31:1-9). But the big section of the "sayings" (all the rest of the book) is mostly in the "third person".

Proverbs' value to us who live in the Christian Age is greatly enhanced by the fact that it is basically non-dispensational wisdom.

When given the writing assignment, we were asked to write on the level of a sophomore in Bible training. This pleased me because I did not want to take all of the time (between 3 and 4 years of composition) and spend all of this effort to write a dry, boring book that would be consulted by a mere handful of dry intellectuals when I could hopefully write something that would be read by and appreciated by many more.

We have broken the material up into more or less 10 to 12 verse sections—about the length that might be covered in a Sunday morning or mid-week class. Each section begins with the "*Text* (from the American Standard version), is followed by "*Study Questions*" (which are meant to be answered before going to the helps of this book), then the"*Paraphrase*" (from "Living Bible" which in reality is not strictly a translation and should not be looked upon nor used as another version but as a "paraphrase" or the author's own rewording of the text—his own interpretation put into present-day expressions, making it somewhat of a small, concise commentary within this book), and the "*Comments*" by your present writer (which contains the heart of what your author can contribute to your understanding of this book), and finally the "*Test Questions*" (which cover both the "*Text*" and the "*Comments*"). "*Noticeable Groupings*' within the chapter is found at the end of Chapters 10-29 (the chapters that lend themselves to such—you should find some good use for the "*Groupings*" material proportionate to the time you spend studying through them).

Your author has employed many cross-references within his comments as he has always had a great interest in tying the Scriptures together. He has also quoted from earlier commentaries where they seemed to say it better than he thought he could, and to give you the value of others who have studied and written.

When asked to include a "*Subject Index*", your author was pleased, for he had several years ago spent a full year of work cataloging the book of Proverbs, and thus it took only five recent weeks to make use of that previous work and to pass on to you something that has many study, teaching, and sermonic possibilities. Please give some time to the *"Index"* from these standpoints.

The noted and respected Thomas Campbell believed that Proverbs contained so much material that would help a person through life that he had his children memorize the entire book. His children had more time on their hands than ours as they lived before public-school days, but at the same time all parents would be wise to go through Proverbs and compile a list of those verses they would like their children to memorize. We have selected and included 52 such as a starter for those of every age to memorize.

Your writer's special interest in the book of Proverbs began when having completed his formal education for the ministry he began working his own way through the Bible. In time he came to the "Poetic" section of the Old Testament on which he spent an estimated five years of special study. At first I was attracted by some of the witty sayings and comparisons in Proverbs (like 26:17: "He that passeth by, and vexeth himself with strife belong not to him, is like one that taketh a dog by the ears"). Then I began using various Proverbs in my messages. A lady who attended one of our Sacramento Gatherings about that time (back in the 1950's) said, "I'm going to have to study into the book of Proverbs. I didn't know that that book was so good." In the 1960's I wrote a book entitled, "Simple, Stimulating Studies in the Proverbs," which contains full-length studies (with only Proverb Scriptures used) on the following important subjects: "The Place of Wisdom"; "The Human Tongue;" "Lazy People;" "The Cry of the Needy;" "The Problem of Pride;" "Anger Outlawed;" "Riches Discussed;" "Fools Considered;" "Lascivious Conduct;" "View of God;" "The Fear of the Lord;" "Correction;" "Parenthood;" "Two Kinds of Wives;" "Psychological Outlook;" "Things Abominable;" "Things Preferable;" and "Honor as a Goal".

Since writing that book invitations have come to teach "Proverbs" in various camps, then the year of special index-work (previously mentioned) and then came the invitation to write this book for you. In receiving this invitation, I felt somewhat like David when offered King Saul's daughter Michael in marriage, "Seemeth it to you a light thing to be the king's son-in-law?" (I Sam. 18:23). And I say, "Seemeth it you a light thing to be chosen from all the possible writers to write this commentary?" And while writing it, the additional thought has occurred that it is not known that any previous "Restoration" writer has ever compiled a "Commentary on Proverbs".

"When does a busy man find the time to write a commentary like this," one might ask. Usually in those early-morning hours when many others are still asleep. Most of the special research work, note-making, and actual writing have been done before breakfast. Rising at 5:00 a.m. (often at 4:00 a.m. down the "home-stretch"), he has studied and written before the rest of the family was up at 6:00 a.m. and before he became otherwise involved with the duties and thoughts of the day. He can well understand the same value placed upon this fresh part of the day by Alexander Campbell, Albert Barnes, and others who have written.

Though the "Introduction" is always in the front of a book, it is customarily the last thing written. That is as it should be, for one needs to have the material written before attempting to introduce it to his readers. In closing, a favorite Proverb again comes to mind that usually has at the completion of each school year of teaching, at the completion of meetings and large-scale rallies, and at the completion of various church building and home-remodeling projects with which I have been associated. At the end of this 3 to 4 year project, now in its last sentence, I agree, "The desire accomplished is sweet to the soul" (Prov. 13:19).

Ottumwa, Iowa, February 6, 1974

CHAPTER 1

TEXT — 1:1-9

1. The proverbs of Solomon the son of David, king of Israel:
2. To know wisdom and instruction;
   To discern the words of understanding;
3. To receive instruction in wise dealing,
   In righteousness and justice and equity;
4. To give prudence to the simple,
   To the young man knowledge and discretion;
5. That the wise man may hear, and increase in learning;
   And that the man of understanding may attain unto sound counsels;
6. To understand a proverb, and a figure,
   The words of the wise, and their dark sayings.
7. The fear of Jehovah is the beginning of knowledge;
   But the foolish despise wisdom and instruction.
8. My son, hear the instruction of thy father,
   And forsake not the law of thy mother:
9. For they shall be a chaplet of grace unto thy head,
   And chains about thy neck.

STUDY QUESTIONS OVER 1:1-9

1. Compile background informatin on Solomon besides the 2 things mentioned in v. 1.
2. What other books of the Bible did Solomon write?
3. The first purpose of Proverbs is to help one know .... (vs. 2-6).
4. What is the meaning of "discern" (v. 2)?
5. What is meant by "wise dealing" (v. 3)?
6. What is the meaning of "equity" (v. 3)?
7. What does "prudence" mean (v. 4)?
8. What would be the purpose of Proverbs to one who is already wise (v. 5)?
9. What is meant by "dark sayings" (v. 6)?
10. What is the first proverb (or wise saying) in the book v. 7?
11. What in v. 8 shows that mothers should join fathers in laying down the law to their children?
12. What was a "chaplet" (v. 9)?
13. What New Testament passages also describe virtues as ornaments (v. 9)?

PONDERING THE PROVERBS

PARAPHRASE OF 1:1-9

1. These are the proverbs of King Solomon of Israel, David's son:

2-6. He wrote them to teach his people how to live--how to act in every circumstance, for he wanted them to be understanding, just and fair in everything they did. "I want to make the simple-minded wise!" he said. "I want to warn young men about some problems they will face. I want those already wise to become the wiser and become leaders by exploring the depths of meaning in these nuggets of truth."

7-9. How does a man become wise? The first step is to trust and reverence the Lord! Only fools refuse to be taught. Listen to your father and mother. What you learn from them will stand you in good stead; it will gain you many honors.

COMMENTS ON 1:1-9

V. 1. A "proverb" is a wise saying. Solomon (the author of all the book except the final chapters) was famous for the proverbs that he spoke--and he spoke 3,000 of them (I Kings 4:32), which is more than we have in this book. "Solomon is the first of the sacred writers whose name stands at the head of his "works" ("Clarke"). Because the first 9 chapters of the book are extended material (chiefly on wisdom) rather than short sayings, though the title of the book is "Proverbs", 10:1 is where the actual "sayings" themselves begin (note that verse). Solomon was David's son by Bathsheba, who had been the wife of Uriah (Matt. 1:6). He became king of Israel during his father's final days of infirmity even though his brother Adonijah (Adonijah had a different mother than Solomon) had tried to beat him out of the kingship (I Kings 1:5-40).

V. 2. The purpose of this divine book is spelled out in a series of infinitives. "Wisdom" is the goal, and "instruction" is the method of gaining it. The end-result is that the listener himself will be able "to discern the words of understanding" by having this divine wisdom laid up in his mind and heart.

V. 3. The instruction to be given was to teach "wise dealing" (wisdom and prudence), "righteousness" (not show how to "beat somebody out of what was rightfully his"), and "justice and equity" (what is fair and honest). Oh, that all our education were bent on making men right, honest, and upright and not merely to make them richer by whatever means they may follow to become such!

V. 4. Sayings (whether Biblical sayings or otherwise) are made by older, wiser people who have been over many of the roads of life and who desire to pass on portions of their knowledge to the younger and to the lesser experienced. Actually, then, when one knows, quotes, and follows time-honored sayings, he is actually speaking and being guided by a knowledge superior to that which he would know on his own.

V. 5. This verse goes a step farther: it shows that the wise and experienced also profit by the wisdom and sayings of others. Nobody is a first-hand expert in all fields so that he cannot profit by the wisdom of others in those fields in which he has not the opportunity to turn his special attention. But even if he has, he may still profit by the wisdom couched in such sayings of others. In fact, it is the wise who are always seeking to advance their knowledge, and a wise man is a joy to teach: "Give instruction to a wise man, and he will be yet wiser: Teach a righteous man, and he will increase in learning" (Prov. 9:9).

V. 6. We live in a world where figures of speech, informed comparisons, big and technical words, etc. are often heard. If we are not posted in the understanding and handling of such, we can draw wrong conclusions, misuse words, and in general betray our ignorance. Thus, 26:7,9 both speak of a "parable in the mouth of fools". The Bible also employs the parabolic in its teachings ("I will open my mouth in a parable; I will utter dark sayings of old"--Psa. 78:2). Jesus spoke many things in parables and at times used language that confounded His hearers. Even the disciples were able to grasp the meaning of other forms of expression more readily: "Lo, now speakest thou plainly, and speakest no dark saying" (John 16:29). Prophecy (especially the book of Revelation) is written in such a way that one needs a good knowledge of history to understand its symbols and predictions. Peter acknowledges that Paul's writings contain "some things hard to be understood, which the ignorant and unstedfast wrest" (II Peter 3:16).

V. 7. We might say that this verse contains the first actual proverb or saying in the book, and it rightfully begins where the whole Bible itself begins--with God (Jehovah). "The fear of the Lord signifies that religious reverence which every intelligent being owes to his Creator...No man can ever become truly wise who does not begin with God" ("Clarke"). Other like passages of the fear of Jehovah as the beginning of wisdom: Prov. 9:10; Psa. 111:10; Job 28:28. The implied contrast within our verse is that the "foolish" do not "fear" Jehovah and, therefore, "despise wisdom and instruction." Note v. 1 for the connection between "wisdom" and "instruction". Those who do not fear come to despise. II Pet. 2:10 shows this: "...despise dominion. Daring, self-willed, they tremble not to rail at dignities." Special instructions, both in the Old and New Testaments, grow out of this fact: "Speak not in the hearing of a fool; For he will despise the wisdom of thy words" (Prov. 23:9): "Neither cast your pearls before swine, lest haply they trample them under their feet, and turn and rend you." (Matt. 7:6).

V. 8. Though Solomon had many wives and concubines (700 of the first and 300 of the second--I Kings 11:3), and we consequently assume numerous sons, it is a surprising fact that we know the name of only one of his sons (Rehoboam, who succeeded him on the throne in Jerusalem). It is likely that the material presented in Proverbs that says, "My son" (this verse: v. 15, 2:1; 3:1,3; 3:11; etc.), was orginially Solomon's material to his son Rehobaom. However, the expression, "My sons" (plural), occurs four times in the book (4:1; 5:7; 7:24; 8:32), in which we have Solomon's teaching to all of his sons. Solomon employed "my son" in two noticeable ways: to begin with a section to make the teaching more personal to the son (as in 1:15; 6:3; and others. When he uses the expression to begin a section of material, he usually tells what listening to his instruction will mean to his life (see vs. 8,9; 3:1,2; 4:10; and others) before actually proceeding to present the section of material. One final thought on our verse: Both parents have important parts in a child's rearing--the "instruction of thy father", the "law of thy mother". In far too many homes the instruction and rearing of the children becomes the responsibility of but one instead of both, or the mother does the instructing, but the father is the disciplinarian who lays down the "law."

V. 9. A chaplet is a wreath or garland that the victor wore on his head. When Joseph was promoted to a ruler in Egypt, they "put a gold chain about hs neck", he rode in Egypt's "second chariot", and they cried before him, "Bow the knee" (Gen. 41:43). Following the sound teachings of the father would bring the son to great dignity as well as give a beauty to his life. The elements of good character are likened to spiritual ornaments. Women particularly are warned in physical charm: "Whose adorning let it not be the outward adorning of braiding the hair, and of wearing of jewels of gold, or of putting on apparel; but let it be the hidden man of the heart, in the incorruptible apparel of a meek and quiet spirit, which is in the sight of God of great price" (I Pet. 3:3,4). See I Tim. 2:9,10 and Prov. 3:22.

TEST QUESTIONS OVER 1:1-9

1. What is a "proverb" (v. 1)?
2. How many proverbs did Solomon speak (v. 1)?
3. What is the relation between "wisdom" and "instruction" (v. 2)?
4. What might be said of the character of the wisdom that Solomon was teaching to his son (v. 3)?
5. What can wise sayings do for a "young man" (v. 4)?
6. Who besides young men can also profit by wise sayings (v. 5)?
7. What are some Bible examples of "dark sayings" (v. 6)?
8. Comment on fools despising wisdom and instruction (v. 7).
9. Discuss "my son" as included in v. 8.
10. What does v. 9 say that following a father's instruction will bring?

TEXT — 1:10-19

10. My son, if sinners entice thee,
Consent thou not.
11. If they say, Come with us,
Let us lay in wait for blood;
Let us lurk privily for the innocent without cause;
12. Let us swallow them up alive as Sheol,
And whole, as those that go down into the pit;
13. We shall find all precious substance;
We shall fill our houses with spoil;
14. Thou shalt cast thy lot among us;
We will all have one purse:
15. My son, walk not thou in the way with them;
Refrain thy foot from their path:

16. For their feet run to evil,
And they make haste to shed blood.
17. For in vain is the net spread
In the sight of any bird:
18. And these lay wait for their own blood;
They lurk privily for their own lives.
19. So are the ways of every one that is greedy of gain;
It taketh away the life of the owners thereof.

STUDY QUESTIONS OVER 1:10-19

1. Why will sinners entice innocent people (v. 10)?
2. What are the three big words in v. 10?
3. What does "lurk privily" mean (v. 11)?
4. What does "Sheol" mean (v. 12)?
5. Is the second statement in v. 12 different from its first, or is it a restatement of it?
6. To what extent will selfishness go (v. 13)?
7. What does "cast thy lot" in v. 14 mean?
8. V. 15 is but an enlargement of what three important words already given?
9. What two words in v. 16 show their eagerness to do wrong?
10. What is the connection of v. 17 with this section of material?
11. Why for their "own" blood and lives (v. 18)?
12. Does sin end up the way it was planned (v. 19)?

PARAPHRASE OF 1:10-19

10-14. If young toughs tell you, "Come and join us"--turn your back on them! "We'll hide and rob and kill," they say; "Good or bad, we'll treat them all alike! And the loot we'll get! All kinds of stuff! Come on, throw in your lot with us; we'll split with you in equal shares."

15-19. Don't do it, son! Stay far from men like that, for crime is their way of life, and murder is their specialty. When a bird sees a trap being set, it stays away, but not these men; they trap themselves! They lay a booby trap for their own lives. Such is the fate of all who live by violence and murder. They will die a violent death.

COMMENTS ON 1:10-19

V. 10. This verse breaks down into two parts: sinners' attempt to mislead a young man and what he should do about it. Be assured that the world (sinners) will put pressure on every person to join them. Oh, the rosy picture that they can paint in the fantisies of a young person's mind! And to be different from the world would be to be "out of steps", "odd", and all that a young person does not really want to be. And so the invitation becomes inticement, and their urging becomes irresistible temptation. The only way a young person (or anybody else) can resist and overcome these pressures from the outside is by that which he has on the inside (parental instruction that has become personal conviction, faith in God, reverential fear, etc.). Oh, how Solomon pleads with his son, "Consent thou not." What important three words they are! This is what Joseph did when urged by Potiphar's wife: "he refused" and said, "How then can I do this great wickedness, and sin against God?" (Gen., 39:8,9). Oh, for more young men with the conviction, native honesty, and courage of Joseph! Daniel did the same (Dan. 1:8); so did Shadrach, Meshach, and Abednego (Dan. 4:17,18). We, too, are commanded to abstain from the world's evil: Eph. 5:7,11; I Thess. 5:22; II Tim. 2:19; Jas. 1:27.

V. 11. Often throughout the book Solomon warns against both evil men and evil women (both are mentioned in 2:12-17). The evil men are wicked oppressors out to get ill-gotten gain, and the evil women are immoral adulteresses. This chapter 1 warning is concering going in with evil men to become an oppressor. This verse and the ones following put the enticement of v. 10 into words. Notice that the people to be hurt by them wouldn't deserve it ("the innocent"), nor would they expect or suspect it ("Let us lay in wait...let us lurk privily").

V. 12. "Sheol" is Hebrew, and "Hades" is Greek for the place of departed spirits. This verse employs Hebrew parallelism in which the two statements mean the same thing; that is, "Sheol" and "pit" are the same; "alive" and "whole" are the same; and "swallow" and "go down" are the same. Death is spoken of as "going down into the pit" in Psa. 28:1: "Unto thee, O Jehovah, will I call: My rock, be not thou deaf unto me; Lest if thou be silent unto me, I become like them that go down into the pit." Sheol is pictured in Prov. 30:15,16 as one of four things personified as never satisfied, that never says, "It is enough."

So, it was no small damage that these evil men planned to inflict and in which they were inviting the young man to participate.

V. 13. This is the part that was luring them on--the hope of gain. The love of money is the root of all kinds of evil (see I Tim. 6:10). As they passed from one robbery and murder to another, all they were thinking about was themselves. The "innocent" (v. 11) had worked to obtain the precious substance; the innocent had not found it amassed in one place as his robbers wanted to. They had patiently seen it grow and accumulate though hard work and saving ways; the robbers were wanting to "fill" their houses with it immediately.

V. 14. "Cast thy lot among us" meant that he would decide to go with them, he would trust his future and his outcome to their way of doing. "We will all have one purse" meant that he would share equally with them. But people who do will lie and cheat and rob and kill others might be untrue to their promise to him too. This was their final appeal to him to join them. What would his decision be?

V. 15. Oh, the concern of the father at this point! He realizes it is a decision-time for his son. Will he fall for their line, or will he go the way he has been taught from youth? He pleads, "My son, walk not thou in the way with them," and restated for emphasis and additional appeal: "Refrain thy foot from their path." This verse is really an enlargement upon "Consent thou not" in v. 10. Other verses on this subject: "Blessed is the man that walketh not in the counsel of the wicked" (Psa. 1:1); "Enter not into the path of the wicked, And walk not in the way of evil men" (Prov. 4:14); "I have refrained my feet from every evil way" (Psa. 119:101).

V. 16. A good reason for Solomon's not wanting his son to take up with such "toughs". They "run" to evil; they "make haste" to shed blood. Ever notice that man is quick to get into inquity, but he wants to take his time to get out of it? The reverse should be true. Two other passages say much the same thing: "Their feet run to evil, they make haste to shed innocent blood" (Isa. 59:7); "Their feet are swift to shed blood" (Rom. 3:15).

V. 17. The wicked are represented as lurking privily for the innocent. It is in this way alone that they can hope to destroy them and take their substance; for if their designs were known, proper precautions would be taken against them" ("Clarke"). In other words, "Son, can't you see what they are doing? Don't get caught!"

V. 18. Their intention would be to hurt others, and they do for awhile, but in time justice catches up with them, and they pay with their lives! The father would have his son view his final outcome from the beginning, and the enticement to join up with the oppressors would not be so strong.

V. 19. Other passages also teach the sorrows and losses to be reaped by those greedy of gain: "He that is greedy of gain troubleth his own house" (Prov. 15:27); "...which some reaching after have been led astray from the faith, and have pierced themselves through with many sorrows" (I Tim. 6:10). Instead of "getting", there is "losing". We note too that the "important" (his own life) is lost trying to gain the "unimportant" (material gain).

TEST QUESTIONS OVER 1:10-19

1. What are the two parts of v. 10?
2. What sin usually characterized "evil men" of Proverbs (v. 11)?
3. Cite the three parallels in v. 12.
4. What does I Tim. 6:10 say about the love of money (v. 13)?
5. Comment on the two parts of v. 14.
6. Why is the father so earnest in v. 15?
7. What should men reverse (v. 16)?
8. What should the son be able to see that evil men are actually doing when they paint such a rosy picture (v. 17)?
9. What would keep the enticement from being so strong (v. 18)?
10. What do oppressors "get", and what do they "lose" (v. 19)?

TEXT — 1:20-33

20. Wisdom crieth aloud in the street;
She uttereth her voice in the broad places;
21. She crieth in the chief place of concourse;
At the entrance of the gates,
In the city, she uttereth her words:
22. How long, ye simple ones, will ye love simplicity?
And scoffers delight them in scoffing,

And fools hate knowledge?
23. Turn you at my reproof:
Behold, I will pour out my spirit upon you;
I will make known my words unto you,
24. Because I have called, and ye have refused;
I have stretched out my hand, and no man hath regarded.
25. Be ye have set at nought all my counsel,
And would none of my reproof:
26. I also will laugh in the day of your calamity;
I will mock when your fear cometh;
27. When your fear cometh as a storm,
And your calamity cometh on as a whirlwind;
When distress and anguish come upon you.
28. Then will they call upon men, but I will not answer;
They will seek me diligently, but they shall not find me.
29. For that they hated knowledge,
And did not choose the fear of Jehovah.
30. They would none of my counsel,
They despised all my reproof.
31. Therefore shall they eat of the fruit of their own way,
And be filled with their own devices.
32. For the backsliding of the simple shall slay them,
And the careless ease of fools shall destroy them.
33. But whoso hearkeneth unto me shall dwell securely,
And shall be quiet without fear of evil.

STUDY QUESTIONS OVER 1:20-33

1. How does wisdom "cry" (v. 20)?
2. What does "concourse" mean (v. 21)?
3. Are the "simple ones", "scoffers," and "fools" different groups or the same group under different words (v. 22)?
4. Is v. 23 speaking of inspiration?
5. What is the antecedent of "I", "my", and "me" from v. 24 to the end of the chapter?
6. What does "set at nought" mean (v. 25)?
7. Will such a day as pictured in v. 26 come to the foolish?
8. How serious will things become for the foolish (v. 27)?
9. What sad news does v. 28 bear?
10. They should have .... knowledge instead of hated it (v. 29)?

11. The fear of Jehovah is something to be .... (v. 29)?
12. V. 30 is a restatement of what previous verse?
13. What is the meaning of "eat" in v. 31?
14. Find three parallel expressions in the two statements of v. 32.
15. What contrast belongs to those who will listen (v. 33)?

PARAPHRASE OF 1:20-33

20-28. Wisdom shouts in the streets for a hearing. She calls out to the crowds along Main Street, and to the judges in their courts, and to everyone in all the land. "You simpletons!" she cries, "how long will you go on being fools? How long will you scoff at wisdom and fight the facts? Come here and listen to me! I'll pour out the spirit of Wisdom upon you, and make you wise. I have called you so often but still you won't come. I have pleaded, but all in vain. For you have spurned my counsel and reproof. Some day you'll be in trouble, and I'll laugh! Mock me, will you?--I'll mock you! When a storm of terror surrounds you, and when you are engulfed by anguish and distress, then I will not answer your cry for help. It will be too late though you search for me ever so anxiously.

29-33. "For you closed your eyes to the facts and did not choose to reverence and trust the Lord, and you turned your back on me, spurning my advice. That is why you must eat the bitter fruit of having your own way, and experience the full terrors of the pathway you have chosen. For you turned away from me--to death; your complacency will kill you, Fools! But all who listen to me shall live in peace and safety, unafraid."

COMMENTS ON 1:20-33

V. 20. From here to the end of the chapter (yes, and on beyond that) wisdom is personified as talking, teaching, crying, watching, and turning a deaf ear to people's cries when suffering from refusing her. Virtue itself is usually represented as a woman; so is wisdom here (note the "her"). Other verses that have wisdom crying or speaking: Prov. 8:1,3,4,6,7. Our verse tells of wisdom uttering her voice and crying aloud in the street and the broad places. Their streets were very narrow. Where two streets met, they made a broad place (see Mark 11:4). Actually wisdom speaks everywhere if people will but listen. What have you learned today from life?

V. 21. "The chief place of concourse" is translated "at the head of the multitudes" ("Young's Literal") and "at the head of the thronged ways" ("American Bible Union Version"). "The entrance of the gates" would be where people entered or left the city and where legal transactions were conducted (Ruth 4:1-11). "In the city" would be where people lived. Vs. 20,21 shows that wisdom spoke to the ancients from every place (the street, the broad places, the chief place of concourse, the entrance of the gates, and in the city). Today wisdom also speaks to us from many places: it speaks from the juvenile court (on child-rearing;, from the curse of alcholicism (asking, "Was Prohibition a failure after all?"), from tobacco-statistics, etc. What do tabacco statistics say? "Don't smoke!" Wisdom tells us it is a foolish habit (look at the effect upon your health); it is a wasteful habit (in outlay of money and in costs in minutes of life when added together; it is a bad habit (bad breath, spreading foul smell wherever one goes, causing others to cough from smoke, etc.).

V. 22. There are those who "love" simplicity (ignorance), some who "delight" in scoffing at the truth and at righteousness and at those who hold them, and some who "hate" knowledge. Wisdom, God, parents, and godly people cannot help wondering, "How much longer will such people live that way?"

V. 23. The very question, "How long...will ye love simplicity...delight in scoffing...hate knowledge?" of v. 22 was itself a "reproof" to those addressed, the hope being to get them to "turn" or change. The height of wisdom which men have sometimes scoffed at and hated is Inspired Wisdom found within the Word of God. The language, "I will pour out my spirit," sounds like a parallel prediction with Joel 2:28, which was fulfilled in God's sending the Holy Spirit to inspire the apostles and prophets of New Testament times. Old Testament writers often "jumped in" such long-range prophecies without elaboration and sometimes without a close topic-connection with its surroundings. Thus, we take this to be a prediction of New Testament inspiration.

V. 24. Wisdom again speaks. "A pause may be imagined, and seems to be impiled between this and the preceding verses (22 and 23), when the address passes into a new phase--from that of invitation and promise to that of judgment and stern denunciation" ("Pulpit Commentary"). Other passages on God calling and speaking but men refusing to hearken: Isa. 65:12; Isa. 66:4; Jer. 7:13; Zech. 7:11.

V. 25. "Set at nought" means to treat as nothing. Men who reject God's "counsel" (His instructions, commandments, and prohibitions) usually do not listen to His "reproof" (correction of their ways) either. This verse's last statement is also found in v. 30. Luke 7:30 says, "The Pharisees and the lawyers rejected for themselves the counsel of God, being not baptized of him (John the Baptist)." Why do men act as if they know more than God? Or, as if they don't have to bow down to God? Whatever the reason, it is both wrong and ruinous!

V. 26. That such a day of calamity is coming for the wicked is rightfully assumed. It is coming! Those who lack the fear of Jehovah and the wisdom that it brings (v. 7) will finally end up in a "fear" that they cannot escape! "The terrific nature of the punishment of the wicked is marked by a succession of terms all of terrible import--calamity, fear, desolation, destruction, distress and anguish (vs. 26,27)" ("Pulpit Commentary"). Wisdom here (and Jehovah in Psa. 2:4) is represented as laughing and mocking when such deserved calamity comes. Actually judgment will but return men's laughing and mocking upon them.

V. 27. What can be more fearful than overpowering storms in nature? These are used to depict the fear, distress, and anguish that will come upon those who have refused to follow wisdom's counsel. All of this was unforeseen when they were scoffing and refusing to listen to sound instruction.

V. 28. Now they will "turn" by the hardships that come upon them even though they wouldn't "turn" in obedience to v. 23. When men begin to reap the results of their own foolish choices, it does very little good to cry to God in the day of judgement! Other passages on His not listening to them and their cries: Job. 27:9; Isa. 1:15; Jer. 11:11; Jer. 14:12; Eze. 8:18. Oh, the desperation of calling when no one will answer! Had they sought God and wisdom diligently, they would have found a rich reward (Heb. 11:6).

V. 29. The reasons for their calamities are here given: they had "hated knowledge", and this helped bring the downfall of the Northern Kingdom ("My people are destroyed for lack of knowledge: because thou has rejected knowledge, I will also reject thee"--Hos. 4:6), and they "did not choose the fear of Jehovah" (Job said the wicked say to God, "Depart from us; For we desire not the knowledge of thy ways"--Job 21:14). V. 22 also spoke of their hating knowledge.

V. 30. Further reasons for their calamities: they had refused God's way ("counsel") and had despised all the "reproof" He had sent them because of their disobedient ways. This verse is a restatement of v. 25.

V. 31. Just as Gal. 6:7 says people will reap what they have sown, so this verse says the wicked will eat what they have planted (v. 22); in judgment God will laugh, God will mock (v. 26). "When we are punished, the blameworthiness lies not with God, but with us sinners" ("Pulpit Commentary").

V. 32. The "simple" referred to in v. 22 are here pictured as "backsliding"--as "fools" they will return to their folly ("as a dog that returneth to his vomit, So is a fool that repeateth his folly"--Prov. 26:11; "If, after they have escaped the defilements of the world through the knowlede of the Lord and Saviour Jesus Christ, they are again entangled therein and overcome, the last state is become worse with them than the first...It has happened unto them according to the true proverb, The dog turneth to his own vomit again, and the sow that had washed to wallowing in the mire"--II Pet. 2:20-22). For "careless ease" destroying one, consider the Rich Fool of Luke 12:19,20: "I will say to my soul, Soul, thou hast much goods laid up for many years; take thine ease, eat, drink, be merry. But God said unto him, Thou foolish one, this night is thy soul required of thee"). The beginning of sin is "confidence" (v. 13); the end of sin is destruction (this verse).

V. 33. In contrast to the wicked this verse sets forth the security of the righteous who have hearkened to wisdom: "The world passeth away, and the lust thereof: but he that doeth the will of God abideth for ever" (I John 2:17); "What man is he that feareth Jehovah? He shall be instructed in the way that he shall choose. His soul shall dwell at ease; And his seed shall inherit the land" (Psa. 25:12,13); "He shall never be moved; The righteous shall be had in everlasing remembrance. He shall not be afraid of evil tidings: His heart is fixed, trusting in Jehovah" (Psa. 112:6,7). "Evil" here is used in the sense of "trouble."

STUDY QUESTIONS OVER 1:20-33

1. What is wisdom as personified busy doing (v. 20)?
2. What are some of the places where wisdom is crying today (v. 21)?
3. What question was raised in v. 22?
4. In v. 23 what was wisdom trying to get the disobedient to do?
5. Cite a passage where God called, but they did not listen (v. 24).
6. What is the difference between "counsel" and "reproof" (v. 25)?
7. Why will wisdom laugh and mock in the day of the foolish people's calamities (v. 26)?
8. How is the fear that comes upon the disobedient pictured (v. 27)?
9. Will these who once mocked in time "call" (v. 28)?
10. What reasons are given in vs. 29,30 for their destruction?
11. According to v. 31 their judgment will only visit what upon them?
12. In what other verse are "fools" and "backsliding" put together (v. 32)?
13. On what subject does the chapter close (v. 33)?

THE HUMAN TONGUE

Of all the subjects that can be named, the subject of the tongue is one that needs to be considered the most. This important part of our bodies can get so far out of line at times, and the terrible havoc that the tongue has done cannot be completely recorded. On the other hand, the good that has been done through words is likewise inestimable.

Exclusive of Proverbs, when preachers go to the Bible to prepare messages on the tongue, the book of James, the book of Ephesians, and the book of Matthew are among the chief sources of material. But, Proverbs discusses this subject more fully than any other book of the Bible—so much that all the material found elsewhere in the Bible does not nearly equal the material found alone in it.

FROM THE 7th CHAPTER

The writer tells of a sad scene that he once beheld: "For at the window of my house I looked through my casement, and beheld among the simple ones, I discerned among the youths, a young man void of understanding, passing through the street near her corner and he went the way to her house, in the twilight, in the evening, in the black and dark night: and, behold, there met him a woman with the attire of an harlot and subtil of heart...She caught him, and kissed him, and with an impudent face said unto him, I have peace offerings with me; this day have I payed my vows. Therefore came I forth to meet thee, diligently to seek thy face, and I have found thee" (verses 6-15), and the following verses show her enticing words, "I have decked my bed with coverings of tapestry, with carved works, with fine linen of Egypt. I have perfumed my bed with myrrh, aloes, and cinnamon. Come, let us take our fill of love until the morning: let us solace ourselves with loves" (verses 16-18). Then she goes on to assure him that he need not fear about her husband coming home: "For the goodman is not at home, he is gone a long journey: he hath taken a bag of money with him, and will come home at the day appointed" (verses 19,20). Oh the sadness in the next verses: "With her much fair speech she caused him to yield, with the flattering of her lips she forced him. He goeth after her straightway, as an ox goeth to the slaughter, or as a fool to the correction of the stocks; till a dart strike through his liver; as a bird hasteth to the snare, and knoweth not that it is for his life" (verses 21-23). What is the lesson? Listen to the next verses: "Hearken unto me now therefore, O ye children, and attend to the words of my mouth. Let not thine heart decline to her ways, go not astray in her paths. For she hath cast down many wounded: yea, many strong men have been slain by her. Her house is the way to hell, going down to the chambers of death."

CHAPTER 2

TEXT — 2:1-9

1. My son, if thou wilt receive my words,
   And lay up my commandments with thee;
2. So as to incline thine ear unto wisdom,
   And apply thy heart to understanding;
3. Yea if thou cry after discernment,
   And lift up thy voice for understanding;
4. If thou seek her as silver,
   And search for her as for hid treasures:
5. Then shalt thou understand the fear of Jehovah,
   And find the knowledge of God.
6. For Jehovah giveth wisdom;
   Out of his mouth cometh knowledge and understanding:
7. He layeth up sound wisdom for the upright;
   He is a shield to them that walk in integrity;
8. That he may guard the paths of justice,
   And preserve the way of his saints.
9. Then shalt thou understand righteousness and justice,
   And equity, yea, every good path.

STUDY QUESTIONS OVER 2:1-9

1. Would you draw a distinction between "my words" and "my commandments" in v. 1?
2. What is heard by the ear must be considered in the .... (v. 2).
3. What words in v. 3 show earnestness in seeking knowledge?
4. How earnestly should knowledge be sought (v. 4)?
5. What knowledge should fathers especially want their sons to have (v. 5)?
6. Do the words of understanding come to man from God's mouth directly or by inspiration (v. 6)?
7. What does "integrity" mean (v. 7)?
8. What word in v. 7 goes along with "guard" and "preserve" in v. 8?
9. How different would the world be if everybody understood these things (v. 9)?

PARAPHRASE OF 2:1-9

1-5. Every young man who listens to me and obeys my instructions will be given wisdom and good sense. Yes, if you want better insight and discernment, and are searching for them as you would for lost money or hidden treasure, then wisdom will be given you and knowledge of God Himself; you will soon learn the importance of reverence for the Lord and of trusting Him.

6-9. For the Lord grants wisdom! His every word is a treasure of knowledge and understanding. He grants good sense to the godly--His saints. He is their shield, protecting them and guarding their pathway. He shows how to distinguish right from wrong, how to find the right decision every time.

COMMENTS ON 2:1-9

V. 1. Other chapters that begin with "My son": Chapters 3,5,6,7. We will point out the doublets as they occur in this and the following 4 verses: (receive my words; and (2) hide my commandments. Other passages on laying up parental instructions in one's heart: Prov. 4:21; 7:1. "The...'if' is conditional, and serves to introduce the series of clauses (vs. 1-4) which lay down the conditions upon which the promises depend...There is a gradation in emphasis in the various terms here used...Just as 'commandments' is stronger than 'words,' so 'hide' is stronger than 'receive'...The Divine commands...are to be hidden in safe custody in the memory, in the understanding, in the conscience, and in the heart...The psalmist expresses the same idea in Psa. 119:11: 'Thy word have I hid in my heart'" ("Pulpit Commentary").

V. 2. Doublet: (1 incline thine ear unto wisdom; and (2) apply thy heart to understanding. Solomon wanted his son to develop an inclination for wisdom ("incline"). Just as a ball will roll down an "incline", so if one is inclined toward wisdom will he assuredly "apply" his heart (put himself into getting understanding).

V. 3. Doublet: (1) cry after discernment; and (2) lift up thy voice for understanding. The picture in this verse is even stronger than "incline" in v. 4. Here the son is urged to "cry after", to "lift up" his voice for "discernment (the ability to distinguish between right and wrong, truth and error, wisdom and foolishness).

V. 4. The "ifs" in these first 4 verses might be thought of

as progressive as follows: if you receive and lay up my commandments (as a child); if you develop an inclination toward wisdom and develop an understanding heart (in youth); and if you cry after and seek for discernment and understanding (as an adult), v. 5 says it will be yours. "The comparison here made between the search for wisdom and the search for the hidden treasures of the earth was not unfamiliar to the Hebrew mind as it is found worked out with great beauty of detail in Job 28" ("Pulpit Commentary"). Prov. 3:14: "For the gaining of it is better than the gaining of silver, And the profit thereof than fine gold. She is more precious than rubies: And none of the things thou canst desire are to be compared unto her" (Prov. 3:14,15).

V. 5. If the conditions of vs. 1-4 are met, then this wonderful promise will apply: the son will understand the fear of Jehovah and will find the knowledge of God. And this fear of Jehovah will then lead to even more wisdom and knowledge (Prov. 1:7).

V. 6. If one seeks for wisdom according to vs. 1-4, then God will give it to him. Involved in this quest is to acknowledge God as the source of all wisdom and to go to Him for it: "If any of you lacketh wisdom, let him ask of God, who giveth to all liberally and upbraideth not; and it shall be given him" (Jas. 1:5). This is what Solomon did ("Give thy servant therefore an understanding heart to judge thy people, that I may discern between good and evil"—I Kings 3:9), and God gave it to him ("Behold, I have done according to thy word: lo, I have given thee a wise and an understanding heart; so that there hath been none like thee before thee, neither after thee shall any arise like unto thee"—I Kings 3:12). In our section Solomon is merely teaching his son from his own experience.

V. 7. God gives wisdom as well as other blessings to the upright: "No good thing will he withhold from them that walk uprightly" (Psa. 84:11). As to God's being a shield to those who walk in integrity, Prov. 20:5 says, "He is a shield unto them that take refuge in him." "God is Himself a buckler or shield...This aspect of God's direct protecting power is met with in other parts of Scripture: Gen. 15:1; Psa. 33:20; Psa. 84:11; Psa. 89:18; Psa. 144:2" ("Pulpit Commentary").

V. 8. Yes, Jehovah guards the "paths of justice". Is it not remarkable that even though men themselves do not always do what is right that the old basics of what is right and wrong still survive (such as love, kindness, truth-telling, the wrongness of killing, stealing, etc.)? He not only guards the paths of justice but particularly preserves the way of those who walk in those paths: "The eyes of the Lord are upon the righteous" (I Pet. 3:12); "He will not suffer thy foot to be moved: He that keepeth thee will not slumber...Jehovah is thy keeper...Jehovah will keep thee from all evil; He will keep thy soul. Jehovah will keep thy going out and thy coming in" (Psa. 121:3-8); "He will keep the foot of his holy ones" (I Sam. 2:9). Note that even God's Old Testament people were called "saints", which means "holy ones".

V. 9. Here are things that every person should understand and not be confused about. If one so applies himself to get wisdom, God will bless him with it, and that will include an understanding of these basic things.

STUDY QUESTIONS OVER 2:1-9

1. What other chapters begin with "my son" (v. 1)?
2. How many of these opening verses contain doublets (v. 1)?
3. Comment upon "incline" and "apply" in v. 2.
4. Comment on the stronger words used in v. 3 than those used in v. 2.
5. Comment on the possible progressiveness of the "ifs" in vs. 1-4.
6. What great promise is found in v. 5?
7. How did Solomon himself get wisdom (v. 6)?
8. God gives wisdom to what group in v. 7?
9. Comment on God guarding the "paths of justice" (v. 8).
10. What will one understand if God blesses him with wisdom (v. 9)?

TEXT — 2:10-22

10. For wisdom shall enter into thy heart,
And knowledge shall be pleasant unto thy soul;
11. Discretion shall watch over thee;
Understanding shall keep thee:
12. To deliver thee from the way of evil,
From the men that speak perverse things;
13. Who forsake the paths of uprightness,
To walk in the ways of darkness;

14. Who rejoice to do evil,
And delight in the perverseness of evil;
15. Who are crooked in their ways,
And wayward in their paths:
16. To deliver thee from the strange woman,
Even from the foreigner that flattereth with her words;
17. That forsaketh the friend of her youth,
And forgetteth the covenant of her God:
18. For her house inclineth unto death,
And her paths unto the dead;
19. None that go unto her return again,
Neither do they attain unto the paths of life:
20. That thou mayest walk in the way of good men,
And keep the paths of the righteous.
21. For the upright shall dwell in the land,
And the perfect shall remain in it.
22. But the wicked shall be cut off from the land,
And the treacherous shall be rooted out of it.

STUDY QUESTIONS OVER 2:10-22

1. Knowledge should be .... (v. 10).
2. What is "discretion" (v. 11)?
3. Does true knowledge trust all persons indiscriminately (v. 12)?
4. What double sin were they guilty of (v. 13)?
5. What about their rejoicing (v. 14)?
6. Why do we speak of dishonest people as "crooked" (v. 15)?
7. Young men should be strongly warned to watch out for dishonest men and .... women (vs. 12,16).
8. What "covenant" (v. 17)?
9. Why mention her "house" (v. 18)?
10. They don't "return" in what sense (v. 19)?
11. What kind of men avoid such women (v. 20)?
12. What are the parallel words in v. 21?
13. What are the parallel words in v. 22?

PARAPHRASE OF 2:10-22

10-15. For wisdom and truth will enter the very center of your being, filling your life with joy. You will be given the sense to stay away from evil men who want you to be their partners in crime--men who turn from God's ways to walk down dark and evil paths, and exult in doing wrong, for they thoroughly enjoy their sins. Everything they do is crooked and wrong.

16-19. Only wisdom from the Lord can save a man from the flattery of prostitutes; these girls have abandoned their husbands and flouted the laws of God. Their houses lie along the road to death and hell. The men who enter them are doomed. None of these men will ever be the same again.

20-22. Follow the steps of the godly instead, and stay on the right path, for only good men enjoy life to the full; evil men lose the good things they might have had; and they themselves shall be destroyed.

COMMENTS ON 2:10-22

V. 10. "'Shall enter' in the sense of permanent residence in the heart" ("Pulpit Commentary"). Col. 3:15 uses the same figure of speech concerning the Word of Christ and our hearts: "Let the word of Christ dwell in you richly." "Dwell" in this verse means to "make a home for". The heart that has made wisdom its permanent inhabitant will be a soul blessed with pleasantness and satisfaction.

V. 11. When blessed with wisdom, "discretion" will be there to guard what we say, what we do, the policies we adopt, etc., and "understanding" will be there to keep us from small embarrassments and costly mistakes. Prov. 6:22 similarly says, "When thou wakest, it shall lead thee; When thou sleepest, it shall watch over thee."

V. 12. Wisdom will keep one from taking up with evil men (this verse) and with evil women (v. 16). The word "deliver" suggests that evil men are out to snare such young men into their plots and ways. The "perverse" speech of evil men is pointed out. There is a certain speech that goes with evil men—usually coarse words, vulgar words, irreverent words.

V. 13. Some of those now evil were once on the right road, for they forsook the "paths of uprightness". Probably as children they were taught the right way. Oh, how many drift from their childhood teachings into the "ways of darkness" (sin)! Those who walk in evil ways always try to get others to fall as they have, but how foolish to listen to them!

V. 14. The wicked become perverted: instead of grieving over evil, they rejoice in doing it. "It is as sport to a fool to do wickedness" (Prov. 10:23); "When thou doest evil, then thou rejoicest" (Jer. 11:15); "Who, knowing the ordinance of God, that they that practice such things are worthy of death, not only do the same, but also consent with them that practise them" (Rom. 1:32). We are forbidden to desire evil: "Abhor that which is evil" (Rom. 12;&); "Love not the world...the lust of the flesh and the lust of the eyes and the vain-glory of life" (I John 2:15,16).

V. 15. Instead of walking a straight and right course, they are further described as "crooked", and instead of staying on the right way, they are said to be "wayward" in their paths. Psa. 125:5 speaks of those who "turn aside unto their crooked ways". It is from this crookedness and waywardness that true wisdom will deliver a young man.

V. 16. A "strange" woman means one who is not his wife; she is a "foreigner" to him because she is not related to him in marriage. This is a warning against loose, lascivious living that ends in sexual misbehavior. Several chapters (or extended sections) are devoted to warning against such involvements (here; 5:1-23; 6:23-25; 7:4-27; 9:13-18). Our verse warns of her enticing words ("flattereth with her words"). Other verses do the same: "The lips of a strange woman drop honey, And her mouth is smoother than oil" (Prov. 5:3); "To keep thee from the evil woman, From the flattery of the foreigner's tongue" (Prov. 6:24); "With her much fair speech she causeth him to yield; with the flattering of her lips she forceth him along" (Prov. 7:21).

V. 17. Such a woman was once married, but she has forsaken her husband (here called "the friend of her youth"). What a poor one to get mixed up with! She is not only untrue to man (her husband), but she "forgetteth the covenant of her God" (God's covenant or law forbids her to leave her husband and live as she is living). But her actions show that she doesn't care what God says.!

V. 18. Her "house" is referred to because this is where she "operates" her dirty business. Other passages on immorality and death: "Her feet go down to death; Her steps take hold on Sheol" (Prov. 5:5); "Her house is the way to Sheol, Going down to the chambers of death" (Prov. 7:27). The results are a bold contrast to her enticing promises: "As for him that is void of understanding, she saith to him, stolen waters are sweet, And bread eaten in secret is pleasant. But he knoweth not that the dead are there; that her guests are in the depths of Sheol" (Prov. 9:16-18).

V. 19. "The difficulty which they who give themselves up to the indulgence of lust and passion encounter in extricating themselves makes the statement...an almost universal truth...It is as difficult to bring back a libidinous person to chastity as a dead man to life. This passage led some...to declare that the sin of adultery was unpardonable. Fornication was classed by the scholastic divines among the seven deadly sins" ("Pulpit Commentary").

V. 20. The "good men" of this verse are to be contrasted with the evil men of v. 12, and their good lives with the evil men who indulge with evil women.

V. 21. In contrast with "death" resulting from the indulgent life, this verse speaks of the good men getting to live on. Psa. 37 stresses this blessing of godliness: Those that wait for Jehovah, they shall inherit the land" (v. 9); "The meek shall inherit the land" (v. 11); "Such as are blessed of him shall inherit the land" (v. 22); "The righteous shall inherit the land, And dwell therein for ever" (v. 29).

V. 22. The doom of the wicked is again mentioned. This fact is also stressed in Psa. 37: "They shall soon be cut down like the grass" (v. 2); "Evil-doers shall be cut off" (v. 9); "Yet a little while, and the wicked shall not be" (v. 10); "The arms of the wicked shall be broken" (v. 17); "The wicked shall perish, And the enemies of Jehovah shall be as the fat of lambs: They shall consume; in smoke shall they consume away" :v. 20); "They that are cursed of him shall be cut off" (v. 22); "The seed of the wicked shall be cut off" (v. 28); "I have seen the wicked in great power, And spreading himself like a green tree in its native soil. But one passed by, and, lo, he was not: Yea, I sought him, but he could not be found" (vs. 35,36); "As for the transgressors, they shall be destroyed together: The end of the wicked shall be cut off" (v. 38).

TEST QUESTIONS OVER 2:10-22

1. What does "shall enter" in v. 10 signify about wisdom?
2. From what will discretion and understanding keep us (v. 11)?

3. Comment on the perverse speech of evil men (v. 12).
4. Are there wicked men who once walked in the paths of uprightness (v. 13)? When?
5. How perverted do the wicked become (v. 14)?
6. "Crooked" is the opposite of what way to walk (v. 15)?
7. Comment on the wicked woman's use of words to ensnare men (v. 16).
8. To what two parties is such a woman untrue (v. 17)?
9. What other passages besides v. 18 say that her house leads to death?
10. What does v. 19 say about the difficulty involved in freeing oneself from such behavior once that he has begun it?
11. Who are the "good men" of v. 20?
12. What chapter has much to say about the long life of the righteous (v. 21)?
13. What chapter has much to say about the short life of the wicked (v. 22)?

FOOLS ARE KNOWN BY THEIR SPEECH

Listen to 15:14: "The heart of him that hath understanding seeketh knowledge: but the mouth of the fools feedeth on foolishness." If you need any commentary on this verse, just go down to the corner store or to the garage or to the barber shop—just anywhere that men with time on their hands gather—and listen to them for ten minutes, and you will well understand the statement, "The mouth of fools feedeth on foolishness". The chances are, you will not hear one thing that will build you up or do you any good, but will hear a lot of vocal drivel that depicts nothing but shallowness of thought, and such will go on all day long!

Another vocal mark of a fool is that he tells everything he knows. 29:11 says, "A fool uttereth all his mind." He will freely talk concerning his financial matters or his business dealings. He will not hestitate to tell you how much money he has or how much he made or how much he sold his car for. For some reason, he wants everyone to know everything about him, so he tells everything he knows.

But, not only does he talk about his own things—he talks about everybody else's things too. And this gets him into trouble. 18:7 says, "A fool's mouth is his destruction."

Furthermore, a fool weaves into his conversation all the rude words, all the vulgar words, and all the latest delinquents' expressions. His speech is marked by all kinds of grammatical errors. Nothing of good literature is ever upon his tongue. No statement from the pen of David or from the pens of the great secular writers ever is upon his lips. In short, 17:7 says, "Excellent speech becometh not a fool."

"TEACHING PARENTS"

Proverbs shows us parents who teach and warn their children. "My son," the writer says, "if sinners entice thee, consent thou not." And then he goes on to forewarn his son of the way they will approach him to get him to go with them. But, the father adds, "Walk not thou in the way with them; refrain thy foot from their path" (1:10-15).

There was ever the instruction to trust in God. "My son, let not them depart from thine eyes: keep sound wisdom and discretion: so shall they be life unto thy soul, and grace to thy neck. Then shalt thou walk in thy way safely, and thy foot shall not stumble. When thou liest down, thou shalt not be afraid: yea, thou shalt lie down, and thy sleep shall be sweet. Be not afraid of sudden fear, neither of the desolation of the wicked, when it cometh. For the Lord shall be thy confidence, and shall keep thy foot from being taken" (3:21-26).

The writer tells his son, "I was my father's son, tender and only beloved in the sight of my mother. He taught me also, and said unto me, Let thine heart retain my words: keep my commandments, and live" (4:3,4), and the writer was turning around and doing the same thing to his son—teaching him.

Some fathers do little more than bring the children into the world and bring the money home for their livelihood. Proverbs shows that a father is to be teacher too, not expecting the mother to do all the talking and all the rearing of the children. On the other hand, the woman is to be a teacher also: "Forsake not the law of thy mother" (1:8). She doesn't always wait till Dad comes home from work to tend to the disobedience of the children. She is strict with them also.

CHAPTER 3

TEXT — 3:1-12

1. My son, forget not my law;
   But let thy heart keep my commandments:
2. For length of days, and years of life,
   And peace, will they add to thee.
3. Let not kindness and truth forsake thee:
   Bind them about thy neck;
   Write them upon the tablet of thy heart:
4. So shalt thou find favor and good understanding
   In the sight of God and man.
5. Trust in Jehovah with all thy heart,
   And lean not upon thine own understanding:
6. In all thy ways acknowledge him,
   And he will direct thy paths.
7. Be not wise in thine own eyes;
   Fear Jehovah, and depart from evil:
8. It will be health to thy navel,
   And marrow to thy bones.
9. Honor Jehovah with thy substance,
   And with the first-fruits of all thine increase:
10. So shall thy barns be filled with plenty,
   And thy vats shall overflow with new wine.
11. My son, despise not the chastening of Jehovah;
   Neither be weary of his reproof:
12. For whom Jehovah loveth he reproveth,
   Even as a father the son in whom he delighteth.

STUDY QUESTIONS OVER 3:1-12

1. Is remembering what parents said a part of obedience (v. 1)?
2. How desirable are the blessings of obedience mentioned in v. 2?
3. How would kindness and truth "forsake" one (v. 3)?
4. What Bible persons were said to have the favor of both God and man (v. 4)?
5. How would you relate the two statements of v. 5 to each other?
6. How can we "acknowledge" God (v. 6)?
7. What feelings does v. 7 reveal about those who are wise in their own eyes?

8. Apply the illustrations in v. 8.
9. Why does giving honor God (v. 9)?
10. Should God be given the first of our paycheck or what is left over from it (v. 9)?
11. What are "vats" (v. 10)?
12. Where is v. 11 quoted in the New Testament?
13. What motivates God to reprove (v. 12)?

PARAPHRASE OF 3:1-12

1-6. My son, never forget the things I've taught you. If you want a long and satisfying life, closely follow my instructions. Never forget to be truthful and kind. Hold these virtues tightly. Write them deep within your heart. If you want favor with both God and man, and a reputation for good judgment and common sense, then trust the Lord completely; don't ever trust yourself. In everything you do, put God first, and He will direct you and crown your efforts with success.

7,8. Don't be conceited, sure of your own wisdom. Instead trust and reverence the Lord, and turn your back on evil; when you do that, then you will be given renewed health and vitality.

9,10. Honor the Lord by giving Him the first part of all your income, and He will fill your barns with wheat and barley and overflow your vats with the finest wines.

11,12. Young man, do not resent it when God chastens and corrects you, for His punishment is proof of His love. Just as a father punishes a son he delights in to make him better, so the Lord corrects you.

COMMENTS ON 3:1-12

V. 1. In this and succeeding verses the material divides itself into 2-verse thoughts, the first verse giving the commandment and the second verse the promise or explanation. Check this for yourself. Too many children instead of not forgetting their parent's law and keeping the commandments get it backwards: they "keep forgetting" what they were told. If one remembers his father's instruction, his father should not have to keep reminding him of his duty. Remembering what one is told is a necessary part of obedience.

V. 2. The long life promised to the righteous is contrasted

with the shorter life of the wicked as set forth over and over again in Psa. 37. That it is natural to want to live is seen in the fact that people seek to extend their lives by medical and surgical means. "Peace" meant even more to them because of the warring world in which they lived. The blessings that come to the obedient, then, are major in importance.

V. 3. Being kind and always telling the truth would especially make for the life of peace promised in v. 2 (as far as the individual was concerned). If one loves, he is kind (I Cor. 13:4). "Brotherly kindness" is to be added to one's character (II Pet. 1:7; Eph. 4:32). Concerning "truth", "Pulpit Commentary" says it is that "absolute integrity of character, both in word and deed, which secures the unhesitating confidence of all." The son was to grace his life with them ("bind them about thy neck"), and he was to imbed them in the very fibre of his character ("write them upon the tablet of thy heart"). The heart is like a table or tablet on which can be written either good (II Cor. 3:3) or bad (Jer. 17:1).

V. 4. Both God and man will approve and appreciate one who follows kindness and truth. Concerning having the favor of both God and man, notice these passages: "The child Samuel grew on, and increased in favor both with Jehovah, and also with men" (I Sam. 2:26); "And Jesus advanced in favor with God and men" (Luke 2:52); "He that herein serveth Christ is well-pleasing to God, and approved of men" (Rom. 14:18). Man's greatest happiness is attained when he has the favor of God and the respect of his fellowmen.

V. 5. Other commands to trust Jehovah: "Trust in Jehovah" (Psa. 37:3); "Commit thy way unto Jehovah; Trust also in him" (Psa. 37:5). "Trust" means to rely upon, put confidence in. This we need to do toward God and not to suppose that we are self-contained and self-sufficient of ourselves. Man makes a grave mistake when he does not pray, does not commit his way to God, and does not depend upon God. So often, though, men turn earthly assets and strong-points into occasions of pride and as a result fail to think of God. Thus, Jer. 9:23,24 says, "Thus saith Jehovah, Let not the wise man glory in his wisdom, neither let the mighty man glory in his might, let not the rich man glory in his riches; but let him that glorieth glory in this, that he hath understanding, and knoweth me." And I Tim. 6:17 says, "Charge them that are rich in this present world, that they be not highminded, nor have their hope set on the uncertainty of riches, but on God." See also Isa. 31:1; Psa. 20:7; Psa. 44:1-8; Psa. 118:8,9.

V. 6. "This expression covers the whole area of life's action...It guards against our acknowledging God in great crises and solemn acts of worship only...To acknowledge God is, therefore, to recognize in all our dealings and undertakings God's overruling providence" ("Pulpit Commentary"). "Begin, continue and end every work, purpose, and device with God. Earnestly pray for His direction at the commencement; look for His continual support in the progress; and so begin and continue that all may terminate in His glory...The great sin of the human race is their continual endeavor to live independently of God" ("Clarke"). Man's need of acknowledging God is well stated by Jeremiah in Jer. 10:23: "O Jehovah, I know that the way of man is not in himself; it is not in man that walketh to direct his steps." By praying at the outset of the day, we acknowledge that a good day is dependent upon Him. By thanking God before we eat, we acknowledge that He has made the possession of food possible. By praying before we begin a trip, we acknowledge that His help is important in making the trip safely. And there are many other such examples of acknowledging Him in all our various ways, which carries His promise to direct our paths.

V. 7. Rom. 12:16 similarly warns, "Be not wise in your own conceits." Man doesn't have to possess very much knowledge, it seems, until it goes to his head: "Knowledge puffeth up" (I Cor. 8:1). Instead of thinking how great we are, we should be thinking of how great God is and how small we are and as a result "fear" Him and "depart from evil" instead of proudly living in sin. Job was one who "feared God, and turned away from evil" (Job 1:1). After enumerating some of man's sins in Rom. 3:10-17, the next verse (v. 18) seems to explain the whole matter: "There is no fear of God before their eyes". Verses 5-7 hang together: "trust" Jehovah (v. 5), "acknowledge" Him (v. 6), "fear" Him (v. 7) and don't lean on your "own understanding" (v. 5), don't be wise in your "own eyes" (v. 7).

V. 8. The results of obeying the parental instructions contained in vs. 5-7 are contained in those verses and in the 3 that follow: God will "direct" your paths (v. 6); you will "depart" from evil (v. 7); it will be "health" to you (this verse). The "marrow" in one's bones plays a very important part in one's overall health. We may be ignorant of some lasting connection that the navel has with one's health after one's birth that it is spoken of so prominently. Could it here be used as a symbol of utter dependence upon God (raised in previous verses) that we must maintain in a spiritually healthy condition? "Clarke" explains the problem thus: "The central region of the body is taken as the representative of all the vital organs."

V. 9. "The injunctions also show that the honoring of God does not consist simply of lip-service, of humility and confidence in Him, but also of external worship, and incorporeal things" ("Pulpit Commentary"). Yes, God can be honored with substance (Material gain) if it be presented in the right spirit and in proportion to one's material blessings. Other passages on giving God the "first-fruits" of the harvest: Exo. 23:19; Deut. 26:1,2. Just as the Lord claims the first day of each week as His day (Rev. 1:10; Acts 20:7; I Cor. 16:2), even so He claims the first portion of man's produce and earnings. Abel's acceptable sacrifice was the "firstlings" and the "fat" of his flock (Gen. 4:4). People who spend and spend and spend out of their paychecks and then give "something" out of what is left to God are likely to dishonor rather than "honor" Him with their gift. Tithers always give of the "first-fruits" rather than of the "left-overs"!. Remember, too, that the first thing Noah did after the flood was not build a house for himself but an altar to God (Gen. 8:20); those who were scattered from Jerusalem are reported in their "preaching the word" rather than in their finding jobs for the support of themselves (Acts 8:1,4); and Jesus taught all of us to seek "first" the kingdom of God and its righteousness before what we are going to eat, drink, or wear (Matt. 6:31-33).

V. 10. Man is concerned about his own things and often leaves God out of his life and concerns or subordinates Him to an inferior place (second, third or fourth place). Here God promises to give man what he wants ("barns be filled with plenty...vats overflow") if he puts God first in his life. The "vats" were olive-oil vats or grape-juice vats. Similarly Deut. 28:8-12 says "Jehovah will command the blessing upon thee in thy barns, and in all that thou puttest thy hand unto...And Jehovah will make thee plenteous for good...in the fruit of thy ground...Jehovah will open unto thee his good treasure the heavens, to give the rain of thy land in its season, and to bless all the work of thy hand." In Mal. 3:10,11 God promised agricultural blessings if they would honor Him with their tithes: "Bring ye the whole tithe into the store-house...and prove me now herewith, saith Jehovah of hosts, if I will not open you the windows of heaven, and pour you out a blessing, that there shall be not room enough to receive it. And I will rebuke the devourer for your sakes, and he shall not destroy the fruits of your ground; neither shall your vine cast its fruit before the time in the field."

V. 11. Immediately after telling of all the joyous blessings that God sends, we have another blessing listed, a blessing of a different nature, a blessing in disguise--chastening. Unlike the other blessings, it comes not because of obedience but disobedience; nor is it like other blessings, joyous at the time, but grievous, but it proves to be a blessing in the peaceful fruit that it brings to those who are corrected by it. "All chastening seemeth for the present not to be joyous but grievous; yet afterward it yieldeth peaceable fruit unto them that have been exercised thereby, even the fruit of righteousness" (Heb. 12:11); "For they indeed for a few days chastened us as seemed good to them; but he for our profit, that we may be partakers of his holiness" (Heb. 12:10); "We are chastened of the Lord, that we may not be condemned with the world" (I Cor. 11:32). Our verse is similar to Job 5:17 ("Behold, happy is the man whom God correcteth: Therefore despise not thou the chastening of the Almighty") and is quoted in Heb. 12:5,6. Solomon urges his son not to "despise" or belittle, not to disregard or misunderstand God's chastening nor to be weary of it, for it will bring blessings (Psa. 94:12).

V. 12. Satan tempts us because he seeks our destruction (I Pet. 5:8), and wicked people persecute us because they hate us (Luke 6:22), but God brings His hardship of chastening upon us because He loves us (this verse; Heb. 12:6; Rev. 3:19). His chastening is compared to the correction of our earthly parents (this verse; Deut. 8:5; Heb. 12:7-9). Solomon has to tell us that it is God's love that causes Him to chasten. People's idea of "love" is not always right. The preacher who forcefully condemns sin and falsehood is accused of having an unloving attitude (Yet he is working to save people). The parent who corrects his children is criticized as harsh and unloving, but both God who corrects His children and parents who correct theirs do so because of love and concern ("He that spareth the rod hateth his son; But he that loveth him chasteneth him betimes"--Prov. 13:24).

TEST QUESTIONS OVER 3:1-12

1. What about the child who says to his parent, "I forgot that I was supposed to do that" (v. 1)?
2. What promises does v. 2 spell out for the obedient child?
3. To what is the heart likened in v. 3?
4. What two blessings come from being kind and always telling the truth (v. 4)?
5. In what does man have a tendency to trust instead of God (v. 5)?
6. What is the promise connected with acknowledging God in all our ways (v. 6)?
7. What does man often allow his little bit of knowledge to do to him (v. 7)?
8. What is the promise connected with fearing God and departing from evil instead of being wise in one's own conceit (v. 8)?
9. Comment upon v. 9.
10. What is the promise connected with giving God the first-fruits (v. 10)?
11. In what sense is chastening also a blessing (v. 11)?
12. Show how love is involved both in God's chastening of His children and in earthly parents' chastening of theirs (v. 12).

TEXT — 3:13-26

13. Happy is the man that findeth wisdom,
And the man that getteth understanding.
14. For the gaining of it is better than the gaining of silver,
And the profit thereof than fine gold.
15. She is more precious than rubies:
And none of the things thou canst desire are to be compared unto her.
16. Length of days is in her right hand;
In her left hand are riches and honor.
17. Her ways are ways of pleasantness,
And all her paths are peace.
18. She is a tree of life to them that lay hold upon her:
And happy is every one that retaineth her.

19. Jehovah by wisdom founded the earth;
By understanding he established the heavens.
20. By his knowledge the depths were broken up,
and the skies drop down the dew.
21. My son, let them not depart from thine eyes;
Keep sound wisdom and discretion:
22. So shall they be life unto thy soul,
And grace to thy neck.
23. Then shalt thou walk in thy way securely,
And thy foot shall not stumble.
24. When thou liest down, thou shalt not be afraid:
Yea, thou shalt lie down, and thy sleep shall be sweet.
25. Be not afraid of sudden fear,
Neither of the desolation of the wicked, when it cometh:
26. For Jehovah will be thy confidence,
And will keep thy foot from being taken.

STUDY QUESTIONS OVER 3:13-26

1. Why is the man who gets wisdom "happy" (v. 13)?
2. Why is the getting of wisdom better than the getting of treasures (v. 14)?
3. Give a synonym for "precious" as used in v. 15.
4. Compare the blessings mentioned in v. 16 with those mentioned in v. 2.
5. What two additional blessings of wisdom are promised in v. 17?
6. What is meant by "tree of life" in v. 18?
7. How is God's wisdom reflected in His creation (v. 19)?
8. What breaking up of depths is referred to in v. 20?
9. What does "keep" mean in v. 21?
10. Comment upon "grace" as used in v. 22.
11. What Hebrew parallelism do we have in v. 23?
12. What is there to fear about the night (v. 24)?
13. Why can a godly person be safe and secure from all alarms as the song, "Leaning on the Everlasting Arms" says (v. 25)?
14. Where is a godly person's confidence placed (v. 26)?

PARAPHRASE OF 3:13-26

13-18. The man who knows right from wrong and has good judgment and common sense is happier than the man who is immensely rich! For such wisdom is far more valuable than precious jewels. Nothing else compares with it. Wisdom gives a long, good life; riches; honor; pleasure; and peace. Wisdom is a tree of life to those who eat her fruit; happy is the man who keeps on eating it.

19. The Lord's wisdom founded the earth; his understanding established all the universe and space.

20. The deep foundations of the earth were broken open by His knowledge, and the skies poured down rain.

21-26. Have two goals--wisdom--that is, knowing and doing right--and common sense. Don't let them slip away, for they fill you with living energy and are a feather in your cap. They keep you safe from defeat and disaster and stumbling off the trail. With them on guard you can sleep without fear; and you need not be afraid of disaster or the plots of wicked men; for the Lord is with you; He protects you.

COMMENTS ON 3:13-26

V. 13. Vs. 13-20 go together, bidding the son to get wisdom and understanding for the rich blessings they bestow and reminding him that the Highest Himself employed wisdom in laying out the universe. He who finds wisdom gets understanding, and the finding is not so likely by accident as by searching. The whoso "findeth" wisdom of Prov. 8:35 is the one who has heard "instruction" (Prov. 8:33). Yes, a wise, an informed, an understanding person is a "happy" person, for he is blessed with the light of knowledge.

V. 14. God would have men seek wisdom as they seek earthly treasures: "If thou seek her as silver, And search for her as for hid treasurers: Then shalt thou understand the fear of Jehovah, And find the knowledge of God" (Prov. 2:4,5); "My fruit is better than gold, yea, than fine gold; And my revenue than choice silver" (Prov. 8:19). Especially is the knowledge of God's Word so valuable: "I rejoice at thy word, As one that findeth great spoil" (Psa. 119:162); "The ordinances of Jehovah are true, and righteous altogether. More to be desired are they than gold, yea, than much fine gold" (Psa. 19:9,10).

V. 15. A similar passage comparing rubies and the value of wisdom: "Wisdom is better than rubies; And all the things that may be desired are not to be compared unto it" (Prov.

8:11). "Pulpit Commentary": "There is nothing--neither silver, gold, precious stones, nor anything precious--which is an equivalent to wisdom in value...When everything is put before us to choose from...like Solomon at Gibeon, we should prefer wisdom (I Kings 3:11-13)!"

V. 16. Both hands are full of great things and are stretched out to the person of true understanding. "The two hands, the right and the left, signify the abundance of Wisdom's gifts" ("Pulpit Commentary"). Wisdom claims, in Prov. 8:18, to have "riches and honor" to bestow. Long life, then, can be a result of wisdom. Riches, then, can be a product of wisdom. Honor, then, can come to those with wisdom.

V. 17. Here are two more great blessings of wisdom: "pleasantness" and "peace". Add these to riches and honor and long life, and who could ask for more as far as earthly life is concerned? Contrast such a life with one's life that is void of wisdom and is characterized by foolish ways.

V. 18. Like "Fountain of Youth" in our language, so "Tree of Life" in Bible days stood for something very desirable. The name was first used for one of the trees in the midst of the Garden of Eden (Gen. 2:9). God did not allow Adam and Eve to eat of this tree after they sinned (Gen. 3:22-24). In Rev. 2:7 it is said to be in the Paradise of God. The blessings of having wisdom are compared to eating from the tree of life! Our verse points out the importance both of laying hold upon (obtaining) wisdom and then of retaining it. Unfortunately, many never obtain it, and sadly some who have had it have not retained it later. So, we should work to possess it, and we should be careful not to let it get away from us. Even a small amount of folly can undo one's wisdom: "Dead flies cause the oil of the perfumer to send forth an evil odor; so doth a little folly outweigh wisdom and honor" (Eccl. 10:1).

V. 19. Always is man urged to be like God. The same is true concerning wisdom. After all these instructions on wisdom, Solomon now points out that God Himself is guided by wisdom. Other passages showing that God employed wisdom in creating the universe and life upon it: "O Jehovah, how manifold are thy works! In wisdom hast thou made them all" (Psa. 104:24); Wisdom says, "When he established the heavens, I was there: When he set a circle upon the face of the deep, When he made the firm skies above, When the fountains of the deep became strong, When he gave to the sea its bound, That the waters should not transgress his commandment, When he marked out the foundations of the earth; Then I was by him, as a master workman" (Prov. 8:27-30); "He hath established the world by his wisdom, and by his understanding hath he stretch out the heavens" (Jer. 10:12). The marvels of creation continue to mystify the greatest minds in their depth and accuracy.

V. 20. The watering of the earth, so necessary to its vegetation and its support of both human and animal life, is here under consideration. Only God would know how to lay out and operate such a vast, continual system. There may be an illusion to the breaking up of the deep at the time of the Flood (Gen. 7:11); if so, it would still be saying that only God would know how to do such.

V. 21. Both statements mean the same: "them" is identified as "sound wisdom and discretion", and "let them not depart from thine eyes" is boiled down to the word "keep". It was the father's strong desire that his son would always keep his eyes upon the way of true wisdom both as a young man growing up and as a grown man. This good verse introduces material that runs through v. 26.

V. 22. The rewards of living by wisdom dominate this 6-verse section. This verse mentions two: "life" and "grace." "Life is used here in an all-inclusive sense of embracing more than lengthy existence a blessed and a spiritual life here. Other passages on an ornamented neck: "They shall be a chaplet of grace unto thy head, And chains about thy neck" (Prov. 1:9); "Bind them about thy neck" (Prov. 3:3); "Tie them about thy neck (Prov. 6:21). Prominent men wore golden chains around their necks: Belshazzar said, "Whosoever shall read this writing, and show me the interpretation thereof, shall be clothed with purple, and have a chain of gold about his neck, and shall be the third ruler in the kingdom" (Dan. 5:7); "Pharaoh took off his signet ring from his hand, and put it upon Joseph's hand, and arrayed him in vestures of fine linen, and put a gold chain about his neck" (Gen. 41:42).

V. 23. The promised rewards continue in this verse, this being a promise of safety and security. "As he who is accompanied by an escort proceeds on his way in safety, so you protected by God will pass your life in security; or, as Trapp, 'Thou shalt ever go under a double guard, 'the peace of God within thee (Phil. 4:7) and the 'power of God' without thee (I Pet. 1:5)'" ("Pulpit Commentary"). Prov. 10:9 speaks similarly:

"He that walketh uprightly walketh surely". Psa. 37:31 says, "The law of his God is in his heart; None of his steps shall slide." But contrast the ways of the wicked: Their way shall be unto them as slippery places in the darkness" (Jer. 23:12).

V. 24. One's safety and the resulting peace of mind are again stressed. Other passages on this peaceful condition: "I will give peace in the land, and ye shall lie down, and none shall make you afraid" (Lev. 26:6); "In peace will I both lay me down and sleep; For thou, Jehovah, alone makest me dwell in safety" (Psa. 4:8. Such lying down in peace and safety is employing the figure of sheep (Psa. 23:2). Words of a song: "Anywhere with Jesus I can safely go to sleep When the dark'ning shadows round about me creep."

V. 25. Again the blessing of safety, peace, and lack of fear is emphasized. "Sudden fear" would be that which strikes instantly, immediately, without advanced warning. Their world, even more than ours, was one of uncertainty: anything could happen at any time. Psa. 91:5,6 tunes us in on some of their uncertainties: "Thou shalt not be afraid for the terror by night, Nor for the arrow that flieth by day; Nor the pestilence that walketh in darkness, Nor for the destruction that wasteth at noonday." As Christians we can sing, "What have I to dread? What have I to fear? Leaning on the everlasting arms. I have blessed peace with my Lord so near; Leaning on the everlasting arms."

V. 26. Jehovah will be the One in whom the believer places his confidence--he commits his way unto Him (Psa. 37:5). All the great "heroes of faith" in Heb. 11 had this one thing in common: their faith, their confidence, was in God. One with true wisdom, such as is urged in the previous verse of this chapter, will include God in everything (vs. 5,6). If one is wise at all, wisdom will teach him not to trust in his own wisdom, strength, or perfection but in the guidance, help, and mercy of God. Can we not say that confidence in God is never misplaced, but confidence apart from Him is always a false confidence that in time will let us down? The promise of our verse: He will "keep thy foot from being taken" shows there are many traps and snares along the way that God will keep us from getting into. After saying, "My help cometh from Jehovah" (Psa. 121:2), the Psalmist goes onto emphasize the "Keeping" work of God: "Jehovah is thy keeper...Jehovah will keep thee from all evil; He will keep thy soul. Jehovah will keep thy going out and thy coming in From this time forth and for evermore" (Psa. 121:5-8). God's promise again: "A thousand shall fall at thy side, And ten thousand at thy right hand; But it shall not come nigh to thee" (Psa. 91:7).

TEST QUESTIONS OVER 3:12-16

1. Who is said in v. 13 to be the happy person?
2. Comment upon v. 14.
3. When did Solomon himself show that he placed the value of wisdom above everything else that he might have desired (v. 15)?
4. What does the mentioning of both hands in v. 16 signify?
5. Contrast the blessings of wisdom mentioned in v. 17 with the life of one who lacks wisdom.
6. What two thoughts are set forth by the two verbs in v. 18?
7. What is the purpose of switching from talking about the wisdom that human beings need to the wisdom that God employed in creating the universe (v. 19)?
8. What great work is mentioned in v. 20 that only God could do?
9. V. 21 introduces material that runs through what verse?
10. What all does the word "life" in v. 22 embrace?
11. What great promise is contained in v. 23?
12. What is again stressed in v. 24?
13. What would cause "sudden fear" (v. 25)?
14. What passage in Psa. emphasizes God's "keeping" work (v. 26)?

TEXT — 3:27-35

27. Withhold not good from them to whom it is due,
When it is in the power of thy hand to do it.
28. Say not unto thy neighbor, Go, and come again,
And to-morrow I will give;
When thou hast it by thee.
29. Devise not evil against thy neighbor,
Seeing he dwelleth securely by thee.
30. Strive not with a man without cause,
If he have done thee no harm.
31. Envy thou not the man of violence,
And choose none of his ways.

32. For the perverse is an abomination to Jehovah;
But his friendship is with the upright.
33. The curse of Jehovah is in the house of the wicked;
But he blesseth the habitation of the righteous.
34. Surely he scoffeth at the scoffers;
But he giveth grace unto the lowly.
35. The wise shall inherit glory;
But shame shall be the promotion of fools.

STUDY QUESTIONS OVER 3:27-35

1. Where did Jesus teach that to withhold good is actually evil (v. 27)?
2. Why would one put off to tomorrow giving help that he is able to give today (v. 28)?
3. Should a neighbor's security be one of our concerns (v. 29)?
4. Who especially needs the instruction found in v. 30?
5. What is listed in v. 31 as a possible cause of strife?
6. How are the violent of v. 31 described in v. 32?
7. According to v. 33 what does God do to those who are wicked?
8. Where in the New Testament is v. 34 quoted?
9. What do the wise have to look forward to (v. 35)?
10. What do fools have to look forward to (v. 35)?

PARAPHRASE OF 3:27-35

27-32. Don't withhold repayment of your debts. Don't say, "Some other time," if you can pay now. Don't plot against your neighbor; he is trusting you. Don't get into needless fights. Don't envy violent men. Don't copy their ways. For such men are an abomination to the Lord, but He gives His friendship to the godly.

33-35. The curse of God is on the wicked, but His blessing is on the upright. The Lord mocks at mockers, but helps the humble. The wise are promoted to honor, but fools are promoted to shame!

COMMENTS ON 3:27-35

V. 27. Beginning with this verse Solomon discusses our relationship with those about us. First of all, he says we should pay what we owe just as soon as we are able to do so. But this verse is not limiting the subject to paying debts: it is talking about doing "good" to those about us—a subject set forth in several important places in the Bible: "Do good"—Psa. 37:3; "As we have opportunity, let us work that which is good toward all men, and especially toward them that are of the household of faith"—Gal. 6:10; Jesus "went about doing good, and healing all that were oppressed of the devil"—Acts 10:38. To learn the E, G, B, D, F, A lines of the musical staff, elementary teachers have long used the significant statement: "Every Good Boy Does Fine Always"—and it is true! A careful study of Mark 3:4 and its surrounding verses will show that it was "lawful" to do good on the Jewish sabbath (to heal a sick man) but harmful (or evil) not to. Jesus had the power to heal him, and He affirmed it would have been wrong not to do so. Everyone needs a growing conviction that what God has given him is to be used wherever needed and not merely squandered for his own selfish wants.

V. 28. This instruction refers back to v. 27. How many times people in urgent need have gone to someone of means and ability for help only to be put off until "tomorrow" or "next week" when it was only the slightest matter that could have been taken care of easily that kept them from giving the help that very day. God tells us not to dally with duty! We have a saying that says, "Don't put off to tomorrow what you can do today."

V. 29. At the bottom of every case of trouble, there is someone who got things mixed up or who purposely did wrong to begin it. Here is a commandment against purposely, knowingly devising evil and trouble for someone else. We have sayings that remind us to drive carefully and to live carefully, for the life we save may be our own. This verse, though, appeals strictly to our feelings of responsibility for the other person: take care of your neighbor, for he dwells securely through your dealings. But don't forget that trouble can be a two-way street: there is a sense in which you dwell securely by him.

V. 30. If everybody heeded this, there could be no strife except that which might arise from some misunderstanding. Remember that it takes somebody to start trouble before there can be trouble. Some people who seem to live in a state of strife really need this instruction, for they are chief offenders.

V. 31. Other similar passages: "Fret not thyself because

of evil-doers, Neither be thou envious against them that work unrighteousness" (Psa. 37:1); "I was envious at the arrogant, When I saw the prosperity of the wicked" (Psa. 73:3); "Be not thou envious against evil men; Neither desire to be with them" (Prov. 24:1). It is too bad that so many choose wrong models to follow. In this verse the father continues to warn his son about joining in with a life of violence (See Prov. 1:10-19; Prov. 2:12-15).

V. 32. One who "devises evil" against his neighbor (v. 20), one who "strives" with a man who has done him no wrong (v. 30), one who "envies" the wicked (v. 30) is said in this verse to be "perverted"—he is doing what God never planned for a person to do. This verse tells of two contrasting classes of persons (the "perverse" and the "upright") and of God's contrasting attitudes toward them ("abomination" for the perverse and "friendship" with the upright). Passages on God's pleasure with the righteous: "The friendship of Jehovah is with them that fear him; And he will show them his covenant" (Psa. 25:14); "Ye are my friends, if ye do the things which I command you" (John 15:14); "The eyes of the Lord are upon the righteous, And his ears unto their supplication" (I Pet. 3:12). Passages on God's displeasure with the wicked: "Know ye not that the friendship of the world is enmity with God? Whosoever therefore would be a friend of the world maketh himself an enemy of God" (Jas. 4:4); "Alienated and enemies in your mind in your evil works" (Col. 1:21); "He that obeyeth not the Son shall not see life, but the wrath of God abideth on him" (John 3:36).

V. 33. Another verse contrasting God's treatment of the wicked and the righteous. The law that they were under had a long list of curses in Deut. 26:15-26 and a long list of blessings in Deut. 27:3-6. God can send blessings upon people, or He can bring curses upon them. The basis on which God gives to each is set forth in Deut. 11:26-28: "Behold, I set before you this day a blessing and a curse: the blessing, if ye shall hearken unto the commandments of Jehovah your God...and the curse, if ye shall not hearken unto the commandments of Jehovah your God." Psa. 37:22 says, "Such as are blessed of him shall inherit the land; And they that are cursed of him shall be cut off." One's relationship to God and His consequent attitude toward us is the main issue of life.

V. 34. A double contrast: "scoffeth" vs. "giveth" and "scoffers" vs. "the lowly". Scoffers are those who act as if they "know it all"; the lowly are those who recognize their deficiencies and who, as a result, trust" in God and do not lean to their "own understanding" but who "acknowledge Him" in all their ways (vs. 5,6). Jas. 4:6 refers to this verse ("He giveth more grace. Wherefore the scripture saith, God resisteth the proud, but giveth grace to the humble" as does I Pet. 5:5 ("God resisteth the proud, but giveth grace to the humble").

V. 35. A double contrast: "wise" vs. "fools" and "glory" vs. "shame." "The wise shall inherit glory"—what an inheritance to come into! Abraham was wise in following God's directions, and think of the glory he inherited as a result! Daniel was wise in his decision concerning the king's wine and dainties, and think of the glory he had before the book of Daniel closed! The Christian is the wise builder who builds his house upon the rock (Matt. 7:24-25), and the resulting Christian life is one of glory ("Ye rejoice greatly with joy unspeakable and full of glory"—I Pet. 1:8), and he will have his eternity in glory! On the other hand "shame shall be the promotion of fools"—what a "promotion" to get! We detect irony in the use of "promotion" here. The fool has nothing to look forward to but "shame". A fool lives a shameful life, and his eternity will be one of "shame and everlasting contempt" (Dan. 12:2). That which both the wise and the foolish come to will be because God will make it so!

TEST QUESTIONS OVER 3:27-35

1. Where else besides v. 27 does the Bible talk about doing good?
2. What is v. 28 condemning?
3. What reason is cited in v. 29 for not devising evil against one's neighbor?
4. Who especially needs the instruction in v. 30?
5. Whom does the father not want his son to envy (v. 31)?
6. Cite the double contrast in v. 32.
7. What chapter of the Old Testament contained lists of both blessings and curses (v. 33)?
8. What is the double contrast in v. 34?
9. How is the word "promotion" used in v. 35?

NOTICING THE NEEDS OF THE NEEDY

29:7 says, "The righteous considereth ('taketh knowledge of'—R.V.) the cause of the poor: but the wicked regardeth not to know it." There are those who have never known what real shortage is. They have always had plenty. It is hard for them to realize how "hard put" people can be and how helpless they are before such conditions. So they go their ways, not bothering themselves to look into people's conditions. But, 29:7 says the righteous look into their cases.

It is too easy for some people to be like the priest and the Levite, who did not want to be bothered with the needs of the needy. It takes time, it takes money, and it may even give one a headache to get next to the condition of the needy. No wonder, then, that is "the righteous" who considers the cause of the needy.

In the fast pace of present-day living, let us not permit sickness to go on in our communities, and we not know anything about it. Let us not permit death to strike, and we not be there to help. Let us not permit tragedies to happen, and we not concern ourselves.

DISCRETION IN SPEAKING

I marvel not that some people have trouble. Their customary way of speaking is loud, thoughtless, and rough. Unless one controls his speech, the other person will have a time controlling his temper.

Listen to this great memory verse: "A soft answer turneth away wrath: but grievous words stir up anger" (15:1). A "soft" answer is just the opposite of a "harsh" answer. Like the virtuous woman, "the law of kindness" should be in our mouths. Oh, the cutting things that people sometimes say to the man at the store! It may be a neighbor. It may be to some person in the church. And yet they claim to be Christians. There isn't much Christianity to a person who has an unbridled tongue.

All it takes sometimes to get into a real fight is to say the wrong word. Many times everything is all set for trouble, and if you do not guard your speech, you are going to stir up anger rather than turn it away.

CHAPTER 4

TEXT — 4:1-9

1. Hear my sons, the instruction of a father,
   And attend to know understanding:
2. For I give you good doctrine;
   Forsake ye not my law.
3. For I was a son unto my father,
   Tender and only beloved in the sight of my mother.
4. And he taught me, and said unto me:
   Let thy heart retain my words;
   Keep my commandments, and live;
5. Get wisdom, get understanding;
   Forget not, neither decline from the words of my mouth;
6. Forsake her not, and she will preserve thee;
   Love her, and she will keep thee.
7. Wisdom is the principal thing; therefore get wisdom;
   Yea, with all thy getting get understanding.
8. Exalt her, and she will promote thee;
   She will bring thee to honor, when thou dost embrace her.
9. She will give to thy head a chaplet of grace;
   A crown of beauty will she deliver to thee.

STUDY QUESTIONS OVER 4:1-9

1. Why the change from the usual "son" to "sons" in v. 1?
2. What does "doctrine" mean?
3. What does v. 3 show to be the way parents should feel concerning their children?
4. What kind of parent is described in v. 4?
5. How many times is "get" used in the book of Proverbs (v. 5)?
6. Reword v. 6.
7. Connect the thought of v. 7 with the author of Proverbs.
8. What will wisdom do for its possessor (v. 8)?
9. What was a chaplet (v. 9)?

PARAPHRASE OF 4:1-9

1-6. Young men, listen to me as you would to your fahter. Listen, and grow wise, for I speak the truth--don't turn away. For I, too, was once a man, tenderly loved by my mother as an only child, and the companion of my father. He told me never to forget his words. "If you follow them," he said, "you will have a long and happy life." "Learn to be wise," he said, "and develop good judgment and common sense! I cannot over-emphasize this point." Cling to wisdom--she will protect you. Love her--she will guard you.

7-9. Determination to be wise is the first step toward becoming wise! And with your wisdom, develop common sense and good judgment. If you exalt wisdom, she will exalt you. Hold her fast and she will lead you to great honor; she will place a beautiful crown upon your head.

COMMENTS ON 4:1-9

V. 1. Only three times in the entire book does the author address his material to his "sons" (plural) instead of to his "son" (singular): here; 5:7; 7:24. No reason is easily discernible for the change at this and the other places. "Hear" is used many times in Proverbs as are "instruction" and "understanding". Similar passages: "My son, hear the instruction of thy father" (Prov. 1:8); "Come, ye children, hearken unto me" (Psa. 34:11); "Fathers...nuture them in the chastening and admonition of the Lord" (Eph. 6:4).

V. 2. "Doctrine" means "teaching". The father is sure that his teaching is "good", for he has been over the road, has experienced much, has observed a lot, and has come to sound and studied conclusions, and he has the welfare of his children at heart. For the most part children normally accept their parents' teachings as good. Because what he was teaching was good, he insists that they not forsake his law.

V. 3. As Solomon instructs his own children, he recalls that he too was once a child, a son of his father David (who picked him to be his successor: I Kings 1:32-35) and tender and beloved in the sight of his mother (Bathsheba). Every grown-up should be able to look back upon his childhood days and feel this way about his parents. Our verse reminds us that those who are now fathers were once sons, and those who now teach were once taught.

V. 4. David took time to teach and prepare Solomon for the great task that was before him in life. Such a constant, several-years' task takes a father's time and attention, and it involves a recognition of divine responsibility and a desire to see one's son grow up to be what he ought to be. Fathers should be more than sires and material providers for their children: "Fathers...nuture them in the chastening and admonition of the Lord" (Eph. 6:4). The direct quotation begins in this verse, but it is debatable just where the quotation ends. Some say the quotation runs to the end of the chapter; some say through v. 9 (where the Hebrew paragraph ends). As a conjecture we would place the end quotation at the conclusion of v. 9. David urged Solomon to keep his teachings within his heart, and he assured him of "life" as a result. Prov. 7:1,2 is very similar: "My son, keep my words, And lay up my commandments with thee. Keep my commandments and live."

V. 5. "Get" is used many times in the book of Proverbs. In English we might make a play on words within this verse by saying, "Get wisdom and understanding and forget not what I am teaching you." Good parents are ambitious for what their children will grow out to become--actually more so than the children themselves at the time.

V. 6. That which we "love", we do not "forsake". Therefore, David called upon Solomon to love wisdom, "forsake her not", and his promise was that wisdom would "preserve" and "keep" him. Wisdom would keep him from evil, from evil men, from evil women, from mistakes, from sorrows and disappointments, and from a sad ending. And it will do the same for each of us today! The forgetting in v. 5 would be unintentional while the forsaking in this verse could be done while realizing what one was doing.

V. 7. With all of thy getting of various things in life, be sure to get wisdom, and this Solomon did (I Kings 4:29-34; I Kings 10:1-7). The New Testament would teach that the salvation of one's soul is the principal thing in life, but Proverbs, preceding the Christian age, makes wisdom the principal thing, and yet there need not be a clash, for wisdom--true wisdom--will cause one to be saved: the "wise" man builds his house upon the rock of Christ (Matt. 7:24,25); a knowledge of God's Word causes one to be "wise unto salvation" (II Tim. 3:15). But how does one go about getting wisdom? First of all it must be sought by prayer (Jas. 1:5; I Kings 3:5-12), and then man must constantly sit at the feet of the three great "teachers". They are: (1) instruction (learning by listening to what others would teach us--Prov. 9:9); (2)

observation (learning by keeping one's eyes open, learning from the experiences of others--Psa. 37:25; Prov. 24:30-34); and (3) experience--learning from your own experiences--Phil. 4:10-12).

V. 8. The son would "exalt" wisdom by making it his chief concern, and his love for wisdom is couched in the words, "When thou dost embrace her." If he would exalt wisdom, wisdom would exalt him just as if he turned his back on wisdom, wisdom would turn her back upon him (Prov. 1:24-31). Learning cannot be over-emphasized unless one learns the wrong thing (Col. 2:8), unless one fails to add the other essentials to character-development (II Pet. 1:5-7), and unless one becomes conceited over his knowledge (Rom. 12:16). "Knowledge is power; and it is truly astonishing to see what influence true learning has. Nothing is so universally respected" ("Clarke").

V. 9. Wisdom will (in time) give or deliver to one's head a chaplet (wreath or garland) of grace, a crown of beauty. Similar passages: Prov. 1:9; Prov. 3:22. These promotions and honors among men is the exalting referred to in v. 8.

TEST QUESTIONS OVER 4:1-9

1. How many times does the author of Proverbs address his material to "sons" (plural) instead of to "son" (singular) (v. 1)?
2. How does the father know that his teaching is "good" (v. 2)?
3. Who were Solomon's father and mother (v. 3)?
4. What did David take time to do with reference to his Solomon (v. 4)?
5. What word in v. 5 is used many times in Proverbs?
6. What are some of the things David realized that wisdom would keep Solomon from (v. 6)?
7. Does there have to be a clash between "salvation" and "wisdom" (v. 7)?
8. What are man's 3 great "teachers" (v. 7)?
9. What commandment concerning wisdom is found in v. 8?
10. When will wisdom deliver chaplets and crowns to one's head (v. 9)?

TEXT — 4:10-19

10. Hear, O my son, and receive my sayings;
And the years of thy life shall be many.

11. I have taught thee in the way of wisdom;
I have led thee in paths of uprightness.
12. When thou goest, thy steps shall not be straitened;
And if thou runnest, thou shalt not stumble.
13. Take fast hold of instruction; let her not go:
Keep her; for she is thy life.
14. Enter not into the path of the wicked,
And walk not in the way of evil men.
15. Avoid it, pass not by it;
Turn from it, and pass on.
16. For they sleep not, except they do evil;
And their sleep is taken away, unless they cause some to fall.
17. For they eat of the bread of wickedness,
And drink the wine of violence.
18. But the path of the righteous is as the dawning light,
That shineth more and more unto the perfect day.
19. The way of the wicked is as darkness:
They know not at what they stumble.

STUDY QUESTIONS OVER 4:10-19

1. Tie v. 10 in with the first commandment of the Ten Commandments that contains a promise.
2. What is the difference between "taught" and "led" in v. 11?
3. What does "straitened" mean (v. 12)?
4. What is the significance of taking "fast hold" of instruction (v. 13)?
5. What was the practical value of the Horatio Alger, Jr. books for boys years ago (v. 14)?
6. What 4 pointed instructions are given in v. 15?
7. According to v. 16 how perverse can some people get?
8. What is the "diet" of perverse people (v. 17)?
9. Comment upon "beautiful" in v. 18.
10. Living in sin is like walking in .... (v. 19).

PARAPHRASE OF 4:10-19

10. My son, listen to me and do as I say, and you will have a long, good life.

11-13. I would have you learn this great fact: that a life of doing right is the wisest life there is. If you live that kind of life, you'll not limp or stumble as you run. Carry out my instructions; don't forget them, for they will lead you to real living.

14-17. Don't do as the wicked do. Avoid their haunts--turn away, go somewhere else, for evil men don't sleep until they've done their evil deed for the day. They can't rest unless they cause someone to stumble and fall. They eat wickedness and violence!

18,19. But the good man walks along in the ever brightening light of God's favor; the dawn gives way to morning splendor, while the evil man gropes and stumbles in the dark.

COMMENTS ON 4:10-19

V. 10. If our conjecture is right, the direct quotation of David's words to Solomon ended with v. 9, in which case we return to this verse in Solomon's words to his son. Just as Solomon had received the "sayings" of his father and had passed some of them on in vs. 4-9, so now he calls upon his son to receive his sayings. While his son Rehoboam did not demonstrate wisdom in I Kings 12:13,14, he was probably wise as a rule. Honoring one's parents by listening to them and doing as they teach carry the promise of length of life: here and in Exo. 20:12; Eph. 6:1-3; Prov. 3:2. Wisdom itself can be the means of lengthening one's life just as folly can shorten it. The promise of God can of itself lengthen it just as disobedience to His will can nullify the promise. But so can sin enter into the length of one's life: "Vice and intemperance impair the health and shorten the days of the wicked; while true religion, sobriety, and temperance prolong them. The principal part of our diseases spring from indolence, intemperance, and disorderly passions. Religion excites to industry, promotes sober habits, destroys evil passions, and harmonizes the soul; and thus, by preventing many diseases, necessarily prolongs life" ("Clarke").

V. 11. As a father he had "taught" with words, and he had "led" with example, and unless the latter combines with the former, a father is wasting his words. The inspired Luke was as much interested in what Jesus did as he was in what He said (Acts 1:1). Paul both taught and set an example (Acts 20:20,35).

Our verse indicates that the wisdom contained in teaching leads to uprightness of living.

V. 12. "Straitened" means "limited". Following the wisdom of parental teaching will lead to a full and not a limited life; life will open itself to a wise person. He may be born in obscurity but become a well known person of renown. He may begin at the bottom and end up on top. "Runnest" would signify "going fast"; "stumble" would signify an "abrupt stopping of that progress". Wisdom would keep one from becoming broken and ruined at the height of progress. Psa. 18:36 is a similar verse: "Thou hast enlarged my steps under me, And my feet have not slipped."

V. 13. Do not dilly-dally about the matter of learning. Be in earnest about it. The wording of this verse shows how important instruction is. It is about like saying to a man overboard who cannot swim, "Take fast hold of the lifeline; let it not go; keep a tight hold on it, for it is thy life." How many of us fully grasp as we should the importance of learning?

V. 14. Neither begin ("enter not") nor continue ("walk not") in the way of the wicked. "Blessed is the man that walketh not in the counsel of the wicked" (Psa. 1:1). "My son, walk not thou in the way with them; Refrain thy foot from their path" (Prov. 1:15). "Clarke": "Never associate with those whose life is irregular or sinful; never accompany them in any of their acts of transgression." One will never walk the way of an evil man unless he enters their path; to do so is to prefer their way to God's way. The Horatio Alger, Jr. series of books for boys was good for sounding the same warning, and they were good reading matter for growing, developing minds.

V. 15. How can one keep from entering the wrong path? Know that it is wrong, and then "avoid" it--stay away from it, stay as far away from it as you can (like you would a rattlesnake den or a vicious dog). Adam and Eve walked with God as long as they did not go near the forbidden tree. The careful Joseph tried never to be with the wicked wife of Potipher (Gen. 39:10). Prov. 5:8 says, "Remove thy way from her, And come not nigh the door of her house."

V. 16. Some are so wicked that they live just as this verse says. Instead of living as a Christian ("To me to live is Christ"--Phil 1:21), to them to live is to "do evil" and to "cause some to fall" (others to join them in the sin-game). When an older Christian woman was asked about the two men she was caring for, she said, "All they do is sit in front of the television all day, smoke their cigarettes, and run down the church of Christ." What a way to live! They know not God, and they are not obedient to the gospel; therefore, they will be punished with everlasting destruction: "...the revelation of the Lord Jesus from heaven with the angels of his power in flaming fire, rendering vengeance to them that know not God, and to them that obey not the gospel of our Lord Jesus: who shall suffer punishment, even eternal destruction from the face of the Lord and from the glory of his might" (II Thess. 1:7-9).

V. 17. "Violence" is the only item in some people's "diet" of life--this is what they "eat" and "drink" everyday. With such perverted "appetites", they have no "hunger" for God and no "thirst" for righteousness.

V. 18. "But" is set in contrast with the foregoing verse. Besides the way the wicked life, there is also a "path" that the righteous follow. This good path is illuminated with the light of God. When we begin in that path, it is like beholding the first rays of dawn; as we follow, the day gets brighter and brighter, and we can see the righteousness of God's way more and more; in time this path will bring us to the "perfect day" (eternity with God). "This verse contains a fine metaphor; it refers to the sun rising above the horizon and the increasing twilight till its beams shine full upon the earth" ("Clarke").

V. 19. In this verse about the wicked we are back in "darkness". Living in sin is like walking in darkness in which one can stumble and fall to his hurt because he could not see what there was to trip over. Jer. 23:12 talks of the wicked walking in "slippery places in the darkness" (can you think of anything more "scary"?). Jesus urged men to walk in His light to avoid the darkness that would come upon them if they didn't; He also said that "he that walketh in the darkness knoweth not whither he goeth" (John 12:35).

TEST QUESTIONS OVER 4:10-19

1. What promise does honoring one's parents and their teachings carry (v. 10)?
2. How important is example in a parent (v. 11)?
3. Comment on "runnest" in v. 12.
4. What comparison did the comments on v. 13 make?

5. What double prohibition is laid down in v. 14?
6. What young man in Gen. was careful to avoid the way of evil (v. 15)?
7. What will happen to those who are evil and do not know God in their lives (v. 16)?
8. How do the wicked show their perverted "appetites" (v. 17)?
9. What is the "perfect day" to which we hope someday to arrive (v. 18)?
10. What did Jesus say about the wicked and "darkness" (v. 19)?

TEXT — 4:20-27

20. My son, attend to my words;
Incline thine ear unto my sayings.
21. Let them not depart from thine eyes;
Keep them in the midst of thy heart.
22. For they are life unto those that find them,
And health to all their flesh.
23. Keep thy heart with all diligence;
For out of it are the issues of life.
24. Put away from thee a wayward mouth, deceitful
And perverse lips put far from thee. devious
25. Let thine eyes look right on,
And let thine eyelids look straight before thee.
26. Make level the path of thy feet,
And let all thy ways be established.
27. Turn not to the right hand nor to the left:
Remove thy foot from evil.

STUDY QUESTIONS OVER 4:20-27

1. Why does the father go over the same thought so often (v. 20)?
2. What 2 parts of a person are spoken of in v. 21?
3. Is v. 22 speaking literally or figuratively?
4. Memorize v. 23.
5. Find the parallels in v. 24.
6. What is the meaning of v. 25?
7. In life what should one be interested in as brought out in v. 26?
8. How much deviation from the proper path is allowed (v. 27)?

PARAPHRASE OF 4:20-27

20-22. Listen, son of mine, to what I say. Listen carefully. Keep these thoughts ever in mind; let them penetrate deep within your heart: for they will mean real life for you, and radiant health.

23-27. Above all else, guard your affections. For they influence everything else in your life. Spurn the careless kiss of a prostitute. Stay far from her. Look straight ahead; don't even turn your head to look. Watch your step. Stick to the path and be safe. Don't side-track; pull back your foot from danger.

COMMENTS ON 4:20-27

V. 20. Oh, the earnestness of the father's instructions and entreaties as he thinks upon these matters!

V. 21. That Rehoboam would keep what his father was teaching him ever before his eyes and ever in his heart was so important that Solomon mentions it so often in this section of the book. Prov. 3:21 is similar: "My son, let them not depart from thine eyes; Keep sound wisdom and discretion."

V. 22. The great physical blessings of "life" and "health" are promised if the son will follow the father's good teachings throughout life. Several times is "life" promised on this basis: "Length of days, and long life...shall they add to thee" (Prov. 3:2); "Length of days is in her right hand" (Prov. 3:16); "Hear, O my son, and receive my sayings; and the years of thy life shall be many" (Prov. 4:10). Prov. 3:8 also promises "health" on this basis: "It shall be health to thy naval and marrow to thy bones."

V. 23. Here is one of the best known, most memorized verses in all of Proverbs. The reason is obvious: the outward words and deeds and course of life are but the manifestation of what is in one's heart. Other passages: "Out of the abundance of the heart the mouth speaketh. The good man out of his good treasure bringeth forth good things: and the evil man out of his evil treasure bringeth forth evil things" (Matt. 12:34,35); "The things which proceed out of the mouth come forth out of the heart...Out of the heart come forth evil thoughts, murders, adulteries, fornications, thefts, false witness, railings" (Matt. 15:18,19); "Let each man do as he hath purposed in his heart" (II Cor. &;7). The Pharisees kept the outside but neglected the inside. Jesus pointed out that if they cleaned the inside, the outside would automatically be all right: "Woe unto you, scribes and Pharisees, hypocrites! for ye make clean the outside of the cup and of the platter, but within they are full of extortion and excess. Thou blind Pharisee, cleanse first that which is within the cup and platter, that the outside of them may be clean also" (Matt. 23:25,26).

V. 24. A "wayward" person is one who has gone astray, so a "wayward" mouth is a mouth that speaks wrong things. "Perverse lips" is but a repetition of the same type of mouth. Wrong speech is so detrimental and out of place that our verse says it should be "put away", "put far" away! So, say nothing wrong--don't even come close. In other words, use nothing that is out-and-out wrong and not even that which is "shady". One will be judged by his speech: "Every idle word that men shall speak, they shall give account thereof in the day of judgment. For by thy words thou shalt be justified, and by thy words thou shalt be condemned" (Matt. 12:36,37).

V. 25. After urging the son's care of his "heart" in v. 23 and bidding him to put away "perverse lips" in v. 24, he now calls upon him to direct his "eyes" and not let them wander upon sights that would be detrimental. In the next 2 verses he will speak of his "feet". Especially when it comes to "women", this is such an important and right way to keep from lusting in one's heart (Matt. 5:28; II Pet. 2:14). Job said, "I made a covenant with mine eyes; How then should I look upon a virgin?" (Job 31:1). This is a covenant that every man needs to make with his eyes. Let his own wife be the "desire of" his "eyes" even as Ezekiel's wife was to his (Eze. 24:16,18).

V. 26. In everday life we try to keep from falling. Every irregularity in the sidewalk and every object in the pathway is a potential stumblingblock that could result in a fall. In life we should avoid everything that would cause us to stumble and fall; we should want our ways to be "established."

V. 27. Don't deviate from the right path in either way. We have to be careful of ditches on both sides of the road. One who is in the ditch is going nowhere. Other passages: "Ye shall observe to do therefore as Jehovah your God hat commanded you: ye shall not turn aside to the right hand or to the left" (Deut. 5:32); "Thou shalt hearken unto the commandments of Jehovah thy God...to observe them and do them, and shalt not turn aside from any of the words which I command you this day, to the right hand, or to the left" (Deut. 28:13,14); "Observe to do according to all the law...turn not from it to the right hand or to the left" (Josh. 1:7). In putting away pride, we must be careful not to become sloven; in putting away rashness, we should not become soft; etc.

TEST QUESTIONS OVER 4:20-27

1. Find the parallels in v. 20.
2. Rehoboam was to keep his father's instructions before his .... and in the midst of his .... (v. 21).
3. What 2 blessings of obedience are promised in v. 22?
4. What great fact of life is contained in v. 23?
5. How seriously important is one's speech (v. 24)?
6. What was Job's covenant with his eyes (v. 25)?
7. Comment on v. 26.
8. What do you get from turning not to the "right hand" nor to the "ieft" (v. 27)?

LAZINESS IS WASTEFULNESS

The Bible reveals waste to be a terrible thing. This is not a saying from the Bible, but it is surely true: "Wilful waste makes woeful want." We see that in the prodigal son. But, listen to what 18:9 says, "He also that is slothful in his work is brother to him that is a great waster." You can see how that would be: the waster destroys that which is produced while the slothful man fails to produce it in the first place.

There are those who are ambitious, but wasteful, and they think it is so terrible when people are lazy. On the other hand, there are those who talk about how wasteful some people are, but they themselves are too lazy to work. Proverbs says in the final analysis, both are brothers.

CHAPTER 5

TEXT — 5:1-14

1. My son, attend unto my wisdom;
Incline thine ear to my understanding:
2. That thou mayest preserve discretion,
And that thy lips may keep knowledge.
3. For the lips of a strange woman drop honey,
And her mouth is smoother than oil:
4. But in the end she is bitter as wormwood,
Sharp as a two-edged sword.
5. Her feet go down to death;
Her steps take hold on Sheol;
6. So that she findeth not the level path of life:
Her ways are unstable, and she knoweth it not.
7. Now therefore, my sons, hearken unto me,
And depart not from the words of my mouth.
8. Remove thy way far from her,
And come not nigh to the door of her house;
9. Lest thou give honor unto others,
And thy years unto the cruel;
10. Lest strangers be filled with thy strength,
And thy labors be in the house of an alien,
11. And thou mourn at thy latter end,
When thy flesh and thy body are consumed,
12. And say, How have I hated instruction,
And my heart despised reproof;
13. Neither have I obeyed the voice of my teachers,
Nor inclined mine ear to them that instructed me!
14. I was well-nigh in all evil
In the midst of the assembly and congregation.

STUDY QUESTIONS OVER 5:1-14

1. Why should a father teach his son (v. 1)?
2. How does v. 2 say wisdom will show up?
3. Comment on the 2 figures used in v. 3.
4. How is the "end" in v. 4 different from what we read in v. 3?
5. Where does the evil woman's way go (v. 5)?
6. What kind of person is this woman (v. 6)?
7. What is the purpose of v. 7 being where it is?
8. Why is the instruction in v. 8 so pertinent?
9. How deeply does such a person usually get involved (v. 9)?

10. How would strangers be filled with his strength (v. 10)?
11. What does such living often do to one's body (v. 11)?
12. Whose instructions had not been heeded (v. 12)?
13. People learn, but sometimes it is too .... (v. 13).
14. What is the meaning of v. 14?

PARAPHRASE OF 5:1-14

1-6. Listen to me, my son! I know what I am saying; listen! Watch yourself, lest you be indiscreet and betray some vital information. For the lips of a prostitute are as sweet as honey, and smooth flattery is her stock in trade. But afterwards only a bitter conscience is left to you, sharp as a double-edged sword. She leads you down to death and hell. For she does not know the path to life. She staggers down a crooked trail, and doesn't even realize where it leads.

7-14. Young men, listen to me, and never forget what I'm about to say: Run from her! Don't go near her house, lest you fall to her temptation and lose your honor, and give the remainder of your life to the cruel and merciless; lest strangers obtain your wealth, and you become a slave of foreigners. Lest afterwards you groan in anguish and in shame, when syphilis consumes your body, and you say, "Oh, if only I had listened! If only I had not demanded my own way! Oh, why wouldn't I take advice? Why was I so stupid? For now I must face public disgrace."

COMMENTS ON 5:1-14

V. 1. Life's experiences and learning bring to a father a degree of wisdom and understanding that he passes onto this children. Here is the same instruction found variously worded in Prov. 1:8; 2:1,2; 3:1; 3:21; 4:1,2; 4:10-13; 4:20,21; 6:20,21; 7:1-3; 7:24.

V. 2. "Discretion" is "good judgment in conduct and especially in speech". "Preserve" and "keep" are interchangable in the two statements of this verse. Great care should be exercised in our speech so that it always reflects discretion and knowledge.

V. 3. Several lengthy sections of the first chapters of Proverbs are given to warning against immorality. Immorality has proven to be one of people's greatest pitfalls. Psa. 55:21 also speaks of wicked people's "smooth" speech ("smooth as butter," "softer than oil"). False teachers also employ "smooth and fair speech" to succeed at their perverse ways (Rom. 16:17,18). The warning of our verse about this woman's "lips" and "mouth" may be relative to her flattering words (see Prov. 2:16; Prov. 6:24), or it may be relative to her kisses (Prov. 7:13).

V. 4. Sinners fall for the pleasure involved while wisdom (the father in this verse) sees the "end". The bitter end of such indulgence ("bitter as wormwood", "sharp as a two-edged sword") is to be contrasted with the "honey" and "oil" of v. 3. Solomon said, "I find more bitter than death the woman whose heart is snares and nets and whose hands are bands: whoso pleaseth God shall escape from her; but the sinner shall be taken by her" (Eccl. 7:26).

V. 5. A triple parallel: "her feet" and "her steps", "go down" and "take hold on", and "death" and "Sheol". Before we go with somebody, it is the part of wisdom to find where she is going. Sin always leads to death: "In the day that thou eatest these of thou shalt surely die" (Gen. 2:17); "They that practice such things are worthy of death" (Rom. 1:32); "As through one man sin entered the world, and death through sin; and so death passed unto all men, for that all have sinned" (Rom. 5:12); "the end of these things is death" (Rom. 6:23); "Sin and death" (Rom. 8:2); "Sin, when it is full grown, bringeth forth death" (Jas. 1:15). The body would come to "death" at which time the spirit would depart to "Sheol" (Hades). Prov. 7:27 says, "Her house is the way to Sheol, Going down to the chambers of death."

V. 6. Consider Prov. 4:26 in connection with this verse: "Make level the path of thy feet, And let all thy ways be established." Our verse says such a woman never knows this way: she is "unstable", undependable, and has nothing that she can hold onto. Man likes level ways to travel (they are so much easier than to be going up and going down hills), but such a woman knows nothing of the good road of life. And yet her kind has never neared extinction!

V. 7. Another return to "my sons" (plural) instead of the customary "my son" (singular). The plural is used 3 times in Proverbs: here, 4:1; 7:24. "Hearken to me," says the father and not to "her"! "Depart" from her but not from the "words of my mouth".

V. 8. The best way to keep from getting caught is to stay away from the trap. Quarantines are to keep people isolated from the problem. Eve said they were not even to "touch" the tree (Gen. 3:3). We are told to "come...out from among them", to be "separate", not even to "touch" the unclean thing (II Cor. 6:17). The pure Jospeh did not even want to be around the seductive Potipher's wife (Gen. 39:10).

V. 9. Fornication is seldom a one-time matter (unless one repents). Usually (like with alcohol) one gets involved for "years", and his good name ("honor") is sacrificed. Immorality is "cruel" in what it does to the guilty, to his mate, and to his family.

V. 10. Others will have the substance earned through strength and labor. Prov. 6:26 says, "On account of a harlot a man is brought to a piece of bread." The Prodigal Son had devoured his inheritance with harlots (Luke 15:13,30).

V. 11. God has seen fit to visit immorality with the plague of various social diseases (veneral diseases such as syphilis, gonorrhea, and lymphogranuloma). The father had forseen the mourning sure to come, but a young man might not consider it because of the sinful pleasure that precede it.

V. 12. A man suffering his last would have learned, but it would be too late to profit him. His father would probably be dead and gone by the time the prodigal wakened up to reality with a disease-ridden and ruined body, but his father's words would return to his mind with greater meaning. As he looks back, he sees that he actually "hated" and "despised" his father's instruction. Other instances of such: Prov. 1:25,29; Prov. 12:1.

V. 13. "Teachers" implies that others besides his father had tried to counsel him. Surely his mother would have been one of them ("Forsake not the law of thy mother"--Prov. 1:8). He had had good teachers (like many), but he was "smarter" than his teachers--he followed his own ways!

V. 14. "Such was my shamelessness that there was scarcely any wickedness which I did not commit, unrestrained even by the presence of the congregation and assembly. The fact which the ruined youth laments is the extent and audacity of his sins" ("Pulpit Commentary").

TEST QUESTIONS OVER 5:1-14

1. Where else in Proverbs is such instruction given (v. 1)?
2. What 2 words in v. 2 are interchangable in meaning?
3. Where else besides v. 3 does the Bible warn about

"smooth" talk put out by evil people?

4. What in v. 4 is different from something in v. 3?
5. Where else besides v. 5 does the Bible connect death with sin?
6. Comment upon v. 6.
7. The father bids his son to hearken to him instead of to .... (v. 7).
8. The father bids the son to forsake .... instead of his instruction (v. 7).
9. How is the best way to keep from getting caught in a trap (v. 8)?
10. Comment on "years" in v. 9.
11. Comment on "honor" in v. 9.
12. Comment on "cruel" in v. 9.
13. Who wasted his substance with harlots (v. 10)?
14. What divine outcry against immorality shows forth in v. 11?
15. What mistake did the son make as he reflected on his case (v. 12)?
16. Comment on "teachers" (plural) (v. 13).
17. What is v. 14 talking about?

TEXT — 5:15-23

15. Drink waters out of thine own cistern,
And running waters out of thine own well.
16. Should thy springs be dispersed abroad,
And streams of water in the streets?
17. Let them be for thyself alone,
And not for strangers with thee.
18. Let thy fountain be blessed;
And rejoice in the wife of thy youth.
19. As a loving hind and a pleasant roe,
Let her breasts satisfy thee at all times;
And be thou ravished always with her love.
20. For why shouldest thou, my son, be ravished with a strange woman,
And embrace the bosom of a foreigner?
21. For the ways of men are before the eyes of Jehovah;
And he maketh level all his paths.
22. His own inquities shall take the wicked,
And he shall be holden with the cords of his sin.

23. He shall die for lack of instruction;
And in the greatness of his folly he shall go astray.

STUDY QUESTIONS OVER 5:15-23

1. What does v. 15 mean?
2. What is the meaning of v. 16?
3. Is it all right for a man to share his wife with others (v. 17)?
4. V. 18 is a restatement of what previous verse?
5. What is a "hind", and what is a "roe" (v. 19)?
6. Why should one embrace the bosom of a foreigner and be ravished with a strange woman (v. 20)?
7. What does v. 21 mean?
8. How is the bondage of sin brought out in v. 22?
9. What is sin called in v. 23?

PARAPHRASE OF 5:15-23

15-21. Drink from your own well, my son--be faithful and true to your wife. Why should you beget children with women of the street? Why share your children with those outside your home? Let your manhood be a blessing, rejoice in the wife of your youth. Let her charms and tender embrace satisfy you. Let her love alone fill you with delight. Why delight yourself with prostitutes, embracing what isn't yours? For God is closely watching you, and He weighs carefully everything you do.

22,23. The wicked man is doomed by his own sins; they are ropes that catch and hold him. He shall die because he will not listen to the truth; he has let himself be led away into incredible folly.

COMMENTS ON 5:15-23

V. 15. Instead of carrying on immorally, he counsels his son to get married, have his own mate, and partake of his own well and cistern. This is what he will do in other fields of life. He will have his own garden--he will not steal out of his neighbor's garden. He will have his own flowers--he won't steal from his neighbor's flower garden. Heb. 13:4 says, "Let marriage be had in honor among all, and let the bed be undefiled"--that which is sin outside of marriage is innocent within the bounds of marriage--"for fornicators and adulterers God will judge"--those who carry on immorally apart from or outside of the marriage bounds.

V. 16. "The figurative language is still continued, and under the terms 'fountains' and 'rivers of waters' are to be understood children, the legitimate issue of lawful marriage...The meaning appears to be: 'Let thy marriage be blessed with many children, who may go abroad for the public good" ("Pulpit Commentary"). Psa. 127:3-5 pictures such: "Children are a heritage of Jehovah; And the fruit of the womb is his reward. As arrows in the hand of a mighty man, So are the children of youth. Happy is the man that hath his quiver full of them." And Psa. 128:3: "Thy wife shall be as a fruitful vine, In the innermost parts of thy house; Thy children like olive plants, Round about thy table." The question form of our verse shows that a man should not beget illegitimate children.

V. 17. Do not consent to living with a wife who is unfaithful. This verse puts the thought into commandment form: it says, "Don't share your mate with anybody else;" and observation confirms that it seldom works out to keep living with an unfaithful mate in the hope that everything will ultimately turn out all right. Mate-trading is not only forbidden by this, but it is inevitably the ruin of marraige.

V. 18. This carries the same thought as v. 15, only in more explicit language. God has created you so you have all the possibilities of love and enjoyment at home. Eccl. 9:9 says, "Live joyfully with the wife whom thou lovest." But people who lacked the character, conviction and conscience to behave themselves during their courtships often tire of one another during the years of marriage, and then the same lack of character and control causes them to become "grumpy" with each other and to seek immoral connections with others.

V. 19. "Pulpit Commentary" says, "The loving hind and pleasant roe...descriptive of the grace and fascinating charms of the young wife...She is to be the object of thy love and devotion, the one in whom thine affections are to find the fulfillment of their desires." The correctness of the above is brought out by the fact that the "hind" and the "roe" enter often into the erotic poetry of the East.

V. 20. Two great thoughts involved here: (1) Be ravished with your own wife; embrace your own sweet wife; who should be dearer to you than the one who is for you alone? (2) Don't be ravished by and don't embrace any other; it is wrong to do so; and the whole affair will let you down in time.

V. 21. Many passages show that no man, though he may try to slip around behind the back of his wife and carry on with some other woman, can conceal his deeds from God: "The eyes of Jehovah run to and fro throughout the whole earth" (II Cron. 16:9); "Doth not he see my ways?" (Job 31:4); "His eyes are upon the ways of a man, And he seeth all his goings" (Job 34:21); "The eyes of Jehovah are in every place, Keeping watch upon the evil and the good" (Prov. 15:3); "Mine eyes are upon all their ways; they are not hid from my face, neither is their iniquity concealed from mine eyes" (Jer. 16:17); "...whose eyes are open upon all the ways of the sons of men, to give every one according to his ways, and according to the fruit of his doings" (Jer. 32:19); "They consider not in their hearts that I remember all their wickedness; now have their own doings beset them about; they are before my face" (Hos. 7:2). For the statement, "he maketh level all his paths," the Margin seems to fit the context and sense better: He "weigheth carefully" all his paths.

V. 22. "Most people who follow unlawful pleasures think they can give them up whenever they please, but sin repeated becomes customary, custom soon engenders habit, and habit in the end assumes the form of necessity; the man becomes bound with his own cords and so is led captive by the devil at his will" ("Clarke"). Iniquity is like an outlaw who overpowers a person and then keeps him by chaining him. Christ came to release all such: "He hath sent me to proclaim release to the captives" (Luke 4:18).

V. 23. Not that he didn't have instruction but that he had instruction that he didn't heed, for in v. 12 he admitted, "How have I hated instruction, And my heart despised reproof; Neither have I obeyed the voice of my teachers, Nor inclined mine ear to them that instructed me!" Sin is here called "folly" (a "great" folly) that takes one out of the path ("astray") like a lost and wandering sheep and gets one off-course (like a wandering star for whom the blackness of darkness is reserved forever--Jude 13). Both God and decent people have always considered fornication and adultery a "great" sin.

TEST QUESTIONS OVER 5:15-23

1. Is it wrong for husband and wife to enjoy the affectionate life (v. 15)?
2. What does v. 16 forbid in question-form?
3. Does God say it is all right to continue living with an unfaithful mate (v. 17)?
4. What previous verse in this chapter is saying the same as v. 18?
5. In what other literature were "hind" and "roe" used as symbolic of the grace and fascinating charms of love (v. 19)?
6. What is forbidden in v. 20?
7. Cite some other passages besides v. 21 that tell of God's all-seeing eye.
8. What does v. 22 emphasize about sin?
9. Why is fornication called "folly" in v. 23?

POSSESSION OF HAPPINESS

A man's own success has much to do with his possession of happiness. Listen to three verses upon this subject: "A man shall be satisfied with good by the fruit of his mouth: and the recompense of a man's hands shall be rendered unto him" (12:14). When a person has said the right thing and has done the right thing, it brings him personal satisfaction, and he enjoys the reward of right doing. A second passage states it so well, when it says, "The desire accomplished is sweet to the soul" (13:19). When a person has launched out into a project and has accomplished it, how good it feels. To spend a day in carrying out well-laid-out plans is one of life's greatest joys, and for the most part, it is an everyday privilege. A third passage reads: "Hope deferred maketh the heart sick: but when the desire cometh, it is a tree of life" (13:12). When a person has planned for something and then finds that its realization cannot be at the time expected, it brings a letdown that is well described by the words, "maketh the heart sick." All of us have sometime known what it is to be sick of heart over a deferred hope. But, the passage says it is a tree of life to us when that desire is realized. So, our successes and failures have much to do with our happiness or our lack of it.

But, there are other things that enter in also. 15:30 says, "A good report maketh the bones fat," after it says, "The light of the eyes rejoiceth the heart." Similarly does 25:25 report, "As cold waters to a thirsty soul, so is good news from a far country, when one has been eagerly awaiting news, is just as exhilarating to his spirits.

Then, when one's spirit is bowed in sorrow, how good it is to have the comfort of another! 12:25 says, "Heaviness in the heart of man maketh it stoop: but a good work maketh it glad." And 16:24 says, "Pleasant words are as any honeycomb, sweet to the soul, and health to the bones." Such words, either uttered to us when our spirits need refreshment or uttered in the normal course of conversation, cast a spirit of cheerfulness about us which we all appreciate. Unpleasant words do quite the opposite.

A life of trust in God also brings happiness to a person. "He that handleth a matter wisely shall find good: and whoso trusteth in the Lord, happy is he" (16:20).

CHAPTER 6

TEXT — 6:1-11

1. My son, if thou art become surety for thy neighbor,
If thou hast striken thy hands for a stranger;
2. Thou art snared with the words of thy mouth,
Thou art taken with the words of thy mouth.
3. Do this now, my son, and deliver thyself,
Seeing thou art come into the hand of thy neighbor:
Go, humble thyself, and importune thy neighbor;
4. Give not sleep to thine eyes,
Nor slumber to thine eyelids;
5. Deliver thyself as a roe from the hand of the hunter,
And as a bird from the hand of the fowler.
6. Go to the ant, thou sluggard;
Consider her ways, and be wise:
7. Which having no chief,
Overseer, or ruler,
8. Provideth her bread in the summer,
And gathereth her food in the harvest.
9. How long wilt thou sleep, O sluggard?
When wilt thou arise out of thy sleep?
10. Yet a little sleep, a little slumber,
A little folding of the hands to sleep:
11. So shall thy poverty come as a robber,
And thy want as an armed man.

STUDY QUESTIONS OVER 6:1-11

1. What does it mean to "strike thy hands" (v. 1)?
2. What is the figure of being "snared" (v. 2)?
3. How does one "deliver" himself in this setting (v. 3)?
4. What does "importune" mean (v. 3)?
5. Give "no sleep" or give "not excessive sleep" to thy eyelids (v. 4)?
6. Who is a "fowler" (v. 5)?
7. For what is ant especially known (v. 6)?
8. Do ants have no leader (v. 7)?
9. Comment on the strange habits of ants (v. 8).
10. Is late-sleeping for healthy people encouraged in the Bible (v. 9)?
11. What word in v. 10 is emphatic?
12. Comment on the possessions of an armed man and a robber in the Bible days (v. 11).

PARAPHRASE OF 6:1-11

1-5. Son, if you endorse a note for someone you hardly know, guaranteeing his debt, you are in serious trouble. You may have trapped yourself by your agreement. Quick! Get out of it if you possibly can! Swallow your pride; don't let embarrassment stand in the way. Go and beg to have your name erased. Don't put it off. Do it now. Don't rest until you do. If you can get out of this trap you have saved yourself like a deer that escapes from a hunter, or a bird from the net.

6-11. Take a lesson from the ants, you lazy fellow. Learn from their ways and be wise! For though they have no king to make them work, yet they labor hard all summer, gathering food for the winter. But you--all you do is sleep. When will you wake up? "Let me sleep a little longer!" Sure, just a little more! And as you sleep, poverty creeps upon you like a robber and destroys you; want attacks you in full armor.

COMMENTS ON 6:1-11

V. 1. "Pulpit Commentary": "The sixth chapter embraces four distinct discourses, each of which is a warning. The subjects treated of are: (1) suretyship--vs. 1-5; (2) sloth--vs. 6-11; (3) malice--vs. 12-19; and (4) adultery--vs. 20 to the end." Our judgment would make "perverseness" the subject of vs. 12-19 instead of "malice". At first it would appear that the subject being treated in Chapter 5 and to which the author returns to in the last part of this chapter has been abruptly interrupted by these three non-related subjects. But "Pulpit Commentary" says, "The subject treated of in the preceding chapter is the happiness of the married life, and this is imperilled by incautious undertaking of suretyship, and suretyship, it is maintained induces sloth, while sloth leads to maliciousness. After treating of suretyship, sloth, and malice in succession, the teacher recurs to the former subject of his discourse, viz. impurity of life." "Clarke": "If thou pledge thyself in behalf of another, thou takest the burden off him, and placest it on thine own shoulders; and when he knows he has got one to stand between him and the demands of law and justice, he will feel little responsibility; his spirit of exertion will become crippled, and listlessness as to the event will be the consequences. His own character will suffer little; his property nothing, for his friend bears all the burden." Other passages on suretyship: Prov. 11:15; 17:18; 20:16; 22:26; 27:13. From studying all of these verses "Clarke" comes to this conclusion on "suretyship": "Give what thou canst; but, except in extreme cases, be surety for no man."

V. 2. "Striking hands" then was like signing a contract now. Sometimes one later sees his mistake of going surety for a party.

V. 3. "My son" here shows the earnestness of the father's entreaty. He was to go to the creditor and agree to some kind of settlement that would release him from any further or future obligation. "Do it now!" says the father, and v. 4 continues the urgency of doing it immediately--do it before you have to stand good for your friend's debt.

V. 4. Don't spend any time sleeping--not even one night--until you have cleared youself in the matter. This expression for doing something immediately is also used in Psa. 132:4,5: "I will not give sleep to mine eyes, Or slumber to mine eyelids; Until I find out a place for Jehovah."

V. 5. Continuing the figure of a "snare" raised in v. 2, he urges the son to take a lesson from the hunted roe or bird: they sense danger, they seek safety; they lose no time in doing so.

V. 6. Ants are well distributed and are everywhere known for ambitious activity. To speak of his sleep-loving son as a "sluggard" was not complementary (it means "lazy one"), but it was fitting. Solomon's use of animals ("roe" and "bird" in v. 5 and "ant" in this verse) is in keeping with Job 12:7: "Ask now the beasts, and they shall teach thee; And the birds of the heavens, and they shall tell thee."

V. 7. The ant is a fitting representative of true ambition, for an ant does not have to have a boss to make her work. And when did you ever see one that wasn't working? Remember Aesop's fable about the ant and the grasshopper?

V. 8. While some who live in cold climates where ants become dormant during winter have argued that Proverbs is in error here in its representation of the habit of the ant, "Tristrum" in "Pulpit Commentary" says, "Contrary to its habits in colder climates, the ant is not there dormant through the winter; and among the tamarisks of the Dead Sea it may be seen in January actively engaged in collecting the aphides and saccharine exudations...Two of the most common species of the Holy Land...are strictly seed-feeders and in summer lay up large stores of grain for winter use."

V. 9. The same words as v. 9,10 are found in Prov. 24:33,34. Again he refers to his son as a sleeping "sluggard". He is such a contrast to the industrious ant. "Early to bed, early to rise Makes a man healthy, wealthy, and wise" is an old saying not too well practiced by many modern youth who neither want to go to bed at night nor get up in the morning! Our verse is not arguing against a proper amount of sleep but against that over-sleeping that youth is sometimes guilty of (sleeping all morning if not called and made to get up). This is a good way to waste one's life and have little to show by way of accomplishment.

V. 10. The emphasis is on "little". Have you ever known an ambitionless young person to say, "Let me sleep a little longer;" or, "I'll get up in a little while"? But if left to him/her, the "little" becomes a "lot".

V. 11. A sluggard's poverty is also referred to in other passages: "He becometh poor that worketh with a slack hand" (Prov. 10:4); "The soul of the sluggard desireth, and hath nothing" (Prov. 13:4); "The sluggard will not plow by reason of the winter; Therefore he shall beg in harvest, and have nothing" (Prov. 20:4). A "robber" was always in need, and an armed man was a poorly-paid man (compare Luke 3:14). In other words, a little sleep, a little slumber, and a little folding of the hands lead to a lot of poverty! "The expression, 'thy poverty' and 'thy want', represent the destitution of the sluggard as flowing directly from his own habit of self-indulgence" ("Pulpit Commentary").

TEST QUESTIONS OVER 6:1-11

1. Is there really a change of subjects beginning in v. 1?
2. Striking hands then was like .... now (v. 2).
3. What does "my son" in v. 3 indicate?
4. How soon was the son to go to the creditor (v. 4)?
5. What 3 things do the roe and bird do when the hunter comes around (v. 5)?
6. What uncomplimentary name did the father call his sleeping son (v. 6)?
7. What fable of Aesop does v. 7 recall to one's mind?
8. What discussion has arisen over what v. 8 says about the habit of the ant?

9. What about many modern youth and late-morning sleeping (v. 9)?
10. Give a modern statement or 2 of modern-day sleepers using "little" (v. 10).
11. Does the Bible represent a sluggard as one likely to become rich or to have to live in poverty (v. 11)?

TEXT — 6:12-22

12. A worthless person, a man of iniquity,
Is he that walketh with a perverse mouth;
13. That winketh with his eyes, that speaketh with his feet,
That maketh signs with his fingers;
14. In whose heart is perverseness,
Who deviseth evil continually,
Who soweth discord.
15. Therefore shall his calamity come suddenly;
On a sudden shall he be broken, and that without remedy.
16. There are six things which Jehovah hateth;
Yea, seven are which are an abomination unto him:
17. Haughty eyes, a lying tongue,
And hands that shed innocent blood;
18. A heart that deviseth wicked purposes,
Feet that are swift in running to mischief,
19. A false witness that uttereth lies,
And he that soweth discord among brethren.
20. My son, keep the commandment of thy father,
And forsake not the law of thy mother:
21. Bind them continually upon thy heart;
Tie them about thy neck.
22. When thou walkest, it shall lead thee;
When thou sleepest, it shall watch over thee;
And when thou awakest, it shall talk with thee.

STUDY QUESTIONS OVER 6:12-22

1. "Worthless" is what sense (v. 12)?
2. Does v. 13 make winking a sin?
3. What is "discord" (v. 14)?
4. Where is the emphasis in v. 15?
5. Why not say "seven things" to begin with instead of the way v. 16 words it?

6. Comment on each item in v. 17.
7. Comment on each item in v. 18.
8. Comment on each item on v. 19.
9. What does "keep" mean in v. 20?
10. Comment on "bind" and "tie" as used in v. 21.
11. What within a person will do the 3 things mentioned in v. 22?

PARAPHRASE OF 6:12-22

12-15. Let me describe for you a worthless and a wicked man; first, he is a constant liar; he signals his true intentions to his friends with eyes and feet and finger. Next, his heart is full of rebellion. And he spends his time thinking of all the evil he can do, and stirring up discontent. But he will be destroyed suddenly, broken beyond hope of healing.

16-19. For there are six things which the Lord hates--no, seven: haughtiness, lying, murdering, plotting evil, eagerness to do wrong, a false witness, and sowing discord among brothers.

20-22. Young man, obey our father and your mother. Tie their instructions around your finger so you won't forget. Take to heart all of their advice. Every day and all night long their counsel will lead you and save you from harm; when you wake up in the morning, let their instructions guide you into the new day.

COMMENTS ON 6:12-22

V. 12. One with a perverse mouth is doubly described as a "man of iniquity" and a "worthless person". He is the former in that perverse speech is sinful; he is the latter in that he does neither God nor man good with his speech.

V. 13. One who gives you signals with his eyes, feet, and fingers to "speak" to some but to conceal what he is saying from others is a character to be on guard against. He too is described as being a "man of iniquity" and a "worthless person". Other references to this type of "winking": Psa. 35:19; Prov. 10:10.

V. 14. Such a "worthless", "iniquitious" man is further described as having a perverse heart, a heart that is continually devising some kind of evil (in this verse, "discord"). On Pentecost the apostles were all together with "one accord" (Acts

2:1)--unity, harmony. "Discord" is just the opposite. It can be "sown" among very dear friends by subtle-hearted person. Such takes time to grow, but in time it will produce such a crop. V. 19 also refers to sowing discord among brethren.

V. 15. He has plotted the downfall of others; he himself will meet his own destruction. The destruction is described in two ways: "suddenly" and "without remedy". Other passages on being ruined without any hope of remedy: II Chron. 36:16; Prov. 29:1; Jer. 19:11.

V. 16. God may love the world--the people (John 3:16), but there are things that He "hates". In fact, His hatred can run to holding things in "abomination" (detestable). Why the unusual construction here? Evidently not only to give emphatic position to sowing discord among brethren but to call particular attention to it.

V. 17. This verse shows that eyes, tongue, and hands can and do sin, and that God hates and holds in abomination sinful things done by them. "Haughty eyes" are also condemned in Psa. 18:27 and Psa. 101:5. A "lying tongue" is called a "deceitful tongue" in Psa. 120:2,3. "Pulpit Commentary" aptly observes, "Lying is the wilful perversion of truth, not only by speech but by any means whatever whereby a false impression is conveyed to the mind."

V. 18. Two more ways that one can displease God to the fullest: to have a heart that thinks up evil (evil intentions, evil plots against people, etc.) and to have feet that are quick to carry the above out. With so much evil in the world (I John 5:19)--all stemming, of course, from the devil--there are many such wicked hearts through which the devil works to cause it. Jer. 17:9 speaks of the heart being "corrupt". Prior to the Flood (and bringing it on) was the fact that "every imagination of the thoughts of his heart was only evil continually" (Gen. 6:5). The implication of John 2:23-25 is that what is "in man" is not good. On the last part of our verse Isa. 59:7 and Rom 3:15 say the same: "Their feet run to evil" and "Their feet are swift to shed blood".

V. 19. These two are "twins": bearing false witness and sowing discord among brethren. What an act (to utter lies about a person)! What an achievement (to divide good friends)! Jesus pronounces a blessing upon the "peacemaker" (Matt. 5:9), and this section shows the utter contempt that God has for the opposite of the peacemaker--the discord-sower. The 9th

Commandment (Exo. 20:16) forbade bearing false witness against one's neighbor, and yet is has often been done.

V. 20. The important instructions in v. 24-35 are introduced by vs. 20-23. Our verse is reminiscent of Prov. 1:8 ("My son, hear the instruction of thy father, And forsake not the law of thy mother") and parallel in instruction with Eph. 6:1 ("Children, obey your parents").

V. 21. "Bind" them and "tie" them would be to secure them in your heart and mind; don't let them get away. The "continually" would assure him of always having them to bless his life. Similarly does Prov. 3:3 say, "Bind them about thy neck; Write them upon the tablet of thy heart," and Prov. 7:3 says, "Bind them upon thy fingers; Write them upon the tablet of thy heart."

V. 22. Such binding and tying would cause the understanding imparted to him to do three things for him: (1) lead him when he walked; (2) watch over him when he slept; and (3) talk with him when he awoke. In other words one's childhood teachings should accompany him at all times to instruct him constantly as to what to do (compare Prov. 3:23,24; Prov. 2:11). Even when one is older in life, memory and conscience will combine to say to him, "Dad always told me such-and-such;" and, "I can still hear Mother say such-and-such."

TEST QUESTIONS OVER 6:12-22

1. Comment on the person with a perverse mouth (v. 12).
2. What kind of person is v. 13 describing?
3. What kind of heart sows discord (v. 14)?
4. How is such a person's downfall described in v. 15?
5. What does God not love (v. 16)?
6. What all does "lying" include (v. 17)?
7. What other verses of Scripture go along with what is said in v. 18?
8. What commandment would be violated by bearing false witness (v. 19)?
9. What previous verse in Proverbs is v. 20 like?
10. What is the significance of "bind" and "tie" in v. 21?
11. How long will some childhood teachings remain with a person (v. 22)?

TEXT — 6:23-35

23. For the commandment is a lamp; and the law is light;
And reproofs of instruction are the way of life:
24. To keep thee from the evil woman,
From the flattery of the foreigner's tongue.
25. Lust not after her beauty in thy heart;
Neither let her take thee with her eyelids.
26. For on account of a harlot a man is brought to a piece of bread;
And the adulteress hunteth for the precious life.
27. Can a man take fire in his bosom,
And his clothes be not burned?
28. Or can one walk upon hot coals,
And his feet not be scorched?
29. So he that goeth in to his neighbor's wife;
Whosoever toucheth her shall not be unpunished.
30. Men do not despise a thief, if he steal
To satisfy himself when he is hungry:
31. But if he be found, he shall restore sevenfold;
He shall give all the substance of his house.
32. He that committeth adultery with a woman is void of understanding:
He doeth it who would destroy his own soul.
33. Wounds and dishonor shall he get;
And his reproach shall not be wiped away.
34. For jealousy is the rage of a man;
And he will not spare in the day of vengeance.
35. He will not regard any ransom;
Neither will he rest content, though thou givest many gifts.

TEST QUESTION OVER 6:23-35

1. What is there about parental teachings that are like a lamp or light (v. 23)?
2. How many times (different sections) in Proverbs does the author warn of wicked women (v. 24)?
3. What is "lust" (v. 25)?
4. What does "precious life" in v. 26 mean?
5. What does v. 27 mean?
6. Does v. 28 teach the same as v. 27?

7. Has society been right in thinking that adultery is a terrible sin (v. 28)?
8. Does v. 30 condone stealing?
9. What did the law of Moses teach about restitution (v. 31)?
10. What reflects such a man's lack of understanding (v. 32)?
11. What about an adulterer's reputation (v. 33)?
12. Who is the angry man of v. 34?
13. Whose gifts will such a man refuse (v. 35)?

PARAPHRASE OF 6:23-35

23,24. For their advice is a beam of light directed into the dark corners of your mind to warn you of danger and to give you a good life. Their counsel will keep you far away from prostitutes with all their flatteries.

25-31. Don't lust for her beauty. Don't let her coyness seduce you. For a prostitute will bring a man to poverty, and an adulteress may cost him his very life. Can a man hold fire against his chest and not be burned? Can he walk on hot coals and not blister his feet? So it is with the man who commits adultery with another man's wife. He shall not go unpunished for this sin. Excuses might even be found for a thief, if he steals when he is starving! But even so, he is fined seven times as much as he stole, though it may mean selling everything in his house to pay it back.

32-35. But the man who commits adultery is an utter fool, for he destroys his own soul. Wounds and constant disgrace are his lot, for the woman's husband will be furious in his jealousy, and he will have no mercy on you in his day of vengeance. You won't be able to buy him off no matter what you offer.

COMMENTS ON 6:23-35

V. 23. The three statements of the verse are progressive: the commandment is a "lamp"; the law is "light"; and reproofs of instruction are the "way of life". The truth is always enlightening and shows the way to go: "The commandment of Jehovah is pure, enlightening the eyes" (Psa. 19:8); "The opening of thy words giveth light" (Psa. 119:130); "Thy word is a lamp unto my feet, And light unto my path" (Psa. 119:105); Jesus said, "I am the light of the world: he that followeth me shall not walk in the darkness, but shall have the light of life" (John 8:12).

V. 24. Oh, the importance of the young man growing up and not being taken in by the "evil woman" and her flattering tongue! Her "flattery" is warned against several times: "To deliver thee from the strange woman, Even from the foreigner that flattereth with her words" (Prov. 2:16); "The lips of a strange woman drop honey, And her mouth is smoother than oil" (Prov. 5:3); "That they may keep thee from the strange woman, From the foreigner that flattereth with her words" (Prov. 7:5).

V. 25. "Lust" in this passage is that burning desire for intimacies with her. It is that which gets into the "heart", and it reminds us of Jas. 1:14,15, which says that "a man is tempted, when he is drawn away by his own lust, and enticed. Then the lust, when it hath conceived, beareth sin." It was "lust" in Amnon's heart for his half-sister Tamar that caused him to do what he did (II Sam. 13:1-14). Because of this Job made a covenant with his "eyes" so that he would not think on a maid (Job 31:1). "Pulpit Commentary" says, "The admonition is a warning to repress the very first inclination to unchaste desires." To harbor such lustful, unchaste thoughts and feelings in one's heart is to be guilty of adultery-in-the-heart before God (Matt. 5:28). To create this lust in men's hearts there are women who both subtly and openly go out of their way to attract the attention of men. The wicked Jezebel "painted her eyes" in an attempt to buy Jehu off from his military designs about her and her family (II Kings 9:30).

V. 26. "From this verse onward to the end of the chapter the discourse consists of a series of arguments...exhibiting the evil consequences of such indulgence" ("Pulpit Commentary"). Many sinful habits have cost men a lot of money over the years (prostitution, gambling, drunkenness, smoking, etc.). Bible passages showing the financial outlay of immoral living: Prov. 29:3; Luke 15:13,30; Gen. 38:13-17. The evil consequences brought to mankind by a money-making harlot are of no concern to her (she "hunteth for the precious life").

V. 27. The answer is "no". Just as getting too close to a fire is inviting destruction by blaze, so getting involved with an immoral woman is a sure way to absolute ruin! This is a sin that no person can get away with. See v. 29 where the word "so" leads to the application of this question's answer.

V. 28. The answer again is "no", and v. 29 applies to this

verse just as it does to v. 27.

V. 29. One can no more commit adultery with his neighbor's wife and get away with it unpunished than one can take fire into his bosom and his clothes not be burned or walk upon hot coals and his feet not be scorched. Who will punish him? (1) her husband: "Jealousy is the rage of a man; and he will not spare in the day of vengeance. He will not regard any ransom; neither will he rest content, though thou givest many gifts" (Prov. 6:34,35); (2) society: "Wounds and dishonor shall he get; And his reproach shall not be wiped away" (Prov. 6:33); and (3) God: "They which do such things shall not inherit the kingdom of God" (Ga. 5:19-21).

V. 30. Even though a thief will be punished upon being caught (v. 31), yet men are somewhat understanding if he stole out of extreme hunger.

V. 31. But even then he will still be punished. The law of Moses required a fourfold restitution of stolen sheep and a fivefold restitution for stolen oxen (Exo. 22:1). Zacchaeus spoke of restoring fourfold (Luke 19:8). Possibly in Solomon's day they had increased the penalty to a sevenfold restitution. Actually one might lose everything he had making the restitution ("he shall give all the substance of his house"). V. 35 shows that the injured husband of the woman will not take any form of restitution for a man having taken her.

V. 32. Adultery is "an unwarrantable invasion of his neighbor's rights" ("Pulpit Commentary"). Other passages connect such action with a lack of understanding: Prov. 7:7; Prov. 9:4; Prov. 9:16. "Lust has displaced right reason" ("Pulpit Commentary"). God's displeasure with adultery is seen in His commanding the guilty parties to be put to death under the Old Testament (Lev. 20:10; Deut. 22:22) and in His condeming the same to everlasting destruction today (I Cor. 6:9-10; Rev. 22:15).

V. 33. "Wounds" may be those inflicted by the enraged husband as mentioned in v. 34; they may be referring to the wounds received by being stoned to death according to the law of Moses; or they may be associated with "dishonor" with which it is joined by "and". People will "talk" about such a person, and the guilty may deplore that fact, but it is right here in the Bible that those guilty of adultery get themselves a reproach, and that reproach will not cease. Even after a person is dead or has settled down to a proper behavior, people will still remember him as "the man who stole So-and-so's wife". God Himself was still talking about David's sin with Bathsheba in Matt. 1:6.

V. 34. The worst feelings of anger are kindled in the man whose wife has been taken by someone else. Because of this there have been vicious fist fights, knife-stabbings, and shootings.

V. 35. Nothing that the guilty man can do to try to make amends or to appease the man whose wife he took will work. We must face the fact that there is something about adultery that is different from any other sin that man can commit, and it's that way whether people like it or not!

TEST QUESTIONS OVER 6:23-35

1. Comment upon v. 23.
2. What does v. 24 warn the young man about?
3. What 2 things does v. 25 warn him about?
4. What does v. 26 warn him about?
5. What is the answer to vs. 27,28?
6. From what 3 sources can a man expect punishment for his adultery (v. 29)?
7. From vs. 30-35 show that society looks upon adultery as worse than stealing.
8. What 2 things does v. 32 affirm about the man who commits adultery?
9. Comment upon the truthfulness of v. 33.
10. Comment upon the truthfulness of vs. 34,35.

CHILDREN RECEIVE INSTRUCTION

"Hear, ye children, the instruction of a father, and attend to know understanding. For I give you good doctrine, forsake ye not my law" (4:1,2). A good father gives good doctrine—good teaching. His ways are right, and he is not going to misguide his child. 3:1 says "My son, forget not my law; but let thine heart keep my commandments." Remembering what they are told is just as important in the home as remembering what God has commanded us. People forget what God says and disobey; children forget what parents say and disobey. "I forgot," they say so often. They need to be taught to remember what they are told, and parents whose regulations are regularly kicked around with this "I forgot" business are weak parents, who are in the process of failing already with their children.

How important are parental instructions? Listen to 6:21: "Bind them continually upon thine heart, and tie them about thy neck." Listen again: "Bind them upon thy fingers, write them upon the table of thine heart" (7:3). "Bind" is a strong word. Children should "bind" their parents' teachings upon their hearts, fingers, and all to remind them of what they are to do.

But, there are some children who will not listen. "A fool despiseth his father's instruction: but he that regardeth reproof is prudent" (15:5). Children who will not listen usually shows them to be such. While a wise son maketh "a glad father, a foolish man despiseth his mother" (15:20). 13:1 tells of the way that a wise son will listen to his father's instruction, and that there are sons who scorn every rebuke given. Yes, there will be outside forces, outside influences, that will seek to tear down our children. That is why the Proverb writer said, "Cease, my son, to hear the instruction that causeth to err from the words of knowledge" (19:27). What a text! Such sons and daughters come to no good end.

CHAPTER 7

TEXT — 7:1-12

1. My son, keep my words,
And lay up my commandments with thee.
2. Keep my commandments and live;
And my law as the apple of thine eye.
3. Bind them upon thy fingers;
Write them upon the tablet of thy heart.
4. Say unto wisdom, Thou art my sister;
And call understanding thy kinswoman;
5. That they may keep thee from the strange woman,
From the foreigner that flattereth with her words.
6. For at the window of my house
I looked forth through my lattice;
7. And I beheld among the simple ones,
I discerned among the youths,
A young man void of understanding,
8. Passing through the street near her corner;
And he went the way to her house,
9. In the twilight, in the evening of the day,
In the middle of the night and in the darkness.
10. And, behold, there met him a woman
With the attire of a harlot, and wily of heart.
11. (She is clamorous and wilful;
Her feet abide not in her house:
12. Now she is in the streets, now in the broad places,
And lieth in wait at every corner.)

STUDY QUESTIONS OVER 7:1-12

1. Contrast the child who regards his parents' teachings with one who does not (v. 1).
2. What is the "apple" of the eye (v. 2)?
3. Why is "heart" used for "mind" so many times in the Bible (v. 3)?
4. Why are graces and virtures often misrepresented in sculpturing, art, and literature as women (v. 4)?
5. Yet v. 5 shows that women may be .... as well as virtuous.
6. Describe such a window of their times as is suggested in v. 6.
7. Are we all "simple" when young (v. 7)?

8. What verse in Proverbs says to stay completely away from her (v. 8)?
9. What does the Bible say about sinning and "darkness" (v. 9)?
10. Why is her heart described as "wily" (v. 10)?
11. Why is she also described as "clamorous" (v. 11)?
12. What were their "broad places" (v. 12)?

PARAPHRASE OF 7:1-12

1-5. Follow my advice, my son; always keep it in mind and stick to it. Obey me and live! Guard my words as your most precious possession. Write them down, and also keep them deep within your heart. Love wisdom like a sweetheart; make her a beloved member of your family. Let her hold you back from visiting a prostitute, from listening to her flattery.

6-12. I was looking out the window of my house one day, and saw a simple-minded lad, a young man lacking common sense, walking at twilight down the street to the house of this wayward girl, a prostitute. She approached him, saucy and pert, and dressed seductively. She was the brash, coarse type, seen often in the streets and markets, soliciting at every corner for men to be her lovers.

COMMENTS ON 7:1-12

V. 1. Before the father begins this lengthy warning against his son's getting involved with a wicked woman, he urges him to be obedient to what he is teaching him. Why does the father go over and over this warning in Proverbs? Because he is "training up" his son in the way that he should go the promise for which is, "He will not depart from it" (Prov. 22:6).

V. 2. The "apple" of the eye is the pupil of the eye ("Zondervan Pictorial Bible Dictionary"). To keep something "as the apple of thine eye" was a proverbial expression for anything particularly precious and liable to be injured unless guarded with scrupulous care" ("Pulpit Commentary"). The expression is used also in Deut. 32:10; Psa. 17:8; Zech. 2:8. What does one guard or keep any more than his eye? The father's promise was that if his son would keep his commandments as he would his eye, he would "live" and not be cut off from the living as a wicked person (Psa. 37:1,2).

V. 3. "Bind" means to "tie". The thought of his binding his father's instructions upon his fingers seems similiar to our talk of "tying a string on our finger" when we don't want to forget something. The heart is here spoken of as a "tablet", a writing surface. And indeed the heart is a place to lay up things precious and dear: Mary did so concerning many things said about her son Jesus and said by Him (Luke 2:19; Luke 2:51); we are told to write God's Word upon our hearts (Heb. 8:10; Psa. 119:11).

V. 4. Claim a close relationship with those women "Wisdom" and "Understanding", and such relationship will keep one from any relationship with the wicked, immoral woman about to be discussed (beginning in the next verse--v. 5). Note that the young man who got involved with her did not make "Understanding" his close relative, for v. 7 says he was "void of understanding". From antiquity many virtues have been portrayed in sculpturing, art, and literature as women. It does seem that many virtues can reach their highest pinnacle in womanhood or if lacking can be sacrificied the most my womanhood.

V. 5. "Keep my words," says the father in v. 1, "that they may keep thee from the strange woman" (this verse). "Pulpit Commentary" aptly observes: "When the heart is filled with the love of what is good, it is armed against the seductions of evil pleasure or whatever may entice the soul from God and duty." Prov. 2:16 and Prov. 6:24 also speak of being kept from the evil woman--she is someone to avoid!

V. 6. "To show the greatness of the danger presented by the seductions of the temptress, the writer introduces...an actual example of what had passed before his own eyes" ("Pulpit Commentary"). Latticework was used over windows and other areas by crossing laths over each other for privacy (so one could look out without being seen), to keep the welcome flow of breeze coming in while keeping the hot rays of the sun out, and for decorative purposes. It was through such that the father had looked out upon the sad spectacle that he mentions.

V. 7. "The 'simple' are the inexperienced, who are easily led astray" ("Pulpit Commentary"). Other passages connecting the "simple" and those "void of understanding" with immorality: "He that commiteth adultery with a woman is void of understanding" (Prov. 6:23); "Whoso is simple, let him turn in hither: As for him that is void of understanding, she saith to him, Come, eat ye of my bread, And drink of the wine which I have mingled. Leave off, ye simple ones, and live; And walk in the way of understanding" (Prov. 9:4-6); "Whoso is simple, let him turn in hither; And as for him that is void of understanding, she saith to him, Stolen waters are sweet" (Prov. 9:16,17). This verse shows that what one does is known and read by others.

V. 8. He wasn't aware of how dangerous it was to him to be found in her area. This verse sounds like he purposely went to her house with the idea of immorality, but the pressure she put on him (beginning in v. 13) does not bear this out.

V. 9. Wickedness seems to "come to life" when darkness begins to set in: "The eye also of the adulterer waiteth for the twilight, Saying, No eye shall see me" (Job 24:15); "They that are drunken are drunken in the night" (I Thess. 5:7). The devil's dens of iniquity are all open at night.

V. 10. "Her attire catches the eye at once and identifies her--compare Gen. 38:14. In Rev. 17:4 the harlot is arrayed in purple and scarlet and decked with gold and precious stones and pearls; and in the present case the female is dressed in some conspicuous garments, very different from the sober clothing of the pure and modest" ("Pulpit Commentary"). "Wily" means "subtle". She cannot be believed: her "lures" are in reality all "lies"!

V. 11. Prov. 9:13 also mentions her being "clamorous", meaning loud and boisterous--something that a good woman is not (I Pet. 3:4). This is why she is so forward. Being "wilful" means she is stubborn and disobedient. "Ungovernable...In Hos. 4:16...the same word is used of a wild heifer that will not submit its neck to the yoke" ("Lange"). She does not stay in the house, for she is out working her dirty trade.

V. 12. She knows no shame. She goes out where people are to snare men.

TEST QUESTIONS OVER 7:1-12

1. Why does the father go over and over this warning in Proverbs (v. 1)?
2. On what basis does the father promise "life" to his son in v. 2?
3. What expression do we have that sounds like v. 3?

4. Who made a "tablet" out of her heart (v. 3)?
5. What relationship should the son develop (v. 4)?
6. What relationship should he avoid (v. 4)?
7. Keeping his father's words should keep the son from .... (v. 5).
8. Why does the father introduce an actual example beginning in v. 6?
9. What other passages connect a lack of understanding with committing immoral acts (v. 7)?
10. Interpret the simple youth's being in her area (v. 8).
11. What about wickedness and night (v. 9)?
12. How did a harlot dress (v. 10)?
13. Comment on her being "wilful" (v. 11).
14. Why is she out in the streets and broad places (v. 12)?

TEXT — 7:13-27

13. So she caught him, and kissed him,
And with an impudent face she said unto him:
14. Sacrifices of peace-offerings are with me;
This day have I paid my vows.
15. Therefore came I forth to meet thee,
Diligently to seek thy face, and I have found thee.
16. I have spread my couch with carpets of tapestry,
With striped cloths of the yarn of Egypt.
17. I have perfumed my bed
With myrrh, aloes, and cinnamon.
18. Come, let us take our fill of love until the morning;
Let us solace ourselves with loves.
19. For the man is not at home;
He is gone a long journey:
20. He hath taken a bag of money with him;
He will come home at the full moon.
21. With her much fair speech she causeth him to yield,
With the flattering of her lips she forceth him along.
22. He goeth after her straightway,
As an ox goeth to the slaughter,
Or as one in fetters to the correction of the fool;
23. Till an arrow strike through his liver;
As a bird hasteth to the snare,
And knoweth not that it is for his life.
24. Now therefore, my sons, hearken unto me,

And attend to the words of my mouth.
25. Let not thy heart decline to her ways;
Go not astray in her paths.
26. For she hath cast down many wounded:
Yea, all her slain are a mighty host.
27. Her house is the way to Sheol,
Going down to the chambers of death.

STUDY QUESTIONS OVER 7:13-27

1. Why is face described as "impudent" (v. 13)?
2. What is v. 14's connection with the subject under consideration (v. 14)?
3. Was she really looking for him personally (v. 15)?
4. Why all of this (v. 16)?
5. Would we put cinnamon in our beds (v. 17)?
6. What young man in the Bible successfully resisted such talk (v. 18)?
7. Was she, then, a married woman (v. 19)?
8. Why tell him what she did in v. 20?
9. Does the fact that he did not give in easily indicate that he knew it was wrong (v. 21)?
10. Was this his view at the moment (v. 22)?
11. When would this have been (v. 23)?
12. Would the father's words help the young man resist such (v. 24)?
13. The act of sin is preceded by the .... to sin (v. 25).
14. Was he the first to fall for her talk and to suffer the consequences (v. 26)?
15. What does sin lead to (v. 27)?

PARAPHRASE OF 7:13-27

13-20. She put her arms around him and kissed him, and with a saucy look she said, "I've decided to forget our quarrel! I was just coming to look for you and here you are! My bed is spread with lovely, colored sheets of finest linen imported from Egypt, perfumed with myrrh, aloes and cinnamon. Come on, let's take our fill of love until morning, for my husband is away on a long trip. He has taken a wallet full of money with him, and won't return for several days."

21-23. So she seduced him with her pretty speech, her

coaxing and her wheedling, until he yielded to her. He couldn't resist her flattery. He followed her as an ox going to the butcher, or as a stag that is trapped, waiting to be killed with an arrow through its heart. He was as a bird flying into a snare, not knowing the fate awaiting it there.

24-27. Listen to me, young men, and not only listen but obey. Don't let your desires get out of hand; don't let yourself think about her; don't go near her; stay away from where she walks, lest she tempt you and seduce you. For she has been the ruin of multitudes--a vast host of men have been her victims. If you want to find the road to hell, look for her house.

COMMENTS ON 7:13-27

V. 13. Very reminiscent of Potiphar's wife: "She caught him by his garment saying, Lie with me" (Gen. 39:12). On "impudent face" the Hebrew indicates that "she strengthened her countenance, assumed the most confident look she could, endeavored to appear friendly and sincere" ("Clarke").

V. 14. When one had made a peace-offering to God, he (she) was allowed to take of portion of the meat home (Lev. 3:1-5). She was planning a delicious meal (a banquet for two) to which she invites the young man. "The religious nature of the feast is utterly ignored or forgotten. The shameless woman uses the opportunity simply as a convenience for her sin ("Pulpit Commentary").

V. 15. Here is an instance of "flattery" that is so characteristic of her and which is warned against several times: "That flattereth with her words" (Prov. 2:16); "To keep thee from the evil woman, From the flattery" (6:24). Notice that "flattery" is always connected with the early part of each instance--with the alluring phase of her operation.

V. 16. Wicked women have employed every means involving beauty, fragrance, etc., beautifying themselves, their clothing, and their quarters to entice men. Bait for the trap!

V. 17. And here comes the fragrance!

V. 18. All of this is to get him to "come". Dealing with the Hebrew, "Clarke" says, "Let us revel in the breasts," for the first statement; for the second: "Let us gratify each other with loves, with the utmost delights." And then he remarks: "This does not half express the original, but I forbear...The original itself is too gross to be literally translated, but quite in character as coming from the mouth of an abandoned woman."

V. 19. She takes care of any fear that he might have of her "husband". The young man would realize that "Jealousy is the rage of a man; And he will not spare in the day of vengeance. He will not regard any ransom; Neither will he rest content though thou givest many gifts" (Prov. 6:34,35). But she begins assuring him that her husband will know nothing about the matter: he is "not at home"; he has gone on a "long journey".

V. 20. The assurances continue: he has plenty of "money" with him for his long trip (probably a merchandising trip); he will not be home again until the "full moon". Sinners always have everything taken care of, they think, but have you not noticed that they still get caught every so often? The trouble is, they think no further than not getting caught by people. But all the while God is watching and on judgment will open the book of each person's life and judge him (or her) out of those books according to one's works (Rev. 20:12).

V. 21. What about her flattery of him? What about her tapestried couch? What about her perfumed bed? What about her assurances that it was safe? All this caused him to "yield". "The lips of a strange woman drop honey, And her mouth is smoother than oil" (Prov. 5:3). The young man evidently didn't give in easily, knowing it would be wrong. But how many times temptation wins over knowledge! "Clarke" observes, "With her blandishments and lascivious talk, she overcame all his scruples and constrained him to yield." This would appear to be the first time he had yielded to this temptation--but it would it be the last time? But he isn't the only one: "She hath cast down many wounded" (v. 26).

V. 22. Once a person has given in inwardly, there is nothing to keep him from proceeding to the evil act itself: "He goeth after her straightway". But how does he go? He sees himself as one on the verge of satisfying his curiosity concerning what happens in sex, of one who is about to experience life's greatest thrill in an exciting setting. The pleasure, not the punishment, of sin is uppermost in his mind at the moment. But in reality he is going as an "ox goeth to the slaughter" ("Her house inclineth unto death, And her paths unto the dead" (Prov. 2:18); "Her mouth is smoother than oil: But in the end she is bitter as wormwood, Sharp as a two-edged sword. Her feet go down to death; Her steps take hold on Sheol" (Prov. 5:3-5); "He knoweth not that the dead are there; That her guests are in the depths of Sheol" (Prov. 9:18). Our verse also indicates that he is in for a "beating", for he goes after her "as one in fetters to the correction of the fool".

V. 23. Other figures of suffering and death continue: an arrow through the liver, a bird caught in a trap. With all the promises that sin makes and with what actually follows, no wonder Heb. 3:13 speaks of the "deceitfulness" of sin, and the devil (who is behind every temptation) is proven to be the "liar" that Jesus said he was (John 8:44). The mess he is getting his life into, the shame that he will bear in honorable society, the trouble he will involve himself in with sinned-against husbands throughout the years, the danger he will bring to the stability of his own house, the disease he will encounter in his own body, the early death he will bring upon himself, and the eternal Hell in which he will suffer forever and ever are the real outcomes of such sin.

V. 24. Here Solomon speaks to all of his "sons". He wants all of them to listen to the urgent appeal he is about to make in the succeeding verses.

V. 25. Keep this type of thinking out of your "heart", and then you will not "go" after her. If you let your heart, it will decline to her ways and go in her paths. Only the strong teaching of parents can save young men from getting involved with such a woman sometime in life. Note the words "decline" (down) and "astray" (lost); to go that way is to go down and to lose one's way in life.

V. 26. One woman, but she has ruined many men; her slain are a mighty host; "The harlot...as a ruthless conqueror leaves a field of battle strewn with corpses" ("Pulpit Commentary"). If you do not realize the power that women can have over men, think of how this very thing overcame the strong man Samson (Judg. 16:1), how it was a pitfall for the great David on one occasion (II Sam. 11:2-4), and what Neh. 13:26 says about Solomon: "Did not Solomon king of Israel sin by these things? yet among many nations was there no king like him, and he was beloved of his God, and God made him king over all Israel: nevertheless even him did foreign women cause to sin." The author took nothing for granted as he warned his sons, and today "let him that thinketh he standeth take heed lest he fall" (I Cor. 10:12). So keep your eyes where they belong; keep your hands to yourself; don't flirt; don't think upon women; don't read about romance; don't be entertained by it.

V. 27. In deep-shaft coal mines there is a house built over the elevator. When one enters that house and gets on the elevator, it goes only one direction--down. And that's the way it is when one goes to the harlot's house. Other passages on this fact: Prov. 2:18; Prov. 5:5; Prov. 9:18.

TEST QUESTIONS OVER 7:13-27

1. What shows the unfeminine forwardness of this woman (v. 13)?
2. Was her religion helping her conduct (v. 14)?
3. In this instance what won out over knowledge (v. 14)?
4. V. 15 is an instance of .... warned against several times.
5. What "bait" does she throw at out in v. 16?
6. What "bait" in v. 17?
7. What does "Clarke" say about the Hebrew wording of v. 18?
8. What fear of his does she seek to allay in v. 19?
9. What additional assurance does she give in v. 20?
10. Did the young man survive her talk (v. 21)?
11. Was this probably his first time to be led into this sin (v. 21)?
12. Would it probably be his last (v. 21)?
13. Before he gave in outwardly, where did he give in (v. 22)?
14. What was uppermost in his mind at his moment of yielding (v. 22)?
15. His going after her is likened to what in v. 22?
16. To what in v. 23?
17. What word shows up in the plural in v. 24?
18. Comment on the words "decline" and "astray" in v. 25.
19. One woman, but .... victims (v. 26).
20. Who were some men who fell before this sin (v. 26)?
21. Her house is the way to .... (v. 27).

TEXT — 8:1-11

1. Doth not wisdom cry,
And understanding put forth her voice?
2. On the top of high places by the way,
Where the paths meet, she standeth;
3. Beside the gates, at the entry of the city,
At the coming in at the doors, she crieth aloud:
4. Unto you, O men, I call:
And my voice is to the sons of men.
5. O ye simple, understand prudence;
And, ye fools, be of an understanding heart.
6. Hear, for I will speak excellent things;
And the opening of my lips shall be right things.
7. For my mouth shall utter truth;
And wickedness is an abomination to my lips.
8. All the words of my mouth are in righteousness;
There is nothing crooked or perverse in them.
9. They are all plain to him that understandeth,
And right to them that find knowledge.
10. Receive my instruction, and not silver;
And knowledge rather than choice gold.
11. For wisdom is better than rubies;
And all the things that may be desired are not to be compared unto it.

STUDY QUESTIONS OVER 8:1-11

1. What is the relationship between wisdom and understanding (v. 1)?
2. What is meant by "high places" here (v. 2)?
3. How does wisdom "cry" in these high places (v. 3)?
4. Why do men need great wisdom and understanding (v. 4)?
5. Would having an understanding heart raise these from being simpletons and fools (v. 5)?
6. Is true wisdom ever wrong (v. 6)?
7. Does wisdom ever compromise with wickedness (v. 7)?
8. How would a student of logic designate the two statements in v. 8?
9. Are some things plain to one person that are not to others (v. 9)?

10. In what other passages is wisdom valued greater than earthly treasures (v. 10)?
11. How were rubies used in those days (v. 11)?

PARAPHRASE OF 8:1-11

1-11. Can't you hear the voice of wisdom? She is standing at the city gates and at every fork in the road, and at the door of every house. Listen to what she says: "Listen, men!" she calls. "How foolish and naive you are! Let me give you understanding. O foolish ones, let me show you common sense! Listen to me! For I have important information for you. Everything I say is right and true, for I hate lies and every kind of deception. My advice is wholesome and good. There is nothing of evil in it. My words are plain and clear to anyone with half a mind--if it is only open! My instruction is far more valuable than silver or gold." For the value of wisdom is far above rubies; nothing can be compared with it.

COMMENTS ON 8:1-11

V. 1. Wisdom is again personified and is again feminine. Here is Hebrew parallelism in which the second line is a restatement of the first: "wisdom" and "knowledge" go together as do "cry" and "put forth her voice". This section is very similar to Prov. 1:20-22: "Wisdom crieth aloud in the street; She uttereth her voice in the broad places; She crieth in the chief place of concourse; At the entrance of the gates, In the city, she uttereth her words: How long, ye simple ones, will ye love simplicity? And scoffers delight them in scoffing, And fools hate knowledge?" In 1:20,21 the material is set forth in the declarative mood while 8:1 introduces the material with the interrogative mood. "The interrogative form, which expects an affirmative answer, is a mode of asserting a truth" ("Pulpit Commentary"). However, it is just the opposite in 1:22 and 8:5--Chapter 1 being interrogative and Chapter 8 exclamatory.

V. 2. "She takes her stand...in the most open and elevated parts of the city where she may be best seen and heard by all who pass by...where many paths converge, and where people meet from different quarters" ("Pulpit Commentary").

V. 3. By lifting up her voice in the gates and doors to the city, she would be heard by all who were coming in and by all who were going out. It would be for the great who entered and for the lowly who entered. Nor does wisdom speak feebly--she crieth aloud! Most people know what is right and wrong, what is wise and foolish, what should and shouldn't be done. How thankful we should be that wisdom is that prominent!

V. 4. Wisdom and understanding were being spoken about in v. 1-3; now they themselves begin to speak, and their direct quotation runs from this verse through v. 10.

V. 5. More parallelism: "ye simple" and "ye fools" go together, and "understand prudence" and "be of an understanding heart" are parallels. The simple are "those not yet perverted but easily influenced for good or evil". This is where each peson begins. If people do not acquire wisdom later on, then they are considered "fools". The interjection form (introduced by "O") shows the urgency of being directed in the right way. "Webster" says of "prudence": "Ability to regulate and discipline oneself through the exercise of the reason."

V. 6. Wisdom also claims to have imparted "excellent" things in Prov. 22:20: "Have I not written unto thee excellent things of counsels and knowledge?" Wisdom is never wrong but always "right". Those who would "excel" must always exalt wisdom.

V. 7. And "truth" is tied in with wisdom and excellence and righteousness. Wisdom always speaks the truth because wickedness (lying, deceit, etc.) is not only foreign to wisdom but is actually abominable to it. Oh, that each of us might be so wise that wickedness is abominable to our lips! Remember this when you find yourself involved in some church-trouble.

V. 8. Yes, and here comes "righteousness" to go along with or be a stronger expression of the "right things" of v. 6. And it is set over against or in contrast to "wickedness" in v. 7. The "all are" of the first statement is what logic calls a "universal positive", and the "nothing is" of the second statement is called a "universal negative". Both of these statements are "absolutes", showing that everything about wisdom is righteous, and nothing about it is wicked.

V. 9. While wisdom may be "too high for a fool" (Prov. 24:7), it is certainly obtainable to one who wishes to see and understand. Our verse describes the type of person we should all be: one who understands because he has been looking for knowledge. To all such, wisdom is "plain", clear, not difficult.

V. 10. With this verse closes the statement by wisdom and understanding that began in v. 4. More parallelism in this verse (find it). The opportunity to learn through "instruction" might be said to be a "silver" opportunity while the actual acquisition of "knowledge" through that instruction may be said to be a "golden" possession. Notice that a knowledge of the true and the right is here said to be a higher goal and a greater possession than wealth.

V. 11. The author of Proverbs here comments on the truthfulness of what wisdom and understanding affirmed in v. 10. He says the possession of wisdom is greater than possessing rubies--or anything else! Similar statements of such evaluation of wisdom: "How much better it is to get wisdom than gold! Yea, to get understanding is rather to be chosen than silver" (Prov. 16:16); "The gaining of it is better than the gaining of silver, And the profit thereof than fine gold. She is more precious than rubies: And none of the things thou canst desire are to be compared unto her" (Prov. 3:14,15); "Wisdom is the principal thing; therefore get wisdom; Yea, with all thy getting get understanding" (Prov. 4:7). As valuable as wisdom is, it is not something that can be acquired by money (like some commodity): "It cannot be gotten for gold, Neither shall silver be weighed for the price thereof" (Job 28:15). Euclid of Alexandria was right of long ago. Called the "father of Geometry", when his "king asked if there were not an easier way to learn geometry than by the study of the 'Elements' (Euclid's set of books), Euclid answered, 'There is no royal road to geometry' ("World Book Encyclopedia").

TEST QUESTIONS OVER 8:1-11

1. These first verses are very similar to what earlier section in Proverbs?
2. Comment on v. 2.
3. By whom would wisdom and understanding be heard, according to v. 3?
4. What begins in v. 4?
5. Comment on "ye simple" (v. 5).
6. Comment on "ye fools" (v. 5).
7. Can you find a quartet of qualities in vs. 6-8 that go together?
8. Comment upon those 4 qualities in their desirableness in

our lives.

9. Contrast v. 9 with Prov. 24:7.
10. What great comparative value is placed upon wisdom and understanding in vs. 10,11, both by their own statement and by the writer's comment?

TEXT – 8:12-21

12. I wisdom have made prudence my dwelling,
And find out knowledge and discretion.
13. The fear of Jehovah is to hate evil:
Pride, and arrogancy, and the evil way,
And the perverse mouth, do I hate.
14. Counsel is mine, and sound knowledge:
I am understanding; I have might.
15. By me kings reign,
And princes decree justice.
16. By me princes rule,
And nobles, even all the judges of the earth.
17. I love them that love me;
And those that seek me diligently shall find me.
18. Riches and honor are with me;
Yea, durable wealth and righteousness.
19. My fruit is better than gold, yea, than fine gold;
And my revenue than choice silver.
20. I walk in the way of righteousness,
In the midst of the paths of justice;
21. That I may cause those that love me to inherit substance,
And that I may fill their treasuries.

STUDY QUESTIONS OVER 8:12-21

1. Whom did Paul say should be discreet (v. 12)?
2. What other passages show God to have likes and dislikes (v. 13)?
3. Show that understanding is power (v. 14).
4. Do people accept leadership whose wisdom they do not respect (v. 15)?
5. Does v. 16 mean there has never been a noble or judge who was not wise?
6. What is the adverb modifying "seek" in v. 17?
7. What are the parallel words within v. 18?

8. How did "gold", "fine gold," and "choice silver" sound to the ancients (v. 19)?
9. Is there any difference between "righteousness" and "justice" (v. 20)?
10. Cite an example in your own community of one to whom wisdom brought wealth (v. 21).

PARAPHRASE OF 8:12-21

12,13. Wisdom and good judgment live together, for wisdom knows where to discover knowledge and understanding. If anyone respects and fears God, he will hate evil. For wisdom hates pride, arrogance, corruption and deceit of every kind.

14-21. "I, Wisdom, give good advice and common sense. Because of my strength, kings reign in power. I show the judge who is right and who is wrong. Rulers rule well with my help. I love all who love me. Those who search for me shall surely find me. Unending riches, honor, justice and righteousness are mine to distribute. My gifts are better than the purest gold or sterling silver! My paths are those of justice and right. Those who love and follow me are indeed wealthy. I fill their treasuries.

COMMENTS ON 8:12-21

V. 12. Again personified wisdom speaks after a one-verse break. Its personification is carried a step farther by speaking of her as "dwelling" in prudence. Her quest for "knowledge" and "discretion" are successful.

V. 13. One hates evil who fears Jehovah because he views evil from God's viewpoint: he knows how wrong it is, how contrary to God, and what it will result in. Prov. 16:6 says, "By the fear of Jehovah men depart from evil." That God hates "pride and arrogancy", Prov. 6:16,17 says, "There are six things which Jehovah hateth; Yea, seven which are an abomination unto him: Haughty eyes..." The "evil way", by virtue of its location in the sentence, must be the wicked things that grow out of pride and arrogancy (like Prov. 13:10: "By pride cometh only contention"). A "perverse" mouth is a mouth that is perverted from its intended speech. That God also hates such a mouth, Prov. 4:24 says, "Perverse lips put far from thee".

V. 14. Wisdom's "counsel" should be heard because wisdom has "sound knowledge". Pardon us, but many who counsel with young people and others sometimes give the wierdest advice. In short, such should not be counselors at all. Understanding claims to possess "might", and indeed it does; it is power. With it, one is prepared; without it, one is defeated. "Clarke" observes: "It enables man to bring everything to his aid: to construct machines by which one man can do the work of hundreds." No wonder that "Bacon" said, "Knowledge is power."

V. 15. Saul may have been king, but when he was going so absolutely against wisdom in a case involving Jonathan, he found out that the people--not he--reigned under that condition (I Sam. 14:23-45). When Rehoboam was not wise in not listening to the advice of his elders, he did not rule the whole kingdom but lost control of ten-twelfths of it (I Kings 12:16,17).

V. 16. The thought of this verse is mostly a repetition of the thought in v. 15. Even parents will find out in time that unless their decisions make sense, their children will rebel and not submit to their rule.

V. 17. Wisdom is good to those who love it. Wisdom is something to be sought and to be sought diligently. This is the way Solomon sought it, and God answered his prayer for it (I Kings 3:9).

V. 18. Wisdom is more valuable than silver and gold (vs. 10,11) and cannot be purchased with gold or silver (Job 28:15), and yet credit it with bringing both riches and honor to its possessor. Since the wealth is spoken of in connection with "righteousness", it is spoken of as "durable" or enduring and not passing.

V. 19. While "gold", "fine gold", and "silver" are among the products of wisdom (see "riches" and "wealth" in v. 18), they must be among the lesser valued "fruit" of wisdom. Other fruits of wisdom must be considered greater. Some of them are mentioned in the next verse.

V. 20. One who walks with and by wisdom will walk in the way of "righteousness" and in the paths of "justice".

V. 21. Again the acquisition of wealth can be one of the results of having wisdom. "Fools" and "money" don't go together ("A fool and his money are soon parted," says an old saying), but wisdom and money do.

TEST QUESTIONS OVER 8:12-21

1. Note the personification of wisdom in v. 12.
2. Why does one who fears God hate evil (v. 13)?
3. What makes wisdom a good counselor (v. 14)?
4. How was King Saul unwise in dealing with his son Jonathan (v. 15)?
5. What about parents and unwise decisions (v. 16)?
6. To whom is wisdom good (v. 17)?
7. Can one be both righteous and wealthy (v. 18)?
8. Is wealth the greatest fruit of wisdom (v. 19)?
9. What way and paths does wisdom walk (v. 20)?
10. Comment on wisdom and wealth going together (v. 21).

TEXT — 8:22-36

22. Jehovah possessed me in the beginning of his way,
Before his works of old.
23. I was set up from everlasting, from the beginning,
Before the earth was.
24. When there were no depths, I was brought forth,
When there were no fountains abounding with water.
25. Before the mountains were settled,
Before the hills was I brought forth;
26. While as yet he had not made the earth, nor the fields,
Nor the beginning of the dust of the world.
27. When he established the heavens, I was there:
When he set a circle upon the face of the deep,
28. When he made firm the skies above,
When the fountains of the deep became strong,
29. When he gave to the sea its bound,
That the waters should not transgress his commandment,
When he marked out the foundations of the earth;
30. Then I was by him, as a master workman;
And I was his daily delight,
Rejoicing always before him.
31. Rejoicing in his habitable earth;
And my delight was with the sons of men.
32. Now therefore, my sons, hearken unto me;
For blessed are they that keep my ways.
33. Hear instruction, and be wise,
And refuse it not.
34. Blessed is the man that heareth me,

Watching daily at my gates,
Waiting at the posts of my doors.
35. For whoso findeth me findeth life,
And shall obtain favor of Jehovah.
36. But he that sinneth against me wrongeth his own soul:
All they that hate me love death.

STUDY QUESTIONS OVER 8:22-36

1. Comment on God's wisdom (v. 22).
2. Are we to conceive of "everlasting" as having existed before time was (v. 23)?
3. What "fountains" are referred to in v. 24?
4. What is meant by the mountains being "settled" in v. 25?
5. Where else does the Bible tell of God's creating the universe (besides here in this section)?
6. What word in v. 27 is especially noticeable?
7. What is meant by "firm" in v. 28?
8. Is there a definite line where the ocean stops (v. 29)?
9. Who is the "master workman" in v. 30--wisdom or God?
10. Does "daily" refer to the creation-days of Gen. 1 (v. 30)?
11. What is the force of "habitable" in v. 31?
12. In what ways "blessed" (v. 32)?
13. Hear and be wise, but don't refuse and be .... (v. 33).
14. How does "watching" enter in (v. 34)?
15. What two blessings are promised in v. 35?
16. How can one sin against wisdom (v. 36)?

PARAPHRASE OF 8:22-36

22-26. The Lord formed me in the beginning, before He created anything else. From ages past, I am. I existed before the earth began. I lived before the oceans were created, before the springs bubbled forth their waters onto the earth; before the mountains and the hills were made. Yes, I was born before God made the earth and fields, and high plateaus.

27-32. I was there when He established the heavens and formed the great springs in the depths of the oceans. I was there when He set the limits of the seas and gave them His instructions not to spread beyond their boundaries. I was there when He made the blueprint for the earth and oceans. I was always at His side like a little child. I was His constant delight, laughing and playing in His presence. And how happy I was with what He created--His wise world and all His family of mankind! And so, young men, listen to me, for how happy are all who follow my instructions.

33-36. Listen to my counsel--oh, don't refuse it--and be wise. Happy is the man who is so anxious to be with me that he watches for me daily at my gates, or waits for me outside my home! For whoever finds me finds life and wins approval from the Lord. But the one who misses me has injured himself irreparably. Those who refuse me show that they love death.

COMMENTS ON 8:22-36

V. 22. Wisdom is still speaking. Wisdom is not something new, something that only recently came along. It takes precedence in value over other things by virtue of its existence before there was anything here and because it is an attribute of God.

V. 23. Wisdom is "from everlasting", "from the beginning," "before the earth was." What else can claim existence that far back? Only those things that are other attributes of God (such as His "power"), for He alone existed.

V. 24. The Bible often divides the creation of the universe into three parts: heaven, earth and sea (Neh. 9:6; Exo. 20:11; Rev. 14:7; and others). Beginning with this verse these three are considered with being of shorter duration than wisdom: sea (this verse), earth (vs. 25,26), and heaven (v. 27).

V. 25. We use the mountains and hills as a gauge for comparing something that is old in our saying, "As old as the hills." But wisdom existed even before there were any hills!

V. 26. If wisdom had not been an attribute of God, earth would have been uninhabitable by man, there would have been nothing for him to eat or wear, etc.

V. 27. Isa. 40:22 also speaks of the "circle" of the earth.

V. 28. Ever hear a child ask, "What if the sky fell down upon us?" God made it "firm" over our heads. The "fountains of the deep" are the "springs of the sea" mentioned in Job 38:16. Their strength mentioned here was manifested in the days of

Noah when they burst forth at the special decree of God and, joined with the water that poured down for forty days and nights when the "windows of heaven" were opened, helped flood the earth until even the mountains were covered (Gen. 7:11,19).

V. 29. Go to any beach or seacoast, and you can observe the definite line where the ocean waters stop in their ebb and flow and in their swellings during great storms. Similarly does Job 38:8,10,11 say that God "shut up the sea with doors" and "marked out for it a bound, and set bars and doors, and said, Hitherto shalt thou come, but no further; and here shall thy proud waves by stayed." The "foundation" of the earth (or "foundations" of the earth in Job 38:4) is evidently to be taken figuratively and not literally since the Bible speaks of God's hanging the earth on nothing--suspended it in space (Job 26:7). What, then, is meant by the foundation or foundations of the earth? "Clarke" takes a stab at the subject: "Those irreversible laws by which all motions are governed...the principles on which it is constructed, and the laws by which it is governed."

V. 30. God has His wisdom "with" Him in all of His creative acts. This is what made everything "good" that He created. See the reference to this after the various days of creation (Gen. 1:10,12, etc.). "Daily" in our verse is reminiscent of the creative days of Gen. 1.

V. 31. God made the earth as a dwellingplace (Isa. 45:18) whereas, as far as we know, the other planets were not so prepared. The finale of God's creation, the climax of it all, was the creation of man (Gen. 1:26), mentioned in our verse.

V. 32. If wisdom is that ancient; if wisdom is an eternal attribute of God; if wisdom was back there with God when everything was being created, then people should listen when wisdom speaks. In our verse wisdom says, "Hearken unto me...keep my ways," and a blessing is pronounced upon those who do.

V. 33. Another verse connecting our being wise with hearing, and not refusing, instruction. It is the foolish, not the wise, who refuse wisdom and instruction (Prov. 1:8).

V. 34. One who seeks wisdom lives in a state of expectation and anticipation. He watches and waits. "Waiting" is often involved in "watching" as in the cat patiently watching for a mouse or as in Christians watching for their Lord's return.

V. 35. A double blessing ultimately comes to those who through watching and waiting find wisdom: "life" (both here and hereafter, both spiritual and eternal) and the "favor of Jehovah" (the greatest possession that one can have).

V. 36. One can sin against wisdom in several ways: by not desiring it, by not seeking after it, by not listening when it speaks, by not believing what it says, by not doing what it commands, by not desiring what it promises, and by not heeding its warnings. In which ever way or if in all ways one sins against wisdom, he is not merely wronging wisdom: he is wronging his own soul--he will be the one who suffers for it. Put very bluntly wisdom summarizes: "All they that hate me love death." This statement exemplifies the fact that truth itself is blunt, unflinching, unbending, no respector of persons.

TEST QUESTIONS OVER 8:22-36

1. Wisdom is not something .... (v. 22).
2. In order to have existed as far back as wisdom, something had to be an attribute of .... (v. 23).
3. The Bible often divides the creation of the universe into what three divisions (v. 24)?
4. What is older than the hills (v. 25)?
5. Would the earth have been habitable by man if wisdom had not been with God in creating it (v. 26)?
6. What other passage speaks of the "circle" of the earth (v. 27)?
7. What does v. 28 assure us about the sky?
8. Where else are the "fountains of the deep" mentioned (v. 28)?
9. Cite the proof of the truth in v. 29 about the sea.
10. Is "foundation" in v. 29 to be taken literally or figuratively?
11. Tie up v. 30 with Gen. 1.
12. Comment on v. 31.
13. According to v. 32, why should we listen to wisdom?
14. Who receive and who do not receive instruction (v. 33)?
15. Give an example of "waiting and watching" (v. 34).
16. According to v. 35, why should we seek wisdom?
17. What two blunt statements does wisdom make in v. 36?

TEXT — 9:1-9

1. Wisdom hath builded her house;
She hath hewn out her seven pillars:
2. She hath killed her beasts; she hath mingled her wine;
She hath also furnished her table:
3. She hath sent forth her maidens;
She crieth upon the highest places of the city:
4. Whoso is simple, let him turn in hither:
As for him that is void of understanding, she saith to him
5. Come, eat ye of my bread,
And drink of the wine which I have mingled.
6. Leave off, ye simple ones, and live;
And walk in the way of understanding.
7. He that correcteth a scoffer getteth to himself reviling; and he that reproveth a wicked man getteth himself a blot.
8. Reprove not a scoffer, lest he hate thee:
Reprove a wise man, and he will love thee.
9. Give instruction to a wise man, and he will be yet wiser:
Teach a righetous man, and he will increase in learning.

STUDY QUESTIONS OVER 9:1-9

1. What are the seven pillars of wisdom's house (v. 1)?
2. Does wisdom believe in mixed wine (v. 2)?
3. Who are wisdom's maidens (v. 3)?
4. Is wisdom beckoning the simple to sin like the harlot woman (v. 4)?
5. What is her bread and her wine (v. 5)?
6. "Leave off" what (v. 6)?
7. Who gives such a righteous man a blot (v. 7)?
8. What are the opposite results of reproving a scoffer and a wise man (v. 8)?
9. Who profits from instruction (v. 9)?

PARAPHRASE OF 9:1-9

1-6. Wisdom hath built a palace supported on seven pillars, and has prepared a great banquet, and mixed the wines, and sent out her maidens inviting all to come. She calls from the busiest intersections in the city, "Come, you simple ones without good judgment; come to wisdom's banquet and drink the wines that I have mixed. Leave behind your foolishness and begin to live; learn how to be wise.

7-9. If you rebuke a mocker, you will only get a smart retort; yes, he will snarl at you. So don't bother with him; he will only hate you for trying to help him. But a wise man, when rebuked, will love you all the more. Teach a wise man, and he will be the wiser; teach a good man, and he will learn more.

COMMENTS ON 9:1-9

V. 1. "The same wisdom speaks here who spoke in the preceding chapter. There she represented herself as manifest in all the works of God in the natural world--all being constructed according to counsels proceeding from an infinite understanding. Here she represents herself as the great potentate who was to rule all that she had constructed; and having an immense family to provide for had made an abundant provision and calls all to partake of it. This is the continuation of the parable begun in the preceding chapter, where wisdom is represented as a venerable lady whose real beauties and solid promises are opposed to the false allurements of pleasure, who was represented in the seventh chapter under the idea of a debauched and impudent woman. This one, to draw young men into her snares, describes the perfumes, the bed, and the festival which she had prepared. Wisdom acts in the same way but instead of the debauchery, the false pleasures, and the criminal connections which pleasure had promised offers her guests a strong, well-built, magnificient palace, chaste and solid pleasures, salutary instructions, and a life crowned with blessedness" ("Clarke"). Consider the contrast between the lady "wisdom" in vs. 1-12 and the "foolish woman" of vs. 13-18. Wisdom "builds" (v. 1), but immorality tears down. Both are inviting guests to come in (vs. 3-5 and vs. 14-17). Within their invitations both used the exact words at one point: "Whoso is simple, let him turn in hither: and as for him that wanteth understanding, she saith to him..." (v. 4 and v. 16). the wicked woman offers "stolen waters" and "bread eaten in secret" (v. 17), showing the illegitimacy of what she is offering while wisdom operates in legitimate wares and ways (in the open). The pleasure of sin is said to be "sweet" and "pleasant" (v. 17) while wisdom may impart some of its knowledge through reproof (v.

8). The guests of the immoral woman end in death (v. 18) while wisdom leads to life (v. 6). The "seven" pillars of wisdom may be the seven things mentioned in Jas. 3:17 concerning heavenly wisdom: (1) pure; (2) peaceable; (3) gentle; (4) easy to be entreated; (5) full of mercy and good fruits; (6) without variance; and (7) without hyprocisy, or "seven" may be used here as it so often is in the book of Revelation as an ideal number.

V. 2. In the preparation of her feast of good things, she had prepared her food and her beverage and had set the table. By "mingled her wine" is probably meant the mixing of the straight grape juice with the proper amount of water to make it a better tasting beverage (which the ancients among the Jews, Greeks, and Romans did). Since we are dealing with wisdom, the preceding seems more likely than that she added drugs to give it more potency.

V. 3. With everything ready she sends forth the maidens to call the guests to the feast. There have been times when maidens were employed to beckon the guests that the hour of banqueting had come.

V. 4. The wicked woman of v. 16 uses the same words in her invitation. Wisdom is pleased to call those who lack it, calling them to begin a life of wisdom. In a sense we all start "simple".

V. 5. We are told in Prov. 4:5 to "get wisdom", and this verse compares the gaining of wisdom as desirable and not miserable by using the figure of dining, something that people enjoy doing. For "mingled wine" see comments on v. 2.

V. 6. Put an end to living without wisdom; cease ignorance and folly. Adopt a new way: the way of understanding. All who make this change are glad they did.

V. 7. A triple parallel: "correcteth" and "reproved"; "scoffer" and "Wicked man"; and "getteth to himself reviling" and "getteth himself a blot". A scoffer will neither appreciate your sincere intention to help him nor allow himself to see the correctness of what you are saying to him. Instead of straightening up as a result of your proper rebuke, he will say all manner of evil about you, and you (the innocent) end up with a "blot".

V. 8. Reprove the wise but not the scoffer. The one will love you for it; the other will hate you. In harmony with this verse the Lord reproved Saul of Tarsus (Acts 9:4) and chastens His children (Heb. 12:6), but He teaches us not to cast our pearls before swine--scoffers (Matt. 7:6).

V. 9. The same good qualities of the wise man who accepted rebuke in v. 8 show up in this verse and justify the time and effort that it takes to instruct him. As a result of your efforts he will be "yet wiser" and "will increase in learning". This is satisfying to any instructor. Jesus' parabolic teaching resulted in "whosoever hath, to him shall be given, and he shall have abundance" (Matt. 13:12).

TEST QUESTIONS OVER 9:1-9

1. Cite some of the contrasts between the woman Wisdom and the wicked woman in this chapter?
2. What three preparations are mentioned in v. 2?
3. What was probably involved in wisdom's "mixed wine" (v. 2)?
4. What phase of things is mentioned in v. 3?
5. In a sense do we all begin life "simple" (v. 4)?
6. What is gaining wisdom likened to doing in v. 5?
7. What important change is called for in v. 6?
8. Cite the triple parallel in v. 7.
9. How does the New Testament follow the instructions found in v. 8?
10. What is a teacher's joy (v. 9)?

TEXT — 9:10-18

10. The fear of Jehovah is the beginning of wisdom;
And the knowledge of the Holy One is understanding.
11. For by me thy days shall be multiplied,
And the years of thy life shall be increased.
12. If thou are wise, thou art wise for thyself;
And if thou scoffest, thou alone shall bear it.
13. The foolish woman is clamorous;
She is simple, and knoweth nothing.
14. And she sitteth at the door of her house,
On a seat in the high places of the city,
15. To call to them that pass by,
Who go right on their ways:
16. Whoso is simple, let him turn in hither;
And as for him that is void of understanding, she saith to him,
17. Stolen waters are sweet,

And bread eaten in secret is pleasant.
18. But he knoweth not that the dead are there;
That her guests are in the depths of Sheol.

STUDY QUESTIONS OVER 9:10-18

1. Where is the opening statement of v. 10 first mentioned in Proverbs?
2. Where else in Proverbs is the truth in v. 11 found?
3. The "foolish woman" of v. 13 is to be contrasted with what other woman?
4. Is this low-down woman ashamed of herself and her business (v. 14)?
5. Are wicked people "evangelistic" for sin (v. 15)?
6. Who will get caught by such a wicked woman (v. 16)?
7. Do sinners believe what v. 17 says?
8. Why does v. 18 begin with "but"?

PARAPHRASE OF 9:10-18

10-12. For the reverence and fear of God are basic to all wisdom. Knowing God results in every other kind of understanding. Wisdom will make the hours of your day more profitable and the years of your life more fruitful. Wisdom is its own reward, and if you scorn her, you may only hurt yourself.

13-18. A prostitute is loud and brash, and never has enough of lust and shame. She sits at the door of her house or stands at the street corners of the city, whispering to men going by, and to those minding their own business. "Come home with me," she urges simpletons, "stolen melons are the sweetest; stolen apples taste the best!" But they don't realize that her former guests are now citizens of hell.

COMMENTS ON 9:10-18

V. 10. Other passages agreeing with the first statement: "The fear of the Lord, that is wisdom" (Job 28:28); "The fear of Jehovah is the beginning of wisdom" (Psa. 111:10); "The fear of Jehovah is the beginning of knowledge" (Prov. 1:7). No one can be a person of real understanding who does not know the holy One in whom alone originally resided wisdom, knowledge, and understanding. The Greeks were famous for their knowledge, but the Greeks through their philosophies "knew not God" (I Cor. 1:21). Paul (the writer of I Cor. 1:21) knew, for he had been to Athens and had beheld the famous city "full of idols" (Acts 17:16). Is it any wonder, then, that when he preached there the resurrection of the dead "some mocked" (Acts 17:32)? Nor do present-day philosophies that disregard the revelation of God in the Bible have an understanding of our holy God.

V. 11. "The parenthetical explanation being concluded in which wisdom has intimated why it is useless to appeal to the scorner and the wilful sinner, she now resumes the direct address interrupted at v. 7, presenting a forcible reason for the advice given in v. 6, though there is still some connection with v. 10 as it is from the wisdom that comes from the fear of the Lord that the blessings now mentioned spring" ("Pulpit Commentary"). Other passages on what imparts long life: "My son...let thy heart keep my commandments: For length of days, and years of life, And peace, will they add to thee" (Prov. 3:1,2); "The fear of Johovah prolongeth days; But the years of the wicked shall be shortened" (Prov. 10:27).

V. 12. "Though thy example may be very useful to thy neighbors and friends, yet the chief benefit is to thyself. But if thou scorn--refuse to receive--the doctrines of wisdom, and die in thy sins, thou alone shalt suffer the vengeance of an offended God" ("Clarke"). There is a sense in which others let you be wise if it is your choice to be wise, and others let you scoff if that be your choice. Whatever your choice, the non-committee multitude will not join you. In other words, the scholar who is right tries to tell the others and is not always believed (at least, is not always "joined"), and the scoffer who is wrong tries to gain adherents to his way of thinking, and he runs into a similar reception.

V. 13. The "foolish woman" of this and following verses is in contrast to the woman "wisdom" of vs. 1-6. As this wicked woman has been fully identified in previous sections (2:16-19; 5:3-23; 6:24-35; 7:5-27), this section is speaking of the immoral woman. Our verse says she is "foolish", "clamorous", "simple", and "knoweth nothing". The Bible has no compliments for the adulteress (or the adulterer). She is "foolish" instead of wise, for it is much wiser to be happily married to a good man than to sell yourself for a few minutes to any man who comes along. She is "clamorous" (boisterous, loud, forward), which was pointed out in Prov. 7:11-13 wherein she was said not to remain in her house but to get out on the street and aggressively proposition men. She is "simple", for her trade does not necessitate her to develop her mind, and little is a harlot concerned or involved in the concerns and the involvements of the community. She "knoweth nothing", for she either doesn't know or doesn't care what she is doing, how she is looked upon, what harm she is bringing to the homes and bodies and souls of others, and of what she is robbing herself of and ultimately bringing upon herself.

V. 14. She is forward, not bashful, in pushing her trade. She is bold and not ashamed.

V. 15. She gets out in the passing crowd and tries to get customers. But thank God, most people have enough sense to keep going "right on their ways" instead of stopping and getting involved with her. Those who do not fall for her are men who have been taught from youth to fear adultery, or who are happily married to good wives and have righteous children at home to whom they are examples, or who have committed themselves to a godly life that even if once guilty of such behavior will have no part in it.

V. 16. Anyone who will listen to her and go with her really isn't any wiser than she was described as being in v. 13. She employs the same words as wisdom uses (see v. 4); she is going to "educate" the "simple" who are "void of understanding". They will "learn" all right, but it will be the wrong thing, and the time will come when they will see that they listened to the wrong person: "Thou mourn at thy latter end, When thy flesh and thy body are consumed, And say, How have I hated instruction, And my heart despised reproof; Neither have I obeyed the voice of my teachers, Nor inclined mine ear to them that instructed me!" (Prov. 5:11-13).

V. 17. Hers is an invitation to commit adultery with her. She is referred to as "stolen waters", for she does not really belong to those who accept her invitation, for is she is married (as in Prov. 6:29 and as in Prov. 7:19,20), she belongs to her husband, and if she is unmarried she should belong to and save herself for the man whom she will later marry. God never intended that any woman would be to society like the old town-well of years ago or like the block of stock-salt in the cow pasture. A woman who does not save herself (or a man who does not save himself) for the mate that she (or he) will later marry really does not deserve a pure mate in marriage! It is only a saying that "stolen melons are sweeter". Why should any man choose the arms and the bosom and the intimacies of an impure, ungodly woman to the sweet and attractive and good wife whom he has personally chosen and shared life with over the years? No, "stolen waters" are not better! Therefore, "drink waters out of thine own cistern, And running waters out of thine own well...Rejoice in the wife of thy youth. As a loving hind and a pleasant doe, Let her breasts satisfy thee at all times; And be thou ravished always with her love" (Prov. 5:15-19).

V. 18. The "sweetness" and the "pleasantness" that she promised in v. 17 end in "death"--just like all sin. Other passages connecting immorality with death: Prov. 2:18; Prov. 7:27. Other passages connecting sin with death: Rom 6:23; Jas. 1:15.

TEST QUESTIONS OVER 9:10-18

1. What success do philosophies of men have in common to a knowledge of God (v. 10)?
2. What great promise is contained in v. 11?
3. Comment on v. 12.
4. In what way is an immoral woman "foolish" (v. 13)?
5. In what way "simple" (v. 13)?
6. In what way "clamorous" (v. 13)?
7. In what way "knoweth nothing" (v. 13)?
8. What shows her forwardness (v. 14)?
9. Do most men of the crowd stop with her or pass right on (v. 15)?
10. Why will they do this (v. 15)?
11. What kind of "education" does the immoral woman give to the "simple" (v. 16)?
12. Why is she "stolen waters" if married (v. 17)?
13. Why also "stolen waters" if yet unmarried (v. 17)?
14. How does her praise of "sweetness and pleasantness" turn out (v. 18)?

TEXT — 10:1-11

1. The Proverbs of Solomon.
A wise son maketh a glad father;
But a foolish son is the heaviness of his mother.
2. Treasures of wickedness profit nothing;
But righteous delivereth from death.
3. Jehovah will not suffer the soul of the righteous to famish;
But he thrusteth away the desire of the wicked.
4. He becometh poor that worketh with a slack hand;
But the hand of the diligent maketh rich.
5. He that gathereth in summer is a wise son;
But he that sleepeth in harvest is a son that causeth shame.
6. Blessings are upon the head of the righteous;
But violence covereth the mouth of the wicked.
7. The memory of the righteous is blessed;
But the name of the wicked shall rot.
8. The wise in heart will receive commandments;
But a prating fool shall fall. — Babbling
9. He that walketh uprightly walketh surely;
But he that perverteth his ways shall be known.
10. He that winketh with the eye causeth sorrow;
But a prating fool shall fall.
11. The mouth of the righteous is a fountain of life;
But violence covereth the mouth of the wicked.

STUDY QUESTIONS OVER 10:1-11

1. Why say, "The proverbs of Solomon," here in the middle of the book (v. 1)?
2. Exemplify how wise children make glad parents (v. 1).
3. Exemplify how foolish children make sad parents (v. 1).
4. In what sense do treasures of wickedness profit nothing when many wicked are wealthy (v. 2)?
5. When does righteousness deliver one from death (v. 2)?
6. What does "soul" mean in v. 3?
7. What is a "slack hand" (v. 4)?
8. Why even bring "hand" into this verse (v. 4) that uses it twice?
9. Causeth shame to whom (v. 5)?
10. Whose "blessings" are upon the righteous (v. 6)?
11. How does violence cover the mouth of the wicked (v. 6)?

12. What is the significance of the word "rot" here in v. 7?
13. What does "prating" mean (v. 8)?
14. List ways that one might pervert his ways and be found out (v. 9).
15. In v. 10 what is wrong with winking?
16. How can one's mouth be a "fountain of life" (v. 11)?

PARAPHRASE OF 10:1-11

1. These are the proverbs of Solomon. Happy is the man with a level-headed son; sad the mother of a rebel.
2. Ill-gotten gain brings no lasting happiness; right living does.
3. The Lord will not let a good man starve to death, nor will He let the wicked man's riches continue forever.
4. Lazy men are soon poor; hard workers get rich.
5. A wise youth makes hay while the sun shines, but what a shame to see a lad who sleeps away his hour of opportunity.
6. The good man is covered with blessings from head to foot, but an evil man inwardly curses his luck.
7. We all have happy memories of good men gone to their reward, but the names of wicked men stink after them.
8. The wise man is glad to be instructed, but a self-sufficnent fool falls flat on his face.
9. A good man has firm footing, but a crook will slip and fall.
10. Winking at sin leads to sorrow; bold reproof leads to peace.
11. There is living truth in what a good man says, but the mouth of the evil man is filled with curses.

COMMENTS ON 10:1-11

V. 1 After 9 chapters in this book called "Proverbs," aren't you surprised to see the heading, "The proverbs of Solomon," here? The explanation: a "proverb" is a wise saying. The first 9 chapters, while exalting and containing "wisdom", are not "sayings" but are extended topical material. The actual "sayings" begin here and will continue through chapter 29. The message of the verse: What we do as sons can affect the happiness or the heaviness of our parents, both while under their roof and after we leave it. The Prodigal Son (Luke 15:11-32) surely brought heaveniness upon his foolish departure and throughout his waywardness and indulgence, but he brought happiness upon his penitent return. Other passages containing the same truth: Prov. 15:20; 17:21, 25; 19:13; 29:3,15. Thought for parents: The way you are now rearing your children will have much to do with your own future happiness or heaviness.

V. 2. Treasures of wickedness are riches gotten by wrong means. A Christian must follow only acceptable vocations: Eph. 4:28; marginal note on Tit. 3:8. "Better is a little, with righteousness, Than great revenues with injustice" (Prov. 16:8). Other similar references: Prov. 11:4; Psa. 34:10; 37:25; Dan. 4:27. And yet communities and families are usually more proud of their rich than they are of their righteous!

V. 3. "American Bible Union version": "Jehovah will not let the spirit of the righteous famish; But he repels the longing of the wicked." God so blesses the righteous that they do not faint. Consider David's praise of God in Psa. 23:1-6. And so states Paul in II Cor. 4:16. But equally so is God's face against those who do evil (I Pet. 3:12).

V. 4. The proper result of shiftlessness is to have nothing. God has willed that if a person will not work, he should not have things to eat (II Thess. 3:10). Some may become rich through crooked dealings, but others are prosperous through diligence. For similar material see Prov. 12:24; 13:4; 19:15; 21:5. In calling men to serve Him God has always called the busy people: Elisha plowing (I Kings 19:19-21), fishermen working (Matt. 4:18-22), Matthew sitting at his place of toll (Matt. 9:9), and Saul of Tarsus busy persecuting (Acts 26:10-18).

V. 5. This is related in content to v. 4. Also to v. 1. In life our actions commend others or embarrass them.

V. 6. "Clarke" comments: "As blessings shall be on the head of the just, so the violence of the wicked shall cover their face with shame and confusion. Their own violent dealings shall be visited upon them." V. 11 talks again of violence covering the mouth of the wicked.

V. 7. This verse speaks of the deceased. "The righteous shall be had in everlasting remembrance" (Psa. 112:6). Their virtues are extolled (Acts 9:36-39). But the bad things that a wicked person did are remembered long after he is dead. His name "rots" (gets worse) because that is the only side of him seemingly remembered and passed onto others. While we may call our children "Timothy", "Matthew", and other good Bible characters' names, yet we do not name them "Cain", "Ahab", or "Jezebel".

V. 8. Jesus also likened the obedient to the wise (Matt. 7:26, 27(. Webster on "prate": "To talk, especially much and to little purpose; to chatter." Thus Young translates "a talkative fool". Diotrophes prated against the apostle John (III John 10). Such will "fall," sometimes as a consequence of his words even before he falls at the final judgment. V. 10 repeats the statement.

V. 9. Walks in "integrity" says "Young's Literal" and "Amplified." One who is walking in righteousness knows what he is doing, has assurance, and is safe. To pervert one's way is to divert it from what is right. One cannot do this without being found out, at least ultimately (dishonesty, adultery, embezzlement, etc.). Want to be known and noticed? Do wrong, and you will be. The righteous settle for "walketh surely". Prov. 28:18 is a parallel passage.

V. 10. This ends the same as v. 8. "Pulpit Commentary": Winking with the eye "is a sign of craft, malice, and complicity with other wicked comrades." Study Prov. 6:12-14 also. The first statement shows that wrongdoing brings sorrow to others; the second shows that it brings destruction to oneself.

V.11. The blessings brought by the mouth of the righteous is set in contrast to the sorrow and destruction brought by the wicked in v. 10. Psa. 37:30 also speaks of the "mouth of the righteous". People are helped by what good people say. This verse ends the same as v. 6.

TEST QUESTIONS OVER 10:1-11

1. What does a wise son make (v. 1)?
2. What does a foolish son make (v. 1)?
3. What was said about treasures of wickedness (v. 2)?
4. To what does a slack hand lead (v. 4)?
5. What was said about the hand of the diligent, (v. 4)?
6. What about the memory of the righteous (v. 7)?
7. What about the name of the wicked (v.7)?
8. What does "prating" mean (v. 8)?
9. Comment on "winking" as used in v. 9.
10. Of which are communities and families more proud--of their rich or their righteous (v. 9)?
11. Which spreads faster and farther--news of one's good deeds or bad deeds (v. 9)?
12. Which verse did the Paraphrase help you with the most?
13. Which verse did the Comments help you with the most?

TEXT — 10:12-22

12. Hatred stirreth up strifes;
But love covereth all transgressions.
13. In the lips of him that hath discernment wisdom is found;
But a rod is for the back of him that is void of understanding.
14. Wise men lay up knowledge;
But the mouth of the foolish is a present destruction.
15. The rich man's wealth is his strong city:
The destruction of the poor is their poverty.
16. The labor of the righteous tendeth to life;
The increase of the wicked, to sin.
17. He is in the way of life that heedeth correction;
But he that forsaketh reproof erreth.
18. He that hideth hatred is of lying lips;
And he that utterth a slander is a fool.
19. In the multitude of words there wanteth not transgression;
But he that refraineth his lips doeth wisely.
20. The tongue of the righteous is as choice silver:
The heart of the wicked is little worth.
21. The lips of the righteous feed many;
But the foolish die for lack of understanding.
22. The blessing of Jehovah, it maketh rich;
And he addeth no sorrow therewith.

STUDY QUESTIONS OVER 10:12-22

1. How does love "cover" transgressions (v. 12)?
2. What is meant by one having "discernment" (v. 13)?
3. Why don't more people "lay up knowledge" (v. 14)?
4. To whom is the mouth of fools a present destruction--to themselves or others (v. 14)?
5. What is meant by one's wealth being his "strong city" (v. 15)?
6. What kind of "life" does righteous labor lead to (v. 16)?
7. What is meant by the "increase" of the wicked (v. 16)?
8. What is meant by the "way of life" (v. 17)?
9. Name several persons in the Bible who forsook reproof (v. 17).
10. What might one say ("lying lips") who is concealing his hatred (v. 18)?

11. What two words in v. 18 are contrasts?
12. Why do a multitude of words result in transgression (v. 19)?
13. How is the tongue of the righteous like choice silver (v. 20)?
14. What other Bible passages speak of words' feeding people (v. 21)?
15. What kind of death does v. 21 have in mind?
16. Does the blessing of Jehovah make some people or all people rich (v. 22)? Explain.
17. What is implied by some riches when it says, "He addeth no sorrow therewith" (v. 22)?

PARAPHRASE OF 10:12-22

12. Hatred stirs old quarrels, but love overlooks insults.
13. Men with common sense are admired as counselors; those without it are beaten as servants.
14. A wise man holds his tongue. Only a fool blurts out everything he knows; that only leads to sorrow and trouble.
15. The rich man's wealth is his only strength. The poor man's poverty is his only curse.
16. The good man's earnings advance the cause of righteousness. The evil man squanders his on sin.
17. Anyone willing to be corrected is on the pathway to life. Anyone refusing has lost his chance.
18. To hate is to be a liar; to slander is to be a fool.
19. Don't talk so much. You keep putting your foot in your mouth. Be sensible and turn off the flow!
20. When a good man speaks, he is worth listening to, but the words of fools are a dime a dozen.
21. A godly man gives good advice, but a rebel is destroyed by lack of common sense.
22. The Lord's blessing is our grestest wealth. All our work adds nothing to it!

COMMENTS ON 10:12-22

V. 12. Hatred does not desire the fellowship of the one hated, does not wish the peace and the welfare of the one hated. Hatred must show itself, and the result is trouble and strife. Hatred will stir up strife by picking on all the small "talking points" that love would have overlooked (I Cor. 13:4). The soft answer (of love) will turn away wrath, but the grievous words (of hatred) will stir up strife (Prov. 15:1). Other Scriptures on love's covering or concealing faults: Prov. 17:9; I Pet. 4:8.

V.13 One who is wise has "discerning lips"; that is, he knows what to say and what not to say, when to say it and when not to, how to say it and how not to, how much to say, where to say it and where not to, etc. Jesus' perfection was also seen in this. Peter's imperfection often exhibited itself in this (Matt. 16: 21-23; Luke 9:32-35; John 21:19-22. Proper speech is a crowning virtue (Jas. 3:2). During World War II Uncle Sam was shown on posters with his finger saying, "Sh-h-h." Another government poster during that war showed a big ship sinking and included these few words, "Somebody talked!" No wonder Prov. 26:3 says, "A whip for the horse, a bridle for the ass, and a rod for the back of fools."

V. 14. A wise man does more listening (taking in, "laying up") than he does talking; the fool, just the opposite. See Prov. 18:7; 21:23. Christians are taught to be "swift to hear" but "slow to speak" (Jas. 1:19).

V. 15. The opening statement is also in Prov. 18:11. "Strong city" means that in which he trusts. There are those who trust in their riches (Psa. 52:7). I Tim. 6:17 forbids it, and Jesus said such cannot enter heaven (Mark 10:24). Job recognized that to make riches one's "confidence" is to "deny" God (Job 31:24-28).

V. 16. The labor of the righteous is good for him: he enjoys his food, he sleeps well, he is healthy, and his mind is not troubled. Ecc. 5:12 says, "The sleep of a laboring man is sweet, whether he eat little or much; but the fulness of the rich will not suffer him to sleep." The increase of the wicked is not good for him, for it but leads to sin. Luxury and licentious living often go together. Kings as a group (the wealthies in the land) were usually not godly. Eccl. 10: 17 says, "Happy art thou, O land, when thy king is the son of nobles, and thy princes eat in due season, for strength, and not for drunkenness!"

V. 17. In v. 16 labor led to "life"; in this verse heeding correction does. All people make mistakes and will be corrected: as children by parents (Heb. 12:9), school teachers, and other adults; later in life by employers, neighbors, mates, God's leaders, and even God through chastening (Heb. 12:5,6). David listened to what Abigail had to say, saw the wisdom of it, and wisely changed his course (I Sam. 26:32,33). For other passages on heeding correction see Prov. 12:1; 13:18; 15:5, 31, 32. But there will always be those who forsake reproof, and they will not prosper (Prov. 15:10). See also Prov. 1:25, 26.

V. 18. "Hideth" and "uttereth" are obvious contrasts. Those who seek to hide their true feelings will lie. When asked, "What's the matter?" or "What have I done that's wrong?" they will reply, "Nothing." When asked, "Why are you upset?" they will say, "I'm not upset." See also Prov. 20:24-26. On the other hand to slander (defame) is foolish and wrong (Matt. 5:21,22). The word "devil" means "slanderer". We must be careful not to be guilty of doing the same thing (I Tim. 3:11). We should neither hide hatreds nor utter slanders. We can only avoid such a dilemma by getting hatred out of our hearts, which we are commanded to do (Eph. 4:31).

V. 19. Eccl. 5:3 says a fool's voice is known, is recognized, by its multitude of words. Jas. 1:19 says we are to be "slow to speak". See also Prov. 17:28. Those who speak incessantly will surely sometime speak when they should be listening, will say some things that shouldn't be said, and will sometime speak before they think. "Speak little, because for one sin which we may commit by keeping silence where it would be well to speak, we commit a hundred by speaking upon all occasions" (Pinart).

V. 20. A triple contrast: "tongue" vs. "heart"; "the righteous" vs. "the wicked"; "choice silver" vs. "little worth". The "little worth" of the wicked person's heart is seen in that contains no praise for God and no love for his fellowman.

V. 21. In this verse "feed" is set over against "die". "The lips of the wise disperse knowledge" (Prov. 15:7). Jesus "fed" multitudes with His teachings. Teachers of God's Word "feed" the flock of God (Acts 20:28). Paul "fed" many people in many places. We too can edify (build people up) with our lips (Eph. 4:29). People need this knowledge, for they will die for lacking it or for disregarding it (Hos. 4:6). Why does a mouse die in a trap or a fish die on the end of a hook? Because they "didn't know" what would happen by biting the bait.

V. 22. When Israel did right, God blessed them and enriched them. They were not made rich by their own power but by God's (Deut. 8:17, 18). Compare Gen. 24:35; 26:12; Psa. 37:22. Those who gain riches without regard for God both err from the faith and pierce themselves through with many sorrows (I Tim. 6:9, 10). When people get money in their own way, they often resort to crookedness, and all kinds of troubles follow.

"Unsanctified riches bring only trouble and vexation" (Pulpit Commentary"). God's riches are a blessing all the way ("no sorrow therewith").

TEST QUESTIONS OVER 10:12-22

1. Why does hatred stir up strife (v. 12)?
2. In what way does love cover transgression (v. 12)?
3. How does one show that he/she has discerning lips (v. 13)?
4. What two verses extolled listening and condemned excessive talking?
5. Why is a rich man's riches referred to as his "strong city" (v. 15)?
6. What did Jesus say about those who trust in riches (v. 15)?
7. In what ways is the labor of the righteous good for him (v. 16)?
8. What often happens when the wicked increase in riches (v. 16)?
9. What are some of the groups or individuals who will correct us throughout life (v. 17)?
10. What is better than hiding hatred within or uttering slander without (v. 18)?
11. How do we know that slander is of the devil (v. 18)?
12. Whose voice is known by its multitude of words (v. 19)?
13. How does v. 20 describe the worth of the righteous person's tongue?
14. How does v. 20 describe the worth of the wicked person's heart?
15. How can we "feed" people with words (v. 21)?
16. What often happens when people obtain riches for themselves without regard for God (v. 22)?
17. How do riches gained from God's blessings differ (v. 22)?

TEXT — 10:23-32

23. It is as sport to a fool to do wickedness;
And so is wisdom to a man of understanding.
24. The fear of the wicked, it shall come upon him;
And the desire of the righteous shall be granted.
25. When the whirlwind passeth, the wicked is no more;
But the righteous is an everlasting foundation.
26. As vinegar to the teeth, and as smoke to the eyes,

So is the sluggard to them that send him.
27. The fear of Jehovah prolongeth days;
But the years of the wicked shall be shortened.
28. The hope of the righteous shall be gladness;
But the expectation of the wicked shall perish.
29. The way of Jehovah is a stronghold to the upright;
But it is a destruction to the workers of iniquity.
30. The righteous shall never be removed;
But the wicked shall not dwell in the land.
31. The mouth of the righteous bringeth forth wisdom;
But the perverse tongue shall be cut off.
32. The lips of the righteous know what is acceptable;
But the mouth of the wicked speaketh perverseness.

STUDY QUESTIONS OVER 10:23-32

1. Cite illustrations of people who make sport of wickedness (v. 23).
2. Does v. 23 mean that wisdom is "sport" to the man of understanding?
3. According to v. 24 what will come upon the wicked, and what will come upon the righteous?
4. What "whirlwind" will take away the wicked (v. 25)?
5. How are the righteous an "everlasting foundation" (v. 25)?
6. What do the three things mentioned in v. 26 have in common?
7. How does the fear of Jehovah "prolong days" (v. 27)?
8. What shortens the years of the wicked (v. 27)?
9. What is meant by the expectation of the wicked perishing (v. 28)?
10. What is meant by the "way of Jehovah" in v. 29?
11. Why say the righteous shall "never" be removed when all must die (v. 30)?
12. Why say the wicked shall not dwell in the land when there are many wicked people living (v. 30)?
13. In what sense will the perverse tongue be "cut off" (v. 31)?
14. Why say the "lips" know when it is the "mind" that knows (v. 32)?
15. Which verse did the Paraphrase help you with the most?
16. Which verse did the Comments help you with the most?

PARAPHRASE OF 10:23-32

23. A fool's fun is being bad; a wise man's fun is being wise!
24. The wicked man's fears will all come true, and so will the good man's hopes.
25. Disaster strikes like a cyclone and the wicked are whirled away. But the good man has a strong anchor.
26. A lazy fellow is a pain to his employers--like smoke in their eyes or vinegar that sets the teeth on edge.
27. Reverence for God adds hours to each day; so how can the wicked expect a long, good life?
28. The hope of good men is eternal happiness; the hopes of evil men are all in vain.
29. God protects the upright but destroys the wicked.
30. The good shall never lose God's blessings, but the wicked shall lose everything.
31. The good man gives wise advice, but the liar's counsel is shunned.
32. The upright speak what is helpful; the wicked speak rebellion.

COMMENTS ON 10:23-32

V. 23. To do mischief is sport or fun to a fool. Heb. 11:25 speaks of the "pleasures of sin". Godliness would be boredom to him until converted. He is sure he is living the only way to be lived. He thinks he is smart, and that everybody else is missing out on the main thing of life. But don't forget that the man of understanding enjoys the way of wisdom too. Fools are not the only ones who enjoy themselves. Yes, godly people are happy too!

V. 24. Many know they are not right, but outwardly they seem to act as if there is nothing to worry about. Yet, within them are lurking fears that come to the surface when they think they are going to die. As instantly as men cry out for God's mercy when they think they may suddenly die shows they have done some thinking ahead of time about their manner of life knowing it was not right. Their way of life finally catches up with them, but the righteous have hope as they look to the future, and that hope will be granted whether in answer to prayer for things here or in heaven in eternty. Notice the same truth in Psa. 145:19; I John 5:14, 15.

V. 25. Finally God's patience with the wicked comes to an end, and He sweeps them away with the suddenness of a whirlwind. After such a storm has passed, oftentimes it is only the foundation of a building that is left. The righteous are like that foundation, the wicked like the building that was carried away. Psa. 37 is a psalm that says the same thing over and over. Read it, noting the sudden destruction of the wicked and the continuation and blessing of the righteous.

V. 26. See the "Paraphrase" on this verse. The teeth do not like vinegar nor the eyes smoke, and neither does an employer like a sluggard. Pulpit Commentary: "In a country where chimneys are unknown...the eyes must have often been painfully affected by the household fire."

V. 27. As a rule a person or a people given to sin will not live as long as a godly person or people. Sin soon burns its victims out like a roaring fire does the wood. Read Prov. 9:11 and Psa. 55:23 in connection with this verse.

V. 28. Several times does this chapter state this same truth. The righteous have much to hope for, and God does not disappoint them. The hopes of the wicked will be dashed to the ground as they perish. Psa. 112:10 and Prov. 11:7 also speak of the expectation of the wicked perishing. Sin, then, is a losing game. Don't play it!

V. 29. The way of Jehovah is followed by two statements: it is a stronghold (the utmost is protection) to the upright, but it is destruction to the workers of iniquity. When God rises to sift a people, not one kernel will be lost, but all the sinners will be destroyed (Amos 9:9). For God's special care of the righteous, see Psa. 91:1-12. It pays to do right. The backslidden people of Malachi's day said it didn't (Mal. 3:14, 15), but look what Mal. 3:16-4:2 goes on to record.

V. 30. And again the same lesson is emphasized. "Never be removed" is said of the righteous, but "not dwell" of the wicked. For the security of the godly see Psa. 125:1,2.

V. 31. The good mouth brings forth good things like praise (Eph. 5:4), edifying things (Eph. 4:29), and truth (Eph. 4:25) while the wicked mouth brings forth just the opposite, for which it will be destroyed.

V. 32. The lips of the righteous know what to say, when, where, etc. The mouth of the wicked speaks the wrong thing. Proverbs, Ephesians, and James all have much to say on the use and the abuse of the tongue.

TEST QUESTIONS OVER 10:23-32

1. What is fools' attitude toward mischief? Toward godliness (v. 23)?
2. Do godly people have any fun in life (v. 23)?
3. Do the wicked ever have any inward fears? When do they come to the surface (v. 24)?
4. What about the wicked when the whirlwind passes? What about the righteous (v. 25)?
5. Who is compared with vinegar to the teeth and smoke to the eyes (v. 26)?
6. What can shorten the life-span of sinners (v. 27)?
7. What often keeps the expectation of the wicked from coming to pass (v. 28)?
8. The way of Jehovah is what two different things to the upright and to the workers of iniquity.. (v. 29)?
9. How is the security of the godly and the insecurity of the wicked set forth in v. 30?
10. What are some of the good things that issue from the mouth of the righteous? What are some of the bad things that issue from the mouth of the wicked (v. 31)?
11. What three Bible books have much to say about the use and the abuse of the tongue (v. 32)?

NOTICEABLE GROUPINGS IN CHAPTER 10

"The righteous"--

"The memory of the righteous" (v. 7).
"The mouth of the righteous" (v. 11, 31).
"The labor of the righteous" (v. 16).
"The tongue of the righteous" (v. 20).
"The lips of the righteous" (v. 21).
"The desire of the righteous" (v. 24).
"The hope of the righteous" (v. 28).
"The lips of the righteous" (v. 32).

"The wicked"--

"The name of the wicked" (v. 7).
"The heart of the wicked" (v. 20).
"The fear of the wicked" (v. 24).
"The years of the wicked" (v. 27).
"The expectation of the wicked" (v. 28).
"The mouth of the wicked" (v. 32).

"Fools"--

"A foolish son is the heaviness of his mother" (v. 1).
"A prating fool shall fall" (vs. 8, 10).
"The mouth of the foolish is a present destruction" (v. 14).
"He that uttereth a slander is a fool (v. 18).
"The foolish die for lack of understanding" (v. 21).
"It is as sport to a fool to do wickedness" (v. 23).

Laziness"--

"He becometh poor that worketh with a slack hand" (v. 4).
"He that sleepeth in harvest is a son that causeth shame" (v. 5).
"As vinegar to the teeth, and as smoke to the eyes, so is a sluggard to them that send him" (v. 26).

"Diligence"--

"The hand of the diligent maketh rich" (v. 4).
"He that gathereth in summer is a wise son" (v. 5).
"The labor of the righteous tendeth to life" (v. 16).

"Speech"--

"Violence covereth the mouth of the wicked" (vs. 6, 11).
"In the lips of him that hath discernment wisdom is found" (v. 13).
"The mouth of the foolish is a present destruction" (v. 14).
"He that hideth hatred is of lying lips" (v. 18).
"He that uttereth a slander is a fool" (v. 18).
"In the multitude of words there wanteth not transgression" (v. 19).
"He that refraineth his lips doeth wisely" (v. 19).
"The tongue of the righteous is as choice silver" (v. 20).
"The lips of the righteous feed many" (v. 21).
"The mouth of the righteous bringeth forth wisdom" (v. 31).
"The perverse tongue shall be cut off" (v. 31).
"The lips of the righteous know what is acceptable" (v. 32).
"The mouth of the wicked speaketh perverseness" (v. 32).

TEXT — 11:1-11

1. A false balance is an abomination to Jehovah;
   But a just weight is his delight.
2. When pride cometh, then cometh shame;
   But with the lowly is wisdom.
3. The integrity of the upright shall guide them;
   But the perverseness of the treacherous shall destroy them.
4. Riches profit not in the day of wrath;
   But righteousness delivereth from death.
5. The righteousness of the perfect shall direct his way;
   But the wicked shall fall by his own wickedness.
6. The righteousness of the upright shall deliver them;
   But the treacherous shall be taken in their own iniquity.
7. When a wicked man dieth, his expectation shall perish;
   And the hope of iniquity perisheth.
8. The righteous is delivered out of trouble;
   And the wicked cometh in his stead.
9. With his mouth the godless man destroyeth his neighbor;
   But through knowledge shall the righteous be delivered.
10. When it goeth well with the righteous, the city rejoiceth;
    And when the wicked perish, there is shouting.
11. By the blessing of the upright the city is exalted;
    But it is overthrown by the mouth of the wicked.

STUDY QUESTIONS OVER 11:1-11

1. What is meant by "balance" (v. 1)?
2. Name two Bible characters whose perverseness brought their destruction (v. 3).
4. What is meant by the "day of wrath" (v. 4)?
5. Give a Biblical illustration of the righteousness of the perfect directing his way (v. 5).
6. How much is v. 6 like v. 5?
7. What dies besides a wicked person's body (v. 7)?
8. What is meant by "the wicked cometh in his stead" (v. 8)?
9. Why would a man destroy his neighbor (v. 9)?
10. Illustrate both truths in v. 10 with kings of the Old Testament.
11. Does "blessing" mean "prayers for the city" or the blessings of God upon the righteous (v. 11)?

12. How could a city be overthrown by the mouth of the wicked (v. 11)?

PARAPHRASE OF 11:1-11

1. The Lord hates cheating and delights in honesty.
2. Proud men end in shame, but the meek become wise.
3. A good man is guided by his honesty; the evil man is destroyed by his dishonesty.
4. Your riches won't help you on Judgment Day; only righteousness counts then.
5. The upright are directed by their honesty; the wicked shall fall beneath their load of sins.
6. The good man's goodness delivers him; the evil man's treachery is his undoing.
7. When an evil man dies, his hopes all perish, for they are based upon this earthly life.
8. God rescues good men from danger while letting the wicked fall into it.
9. Evil words destroy. Godly skill rebuilds.
10. The whole city celebrates a good man's success--and also the godless man's death.
11. The good influence of godly citizens causes a city to prosper, but the moral decay of the wicked drives it downhill.

COMMENTS ON 11:1-11

V. 1. A perusal of this chapter will show that its sayings deal principally with honesty, integrity and uprightness in human relationships. A "false balance" was a set of dishonest scales. That God is concerned about honesty in business is evident from this verse and from Lev. 19:35,36; Deut. 25:13-16; Prov. 20:10, 23.

V. 2. A double contrast: "pride" vs. "lowly" and "shame" vs. "wisdom". Pulpit Commentary: "Self-assertion and self-confidence shall meet with mortification and disgrace in the end."

V. 3. A triple contrast: "integrity" vs. "perverseness"; "the upright" vs. "the treacherous"; and "guide" vs. "destroy". The integrity of Joseph "guided" him with reference to Potiphar's wife (Gen 39:7-12), and the perverseness of Absalom "destroyed" him (II Sam. 15-18).

V. 4. "Clarke": "Among men they can do all things; but they cannot purchase the remission of sins, nor turn aside the wrath of God when that is poured out." Observe this fact in I Pet. 1:18; Prov. 10:2; Eze. 7:19; Zeph. 1:18. If one could gain the whole world, he could not redeem his lost soul by offering it to God at judgment (Mark 8:36, 37). But righteousness has a great bearing on one's being delivered when God raises to punish (Gen. 7:1; II Pet. 2:5,7).

V. 5. This saying is similar to v. 3. We observe that a person spends a lifetime developing his righteousness, and all the while it is the directing force of his life. Remember the wickedness of Judas and the downfall it brought him (Matt. 26:14-16; Matt. 27:3-5).

V. 6. One's righteousness that has directed him (v. 5) also delivers him from many a destruction. A treacherous person is one bent on injuring another for his own sinful gain. But such are often taken in the plot they laid for others: Psa. 9:15; Prov. 5:22; Eccl. 10:8.

V. 7. Compare with Prov. 10:28. Get this lesson: there is nothing good beyond death for the wicked. Death dashes his earthly hopes to the ground, and eternity holds nothing good for him.

V. 8. God's providential leadership and His answer of the righteous people's prayers brings about this deliverance (II Kings 18:28--19:19, 35). On the wicked coming in his stead, "Young" translates: "The righteous from distress is drawn out, And the wicked goeth in instead of him." "American Bible Union version:" "The righteous was delivered out of trouble; And the wicked came into his place." Amplified speaks of the wicked getting into trouble instead of the righteous.

V. 9. This verse well fits a court scene where the false witness can destroy his neighbor and where the faithful witness can deliver the innocent. Naboth was destroyed through false witnesses (I Kings 21:1-13).

V. 10. This verse and the one following have sayings about the "city". Good kings were honored because of their successful reigns (IIChron. 32:33; 35:24, 25); not so with the bad kings (II Chron. 24:25). Consider also Prov. 28:12-18. There must have been much rejoicing when both Athaliah and Herod the Great died.

V. 11. Prov. 29:8 says, "Scoffers set a city in a flame" (mighty cities, after being conquered, were often burned--Josh. 6:24; 8:19); "But wise men turn away wrath" (by submitting rather than resisting an over-powering enemy--Jer. 27:4-11).

TEST QUESTIONS OVER 11:1-11

1. The sayings in this chapter mainly have to do with what?
2. How strongly does God express His feelings about dishonesty in business (v. 1)?
3. What precedes destruction?
4. What precedes honor?
5. How did Joseph's integrity guide him in the Potiphar's-wife situation (v. 2)?
6. How did Absalom's perverseness destroy him (v. 2)?
7. What statement shows that righteousness is actually more powerful than riches (v. 4)?
8. How did Judas's wickedness bring about his downfall (v. 5)?
9. Who is a treacherous person? What often happens to him that he does not expect (v. 6)?
10. What happens to the wicked's hope at death (v. 6)?
11. How did Hezekiah's righteousness deliver him and Jerusalem out of trouble (v. 7)?
12. What is meant in v. 8 by "the wicked cometh in his stead?"
13. How can one's mouth destroy his neighbor (v. 9)?
14. Cite two rulers whose death must have brought rejoicing to their people (v. 10).
15. How could scoffers set their city aflame (v. 11)?
16. How would wise men often turn away wrath from their city (v. 11)?

TEXT — 11:12-21

12. He that despiseth his neighbor is void of wisdom;
But a man of understanding holdeth his peace.
13. He that goeth about as a talebearer revealeth secrets;
But he that is of a faithful spirit concealeth a matter.
14. Where no wise guidance is, the people falleth;
But in the multitude of counsellors there is safety.
15. He that is surety for a stranger shall smart for it;
But he that hateth suretyship is secure.
16. A gracious woman obtaineth honor;
And violent men obtain riches.
17. The merciful man doeth good to his own soul;
But he that is cruel troubleth his own flesh.
18. The wicked earneth deceitful wages;

But he that soweth righteousness hath a sure reward.
19. He that is stedfast in righteousness shall attain unto life;
And he that pursueth evil doeth it to his own death.
20. They that are perverse in heart are an abomination to Jehovah;
But such as are perfect in their way are his delight.
21. Though hand join in hand, the evil man shall not be unpunished;
But the seed of the righteous shall be delivered.

STUDY QUESTIONS OVER 11:12-21

1. Is lack of respect equivalent to "despising," or is "despising" always active (v. 12)?
2. Is a talebearer one who bears falsehoods, or is he also one who reveals truths that ought to be kept secret (v. 13)?
3. "Faithful" to whom or to what in v. 13?
4. According to v. 14 one should have both .... and .... counselors.
5. What is meant by being "surety" for another (v. 15)?
6. What would be included in being a "gracious" woman (v. 16)?
7. Does society or God (or both) cause the statements in v. 17 to come true?
8. What are "deceitful" wages (v. 18)?
9. "Soweth righteousness" reminds one of what well known New Testament passage (v. 18)?
10. What are the contrasts in v. 19?
11. Name Bible Characters who you consider were "perverse in heart" (v. 20).
12. What is meant by "hand join in hand" (v. 21).
13. What is meant by the "seed of the righteous" (v. 21).

PARAPHRASE OF 11:12-21

12. To quarrel with a neighbor is foolish; a man with good sense holds his tongue.
13. A gossip goes around spreading rumors, while a trustworthy man tries to quiet them.
14. Without wise leadership, a nation is in trouble; but with good counselors there is safety.
15. Be sure you know a person well before you vouch for his credit! Better refuse than suffer later.

16. Honor goes to kind and gracious women, mere money to cruel men.
17. Your own soul is nourished when you are kind; it is destroyed when you are cruel.
18. The evil man gets rich for the moment, but the good man's reward lasts forever.
19. The good man finds Life; the evil man, Death.
20. The Lord hates the stubborn but delights in those who are good.
21. You can be very sure that the evil man will not go unpunished forever. And you can also be very sure that God will rescue the children of the godly.

COMMENTS ON 11:12-21

V. 12. Following Rom. 12:18 is much wiser than despising one's neighbor. Yet many disregard it. Needless or selfish strife is a work of the flesh and not of the Spirit (Gal. 5:19-23). If you say all that can be said, you will have all the trouble that can be had!

V. 13. A double contrast: "talebearer" vs. "faithful spirit" and "reveleth" vs. "concealeth". The first statement is found also in Prov. 20:19. Wisdom dictates that some things should not be told. Both Lev. 19:16 and I Tim. 5:13 show that talebearing is wrong.

V. 14. A double contrast: "no wise guidance" vs. "multitude of counsellors" and "falleth" vs. "safety". The last statement is found also in Prov. 24:6. Kings always had counsellors, and in time of war they depended much upon them. Prov. 15:22 shows that all of us have need of counsel at times. This verse is just the opposite of a know-it-all.

V. 15. Suretyship is when one promises to stand good for the obligation of another if he cannot pay. How many people have "smarted" for co-signing notes of others!

V. 16. A triple contrast; "gracious" vs. "violent"; "woman" vs. "men"; and "honor" vs. "riches." A gracious woman prefers honor to riches, but violent men sacrifice honor to gain riches.

V. 17 The merciful man does good to himself in that others will show mercy to him (Matt. 5:7; Matt. 25:34, 35). On the other hand the cruel are asking for trouble, and it will surely come to him :I Kings 21:17-19).

V. 18. Sometimes it looks like the wicked prosper in this

world (Psa. 37:35), but they will be cut down (Psa. 37:1, 2, 10, 12-15, 17, 20, 38). They have sown to the flesh, and they will reap corruption (Gal. 6:8). "The wages of sin is death" (Rom. 6:23). Sowing to righteousness leads to a sure reward (Hos. 10:12; Jas. 3:18; Psa. 37:3-6, 11, 18, 19, 29-31, 37).

V. 19. A double contrast: "steadfast in righteousness" vs. "pursueth evil" and "life" vs. "death". As sinners pursue evil, godly people forsake evil and follow after righteousness and godliness (I Tim. 6:11; Tit. 2:12). The results? "The world passeth away, and the lust thereof: but he that doeth the will of God abideth for ever" (I John 2:17). See also the great passage, Rom. 2:6-8.

V. 20 A triple contrast: "perverse" vs. "perfect"; "in heart" vs. "in their way"; and "abomination to Jehovah" vs. "his delight". Instances of perverse hearts and God's reaction: Pharisees (Luke 16:14, 15; 18:9-14; Matt. 15:1-9; 23:25-28) and Simon of Samaria (Acts 8:20-22). Instances of good people who pleased the Lord: Job (Job 1:8) and Mary of Bethany (Luke 10:39, 42; Mark 14:3-9). God delights as much in the righteous as He deplores the wicked.

V. 21. The opening statement is also in Prov. 16:5. Clarke: "Let them confederate as they please to support each other, justice will take care that they escape not judgment." Other passages on the deliverance of the righteous: Prov. 16:4,8; Gen. 7:1).

TEST QUESTIONS OVER 11:12-21

1. What two ways is wisdom shown in the neighborhood (v. 12)?
2. Does a faithful person spread rumors and tales or seek to suppress such (v. 13)?
3. What about the person who seeks no counsel or guidance from others (v. 14)?
4. How is "smarting" sometimes connected with suretyship (v. 15)?
5. What are the differing goals of a gracious woman and violent men (v. 16)?
6. How is one being good to himself when he shows mercy to others (v. 17)?
7. How does one trouble his own flesh by being cruel (v. 17)?
8. In what sense are the gains of the wicked "deceitful" (v. 18)?

9. What chapter in Psa. emphasizes the sure reward of the righteous?
10. What are the differing attitudes toward evil and righteousness on the part of the wicked and the righteous (v. 19)?
11. What are the differing outcomes of pursuing evil and righteousness (v. 19)?
12. What group of perverse people of Jesus' day were especially abominable (v. 20)?
13. Does God overlook the righteousness of the righteous (v. 20)?
14. What is meant by "hand join in hand" (v. 21)?

TEXT — 11:22-31

22. As a ring of gold in a swine's snout,
So is a fair woman that is without discretion.
23. The desire of the righteous is only good;
But the expectation of the wicked is wrath.
24. There is that scattereth, and increaseth yet more;
And there is that withholdeth more than is meet, but it tendeth only to want.
25. The liberal soul shall be made fat;
And he that watereth shall be watered also himself.
26. He that withholdeth grain, the people shall curse him;
But blessing shall be upon the head of him that selleth it.
27. He that diligently seeketh good seeketh favor;
But he that searcheth after evil, it shall come unto him.
28. He that trusteth in his riches shall fall;
But the righteous shall flourish as the green leaf.
29. He that troubleth his own house shall inherit the wind;
And the foolish shall be servant to the wise of heart.
30. The fruit of the righteous is a tree of life;
And he that is wise winneth souls.
31. Behold, the righteous shall be recompensed in the earth;
How much more the wicked and the sinner!

STUDY QUESTIONS OVER 11:22-31

1. Illustrate a woman with discretion (v. 22).
2. What is the comparison between her and the hog with a gold ring(v. 22)?
3. Do "desire" and "expectation" in v. 23 stand for "hope" or for what actually results?

4. Find the agricultural setting in v. 24.
5. What is meant by "liberal" in v. 25?
6. What is meant by "fat" (v. 25)?
7. What New Testament passage does the last statement in v. 25 call to mind?
8. How do we know that "withholdeth" in v. 26 means "won't sell?"
9. Why would the owner withhold the grain (v.26)?
10. Whose favor is obtained in v. 27--God's or man's (or both)?
11. Cite instances of people's seeking evil (v. 27)?
12. Show from the Bible that man should not trust in riches (v. 28).
13. What does Psa. 1:3 say about the leaf of the righteous (v. 28)?
14. How does one "trouble his own house" (v. 29)?
15. Give an illustration of the foolish serving the wise (v. 20;.
16. What is meant by "tree of life" in v. 30?
17. In Solomon's day what did "winning souls" mean or involve (v. 30)?
18. What are some of the earthly recompenses upon the righteous (v. 31)?
19. What are some of the earthly recompenses upon the wicked (v. 31)?

PARAPHRASE OF 11:22-31

22. A beautiful woman lacking discretion and modesty is like a fine gold ring in a pig's snout.
23. The good man can look forward to happiness, while the wicked can expect only wrath.
24,25. It is possible to give away and become richer! It is also possible to hold on too tightly and lose everything. Yes, the liberal man shall be rich! By watering others, he waters himself.
26. People curse the man who holds his grain for higher prices, but they bless the man who sells it to them in their time of need.
27. If you search for good you will find God's favor; if you search for evil you will find His curse.
28. Trust in your money and down you go! Trust in God and flourish as a tree!
29. The fool who provokes his family to anger and resentment will finally have nothing worthwhile left. He shall be the

servant of a wiser man.

30. Godly men are growing a tree that bears lifegiving fruit, and all who win souls are wise.

31. Even the godly shall be rewarded here on earth; how much more the wicked!

COMMENTS ON 11:22-31

V. 22. We might ask, "What is a ring of gold if it be on a swine's snout? Does it make the hog? And what is physical beauty if the woman has no discretion? Is physical beauty all that counts?"

V. 23. Instead of "wrath", "Young's Literal translation" gives "transgression", and the "Septuagint" gives "shall perish". The passage means that the righteous desire only that which is good while the wicked desire that which is wrong ("transgression") or that which brings God's "wrath," causing them to perish." How wonderful to have right desires! And how bad to crave the wrong thing!

V. 24. "Scattereth" here has reference to giving to the needy (Psa. 112:9). Judiciously helping the needy does not impoverish us (God blesses us), but if we withhold from them, God will withhold from us. II Cor. 9:6: "He which soweth sparingly shall reap also sparingly; and he which soweth bountifully shall reap also bountifully." An old epitaph: "What we spent, we had; what we saved, we lost; what we gave, we have."

V. 25. "Liberal" here means "generous"; "fat" means "prosperous". Promised also in Luke 6:38: "Give, and it shall be given unto you; good measure, pressed down, and shaken together, and running over, shall men give into your bosom. For with the same measure that ye mete withal it shall be measured to you again."

V. 26. Often the rich withhold selling grain during shortages to let the price go higher and higher. How the people will curse such a character! But how the same people would bless him for not waiting for higher prices but releasing to their need!

V. 27. One who seeks to do right will obtain the favor of both man and God. As a young man Jesus "advanced...in favor with God and man" (Luke 2:52). So did the child Samuel (I Sam. 2:26). So will a virtuous person (Prov. 31:28-31). Those who traffic in evil will have evil (trouble) come upon them: Esth. 7:10; Psa. 7:15, 16; 9:15, 16; 10:2; 57:6.

V. 28. This man trusts his riches rather than God, something consistently condemned in the Bible: Job 31:24; Psa. 52:8; Mark 10:24; I Tim. 6:17. The righteous are often compared to the flourishing tree or leaf: Psa. 1:3; 52:8; 92:12; Jer. 17:8.

V. 29. God is displeased with one who makes trouble for his parents and brothers and sisters. He will inherit the "wind" (get nothing) rather than be included in the family inheritance. In life the foolish "serve" or work for the "wise". The man wise enough to choose what he wants to succeed in and prepares himself for it gets much farther than the man who idly drifts from job to job and from day to day.

V. 30. Men draw good from the lives of the righteous. To partake of the good from their lives is like eating of the tree of life. The righteous wisely win souls from the wrong to the right. This is a great Old Testament verse on the good influencing the bad over to the right way of life.

V. 31. The New Testament mainly points to the final reaping of what we have sown (Gal. 6:7-9), yet there are earthly as well as eternal consequences of our sowing (Matt. 6:33; I Tim. 4:8). There are two yokes that one can wear in life: Christ's and Satan's. Christ invited those worn out with the terrible load of sin (wearing Satan's yoke) to come to Him and to take His yoke instead, promising them soul-rest and a much better and easier way to live (Matt. 11:28-30). When one considers the sorrows and disappointments and intrigue and distrust that sin brings to a person, truly the way of the transgressor is hard (Prov. 13:15).

TEST QUESTIONS OVER 11:22-31

1. In what way is a beautiful woman with no judgment like a hog with a gold ring in its nose (v. 22)?
2. What do some other versions give instead of "wrath" in v. 23?
3. Tell in your own words what v. 24 means.
4. What are the meanings of "liberal" and "fat" as used in v. 25?
5. "Withholdeth grain" in what sense (v. 26)?
6. What two things are different people seeking, according to v. 27, and what are their prospects at succeeding at their endeavor?
7. "Trusting in riches" is set over against trusting in .... (v. 28)

8. Cite two passages that liken the righteous to a flourishing tree or leaf (v. 28).
9. What will one "inherit" from his family who has caused them endless trouble (v. 20)?
10. In life who serves whom among the wise and the foolish (v. 29)?
11. Discuss the question of the righteous person's influence from v. 30.
12. What are some of the earthly recompenses of the

12. What are some of the earthly recompenses of the righteous right in this life (v. 31)?
13. What are some of the earthly recompenses of the wicked in this life (v. 31)?

NOTICEABLE GROUPINGS IN CHAPTER 11

"What are you doing to yourself?"--

"The wicked will fall by his own wickedness" (v. 5).
"The merciful man doeth good to his own soul" (v. 17).
"He that is cruel troubleth his own house" (v. 17).
"He that pursueth evil doeth it to his own death" (v. 19).
"He that troubleth his own house shall inherit the wind" (v. 29).

"Abomination and delight"--

"A false balance is an abomination to Jehovah; But a just weight is his delight" (v. 1).

"They that are perverse in heart are an abomination to Jehovah; But such as are perfect in their way are his delight" (v. 20).

"Destruction"--

"The perversness of the treacherous shall destroy them" (v. 3)
"With his mouth the godless man destroyeth his neighbor" (v. 9)
"The city....is overthrown by the mouth of the wicked" (v, 11).
"He that pursueth evil doeth it to his own death" (v. 19)
"He that trusteth in his own riches shall fall" (v. 28).

CHAPTER 11

"Deliverance"--

"Righteousness delivereth from death" (v. 4).

"The righteousness of the upright shall deliver them" (v. 6).

"The righteous is delivered out of trouble" (v. 8).

"Through knowledge shall the righteous be delivered" (v. 9).

"The seed of the righteous shall be delivered" (v. 21).

"Righteous"--

"The integrity of the upright shall guide them" (v. 3).

"The righteousness of the perfect shall direct his way" (v. 5).

"The righteous is delivered out of trouble" (v. 8).

"Through knowledge shall the righteous be delivered" (v. 9).

"When it goeth well with the righteous, the city rejoiceth" (v. 10).

"By the blessing of the upright the city is exalted" (v. 11).

"He that soweth righteousness hath a sure reward" (v. 18).

"He that is steadfast in righteousness shall attain unto life" (v. 19).

"The seed of the righteous shall be delivered" (v. 21).

"The desire of the righteous is only good" (v. 23).

"He that diligently seeketh good seeketh favor" (v. 27).

"The righteous shall flourish as the green leaf" (v. 28).

"The fruit of the righteous is a tree of life" (v. 30).

"The righteous shall be recompensed in the earth" (v. 31).

PRIDE IS A TROUBLE-MAKER

"He that is of a proud heart stirreth up strife" (28:25), and 13:10 says, "Only by pride cometh contention."

When one is proud, he is going to try to have his own way no matter what. He will not concede that he has been wrong or that he could even be wrong. He is a self-centered, conceited man who is going to ram-rod his way through anything (or anybody) that would resist him.

It should be easy to admit error when one sees his mistake, but pride will not permit a person to make such an admission. He would rather defend himself though in error than to concede the truth. Thus, trouble arises through pride. And there are other ways too in which pride causes trouble.

PRIDE LEADS DOWN—NOT UP

"A man's pride shall bring him low" (29:23). There is a lot in that simple statement. A man's pride is actually self-exaltation. A proud man lifts himself up. But, this proverb so wisely says that his pride will actually bring him down in time. And it will. As 16:18 says, "Pride goeth before destruction, and a haughty spirit before a fall."

Haman's pride brought his destruction. So did Nebuchadnezzar's make a beast of the field of him for seven years. Peter's trusting in his own moral strength led to his downfall, for he didn't watch and pray as he should have done. And the persons of the Bible, as well as the persons of any community, give one ample examples of this sad fact.

PRIDE CONTRASTED WITH WISDOM

A proud person glories in his exalted or inflated thoughts of himself. He thinks he is "it", or she thinks she is "it". But, Proverbs lists pride as foolish and in a number of passages contrasts it with wisdom. 14:3 says, "In the mouth of the FOOLISH, is a rod of pride: but the lips of the wise shall preserve them." 11:2 says, "When pride cometh, then cometh shame: but with the lowly is wisdom." And 13:10 says, "Only by pride cometh contention: but with the well advised is wisdom." One is not well advised who is proud in heart. He has been using the wrong standard of measure. He is viewing himself in the light of his own thoughts, and they are warped. Anyone is foolish who views himself primarily in the light of his own thoughts. What God thinks of us is always right, and the common consensus of thought concerning us is also to be taken into consideration.

Let us see, then, that pride has no chance to get a start in our hearts. Let us pull out the first appearance of it lest it grow and take possession of our hearts.

TEXT — 12:1-9

1. Whoso loveth correction loveth knowledge;
But he that hateth reproof is brutish.
2. A good man shall obtain favor of Jehovah;
But a man of wicked devices will he condemn.
3. A man shall not be established by wickedness;
But the root of the righteous shall not be moved.
4. A worthy woman is the crown of her husband;
But she that maketh ashamed is as rottenness in his bones.
5. The thoughts of the righteous are just;
But the counsels of the wicked are deceit.
6. The words of the wicked are of lying in wait for blood;
But the mouth of the upright shall deliver them.
7. The wicked are overcome, and are not;
But the house of the righteous shall stand.
8. A man shall be commended according to his wisdom;
But he that is of a perverse heart shall be despised.
9. Better is he that is lightly esteemed, and hath a servant;
Than he that honoreth himself, and lacketh bread.

STUDY QUESTIONS OVER 12:1-9

1. What is the meaning of "loving correction" when Heb. 12:11 says no chastening for the moment seems joyous but grevious (v. 1)?
2. In what sense is one "Brutish" who hates reproof (v. 1)?
3. Among the things that a person might seek, where should obtaining the favor of God rank (v. 2)?
4. Cite some example of people of wicked devices whom God condemned (v. 2)?
5. Apply both parts of v. 3 to David and his contemporaries.
6. According to v. 4 how can a wife affect her husband and his situation in life?
7. Are "thoughts" and "counsels" in v. 5 the same or different? Comment.
8. In what two different ways can the tongue be used (v. 6)?
9. Think of people of your own acquaintance whom you respect for their wisdom (v. 8).
10. What verse in this chapter is similar to v. 7?

11. Think of people of your own acquaintance who are despised because of their perverse heart (v. 8).
12. What does the Bible say about honoring and exalting yourself (v. 9)?

PARAPHRASE OF 12:1-9

1. To learn, you must want to be taught. To refuse reproof is stupid.
2. The Lord blesses good men and condemns the wicked.
3. Wickedness never brings real success; only the godly have that.
4. A worthy wife is her husband's joy and crown; the other kind corrodes his strength and tears down everything he does.
5. A good man's mind is filled with honest thoughts; an evil man's mind is crammed with lies.
6. The wicked accuse; the godly defend.
7. The wicked shall perish; the godly shall stand.
8. Everyone admires a man with good sense, but a man with a warped mind is despised.
9. It is better to get your hands dirty--and eat--than to be to proud to work and starve.

COMMENTS ON 12:1-9

V. 1. This 12th chapter is another entire chapter with two statements per verse, usually contrasting statements and usually a contrast between the righteous and the wicked (as in vs. 2, 3, 5, 6, 7, 10, 12, 13, 17, 20, 21, 22). This verse connects correction and knowledge, showing that we learn through correction. The new worker has everything explained at first; he remembers most of the instructions, but he makes a mistake; the foreman re-shows him the part he had forgotten, and he now knows how to do it. The major league hires batting coaches to help players with their batting (often through correcting something about their present stance, holding the bat, or swing). Yes, correction here means rebuke (see the last statement of the verse). On "brutish" Pulpit Commentary says: "Insensible to higher aspirations, to regret for the past and hope of amendment, as a brute beast." A sad fact: more people hate reproof than love correction (John 3: 19-21; I Kings 22:8; Amos 5:10).

V. 2. A "good" man obtains God's favor, so does a righteous man (Gen. 7:1), and so does a wise man (Prov. 8:35). Rom. 5:7 draws a distinction between a "good" man and a "righteous" man. Righteousness has to do with doing right rather than wrong; goodness has to do with whether one is good to others or not. A man of wicked devices is neither right nor good. The first goal of life should be to obtain God's favor. Abel, Enoch, Noah, Abraham, Joseph, Moses, Daniel, and a host of others did--and we can. Ahab, Jezebel, Judas Iscariot, Ananias and Sapphira didn't--and many today don't.

V. 3. Compare this verse with v. 7 and Prov. 10:25. A tree is something that is "established"; it is there from year to year. So are the righteous, but the wicked are often cut off (Psa. 37:1,2). Saul and his house lost out through disobedience (I Sam. 15:23). David's house was established through obedience (II Sam. 7:12-16). Wickedness may prosper for the moment but not forever (consider Ananias and Sapphira of Acts 5:1-10 ad Haman of Esth. 5:11, 12; 7:8).

V. 4. "Pulpit Commentary:" "A virtuous woman--one whose portrait is beautifully traced in Prov. 31. The term is applied to Ruth in Ruth 3:11...As a crown to her husband, she is an honor to him, adorns and beautifies his life." But there are wives who make their husbands ashamed (maybe by over-spending, maybe their neglect of the house or the children, maybe by their excessive talking, maybe by their immoral conduct, etc.).

V. 5. Everyone has thoughts. The righteous person's thoughts reflect righteous thinking ("just"), but wicked people's thoughts ("counsels expressed in advice") are "deceit" and not sincere.

V. 6. This verse seems to be related to the previous verse. The "Thoughts" of people are put into "words" in which the wicked are out to overthrow, but the righteous are out to deliver. Jezebel used "deceit" and "words" to overthrow Naboth (I Kings 21:7-14). See Prov. 1:10-13 also.

V. 7. Similar in message to v. 3. In v. 6 the wicked were out to overthrow others; in this verse they themselves are overthrown, and the righteous who in v. 6 were out to deliver others are in this verse themselves established. Read the New Testament account of this (Matt. 7:24-27).

V. 8. "David behaved himself wisely, and Saul set him over the men of war" (I Sam. 18:5). A wise person will be looked to for leadership among the relatives, in the community, at work, and in the church. While the righteous and the wise are held in high respect, the wicked are despised (I Sam. 25:17).

V. 9. Instead of "hath a servant", some versions say "Serving himself" ("Septuagint"); "Tills for himself" ("American Bible Union version") "amplified" speaks of working for his own support. "Pulpit Commentary": "it is wiser to look after one's own business and provide for one's own necessities, even if thereby he meets with contempt and detraction, than to be in real want, all the time assuming the airs of a rich and prosperous man."

TEST QUESTIONS OVER 12:1-9

1. What is the result of loving correction (v. 1)?
2. How is one "brutish" who hates reproof (v. 1)?
3. What is the careful distinction between a "righteous" person and a "good" person (v. 2)?
4. What should be one's first goal in life (v. 2)?
5. Who were some in the Bible who were not established because of wickedness (v. 3)?
6. Who were some who were established because of righteousness (v. 3)?
7. What chapter contains extended material on the virtuous woman (v. 4)?
8. How can a wife be a crown to her husband (v. 4)?
9. How can she make him ashamed (v. 4)?
10. How are vs. 5, 6 related?
11. How are vs. 6, 7 related?
12. How did David's case illustrate v. 8?
13. What do some other versions give for "hath a servant" in v. 9?

TEXT — 12:10-19

10. A righteous man regardeth the life of his beast;
    But the tender mercies of the wicked are cruel.
11. He that tilleth his land shall have plenty of bread;
    But he that followeth after vain persons is void of understanding.
12. The wicked desireth the net of evil men;
    But the root of the righteous yieldeth fruit.

13. In the transgression of the lips is a snare to the evil man;
But the righteous shall come out of trouble.
14. A man shall be satisfied with good by the fruit of his mouth;
And the doings of a man's hands shall be rendered unto him.
15. The way of a fool is right in his own eyes;
But he that is wise hearkeneth unto counsel.
16. A fool's vexation is presently known;
But a prudent man concealeth shame.
17. He that uttereth truth showeth forth righteousness;
But a false witness, deceit.
18. There is that speaketh rashly like the piercings of a sword;
But the tongue of the wise is health.
19. The lip of truth shall be established for ever;
But a lying tongue is but for a moment.

STUDY QUESTIONS OVER 12:10-19

1. Does v. 10 teach that a person's righteousness will include the way he treats his animals?
2. What is meant by the "tender mercies of the wicked" (v. 10)?
3. Who are "vain persons" in v. 11?
4. Give the meaning of v. 12 by rewriting in it your own words.
5. Cite Bible instances of the righteous coming out of trouble (v. 10).
6. Cite Bible instances of the doings of men's hands being rendered to them (v. 14).
7. What thought-connection is there between the two statements in v. 15?
8. Is all vexation wrong (v. 16)?
9. In what other Bible passages are both "truth" and "righteousness" found (v. 17)?
10. In v. 18 rash speech is contrasted with what kind of speech?
11. There is a saying that "truth crushed to the ground will .... again" (v. 19).
12. How can v. 19 be a comfort when one has been misrepresented?

PARAPHRASE OF 12:10-19

10. A good man is concerned for the welfare of his animals, but even the kindness of godless men is cruel.
11. Hard work means prosperity; only a fool idles away his time.
12. Crooks are jealous of each other's loot, while good men long to help each other.
13. Lies will get any man into trouble, but honesty is its own defense.
14. Telling the truth gives a man great satisfaction, and hard work returns many blessings to him.
15. A fool thinks he needs no advice, but a wise man listens to others.
16. A fool is quick-tempered; a wise man stays cool when insulted.
17. A good man is known by his truthfulness; a false man by deceit and lies.
18. Some people like to make cutting remarks, but the words of the wise soothe and heal.
19. Truth stands the test of time; lies are soon exposed.

COMMENTS ON 12:10-19

V. 10. A proverb for farmers, some of whom can be very cruel to their animals. Children should be taught not to torture nor abuse animals. As a child I learned:

Be kind to your animal,
For it cannot complain;
Be thoughtful when
Using the whip or the rein.

"Clarke:" "One principal characteristic of a holy man is mercy; cruelty is unknown to him, and his benevolence extends to the meanest of the brute creation. Pity rules the heart of a pious man; he can do nothing that is cruel. He considers what is best for the comfort, ease, health and life of the beast that serves him;" "Pulpit Commentary": "God enacted that the rest of the sabbath should extend to the domestic animals (Exo. 20:10); that a man should help the overburdened beast even of his enemy (Exo. 23:5); that the unequal strength of the ox and ass should not be yoked together in the plough (Deut. 22:10); that the ox should not be muzzled when he was treading out the corn

(Deut. 25:4); that the sitting bird should not be taken from her little brood (Deut. 22:6), nor a kid seethed in its mothers' milk (Exo. 23:19). God was concerned over both man and animals in Nineveh's threatened destruction (Jon. 4:11)." There seems to be irony is speaking of the "tender mercies" of the wicked as it labels them as "cruel". All that some people know is cruelty but no tenderness.

V. 11. Prov. 28:19 is much like this verse. "Plenty" is the expected pay-off of work. The implication is that one who joins "vain fellows" (non-workers in this contrast) lacks understanding and will come to poverty. The elder son in the parable had plenty of bread, but the prodigal son who ran with useless people came to want (Luke 15:11-14, 17, 25, 26).

V. 12. The wicked (thieves, embezzlers, kidnappers, cheaters, etc.) desire and try to obtain by evil ways, but they are usually caught and end up with nothing while the righteous (who honestly work for what they have) are fruitful in their honest labors (Psa. 1:3, 4).

V. 13. The "net of evil" men desired by the wicked in order to get dishonest gain here becomes a "snare" in which one himself is taken. A liar's memory is not always good enough to keep him from contradicting himself and thus getting himself into trouble (Prov. 18:7), but the truthful, forthright speech of the righteous brings them out of difficulties.

V. 14. Compare Prov. 13:2 for a similar statement. One who has answered kindly is satisfied with the peace that results (Prov. 15:1). A good man's "doings" will also bring him blessings (Luke 6:38; Prov. 31:28-31).

V. 15. A fool knows little, actually not enough to know that he might be wrong, actually too little to seek out the advice of one who does know. Both testaments tell us not to be wise in our own eyes (Prov. 3:7, Rom. 12:16). A wise man can (and will) be warned, but a fool will go on his own way, not seeing his error, and will suffer for it (Prov. 22:3; 27:12).

V. 16. A writer has said: "A foolish man, if he is vexed, insulted, or slighted, has no idea of controlling himself or checking the expression of his aroused feelings; he at once....makes his vexation known." The wise man keeps a cool head and copes with the problem rather than cursing. Prov. 29:11 is a companion verse: "A fool uttereth all his anger; But a wise man keepeth it back and stilleth it."

V. 17. Truth and righteousness are properly associated

together (I Kings 3:6; Isa. 48:1; Zech. 8:8). Christians are to have their loins girt about with the "truth" and are to have on the breastplate of "righteousness" (Eph. 6:14). One speaks truth who has an eye to righteousness, but one who is untrue utters deceit (Prov. 14:5). We are commended before God by speaking right words but condemned before Him by speaking wrong words (Matt. 12:37).

V. 18. A double contrast: "Speaketh rashly" vs. "tongue of the wise" and "like the piercings of a sword" vs. "health". Rashness is always opposed to reason, for in rashness one speaks or acts before he thinks or beyond his thinking. Such a tongue can be like a destructive, cutting sword (Psa. 59:7; 64:3). Who hasn't sometime been cut (even cut down) by the thoughtless words of others? And yet speech can perk one up (Prov. 12:25), actually build one up. "Edify" means to "build up", and speech can be edifying (Eph. 4:29).

V. 19. It is always right to speak the truth instead of lying, and in the long run it is profitable to have told the truth, for most lies are ultimately found out. Never misrepresent anybody or anything, and if misrepresented by others, remember and take comfort from the fact that in time the truth will be known. Men may have killed Jesus as if evil, but God raised Him as His own Son (Acts 2:23, 24).

TEST QUESTIONS OVER 12:10-19

1. According to v. 10 what two ways can a person treat animals?
2. Show from the Scriptures that God in His laws was concerned about animals (v. 10).
3. Who are the "vain persons" in v. 11?
4. What well known person in one of Jesus' parables followed vain persons and ended up with nothing (v. 11)?
5. Instead of honest work how do wicked people try to obtain things (v. 12)?
6. What is the double message of v. 13?
7. What will both a good man's words and his doings do for him (v. 14)?
8. What is right in the eyes of a fool (v. 15)?
9. What does a fool not seek nor heed (v. 15)?
10. How does a fool make his vexation known (v. 16)?
11. Eph. 6:14 speaks of being girt with .... and having on the breastplate of ....

12. What is rashness contrasted with (v. 17)?
13. A wicked tongue is likened to a .... in v. 18.
14. What does "edify" mean (v. 18)?
15. We know misrepresentation is not right. Show from v. 19 that it is also not wise.

TEXT — 12:20-28

20. Deceit is in the heart of them that devise evil;
But to the counsellors of peace is joy.
21. There shall be no mischief happen to the righteous;
But the wicked shall be filled with evil.
22. Lying lips are an abomination to Jehovah;
But they that deal truly are his delight.
23. A prudent man concealeth knowledge;
But the heart of fools proclaimeth foolishness.
24. The hand of the diligent shall bear rule;
But the slothful shall be put under taskwork.
25. Heaviness in the heart of a man maketh it stoop;
But a good word maketh it glad.
26. The righteous is a guide to his neighbor;
But the way of the wicked causeth them to err.
27. The slothful man roasteth not that which he took in hunting;
But the precious substance of men is to the diligent.
28. In the way of righteousness is life;
And in the pathway thereof is no death.

STUDY QUESTIONS OVER 12:20-28

1. How many stated and implied truths can you find in v. 20?
2. What is the meaning of "mischief" in v. 21?
3. What is the meaning of "evil" in v. 21?
4. Why does it matter what God thinks of our speech (v. 22)?
5. Cite two contrasts in v. 22.
6. Why would a prudent man "conceal" knowledge (v. 22)?
7. Cite three contrasts in v. 23.
8. What is a "sloth" from which our word "slothful" comes (v. 24)?
9. Find two contrasts in v. 25.

10. If the righteous was a guide to his neighbor in Old Testament times, how is this even more true in New Testament times (v. 26)?
11. By extension could v. 27 be used against killing for sport (v. 27)?
12. Cite other passages besided v. 28 that connect righteousness with life.

COMMENTS ON 12:20-28

V. 20. Deceit in the hearts of those who devise evil is contrasted with the joy that is in the hearts of those whose counsel toward peace. Those who devise evil will do anything (lie, cheat, etc.) in order to accomplish their ends. Those who counsel peace have the good feeling of joy.

V. 21. "Mischief" and "evil" here both mean calamity or difficulty. Other passages using "evil" in this way: Amos 3:6; Eccl. 12:1. Had Jonah obeyed God, he would not have had the nightmarish experience he did (Jon. 1:1-2:6).

V. 22. Strong verses against lying: Prov. 6:17; Col. 3:9; Rev. 21:8; 22:15. God is for truth-telling (Eph. 4:25) and for sincerity (John 1:47).

V. 23. A triple contrast: "prudent" vs. "fools"; "concealeth" vs. "proclaimeth"; and "knowledge" vs. "foolishness." Why would a prudent man conceal knowledge? "He is not wont to utter unadvisedly what he knows but waits for fitting opportunity, either from humility or wise caution" ("Pulpit Commentary"). In contrast "a foolish man cannot help exposing the stupid ideas that arise in his mind" (Pulpit Commentary").

V. 24. The diligent bear rule in the community, in business, in the church, etc. See these two classes in the Parable of the Pounds (Luke 19:12-24). Before Esau and Jacob were born, God predicted that the elder (Esau) would serve the younger (Jacob) (Gen. 25:23). Jacob was diligent (agressive to get ahead, and he used every opportunity and every means at his disposal to do so), but Heb. 12:16 calls Esau a "profane" person, who "for one mess of meat sold his own birthright". What is God's evaluation of diligence and indolence? "I love Jacob; but Esau I hated" (Mal. 1:2, 3).

V. 25. While a person's own grief can make his heart heavy, a good word from someone else can cheer it up (Isa. 50:4; Prov. 12:18). Prov. 15:13 treats both conditions of the heart.

V. 26. Here are two kinds of neighbors: a true neighbor (one who is a guide) and a bad neighbor (one who causes another to err). The second greatest commandment in the law of Moses and one also found in the new covenant: love your neighbor (Matt. 22:36-39; Rom. 13:8). The law of love is to help one another (Gal. 6:2; 5:13); nor will love work injury to a neighbor (Rom. 13:10).

V. 27. The slothful man may kill game, bring it home, lay it down, and not bother to roast it so that it might be eaten. Not so with the diligent to whom everything acquired is "precious" (valuable). Some people will never get ahead because of not taking care of what they have; others get ahead by taking care of everything they have.

V. 28. Often the Hebrew poets restated the same thought in different words, such as here. This form emphasizes the fact that righetousness leads to life, not to death--a fact often taught in the Bible (Psa. 37:9, 11, 18, 29).

TEST QUESTIONS OVER 12:20-28

1. What do devisers-of-evil employ to accomplish their ends (v. 20)?
2. What emotion do counselors of peace receive (v. 20)?
3. Prove that "mischief" and "evil" sometimes mean "difficulties" in the Bible (v. 21.)?
4. What is God's reaction to lying lips (v. 22)?
5. What is the triple contrast in v. 23?
6. What causes a prudent man to "conceal" knowledge (v. 23)?
7. What class gets elevated to ruling (v. 24)?
8. What twin brothers exemplify the two sides of v. 24?
9. What should we do when we find people with heavy hearts (v. 25)?
10. What contrast toward neighbors is found in v. 26?
11. Who does not roast what he shoots (v. 27)?
12. What common practice in Hebrew poetry is observed in v. 28?

NOTICEABLE GROUPINGS IN CHAPTER 12

"*Wicked*"--

"A man of wicked devices will he condemn" (v. 2).
"A man shall not be established by wickedness (v. 3).
"The counsels of the wicked are deceit" (v. 5).

"The words of the wicked are of lying in wait for blood" (v. 6).

"The wicked are overthrown, and are not" (v. 7).

"The tender mercies of the wicked are cruel" (v. 10).

"The wicked desire the net of evil men" (v. 12).

"The wicked shall be filled with evil" (v. 21).

"The way of the wicked causeth them to err" (v. 26).

"Righteous"--

"A good man shall obtain favor of Jehovah" (v. 2).

"The root of the righteous shall not be moved" (v. 3).

"The thoughts of the righteous are just" (v. 5).

"The mouth of the upright shall deliver them" (v. 6).

"The house of the righteous shall stand" (v. 7).

"A righteous man regardeth the life of his beast" (v. 10).

"The root of the righteous yieldeth fruit" (v. 12).

"The righteous shall come out of trouble" (v. 13).

"There shall be no mischief happen to the righteous" (v. 21).

"The righteous is a guide to his neighbor" (v. 26).

"In the way of righteousness is life: And in the pathway thereof is no death" (v. 28).

"Speech"--

"The words of the wicked are of lying in wait for blood; But the mouth of the upright shall deliver them" (v. 6).

"In the transgression of the lips is a snare to the evil man" (v. 13).

"A man shall be satisfied with good by the fruit of his mouth" (v. 14).

"He that uttereth truth showeth forth righteousness; But a false witness deceit" (v. 17).

"There is that speaketh rashly like the piercings of a sword; But the tongue of the wise healeth" (v. 18).

"The lip of truth shall be established for ever; But a lying tongue is but for a moment" (v. 19).

"Lying lips are an abomination to Jehovah" (v. 22).

"The heart of fools proclaimeth foolishness" (v. 23).

"A good word maketh it glad" (v. 25).

"Fools"--

"The way of a fool is right in his own eyes" (v. 15).

"A fool's vexation is presently known" (v. 16).

"The heart of fools proclaimeth foolishness" (v. 23).

CHAPTER 12

"Wisdom"--

"Whoso loveth correction loveth knowledge" (v. 1).

"A man shall be commended according to his wisdom" (v. 8).

"He that is wise hearkeneth unto counsel" (v. 15).

"A prudent man concealeth shame" (v. 16).

"The tongue of the wise is health" (v. 18).

"A prudent man concealeth knowledge" (v. 23).

"Deceit"--

"The counsels of the wicked are deceit" (v. 5).

"A false witness, deceit" (v. 17).

"A lying tongue is but for a moment" (v. 19).

"Lying lips are an abomination to Jehovah" (v. 22).

"The way of the wicked causeth them to err" (v. 26).

"Favor"--

"A good man shall obtain favor of Jehovah" (v. 2).

"A man shall be commended according to his wisdom" (v. 8).

"Better is he that is lightly esteemed, and hath a servant,
Than he that honoreth himself, and lacketh bread" (v. 9).

FOOLS DISREGARD WISDOM

"The fear of the Lord is the beginning of knowledge: but fools despise wisdom and instruction" (1:7). "A fool despiseth his father's instruction: but he that regardeth reproof is prudent" (15:5). Such a person will turn his back on the very instruction that would make something of him. He pays no attention to what others try to tell him. He goes on his way, not realizing he has turned his back upon sound counsel. 24:7 puts it so briefly, but so correctly. "Wisdom is too high for a fool."

12:15 says, "The way of a fool is right in his own eyes: but he that hearkeneth unto counsel is wise." We have all seen living demonstrations of this. We may not always see fit to do everything that everybody tries to get us to do, but we should give sensible consideration to those things we are told. Probably most things we can accept, and we should.

10:8 continues, "The wise in heart will receive commandments: but a prating fool shall fall." And 29:9 says, "If a wise man contendeth with a foolish man, whether he rage or laugh, there is no rest." In this last passage, you will notice the usual responses given by fools to the wise efforts of others in their behalf—they will either get angry (rage) or make fun (laugh). Wisdom is too high for fools, but they don't know it.

CHAPTER 13

TEXT — 13:1-9

1. A wise son heareth his father's instruction;
But a scoffer heareth not rebuke.
2. A man shall eat good by the fruit of his mouth;
But the soul of the treacherous shall eat violence.
3. He that guardeth his mouth keepeth his life;
But he that openeth wide his lips shall have destruction.
4. The soul of the sluggard desireth, and hath nothing;
But the soul of the diligent shall be made fat.
5. A righteous man hateth lying;
But a wicked man is loathsome, and cometh to shame.
6. Righteousness guardeth him that is upright in the way;
But wickedness overthroweth the sinner.
7. There is that maketh himself rich, yet hath nothing:
There is that maketh himself poor, yet hath great wealth.
8. The ransom of a man's life is his riches;
But the poor heareth no threatening.
9. The light of the righteous rejoiceth;
But the lamp of the wicked shall be put out.

STUDY QUESTIONS OVER 13:1-9

1. Is the son wise to hear his father or wise because he hears (v. 1)?
2. Why does a scoffer not listen (v. 1)?
3. What is the meaning of "soul" in v. 2?
4. What are some things that guarded speech will not permit to be said (v. 3)?
5. What does "open wide his lips" mean (v. 3)?
6. From what small animal does our word "sluggard" come (v. 4)?
7. What is the small animal known for (v. 4)?
8. Does "fat" in v. 4 stand for something good or something bad?
9. Cite passages in which both God and godly people hate sin (v. 5).
10. What does "loathsome" mean (v.5)?
11. List the contrasts in v. 6.
12. How can a person emphasize riches and yet have none (v. 7)?
13. How can a person be poor and yet have great wealth (v. 7)?

14. What is meant in v. 8 by riches being the ransom of a man's life?
15. What does v. 8 have in mind when it says the poor hear no threatening?
16. What do "light" and "lamp" in v. 9 stand for?

PARAPHRASE OF 13:1-9

1. A wise youth accepts his father's rebuke; a young mocker doesn't.
2. The good man wins his case by careful argument; the evil-minded only wants to fight.
3. Self-control means controlling the tongue! A quick retort can ruin everything.
4. Lazy people want much but get little, while the diligent are prospering.
5. A good man hates lies; wicked men lie constantly and come to shame.
6. A man's goodness helps him all through life, while evil men are being destroyed by their wickedness.
7. Some rich people are poor, and some poor people have great wealth!
8. Being kidnaped and held for ransom never worries the poor man!
9. The good man's life is full of light. The sinner's road is dark and gloomy.

COMMENTS ON 13:1-9

V. 1. Instruction for the wise, rebuke for the unwise. Wisdom is shown in respecting the age, learning, and office of the father; the scoffer respects nobody. He is wise in his own conceit (Rom. 12:16). Samson did not regard the rebuke of his father (Judg. 14:1-4) nor did Eli's son regard his (I Sam. 2:22-25). If a son will not respect his father enough to follow his instructions, it will not be surprising if he doesn't receive his rebuke. One who scoffs at his father now will scoff at God and sacred things also.

V. 2 Compare Prov. 12:14. Ever hear of eating your own words? What people do and say will determine what they "eat" as a result. What will you eat?

V. 3. Guarding one's mouth suggests that a person should not say just anything that comes into his/her mind. One who opens his lips wide is one who talks too much and consequently says some things he shouldn't. If we keep our mouth, we keep ourselves from many troubles (Prov. 21:23). Let us say with David, "I will take heed to my ways, That I sin not with my tongue" (Psa. 39:1).

V. 4. It is easy to pass somebody's nicely kept farmstead or home and wish to be a farmer or have a well kept home. It is easy to hear somebody speak who knows the Scripture and wish to be able to find things in the Bible. But while desiring is the basis of getting, it takes much work and application to make dreams and desires come true, and this becomes the downfall of the lazy (Prov. 10:4). Pulpit Commentary: "He has the wish, but not the will."

V. 5. The righteous hate all sin (Rom. 12:9). The wicked are loathsome in the eyes of others who deplore their conduct, and they come to no good end.

V. 6. Prov. 11:6 is a companion verse. Righteousness keeps one from getting into trouble, but a sinner is overthrown in his wickedness.

V. 7. Some take the Hebrew for "maketh himself" to mean "feign". If that translation is correct, the verse would be speaking of some who were poor but feigned themselves to be rich while others with great wealth would feign themselves poor. The above are both sometimes done. Another meaning commonly taken on the verse: some who would be rich and who do everything they can to become rich end in poverty while others are always giving away and giving away and yet end up rich. The latter view may be referring to the "nothing" that the wicked rich people will have in eternity (Luke 12:20,21) and to the "great wealth" that the righteous will have who have laid up treasures in heaven (Matt. 6:20). Translations and commentaries seem to favor the first position.

V. 8. "Clarke": "In despotic countries a rich man is often accused of some capital crime, and to save his life, though he may be quite innocent, is obliged to give up his riches; but the poor in such countries are put to no trouble."

V. 9. Various passages refer to the lamp or light of the wicked being put out (Job 18:5,6; 21:17; Prov. 24:20). While applied to the individual and his life, the figure was drawn from their household habit: "No house, however poor, is left without a light burning in it all night; the housewife rising betimes to secure its continuance by replenishing the lamp with oil. If a lamp goes out, it is a fatal omen" ("Geike"). The Septuagint translates: "The light of the righteous is everlasting; but the light of sinners is quenched."

TEST QUESTIONS OVER 13:1-9

1. What about a wise son and his father's instruction (v. 1)?
2. What about a scoffer and rebuke (v. 1)?
3. What does v. 2 say a treacherous man will have to "eat?"
4. What does "guarding one's mouth" imply should be done (v. 3)?
5. Why will the sluggard have nothing (v. 6)?
6. Why will the diligent prosper (v. 4)?
7. What is a righteous man's attitude toward lying (v. 5).
8. Find the triple contrast in v. 6.
9. What two positions have been taken concerning the meaning of v. 7?
10. What did a rich man sometimes have to sacrifice in order to save his life (v. 8)?
11. What was meant by the lamp of the wicked being put out (v. 9)?

TEXT — 13:10-17

10. By pride cometh only contention;
But with the well-advised is wisdom.
11. Wealth gotten by vanity shall be diminished;
But he that gathereth by labor shall have increase.
12. Hope deferred maketh the heart sick;
But when the desire cometh, it is a tree of life.
13. Whoso despiseth the word bringeth destruction on himself;
But he that feareth the commandment shall be rewarded.
14. The law of the wise is a fountain of life,
That one may depart from the snares of death.
15. Good understanding giveth favor;
But the way of the transgressor is hard.
16. Every prudent man worketh with knowledge;
But a fool flaunteth his folly.
17. A wicked messenger falleth into evil;
But a faithful ambassador is health.

STUDY QUESTIONS OVER 13(10-17

1. Does "wisdom" in the last statement of v. 10 mean the

avoidance of contention in the setting of the verse?
2. And how can "pride" produce contention (v. 10)?
3. What is "wealth gotten by vanity" (v.11)?
4. Cite ways that hope can be deferred, making the heart sick (v. 12).
5. What does "tree of life" mean in v. 12?
6. Whose "word" in v. 13? Whose "commandment?"
7. Comment upon "snares of death" (v. 14).
8. Can you cite ten Bible examples that show the way of the transgressor to be hard (v. 15).
9. From everyday life show three ways you have seen fools flaunt folly (v. 16).
10. Who would a "wicked messenger" be in v. 17?

PARAPHRASE OF 13:10-17

10. Pride leads to arguments; be humble, take advice and become wise.
11. Wealth from gambling quickly disappears; wealth from hard work grows.
12. Hope deferred makes the heart sick; but when dreams come true at last, there is life and joy.
13. Despise God's Word and find yourself in trouble. Obey it and succeed.
14. The advice of a wise man refreshes like water from a mountain spring. Those accepting it become aware of the pitfalls on ahead.
15. A man with good sense is appreciated. A treacherous man must walk a rocky road.
16. A wise man thinks ahead; a fool doesn't, and even brags about it!
17. An unreliable messenger can cause a lot of trouble. Reliable communication permits progress.

COMMENTS ON 13:10-17

V. 10. The "King James" puts "only" with pride: "Only by pride cometh contention." Our text puts it with "contention": "By pride cometh only contention." Certainly contentions grow out of pride, one who will not be advised and who will argue back. The reason: a proud person is self-centered. A self-centered person "knows it all", and when anyone tries to advise him, he gets into an argument. On the other hand why is "wisdom" with the well-advised? Because he knows all that he himself has learned plus that which he can pick up from others. He is not proud, so he can listen and learn.

V. 11. "Pulpit Commentary": "Wealth obtained without labor and exertion, or by illegitimate and dishonest means is soon dissipated, is not blessed by God, and has no stability...Quickly won, quickly gone." Our saying: "Easy come, easy go." But those who have obtained through hard work don't "blow" their money.

V. 12. You look forward with anticipation to some day or event only to learn that it has been postponed, and what a letdown! To be put off, to be disappointed, is hard on the heart. Imagine Jacob's letdown when Rachel was not his after working those seven years for her! But when something does come to which one has long looked forward, it is a "tree of life" (health to the heart).

V. 13. Probably referring to God's Word and commandment, although the same principle is in effect concerning any word of wisdom or just commandment. King Saul did not obey God's commandment to destroy the Amalekites and all their possessions so God took the kingship away from his house (I Sam. 15:17-23). Look at Abraham as one who was rewarded for fearing God's commandment enough to have proceeded to sacrifice his son Isaac until God intervened (Gen. 22:1-18).

V. 14. In Proverbs the second statement of a verse is usually a contrast to the verse's first statement. Occasionally it isn't, as in this verse. Pulpit Commentary: "The rules and teaching of wise men are a source of life to those who follow them so that they depart from the snares of death." Jesus is the wise lawgiver of the New Testament (Acts 3:22), and all who follow His teachings will have life (John 8:12) and will escape the snares of the devil (I Tim. 3:7) that bring death (Rom. 6:23). How can one escape traps that are set for him? By following the wisdom of one who knows where those traps are!

V. 15. We honor the person who knows and uses his understanding aright whether he be parent, leader, or neighbor. On the other hand we see the unbearable outcome of sin in Cain's statement, "My punishment is greater than I can bear" (Gen. 4:13), in King Saul's miserable end (I Sam. 28:15-25; 31:1-4), and in Judas Iscariot's suicide (Matt. 27:3-5).

V. 16. Two altogether different kinds of persons: one man works with knowledge; the other shows off his folly. The fool does this because wisdom is too high for him (Prov. 24:7). David showed his prudence in the way he dealt with Saul, with his brothers, with Absalom, and with others. "I wisdom have made prudence my dwelling" and as a result "find out knowledge and discretion" (Prov. 8:12).

V. 17. A "wicked messenger" is one who is not true to the one sending him. He will be called to answer for his unfaithfulness. A curse belongs to one who perverts the gospel (Gal. 1:6-9). One who is a faithful representative brings joy to the one dispatching him. God was pleased with Jesus (Matt. 17:5), and Christ will be pleased with us if we faithfully proclaim His Word (Matt. 28:19,20).

TEST QUESTIONS OVER 13:10-17

1. How does pride bring contention (v. 10)?
2. Why is wisdom with the well-advised (v. 10)?
3. Why is wealth gotten by vanity short-lived (v. 11)?
4. Why is wealth gotten by hard work more enduring (v. 11)?
5. What does hope deferred bring (v. 12)?
6. What is the difference in the end of one who fears God's commandments and one who doesn't (v. 13)?
7. Which verse of this section does not contain a contrast?
8. What does the law of the wise permit a person to escape (v. 14)?
9. Illustrate the truth of good understanding bringing favor (v. 15).
10. Illustrate the truth that the way of the transgressor is hard (v. 15).
11. What two different kinds of persons does v. 16 talk about?
12. What does it say about each (v. 16)?
13. What kind of evil will a wicked messenger fall into (v. 17)?
14. What kind of health does a faithful ambassador bring (v. 17)?

TEXT — 13:18-25

18. Poverty and shame shall be to him that refuseth correction;
But he that regardeth reproof shall be honored.

19. The desire accomplished is sweet to the soul;
But it is an abomination to fools to depart from evil.
20. Walk with wise men, and thou shalt be wise;
But the companion of fools shall smart for it.
21. Evil pursueth sinners;
But the righteous shall be recompensed with good.
22. A good man leaveth an inheritance to his children's children;
And the wealth of the sinner is laid up for the righteous.
23. Much food is in the tillage of the poor;
But there is that is destroyed by reason of injustice.
24. He that spareth his rod hateth his son;
But he that loveth him chasteneth him betimes.
25. The righteous eateth to the satisfying of his soul;
But the belly of the wicked shall want.

STUDY QUESTIONS OVER 13:18-25

1. "Refuseth correction" in the first statement is set over against what words in the second statement (v. 18)?
2. Is there a connection between the thoughts in the first and second statements of v. 19?
3. Name a character in one of Jesus' parables who "smarted" for having been a "companion of fools" (v. 20).
4. What does "evil" mean in v. 21?
5. In what way is the "wealth of the wicked" laid up for the righteous (v. 22).
6. Restate the contrast found in v. 23.
7. In what way does a person "hate" his son if he fails to discipline him properly (v. 24)?
8. What does "betimes" mean (v. 24)?
9. How is "soul" used in v. 25?

PARAPHRASE OF 13:18-25

18. If you refuse criticism you will end in poverty and disgrace; if you accept criticism you are on the road to fame.
19. It is pleasant to see plans develop. That is why fools refuse to give them up even when they are wrong.
20. Be with wise men and become wise. Be with evil men and become evil.
21. Curses chase sinners, while blessings chase the righteous!
22. When a good man dies, he leaves an inheritance to his

grandchildren; but when a sinner dies, his wealth is stored up for the godly.

23. A poor man's farm may have good soil, but injustice robs him of its riches.

24. If you refuse to discipline your son, it proves you don't love him; for if you love him you will be prompt to punish him.

25. The good man eats to live, while the evil man lives to eat.

COMMENTS ON 13:18-25

V. 18. "A wise son heareth his father's instruction" (v. 1) and "shall be honored" (this verse) while "a scoffer heareth not rebuke" (v. 1), and "poverty and shame shall be to him that refuseth correction" (this verse). Reproof is mentioned as a part of everyone's life for no one can be right all the time (Heb. 12:6,9). Sooner or later each of us, somehow or in some way, "pulls a boner" and gets rebuked for it. Are we easily entreated? (Jas. 3:17). Are we exercised by God's chastening? (Heb. 12:11). If so, we will be honored; if not, "poverty and shame" will result.

V. 19. "The desire accomplished" (some worthy goal achieved is brought about because of diligence, v. 4) and is "sweet to the soul" (satisfying). The inventions of Thomas Edison began with an apparent need, followed by a belief that something could be done about it, urged on by a strong desire and determination to see it done, and pursued by his characteristic diligence, and when he ultimately came upon the answer, how gratifying to present its usefulness to his fellowmen! Consider Nehemiah's satisfaction when the wall was completed (Neh. 1:3,5; 2:3-5, 17,18; 6:15). The bigger and the longer a task, the more diligence and patience and desire it takes to accomplish it. If there be a connection between the first and second statements of this verse, it is that while good men dedicate themselves to the accomplishing of their righteous desires, the fool would consider it abominable to give up his sins in order to live that way.

V. 20. A Dutch proverb: "He that lives with cripples learns to limp." A Spanish saying: "He that lies down with dogs shall rise up with fleas." An Oriental saying: "He that takes the raven for his guide shall light upon carrion." The idea of apprenticeship is that we will be the wiser for for having worked with those more advanced than we are. Younger men go to places of study and learning for this purpose. But others are contented with being compaions of "fool." The outcome: they will "smart" for it, like the Prodigal Son (Luke 15:13-16). It is too bad that some would rather "smart" than be "wise". One's native wisdom and ideals are reflected in the compaions that he chooses.

V. 21. "Evil" or trouble is on the trail of sinners; it follows them wherever they go. It will ultimately catch up with everyone of them (on Judgment Day if not earlier). The righteous, on the other hand, will be recompensed for their good.

V. 22. A good man works hard, accomplishes much and takes care of what he had (see last statement in v. 11). He has something to pass onto succeeding generations. His children must also have been taught the lessons of thrift and economy, or there would be nothing left for them to pass onto his grandchildren. As for the wealth of the wicked man, there is an old saying that goes, "The third generation shall not possess the goods that have been unjustly acquired." Sometimes it ends up in the hands of the righteous. Keep your eyes open in life, and you will get to see an example of this.

V. 23. The last statement is variously translated: "But there is that is consumed without judgment" ("Young's Literal"); "But there is that is destroyed for want of judgment" ("King James"). The thought seems to be that work normally produces a good supply, but as "Clarke" observes: "How much of the poverty of the poor arises from their own want of management! They have little or no economy and no foresight. When they get anything, they speedily spend it, and a feast and a famine make the chief varieties of their life." Migrant workers are often a good example.

V. 24. The first statement puts the outcome for the attitude; that is, in view of what will result from sparing the rod, one is not really loving his child by sparing the rod (some claim they "love" their child too much to discipline him with whippings). It is better to "spare" the child from ruination than from the rod! Consider the wisdom of the saying: "Spare the rod and spoil the child." For "chasteneth him betimes" the "Amplified" says he punishes him early; "American Bible Union" says: "gives him timely chastisement;" "early" ("Pulpit Commentary"); others give "diligently". "Immediately" seems to be the thought. A wise parent will not defer punishing, will not put it off and off and really do nothing about his child's disobedience.

V. 25. The righteous may not be wealthy, but they will have enough (Matt. 6:33; Psa. 37:25). The Prodigal Son (Luke

15:14) exemplifies the latter statement.

TEST QUESTIONS OVER 13:18-25

1. What serious personal reapings may result from refusing correction (v. 18)?
2. What is the promised result of regarding reproof (v. 18)?
3. What about a "desire accomplished" (v. 19)?
4. Why do fools not know this satisfaction (v. 19)?
5. What are the contrasting results of choosing wise men and fools for companions (v. 20)?
6. What finally catches up with sinners (v. 21)?
7. What comes to the righteous (v. 21)?
8. Why does a good man leave an inheritance (v. 22)?
9. What sometimes happens to the wealth of the wicked (v. 22)?
10. What are some other translations given for "destroyed by reason of injustice" (v. 23)?
11. What is the meaning of v. 23?
12. What strong language is used in v. 24 for not properly punishing a child?
13. What is the meaning of "betimes" (v. 24)?
14. What is God's material promise to the righteous (v. 25)?
15. What Bible character fulfilled the statement, "The belly of the wicked shall want" (v. 25)?

NOTICEABLE GROUPINGS IN CHAPTER 13

"Destruction"--

"He that openeth wide his lips shall have destruction" (v.3).
"Wickedness overthroweth the sinner" (v. 6).
"Whoso despiseth the word bringeth destruction on himself" (v. 13).
"There is that is destroyed by reason of injustice" (v. 23).

"Speech"--

"A man shall eat good by the fruit of his mouth" (v. 2).
"He that guardeth his mouth keepeth his life; But he that openeth wide his lips shall have destruction" (v. 3).
"A righteous man hateth lying" (v. 5).

"Parent and child"--

"A wise son heareth his father's instruction; But a scoffer heareth not rebuke" (v. 1).

"He that spareth his rod hateth his son; But he that loveth him chasteneth him betimes" (v. 24).

"Righteous"--

"A righteous man hateth lying" (v. 5).

"Righteousness guardeth him that is upright in the way" (v. 6).

"The light of the righteous rejoiceth" (v. 9).

"The righteous shall be recompensed with good" (v. 21).

"A good man leaveth an inheritance to his children's children" (v. 22).

"Wicked"--

"A wicked man is loathsome, and cometh to shame" (v. 5).

"Wickedness overthroweth the sinner" (v. 6).

"The lamp of the wicked shall be put out" (v. 9).

"A wicked messenger falleth into evil" (v. 17).

"Evil pursueth sinners" (v. 21).

"The wealth of the sinner is laid up for the righteous" (v. 22).

"Wisdom"--

"A wise son heareth his father's instruction" (v. 1).

"With the well-advised is wisdom" (v. 10).

"The law of the wise is a fountain of life" (v. 14).

"Good understanding giveth favor" (v. 15).

"Every prudent man worketh with knowledge" (v. 16).

"Walk with wise men, and thou shalt be wise" (v. 20).

"Fools"--

"A fool flaunteth his folly" (v. 16).

"It is an abomination to fools to depart from evil" (v. 10).

"The companion of fools shall smart for it" (v. 20).

CHAPTER 14

TEXT — 14:1-12

1. Every wise woman buildeth her house;
But the foolish plucketh it down with her own hands.
2. He that walketh in his uprightness feareth Jehovah;
But he that is perverse in his ways despiseth him.
3. In the mouth of the foolish is a rod for his pride;
But the lips of the wise shall preserve them.
4. Where no oxen are, the crib is clean;
But much increase is by the strength of the ox.
5. A faithful witness will not lie;
But a false witness uttereth lies.
6. A scoffer seeketh wisdom, and findeth it not;
But knowledge is easy unto him that hath understanding.
7. Go into the presence of a foolish man,
And thou shalt not perceive in him the lips of knowledge.
8. The wisdom of the prudent is to understand his way;
But the folly of fools is deceit.
9. A trespass-offering mocketh fools;
But among the upright there is good will.
10. The heart knoweth its own bitterness;
And a stranger doth not intermeddle with its joy.
11. The house of the wicked shall be overthrown;
But the tent of the upright shall flourish.
12. There is a way which seemeth right unto a man;
But the end thereof are the ways of death.

STUDY QUESTIONS OVER 14:1-12

1. Find the two contrasts in v. 1.
2. Name some blessings of walking uprightly (v. 2).
3. Name some blessings of being perverse (v. 2).
4. Reword the first statement in v. 3 so as to bring out its meaning.
5. What is the meaning of "clean" in v. 4?
6. We talk about, "As strong as an ...." (v. 4).
7. What are some of the reasons why some people bear false witness (v. 5)?
8. Why does a scoffer have trouble learning (v. 6)?
9. Are there people who you judge to be wiser than they prove to be (v. 7)?

10. What does "prudent" mean in v. 8?
11. How could a trespass-offering mock fools (v. 9)?
12. What is "good will" (v. 9)?
13. Write an elaboration on v. 10.
14. Find the triple contrast in v. 11.
15. What other verse in Proverbs restates v. 12?
16. Cite an incident in the Bible, in history, or in your own personal knowledge illustrating v. 12.

PARAPHRASE OF 14:1-12

1. A wise woman builds her house, while a foolish woman tears hers down by her own efforts.
2. To do right honors God; to sin is to despise Him
3. A rebel's foolish talk should prick his own pride! But the wise man's speech is respected.
4. An empty stable stays clean--but there is no income from an empty stable.
5. A truthful witness never lies; a false witness always lies.
6. A mocker never finds the wisdom he claims he is looking for, yet it comes easily to the man with common sense.
7. If you are looking for advice, stay away from fools.
8. The wise man looks ahead. The fool attempts to fool himself and won't face facts.
9. The common bond of rebels is their guilt. The common bond of godly people is good will.
10. Only the person involved can know his own bitterness or joy--no one else can really share it.
11. The work of the wicked will perish; the work of the godly will flourish.
12. Before every man there lies a wide and pleasant road that seems right but ends in death.

COMMENT ON 14:1-12

V. 1. People can either build or pluck down. The wise build (Prov. 24:3-5); the foolish destroy. Owners usually build and take care of things; renters often let everything run down. Rachel and Leah are said to have built the house of Israel (Ruth 4:11). Contrast the virtuous woman of Prov. 31 with the adulterous woman often pictured in the first part of Proverbs with reference to building and destroying.

V. 2. This verse deals with two classes of men just as v. 1

did with two classes of women. What a wonderful life results for both and for their offspring when "he that walketh in his uprightness" (this verse) marries the "wise woman" (v. 1)! When people properly fear God, they keep his commandments (Eccl. 12:13); when people don't fear God, evil results (Rom. 3:15-18; Gen. 20:11). "Jehovah" is the antecedent of "him" in the second statement. Those who are perverse in their ways pay no attention to God, and "the world is full of" them.

V. 3. "American Bible Union version" and "Young's Literal" give, "A rod of pride." Septuagint: "Fom the mouth of fools cometh a staff of insolence." The foolish can have a cruel tongue ("rod"). Other passages compare the wicked tongue to a cutting sword (Psa. 57:4; 64:3).

V. 4. The ox was used for agricultural purposes then (I Kings 19:19; Deut. 25:4). A "clean" crib meant an "empty" crib. We, too, talk of the "strength" of an ox in our saying: "As strong as an ox." Through the wise use of animal power (and now much more of mechanical power), man has been able to increase his agricultural (and other) output. Man shows that he is of a higher sphere than the animal world, for he constantly utilizes the strengths and abilities of lower forms of life to serve him.

V. 5. The one difference between a "faithful" and a "false" witness: one will lie; the other one won't. Some are "false" because it is not always easy to tell the full truth. Others are "false" on purpose (for material gain, to ruin others, etc.). The soldiers who guarded Jesus' tomb lied and were paid for it (Matt. 28:11-14). Men told lies in Jesus' trial to bring about His condemnation (Mark 14:57,58). Other passages against bearing false witness: Exo. 20:16; 23:1; Prov. 6:19; 12:17; 14:25. The apostles would neither lie nor suppress the truth about Jesus (Acts 4:18-20). Such conscientious souls are needed in every age.

V. 6. A "scoffer" is strong on his own ideas and reluctant to take the word of others. Learning is not gullible, but there is still a strong element of trust involved in learning, which the scoffer does not have. Therefore, he cuts himself off from some wisdom that he could have if he were otherwise in attitude. But it is much easier for an humble man of understanding to increase his knowledge, for he has no barrier of pride. One who has understanding easily picks up additional knowledge from what he reads, hears, studies, and is instructed in, for he can understand and comprehend what he comes in contact with. See

Prov. 9:9; 17:24.

V. 7. There is some doubt as to which rendering is correct. The "King James" has: "Go from the presence of a foolish man, when thou perceivest not in him the lips of knowledge." The "American Standard" gives a truism (the foolish man has nothing to give you by his presence), but the "King James" tells you what to do about it (depart from his unprofitable presence). Enroll under teachers who know what they are talking about; doctor with those who know what they are doing; listen to religious teachers who accurately know the Bible. People would save themselves much disillusionment if they would regard this instruction.

V. 8. The prudent wisely watch every aspect of their lives (v. 15). They do not jump and then look for a place to land. They do not shoot and then investigate whether it was a deer or a man. They do not sign the contract and then study to see what they signed. And spiritually they are just as careful (Eph. 5:15). The foolish foolishly suppose they can deceive others, but seldom are they successful in their attempt.

V. 9. A trespass-offering was ordained of God if properly offered (Lev. 6:1-7), but if one thought he would "pull the wool over" God's eyes by such an offering when he intended to keep on in the trespass, he was mocked--not God (Gal. 6:7). For this reason God did not accept the acts of worship mentioned in Isa. 1:11-17. The "upright" gain the good will and favor of God by their honest dealings with themselves before Him.

V. 10. There is a portion of each person's inner-self that no one else can fully enter into. After others have sought to assuage our grief with their words lovingly administered, there is still a portion that they have not touched not known. On the other hand after we have sought to share our joys with others, we have probably enlisted their polite ears more than we have their hearts' feelings. We canot fully communicate our joys, nor can they fully enter into our joys.

V. 11. A triple contrast: "house" vs. "tent"; "wicked" vs. "upright"; and "shall be overthrown" us. "shall flourish". This verse blends the material found is vs. 1,2; study it until you can see this fact.

V. 12. Prov. 16:25 gives the identical statement. The importance of the truth may account for its double appearance in the book. Men are often talked into things that do not end as they expected. Sometimes people do the wrong thing when they think they are doing the wise and desirable thing--like mice eating bait on a trap or fish eating bait on a hook. This is even true religiously (John 16:2; Acts 26:9; Rom. 10:1-3). False teachers may look like sheep even though they are ravening, devouring wolves (Matt. 7:15). Counterfeits are made to resemble the genuine. So the devil pawns off denominations started by men for the church started by Christ.

TEST QUESTIONS OVER 14:1-12

1. The wise woman who builds her house and the foolish woman who tears hers down are likened to what two women in the earlier and the latter chapters of Prov.?
2. V. 2 shows what to be a motivation for uprightness?
3. What is the perverse person's attitude toward God or the idea of God (v. 2)?
4. Some passages liken a wicked tongue to a sword; what does v. 3 liken it to?
5. How was the ox used in Bible days (v. 4)?
6. What saying do we have involving the ox (v. 4)?
7. What was the case where there were no oxen (v. 4)?
8. How has man used his head for greater productive output (v. 4)?
9. How does this fact distinguish him from the animal world (v. 4)?
10. What two kinds of witnesses are there (v. 5)?
11. Why will people bear false witness (v. 5)?
12. Who said, "We cannot but speak the things which we saw and heard" (v. 5)?
13. Why does a scoffer sometimes cut himself off from the opportunity of learning (v. 6)?
14. Why is acquiring knowledge easy for the person who has understanding (v. 6)?
15. How do the King James and American Standard differ on v. 7?
16. How do people bring disillusionment upon themselves by not regarding v. 7?
17. What are the prudent very careful about (v. 8)?
18. Comment upon "the folly of fools in deceit" (v. 8).
19. How does a tresspass-offering mock fools (v. 9)?
20. How do the upright acquire God's good will (v. 9)?
21. Comment upon v. 1.

22. What triple contrast is found in v. 11?
23. Show that v. 11 blends the material found in vs. 1,2.
24. What explanation was suggested for v. 12 and Prov. 16:25 being in the book of Proverbs since they are identical statements?
25. Illustrate the truth of v. 12.

TEXT — 14:13-24

13. Even in laughter the heart is sorrowful;
And the end of mirth is heaviness.
14. The backslider in heart shall be filled with his own ways;
And a good man shall be satisfied from himself.
15. The simple believeth every word;
But the prudent man looketh well to his going.
16. A wise man feareth, and departeth from evil;
But the fool beareth himself insolently, and is confident.
17. He that is soon angry will deal foolishly;
And a man of wicked devices is hated.
18. The simple inherit folly;
But the prudent are crowned with knowledge.
19. The evil bow down before the good;
And the wicked, at the gates of the righteous.
20. The poor is hated even of his own neighbor;
But the rich hath many friends.
21. He that despiseth his neighbor sinneth;
But he that hath pity on the poor, happy is he.
22. Do they not err that devise evil?
But mercy and truth shall be to them that devise good.
23. In all labor there is profit;
But the talk of the lips tendeth only to penury.
24. The crown of the wise is their riches;
But the folly of fools is only folly.

STUDY QUESTIONS OVER 14:13-24

1. Are there people who try to act happy when they really aren't, or is life an admixture of happiness and sorrow (v. 13)?
2. In the Bible whose "mirth" ended in "heaviness" (v. 13)?
3. A blackslider in heart is filled with his own ways instead of whose ways (v. 14)?
4. At what stage of life is one of the most apt to believe

every word (v. 15)?
5. Cite other passages connecting fear with departing from sin (v. 16).
6. What does "insolent" mean (v. 16)?
7. Who hates a man of wicked devices (v. 17)?
8. Does life become better for the simple (18)?
9. What are some Bible instances of v. 19?
10. Why do people not want to be companions of the extremely poor (v. 20)?
11. Do you see in v. 21 a man despising his neighbor because he is poor, or is the first clause to be so limited?
12. What are illustrations of devising evil (v. 22)?
13. What are illustrations of devising good (v. 22)?
14. What does "penury" mean (v. 23)?
15. What is meant by "crown" in v. 24?

PARAPHRASE OF 14:13-24

13. Laughter cannot mask a heavy heart. When the laughter ends, the grief remains.
14. The backslider gets bored with himself; the godly man's life is exciting.
15. Only a simpleton believes what he is told! A prudent man checks to see where he is going.
16. A wise man is cautious and avoids danger; a fool plunges ahead with great confidence.
17. A short-tempered man is a fool. He hates the man who is patient.
18. A simpleton is crowned with folly; the wise man is crowned with knowledge.
19. Evil men bow before the godly.
20. Even his own neighbors despise the poor man, while the rich have many "friends."
21. To despise the poor is to sin. Blessed are those who pity them.
22. Those who plot evil shall wander away and be lost, but those who plan good shall be granted mercy and quietness.
23. Work brings profit; talk brings poverty!
24. Wise men are praised for their wisdom; fools are despised for their folly.

COMMENTS ON 14:13-24

V. 13. Fun and sorrow are found in both statements. Many who laugh may have inward sorrows they are either trying to suppress or cover up (first statement). Some who laugh easily cry just as easily. An old saying: "Laugh before breakfast, and you will cry before night" (probably superstition). Mirth sometimes precedes heaviness, like Belshazzar's feast (Dan. 5:1-6) and loose living (Prov. 5:4).

V. 14. A backslidden life is no longer filled with God's ways but with one's own. A backslider is one who has returned to selfish living. Clarke: "Who is the backslider? 1. The man who once walked in the ways of religion but has withdrawn from them. 2. The man who once fought manfully against the world, the devil, and the flesh but has retreated from the battle or joined the enemy. 3. The man who once belonged to the congregation of the saints but is now removed from them and is set down in the synagogue of Satan." One backslides "in heart" before he does in his "ways": people cease enjoying the assembly before they actually quit attending; they lose their touch with God in prayer before they drop the practice of prayer; etc. A "good man" (contrasted with the backslider) will be satisfied from himself because he is actually filled with God's good and holy ways which bring blessings and satisfaction.

V. 15. Such are like children (Eph. 4:14). Older people often amuse themselves by taking advantage of an innocent child's gullibility by telling him all kinds of yarns and tales. And some people grow up and never doubt anything they hear. In contrast "the prudent man considers whither the advice given will lead him; he always acts with deliberation" ("Pulpit Commentary").

V. 16. A wise man does not take dangerous chances, but a foolish man will (Prov. 22:3). Joseph was a "wise man" who feared God and "departed" from the evil in which Potiphar's wife would have ensnared him (Gen. 39:9-12).

V. 17. The Bible is against quick-temperedness: Tit. 1:7; Jas. 1:19; Prov. 15:18; 16:32. An angry man will deal foolishly because anger momentarily blurs one's judgment (a good reason for not losing one's temper). Jokingly, keep your temper--nobody wants it. A man of wicked devices is hated of God (Prov. 12:2), but two human groups who hate or abhor him are those who are hurt by his devices (like people who get robbed or cheated by some slick maneuver) and those who do not approve of them (Rev. 2:2).

V. 18. Those at the low end of wisdom (the simple) participate or know only folly (foolishness) (Prov. 18:2; Eccl. 7:5,6); those at the top end (the prudent) are blessed with knowledge (Prov. 9:9). A Stoic saying: "The wise is the only king."

V. 19. "Pulpit Commentary": "The final victory of good over evil is here set forth. However triumphant for a time and apparently prosperous the wicked may be, their success is not lasting; they shall in the end succumb to the righteous even as the Canaanite kings crouched before Joshua's captains (Josh. 10:24) and, hurled from their high estate, they shall stand humbly at the good man's door begging for bread to support their life (I Sam. 2:36). The contrast here indicated is seen in our Lord's report of the rich man and Lazarus when the beggar is comforted and the rich man is tormented, and when the latter urgently sues for the help of the once despised outcast to mitigate the agony which he is suffering" (Luke 16:24). When troubles hit the wicked and ungodly (those who never go to church;, they often turn to the righteous for sympathetic help and comfort (a preacher, the church, or some good Christian). Ultimately the wicked will bend (Dan. 3:24-26, 28-30; 5:13,16; Rev. 3:9).

V. 20. There is a certain shame and disgrace to extreme poverty that causes even neighbors not to be associated with such in people's minds. This is why people are often ashamed of their poor relatives (Prov. 10:7), their clothes, their car, their home, their ways, etc. But people are usually glad to claim relationship and friendship with the financially successful (a saying: "Success makes false friends and true enemies"). The rich have many friends, especially if they are generous with their gifts or have powers and offices to bestow.

V. 21. But we are not to despise our neighbor (even if he is poor, as in v. 20). Some have no sense of respect or honor, seemingly despising, belittling, and running down everyone continually. Let us not thus violate the "second commandment" (Mark 12:31), but let us have pity upon the poor (Gal. 2:10; Matt. 25:35,36), for those who do will be blessed of God (Psa. 41:1; Acts 20:35; Prov. 19:17; Luke 14:13,14).

V. 22. Such a question is an emphatic way to state truth. The man who invented the atomic bomb went out of his mind after it was used on the Japanese, and the widow of the man who invented television is extremely remorseful because of the evil it has become associated with and promotes. This verse speaks of two devisings (evil and good). Some are devising evil (the wicked), and some are devising good (the godly). What are you devising? Mercy and truth belong together (Prov. 3:3; Psa. 61:7; John 1:17; I Tim. 1:2).

V. 23. There is often a difference between being a talker and a worker. It is not those who talk about what they are going to do but those who go out and get it done that counts. Sometimes children come to look down upon their lazy, wind-bag, good-for-nothing dads who are always talking about the trip the family is going to take, the house they are going to build, etc. but who never get any of it done. This verse has two contrasts: "talk" vs. "labor" and "penury" vs. "profit". "Penury" means to want or to suffer need.

V. 24. Notice "folly" all the way in this triple contrast: "The crown" vs. "the folly"; "of the wise" vs. "of fools"; and "is their riches" vs. "is only folly". Pulpit Commentary: "Decorate folly as you may, deck it out in gaud and ornament, it is still nothing but folly and is discerned as such, and that all the more for being made conspicuous."

TEST QUESTIONS OVER 14:13-24

1. Comment upon v. 13.
2. Who is a backslider (v. 14)?
3. Why is a good man satisfied from himself (v. 14)?
4. What is v. 15's contrast between the simple and the prudent?
5. What is v. 16's contrast between the wise and the foolish?
6. What does the Bible say about being quick-tempered (v. 17)?
7. What is v. 18's contrast between the simple and the prudent?
8. Cite examples of the truth set forth in v. 19.
9. Why do people disdain the poor (v. 20)?
10. Why do many want to claim the rich for friends (v. 20)?
11. What commandment is violated by despising your neighbor (v. 21)?
12. Where else are we taught to have pity (help) the poor (v. 21)?
13. Have people ever lived to regret evil they one time devised (v. 22)?

14. What two contrasts are found in v. 23?
15. What does "penury" mean (v. 23)?
16. Cite the triple contrast in v. 24.

TEXT — 14:25-35

25. A true witness delivereth souls;
But he that uttereth lies causeth deceit.
26. In the fear of Jehovah is strong confidence;
And his children shall have a place of refuge.
27. The fear of Jehovah is a fountain of life,
That one may depart from the snares of death.
28. In the multitude of people is the king's glory;
But in the want of people is the destruction of the prince.
29. He that is slow to anger is of great understanding;
But he that is hasty of spirit exalteth folly.
30. A tranquil heart is the life of the flesh;
But envy is the rottenness of the bones.
31. He that oppresseth the poor reproacheth his Maker;
But he that hath mercy on the needy honoreth him.
32. The wicked is thrust down in his evil-doing;
But the righteous hath a refuge in his death.
33. Wisdom resteth in the heart of him that hath understanding;
But that which is in the inward part of fools is made known.
34. Righteousness exalteth a nation;
But sin is a reproach to any people.
35. The king's favor is toward a servant that dealeth wisely;
But his wrath will be against him that causeth shame.

STUDY QUESTIONS OVER 14:25-35

1. A true witness "delivereth souls" from what (v. 25)?
2. How is "fear" used in v. 26?
3. What is meant by "fountain of life" in v. 27?
4. Give a synonym for "want" in v. 28.
5. Give illustrations of "hasty of spirit" exalting folly (v. 29).
6. What is a "tranquil" heart (v. 30)?
7. What passage in Matt. does v. 31 remind one of?
8. What is the righteous person's "refuge" when death comes (v. 32)?

9. What is the meaning of "resteth" in v. 33?
10. Trace the truthfulness of v. 34 in Israel's up-and-down history.
11. Cite the double contrast in v. 35.

PARAPHRASE OF 14:25-35

25. A witness who tells the truth saves good men from being sentenced to death, but a false witness is a traitor.
26. Reverence for God gives a man deep strength; his children have a place of refuge and security.
27. Reverence for the Lord is a fountain of life; its waters keep a man from death.
28. A growing population is a king's glory; a dwindling nation is his doom.
29. A wise man controls his temper. He knows that anger causes mistakes.
30. A relaxed attitude lengthens a man's life; jealousy rots it away.
31. Anyone who oppresses the poor is insulting God who made them. To help the poor is to honor God.
32. The godly have a refuge when they die, but the wicked are crushed by their sins.
33. Wisdom is enshrined in the hearts of men of common sense, but it must shout loudly before fools will hear it.
34. Godliness exalts a nation, but sin is a reproach to any people.
35. A king rejoices in servants who know what they are doing; he is angry with those who cause trouble.

COMMENTS ON 14:25-35

V. 25. V. 5 of this chapter speaks of the faithful witness and of the lying witness mentioned in this verse. A true witness "delivereth" souls or persons from their false accusers in court; a false witness, on the other hand, will tell lies of deceit in order to bring about one's condemnation. This verse has a ready application today to the true gospel preacher who delivers souls from the clutch of sin and the doom it would bring upon him and to the false teacher who utters falsehood deceitfully (Eph. 4:14). The tongue of man is either a mighty instrument for good or a mighty monster for bad (Prov. 18:21).

V. 26. This and the following verse both refer to the "fear

of Jehovah". The "fear of Jehovah" here is that reverence for Him that causes one to commit one's whole self to Him, and when this is done, both he and his children are blessed: he has strong confidence or assurance that God will take care of Him (Heb. 13:5,6; Psa. 23:1-6), and his children (brought up to live the same way) will be likewise blessed.

V. 27. This verse and Prov. 13:14 strongly resemble. Also compare it with v. 16. One who fears Jehovah departs from evil that he may escape the "snares of death" (this verse), which characterizes him as "wise" (v. 16). Instead of death he is drinking of the fountain of life. Because Adam and Eve sinned, they were banned from the tree of "life", and they brought "death" upon themselves (Gen. 2:17; 3:22-24).

V. 28. To be too small in number was to invite invasion, and the rule was that the lesser-in-number lost to the greater-in-number. This is why the men of Gideon's army were so fearful (Judg. 6:33; 7:3). In somewhat a different thought Pulpit Commentary says, "This maxim is not in accordance with the views of Oriental conquerors and despots, who in their selfish lust of aggrandizement cared not what suffering they inflicted or what blood they shed...The reign of Solomon, the peaceful, gave an intimation that was and conquest were not a monarch's highest glory; that a happy and numerous people, dwelling securely and increasing in numbers, was a better honor for a king and more to be desired" (I Kings 4:24,25,20).

V. 29. V. 19 of this chapter deals with the man who is "soon angry" while this verse deals with one who is "slow to anger". The quick-tempered man will "deal foolishly" (v. 17), while the calm-headed man is of "great understanding" (this verse). The man of understanding does not burst into a rage, for to do so is to exalt "folly", for an angry man will say and do things before he thinks, which are both unwise and often disastrous. Compare Prov. 16:32 and Jas. 1:19 with this teaching.

V. 30. There is nothing better for the health of one's body than a tranquil, calm, and peaceful heart. Oh, the health disturbances that are brought on through a distraught mind and heart! All the doctor's prescriptions and all the doctor's operations cannot put one's health together again. God wants us to live right that we might be at peace with Him (Num. 6:24-26. He wants us to live at peace with our fellowmen (Heb. 12:14). When our consciences are void of offence toward both God and men :(Acts 24:16), what a blessing of peace follows (Col. 3:15; Phil. 4:7; Rom. 8:6) Psa. 37:37) I Pet. 3:11), one of which is "the life of the flesh" (this verse). Prov. 12:4 also speaks of "the rottenness of the bones". When one's very framework is thus deteriorated, one's health is in an extremely bad way.

V. 31. One's action toward the poor and needy is here judged in relation to God (Matt. 25:44,45), who is the Maker of the poor as well as any other (Prov. 22:2). Prov. 17:5 speaks of mocking the poor, which also results in reproaching their Maker. V. 21 of this chapter speaks of having pity on the poor which he does by having mercy upon him (this verse). People of Job's day understood this teaching (Job 31:13-15). In life there are some who help make people poor (like the thieves in the Good Samaritan parable, Luke 10:30) and others who help the needy (like the Good Samaritan himself, Luke 10:33,34); and then there are also many (like the priest and levite of that parable) who neither made the man poor nor help him get better (Luke 10:31,32). In which class are you?

V. 32. The wicked are cut off because of their sins (Psa. 37:1,2), sometimes right while they are committing it (Acts 5:1-10; Lev. 10:1,2; Num. 11:33). The godly have always had the refuge of hope and God's help in death (Psa. 23:4; Phil. 1:21,23; II Cor. 5:8). Even wicked men, like Balaam, have wished to die the death of the righteous (Num. 23:10). "Thus the Christian martyrs went joyfully to the stake, and gentle women and little children smiled on the sword which sent them home. It is natural to see in this clause a belief in a future life, and a state of rewards and punishments" ("Pulpit Commentary"). This verse causes us to ask, "Which is really more important--to enjoy the pleasures of sin for a season and be rejected and punished of God forever or to live the way that is always right and that will end right?"

V. 33. A triple contrast: "Wisdom" vs. "that which is in the inward part of fools"; "him that hath understanding" vs. "fools"; and "resteth" vs. "is made known". From the contrast we understand the word "rest" as meaning it quietly resides. Therefore, a wise, informed, and knowledgeable person is not always telling all he may know (he couldn't, and he has no disposition to flaunt his knowledge;. But with fools it is different: they are always talking, and they will tell you everything (Prov. 29:11; 12:16). For the last clause a few Hebrew copies give, "In the midst of fools it maketh itself known."

V. 34. An oft-quoted verse because its message is pertinent. God sees that righteousness does build up, bless, and make a great nation, and history surely shows that sin deteriorates a nation (many nations have fallen from the inside through moral degradation). Who could better understand this verse than the Israelites themselves who could certainly see that when they had good kings and were following God's way, the nation was "up", and that when they had bad kings and were following wickedness, the nation was "down"? This is observable throughout Kings and Chronicles.

V. 35. Every leader that Joseph was under (Potiphar, the jailer, and Pharoah) could see that he was wise, and they respected that wisdom and showed favor toward him (Gen. 39:3-6, 21-23; 41:39-43). Daniel, too, though a part of a captured people, was in every king's favor and service that he was under (Dan. 1:19,20; 2:46-48; 5:29; 6:1-3). For the promotion of the wise see Matt. 24:45,47. Even heathen governments have punished those who did things contrary to its laws and things against its best interest. In this age of softening-punishments (in the government, at work, at school, in the home, etc.) there is a need to return to stricter trials and just punishments.

TEST QUESTIONS OVER 14:25-35

1. How might v . 25 apply to preachers?
2. What does the fear of Jehovah cause one to do (v. 26)?
3. What else does one do who fears Jehovah (v. 27)?
4. Why was Gideon's army so fearful in Judg. 6,7 (v. 28)?
5. How does one hasty of spirit exalt folly (v. 29)?
6. Relate both a peaceful heart and an envious heart to one's health (v. 30).
7. What are three classes of people in relation to the poor (v. 31)?
8. Name some wicked people who were cut down right while doing their sin (v. 32).
9. State the contrast in v. 33 concerning the understand and the fools.
10. How was the nation of Israel in a good position to understand v. 34?
11. What Bible heroes served their governmental superiors well (v. 35)?

NOTICEABLE GROUPINGS IN CHAPTER 14

"Fools"--

"The foolish plucketh it down with her own hands" (v. 1).
"In the mouth of the foolish is a rod for his pride" (v. 3).
"Go into the presence of a foolish man, And thou shalt not perceive in him the lips of knowledge" (v. 7).
"The folly of fools is deceit" (v. 8;.
"A trespass-offering mocketh fools" (v. 9).
"The fool beareth himself insolently, and is confident" (v. 16).
"He that is soon angry will deal foolishly" (v. 17).
"The simple inherit folly" (v. 18).
"The folly of fools is only folly" (v. 24).
"He that is hasty of spirit exalteth folly" (v. 29).
"That which is in the inward part of fools is made known" (v. 33).

"The simple"--

"The simple believe every word" (v. 15).
"The simple inherit folly" (v. 18).

"The wise"--

"Every wise woman buildeth her house" (v. 1).
"The lips of the wise shall preserve them" (v. 3).
"Knowledge is easy unto him that hath understanding." (v. 6).
"The wisdom of the prudent is to understand his way" (v. 8).
"The prudent man looketh well to his going" (v. 15).
"A wise man feareth, and departeth from evil" (v. 16).
"The prudent are crowned with knowledge" (v. 18).
"The crown of the wise is their riches" (v. 24).
"He that is slow to anger is of great understanding" (v. 29).
"Wisdom resteth in the heart of him that hath understanding" (v. 33).
"The king's favor is toward a servant that dealeth wisely" (v. 35).

"Fear"--

"He that walketh in his uprighteness feareth Jehovah" (v. 2).
"A wise man feareth, and departeth from evil" (v. 16).
"In the fear of Jehovah is strong confidence" (v. 26).

CHAPTER 14

"The fear of Jehovah is a fountain of life" (v. 27).

"Speech"--

"In the mouth of the foolish is a rod for his pride; But the lips of the wise shall preserve them" (v. 3).

"A faithful witness will not lie; But a false witness uttereth lies" (v. 5).

"A foolish man, And thou shalt not perceive in him the lips of knowledge" (v. 7).

"The talk of the lips tendeth only to penury" (v. 23).

"A true witness delivereth souls; But he that uttereth lies causeth deceit" (v. 25).

"The righteous"--

"He that walketh in his uprightness feareth Jehovah" (v. 2).

"Among the upright there is good will" (v. 9).

"The tent of the upright shall flourish" (v. 11).

"A goodman shall be satisfied from himself" (v. 14).

"Mercy and truth shall be to them that devise good" (v. 22).

"The righteous hath a refuge in his death" (v. 32).

"The wicked"--

"The house of the wicked shall be overthrown" (v. 11).

"A man of wicked devices is hated" (v. 17).

"The evil bow down before the good; And the wicked, at the gates of the righteous" (v. 19).

"Do they not err that devise evil?" (v. 22).

"The wicked is thrust down in his evil-doing" (v. 32).

"Knowledge"--

"Knowledge is easy unto him that hath understanding" (v. 6).

"Thou shalt not perceive in him the lips of knowledge" (v. 7).

"The wisdom of the prudent is to understand his way" (v. 8).

"The prudent are crowned with knowledge" (v. 18).

"Wisdom resteth in the heart of him that hath understanding" (v. 33).

GOD CREATED US ALL

"The rich and poor meet together: the Lord is the maker of them all" (22:2). The rich may feel superior to the poor, but they need to remember that God is the poor man's God just as much as He is their God. They should not overlook the fact that the poor man is rich in the fact that he too is a recipient of God's love and concern. On the other hand, the poor many times hate the rich, but they need to remember that God is just as much concerned about the soul of the rich as He is their souls. All have been created in the image of God, and we have gone a long way in living right in the earth when we come to regard each person as one who bears the image of God. Because of this fact, we are to have a regard and a love for each individual.

"The poor and the deceitful man meet together: the Lord lighteneth both their eyes" (29:13). God does not rejoice in their deceitfulness, but He bears with them in His great longsuffering and loving kindness, hoping that the time will come when they will be what they should be. That we too might not abandon people without any future hope whom God continues to sustain!

GOD CREATED AND SUSTAINS THE UNIVERSE

The thought that all things came into existence through millions of years of struggle via the evolutionary route is all too common today. That all things merely govern themselves in a natural way without any personal God behind it all seems even more common. But, both concepts are wrong. Proverbs is strong on the fact of God's creation, and it also shows that He governs His universe today: "The Lord by wisdom hath founded the earth; by understanding hath he established the heavens. By his knowledge the depths are broken up, and the clouds drop down the dew" (3:19:20).

CHAPTER 15

TEXT 15:1-11

1. A soft answer turneth away wrath;
   But a grevious word stirreth up anger.
2. The tongue of the wise uttereth knowledge aright;
   But the mouth of fools poureth out folly.
3. The eyes of Jehovah are in every place,
   Keeping watch upon the evil and the good.
4. A gentle tongue is a tree of life;
   But perverseness therein is a breaking of the spirit.
5. A fool despiseth his father's correction;
   But he that regardeth reproof getteth prudence.
6. In the house of the righteous is much treasure;
   But in the revenues of the wicked is trouble.
7. The lips of the wise disperse knowledge;
   But the heart of the foolish doeth not so.
8. The sacrifice of the wicked is an abomination to Jehovah;
   But the prayer of the upright is his delight.
9. The way of the wicked is an abomination to Jehovah;
   But he loveth him that followeth after righteousness.
10. There is grievous correction for him that forsaketh the way;
    And he that hateth reproof shall die.
11. Sheol and Abaddon are before Jehovah;
    How much more then the hearts of the children of men!

STUDY QUESTIONS OVER 15:1-11

1. Find the double contrast in v. 1.
2. Does "fools" mean "simpleton" or "unwise" in v. 2?
3. Cite other passages besides v. 3 that show either the omnipresence of the omniscience of God.
4. The breaking of what "spirit" (v. 4)?
5. Locate other passages besides v. 5 that speak of despising correction.
6. Locate other passages on regarding reproof (v. 5).
7. Who was a righteous man in the Bible who was rich (v. 6)?
8. Who was a wicked rich man who had trouble (v. 6)?
9. What does "disperse" mean (v. 7)?
10. What makes the sacrifice mentioned in v. 8 abominable to God?

11. Compare vs. 8,9.
12. Forsaketh what "way" (v. 10)?
13. What is "Sheol" (v. 11)?
14. Where else is "Abaddon" used in the Bible (v. 11)?

PARAPHRASE OF 15:1-11

1. A soft answer turns away wrath, but harsh words cause quarrels.
2. A wise teacher makes learning a joy; a rebellious teacher spouts foolishness.
3. The Lord is watching everywhere and keeps His eye on both the evil and the good.
4. Gentle words cause life and health; griping brings discouragement.
5. Only a fool despises his father's advise; a wise son considers each suggestion.
6. There is treasure in being good, but trouble dogs the wicked.
7. Only the good can give good advice. Rebels can't.
8. The Lord hates the gifts of the wicked, but delights in the prayers of His people.

9,10. The Lord despises the deeds of the wicked, but loves those who try to be good. If they stop trying, the Lord will punish them; if they rebel against that punishment, they will die.

11. The depths of hell are open to God's knowledge. How much more the hearts of all mankind!

COMMENTS ON 15:1-11

V. 1 The setting of the verse: someone has spoken angrily to us. What kind of answer shall we give? We can return a "soft" (gentle) answer, which will tone down the other's wrath, or we can answer in the same tone in which he spoke to us, and full-fledged trouble flares. "Pulpit Commentary: "Two things are here observed: an answer should be given--the injured person should not wrap himself in sullen silence; and that answer should be gentle and conciliatory." A medieval rhyme: "Anger, however great, is checked by answer sweet." This instruction is necessary for maintaining good human relations. Even strange animals are often calmed by a gentle voice. Giving a "soft" answer is part of obeying Rom. 12:18. An instance of the "soft" answer working (I

Sam 25:23-33). Instances of "grievous" words stirring up strife (Judg. 8:1-3; Prov. 25:15; I Sam. 25:10-13; I Kings 12:13-16).

V. 2. A "wise" person has the knowledge to utter; he also knows when, where, and how to speak; and he studies or thinks before he speaks (v. 28). Jesus' speech was always superior, beginning with Luke 2:46,47. But fools pour out folly (Prov. 12:23; 13:16). A fool's voice is known by its words (Eccl. 5:3).

V. 3. Both the omnipresence and the omniscience of God are implied in this statement: He is everywhere, and He knows everything (Psa. 139:1-12; Prov. 5:21; Jer. 16:17; Heb. 4:13). Such knowledge is necessary if God is to be our judge (Jer. 32:19). Since He beholds both the evil and the good, God is not human, for human beings tend to see only the evil of their enemies and critics and to by-pass the evil in their friends and close relatives. This verse backs up our song, "You Cannot Hide from God." Jonah (Jon. 1:3) tried it; so did Achan (Josh. 7:1,11,16-21); so did Ananias and Sapphira (Acts 5:1-9); so did many others.

V. 4. A "tree of life" to everyone: to the one who has spoken and to those who have heard. The perverse tongue is a "breaking of the spirit" to all involved: the speaker himself is often hurt; so are those who have been spoken to. A kind tongue was a part of the virtuous woman (Prov. 31:26).

V. 5. A fool is wrong twice: first, he disobeys, and then he will not accept correction--much like King Asa (II Chron. 16:7-10). Some will accept correction, and some won't (Prov. 10:1). Those who do are "wise" (Prov. 10:1); those who don't aren't. See these passages (Prov. 13:18; 15:10,12,31,32).

V. 6. This was especially true of Israel's and Judah's kings. Those who were good gained cities and amassed wealth through the blessing of God, and those who were wicked often lost cities and had to pay off their enemies to keep from being destroyed.

V. 7. Another contrast between the "wise" and "foolish". The wise's lips "disperse" (disseminate, give out) knowledge (Prov. 10:21), but the foolish's heart has no inclination to do so. These two groups live "poles apart". They live in the same material world, yet they live in two different "worlds" while here.

V. 8. Sometimes the wicked sacrifice, pray, and keep up a "front" of religion, but it does them no good (Prov. 21:27; 28:9; Gen. 4:5; Isa. 1:11; Jer. 6:20; Amos 5:22: Mark 7:7; Luke 18:11-14). God is pleased to hear the prayers of the godly (I Pet.

2:12; John 9:31; I John 3:22).

V. 9. This verse goes closely with v. 8. Sinners often look down upon others who do not live as they live, go where they go, and indulge in what they indulge in. They seem to be very "sold" on themselves and their ways, even thinking it strange that others do not run with them to the same excess of riot and speaking evil of them (I Pet. 4:4); but their ways are abominable to God (this verse;. And Psa. 1:1 says, "Blessed is the man that walketh not in the counsel of the wicked, Nor standeth in the way of sinners, Nor sitteth in the seat of the scoffers." Righteousness is something to be followed (pursued). and we are to follow wherever it may lead (Prov. 21:21; I Tim. 6:11). There are "paths of righteousness" (Psa. 23:3) where the Good Shepherd has led His sheep throughout the centuries of time.

V. 10. Those who are in the "way of the wicked" (v. 9) are in for grievous correction, both by God and man (God's chastening and man's courts and personal dealings). And while such are famous for not regarding reproof, not listening, not amending their ways, they had better, for "he that hateth reproof shall die" (sometimes by execution, sometimes by God's cutting him off, and by ultimately the second death). Other passages: Vs. 5,12,32; Prov. 5:12; 10:17; Heb. 21:11.

V. 11. "Sheol" is the Hebrew word for the place of departed spirits (the same as "Hades" in Greek). "Abaddon" is the Hebrew word for destruction (the same as "Apollyon" in Greek). Both forms of the latter are used in Rev. 9:11 "Sheol and Abaddon" are used together in Job 26:6 and Prov. 27:20. The omniscience of God, then, extends to those who have perished (this verse; Psa. 139:8), and so does it also to the hearts of men (I Sam. 16:7; II Chron. 6:30; Psa. 7:9; 44:21; John 2:24,25; Acts 1:24; 8:21).

TEST QUESTIONS OVER 15:1-11

1. In what two ways can we respond to cutting words (v. 1)?
2. Give the outcome of the two different answers (v. 1)?.
3. Comment upon a wise person's uttering knowledge (v. 2).
4. What comes forth from a fool's mouth (v. 2)?
5. Cite two passages showing God's omniscience (v. 3).
6. Why is God's omniscience necessary to His righteous judgment (v. 3)?
7. Who all are blessed by the gentle tongue (v. 4)?
8. Who all are hurt by the perverse tongue (v. 4)?

9. What two times is the fool of v. 5 wrong?
10. Illustrate v. 6 by some of the kings of Israel and Judah.
11. What is the contrast between the wise and foolish in v. 7?
12. Why would the wicked bother to sacrifice to God (v. 8)?
13. What about the sacrifice of the wicked (v. 8)?
14. How does sinners' view of the ungodly life differ from God's view of it (v. 8)?
15. What does it mean to "follow" righteousness (v. 9)?
16. Who will correct the person who forsakes the right way (v. 10)?
17. Why should people listen to reproof (v. 10)?
18. What is "Sheol" (v. 11)?
19. What Greek word means the same (v. 11)?
20. What does "Abaddon" mean (v. 11)?
21. What Greek word means the same (v. 11)?
22. According to v. 11 what is before the eyes of God?

TEXT — 15:12-22

12. A scoffer loveth not to be reproved;
He will not go unto the wise.
13. A glad heart maketh a cheerful countenance;
But by sorrow of heart the spirit is broken.
14. The heart of him that hath understanding seeketh knowledge;
But the mouth of fools feedeth on folly.
15. All the days of the afflicted are evil;
But he that is of a cheerful heart hath a continual feast.
16. Better is little, with the fear of Jehovah,
Than great treasure and trouble therewith.
17. Better is a dinner of herbs, where love is,
Than a stalled ox and hatred therewith.
18. A wrathful man stirreth up contention;
But he that is slow to anger appeaseth strife.
19. The way of the sluggard is as a hedge of thorns;
But the path of the upright is made a highway.
20. A wise son maketh a glad father;
But a foolish man despiseth his mother.
21. Folly is joy to him that is void of wisdom;
But a man of understanding maketh straight his going.
22. Where there is no counsel, purposes are disappointed;
But in the multitude of counsellors they are established.

STUDY QUESTIONS OVER 15:12-22

1. Is there a relationship between a scoffer's not loving to be reproved and his not going to the wise (v. 12)?
2. What characterizes a "cheerful countenance" (v. 13)?
3. What characterizes a "broken spirit" (v. 13)?
4. Why does a man of understanding seek knowledge when people who are sadly deficient in understanding don't (v. 14)?
5. What is meant by the mouth of fools' feeding on folly (v. 14)?
6. What does "evil" mean in v. 15?
7. A "continual feast" of what kind (v. 15)?
8. Find the double contrast in v. 16.
9. Find the double contrast in v. 17.
10. A "wrathful man" is contrasted with what kind of person in v. 18?
11. What does "appeaseth" mean (v. 18)?
12. How is the way of a sluggard like a "hedge of thorns" (v. 19)?
13. How is the path of the upright like a "highway" (v. 19)?
14. What earlier verse in Proverbs is much like v. 20?
15. What would you include under "folly" in v. 21?
16. What is meant by a man making "straight his going" (v. 21)?
17. Reword the thought found in v. 22.

PARAPHRASE OF 15:12-22

12. A mocker stays away from wise men because he hates to be scolded.
13. A happy face means a glad heart; a sad face means a breaking heart.
14. A wise man is hungry for truth, while the mocker feeds on trash.
15. When a man is gloomy, everything seems to go wrong; when he is cheerful, everything seems right!
16. Better a little with reverence for God, then great treasure and trouble with it.
17. It is better to eat soup with someone you love than steak with someone you hate.
18. A quick-tempered man starts fights; a cool-tempered man tries to stop them.

19. A lazy fellow has trouble all through life; the good man's path is easy!
20. A sensible son gladdens his father. A rebellious son saddens his mother.
21. If a man enjoys folly, something is wrong! The sensible stay on the pathways of right.
22. Plans go wrong with too few counselors; many counselors bring success.

COMMENTS ON 15:12-22

V. 12. A scoffer is a proud, know-it-all person, self-willed, opinionated, and usually wrong. He will not go to the wise to ask or to learn, and he doesn't like people coming to him with their corrections of him. Many deplore being reproved (I Kings 22:8; Amos 5:10; John 3:19,20). For hating and despising reproof see also vs. 5,10,32 of this chapter.

V. 13. A "glad heart" (on the inside) makes a "cheerful countenance" (on the outside). The reverse is also true (a sad heart will show up in a sad countenance--Neh. 1:1-4; 2:1,2). "Pulpit Commentary": "The face is the index of the condition of the mind." "Septuagint" translates: "When the heart is glad, the face bloometh." See also Prov. 17:22; 12:25.

V. 14. The person who has knowledge wants more, and he gets it. Solomon desired wisdom that he might rule God's great people and follow his famous father upon the throne of Israel (I Kings 3:5-9). Note the vastness of his growing wisdom and understanding (I Kings 4:29-34). "Pulpit Commentary": "The wise man...is always seeking to learn more...The fool is always gaping and devouring every silly, or slanderous, or wicked word that comes in his way, and in his turn utters and disseminates it."

V. 15. To the person suffering, no day seems physically good: they are all "evil" (like those referred to in Eccl. 12:1). To the healthy and the happy every day is good (a "continual feast"). Oh, the great blessing of good health and favorable conditions that make one happy!

V. 16. Sometimes "treasure and trouble" go together--are twins (I Tim. 6:9,10). It is really better and the part of wisdom to take a lesser-paying job with which God is pleased than to take a big-paying job with which He is not pleased (Mark 8:36). What is great or true gain? See I Tim. 6:6. Other verses with much of the same truth in them are v. 17 of this chapter; Psa.

37:16; Prov. 16:8; 17:1.

V. 17. A "dinner of herbs" represents a meatless meal (a poor man's meal); "stalled ox" represents a luxurious meal. Note the double contrast: "dinner of herbs" vs. "stalled ox" and "where love is" vs. "hatred". People can have a good fare of food and love at the same time just the same as people can have hatred with their dinner of herbs. This verse does teach that love in the home is better than luxury in the home if there is to be only one and not both.

V. 18. A wrathful man stirs up contention because he wants things stirred up. What a perverted outlook! But men who are slow to anger try to keep things calm. And they are doing what they should. "Hot heads" and "cold hearts" often go together. See also Prov. 26:21; 29:22. "Pulpit Commentary": "It requires two to make a quarrel, and where one keeps his temper and will not be provoked, anger must subside."

V. 19. Try to walk down an old road that has gotten grown over with thornbushes. Progress is slow and difficult. Such is the way of the sluggard of lazy person (Prov. 22:5). In contrast the path of the upright is clear and open (like a highway). Prov. 4:18 also speaks of the path of the righteous.

V. 20. Read Prov. 10:1; 29:3 also. Nothing makes a father happier than the good ways of his children (III John 4). "Despising" one's mother is just the opposite of the Fifth Commandment (Exo. 20:12). A child who is brought up to honor his parents will usually grow up and bring honor and gladness to them.

V. 21. Compare the first statement with the first statement in Prov. 10:23. Putting the two together, "folly" (or "wickedness") is "joy" (or "sport") to the fool. And so it is. Many live this way (consider Tit. 3:3). They may live in the same world, but the wise person lives so differently from the fool who is void of wisdom. The wise man makes his going "straight" (see Eph. 5:15 also).

V. 22. A double contrast: "no counsel" vs. "multitude of counsellors" and "purposes are disappointed" vs. "they are established". Compare Prov. 11:14. "Counsel" in Proverbs' day had to do mostly with war (Prov. 20:18).

TEST QUESTIONS OVER 15:12-22

1. Describe a "scoffer" (v. 12).

2. How does a "glad heart" show up (v. 13)?
3. What does "sorrow of heart" do (v. 13)?
4. Who was a man of understanding who constantly sought more knowledge (v. 14)?
5. Contrast the day of the "afflicted" and the person with a "cheerful heart" (v. 15).
6. What often accompanies a quest for "treasure" (v. 16)?
7. What is better than great treasure and trouble (v. 16)?
8. What kind of home is better than one with the finest of fare if it has trouble (v. 17)?
9. What is the double contrast in v. 18?
10. How is the way of the wicked contrasted with the path of the upright (v. 19)?
11. What is it that makes a happy father (v. 20)?
12. What other verse in Proverbs is similar to the first part of v. 21?
13. When especially did they rely upon "counselors" in olden times (v. 22)?

TEXT — 15:23-33

23. A man hath joy in the answer of his mouth;
And a word in due season, how good is it!
24. To the wise the way of life goeth upward,
That he may depart from Sheol beneath.
25. Jehovah will root up the house of the proud;
But he will establish the border of the widow.
26. Evil devices are an abomination to Jehovah;
But pleasant words are pure.
27. He that is greedy of gain troubleth his own house;
But he that hateth bribes shall live.
28. The heart of the righteous studieth to answer;
But the mouth of the wicked poureth out evil things.
29. Jehovah is far from the wicked;
But he heareth the prayer of the righteous.
30. The light of the eyes rejoiceth the heart;
And good things make the bones fat.
31. The ear that hearkeneth to the reproof of life
Shall abide among the wise.
32. He that refuseth correction despiseth his own soul;
But he that hearkeneth to reproof getteth understanding.
33. The fear of Jehovah is the instruction of wisdom;
And before honor goeth humility.

STUDY QUESTIONS OVER 15:23-33

1. What is meant by a "word in due season" (v. 23)?
2. Does "upward" in v. 24 imply heaven or the better life here?
3. Cite other passages besides v. 25 condemning the proud.
4. Cite other passages besides v. 25 showing God's concern for the widow?
5. What is meant by "border" in v. 25?
6. What would be some examples of "evil devices" (v. 26)?
7. Comment on pleasant words being "pure" (v. 26).
8. How does a greedy person "trouble" his house (v. 27)?
9. What connection is there between hating bribes and living (v. 27)?
10. Will a person remain righteous who speaks the first thing that comes into his or her mind (v. 28)?
11. What are some kinds of evil speech coming from the evil (v. 28)?
12. In what sense is Jehovah "far" from the wicked (v. 29).
13. Why does God hear the prayer of the righteous (v. 29)?
14. What is the "light of the eyes" (v. 30)?
15. What is meant by "make the bones fat" (v. 30)?
16. What is meant by the reproof of "life" (v. 31)?
17. Cite a Biblical character who refused correction (v. 32).
18. In the Bible who was humble before he was honored (v. 33)?

PARAPHRASE OF 15:23-33

23. Everyone enjoys giving good advice, and how wonderful it is to be able to say the right thing at the right time!
24. The road of the godly leads upward, leaving hell behind.
25. The Lord destroys the possessions of the proud but cares for the widows.
26. The Lord hates the thoughts of the wicked but delights in kind words.
27. Dishonest money brings grief to all the family, but hating bribes brings happiness.
28. A good man thinks before he speaks; the evil man pours out his evil words without a thought.
29. The Lord is far from the wicked, but He hears the prayers of the righteous.
30. Pleasant sights and good reports give happiness and

health.

31,32. If you profit from constructive criticism you will be elected to the wise men's hall of fame. But to reject criticism is to harm yourself and your own best interests.

33. Humility and reverence for the Lord will make you both wise and honored.

COMMENTS ON 15:23-33

V. 23. A person does not have joy from just any answer of his mouth but by a right answer or a good answer or a timely answer. "The heart of the righteous studieth to answer" (v. 28). "Let your speech be always with grace, seasoned with salt, that ye may know how ye ought to answer each one" (Col. 4:6). "Being ready always to give answer to every man that asketh you a reason concerning the hope that is in you" (I Pet. 3:15). "All that heard him were amazed at his understanding and his answers" (Luke 2:47). "A word fitly spoken is like apples of gold in network of silver" (Prov. 25:11).

V. 24. The wise choose the way that leads to life rather than destruction ("Sheol"): "Enter ye in by the narrow gate: for wide is the gate, and broad is the way that leadeth to destruction, and many are they that enter in thereby. For narrow is the gate, and straitened the way, that leadeth unto life, and few are they that find it" (Matt. 7:13,14). Wisdom makes the decision now that will end right later: "If thy hand cause thee to stumble, cut it off: it is good for thee to enter into life maimed, rather than having thy two hands to go into hell, into the unquenchable fire" (Mark 9:43). Are you "pressing on the upward way"? Are you "gaining new heights every day"?

V. 25. A double contrast: "root up" vs. "establish" and "the proud" vs. "the widow" (and maybe a third: "house" vs. "border"). For similar passages see Prov. 12:7; 14:11; Psa. 146:9. This is a great warning against arrogancy, self-sufficiency, and being independent in attitude. Concerning the "border" (or boundary) of the widow: "In a country where property was defined by landmarks--stones or some such objects--nothing was easier than to remove these altogether, or to alter their position. That this was a common form of fraud and oppression we gather from the stringency of the enactments against the offence (see Deut. 19:14; 27:17; and compare Job 24:2 and Prov. 22:28). In the Babylonian and Assyrian inscriptions...there are many invoking curses, curious and multifarious, against the distrubers of boundaries" ("Pulpit Commentary").

V. 26. "Evil devices" would include everything from the simplest plot to outsmart somebody to the most complex invention for the production of evil. Such inventers may be lauded, and such devisers may think themselves shrewd, but such is not God's view. God is against "evil" and everything and everybody multiplying it. Words that are "pleasant" (or pleasing) are "pure" and not evil.

V. 27. One "greedy of gain" was violating the Tenth Commandment (Exo. 20:17). But instead of building up one's own house at the expense of others, sometimes one brings ruination to himself and his house, such as did Achan (Josh. 7:21,24,25), Naboth (I Kings 21:1-24), Ananias and Sapphira (Acts 5:1-10), and Lot and others. Other Scriptures: Isa. 5:8; Jer. 17:11; I Tim. 6:9,10. One who hates bribes is one who refuses to accept them (to enrich himself) or one who offers them (In hopes of profiting himself). There is far more of this in government than we realize.

V. 28. "Clarke": "His tongue never runs before his wit; he never speaks rashly, and never unadvisedly; because he studies--ponders--his thoughts and his words." A wise person is "slow to speak" (Jas. 1:19) so as to tell the exact truth and to say what should be said. The chief priests and elders deliberated in answering Jesus (they studied before answering), but it was not righteous (Matt. 21:23-27). The mouth of wicked "poureth out" evil things suggests that they speak with ease, giving no forethought to what they are about to say. And, oh, the wrong things that get said in this way!

V. 29. Man's wickedness puts "distance" between himself and God (Isa. 59:2). God hears the prayer of the righteous, but His face is against the wicked (Psa. 34:15-18; I Pet. 3:12; Psa. 145:18-20). The godly person finds joy in walking with God, and when he needs special help, he can call upon Him. The ungodly relinquish all this to their sin.

V. 30. The sunlight and other beautiful things that man sees bring joy to his heart, and the good news that he hears makes him feel good and results in good health. What one sees and hears, then, affects the way he feels, and the way he feels affects the functions of his body. People who trust instead of fret, who pray instead of worry, who thank God rather than complain, etc. are bound to have better health than those who do otherwise.

V. 31. V. 5 said that the person who regarded reproof would get wisdom. This verse says that such will abide among the wise. See vs. 10,12 also. An old proverb: "Advice is for them that will take it." Stephen referred to his hearers' ears as "uncircumcised" (Acts 7:51). The ear cannot always hear what is pleasing and commendatory, as much as we would like it that way. Praise may be pleasing, but reproof may be more profitable. All of us need both.

V. 32. This verse treats both responses to reproof. One refusing correction may appear to be despising the one reproving him, but in reality he is despising his own best interests; he is hurting himself. The inclusion of so many sayings on correction indicates the amount of this that will come to us in life. Their purpose is to get us to accept it for our own betterment.

V. 33. Compare with Prov. 1:7. To learn true reverence for God is true wisdom. Wisdom would instruct us to this fear through parents, through the Scriptures, and through our religious leaders and religious associates. Honor does precede humility: it was so with Jesus (Phil. 2:7-11); it was so with the penitent publican (Luke 18:13,14); and we must be converted (humbled) before we become Christians (honor).

TEST QUESTIONS OVER 15:23-33

1. What are some other verses besides v. 23 on giving a right answer?
2. What famous statement of Jesus tells us to choose the way that leads to life (v. 24)?
3. What was stated about borders or boundaries (v. 25)?
4. What all would be included under "evil devices" (v. 26)?
5. Who were some Bible characters who troubled their own house through greed (v. 27)?
6. In what area of life are "bribes" the most apt to occur (v. 27)?
7. What is the contrast in speech between the righteous and the wicked in v. 28?
8. In what sense is God "far" from the wicked (v. 29)?
9. What is said of both sight and hearing in v. 30?
10. Who accused his hearers of having "uncircumcised ears" (v. 31)?
11. Who is hurt the more when one refuses correction--the reprover or the reproved (v. 32)?

12. Who in the Bible were humble before they were honored (v. 33)?

NOTICEABLE GROUPINGS IN CHAPTER 15

"Good speech"--

"A soft answer turneth away wrath" (v. 1).

"The tongue of the wise uttereth knowledge aright" (v. 2).

"A gentle tongue is a tree of life" (v. 4).

"The lips of the wise disperse knowledge" (v. 7).

"A man hath joy in the answer of his mouth; And a word in due season, how good is it!" (v. 23).

"Pleasant words are pure" (v. 26).

"The heart of the righteous studieth to answer (v. 28).

"Bad speech"--

"A grievous word stirreth up anger" (v. 1).

"The mouth of fools poureth out folly" (v. 2).

"Perverseness therein is a breaking of the spirit" (v. 4).

"The mouth of fools feedeth on folly" (v. 14).

"The mouth of the wicked poureth out evil things" (v. 28).

"Wise"--

"The tongue of the wise uttereth knowledge aright" (v. 2).

"He that regardeth reproof getteth prudence" (v. 5).

"The lips of the wise disperse knowledge" (v. 7).

"The heart of him that hath understanding seeketh knowledge" (v. 14).

"A wise son maketh a glad father" (v. 20).

"A man of understanding maketh straight his going" (v. 21).

"To the wise the way of life goeth upward, That he may depart from Sheol beneath" (v. 24).

"The ear that hearkeneth to the reproof of life shall abide among the wise" (v. 31).

"Fools"--

"The mouth of fools poureth out folly" (v. 2).

"A fool despiseth his father's correction" (v. 5).

"The heart of the foolish doeth not so" (v. 7).

"The mouth of fools feedeth on folly" (v. 14).

"A foolish man despiseth his mother" (v. 20).

"Folly is joy to him that is void of wisdom" (v. 21).

CHAPTER 15

"Righteous"--

"In the house of the righteous is much treasure" (v. 6).
"The prayer of the upright is his delight" (v. 8).
"He loveth him that followeth after righteousness" (v. 9).
"The path of the upright is made a highway" (v. 19).
"The heart of the righteous studieth to answer" :v. 28).
"He heareth the prayer of the righteous" (v. 29).

"Wicked"--

"In the revenues of the wicked is trouble" (v. 6).
"The sacrifice of the wicked is an abomination to Jehovah" (v. 8).
"The way of the wicked is an abomination to Jehovah" (v. 9).
"There is grievous correction for him that forsaketh the way" (v. 10).
"The mouth of the wicked poureth out evil things" (v. 28).
"Jehovah is far from the wicked" (v. 29).

"Abomination"--

"The sacrifice of the wicked is an abomination to Jehovah" (v. 8).
"The way of the wicked is an abomination to Jehovah" (v. 9).
"Evil devices are an abomination to Jehovah" (v. 26).

"Rebuke"--

"A fool despiseth his father's correction" (v. 5).
"He that regardeth reproof getteth prudence" (v. 5).
"There is grievous correction for him that forsaketh the way" (v. 10).
"He that hateth reproof shall die" (v. 10).
"A scoffer loveth not to be reproved" (v. 12).
"The ear that hearkeneth to the reproof of life Shall abide among the wise" (v. 31).
"He that refuseth correction despiseth his own soul" (v. 32).
"He that hearkeneth to reproof getteth understanding" (v. 32).

DON'T TAKE UP WITH FOOLS

How true is the statement made in 13:20, "He that walketh with wise men shall be wise: but a companion of fools shall be destroyed." Why does God warn people about becoming a companion of fools? Because there are those who seem to know no better than to throw themselves into the direct influence of those whom God labels as fools. Anybody who has no more judgment than to take up with fools will probably not have enough judgment to preserve him from becoming like them.

Again God warns, "Go from the presence of the foolish man, when thou perceivest not in him the lips of knowledge" (14:7). This is more than a warning; it is a commandment. It shows that we must make judgment of others in order to know with whom to be companions and with whom not to be.

Especially do those who are younger (immature in judgment) and those who are known for being easily affected by their surroundings need to regard these true warnings from Proverbs.

HE IS A GOD WHO CHASTENS

"Whom the Lord loveth he correcteth: even as a father the son in whom he delighteth" (3:11,12).

Just as any wise, loving, concerned parent corrects his child, so does God His. Sometimes we make mistakes in our discipline, but God doesn't. When we do wrong, we can be sure that God is not going to stand idly by and permit us to continue in the way of wrong-doing unchastened. He loves us too much to see us continue that way. When we fail to regard His will, He expects that we will regard His chastening.

TEXT — 16:1-11

1. The plans of the heart belong to man;
But the answer of the tongue is from Jehovah.
2. All the ways of a man are clean in his own eyes;
But Jehovah weigheth the spirits.
3. Commit thy works unto Jehovah,
And thy purposes shall be established.
4. Jehovah hath made everything for its own end;
Yea, even the wicked for the day of evil.
5. Every one that is proud in heart is an abomination to Jehovah:
6. By mercy and truth iniquity is atoned for;
And by the fear of Jehovah men depart from evil.
7. When a man's ways please Jehovah,
He maketh even his enemies to be at peace with him.
8. Better is a little, with righteousness,
Than great revenues with injustice.
9. A man's heart deviseth his way;
But Jehovah directeth his steps.
10. A divine sentence is in the lips of the king;
His mouth shall not transgress in judgment.
11. A just balance and scales are Jehovah's;
All the weights of the bag are his work.

STUDY QUESTIONS OVER 16:1-11

1. In view of v. 1 are all answers of the tongue from Jehovah?
2. What is the implication or insinuation in v. 2?
3. What does "purposes" mean in v. 3?
4. Is "its own end" of the text or "his own purpose" of the footnote the real reading in v. 4?
5. Why does God deplore man's pride so much (v. 5)?
6. What is meant by hand joining in hand in v. 5?
7. How do mercy and truth atone for iniquity (v. 6)?
8. Why do some people not depart from evil (v. 6)?
9. How does Jehovah make even a person's enemies to be at peace with a godly person (v. 7)?
10. If v. 7 be true, how could there ever be any martyrs?
11. What other passages resemble v. 8?
12. What previous verse in this chapter resembles v. 9?

13. Was (and is) a divine sentence in the lips of all kings (v. 10)?
14. What were "weights of the bag" (v. 11)?

PARAPHRASE OF 16:1-11

1. We can make our plans, but the final outcome is in God's hands.
2. We can always "prove" that we are right, but is the Lord convinced?
3. Commit your work to the Lord, then it will succeed.
4. The Lord has made everything for His own purposes--even the wicked, for punishment.
5. Pride disgusts the Lord. Take my word for it--proud men shall be punished.
6. Iniquity is atoned for by mercy and truth; being good comes from reverence for God.
7. When a man is trying to please God, He makes even his worst enemies to be at peace with him.
8. A little, gained honestly, is better than great wealth gotten by dishonest means.
9. We should make plans--counting on God to direct us.
10. God will help the king to judge the people fairly; there need be no mistakes.
11. The Lord demands fairness in every business deal. He established this principle.

COMMENTS ON 16:1-11

V. 1. These first seven verses are all "religious" maxims, for they all contain the name "Jehovah". The "answer of the tongue" appears to be set over against the "plans of the heart". If so, the saying would refer to those times when a person's plans become altered by providence so that he ends up doing something else. There is a marvelous teaching here for those who believe in God's providential leadership. See v. 9 also. When we pray, "Thy will, not mine, be done," God may alter our thoughts either in a minor or a major way. Your writer can testify to this as he had personal well-laid vocational plans in life, and yet he believed that it was God's will for him to say, "Lord, I will devote my life to preaching your Word."

V. 2. Prov. 21:2 is very similar. The heart can be so deceptive (Jer. 17:9) that it often deceives the person himself into thinking he is right when he is wrong (Prov. 30:12). Laodicea had its own estimation of itself, but Christ weighed them and found them wanting (Rev. 3:17,18). If we practice self-justification in the eyes of people (Luke 16:15), in time we may come to deceive ourselves into thinking we are all right even though we have not obeyed God's commandments (Jas. 1:22).

V. 3. This verse is very similar to Psa. 37:5: "Commit thy way unto Jehovah; Trust also in him, and he will bring it to pass." The promise of Psa. 37:4 is: "Delight thyself also in Jehovah: And he will give thee the desires of thy heart." God does not always overrule our purposes (He wouldn't unless they are wrong or unless He had some special plan for us), but it is His blessing that makes our plans and purposes come to pass.

V. 4. Jehovah had something definite in mind for everything He created, and if men do not fulfill His loving will, He will use them in another sense as recipients of His just wrath because of their sins. God was as glorified in His overthrow of Pharaoh as He was in His deliverance of Israel (Exo. 9:16). God is as glorified in the "vessels of wrath" as He is in the "vessels of mercy" (Rom. 9:22,23), only in a different way. Yes, He would much rather be glorified by showing mercy, but if man will not so glorify God, He will be glorified in His just wrath.

V. 5. Again we have a saying showing God's abomination for pride. In comparison to God and His works, man is nothing (Psa. 8:3,4; 39:4,5). Even whole nations of the earth are "nothing" in comparison with Him (Isa. 40:15,17). What each of us has, we should not boast of it, for we have received it (I Cor. 4:7). Regardless of the area of our lives that we might be considering, before God "boasting is excluded" (Rom. 3:27). Other passages against pride: Prov. 6:16,17; Luke 18:11-14; I Pet. 5:5; I John 2:16). The last part of our present verse is found in Prov. 11:21 also, meaning that no matter how many alliances proud man may make, God can overthrow them all. Nor is there safety in "numbers" when God arises to punish the multitude of the wicked.

V. 6. God is in both parts of man's salvation: His fear causes man to depart from evil, and His mercy and truth atone for the sin that has been dropped. "Mercy" is that attribute of God that exhibits itself in our forgiveness; "truth" stands for the way that He has set up for us to come to Him for His forgiveness. "Fear" is a deterrent to sin, to crime, and to misbehavior (Prov. 14:16).

V. 7. It is not normal for enemies to be at peace with those whom they hate. There have been instances where God has so blessed individuals that his enemies so respected him or so feared him that they caused him no trouble. Such was true of Israel in Solomon's days (I Kings 4:20,21,24,25). Such caused the Gibeonites to seek peace with Joshua and Israel (Josh. 9:9-11). Such caused Abimilech and the men of Gerar to seek Isaac's peace (Gen. 26:26-29).

V. 8. This should be a great passage to keep in mind when one is tempted to take a high-paying job or to get into a lucrative business that is not right. We know that taverns, theaters, gambling casinos, and other businesses connected with evil can make their owners or operators sizable sums, but it is better to work at something else that makes less money. Compare this verse with Psa. 37:16 and Prov. 15:16. Christians are commanded to work at divinely-approved jobs (Eph. 4:28; Tit. 3:8--especially the marginal note on the latter). Remember, too, that "righteousness" is to be sought before even the earthly necessities of food, drink, and clothing (Matt. 6:33).

V. 9. This is but one of several passages that bear out the thought that "man proposes, but God disposes." See v. 1; Prov. 19:21; Psa. 37:23; Prov. 20;24; Jer. 10:23. These verses emphasize a most precious truth: the providence and leadership of God in our lives. The song writer has tried to put into words both the belief and the feeling of our hearts when he wrote, "He leadeth me; Oh, blessed thought! Oh, words with heavenly comfort fraught!" We should pray for this leadership, follow it, and thank God for it constantly. It is one of the Christian's greatest treasures.

V. 10. God has both instituted government (Rom. 13:1-7) and commanded that they rule justly (II Sam. 23:3; Deut. 16:18-20; v. 12 of this chapter). When a king does his duty properly, man is being ruled governmentally as God intends, and man should submit to his government's decrees as he would to God (I Pet. 2:13,14). The latter statement of the verse must be understood in this context; namely, that if he is wisely and righteously doing his kingly duty, his verdicts will be true verdicts.

V. 11. God commanded just measurements in business (Lev. 19:36) and declares that He is pleased with just weights and highly displeased with false ones (Prov. 11:1). To be right with God one must be honest in business.

TEST QUESTIONS OVER 16:1-11

1. What word is found in the first seven verses of this chapter?
2. How is the leadership of God shown in v. 1?
3. Cite an example of some who were wrong but thought they were right (v. 2).
4. What wonderful promise is contained in v. 3?
5. How would you explain v. 4 to someone?
6. Why is a proud person so abominable to God (v. 5)?
7. What is meant by hand joining in hand (v. 5)?
8. Comment upon mercy's relationship to atonement (v. 6).
9. Comment upon truth's relationship to it (v. 6).
10. Comment upon fear's relationship to man's departure from evil (v. 6).
11. Cite two Biblical examples of v. 7.
12. What does God say is better than "great revenues with injustice" (v. 8;?
13. "Man proposes, but God ...."
14. In what sense is a "divine sentence" in the lips of a king (v. 10)?
15. What does God say about just and unjust weights (v. 11)?

TEXT — 16:12-22

12. It is an abomination to kings to commit wickedness;
For the throne is established by righteousness.
13. Righteous lips are the delight of kings;
And they love him that speaketh right.
14. The wrath of a king is as messengers of death;
But a wise man will pacify it.
15. In the light of the king's countenance is life;
And his favor is as a cloud of the latter rain.
16. How much better is it to get wisdom than gold!
Yea, to get understanding is rather to be chosen than silver.
17. The highway of the upright is to depart from evil:
He that keepeth his way preserveth his soul.
18. Pride goeth before destruction,
And a haughty spirit before a fall.
19. Better it is to be of a lowly spirit with the poor,
Than to divide the spoil with the proud.

20. He that giveth heed unto the word shall find good;
And whoso trusteth in Jehovah, happy is he.
21. The wise in heart shall be called prudent;
And the sweetness of the lips increaseth learning.
22. Understanding is a wellspring of life unto him that hath it;
But the correction of fools is their folly.

STUDY QUESTIONS OVER 16:12-22

1. Why is it such an abomination for kings to commit wickedness (v. 12)?
2. Why do kings love those who speak truth (v. 13)?
3. Show from v. 14 that the will and the rights of a king were supreme.
4. What is meant by the "light of the king's countenance" (v. 15)?
5. Who asked God for "wisdom" rather than riches (v. 16)?
6. What verse in chapter 15 speaks of the way of the upright being a "highway?"
7. Give a Bible example of one's pride leading to his destruction (v. 18).
8. Why is it better to be lowly and poor than rich and proud (v. 19)?
9. What "word" is meant in v. 20?
10. How does the "sweetness of the lips" increase learning (v. 21)?
11. What is meant by understanding being a "wellspring of life" (v. 22)?

PARAPHRASE OF 16:12-22

12. It is a horrible thing for a king to do evil. His right to rule depends upon his fairness.
13. The king rejoices when his people are truthful and fair.
14. The anger of the king is a messenger of death and a wise man will appease it.
15. Many favors are showered on those who please the king.
16. How much better is wisdom than gold, and understanding than silver!
17. The path of the godly leads away from evil; he who follows that path is safe.
18. Pride goes before destruction and haughtiness before a

fall.
19. Better poor and humble than proud and rich.
20. God blesses those who obey Him; happy the man who trusts in the Lord.
21. The wise man is known by his common sense, and a pleasant teacher is the best.
22. Wisdom is a fountain of life on those possessing it, but a fool's burden is his folly.

COMMENTS ON 16:12-22

V. 12. Another saying concerning kings. "Pulpit Commentary": "When a ruler acts justly and wisely, punishes the unruly, rewards the virtuous, acts as God's vicegerent, and himself sets the example of the character which becomes so high a position, he wins the affection of his people...Law-makers should not be law-breakers." A ruler should desire the success of his nation; then he should lead it into righteousness: "Righteousness exalteth a nation; But sin is a reproach to any people" (Prov. 14:34). A king's rule upon his throne and the power passing to his sons is brought about by a righteous rule upon his and their parts. (Prov. 25:5; 29:14).

V. 13. A ruler is concerned about how things are going in his kingdom. For much of this knowledge he is dependent upon the information of others. Inaccurate reporting on their part can be his undoing. So he loves the person who speaks right. In Bible times a king not only ruled but served much like a high judge today (I Kings 3:16-28). In passing judgment he likewise depended upon the information that he heard from the "witnesses". He had a special appreciation for those who spoke the truth. Every ruler knows, though, that he must sort out the information he hears into true, false, partly true, partly false, etc. Is it any wonder that when Jesus said to the ruler Pilate, "To this end am I come into the world, that I should bear witness unto the truth. Every one that is of the truth heareth my voice" (John 18:37), that Pilate remarked, "What is truth?" (John 18:38).

V. 14. The king's wrath is compared to the rage of a roaring lion in Prov. 19:12; 20:2. Various men in Bible times found this to be true: Agag (I Sam. 15:33); the Amalekite who claimed he had mercifully killed Saul (IISam. 1:14,15); Shemei (I Kings 2:39-46); and many others. "None but a fool will excite the monarch's resentment" ("Pulpit Commentary"). Prov. 15:1 says wrath can be pacified with a "soft answer".

V. 15. Prov. 19:12 likens the king's favor to "dew upon the grass". "The former rain in Palestine falls about the end of October or the beginning of November, when the seed is sown; the latter rain comes in March or April, and is absolutely necessary for the due swelling and ripening of the grain. It is accompanied, of course, with cloud, which tempers the heat, while it brings fertility and vigour" ("Pulpit Commentary"). Queen Esther obtained favor in the sight of King Ahasuerus (Esth. 4:11; 5:1,2). Likewise did Jehoiachin obtain the favor of Evil-merodach, king of Babylon (Jer. 52:31-34).

V. 16. Prov. 8:11,19 contains statements to the same effect. Wisdom builds the man, gold his holdings. One who gets wisdom may get riches as a result. For those who take a deeper look into this passage, there seems to be an additional comparison; namely, that "wisdom" is actually better than "understanding" as "gold" is greater than "silver": "An intimation of the superiority of wisdom over intelligence, the former being the guide of life and including the practice of religion, the latter denoting discernment, the faculty of distinguishing between one thing and another" ("Pulpit Commentary").

V. 17. Prov. 15:19 shows that the path of the upright is a highway and not a place of thorns as is the way of the sluggard. A "highway" leads from one place to another place. The highway of the upright leaves or goes away from evil, making it a the "way of holiness" (Isa. 35:8). And one who stays in this way preserves his soul.

V. 18. Pride is when a person is puffed up (I Cor. 13:4), when one's spirit is unduly lifted up within him (Hab. 2:4), when one is conceited and thinks more highly of himself than he ought to think (Rom. 12:16). Haman (Esth. 5:11,12; 7:3-10) and Nebuchadnezzar (Dan. 4:30-33) are good examples of Prov. 17:19 ("He that raiseth high his gate seeketh destruction") and Prov. 18:12 ("Before destruction the heart of man is haughty"), causing the warning of I Cor. 10:12 to be timely ("Let him that thinketh he standeth take heed lest he fall"). "Herodotus": "Artabanus warned the arrogant Xerxes, 'Seest thou how God strikes with the thunder animals which overtop others, and suffers them not to vaunt themselves, but the small irritate him not? And seest thou how he hurls his bolts always against the mightiest buildings and the loftiest trees? For God is wont to cut short whatever is too highly exalted'."

V. 19. "Better" in two senses: One is more righteous to be lowly than proud, and when destruction hits the proud and reduces him to nothing, it is surely ultimately better.

V. 20. The "word" is the Word of God as the last statement of the verse indicates. To give heed is to pay attention to the Word, to respond properly to the Word. This is to believe its facts, obey its commands, accept its promises, and heed its warnings. Heeding what God says reflects a trust in God, which is the happy, blessed way to live (Psa. 34:8; 125:1; Jer. 17:7). "Trust and obey, for there's no other way to be happy in Jesus, but to trust and obey."

V. 21. One usually deserves the reputation he acquires; thus, the wise are called "prudent". People look to those for leadership and advice whose wisdom they respect and admire. "People listen to instruction at the mouth of one who speaks well and winningly" ("Pulpit Commentary"). The "sweetness" of pleasantness of a person's speech enables him to impart his knowledge to others who willingly listen.

V. 22. The person whose understanding in v. 21 blesses others also has it for his own blessing (this verse). One's understanding is like an ever-flowing spring (well) from which he can ever drink. But over and over again is the foolish person corrected by his own folly. He is going to "show them" only to be shown up. Oh, the usual conceit of an ignorant person!

TEST QUESTIONS OVER 16:12-22

1. How many of these verses deal with kings?
2. What establishes a king and his family upon a throne (v. 12)?
3. Why and when would kings appreciate truthful words (v. 13)?
4. What is a king's wrath compared to in other proverbs (v. 14)?
5. What does Prov. 15:1 say can pacify wrath?
6. What if one did not have the favor of the king (v. 15)?
7. V. 16 says .... is better than gold and .... than silver.
8. What is the sense of "highway" in v. 17?
9. Name two Bible characters whose pride preceded their fall (v. 18).
10. In what two ways is it better to be lowly and poor than rich and proud (v. 19)?

11. How do we know that "word" in v. 20 is the Word of God?
12. What do we do when we give "heed" to God's Word (v. 20)?
13. How does a wise person help others (v. 21)?
14. How does he help himself (v. 22)?
15. How is a fool's folly his downfall (v. 22)?

TEXT — 16:23-33

23. The heart of the wise instructeth his mouth,
And addeth learning to his lips.
24. Pleasant words are as a honeycomb,
Sweet to the soul, and health to the bones.
25. There is a way which seemeth right unto a man,
But the end thereof are the ways of death.
26. The appetite of the laboring man laboreth for him;
For his mouth urgeth him thereto.
27. A worthless man deviseth mischief;
And in his lips there is as a scorching fire.
28. A perverse man scattereth abroad strife;
And a whisperer separateth chief friends.
29. A man of violence enticeth his neighbor,
And leadeth him in a way that is not good.
30. He that shutteth his eyes, it is to devise perverse things:
He that compresseth his lips bringeth evil to pass.
31. The hoary head is a crown of glory;
It shall be found in the way of righteousness.
32. He that is slow to anger is better than the mighty;
And he that ruleth his spirit, than he that taketh a city.
33. The lot is cast into the lap;
But the whole disposing thereof is of Jehovah.

STUDY QUESTIONS OVER 16:23-33

1. How does the heart instruct the mouth (v. 23)?
3. What two qualities of honey are brought out in v. 24?
3. What earlier verse in Proverbs is exactly like v. 25?
4. How does one's appetite labor for him (v. 26)?
5. Show from v. 27 that mischief is worthless.
6. What kind of man is v. 28's "perverse" man?
7. What might v. 28's enticements include?
8. What is meant by shutting the eyes and compressing the

lips in v. 30?
9. What is the "hoary head" of v. 31?
10. What virtue or virtues is v. 32 extolling?
11. What is meant by the lot being cast into the lap (v. 33)?

PARAPHRASE OF 16:23-33

23. From a wise mind comes careful and persuasive speech.
24. Kind words are like honey--enjoyable and healthful.
25. Before every man there lies a wide and pleasant road he thinks is right, but it ends in death.
26. Hunger is good--if it makes you work to satisfy it!
27. Idle hands are the devil's workshop; idle lips are his mouthpiece.
28. An evil man sows strife; gossip separates the best of friends.
29. Wickedness loves company--and leads others into sin.
30. The wicked man stares into space with pursed lips, deep in thought, planning his evil deeds.
31. White hair is a crown of glory and is seen most among the godly.
32. It is better to be slow-tempered than famous; it is better to have self-control than to control an army.
33. We toss the coin, but it is the Lord who controls its decision.

COMMENTS ON 16:23-33

V. 23. The wise person thinks before he speaks, instructing himself as to what to say, how to say it, when to say it, to whom to say it, and even whether to say it. It is this thinking that adds "learning" to his lips that he would not otherwise have. He "studieth to answer" (Prov. 15:28) and is sometimes "slow to speak" (Jas. 1:19). Speaking of the heart and the lips of the good man, Matt. 12:35 beautifully says, "The good man out of his good treasure bringeth forth good things."

V. 24. Another proverb on speech. The ancients' sweetening was from the honey. Pleasant words are "pure" words (Prov. 15:26) and "sweet" words (this verse). Pleasant words come from a "sweet" soul and one who is blessed with a healthy outlook, and they bring sweetness to the soul of the hearer and health to him too. Nothing can destroy this sweetness of soul and the consequent health of the body more than angry, hateful, and untrue words.

V. 25. This same statement is found in Prov. 14:12. It is probably included twice in the book not by error but for emphasis. In life it is possible to think you are right when you are "dead-wrong." Many errors occur this way both in religion and in the everyday things of life. This is why we should always be pleased to recheck our conclusions. Even before pulling onto a highway, take one more look after you are sure it is clear--there may be a car coming after all!

V. 26. A laboring man has an appetite. He needs food for strength and for health. He "goes" on food just as an engine does on duel and a fire on wood. But when people don't work, their food goes to fat, which hinders health. We are told by health authorities to eat more for breakfast and less at night so that we burn up what we eat with work during the day rather than let it go to fat while we sleep at night.

V. 27. Somebody is the originator or deviser (cause) of everything that comes to pass. Prompted and empowered by the devil, such a wicked deviser is here said to be "worthless," and he is as worthless and as destructive with his "lips" as a fire can be to property (Jas. 3:6). Both a "fire" and the "lips" have many useful purposes (fire: heat, cooking, industrial purposes, etc.; the lips: conversation, business, singing, preaching, prayer, etc.); but a person who turns these to wicked, mischievous ends is "worthless" both to God and society. We can get along without them, and God will separate them from himself and from the saved forever.

V. 28. Here is the person of v. 27 in action. He is "perverse" because he is perverting his time and powers to destructive from constructive possibilities. He is creating and scattering strife abroad, which is contrary to the will and desire of God (Prov. 6:14; 15:18; 26:21; 29:22). One of his chief ways of proceeding is to work secretly ("whisperer"). This way he can work quietly, be less detected, and appears to be confiding information to those whom he is approaching. And, oh, the power for evil that this approach has: it separates "chief friends." Quite an accomplishment, wouldn't you say! Prov. 17:9 says that he that "harpeth" on a matter can also separate chief friends.

V. 29. Another proverb on misusing one's power for the harm of others. This time he is inviting his neighbor to join him ("enticeth" him, as if it is a good thing to do). If he joins him, he is being led into a way that is not good; actually he is "misled". It was this very thing that Prov. 1:10 was warning against ("If sinners entice thee, consent thou not"). Notice the "violence" that was planned (1:11-14); it was a program of gain by wrong means. We are told in 1:15: "Walk not thou in the way with them; Refrain thy foot from their path."

V. 30. As you behold one sitting with closed eyes and closed mouth, he does not look like the "factory of evil" that he is. While he looks like he is resting and "taking it easy," he is actually devising "perverse things" and working to bring "evil" to pass.

V. 31. The "hoary" head refers to the white hair of old age. It is said here to be a "crown of glory" (compare Prov. 20:29). White hair, then, is not something to be ashamed of, for it should be a mark of distinction (Lev. 19:32). The latter statement of our verse bears out the fact that many are more righteous in old age than in younger years (especially if they have been given religious training in childhood). Some who are wild and utterly neglectful of God settle down to the serious side of life later. A "Gallup Poll" found that the largest group of Bible-readers were 55 years old and older.

V. 32. A person who is "slow to anger" is a person of good judgment, one who exhausts his ability to overlook and explain the possible "why's" and "wherefore's" of another's displeasing action who finally faces the downright evil that the other person has done. This virtue is praised (Prov. 19:11) and commanded (Jas. 1:19), and one is disqualified from being an elder in the church without it (Tit. 1:7). Such rules his own "spirit", and some who can take cities (conquerors) and do all kinds of physical feats of power (like Samson) cannot rule themselves successfully. "Clarke": "It is much easier to subdue the enemy without than the one within...Alexander, who conquered the world, was a slave to intemperate anger, and in a fit of it slew Clytus, the best and most intimate of all his friends."

V. 33. "Pulpit Commentary": "It is not quite clear what articles the Jews used in their diviations by lot. Probably they employed stones, differing in shape or color or having some distinguishing mark...The Jew...did not feel justified in resorting to this practice on every trivial occasion...The lot was employed religiously in cases where other means of decision were not suitable." The soldiers who crucified Jesus cast lots to determine who got what piece of His clothing (Mark 15:24; John 19:23,24).

The apostles used it in determining who would succeed Judas (Acts 1:26). No more often than we read of this in the Bible (though handy it would have been to use often), we conclude that it was not commonplace even then. This was evidently something that God arranged for His Old Testament people that we do not read about in the New Testament. If we lack wisdom, we are not taught to "draw straws" or use some other method of casting lots but to pray and trust that God's leadership will be had (Jas. 1:5).

TEST QUESTIONS OVER 16:23-33

1. What all does a wise person consider before he speaks (v. 23)?
2. What are two blessings of pleasant words (v. 24)?
3. Why should we recheck our conclusions (v. 25)?
4. Comment on the laboring man and his appetite (v. 26).
5. What does v. 27 call a deviser of mischief?
6. Why does a whisperer often succeed with his whispering (v. 28)?
7. How does v. 29 tie up with Prov. 1:10-15?
8. How does the man of v. 30 fool people?
9. At what stage of life do people read the Bible the most (v. 31)?
10. What did Alexander the Great once do in a fit of rage (v. 32)?
11. What did you learn about lot-using from the comments on v. 33?

NOTICEABLE GROUPINGS IN CHAPTER 16

"Jehovah"--

"The plans of the heart belong to man: But the answer of the tongue is from Jehovah" (v. 1).

"All the ways of a man are clean in his own eyes: But Jehovah weigheth the spirits" (v. 2).

"Commit they works unto Jehovah, And thy purposes shall be established" (v. 3).

"Jehovah hath made everything for its own end; Yea, even the wicked for the day of evil" (v. 4).

"Every one that is proud in heart is an abomination to Jehovah" (v. 5).

"By the fear of Jehovah men depart from evil" (v. 6).

"When a man's ways please Jehovah, He maketh even his

enemies to be at peace with him" (v. 7).

"A man's heart deviseth his way; But Jehovah directeth his steps" (v. 9).

"A just balance and scales are Jehovah's; All the weights of the bag are his work" (v. 11).

"The lot is cast into the lap; But the whole disposing thereof is of Jehovah" (v.33).

"Better"--

"Better is a little, with righteousness, Than great revenues with injustice" (v. 8).

"How much better is it to get wisdom than gold! Yea, to get understanding is rather to be chosen than silver" (v. 16).

"Better it is to be of a lowly spirit with the poor, Than to divide the spoil with the proud" (v. 19).

"He that is slow to anger is better than the mighty; And he that ruleth his spirit, than he that taketh a city" (v. 32).

"Pride"--

"Every one that is proud in heart is an abomination to Jehovah" (v. 5).

"Pride goeth before destruction, And a haughty spirit before a fall" (v. 18).

"Better it is to be of a lowly spirit with the poor, Than to divide the spoil with the proud" (v. 19).

"King"--

"A divine sentence is in the lips of the king; His mouth shall not transgress in judgment" (v. 10).

"It is an abomination to kings to commit wickedness; For the throne is established by righteousness" (v. 12).

"Righteous lips are the delight to kings; And they love him that speaketh right" (v. 13).

"The wrath of a king is as messengers of death; But a wise man will pacify it" (v. 14).

"In the light of the king's countenance is life; And his favor is as a cloud of the latter rain" (v. 15).

"Speech"--

"The answer of the tongue is from Jehovah" (v. 1).

"A divine sentence is in the lips of the king; His mouth shall not transgress in judgment" (v. 10).

"Righteous lips are the delight of kings; And they love him that speaketh right" (v. 13).

"The sweetness of the lips increaseth learning" (v. 21).
"The heart of the wise instructeth his mouth, And addeth learning to his lips" (v. 23).
"Pleasant words are as a honeycomb, Sweet to the soul, and health to the bones" (v. 24).
"In his lips there is a scorching fire" (v. 27).
"A whisperer separateth chief friends" (v. 28).
"He that compresseth his lips bringeth evil to pass" (v. 30).

"Righteous"--
"Better is a little, with righteousness, Than great revenues with injustice" (v. 8).
"The throne is established by righteousness" (v. 12).
"Righteous lips are the delight of kings" (v. 13).
"The hoary head is a crown of glory; It shall be found in the way of righteousness" (v. 31).

TEXT — 17:1-10

1. Better is a dry morsel, and quietness therewith,
   Than a house full of feasting with strife.
2. A servant that dealeth wisely shall have rule over a son that causeth shame,
   And shall have part in the inheritance among the brethren.
3. The refining pot is for silver, and the furnace for gold;
   But Jehovah trieth the hearts.
4. An evil-doer giveth heed to wicked lips;
   And a liar giveth ear to a mischievous tongue.
5. Whoso mocketh the poor reproacheth his Maker;
   And he that is glad at calamity shall not be unpunished.
6. Children's children are the crown of old men;
   And the glory of children are their fathers.
7. Excellent speech becometh not a fool;
   Much less do lying lips a prince.
8. A bribe is as a precious stone in the eyes of him that hath it;
   Whithersoever it turneth, it prospereth.
9. He that covereth a transgression seeketh love;
   But he that harpeth on a matter separateth chief friends.
10. A rebuke entereth deeper into one that hath understanding
    Than a hundred stripes into a fool.

STUDY QUESTIONS OVER 17:1-10

1. What does "quietness" stand for in v. 1?
2. Cite the two contrasts in v. 2.
3. What does Jehovah do when He "trieth the hearts" (v. 3)?
4. Why will a liar give heed to a mischievous tongue (v. 4)?
5. What are some common examples of laughing at calamity (v. 5)?
6. Reproacheth whose Maker (v. 5)?
7. What is meant in v. 6 by "the glory of children are their fathers?"
8. What is "excellent" speech (v. 7)?
9. What does "becometh" mean in v. 7?
10. What is the meaning of a bribe's being a precious stone" to its possessor (v. 8)?

11. What is the "it" in v. 8?
12. Covers his or somebody else's transgression (v. 9)?
13. What is "harping on a matter" (v. 9)?
14. What will help a man if one hundred stripes won't (v. 10)?

PARAPHRASE OF 17:1-10

1. A dry crust eaten in peace is better than steak every day along with argument and strife.
2. A wise slave will rule his master's wicked sons and share their estate.
3. Silver and gold are purified by fire, but God purifies hearts.
4. The wicked enjoy fellowship with others who are wicked; liars enjoy liars.
5. Mocking the poor is mocking the God who made them. He will punish those who rejoice at others' misfortunes.
6. An old man's grandchildren are his crowning glory. A child's glory is his father.
7. Truth from a rebel or lies from a king are both unexpected.
8. A bribe works like magic. Whoever uses it will prosper!
9. Love forgets mistakes; nagging about them parts the best of friends.
10. A rebuke to a man of common sense is more effective than a hundred lashes on the back of a rebel.

COMMENTS ON 17:1-10

V. 1. Because their bread was "dry", they dipped it in water and other softening fluids (Ruth 2:14; John 13:36). And having only a dry morsel to eat could be the sign of extreme poverty. So taken, the verse means that poverty and peace are to be preferred to prosperity and problems (such as "strife"). The rich have troubles and problems that the poor do not have. This statement should be a comfort to people who have only the barest of necessities. Prov. 15:17 is very similar.

V. 2. "Pulpit Commentary": "Here is intimated the supremacy of wisdom over folly and vise...Slaves were often raised to high honor and might inherit their master's possessions. Thus Abraham's servant...was at one time considered the patriarch's heir (Gen. 15:2,3); Ziba, Saul's servant, obtained the inheritance of his lord Mephibosheth (II

Sam. 16:4); Joseph was advanced to the highest post in Egypt." In European history when the sons of Clovis, king of the Franks, did not really care to rule but merely to enjoy the pleasures of the palace, they had "mayors of the palace" who did the actual ruling, and in time the mayors became the heirs of the throne itself. (For further reading consult the "Merovingian" and "Carolingian" dynasties in church history books or encyclopedias.) For "a son that causeth shame", see Prov. 10:5; 19:26.

V. 3. Just as men refine gold and silver (Prov. 27:21), so does God refine men. Through the Word (John 15:3), but especially through chastening :Isa. 48:10; Heb. 12:11) and persecution (I Pet. 1:6,7; Jas. 1:2,3; and the indwelling of the Holy Spirit (II Cor. 3:18), does He refine us. Mal. 3:2,3 aptly predicted this refining in the Christian dispensation.

V. 4. It is common for perverse people to believe the wrong thing about others. They want to. They get enjoyment from it. They derive satisfaction in thinking the righteous are not really righteous. This verse is a case of Hebrew parallelism in which the second line restates the truth of the first statement. Thus the "liar" is the "evil-doer", "giveth ear" is the same as "giveth heed", and a "mischievous tongue" is the same as "wicked lips" The liar will have something more to lie about.

V. 5. Prov. 14:31 talked of oppressing the poor; this verse of mocking the poor. People mock the poor when they make fun of them, laugh at them, mimic them, and make life harder for them. God is the "Maker" of the poor as well as the rich (Prov. 22:2); when we mock them, we mock Him; when we give to them, we are making a loan to the Lord (Prov. 19:17). We should not be glad at any calamity, whether that calamity be poverty (as in this context) or any other. Job said he was free from this (Job. 31:29), but Edom wasn't (Oba. 12). God will punish us if we do (Prov. 24:17).

V. 6. When one's own health begins to fail, and it seems there is less and less purpose for one's earthly life, along come the births of grandchildren to inject a new dimension into one's living. They "crown" one's life near one's bowing-out years. The last statement shows that good children not only respect their parents but actually glory in them. How they will brag about them (sometimes even exaggerate concerning what he can do, what he knows, how much money he has, etc.).
For the blessing that children can be, see Psa. 127:3-5; 128:3.

V. 7. Excellent speech is speaking only the facts, speaking them at the right time, at the right place, to the right person, in the right spirit, and for the right purpose (to mention a few of its characteristics). As we don't expect good speech from a fool, neither should we expect bad speech from a ruler. It is a shame that so many of our present-day ruling-class, even though elected to their offices, are known for being "politicians" (policy-men) more than "statesmen" (doing what is right under all conditions).

V. 8. The various translations face the problem of whether it should be "bribe", "gift," or "stone of grace", and whether the "it" after "whithersoever" should be "it" or "he". Of all the translations the "New World" gives as understandable a message on this verse as any: "The gift is a stone winning favor in the eyes of its grand owner. Everywhere that he turns he has success." If the foregoing is correct, both Prov. 18:16 and 19:6 verify the truth of its statement. If "bribe" is correct, "Living Bible" has, "A bribe works like magic. Whoever uses it will prosper" and it adds this footnote: "This is a fact, but the writer strictly forbids this perversion of justice. See v. 23"

V. 9. "Septuagint": "He who concealeth injuries seeketh friendship." One's sense of love will cause him not to repeat many things he has heard, even if true, if they are not in the best interests of the one involved (Prov. 10:12). Harping on a matter is just the opposite of concealing it, for it utilizes every opportunity to bring it up, to mention it, or to ramble on and on about it. This can be the end of friendship.

V. 10. The contrast here does not mean to elevate "rebuke" (words of correction) and eliminate "stripes" (Physical punishments). It merely shows that some "words" do a wise man more good than "stripes" do a fool. What a pity that there are some whom neither words nor stripes will help! Peter was a man who was helped by rebuke, by both Jesus and Paul (Matt. 16:23; 26:75; Gal. 2:11-15).

V. 11. An "evil" man is one who will not be guided and governed by that which is right. He is a law-breaker, both in heart and in act. He seeks only rebellion against properly constituted authority (parents, school, government, manners, etc.). He, thus, is a liability and not an asset. Because he will not obey, will not respect the rights and property of others, he is often confined in prison at a great outlay of citizens' money. Better for society if he had never been born!

TEST QUESTIONS OVER 17:1-10

1. In v. 1 a "dry morsel" stands in contrast with ...., and "quietness" stands in contrast with ....
2. Cite instances illustrating the truth of v. 2.
3. Men work at refining gold and silver; God works at refining .... (v. 3).
4. Why do evil people give heed to wicked lips (v. 3)?
5. Cite the three parallels in v. 4.
6. Why is mocking the poor tantamount to mocking God V. 5)?
7. What about being glad at others' calamities (v. 5)?
8. What is a great blessing of old age (v. 6)?
9. Comment on the fathers being the glory of children (v. 6)?
10. What is the double contrast in v. 7?
11. What is the problem of understanding v. 8?
12. What will love cause one to do concerning the faults of others (v. 9)?
13. Is v. 10 a contrast between rebuking and whipping or what?

TEXT — 17:11-19

11. An evil man seeketh only rebellion;
Therefore a cruel messenger shall be sent against him.
12. Let a bear robbed of her whelps meet a man,
Rather than a fool in his folly.
13. Whoso rewardeth evil for good,
Evil shall not depart from his house.
14. The beginning of strife is as when one letteth out water:
Therefore leave off contention, before there is quarrelling.
15. He that justifieth the wicked, and he that condemneth the righteous,
Both of them alike are an abomination to Jehovah.
16. Wherefore is there a price in the hand of a fool to buy wisdom,
Seeing he hath no understanding?
17. A friend loveth at all times;
And brother is born for adversity.
18. A man void of understanding striketh hands,
And becometh surety in the presence of his neighbor.
19. He loveth transgression that loveth strife:
He that raiseth high his gate seeketh destruction.

STUDY QUESTIONS OVER 17:11-19

1. Rebellion against what (v. 11)?
2. What is a "whelp" (v. 12)?
3. Cite two Bible examples of people's rewarding evil for good (v. 13).
4. The lesson in v. 14 is "Don't begin .... lest it lead to ....
5. The wicked are to be ...., not .... (v. 15).
6. The righteous are to be ...., not .... (v. 15).
7. Cite two Bible examples of justifying the wicked (v. 15).
8. Cite two Bible examples of condemning the righteous (v. 15).
9. Is "fool" in v. 16 one who is mentally deficient or one who does not use his head?
10. What kind of "friends" did the Prodigal Son have (v. 17)?
11. What is "surety" (v. 18)?
12. What is meant by raising high one's gate (v. 19)?

PARAPHRASE OF 17:11-19

11. The wicked live for rebellion! they shall be severely punished.
12. It is safer to meet a bear robbed of her cubs than a fool caught in his folly.
13. If you repay evil for good, a curse is upon your home.
14. It is hard to stop a quarrel once it starts, so don't let it begin.
15. The Lord despises those who say that bad is good, and good is bad.
16. It is senseless to pay tuition to educate a rebel who has no heart for truth.
17. A true friend is always loyal, and a brother is born to help in time of need.
18. It is poor judgment to countersign another's note, to become responsible for his debts.
19. Sinners love to fight; boasting is looking for trouble.

COMMENTS ON 17:11-19

V. 11. The "rebellion" here under consideration was anarchy against the existing government. With the monarchical form of government of those days, this was common and accounted for may assassinations (see the Northern Kingdom history for numerous instances of this). When any such rebellion was detected, the rebellion was immediately put down ("a cruel messenger shall be sent against him").

V. 12. The fierceness of a bear who has lost her young ("whelps") is also referred to in II Sam. 17:8 and Hos. 13:8. One who is unfortunate enough to come along to become involved in some fool's folly may suffer all the way from embarrassment to being murdered. Thus, one may have his car pelted by rock-throwing children as he drives by, his tires slashed because he lives in a neighborhood of "no-goods", or his life taken by hoodlums who kill him to see what he had in his billfold.

V. 13. It is contrary to nature (an extreme wrong) to reward evil for good. It is bad enough not to receive thanks from those helped, but it is even worse for the blessed to repay evil to the giver of good. When this occurs, the promise is that "evil" will abide upon such a one and his house. Instances of repaying good with evil: I Sam. 25:21; Psa. 109:4,5; Jer. 18:20.

V. 14. "Clarke": "As soon as the smallest breach is made in the dike or dam, the water begins to press from all parts towards the breach; the resistance becomes too great to be successfully opposed, so the dikes and all are speedily swept away. Such is the beginning of contentions, quarrels, lawsuits, etc." "Pulpit Commentary" also interprets the statement "as when one letteth out water". It is possible, though, that the expression referred to is the plain type of talk that they used in those days, talk that our society does not look upon as acceptable. Regardless of the figure and its interpretation, its application is unquestioned: cut off strife before it gets started.

V. 15. In God's books the wicked are to be condemned and the righteous commended (Matt. 25:34-36; 41-43 and many, many others). V. 26 of this chapter says, "To punish the righteous is not good, Nor to smite the noble for their uprightness." Exo. 23:7: "The innocent and righteous slay thou not; for I will not justify the wicked." Prov. 24:24: "He that saith unto the wicked, Thou art righteous, People shall curse him, nations shall abhor him." Isa. 5:20: "Woe unto them that call evil good, and good evil."

V. 16. Why pay out money for books and then not read, study, or use them? Why pay tuition fees to go to school when one does not really want to study and learn? "Pulpit Commentary": "A fool thinks that there is a royal road to wisdom, and that it, like other things, is to be purchased with money." One who has a heart for learning will treasure and value every opportunity for learning (books, lectures, films, travel, etc.), such as Abraham Lincoln, and will rise on the wings of acquired knowledge and bless others with the knowledge he has gained. But pupils are not all students, teachers soon discover.

V. 17. A "friend" is "one who loves". A true friend loves at all times, even in times of adversities and reverses and health-failures. They are contrasted with "fair-weather friends" such as the Prodigal Son had (Luke 15:13-16,30). Ruth represents inseparable love (Ruth 1:16). David and Jonathan also (I Sam. 18:1,4; II Sam. 1:26). Brothers may live at a distance and not get to see each other very often, but times of adversity bring them together to help each other. Prov. 18:24 speaks of the friend that is even closer to us than a brother.

V. 18. "Clarke": "Striking each other's hands, or shaking hands, was anciently the form in concluding a contract." This was just as binding as our "signing" our names to a contract today. "Surety" was when one obligated himself for the debts of others. Proverbs gives strong warnings against this (Prov. 6:1,2; 11:15).

V. 19. One who loves strife must "love" transgression for strife produces many violations of God's law (such as jealousies, envyings, evil surmisings, hatreds, anger, malice, evil speaking, etc.). Such is carnality: "Ye are yet carnal: for whereas there is among you jealousy and strife, are ye not carnal, and do ye not walk after the manner of man?" (I Cor. 3:3). Jas. 3:16: "Where jealousy and faction are, there is confusion and every vile deed." "Pulpit Commentary" on exalting one's gate and its consequent destruction: "He who builds a sumptuous house and lives in a way that his magnificient surroundings demand draws ruin on himself...The entrance to a Palestine house would usually be of humble dimensions and sparse ornamentation; any doorway of great architectural pretensions would be uncommon, and would be regarded as a token of extraordinary wealth or reprehensible pride...which he is unable to support or...provoke reprisals and injurious consequences." A saying: "One who makes an unusual success in life makes many false friends and true enemies." Build something great, and the world will not only notice it, but someone will try to destroy it. See Prov. 16:18 also.

TEST QUESTIONS OVER 17:11-19

1. What kind of "rebellion" does v. 11 have particularly in mind?
2. What existing form of government made that a rather common occurrence (v. 11)?
3. What fierce animal is better to run into than a fool in his folly (v. 12)?
4. What are some examples of personal danger involved in meeting a fool in his folly (v. 12)?
5. What two possibilities are there for the expression, "as when one letteth out water" (v. 14)?
6. What is the lesson of v. 14?
7. Why does God pronounce a woe upon any who condemn the righteous and commend the unrighteous (v. 15)?
8. Why does an opportunity for learning sometimes not profit a person (v. 16)?
9. What is the difference between a true friend and a fair-weather friend (v. 17)?
10. If brothers don't get together often, when are they the most apt to get together (v. 17)?
11. What warnings does Proverbs give about "surety" (v. 18)?
12. What are some of the "transgressions" that grow out of "strife" (v. 18)?
13. Why does exalting one's gate often lead to destruction even in this life (v. 18)?

TEXT — 17:20-28

20. He that hath a wayward heart findeth no good;
And he that hath a perverse tongue falleth into mischief.
21. He that begetteth a fool doeth it to his sorrow;
And the father of a fool hath no joy.
22. A cheerful heart is a good medicine;
But a broken spirit drieth up the bones.
23. A wicked man receiveth a bribe out of the bosom,
To pervert the ways of justice.
24. Wisdom is before the face of him that hath understanding;
But the eyes of a fool are in the ends of the earth.
25. A foolish son is a grief to his father,
And bitterness to her that bare him.

26. Also to punish the righteous is not good,
Nor to smite the noble for their uprightness.
27. He that spareth his words hath knowledge;
And he that is of a cool spirit is a man of understanding.
28. Even a fool, when he holdeth his peace is counted wise;
When he shutteth his lips, he is esteemed as prudent.

STUDY QUESTIONS OVER 17:20-28

1. What is a "wayward Heart" in v. 20?
2. What does "fool" mean in v. 21?
3. How can one's attitude affect one's health (v. 22)?
4. What is meant by "out of the bosom" (v. 23)?
5. Apply the last statement of v. 24 to the Prodigal Son.
6. A foolish son is what two things to his parents (v. 25)?
7. Cite Bible instances of smiting the noble or punishing the righteous (v. 26).
8. What does it mean to spare his words (v. 27)?
9. What does holding one's peace mean (v. 28)?

PARAPHRASE OF 17:20-28

20. An evil man is suspicious of everyone and tumbles into constant trouble.
21. It's no fun to be a rebel's father.
22. A cheerful heart does good like medicine, but a broken spirit makes one sick.
23. It is wrong to accept a bribe to twist justice.
24. Wisdom is the main pursuit of sensible men, but a fool's goals are at the end of the earth!
25. A rebellious son is a grief to his father and bitter blow to his mother.
26. How short-sighted to fine the godly for being good! And to punish nobles for being honest!

27,28. The man of few words and settled mind is wise; therefore, even a fool is thought to be wise when he is silent. It pays him to keep his mouth shut.

COMMENTS ON 17:20-28

V. 20. Another case of Hebrew parallelism in which the second statement is a restatement of the first, using different words. A "wayward heart" and a "perverse tongue" are two liabilities. The wayward heart is one that wandered out of the path that God has intended; it will find no good (no blessing from God). It is not pure so it will not see God (Matt. 5:8). It does not think upon the things listed in Phil. 4:8 so it will not know the peace that Phil. 4:7 mentions. Look at Jer. 17:9's description of the wayward heart. The perverse tongue is perverted; that is, it is speaking contrary to God's intentions for it. Such will get itself and others into much mischief and wrong-doing. See Jas. 3:6,8 for the evil that the perverse tongue can cause.

V. 21. The behavior of one's children can greatly affect his own future happiness or sorrow (v. 25; Prov. 10:1; 19:13). Think of the sorrow that Cain brought to Adam and Eve by killing Abel, that Absalom brought to his father David when he tried to steal his throne, and that Hophni and Phinehas brought to their priestly father Eli.

V. 22. Those who have cheerful hearts and bright outlooks upon life have a physical blessing of health that others do not know. On the other hand "nothing has such a direct tendency to ruin health and waste out life as grief, anxiety, fretfulness, bad tempers, etc. All these work death" ("Clarke"). Other passages: Prov. 12:25; 15:13,15.

V. 23. "Clarke": "Above their girdles the Asiatics carry their purses." A wicked (not a righteous) man receives a bribe and perverts justice as a result. This was forbidden in Exo. 23:8. If officials are not to receive them, we should not give them in our desire to get some kind of preferential treatment.

V. 24. The contrast between the fool and the one with understanding in this verse is that the fool's eyes are a long way off (to the "ends of the earth"), but the wise man sees wisdom right where he is. The fool misses the opportunities at hand and is always supposing that somewhere else, something else, is really better. An old saying: "A rolling stone gathers no moss," meaning that one who is always moving about and not settled down will not accumulate much nor accomplish much. Remember the Prodigal Son in this connection (Luke 15)? See Prov. 6:11 also.

V. 25. V. 21 spoke of the sorrow that a fool brings to his father. This verse speaks of the grief and bitterness he brings to both his parents. It is a tragedy when a son brings "grief" instead of joy to his father, and when he brings "bitterness" instead of satisfaction to his mother. But children must be reared and trained, not merely begotten and born. Similar passages: Prov. 10:1; 15:20; 19:13.

V. 26. See v. 15, also Prov. 18:5. This represents corruption in government, a perversion of justice. God has ordained government, and He says, "Do that which is good, and thou shalt have praise from the same" (Rom. 13:3). Both Jesus and Paul were smitten when innocent (Matt. 26:67; Acts 23:1,2).

V. 27. "Pulpit Commentary": "He shows his common sense, not by rash talk or saying all he knows, but by restraining his tongue." We are to be "slow to speak" (Jas. 1:19). "In the multitude of words there wanteth not transgression; But he that refraineth his lips doeth wisely" (Prov. 10:19). "Cool spirit" means not losing one's temper and is parallel to "slow to wrath" (Jas. 1:19) and is praised in Prov. 16:32 ("He that ruleth his spirit"). This verse teaches us the wisdom of both not being too talkative and not losing one's temper.

V. 28. This verse continues the thoughts begun in v. 27. Eccl. 5:3 connects a "fool's voice" with the "multitude of words". Job exclaimed to his rash critics, "Oh that ye would altogether hold your peace! And it would be your wisdom" (Job 13:5). An old saying: "Be silent, and they will think you are a fool; speak, and they will know it." Occasionally you will get acquainted with a fool who does not advertise it with his speech; it was his lack of talkativeness that caused you to think of him as a normal person until you got better acquainted with him.

TEST QUESTIONS OVER 17:20-28

1. What two things are condemned in v. 20?
2. How do they get their owner into trouble (v. 20)?
3. Cite some Bible examples of sons who brought grief to their parents (v. 21).
4. What is said to be a good medicine that does not come from the store (v. 22)?
5. What two people sin when a bribe is given (v. 23)?
6. What is the contrast in v. 24?
7. Give another passage that tells of the grief that children can bring to their parents (v. 25).
8. Cite a Bible example of one being smitten who was upright :v. 26).
9. Does the Bible commend or condemn talkativeness (v. 27)?
10. What does v. 27 say about one who has a "cool spirit?"
11. By what means is a fool sometimes counted among the wise (v. 28)?

CHAPTER 17

NOTICEABLE GROUPINGS IN CHAPTER 17

"*Wisdom*"--

"A servant that dealeth wisely shall have rule over a son that causeth shame, And shall have part in the inheritance among the brethren" (v. 2).

"Wisdom is before the face of him that hath understanding" (v.24).

"He that spareth his words hath knowledge" (v. 27).

"He that is of a cool spirit is a man of understanding" (v. 27).

"*Fools*"--

"Excellent speech becometh not a fool" (v. 7).

"A rebuke entereth deeper into one that hath understanding Than a hundred stripes into a fool" (v. 10).

"Let a bear robbed of her whelps meet a man, Rather than a fool in his folly" (v. 12).

"Wherefore is there a price in the hand of a fool to buy wisdom, Seeing he hath no understanding?" (v. 16).

"He that begetteth a fool doeth it to his sorrow" (v. 21).

"The father of a fool hath no joy" (v. 21).

"The eyes of a fool are in the ends of the earth" (v. 24).

"A foolish son is a grief to his father, And bitterness to her that bare him" (v. 25).

"Even a fool, when he holdeth his peace is counted wise; When he shutteth his lips, he is esteemed as prudent" (v. 28).

"*Strife*"--

"Better is a dry morsel, and quietness therewith, Than a house full of feasting with strife" (v. 1).

"The beginning of strife is as when one letteth out water: Therefore leave off contention before there is quarrelling" (v. 14).

"He loveth transgression that loveth strife" (v. 19).

"*Wicked*"--

"A servant that dealeth wisely shall have rule over a son that causeth shame" (v. 2).

"An evil-doer giveth heed to wicked lips; And a liar giveth ear to a mischievous tongue" (v. 4).

"An evil man seeketh only rebellion" (v. 11).

"A wicked man receiveth a bribe out of the bosom, To pervert the ways of justice" (v. 23).

"*Evil speech*"--

"An evil-doer giveth heed to wicked lips; And a liar giveth ear to a mischievous tongue" (v. 4).

"Much less do lying lips a prince" (v. 7).

"He that harpeth on a matter separateth chief friends" (v. 9).

"He that hath a perverse tongue falleth into mischief" (v. 20).

"*Bribes*"--

"A bribe is as a precious stone in the eyes of him that hath it; Whithersoever it turneth, it prospereth" (v. 8).

"A wicked man receiveth a bribe out of the bosom, To pervert the ways of justice" (v. 23).

TEXT — 18:1-12

1. He that separateth himself seeketh his own desire,
 And rageth against all sound wisdom.
2. A fool hath no delight in understanding,
 But only that his heart may reveal itself.
3. When the wicked cometh, there cometh also contempt,
 And with ignominy cometh reproach.
4. The words of a man's mouth are as deep waters;
 The wellspring of wisdom is as a flowing brook.
5. To respect the person of the wicked is not good,
 Not to turn aside the righteous in judgment.
6. A fool's lips enter into contention,
 And his lips are the snare of his soul.
7. A fool's mouth is his destruction,
 And his lips are the snare of his soul.
8. The words of a whisperer are as dainty morsels,
 And they go down into the innermost parts.
9. He also that is slack in his work
 Is brother to him that is a destroyer.
10. The name of Jehovah is a strong tower;
 The righteous runneth into it, and is safe.
11. The rich man's wealth is his strong city,
 And as a high wall in his own imagination.
12. Before destruction the heart of man is haughty;
 And before honor goeth humility.

STUDY QUESTIONS OVER 18:1-12

1. What kind of person do you visualize in v. 1?
2. What kind of person do you visualize in v. 2?
3. What does "ignominy" mean (v. 3)?
4. How are words like "deep waters" (v. 4)?
5. What is the "wellspring of wisdom" (v. 4)?
6. What verse in Chapter 17 goes with v. 5?
7. Were these "stripes" public stripes (v. 6)?
8. Cite personal instances where you know people's mouths have cost them jobs, marriage, tranquility, etc. (v. 7).
9. Comment on "dainty morsels" (v. 8).
10. How is a slacker a brother to a destroyer (v. 9)?
11. Comment on "tower" as used in v. 10.
12. Do the rich man's "strong city" and "high wall" ever

fail him (v. 11)?

13. What other passages in Proverbs teach the same as v. 12?

PARAPHRASE OF 18:1-12

1. The selfish man quarrels against every sound principle of conduct by demanding his own way.
2. A rebel doesn't care about the facts. All he wants to do is yell.
3. Sin brings disgrace.
4. A wise man's words express deep streams of thought.
5. It is wrong for a judge to favor the wicked and condemn the innocent.

6,7. A fool gets into constant fights. His mouth is his undoing! His words endanger him.

8. What dainty morsels rumors are. They are eaten with great relish!
9. A lazy man is brother to the saboteur.
10. The Lord is a strong fortress. The godly run to Him and are safe.
11. The rich man thinks of his wealth as an impregnable defense, a high wall of safety. What a dreamer!
12. Pride ends in destruction; humility ends in honor.

COMMENTS ON 18:1-12

V. 1. Selfish and self-centered people isolate themselves from others. And a self-centered person is conceited to the point that he goes into a rage against the sound words and advice of others. This is true in the field of religion also: "Mark them that are causing the divisions and occasions of stumbling, contrary to the doctrine which ye learned: and turn away from them. For they that are such serve not our Lord Christ, but their own belly" (Rom. 16:17,18).

V. 2. A fool does not like to take in, to learn, but only to talk. Facts, figures, and business have no interest for the fool--only to talk, talk, talk, and he really has nothing to say that is worth listening to. How often the Bible represents the fool as contented without learning or improving himself!

V. 3. Another Hebrew parallelism, paralleling "wicked" and "ignominy" (no reputation) and paralleling "contempt" and "reproach". The wicked loses a good name and turns despiser of all that is good and of all who are good. "When the wicked cometh," watch out! He injects into the association contempt and reproach. The rule is, those who deserve no honor themselves are sure to dishonor all others, and those who themselves are good are the last to suspicion others of evil.

V. 4. The verse is not talking about just any mouth but the mouth of "wisdom". A wise man's mouth is likened to a "deep", "flowing" spring. Such is a great blessing to all around him, and to such they turn for counsel and guidance.

V. 5. A "court" verse. Clarke: "We must not, in judicial cases, pay any attention to a man's riches, influence, friends, offices, etc. but judge the case according to its own merits." Many passages teach the same: Lev. 19:15; Deut. 1:17; 16:19; Prov. 24:23; 28:21. A nation's principles are either maintained or crucified by its judicial officials.

V. 6. A fool's lips show that he is a fool. He says the wrong thing or speaks at the wrong time, or he says what he does in the wrong place or to the wrong person. He is like a child who does not know these wise details of speech. Consequently, he gets himself into trouble with others, and his superiors correct him severely for it.

V. 7. This verse continues the topic of v. 6. Similar passages: Prov. 10:14; 12:13; 13:3; Eccl. 10:12. "Soul" means "life" here, showing the serious destruction that his speech is capable of bringing.

V. 8. This saying is carried twice in Proverbs (see 26:22 also), probably for a needed emphasis. A "whisperer" is one who goes behind people's backs in talking about them, saying things that are not in the best interests of the one being spoken about. The verse brings out the sad fact that people are willing to listen to such cowardly, wrong, ruinous talk (They are as "dainty morsels"). They are swallowed without question ("they go down into the innermost parts of the belly").

V. 9. The slacker (one who doesn't work) doesn't produce, and the destroyer destroys what has been produced. The results are the same: there is nothing to show for one's time and efforts. Therefore, they are said to be "brothers". Some who don't take care of what they have, or who are spendthrifts, sometimes look down upon and criticize the person who has no ambition and produces nothing. But this saying relates the two groups.

V. 10. Many passages teach that God is a refuge: sometimes a "tower," sometimes a "rock", sometimes covering "wings" (II Sam. 22:3; Psa. 18:2; 27:1; 61:3,4; 91:2ff; 144:2).

The ancients had their fortified cities with their walls, big gates, and towers. Sometimes the enemy was able to break through the gates and batter down the walls. That left a tower to get up into for their final safety. The Lord is able to take care of us when other helpers fail.

V. 11. The first statement is also in Prov. 10:15. In contrast to the righteous person's God, the rich man makes "wealth" that in which he trusts. This is forbidden in I Tim. 6:17: "Charge them that are rich in this present world, that they be not highminded, nor have their hope set on the uncertainty of riches, but on God." Don't overlook the connection of "high wall", "strong city," and "tower" in vs. 10,11.

V. 12. While the righteous of v. 10 find their "tower" (Jehovah) a place of safety, the rich man of v. 11 finds that his false-trust (His "wealth") did not save him from destruction. The first statement is similar to Prov. 16:18; the last to Prov. 15:33. The present verse actually brings these two contrasting statements found isolated in Proverbs and brings them together in one verse as a contrast, whose truths are witnessed numerous times in the Bible.

TEST QUESTIONS OVER 18:1-12

1. How does selfishness show up in v. 1?
2. According to v. 2 what is and what isn't a fool interested in?
3. When the wicked come, what else comes (v. 3)?
4. Find three words in v. 4 that are related in a natural world?
5. What is the setting of v. 5?
6. How does the fool's mouth prove to be his destruction (v. 7)?
7. Why will people play the role of the "whisperer" (v. 8)?
8. Who besides the "whisperer" is condemned in v. 8?
9. Prove that a slacker and a destroyer are "relatives" (v. 9).
10. Find three things in vs. 10,11 that are related in life.
11. Compare the "strong tower" of the righteous with the "strong city" of the rich (vs. 10,11).
12. What fact was brought out about the two statements in v. 12?

TEXT — 18:13-24

13. He that giveth answer before he heareth,
It is folly and shame unto him.
14. The spirit of a man will sustain his infirmity;
But a broken spirit who can bear?
15. The heart of the prudent getteth knowledge;
And the ear of the wise seeketh knowledge.
16. A man's gift maketh room for him,
And bringeth him before great men.
17. He that pleadeth his cause first seemeth just;
But his neighbor cometh and searcheth him out.
18. The lot causeth contentions to cease,
And parteth between the might.
19. A brother offended is harder to be won than a strong city;
And such contentions are like the bars of a castle.
20. A man's belly shall be filled with the fruit of his mouth;
With the increase of his lips shall he be satisfied.
21. Death and life are in the power of the tongue;
And they that love it shall eat the fruit thereof.
22. Whoso findeth a wife findeth a good thing,
And obtaineth favor of Jehovah.
23. The poor useth entreaties;
But the rich answereth roughly.
24. He that maketh many friends doeth it to his own destruction;
But there is a friend that sticketh closer than a brother.

STUDY QUESTIONS OVER 18:13-24

1. How is it "folly" to him (v. 13)?
2. How is it "shame" to him (v. 13)?
3. What would a doctor get out of v. 14?
4. Locate the parallels in v. 15.
5. Cite Bible examples of such "gifts" (v. 16).
6. What lesson should church leaders learn from the first statement (v. 17)?
7. Why did the lot end contentions (v. 18)?
8. What lesson should Christians gain from the first statement in v. 19?
9. Is the first statement in v. 20 true whether his words are good or bad?

10. Give examples of "death" and "life" resulting from the tongue (v. 21).
11. How have Catholics misapplied verse 22.
12. When do the poor use entreaties (v. 23)?
13. Why do the rich answer roughly (v. 23)?
14. When might the first statement of v. 24 prove to be true?
15. What friend of David's seemed to be closer to him than his brothers (v. 24)?

PARAPHRASE OF 18:13-24

13. What a shame--yes, how stupid!--to decide before knowing the facts.!
14. A man's courage can sustain his broken body, but when courage dies, what hope is left?
15. The intelligent man is always open to new ideas. In fact, he looks for them.
16. A bribe does wonders: it will bring you before men of importance!
17. Any story sounds true until someone tells the other side and sets the record straight.
18. A coin toss ends arguments and settles disputes between powerful opponents.
19. It is harder to win back the friendship of an offended brother than to capture a fortified city. His anger shuts you out like iron bars.
20. Ability to give wise advice satisfied like a good meal!
21. Those who love to talk will suffer the consequences. Men have died for saying the wrong thing!
22. The man who finds a wife finds a good thing; she is a blessing to him from the Lord.
23. The poor man pleads and the rich man answers with insults.
24. Some people are friends in name only. Others are closer than brothers.

COMMENTS ON 18:13-24

V. 13. Pre-judging (judging before the facts are known) gives us our word "prejudice". Many misjudgments are made because of pre-judging: replacing investigation with rumor or making a judgment of a person on the sound of his or her name or where one is from (John 1:45,46), one's looks, or first impressions. Nicodemus said, "Doth our law judge a man, except it first hear from himself and know what he doeth?" (John 7:51). Jesus said, "Judge not according to appearance, but judge righteous judgment" (John 7:24).

V. 14. One who maintains a cherry, hopeful, bright outlook will rebound from his sickness sooner, but one who has a dark, pessimistic outlook does not recover so well. In fact, when one loses the will to live, he often dies. Pulpit Commentary: "The influence of the mind over the body, in a general sense, is here expressed."

V. 15. The heart of the prudent desires knowledge, and it uses the ear as a means of acquisition. Or said again, the ear seeks knowledge, and the heart lays it up. It is too bad that we have many people who have no thirst for useful knowledge.

V. 16. "Pulpit Commentary": "The Oriental custom of offering suitable gifts to one in authority, when a favor or an audience is desired, is here alluded to (I Sam. 10:27; I Kings 4:21; 10:25)." See also Gen. 32:20; I Sam. 25:27. It is also true today that people's gifts have opened doors to them in various realms.

V. 17. Leaders, be careful! The first person to come to you with his side of a story may not be true. See this even in children: "Johnny hit me;" and while he is speaking, in comes another child of the group and says, "And what did you do to Johnny first? You kicked him!" An old maxim is so true: "One story is good till the other is told."

V. 18. The ancients sometimes resorted to this to settle important contentions. Moderns in our land sometimes draw straws and other means to settle minor matters. Pulpit Commentary: "If it were not for the decision by lot, persons... would settle their differences by violent means." The apostle used this method in determining who was to succeed Judas (Acts 1:26). There is no doubt but what God directed the pagans' lot to fall upon Jonah (Jon. 1:7). See comment on Prov. 16:33.

V. 19. When love is lost, bitterness sets in, and the bitterness is as strong and as intense as the love had previously been. "Pulpit Commentary": "Bitter are the quarrels of friends"; and, "Those who love beyond measure also hate beyond measure." "Clarke": "When brothers fall out, it is with extreme difficulty that they can be reconciled." The verse shows an offended brother is hard to be won, but it does not say it is impossible. Paul and Barnabas had a serious break (Acts

15:36-40), but there is evidence that such was not permanent. Paul refused to take Mark (Acts 15:37,38), which no doubt was an offence to Mark, but later Paul wrote, "Take Mark, and bring him with thee; for he is useful to me for ministering" (II Tim. 4:11). Jacob and Esau had a notable falling out (Gen. 27:41-45), but later there was a reconciliation (Gen 33:8-12). This verse gives a strong reason for being careful of what we say and do that may needlessly offend others. Jas. 1:19 says, "Let every man be swift to hear, slow to speak, slow to wrath."

V. 20. This verse likens what a man says to the food he eats. If what he says is good, it is like eating good food: there is no bad after-effect. The verse is speaking of good speech. Prov. 12:14 and 13:2 contain similar statements.

V. 21. The tongue can edify (build up), or it can destroy the heart or the reputation of another. By our words we can bring either the best or the worst out of a person. As Jas. 3:9 says, "Therewith bless we the Lord and Father; and therewith curse we man." The last statement of our verse speaks of good speech and the pleasant results it brings.

V. 22. Marriage is God's plan for the human race (Matt. 19:4-6). His displeasure is against the growing trend in society to by-pass marriage by illicitly living together. A common-law situation is not equal to marriage in God's sight (John 4:16-18). Other passages that show the divine plan includes marriage: Prov. 19:14; 31:10; Heb. 13:4. There are at least two abuses of this verse: (1) Jokers quote this in levity as if to prove that a wife is a "thing"; (2) Catholics have used it as a proof-text that marriage is a sacrament because of the words "obtaineth favor of Jehovah". What the verse really means is that when one marries, he is entering into something good and is carrying out God's will for the human race in that regard. If somebody argues back that many marriages are anything but pleasant and good, it is not God's fault but the people who have made their marriages that way. If they would follow God's instructions for marriage (Eph. 5:22-33), they would find that it is good.

V. 23. The poor man who is behind on his loan payments begs for mercy and consideration, and the rich man who loaned him the money and is afraid he is going to lose that money talks roughly to him. The same is true of the delinquent renter and his landlord. The poor man uses entreaties because he knows he is at a disadvantage and is at the mercy of the rich man, and the rich man answers roughly because he can, because he is afraid he is going to lose some money, and sometimes so that he can take undue advantage of the situation.

V. 24. In what sense is the first statement true? In the many friends that people make, often there is one or a small handful of them that he would have been better off not to have known: the one or the group that turned against him and ruined him. In the long run they proved not to be true friends and are to be contrasted to the true friend who "sticketh closer than a brother", such as Jonathan was to David. Jonathan was closer to David (I Sam. 18:1-4; 19:1-7; 20:17,41,42; 23:15-18) than his own brothers were (I Sam. 17:28).

TEST QUESTIONS OVER CHAPTER 18:13-24

1. What does our word "prejudice" mean (v. 13)?
2. Give examples of people who pass judgment beore they have the facts (v. 13).
3. What is one of the best things for helping a sick person get better?
4. What usually happens when a person gives up and loses his will to live (v. 14)?
5. According to v. 15 what two parts of a person are involved in his getting knowledge?
6. Cite examples verifying the truth of v. 16.
7. Where trouble brews, who is often first to tell his side of it (v. 17)?
8. When have people resorted to using the lot to settle their differences (v. 18)?
9. What happens when love between people dies (v. 19)?
10. Comment upon v. 20.
11. What are two uses of the tongue (v. 21)?
12. How important can what we say prove to be (v. 21)?
13. What is the meaning of v. 22?
14. Cite an example of a poor man using entreaties and a rich man answering roughly (v. 23).
15. Why does a poor man use entreaties (v. 23)?
16. Why does a rich man answer roughly (v. 23)?
17. What may come out of some of the friendships that a man makes (v. 24)?
18. What friend in the Bible was closer than the man's own brothers (v. 24)?

NOTICEABLE GROUPINGS IN CHAPTER 18

"*Speech*"--

"The words of a man's mouth are as deep waters" (v. 4).

"A fool's lips enter into contention, And his mouth calleth for stripes" (v. 6).

"A fool's mouth is his destruction, And his lips are the snare of his soul" (v. 7).

"The words of a whisperer are as dainty morsels, And they go down into the innermost parts" (v. 8).

"He that giveth answer before he heareth, It is folly and shame unto him" (v. 13).

"A man's belly shall be filled with the fruit of his mouth; With the increase of his lips shall he be satisfied" (v. 20).

"Death and life are in the power of the tongue" (v. 21).

"The poor useth entreaties; But the rich answereth roughly" (v. 23).

"*Fools*"--

"A fool hath no delight in understanding, But only that his heart may reveal itself" (v. 2).

"A fool's lips enter into contention, And his mouth calleth for stripes" (v. 6).

"A fool's mouth is his destruction, And his lips are the snare of his soul" (v. 7).

"He that giveth answer before he heareth, It is folly and shame unto him" (v. 13).

"*Rich*"--

"The rich man's wealth is his strong city, And as a high wall in his own imagination" (v. 11).

"The rich answereth roughly" (v. 23).

"*Wicked*"--

"When the wicked cometh, there cometh also contempt" (v. 3).

"To respect the person of the wicked is not good" (v. 5).

"*Wisdom*"--

"The wellspring of wisdom is as a flowing brook" (v. 4).

"The heart of the prudent getteth knowledge; And the ear of the wise seeketh knowledge" (v. 15).

CHAPTER 18

"*Righteous*"--

"Not good...to turn aside the righteous in judgment" (v. 5).

"The righteous runneth into it, and is safe" (v. 10).

"*Destruction*"--

"The fool's mouth is his destruction" (v. 7).

"Before destruction the heart of man is haughty" (v. 12).

"He that maketh many friends doeth it to his own destruction" (v. 24).

THE BLESSINGS OF WISDOM

We should appreciate the splendid words concerning the desirableness of wisdom in 4:5-13: "Get wisdom, get understanding; forget it not; neither decline from the words of my mouth. Forsake her not, and she shall preserve thee: love her, and she shall keep thee. Wisdom is the principal thing; therefore get wisdom; and with all thy getting get understanding. Exalt her, and she shall promote thee: she shall bring thee to honour, when thou dost embrace her. She shall give to thine head an ornament of grace: a crown of glory shall she deliver to thee. Hear, O my son, and receive my sayings; and the years of thy life shall be many. I have taught thee in the way of wisdom; I have led thee in right paths. When thou goest, thy steps shall not be straitened; and when thou runnest, thou shalt not stumble. Take fast hold of instruction; let her not go; keep her; for she is thy life."

2:10-17 is another fine passage showing the usefulness of wisdom: "When wisdom entereth into thine heart, and knowledge is pleasant unto thy soul; discretion shall preserve thee, understanding shall keep thee: to deliver thee from the way of the evil man, from the man that speaketh froward things; who leave the paths of uprightness, to walk in the ways of darkness; who rejoice to do evil, and delight in the frowardness of the wicked; whose ways are crooked, and they froward in their paths: to deliver thee from the strange woman, even from the stranger which flattereth with her words." Nothing like wisdom can preserve a person from crooked men and wicked women.

Consider other smaller passages on the subject of wisdom:

12:8: "A man shall be commended according to his wisdom." Other things being as they should be, a man of wisdom is a well respected man. His advice is often sought, His word carries weight. His very person embodies a dignity.

13:20: "He that walketh with wise men shall be wise: but a companion of fools shall be destroyed." This passage shows the importance of proper association. Choosing fools as one's companions does not lead to great things in one's life, but walking with wise men does.

19:2: "That the soul be without knowledge, it is not good." Here is a real appeal to be an informed soul, to know the things we should, to appreciate the privileges of learning and to take advantage of them.

19:27: "Cease, my son, to hear the instruction that causeth to err from the words of knowledge." There is false knowledge that leads astray. In this passage, the father warns the son about receiving false instruction and counsel.

24:3-5: "Through wisdom is an house builded; and by understanding it is established: and by knowledge shall the chambers be filled with all precious and pleasant riches. A wise man is strong; yea, a man of knowledge increaseth strength." Yes, wisdom is strength, and knowledge leads to many victories.

TEXT — 19:1-10

1. Better is the poor that walketh in his integrity
   Than he that is perverse in his lips and is a fool.
2. Also, that the soul be without knowledge is not good;
   And he that hasteth with his feet sinneth.
3. The foolishness of man subverteth his way;
   And his heart fretteth against Jehovah.
4. Wealth addeth many friends;
   But the poor is separated from his friend.
5. A false witness shall not be unpunished;
   And he that uttereth lies shall not escape.
6. Many will entreat the favor of the liberal man;
   And every man is a friend to him that giveth gifts.
7. All the brethren of the poor do hate him:
   How much more do his friends go far from him!
8. He that getteth wisdom loveth his own soul:
   He that keepeth understanding shall find good.
9. A false witness shall not be unpunished;
   And he that uttereth lies shall perish.
10. Delicate living is not seemly for a fool;
    Much less for a servant to have rule over princes.

STUDY QUESTIONS OVER 19:1-10

1. What is a synonym for "integrity" in v. 1?
2. Why is it not good to remain ignorant (v. 2)?
3. Is all "haste" sinful or just some (v. 2)?
4. When does the heart fret against Jehovah (v. 3)?
5. When is a poor person separated from his friend (v. 3)?
6. What class of persons likes to make friends of the wealthy (v. 4)?
7. Will it be God or man who will do the punishing (v. 5)?
8. If everybody is a friend to one who gives gifts, why don't all people love God because of His gifts (v. 6)?
9. What kind of words does he use as he pursues them (v. 7)?
10. In what sense is "love" used in v. 8?
11. Why would v. 9 and v. 5 both be included in the same chapter?
12. What is "delicate living" (v. 10)?
13. What does "not seemly" mean (v. 10)?

PARAPHRASE OF 19:1-10

1. Better be poor and honest and rich and dishonest.
2. It is dangerous and sinful to rush into the unknown.
3. A man may ruin his chances by his own foolishness and then blame it on the Lord.
4. A wealthy man has man "friends"; the poor man has none left.
5. Punish false witnesses. Track down liars.
6. Many beg favors from a man who is generous; everyone is his friend!
5. Punish false witnesses. Track down liars.
6. Many beg favors from a man who is generous; everyone is his friend!
7. A poor man's own brothers turn away from him in embarrassment; how much more his friends! He calls after them, but they are gone.
8. He who loves wisdom loves his own best interest and will be a success.
9. A false witness shall be punished and a liar shall be caught.
10. It doesn't seem right for a fool to succeed or for a slave to rule over princes!

COMMENTS ON 19:1-10

V. 1. This is very similar to Prov. 28:6. Pulpit Commentary: "The poor man who lives a guileless, innocent life, content with his lot and using no wrong means to improve his fortunes, is happier and better than the rich man who is hypocritical in his words and deceives others and has won his wealth by such means." There is often a connection between being poorer and honest and being dishonest and getting rich. The "fool" in this verse is apparently a rich fool.

V. 2. A double contrast: "Soul without knowledge" vs. "hasteth with his feet" and "not good" vs. "sinneth". It is not good for one to be without knowledge when God has given us minds in which to store and which can use knowledge and many means by which to acquire it. God was pleased that Solomon wanted wisdom (I Kings 3:9,10). See also v. 8. One without knowledge often acts hastily (No sense of caution) and errs as a result.

V. 3. "Clarke": "They get into straits and difficulties

through the perverseness of their ways; and...they fret against God; whereas...they are the causes of their own calamities." Rom. 1:19-32 gives a running account of the way mankind subverted its way: they began with a knowledge of God; there came a time when they did not glorify Him as they should; darkness set in upon their unspiritual hearts; in their conceit they began making idols, and the longer they went the worse representation of God they made; they came to be filled with all kinds of wickedness; God finally gave up on them until Gospel times.

V. 4. Compare v. 7. People like to identify with someone who will be a credit to them in the eyes of men, not with someone who will discredit them. The poorest of families don't have very many real friends: those who will claim them, invite them over, etc. (Prov. 14:20). Sometimes even relatives practically disown extreme poverty cases.

V. 5. Another case of Hebrew parallelism in which the latter statement is a restatement of the first. This verse is almost identical to v. 9. For the punishment of false witnesses, see Prov. 21:28; Deut. 19:16-19.

V. 6. They seek his favor for what he can do for them. A saying: "Be an unusual success, and you will have many false friends and true enemies." This can raise the question: Do people love you or what you can do for them? Let a child show up on the school ground with a sack of candy, and everybody wants some; "you know me," many will say.

V. 7. Compare with v. 5; Prov. 14:20. In v. 6 everybody wants to be a friend of the well-to-do, the one who gives gifts; but in this verse a man's friends and relatives even go away from him, not wanting to have anything to do with him. Even the poor man's words of appeal fall on deaf ears.

V. 8. He loves his soul because wisdom is good for the soul (v. 2). Proverbs pictures wisdom as something to "get" (4:7). We are to "buy the truth" (Prov. 23:23). We are to give wisdom an exalted place in our lives (Prov. 4:8). But this verse also talks about keeping understanding. "Get" it, and then "forget it not" Prov. 4:5 would tell us.

V. 9. A false witness, in those instances of lying about others, would be breaking the 9th Commandment (Exo. 20:16). God says such must be punished (v. 5).

V. 10. "Delicate living" is luxurious living. "Seemly" means "fitting for." Both statements of this verse show somebody out of place: a fool living luxuriously and a servant ruling over princes. Neither one is in order. Appropriately does Prov. 30:21-23 say, "For three things the earth doth tremble, And for four, which it cannot bear: For a servant when he is king; And fool when he is filled with food..." History tells us of a man who wanted to guard against falling into the very things of which this verse speaks. He was Agathocles, ruler of Syracuse. He rose from the lowly occupation of a potter and to remind himself of his lowly origin, he ate off cheap earthenware.

TEST QUESTIONS OVER 19:1-10

1. What kind of "fool" is evidently under consideration in v. 1?
2. Why is the honest poor better off than such a person (v. 1)?
3. Why does one lacking knowledge often act hastily (v. 2)?
4. What Bible character did not want to live without knowledge (v. 2)?
5. Tell of the account in Rom. 1 of mankind subverting its way (v. 3).
6. How does wealth make friends for a person (v. 4)?
7. Sometimes what kind of friends (v. 4)?
8. Why is the poverty-stricken family often ostracized and even disowned by their own relatives (v. 4)?
9. What did God say about punishing false witnesses (v. 5)?
10. What is the problem of friends you make and keep through gifts (v. 6)?
11. Contrast vs. 6,7.
12. The two verbs in v. 8 talk of doing what two things with knowledge?
13. A false witness often violates which of the Ten Commandments (v. 9)?
14. According to v. 10 what two things are out of order?

TEXT — 19:11-20

11. The discretion of a man maketh him slow to anger;
And it is his glory to pass over a transgression.
12. The king's wrath is as the roaring of a lion;
But his favor is as dew upon the grass.
13. A foolish son is the calamity of his father;
And the contentions of a wife are a continual dropping.

14. House and riches are an inheritance from fathers;
But a prudent wife is from Jehovah.
15. Slothfulness casteth into a deep sleep;
And the idle soul shall suffer hunger.
16. He that keepeth the commandment keepeth his soul;
But he that is careless of his ways shall die.
17. He that hath pity upon the poor lendeth unto Jehovah,
And his good deed will he pay him again.
18. Chasten thy son, seeing there is hope;
And set not thy heart on his destruction.
19. A man of great wrath shall bear the penalty;
For if thou deliver him, thou must do it yet again.
20. Hear counsel, and receive instruction,
That thou mayest be wise in thy latter end.

STUDY QUESTIONS OVER 19:11-20

1. What does it mean "to pass over a transgression" (v. 11)?
2. Find the contrasts in v. 12.
3. What two sources of trouble can a man have in his own home (v. 13)?
4. How does a "prudent wife" act (v. 14)?
5. What is "slothfulness" (v. 15)?
6. Comment on "he that is careless of his ways shall die" (v. 16).
7. How and when will God repay him (v. 17)?
8. How does one chasten his child (v. 18)?
9. How would one "set" his heart on his child's destruction (v. 18)?
10. Why do some people get angry so easily (v. 19)?
11. How would you relate Rehoboam's case to v. 20?

PARAPHRASE OF 19:11-20

11. A wise man restrains his anger and overlooks insults. This is to his credit.
12. The king's anger is as dangerous as a lion's. But his approval is as refreshing as the dew on grass.
13. A rebellious son is a calamity to his father, and a nagging wife annoys like constant dripping.
14. A father can give his sons homes and riches, but only the Lord can give them understanding wives.
15. A lazy man sleeps soundly--and goes hungry!

16. Keep the commandments and keep your life; despising them means death.
17. When you help the poor you are lending to the Lord--and He pays wonderful interest on your loan!
18. Discipline your son in his early years while there is hope. If you don't you will ruin his life.
19. A short-tempered man must bear his own penalty; you can't do much to help him. If you try once you must try a dozen times.
20. Get all the advice you can and be wise the rest of your life.

COMMENTS ON 19:11-20

V. 11. Prov. 14:29 says, "He that is slow to anger is of great understanding," very similar to this verse that credits it to his "discretion". Prov. 16:32 credits it to ruling his spirit (self-control). It takes both wisdom and self-control to remain calm and collected and Christian under fire and under pressure. It is this ability that enables him to "pass over a transgression of another", which is said to be a "glory" to him. To lose one's temper is not a "glory" to him but a "shame". When one passes over a transgression, he is like God: "Who is a God like unto thee, that pardoneth iniquity, and passeth over the transgression of the remnant of his heritage?" (Mic. 7:18).

V. 12. Numerous passages compare a king's wrath to a roaring lion: Prov. 20:2; 16:14; 28:15. Prov. 16:25 also compares a king's favor to refreshing moisture. "Geike": "The secret of the luxuriant fertility of many parts of Palestine lies in the rich supply of moisture afforded by the sea-winds which blow inland each night and water the face of the whole land...From May till October rain is unknown, the sun shining with unclouded brightness day after day. The heat becomes intense, the ground hard; and vegetation would perish but for the moist west winds that come each night from the sea. The bright skies cause the heat of the day to radiate very quickly into space so that the nights are as cold as day is the reverse...To this coldness of the night air the indispensable watering of all plant-life is due. The winds, loaded with moisture, are robbed of it as they pass over the land, the cold air condensing it into drops of water, which fall in a gracious rain of mist on every thirsty blade...The amount of moisture thus poured on the thirsty vegetation during the night is very great.

Dew seemed to the Israelites a mysterious gift of Heaven, as indeed it is. That the skies should be stayed from yielding it was a special sign of Divine wrath...The favor of an Oriental monarch could not be more beneficaly conceived than by saying that while his wrath is like the roaring of a lion, his favor is as the dew upon the grass."

V. 13. A man is in a bad way when his children are no good and his wife is a constant nagger. Concerning "calamity" "Pulpit Commentary" says, "Calamity in the Hebrew is in the plural number, as if to mark the many and continued sorrows which a bad son brings upon his father, how he causes evil after evil to harass and distress;" and of the contentions of a wife it says, "The flat roofs of Eastern houses, formed of planks loosely joined and covered with a coating of clay or plaster, were always subject to leakage in heavy rains. The irritating altercations and bickering of a cross-grained wife are compared to this continuous drip of water." A Scotch saying: "A leaky house and a scolding wife are two bad companions." Other passages on the foolish son: Prov. 10:1; 15:20; 17:21,25. Other passages on the contentious wife: Prov. 21:9; 27:15.

V. 14. We may get material inheritances from our parents (II Cor. 12:14), but a wise wife is a gift from God (Prov. 18:22). This saying is a bold contrast to v. 13: in this verse many blessings come to us because of our families ("inheritance from fathers" and a "prudent wife").

V. 15. Slothfulness, idleness, excessive sleep, and poverty are connected in this and other passages in Proverbs (6:9-11; 10:4; 20:13; 23:21). Two apt sayings: "Idleness is a living man's tomb" and "Sloth is the mother of poverty".

V. 16. A double contrast: "He that keepeth the commandment" vs. "he that is careless of his ways" and "keepeth his soul" vs. "shall die". One who is obedient to God is careful about his ways, and God blesses him with the salvation of his soul, but one who is disobedient to God is careless about his ways, and the wages of sin is and has always been death (Gen. 2:17; Isa. 1:19,20; Rom. 6:21,23; 8:6; Phil. 3:19; Jas. 1:15).

V. 17. The wording implies "giving to the poor". To "pity" is to feel for, to make their burden your burden, to be touched enough about their situation to stop what you are doing and help them. This we are taught to do: Luke 11:41; 12:33; Gal. 6:10; I John 3:17; Jas. 1:27; Matt. 25:35-36. Cornelius (Acts 10:2,4; and Dorcas (Acts 9:36) were alms givers. Give to the poor, and God has promised to pick up the debt (Luke 14:12-14). Notice the message of Prov. 28:27.

V. 18. Correction administered in time without which the child's mischief becomes meanness, and the character becomes set in wickedness. Other passages teaching parental correction: Prov. 13:24; 23:13,14; 29:17. A German saying: "It is better that the child weep than the father." "Clarke": "It is better that the child may be caused to cry, when the correction may be healthful to his soul, than that the parent should cry afterwards, when the child is grown to man's estate, and his evil habits are sealed for life." Non-chastening parents finally give up on their children and seem content to await the inevitable (whatever may result in life for them, which in Old Testament days would have been death by stoning: Deut. 21:18-21). But this verse would condemn such parents.

V. 19. A man given to wrath always turns to it when things don't go as he would have them. It is a sign of a character-weakness: the inability to cope with either one's situation or one's limitations. A man who loses his temper is like a man who gets drunk: it won't be the last time. "Pulpit Commentary": "While his disposition is unchanged, all your efforts will be useless, and the help which you have given him will only make him think that he may continue to indulge his anger with impunity."

V. 20. One's wisdom is constituted of what one gains on his own and of what others seek to share. The more one has, the more apt he is to listen to what others would impart to him, and the less wisdom one has, the less apt he is to regard the good advice of others. "Pulpit Commentary": "Wisdom gathered and digested in youth is seen in the prudence and intelligence of manhood and of old age."

TEST QUESTIONS OVER 19:11-20

1. What two qualities does it take to remain calm under pressure (v. 11)?
2. What is the significance of "glory" in v. 11?
3. Comment upon Palestine's "dew" (v. 12).
4. What is the significance of "calamity" being plural in Hebrew (v. 13)?
5. What is a wife's contentions compared to (v. 13)?
6. If one has a prudent wife, he should give .... the credit (v. 14).

7. Find four things in v. 15 that go together.
8. What is the double contrast in v. 16?
9. What does it mean to "pity" the poor (v. 17)?
10. Name one Bible character commended for almsgiving (v. 17).
11. When should chastening be administered (v. 18)?
12. It is better for whom to weep (v. 18)?
13. What is periodic wrath a sign of (v. 19)?
14. Why should a young person especially listen to others (v. 20)?

TEXT — 19:21-29

21. There are many devices in a man's heart;
But the counsel of Jehovah, that shall stand.
22. That which maketh a man to be desired is his kindness;
And a poor man is better than a liar.
23. The fear of Jehovah tendeth to life;
And he that hath it shall abide satisfied;
He shall not be visited with evil.
24. The sluggard burieth his hand in the dish,
And will not so much as bring it to his mouth again.
25. Smite a scoffer, and the simple will learn prudence;
And reprove one that hath understanding, and he will understand knowledge.
26. He that doeth violence to his father, and chaseth away his mother,
Is a son that causeth shame and bringeth reproach.
27. Cease, my son, to hear instruction
Only to err from the words of knowledge.
28. A worthless witness mocketh at justice;
And the mouth of the wicked swalloweth iniquity.
29. Judgments are prepared for scoffers,
And stripes for the back of fools.

STUDY QUESTIONS OVER 19:21-29

1. What does the "counsel of Jehovah" mean in v. 21?
2. Why does kindness make one desired (v. 22)?
3. What is different about the construction of v. 23?
4. Are there actually people this lazy (v. 24), or is this a hyperbole?
5. Who are the "simple" in v. 25?

6. Why would anybody act like this (v. 26)?
7. Why do people accept false counsel (v. 27)?
8. Who is a "worthless witness" (v. 28)?
9. Who are "scoffers" and "fools" in v. 29?

PARAPHRASE OF 19:21-29

21. Man proposes, but God disposes.
22. Kindness makes a man attractive. And it is better to be poor than dishonest.
23. Reverence for God gives life, happiness, and protection from harm.
24. Some men are so lazy they won't even feed themselves!
25. Punish a mocker and others will learn from his example. Reprove a wise man and he will be the wiser.
26. A son who mistreats his father or mother is a public disgrace.
27. Stop listening to teaching that contradicts what you know is right.
28. A worthless witness cares nothing for truth--he enjoys his sinning too much.
29. Mockers and rebels shall be severely punished.

COMMENTS ON 19:21-29

V. 21. It is not what man wants that always comes to pass but what God decrees (or allows). See Psa. 33:10,11; Prov. 16:1,2; Isa. 14:26,27; 46:10; Heb. 6:17. God "worketh all things after the counsel of his will" (Eph. 1:11). Men in a human council meeting thought they could stop Christianity (Acts 4:17), but they passed away, and the Word of God is still living, active, and powerful. Herod of Acts 12 took up against the church, killed James, and intended to kill Peter, but before the chapter was ended, he was dead, and in contrast to him Acts 12:24 says, "But the word of God grew and multiplied."

V. 22. This verse states that which we desire in people, and heading the list is "kindness". We like people who are kind; we like to be around them; their influence upon us is good. We appreciate their thoughtfulness; we appreciate their willingness to be helpful. We are comfortable and at-home in their presence. An unkind person is just the opposite of the above. The Bible says, "Be ye kind" (Eph. 4:32); "Love...is kind" (I Cor. 13:4). Concerning the second statement of the verse, this chapter has already shown that people go from and do not want to claim close connections with the extremely poor (vs. 4,7), yet they prefer a poor man to a liar (compare v. 1). A man who will lie to others will lie to you. He is one you cannot trust, for he is not conscientious before God and with men. He makes a poor friend.

V. 23. This verse departs from Proverbs' customary two-line verses. Notice the three lines here. "Tendeth" shows the usual or general results of fearing Jehovah. It means, other things being equal, that one who fears God will live longer--not only longer, but he will reap more satisfaction from living than those who lack it, the reason being that he will have fewer hardships because of not being visited with evil from God. The "fear of Jehovah" takes us back to the first real saying in Proverbs: "The fear of Jehovah is the beginning of knowledge" (1:7).

V. 24. Proverbs has much to say about lazy people: they spend much time sleeping (6:9; 24:30-34; 20:4; 26:13). This verse "out-lazies" the others as it pictures a man putting his hand into the dish to get something to eat and then being too lazy to lift it to his mouth (Prov. 26:15). When one is too lazy to feed himself, he is as lazy as he can get. Yet, all of life becomes a burden to the ambitionless person, the person with no purpose, no motivation. Arabic proverb: "He dies of hunger under the date tree."

V. 25. A scoffer is out of order whether he scoff at God or is plagued with the spirit of scoffing at people. He should be dealt with (the younger the better). The verse implies that even if he doesn't profit by it, the onlooking who might have taken up his ways will be affected for good (compare Deut. 13:10,11). Reproving a wise person definitely aids him, for he wishes to increase his learning, and he is wise enough to see the rightness of the rebuke (last part of Prov. 9:9). Prov. 21:11 is very similar to this verse in both of its statements: "When the scoffer is punished, the simple is made wise; And when the wise is instructed, he receiveth knowledge."

V. 26. The language suggests that the "son" is a grown son, not a child. It is speaking of gross mistreatment of aged parents. While our present society has many instances of this in comparison to Bible days, this verse indicates that there were some bad offspring in Bible days. Remember that parents are to be honored, not thus dishonored. Such conduct causes "shame" to his suffering parents and "reproach" against his own name in the community. Prov. 17:2 also speaks of a "son that causeth shame."

V. 27. It does no good to be exposed to good instruction if it is not going to be followed. There are those who seem to be listening to what you are telling them, but they are only being polite or do not wish to engage in open disagreement, for when they go their way they have not been changed by what they have heard. In time Christian teachers will cease instructing people if they will not be obedient (Acts 18:5,6).

V. 28. A "worthless witness" would include both a false witness (speaking lies) and one who refused to witness (would not tell what he knew). To do either is to mock rather than further justice. Justice dictates that the verdict be built upon the truth, the whole truth, and nothing but the truth. One the latter part of the verse: "Mischief is the object of his passionate desire: it is a real enjoyment to him to produce calamity; he swallows it eagerly as if it were a sweet fruit (Job 20:12; Isa. 28:4); he "drinketh it in like water" (Job 15:16)—("Lange").

V. 29. Another Hebrew parallelism: "judgments" and "stripes" go together as do "scoffers" and "fools". The verse is picturing an adult rather than a child, the "judgments" and "stripes" being public punishments. A child may be "foolish" (Prov. 22:15), but he is not a full-fledged "fool", but if one grows up, and his foolishness continues, and it is the recognized course of his life, then he is indeed a "fool". Other passages on such punishments: Prov. 10:13; 26:3.

NOTICEABLE GROUPINGS IN CHAPTER 19

"*Poor*"--

"Better is the poor that walketh in his integrity Than he that is perverse in his lips and is a fool" (v. 1).

"The poor is separated from his friend" (v. 4).

"All the brethren of the poor do hate him: How much more do his friends go far from him! He pursueth them with words, but they are gone" (v. 7).

"He that hath pity upon the poor lendeth unto Jehovah" (v. 17).

"A poor man is better than a liar" (v. 22).

"*Rich*"--

"Wealth added many friends" (v. 4).

"House and riches are an inheritance from fathers" (v. 14).

CHAPTER 19

"*Fools*"--

"Better is the poor that walketh in his integrity Than he that is perverse in his lips and is a fool" (v. 1).

"The foolishness of man subverteth his way" (v. 3).

"Delicate living is not seemly for a fool" (v. 10).

"A foolish son is the calamity of his father" (v. 13).

"Stripes for the back of fools" (v. 29).

"*Speech*"--

"Better is the poor that walketh in his integrity Than he that is perverse in his lips" (v. 1).

"A false witness shall not be unpunished; And he that uttereth lies shall not escape" (v. 5).

"A false witness shall not be unpunished; And he that uttereth lies shall perish" (v. 9).

"The contentions of a wife are a continual dripping" (v. 13).

"A poor man is better than a liar" (v. 22).

"A worthless witness mocketh at justice; And the mouth of the wicked swalloweth iniquity" (v. 28).

"*Knowledge*"--

"That the soul be without knowledge is not good" (v. 2).

"He that getteth wisdom loveth his own soul: He that keepeth understanding shall find good" (v. 8).

"Hear counsel, and receive instruction, That thou mayest be wise in they latter end" (v. 20).

"Smite a scoffer, and the simple will learn prudence; And reprove one that hath understanding, and he will understand knowledge" (v. 25).

"*Scoffers*"--

"Smite a scoffer (v. 25).

"Judgments are prepared for scoffers" (v. 29).

"*Anger*"--

"The discretion of a man maketh him slow to anger" (v. 11).

"The king's wrath is as the roaring of a lion" (v. 12).

"A man of great wrath shall bear the penalty; For if thou deliver him, thou must do it yet again" (v. 19).

"*Sons*"--

"A foolish son is the calamity of his father" (v. 13).

"Chasten thy son, seeing there is hope; And set not thy heart on his destruction" (v. 18).

"He that doeth violence to his father, and chaseth away his

mother, Is a son that causeth shame and bringeth reproach" (v. 26).

"*Wife*"--

"The contentions of a wife are a continual dripping" (v. 13).

"A prudent wife is from Jehovah" (v. 14).

"*Slothfulness*"--

"Slothfulness casteth into a deep sleep; And the idle soul shall suffer hunger" (v. 15).

"The sluggard burieth his hand in the dish, And will not so much as bring it to his mouth again" (v. 24).

"*Heart*"--

"His heart fretteth against Jehovah" (v. 3).

"There are many devices in a man's heart; But the counsel of Jehovah, that shall stand" (v. 21).

CHAPTER 20

TEXT — 20:1-10

1. Wine is a mocker, strong drink a brawler;
   And whosoever erreth thereby is not wise.
2. The terror of a king is as the roaring of a lion:
   He that provoketh him to anger sinneth against his own life.
3. It is an honor for a man to keep aloof from strife;
   But every fool will be quarrelling.
4. The sluggard will not plow by reason of the winter;
   Therefore he shall beg in harvest, and have nothing.
5. Counsel in the heart of man is like deep water;
   But a man of understanding will draw it out.
6. Most men will proclaim every one his own kindness;
   But a faithful man who can find?
7. A righteous man that walketh in his integrity,
   Blessed are his children after him.
8. A king that sitteth on the throne of judgment
   Scattereth away all evil with his eyes.
9. Who can say, I have made my heart clean,
   I am pure from my sin?
10. Diverse weights, and divers measures,
    Both of them alike are an abomination to Jehovah.

STUDY QUESTIONS OVER 20:1-10

1. According to v. 1 have we as a nation been "wise" to legalize strong drink?
2. Give a Bible instance of the truth of v. 2.
3. Cite other passages besides v. 3 that teach us to avoid strife.
4. What are other excuses besides v. 4 that sluggards might give for not doing a job?
5. He will draw it out of his own heart or out of the heart of another (v. 5)?
6. What is meant in v. 6 by a "faithful" man?
7. Why are the children of a righteous man blessed (v. 7)?
8. How does a king scatter away evil "with his eyes (v. 8)?
9. What is the evident answer to the questions in v. 9?
10. According to v. 10 with what is God displeased?

PARAPHRASE OF 20:1-10

1. Wine gives false courage; hard liquor leads to brawls; what fools men are to let it master them, making them reel drunkenly down the street!
2. The king's fury is like that of a roaring lion; to rouse his anger is to risk your life.
3. It is an honor for a man to stay out of a fight. Only fools insist on quarreling.
4. If you won't plow in the cold you won't eat in the harvest.
5. Though good advice lies deep within a counselor's heart, the wise man will draw it out.
6. Most people will tell you what loyal friends they are, but are they telling the truth?
7. It is a wonderful heritage to have an honest father.
8. A king sitting as judge weighs all the evidence carefully, distinguishing the true from false.
9. Who can ever say, "I have cleansed my heart; I am sinless"?
10. The Lord despises every king of cheating.

COMMENTS ON 20:1-10

V. 1. "Wine" as used in the Bible is not always intoxicating, but in this instance it is (note its connection with "strong drink" and also with what the verse says about it). It is a "mocker", mocking and making a fool out of its drinker with ridiculous and senseless conduct. Strong drink is a "brawler", leading to many quarrels and fights. One who drinks the stuff "erreth", is making a great mistake, sins, and he is "not wise." One can hardly err worse or be more unwise than to take up with strong drink. Oh, the sorrows, griefs, hardships, miseries, and you-name-it that strong drink has brought to the drinker, to his family, and to those who have been injured and killed just so that he could drink! For other passages see Gen. 9:21,22; Prov. 23:29,30; Isa. 28:7; Hos. 4:4. Strong drink is surely not for kings (Prov. 31:4,5), yet they have often been big drinkers. God was highly displeased at the drinking Belshazzar and his antics at the big party of Dan. 5. Every nation that has turned to wine has only weakened itself. A German saying: "More are drowned in the wine cup than in the ocean." Note the New Testament teaching in Eph. 5:18; Rom. 14:21.

V. 2. Being a king, Solomon included numerous sayings involving kings. He especially liked those that showed the importance of having the king's favor and avoiding his disfavor (Prov. 16:16; 19:12). I Kings 2 shows three men encountering Solomon's wrath and suffering death: Adonijah, Job, and Shemei.

V. 3. This verse shows that fools (not wise people) quarrel and engage in trouble while people of honor seek to avoid strife. "Follow peace with all men" (Heb. 12:14); "If it be possible, as much as in you lieth, be at peace with all men" :Rom. 12:18); "Let there be no strife, I pray thee, between me and thee" :Gen. 13:8). This does not mean we are to compromise God's Word in order to have peace. This is an altogether different field (Luke 14:51-53).

V. 4. The lazy, indolent person can always find an excuse for not working. It may be the cold weather (as in this verse), or it may be "too hot", "rainy," "it's too hard," "I don't know how," "I'm not feeling good," "somebody else will do it," "it's not important," "I'll do it later," etc. This is why some people have nothing.

V. 5. "Counsel" in this verse stands for deep wisdom (like water of a deep well). But "counsel" is no good unless you can get it from its possesser. People with little to offer us are generally free with their advice, but people who really have knowledge tend to be more conservative with giving unsolicited advice. In fact, sometimes it takes just the right person who goes at the right time and approaches the subject in just the right way to get such valuable counsel. This verse shows that where there's a will, a man of understanding will find the way to get it.

V. 6. The tendency of humanity is to tell those things that are personally commendable and to forget those things that are derogatory. As such we tell only a part of the story. A "faithful" man (one who tells it exactly as it is concerning himself) is almost impossible to find, according to the implication of this verse. There is much food for thought here for each of us.

V. 7. Everybody is blessed when a man lives right, but especially himself and his family. Since influence and environment are such strong factors in life, those who are the closest to a righteous person are the ones who receive the greatest blessings from their influence. "Integrity" is honesty, uprightness. Other passages showing that one's offspring is blessed by his righteousness and because of his righteousness: Psa. 37:25,26;

112:2.

V. 8. Not just any king, for some kings (like Ahab) have been the source and the multiplication of evil. But a good king is one who rules with a righteous sceptre, and his government praises the good and punishes the evil (I Pet. 2:13,14; Rom. 13:3).

V. 9. The implied answer is "nobody". We can make our hearts corrupt and our lives sinful, but we cannot dispel the guilt nor cleanse away our sin apart from God's mercy. Let us re-say it: Man cannot direct his own way successfully (Jer. 10:23), nor can he save himself by his own righteousness (Tit. 3:5), nor can he cleanse himself from a single sin (this verse). Notice how this is brought out in song: "Nothing in my hand I bring; simply to thy cross I cling; Naked, come to Thee for dress; helpless, look to Thee for grace; Foul, I to the fountain fly; Wash me, Saviour, or I die."

V. 10. Verse 23 reads similarly. Man employs such means to gain personal advantage even though its disadvantage to his fellowmen equals the advantage that it is to himself. It is unscrupulous gain. It is plain and intentional dishonesty. And it is abomination to God. See Deut. 25:13-16 and Prov. 11:1 also.

TEST QUESTIONS OVER 20:1-10

1. How do we know that "wine" in v. 1 is intoxicating?
2. Comment upon "erreth" (v. 1).
4. Comment upon "not wise" (v. 1).
5. Name three men executed by King Solomon (v. 2).
6. Give some Bible statements showing that God wants us to be peaceable people (v. 3).
7. Why did the sluggard in v. 4 not want to plow?
8. Who is more apt to be free with counsel (v. 5)? Who more conservative with it?
9. Comment upon v. 6.
10. Give other passages besides v. 7 that show the blessings that come to children because of righteous parents.
11. What kind of king fulfills v. 8?
12. If Christ had not died, would there be any fountain for our sin (v. 9)?
13. Show from v. 10 that godliness extends to our business dealings.

TEXT — 20:11-20

11. Even a child maketh himself known by his doings,
    Whether his work be pure, and whether it be right.
12. The hearing ear, and the seeing eye,
    Jehovah hath made even both of them.
13. Love not sleep, lest thou come to poverty;
    Open thine eyes, and thou shalt be satisfied with bread.
14. It is bad, it is bad, saith the buyer;
    But when he is gone his way, then he boasteth.
15. There is gold, and abundance of rubies;
    But the lips of knowledge are a precious jewel.
16. Take his garment that is surety for a stranger;
    And hold him in pledge that is surety for foreigners.
17. Bread of falsehood is sweet to a man;
    But afterwards his mouth shall be filled with gravel.
18. Every purpose is established by counsel;
    And by wise guidance make thou war.
19. He that goeth about as a talebearer revealeth secrets;
    Therefore company not with him that openeth wide his lips.
20. Whoso curseth his father or his mother,
    His lamp shall be put out in blackness of darkness.

STUDY QUESTIONS OVER 20:11-20

1. What is the force of the word "even" in v. 11?
2. Select some of the intricate workings of the eye or ear that would disprove evolution and uphold divine creation (v. 12).
3. While sleep is necessary, can one sleep too much (v. 13)?
4. Why does the buyer say, "It is bad, it is bad" (v. 14)?
5. When he goes his way, of what does he boast (v. 14)?
6. Why are lips of knowledge compared with a precious jewel (v. 15)?
7. Explain v. 16.
8. Show how sin is often "sweet" at the time but not so afterwards (v. 17).
9. Whose false guidance ruined Absalom (v. 18)?
10. Why not company with such a person (v. 19)?
11. What is meant by one's lamp being put out (v. 20)?

PARAPHRASE OF 20:11-20

11. The character of even a child can be known by the way he acts--whether what he does is pure and right.
12. If you have good eyesight and good hearing, thank God who gave them to you.
13. If you love sleep, you will end in poverty. Stay awake, work hard, and there will be plenty to eat!
14. "Utterly worthless!" says the buyer as he haggles over the price. But afterwards he brags about his bargain!
15. Good sense is far more valuable than gold or precious jewels.
16. It is risky to make loans to strangers!
17. Some men enjoy cheating, but the cake they buy with such ill-gotten gain will turn to gravel in their mouths.
18. Don't go ahead with your plans without the advice of others; don't go to war until they agree.
19. Don't tell your secrets to a gossip unless you want them broadcast to the world.
20. God puts out the light of the man who curses his father or mother.

COMMENTS ON 20:11-20

V. 11. The Bible says we can know what a person really is by what he does (Matt. 7:16; 12:35; I John 3:10; 2:29). This verse shows that people begin to take notice of one's behavior and to form an opinion concerning him even when he is a young child.

V. 12. Psa. 94:9 and Exo. 4:11 also affirm that God has made our equipment for seeing and hearing, and when one studies the intricacies of these valuable parts of our bodies, who else but God could make them? The theory of evolution is so inadequate to account for the origin of such sensitive, such intricate, such functional, parts of the human body. This is applicable not only to the eyes and ears but to all the body. R. G. Lee: "The most wonderful camera in all the world is the human eye. The most perfect telephone is the human ear. The most perfect violin is the human larynx. The most perfect telegraph system is the human nerves. The most wonderful chemical laboratory is the intestinal tract. The most wonderful thatch is the human hair. The most perfect filter is the human lung. The most perfect screen is the human eyelid. The most perfect pump is the human is the human heart."

V. 13. We know that a person can sleep too little for good health. But we can also sleep too much to get the necessary things done. Clark: "Sleep...is an indescribable blessing; but how often is it turned into a curse! It is like food: a certain measure of it restores and invigorates exhausted nature; more than that oppresses and destroys life." See Prov. 6:9-11; 19:15 also.

V. 14. If there is something wrong with an object one is seeking to buy, it is not out of place for the buyer to take that into consideration with the seller when making the purchase and agreeing upon the price, but this verse knows human nature all too well: to "knock" the product mercilessly and unrighteously as if it were no good, but when the purchase has been made at a small price, oh how the purchaser does brag to his friends of the deal he made! Beware, traders and buyers!

V. 15. Speaking of wisdom, Job 28:16-19 says, "It cannot be valued with the gold of Ophir, with the precious onyx, or the sapphire. Gold and glass cannot equal it, neither shall it be exchanged for jewels of fine gold. No mention shall be made of coral or of crystal: yea, the price of wisdom is above rubies. The topaz of Ethiopia shall not equal it, neither shall it be valued with pure gold." See Prov. 3:15; 8:11 for similar comparisons. This verse is not speaking of wisdom and knowledge held for oneself but shared with others.

V. 16. Prov. 27:13 is very similar. This is exactly what happens when one has made himself surety for another's debts who cannot pay. Prov. 22:26,27 warns against suretyship as do Prov. 6:1,2; 11:15; 17:18.

V. 17. The pleasures of sin seem great at the moment, but they can lead to very sorrowful consequences, and in the end to divine punishment in the lake of fire. Achan enjoyed much more the stealing of the forbidden from the spoils of Jericho than he did the "afterwards" (Josh. 7:20-25). It seemed "sweet" to Joseph's brothers to sell him and get rid of him, but the "afterwards" of it was not good (Gen. 42:21,22). The philosophy of the evil woman of Prov. 9:17 is that "stolen waters of sweet", but the man who drinks "knoweth not that the dead are there; That her guests are in the depths of Sheol" (9:18). Look beyond the momentary pleasure derived from sin to the fearful consequences to which it leads (Heb. 10:31).

V. 18. This saying was given for those days when God had an earthly nation (Israel) and when their wars with the idolatrous were a part of God's plan (a 1500 year period--from Moses onward). Other verses on the same subject and for the same period: Prov. 15:22; 24:6; Luke 14:31. Absalom was not wise in accepting Hushai's false counsel in preference to Ahithophel's wise counsel from his standpoint (II Sam. 17:1-14; 18:6-15). Just as they looked to "counsel" in their warfare, even so should we seek out good advice in pursuing major proposals.

V. 19. The first statement is found also in Prov. 11:13. A talebearer revealeth secrets whereever he goes. But be assured as he tells you the secrets of others that he in turn will reveal your secrets to the next ones to whom he talks. "Therefore company not with him," says this verse's conclusion, and a good conclusion it is! Proverbs has nothing good to say about the "talebearer" and the "whisperer", and what a poor way to live! Surely there is something far higher to live for than to be a talebearer and a gossip.

V. 20. Other Scriptures about cursing and belittling one's parents: Exo. 21:17; Lev. 20:9; Matt. 15:4. Other passages on one's lamp being put out: Prov. 24:20; Job 18:5,6. They always kept a small light burning in their houses at night, for utter darkness was one of the things they feared the most. The "lamp" of one's life, one's household, one's future lineage, would be cut off if he cursed his parents.

TEST QUESTIONS OVER 20:11-20

1. How early do people begin forming an opinion about us (v. 11)?
2. Why does the theory of evolution fall far short of explaining the abilities of the ear and eye (v. 12)?
3. What are the dangers of getting either too little or too much sleep (v. 13)?
4. Why do traders and buyers need v. 14?
5. How does v. 15 describe the lips of knowledge?
6. What passages besides v. 16 contain teachings on suretyship?
7. What word is so important in v. 17?
8. What kind of "counsel" was v. 18 originally dealing with?
9. Why is it wise not to be a companion of a secret-revealer (v. 19)?
10. Why did the ancients customarily leave a small light burning at night (v. 20)?

TEXT — 20:21-30

21. An inheritance may be gotten hastily at the beginning;
But the end thereof shall not be blessed.
22. Say not thou, I will recompense evil:
Wait for Jehovah, and he will save thee.
23. Diverse weights are an abomination to Jehovah;
And a false balance is not good.
24. A man's goings are of Jehovah;
How then can man understand his way?
25. It is a snare to a man rashly to say, It is holy,
And after vows to make inquiry.
26. A wise king winnoweth the wicked,
And bringeth the threshingwheel over them.
27. The spirit of man is the lamp of Jehovah,
Searching all his innermost parts.
28. Kindness and truth preserve the king;
And his throne is upholden by kindness.
29. The glory of young men is their strength;
And the beauty of old men is the hoary head.
30. Stripes that wound cleanse away evil;
And strokes reach the innermost parts.

STUDY QUESTIONS OVER 20:21-30

1. Give a Bible example of one who misspent his inheritance money (v. 21).
2. Compare v. 22 with Abigail's advice to David in I Sam. 25:9-31.
3. What previous verse in this chapter teaches the same as v. 23?
4. What man in the last part of Genesis could look back and see the truth stated in v. 24?
5. What does Eccl. 5:4,5 say about making vows (v. 25)?
6. What should be any ruler's attitude and action toward wickedness (v. 26)?
7. Is v. 27 referring to the conscience?
8. Are kings usually thought of as "kind" (v. 28)?
9. Illustrate the statement about young men in v. 29.
10. Illustrate the statement about old men in v. 29.
11. Is the statement in v. 30 still true?

PARAPHRASE OF 20:21-30

21. A fortune can be made from cheating, but there is a curse that goes with it.
22. Don't repay evil for evil. Wait for the Lord to handle the matter.
23. The Lord loathes all cheating and dishonesty.
24. Since the Lord is directing our steps, why try to understand everything that happens along the way?
25. It is foolish and rash to make a promise to the Lord before counting the cost.
26. A wise king stamps out crime by severe punishment.
27. A man's conscience is the Lord's searchlight exposing his hidden motives.
28. If a king is kind, honest and fair, his kingdom stands secure.
29. The glory of young men is their strength; of old men, their experience.
30. Punishment that hurts chases evil from the heart.

COMMENTS ON 20:21-30

V. 21. Sometimes an inheritance immediately places into a person's hands more money than he has ever had in his possession at any one time. He didn't work for it; he didn't save it; but now all at once it is his. If the person is wise, it can be a great blessing as he thankfully receives it, as he carefully invests or uses it, and as he realizes the value of it. But "come easy, go easy" is so often the rule, and a short time of luxurious living (while it lasts; can make it a curse to him as he gets himself into a standard of living that he cannot maintain by his own earnings after the inheritance money is blown. A common laborer went through an inheritance of $200,000 in six months. He didn't want to go back to working, so he and a woman teamed up and kidnapped a rich man's son, killed him, and collected the ransom money. They were executed by the state of Missouri. Others, like the Prodigal Son, get involved in sinful, indulgent living that they had never known before.

V. 22. Prov. 24:29 also forbids one saying he will take vengeance. I Thess. 5:15 and I Pet. 3:9 also forbid our vengeance-taking and teaches us to render good for their evil. Deut. 32:35,36 promises that God will take care of executing vengeance on the wrongdoer, saving us the trouble, keeping us from making some mistakes, and being sure the wrongdoer will get just what he should receive. Paul reminds us of this in Rom. 12:19,20, promising that by our doing good to them, some of them will be turned from enmity to friendship (v. 21). Abigail believed this and persuaded David (I Sam. 25:9-34), and thereafter David appeared to be completely convinced of the rightness of this procedure (I Sam. 26:7-10; II Sam. 16:5-12).

V. 23. Similar to v. 10. God's great displeasure with crooked dishonest dealings with one's fellowmen is again expressed.

V. 24. That Jehovah leads in our lives, see Prov. 16:9 and Psa. 37:23. Since we cannot successfully direct our own ways (Jer. 10:23), we should ask God to do it for us (Prov. 3:6; Psa. 37:4,5). At the time we may not see the hand of the Lord at work as we will see it later (consider Gen. 50:20). Paul and Silas must have had this faith, for in answering the Macedonian call of Acts 16:9, they were soon in jail in Macedonia, but we see no complaining in them but praying and singing praises to God (Acts 16:25), and great good came out of their actual imprisonment (Acts 16:26-34).

V. 25. We should always think before acting, and when vowing before God this verse shows that one should be sure he is going to carry through before promising. And so agrees Eccl. 5:4,5. We should work to get people to make sacred decisions, but we do not want to pressure them into saying something that they will not have the faith, reverence, and determination to carry out. Many a persuasive, out-going, personality-man has gotten people baptized who were not really ready on their own to live the Christ-directed life.

V. 26. "Winnoweth" and "threshingwheel" refer to their threshing the grain and by rough-handling their separating the grain from the rest. Whippings (punishments) have often been referred to by the word "threshing". Solomon (and God who inspired his including this statement in the Proverbs) knew that the wicked should be dealt with as such, and so should every ruler of any level (parent, judge, school principal, church leader, etc.). Put "ruler" for "king", and this statement makes sense in an extended way to every realm of leadership.

V. 27. I Cor. 2:11 speaks of this "spirit of man": "Who among men knoweth the things of a man, save the spirit of the man, which is in him?" That which man has from Jehovah that animals are not credited with having and that searches out one's innermost thoughts is the conscience. Man has this important facility within him because God wanted him to have it. When one's conscience operates, his thoughts either "accuse" or "excuse" him for his actions (Rom. 2:15), depending upon whether he has violated or carried out what he understands to be right. The conscience is a "Siamese twin" of one's intellect: whatever one's intellect tells him is right or wrong, his conscience accepts the same position and works accordingly (Acts 26:9-11; 23:1).

V. 28. There have been many unkind kings; in fact, it has been common for man to abuse his place of power. Except for David's unkindness to Uriah, he was a living model of a king who wanted to be kind and good to his subjects, to his men, and to his repentant enemies, and who sought to rule with the absolute truth in mind. Note the similar promise in Prov. 29:14. Such a king, though, is not looked upon as "kind" by those who do wrong (v. 26).

V. 29. It is natural for young men to glory in their strength. Their bodies are young, healthy, working, nimble, capable, etc., and because of this, competitive athletics are common for that age. They wrestle, lift weights, run, play football and other types of ball, etc. And because of this strength sometimes they forget that life can be taken from them without a warning, and sometimes they abuse their bodies to the undoing of their comfort in older years. But in time that strength will naturally be replaced with the gray and then the white hair of old age, which is said by this verse to be beautiful. It symbolizes length of days, rich experiences, knowledge and wisdom, and many years of usefulness, all of which add up to a respect that is normally forthcoming (Prov. 16:31).

V. 30. "Stripes" and "strokes" have to do with correcting and punishing those who have done evil. This verse presents the following parallels: "stripes" and "strokes" go together as do "cleanse away evil" and "reach the innermost parts". When such are applied severely enough ("wound"), they do reach the seat of evil (The "innermost parts"). Words of instruction should always precede the wounds of discipline, but words are too weak to reach some people; the only language that some people can get anything out of at all is that of severe discipline. When a congregation no longer deals with the evil committed within it; when a home does not discipline its disobedient children; and when a government does not punish the wrongdoer, it is bad for everybody; the individual himself, the church, the home, and society.

TEST QUESTIONS OVER 20:21-30

1. Tell how the truth of v. 21 was observed in a man in Missouri?
2. From whom did David learn the truth contained in v. 22?
3. How many times in this chapter has God dealt with crookedness in business (v. 23)?
4. What wonderful assurance does v. 24 bring to us?
5. The comments connected v. 25 with what teaching in Eccl.?
6. According to v. 26 what does a wise king do about wickedness?
7. What is conscience a "Siamese twin" to (v. 27)?
8. King David seems to have been a very kind ruler except when (v. 28)?
9. Give examples of young men glorying in their strength (v. 29)?
10. How many times is punishing the wicked brought up in this chapter (v. 30)?

NOTICEABLE GROUPINGS IN CHAPTER 20

"*King*"--

"The terror of a king is as the roaring of a lion" (v. 2).

"A king that sitteth on the throne of judgment Scattereth away all evil with his eyes" (v.8).

"A wise king winnoweth the wicked, And bringeth the threshingwheel over them" (v. 26).

"Kindness and truth preserve the king; And his throne is upholden by kindness" (v. 28).

"*Laziness*"--

"The sluggard will not plow by reason of the winter; Therefore he shall beg in harvest, and have nothing" (v. 4).

"Love not sleep, lest thou come to poverty; Open thine eyes, and thou shalt be satisfied with bread" (v. 13).

"*Business dishonesty*"--

"Diverse weights, and diverse measures, Both of them alike are an abomination to Jehovah" (v. 10).

"It is bad, it is bad, saith the buyer; But when he is gone

his way, then he boasteth" (v. 14).

"Diverse weights are an abomination to Jehovah; And a false balance is not good" (v. 23).

"*Speech*"--

"Most men will proclaim every one his own kindness; But a faithful man who can find?" (v. 6).

"It is bad, it is bad, saith the buyer; But when he is gone his way, then he boasteth" (v. 14).

"The lips of knowledge are a precious jewel" (v. 15).

"He that goeth about as a talebearer revealeth secrets; Therefore company not with him that openeth wide his lips" (v. 19).

"Whoso curseth his father or his mother, His lamp shall be put out in blackness of darkness" (v. 20).

"It is a snare to a man rashly to say, It is holy, And after vows to make inquiry" (v. 25).

"*Outcome*"--

"The terror of the king is as the roaring of a lion: he that provoketh him to anger sinneth against his own life" (v. 2).

"The sluggard will not plow by reason of the winter; Therefore he shall beg in harvest, and have nothing" (v. 4).

"A righteous man that walketh in his integrity, Blessed are his children after him" (v. 7).

"Bread of falsehood is sweet to a man; But afterwards his mouth shall be filled with gravel" (v. 17).

"Whoso curseth his father or his mother, His lamp shall be put out in blackness of darkness" (v. 20).

"An inheritance may be gotten hastily at the beginning; But the end thereof shall not be blessed" (v. 21).

"*Counsel*"--

"Counsel in the heart of man is like deep water; But a man of understanding will draw it out" (v. 5).

"Every purpose is established by counsel; And by wise guidance make thou war" (v. 18).

"*Great questions*"--

"A faithful man who can find?" (v. 6).

"Who can say, I have made my heart clean, I am pure from my sin?" (v. 9).

"*Jehovah*"--

"Diverse weights, and diverse measures, Both of them alike

are an abomination to Jehovah" (v. 10).

"The hearing ear, and the seeing eye, Jehovah hath made even both of them" (v. 12).

"Say not thou, I will recompense evil: Wait for Jehovah, and he will save thee" (v. 22).

"Diverse weights are an abomination to Jehovah" (v. 23).

"A man's goings are of Jehovah" (v. 24).

"The spirit of man is the lamp of Jehovah" (v. 27).

"*Kindness*"--

"Most men will proclaim every one his own kindness" (v. 6).

"Kindness and truth preserve the king; And his throne is upholden by kindness" (v. 28).

"*Knowledge*"--

"Counsel in the heart of man is like keep water; But a man of understanding will draw it out" (v. 5).

"The lips of knowledge are a precious jewel")v. 15).

LAZINESS LOSES OUT

10:4 says, "He becometh poor that dealeth with a slack hand: but the hand of the diligent maketh rich." Evidently because it is too much bother, "The slothful man roasteth not that which he took in hunting," whereas "the substance of the diligent man is precious" (12:27). The diligent bear the rule, "but the slothful shall be under tribute (Revised Version says 'taskwork')" (12:24). Those who are at the bottom of the ladder are forever making uncomplimentary remarks and holding the worst of feelings toward those who go ahead. But, why are many people where they are today? The Bible tells you. It says, "Slothfulness!" 15:19 says, "The way of the slothful man is as a hedge of thorns" (a rough, difficult way) "but the way of the righteous is made plain (Revised Version says 'a highway'). Notice that the "slothful" are contrasted from the "righteous" in this passage.

Yes, over and over in Proverbs, it says that the slothful man "hath nothing". There is an honorable poverty, and the Bible so recognizes it. But, poverty that comes through slothfulness is not honorable—it is dishonorable in every way.

Women, read about the ambitious woman in Prov. 31, better known to us as the "virtuous woman". What a model of excellence. Make that one of your favorite passages of Scripture. Read it often. Appreciate it. Be that kind of woman yourself.

Men, listen to 22:29: Seest thou a man diligent in his business? he shall stand before kings; he shall not stand before mean (Marginal reading is 'obscure') men." You have much to do with the pace that is set at your house, with the standard of living that is maintained, with the outlook upon life of your family.

Be diligent, not lazy, the Proverbs would say!

TEXT — 21:1-10

1. The king's heart is in the hand of Jehovah as the water-courses:
He turneth it whithersoever he will.
2. Every way of a man is right in his own eyes;
But Jehovah weigheth the hearts.
3. To do righteousness and justice
Is more acceptable to Jehovah than sacrifice.
4. A high look, and a proud heart,
Even the lamp of the wicked, is sin.
5. The thoughts of the diligent tend only to plenteousness;
But every one that is hasty hasteth only to want.
6. The getting of treasures by a lying tongue
Is a vapor driven to and fro by them that seek death.
7. The violence of the wicked shall sweep them away,
Because they refuse to do justice.
8. The way of him that is laden with guilt is exceeding crooked;
But as for the pure, his work is right.
9. It is better to dwell in the corner of the housetop,
Than with a countentious woman in a wide house.
10. The soul of the wicked desireth evil:
His neighbor findeth no favor in his eyes.

STUDY QUESTIONS OVER 21:1-10

1. Is v. 1 always true or only when God specially wills it for the fulfillment of some special purpose?
2. Does v. 2 imply that God draws a different conclusion from us in the matter?
3. Is v. 3 frowning on religious ceremony or stating that such is not a substitute for righteousness but a supplement to it?
4. What does "lamp of the wicked" mean (v. 4)?
5. What is the main contrast in v. 5?
6. How could one get treasures by lying (v. 6)?
7. What are some examples of v. 7 from history?
8. Illustrate v. 8 by Herod and Herodias.
9. How could one live in the corner of a housetop (v. 9)?
10. Is the second clause in v. 10 one of the evils of the first clause, or is it the result of that clause?

PARAPHRASE OF 21:1-10

1. Just as water is turned into irrigation ditches, so the Lord directs the king's thoughts. He turns them wherever He wants to.
2. We can justify our every deed but God looks at our motives.
3. God is more pleased when we are just and fair than when we give Him gifts.
4. Pride, lust, and evil actions are all sin.
5. Steady plodding brings prosperity; hasty speculation brings poverty.
6. Dishonest gain will never last, so why take the risk?
7. Because the wicked are unfair, their violence boomerangs and destroys them.
8. A man is known by his actions; an evil man lives an evil life; a good man lives a godly life.
9. It is better to live in the corner of an attic than with a crabby woman in a lovely home.
10. An evil man loves to harm others; being a good neighbor is out of his line.

COMMENTS ON 21:1-10

V. 1. "Clarke": "There is an allusion here to the eastern method of watering their lands. Several canals are dug from one stream; and by opening a particular sluice, the husbandman can direct a stream to whatever part he pleases." We should not conclude from this that everything any king does is of the Lord (this would make God responsible for the many evils of government); yet when God gets ready to affect a king's heart, He is able to do so (Ezra 1:1; 7:6; 7:27; Neh. 1:11; 2:4-8)."

V. 2. This is very similar to Prov. 16:2. Most people are too quick to claim credit (and are offended if they are not given it) and too slow to accept guilt. That God accurately weighs each person (beginning with the heart) See Prov. 24:12; Luke 16:15; Dan. 5:27.

V. 3. There are all kinds of people in the world: some who are both righteous and religious (the godly); some who seek to be righteous but are not religious (the moralist); some who are not careful about righteousness but do try to be religious (the hypocrite); and some who are neither righteous nor religious (the out-and-out wicked). This verse is dealing with the third-listed group above (the hypocrite). We all fall short of the perfection of God (Rom. 3:23), but with our religion we are to be as righteous and as just as we can be, and if we aren't, God is highly displeased with us (Isa. 1:11,15; Hos. 6:6; Mic. 6:7,8) Prov. 15:8).

V. 4. This verse deals with pride and the prosperity of the proud. A "high look" is one of the outward expressions of a "proud heart". Over and over does God speak His displeasure with man's exalted opinion of himself (Prov. 6:16,17; Dan. 4:29-37). "Pulpit Commentary": "Lamp is...a metaphor for prosperity and happiness (II Sam. 22:29; I Kings 11:36); and it is here said that the sinner's outward prosperity and joyousness, springing from no good source, being founded in self, and not resting in virtue and godliness, are in themselves sinful and displeasing to God."

V. 5. This verse speaks of the "thoughts" of the diligent, Prov. 10:4 of the "hand" of the diligent, and Prov. 13:4 of the "soul" of the diligent, and all three verses testify to their mutual prosperity. "Diligent" (as it stands in contrast with "hasty") evidently means the honest, hard-working, patient person who steadily builds up his holdings; "hasty" evidently applies to the person who is a get-rich-quick-any-way type of person condemned by I Tim. 6:9,10. Even small communities have known examples of those who were out for the "fast-buck" who ended up in poverty and want, and cities contain many such examples.

V. 6. Connect this verse with v. 5. Getting treasures by "lying" would be parallel to "treasures of wickedness" in Prov. 10:2 and "wealth gotten by vanity" in Prov. 13:11. In all three verses the result is similar: "vapor driven to and fro" (this verse), "profit nothing" (10:2), and "shall be diminished" (13:11). Such people come to "seek death" (this verse), and the suicide-rate is exceedingly high among the world's wealthy.

V. 7. Even this verse may be related to vs. 5,6. The "violent" are those who injure others; such refuse to think of "justice". "They that take the sword shall perish with the sword" (Matt. 26:52). Is this not the story of conquerors who later find their own type of violence sweeping them helpless away?

V. 8. "Evil men wax worse and worse" (II Tim. 3:13). Such was the story of King Ahab, Herod and Herodias, and many others. One fellow was said to be so crooked that when he died, they didn't dig a grave for him—they just screwed him into the ground! "Laden" shows that guilt is a terrible load. Jesus said to the sinfully weary, "Come unto me, all ye that...are heavy laden, and I will give you rest...unto your souls" (Matt. 11:28,29). The"pure" present a welcome contrast; Much is said in a few words: "his work is right"--it is like it ought to be. And may such increase!

V. 9. Their housetops were flat. Gathering his few things together and living in the corner of the flat housetop, inconvenient as it would be, is proverbially said to be preferred to living down in the commodious house with a woman who is cantankerous. Prov. 25:24 and v. 19 of this chapter are similar. The unpleasantness of dwelling with a contentious woman is also mentioned in Prov. 19:13 and Prov. 27:15. Some women can be blessed with the very finest of material things and yet be anything but happy; they can be anything but a joy to come home to. In our day of permissive divorce courts such contentions lead to divorces.

V. 10. The wicked man does not respect God's law, for he "desireth evil" instead of good, nor does he respect his fellowman, for "his neighbor findeth no favor in his eyes". The wicked man is not prompted by a reverence for God, by a respect for God's law, by holy aspirations. He has his desire set upon evil. "They that are after the flesh mind the things of the flesh" (Rom. 8:5); "The mind of the flesh is enmity against God; for it is not subject to the law of God" (Rom. 8:7). "The wicked...sleep not, except they do evil; and their sleep is taken away, unless they cause some to fall" (Prov. 4:14-16). The person who has no good word for anyone is not honorable himself; this is why "his neighbor findeth no favor in his eyes".

TEST QUESTIONS OVER 21:1-10

1. What is meant by "watercourses" in v. 1?
2. Cite Bible instances in which God turned the hearts of kings in the direction He wanted them to go (v. 1).
3. Is God's evaluation of a person always the same as the person's own evaluation of himself (v. 2)?
4. What kind of person is v. 3 dealing with?
5. When do the wicked have a "high look" (v. 4)?
6. Contrast "diligent" and "hasty" as used in v. 5.
7. Contrast their outcomes (v. 5).
8. How can v. 6 be related to v. 5 and also to Prov. 10:2 and Prov. 13:11?
7. In keeping with v. 7 what usually happens to con-

querors?
8. Name some "crooked" characters in the Bible (v. 8).
10. Comment on "laden" in v. 8.
11. How could one dwell on a housetop (v. 9)?
12. How terrible does Proverbs show a contentious wife to be (v. 9)?
13. How does a man's wickedness show up in vo. 10?

TEXT — 21:11-20

11. When the scoffer is punished, the simple is made wise;
And when the wise is instructed, he receiveth knowledge.
12. The righteous man considereth the house of the wicked,
How the wicked are overthrown to their ruin.
13. Whoso stoppeth his ears at the cry of the poor,
He also shall cry, but shall not be heard.
14. A gift in secret pacifieth anger;
And a present in the bosom, strong wrath.
15. It is joy to the righteous to do justice;
But it is a destruction to the workers of iniquity.
16. The man that wandereth out of the way of understanding
Shall rest in the assembly of the dead.
17. He that loveth pleasure shall be a poor man:
He that loveth wine and oil shall not be rich.
18. The wicked is a ransom for the righteous;
And the treacherous cometh in the stead of the upright.
19. It is better to dwell in a desert land,
Than with a contentious and fretful woman.
20. There is precious treasure and oil in the dwelling of the wise;
But a foolish man swalloweth it up.

STUDY QUESTIONS OVER 21:11-20

1. What three classes of persons are mentioned in v. 11?
2. From what you know of yourself, in which class are you (v. 11)?
3. Does the truth of v. 12 help keep a righteous man in the way of the righteousness?
4. How is v. 13 a fulfillment of Gal. 6:7?
5. Does v. 14 present parallels at each point in the two clauses?
6. What is the antecedent word or thought of the "it" in the

second clause (v. 15)?

7. What picture do you get from the word "wandereth" in v. 16?
8. Why would pleasure make a man poor in Bible days (v. 17)?
9. How would "oil" enter into the picture in v. 17?
10. When is the wicked a ransom for the righteous (v. 18)?
11. What is meant by the last clause in v. 18?
12. Where else besides a desert is it better to dwell than with a contentious woman (v. 19)?
13. What does "swallow up" mean in v. 20?

PARAPHRASE OF 21:11-20

11. The wise man learns by listening; the simpleton can learn only by seeing scorners punished.
12. The godly learn by watching ruin overtake the wicked.
13. He who shuts his ears to the cries of the poor will be ignored in his own time of need.

14,15. An angry man may be silenced by a bribe, while the good man loves truth and justice. But the evil man fears these beyond all else, for they spell his doom.

16. The man who strays away from common sense will end up dead!
17. A man who lives pleasure becomes poor; wine and luxury are not the way to riches.
18. The wicked will finally lose; the righteous will finally win.
19. Better to live in the desert than with a quarrelsome, complaining women.
20. The wise man saves for the future, but the foolish men spends whatever he gets.

COMMENTS ON 21:11-20

V. 11. Prov. 19:25 sets forth similar truths. Even if punishment doesn't help the scoffer himself (and sometimes it doesn't), it will help the onlooking-simple who might have gotten into the same thing. God even commanded to smite certain sinners with death that others might be helped: Deut. 13:6-11; 17:8-13; 19:16-20; 21:18-21. When God smote Ananias and Sapphira, "great fear came upon the whole church, and upon all that heard these things" (Acts 5:11), and you can be sure that nobody else was even tempted to do what they had done! When

Paul wrote that stern, corrective letter (I Cor.) to the Corinthian church, which resulted in its withdrawing from the incestuous man (I Cor. 5; II Cor. 2:4-7), it also did much for the congregation itself (II Cor. 7:8-11). The latter part of our verse shows that a wise man is easy to instruct and gains much from it (Prov. 14:6). Such is a teacher's joy. But it is hard to instruct those who do not want to listen (Heb. 5:11).

V. 12. In keeping with v. 11 this verse shows that the righteous person is also a wise person who learns not only from instruction (v. 11) but also from observation, not having to go through bitter experiences to learn (like Jonah). He notices what happens to the wicked, and he learns from it because he "considers" it or thinks upon it. Seeing what happens to the wicked is good reason not to choose their way!

V. 13. "Pulpit Commentary": "A two-fold retribution is threatened on the unmerciful man: he himself shall fall into distress, and shall appeal to his neighbors for help in vain." Oh, how quickly the tables of life can be turned! Those who refuse to help others today may stand in need of help tomorrow, but no help will be forthcoming. People who know how such a one has acted will not be touched to help him, and God will not move others to help him either. And oh, how bitter the cries when they are ours and when no one will listen!

V. 14. A triple parallel: "gift" and "present", "in secret" and "in the bosom", and "anger" and "strong wrath". "Pulpit Commentary": "A gift offered secretly to one incensed, whether personal enemy, judge, or prince, averts the consequences of the offence." Concerning "in the bosom" "Pulpit Commentary" remarks, "A present kept handy in the bosom of the petitioner's garment, ready to be transferred at a fitting moment." Though this is the way it often works, it is not right (I Sam. 12:3-5) 8:3; Amos 5:12).

V. 15. Prov. 10:29 sets forth similar truth. The righteous rejoice over justice (as does God), but not the workers of iniquity, for justice is their destruction. Jesus loved righteousness and hated iniquity (Heb. 1:9), and the Bible commands us to "abhor that which is evil; cleave to that which is good" (Rom. 12:9). When we do this, we are for truth (facts) and honesty in dealing with cases brought before the court.

V. 16. "Wandereth out" of the way of understanding characterizes one who leaves, departs, goes astray from the established path. "Shall rest" in the assembly of the dead is used ironically: such probably thought or boasted that he would find the good way, but it didn't end as he had invisioned, for the "rest" to which such departures lead is the rest of death. King Ahab knew better when he allowed Jezebel to acquire Naboth's vineyard for him as she did (I Kings 21:1-16), but it did him no good, leading to his death (I Kings 21:17-22). We should know the right way (Eph. 5:17), walk the right way (Jer. 6:16), and not forsake it (II Pet. 2:20,21). This verse reminds one of Jude's statement of "wandering stars, for whom the blackness of darkness hath been reserved for ever" (Jude 13). Men, like meteors that break off and go flying through space, soon come to their everlasting end!

V. 17. Another parallelism: "loveth pleasure" and "loveth wine and oil" mean the same as do "shall be a poor man" and "shall not be rich". To have "a good time" the world's way has always involved a constant expenditure of money (one cause of becoming poor), and such life also diverts one from his work and business interests (another cause). Oh, the multitude of pleasures for people today to get involved in and sidetracked by!

V. 18. "Ransom" in the first clause and "in the stead of" in the second show that something happens to the wicked that might have happened to the righteous or that results in a better state for the righteous. "Clarke": "God often in his judgments cuts off the wicked in order to prevent them from destroying the righteous. And in general we find that the wicked fall into the traps and pits they have digged for the righteous." Prov. 11:8 says, "The righteous is delivered out of trouble; And the wicked cometh in his stead." As wicked Babylon fell, God's people were blessed with liberation. By punishing the scorner, others are spared from falling into the same sin and suffering the same fate (Prov. 21:11,12).

V. 19. This is very similar to v. 9 and Prov. 25:24. There are some kinds of women who will ruin a man's life: a "contentious" woman (this verse); a "fretful" woman (this verse); and an "odious" woman (Prov. 30:23). Since it is "better" to dwell in a "desert" than with such a woman, is not this proverb saying that it is better not to be married than to be married to such a person? Since there is a noticeable percentage of people so married, should it not be some comfort to the unmarried that at least they are in the class that Proverbs says is "better" than that?

V. 20. Wisdom knows the earthly value of precious

treasure and oil (olive oil, which was so useful in Bible days). Men of God like Job, Abraham, Dvid, and others were blessed with an abundance of these, yet they were apparently not selfish with them (did Abraham appear selfish in offering nephew Lot the choice of the land in Gen. 13:2-12?) but were willing to give to others from their store (Job. 31:16-23). The contrast within our verse shows that the "foolish" devours everything he gets his hands on. Is this not the way with many today? They draw big money per hour, blow it all in, and the slightest emergency proves to be a major calamity financially. The Bible says that we are (1) to labor (2) at honest occupations (3) so that we will have something left over above our own needs to give to those who are in need (Eph. 4:28).

TEST QUESTIONS OVER 21:11-20

1. Who always profits when a scoffer is punished (v. 11)?
2. What is the wise person's response to instruction (v. 12)?
3. According to v. 12 a wise person not only learns from instruction but also from ....
4. Why do the righteous learn from the calamities that come upon the wicked (v. 12)?
5. What double calamity does v. 13 say will come upon the man who is unmerciful to the needy?
6. Comment upon "in the bosom" (v. 14).
7. Is v. 14 justifying bribes or observing why men often resort to them?
8. How do the righteous feel about "justice" (v. 15)?
9. Why do the workers of iniquity not rejoice over "justice" (v. 15)?
10. Cite Bible examples of men who "wandered out" of the way that they knew to be right and suffered the end mentioned in v. 16.
11. Cite the parallels in v. 17.
12. In what two ways can pleasure-lovers be made poor (v. 17)?
13. What did you understand from v. 18?
14. What is the single life of an unmarried person better than (v. 19)?
15. What is the difference between the "wise" and the "foolish" with reference to material things (v. 20)?

TEXT — 21:21-31

21. He that followeth after righteousness and kindness
Findeth life, righteousness, and honor.
22. A wise man scaleth the city of the mighty,
And bringeth down the strength of the confidence thereof.
23. Whoso keepeth his mouth and his tongue
Keepeth his soul from troubles.
24. The proud and haughty man, scoffer is his name;
He worketh in the arrogance of pride.
25. The desire of the sluggard killeth him;
For his hands refuse to labor.
26. There is that coveteth greedily all the day long;
But the righteous giveth and withholdeth not.
27. The sacrifice of the wicked is an abomination;
How much more, when he bringeth it with a wicked mind!
28. A false witness shall perish;
But the man that heareth shall speak so as to endure.
29. A wicked man hardeneth his face;
But as for the upright, he establisheth his ways.
30. There is no wisdom nor understanding
Nor counsel against Jehovah.
31. The horse is prepared against the day of battle;
But the victory is of Jehovah.

STUDY QUESTIONS OVER 21:21-31

1. What was Timothy told to "follow" after (v. 21)?
2. What book tells of a wise man who delivered his city from the enemy (v. 22)?
3. What play is made on the word "keepeth" in v. 23?
4. What five words in v. 24 really belong together?
5. "Killeth" him in what sense (v. 25)?
6. With which action is the righteous identified--being greedy or giving (v. 26)?
7. What is meant in v. 27 by one bringing his sacrifice with a wicked mind?
8. What will cause the false witness to perish (v. 28)?
9. Does v. 29 refer to the momentary look of a wicked man or the permanent hard-looking face that sin develops?

10. What other passages besides v. 31 show that it is God and not horses that make the difference in battle?

PARAPHRASE OF 21:21-31

21. The man who tries to be good, loving and kind finds life, righteousness and honor.
22. The wise man conquers the strong man and levels his defenses.
23. Keep your mouth closed and you'll stay out of trouble.
24. Mockers are proud, haughty and arrogant.
25,26. The lazy man longs for many things but his hands refuse to work. He is greedy to get, while the godly love to give!
27. God loathes the gifts of evil men, especially if they are trying to bribe Him!
28. A false witness must be punished; an honest witness is safe.
29. An evil man is stubborn, but a godly man will reconsider.
30. No one, regardless of how shrewd or well-advised he is, can stand against the Lord.
31. Go ahead and prepare for the conflict, but victory comes from God.

COMMENTS ON 21:21-31

V. 21. "Young's Literal": "Whoso is pursuing righteousness..." This would suggest an earnest following after righteousness and kindness. Prov. 15:9 and I Tim. 6:11 also speak of following righteousness. Matt. 5:6 speaks of hungering and thirsting after righteousness. Matt. 6:33 says we should seek the kingdom of God and righteousness before everything else. Both in the seeking the right thing and in the promise of finding the good things of life, righteousness, and honor, this verse is quite similar to Rom. 2:6,7.

V. 22. This verse shows that wisdom is really might. Eccl. 9:13-16 tells of a single wise man who without great forces or great equipment was able to discomfit a mighty army. That wisdom is greater than might, consider the superior brute force of some of the ferocious animal world that man, who is inferior in physical strength, is able to subdue and handle through his superior wisdom.

V. 23. Prov. 13:3 contains a similar truth. A godly man

will keep his heart (Prov. 4:23), will keep himself in the love of God (Jude 21), will keep himself unspotted from the world (Jas. 1:27), and will keep his tongue (this verse). Would you keep yourself from many troubles? Then keep your mouth and your tongue. Most trouble springs from something that one says!

V. 24. Notice three words that go together: "proud," "haughty," and "arrogance". This verse speaks of his working; but what does he do? He scoffs! He laughs at religion, makes fun of godly people, etc. Peter predicted that such would show up in the last days (II Pet. 3:3,4).

V. 25. Prov. 13:4 also speaks of the "desire of the sluggard", saying that he "hath nothing". This verse explains why: "his hands refuse to labor." On his desire killing him, "Pulpit Commentary" suggests: "The mere wish, combined with no active exertion to secure its accomplishment, is fatal to soul, body, and fortune."

V. 26. This verse reflects two ways to live with reference to material things: (1) how can one get more for himself even at others' expense? and (2) how can one help others who are in need? The first majors on selfishness, the second on service. Psa. 37:26 and Psa. 112:9 blesses the giver.

V. 27. The first statement is also found in Prov. 15:8. God does not want people to substitute religious rites for actual righteousness: "To obey is better than sacrifice" (I Sam. 15:22). Thus, God deplores the sacrifice of people who are not trying to live right (Jer. 6:20; Amos 5:22; Isa. 1:11-15). To bring a sacrifice with a "wicked mind" must be to bring it with some motive to deceive God or to "buy God off" because of some sin being persisted in or because of some illegitimate gain from which he is bringing the sacrifice.

V. 28. Very similar to Prov. 19:5 and Prov. 19:9, both of which say, "A false witness shall not be unpunished." "So as to endure" in the second statement stands over against "shall perish" in the first, meaning that the true witness (one who speaks what he knows through his own seeing and hearing) will not be executed for perverting justice through lying such as will befall the false witness.

V. 29. Another contrast between the wicked and the upright in which the wicked hardens his face instead of repenting and having his ways established like the upright. "Septuagint": "An ungodly man shamelessly withstands with his face." This continued wickedness will bring destruction. After showing the prosperity of the righteous, Psa. 1:4-6 says, "The wicked are not so, But are like the chaff which the wind driveth away. Therefore the wicked shall not stand in the judgment, Nor sinners in the congregation of the righteous. For Jehovah knoweth the way of the righteous; But the way of the wicked shall perish."

V. 30. God may allow many things that are wrong to happen (until judgment), but when there is a known showdown between God and the forces of unrighteousness, His opposition always comes out on the short end. Aaron's rod that miraculously became a snake ate up those of Pharaoh's magicians (Exo. 7:10-12). When they tried to duplicate the plagues brought upon the land by Moses, they finally had to give up and acknowledge the supremacy of God (Exo. 8:19). Baal lost out to Jehovah on Mt. Carmel (I Kings 18:26-39). The people of Samaria could see the difference between Simon the sorcerer's fake miracles and Philip's genuine ones (Acts 8:6-13). Herod of Acts 12 began laying hands on the apostles, killing James and intending to do the same to Peter (vs. 1-3). But before the chapter was over, Herod was dead (vs. 21-23), and the very next verse shows God's triumph: "But the word of God grew and multiplied" (v. 24). As II Cor. 13:8 says, we cannot really do anything against the truth.

V. 31. Horses were used in Bible days for war and not for agricultural purposes. This verse shows that even if horses were used (representing human military might), Israel's victory really came from Jehovah and not the human arrangements. See the following passages that bear on the subject: Psa. 20:7; 33:17; Isa. 31:1; Psa. 3:8.

TEST QUESTIONS OVER 21:21-31

1. How does the Bible represent a good person's quest for righteousness (v. 21)?
2. Give proof that wisdom is superior to brute force (v. 22).
3. What all is a godly person to "keep" (v. 23)?
4. What three words in v. 24 go together?
5. Why will the sluggard have nothing (v. 25)?
6. What two attitudes toward material things are found in v. 26?
7. What kind of people does God not want sacrificing (v. 27)?
8. What will not happen to the man who hardens his face (v. 29)?

9. Tell of instances in which God was purposely opposed to the defeat of His opposition (v. 30).
10. What does the Bible say about relying upon "horses" (v. 31)?

NOTICEABLE GROUPINGS IN CHAPTER 21

"*Righteousness*"--

"To do righteousness and justice is more acceptable to Jehovah than sacrifice" (v. 3).
"The righteous man considereth the house of the wicked, How the wicked are overthrown to their ruin" (v. 12).
"It is joy to the righteous to do justice" (v. 15).
"The wicked is a ransom for the righteous; And the treacherous cometh in the stead of the upright" (v. 18).
"He that followeth after righteousness and kindness Findeth life, righteousness, and honor" (v. 21).
"The righteous giveth and withholdeth not" (v. 26).
"The upright, he establisheth his ways" (v. 29).

"*Jehovah*"--

"The king's heart is in the hand of Jehovah as the watercourses: he turneth it whithersoever he will" (v. 1).
"Every way of a man is right in his own eyes; But Jehovah weigheth the hearts" (v. 2).
"To do righteousness and justice Is more acceptable to Jehovah than sactifice" (v. 3).
"There is no wisdom nor understanding Nor counsel against Jehovah" (v. 30).
"The horse is prepared against the day of battle; But victory is of Jehovah" (v. 31).

"*Heart*"--

"The king's heart is in the hand of Jehovah as the watercourses: He turneth it whithersoever he will" (v. 1).
"Jehovah weigheth the hearts" (v. 2).
"A proud heart...is sin" (v. 4).
"The sacrifice of the wicked is an abomination; How much more, when he bringeth it with a wicked mind!" (v. 27).

"*Tongue*"--

"The getting of treasures by a lying tongue Is a vapor driven to and fro by them that seek death" (v. 6).
"Whoso keepeth his mouth and his tongue Keepeth his soul

from troubles" (v. 23).

"A false witness shall perish; But the man that heareth shall speak so as to endure" (v. 28).

"*Wicked*"--

"The lamp of the wicked, is sin" (v. 4).

"The violence of the wicked shall sweep them away" (v. 7).

"The soul of the wicked desireth evil: His neighbor findeth no favor in his eyes" (v. 10).

"The wicked are overthrown to their ruin" (v. 12).

"To do justice...is a destruction to the workers of iniquity" (v. 15).

"The wicked is a ransom for the righteous" (v. 18).

"The sacrifice of the wicked is an abomination" (v. 27).

"A wicked man hardeneth his face" (v. 29).

"*Sacrifice*"--

"To do righteousness and justice Is more acceptable to Jehovah than sacrifice" (v. 3).

"The sacrifice of the wicked is an abomination; How much more, when he bringeth with a wicked mind!" (v. 27).

"*Pride*"--

"A high look, and a proud heart...is sin" (v. 4).

"The proud and haughty man, scoffer is his name; He worketh in the arrogance of pride" (v. 24).

"*Wisdom*"--

"When the scoffer is punished, the simple is made wise; And when the wise is instructed, he receiveth knowledge" (v. 11).

"There is precious treasure and oil in the dwelling of the wise" (v. 20).

"A wise man scaleth the city of the mighty, And bringeth down the strength of the confidence thereof" (v. 22).

"*Death, destruction*"--

"The getting of treasures by a lying tongue Is a vapor driven to and fro by them that seek death" (v. 6).

"The violence of the wicked shall sweep them away" (v. 7).

"The wicked are overthrown to their ruin" (v. 12).

"Destruction to the workers of iniquity" (v. 15).

"The man that wandereth out of the way of understanding Shall rest in the assembly of the dead" (v. 16).

"A false witness shall perish" (v. 28).

"*Rich*"--

"The thoughts of the diligent tend only to plenteousness" (v. 5).

"The getting of treasures by a lying tongue Is a vapor driven to and fro by them that seek death" (v. 6).

"There is precious treasure and oil in the dwelling of the wise" (v. 20).

"*Poor*"--

"Every one that is hasty hasteth only to want" (v. 5).

"Whoso stoppeth his ears at the cry of the poor, He also shall cry, but shall not be heard" (v. 13).

"He that loveth pleasure shall be a poor man: He that loveth wine and oil shall not be rich" (v. 17).

"SLOW TO ANGER" IS GREAT VIRTUE

Listen to the number of times that Proverbs praises the man "slow to anger": "He that is SLOW TO WRATH is of great understanding: but he that is hasty of spirit exalteth folly" (14:29); "A wrathful man stirreth up strife: but he that is SLOW TO ANGER appeaseth strife" (15:18). "The discretion of a man DEFERRETH his anger" (19:11). "He that is SLOW TO ANGER is better than the mighty; and he that ruleth his spirit than he that taketh a city" (16:32).

Who can read these verses and think a quick temper is something that God will tolerate? He praises and commends the man who is slow to anger, but He condemns the individual whose temper is like the firecracker—just waiting to blow up when someone ignites the fuse.

There are so many who need this teaching from Proverbs. If you are one of them, let the Spirit convict your heart of the terribleness of this sin and its consequences. Make it a real burden of your heart that you may be able to overcome it. Confer with another about your decision, and pray together for a complete victory over it.

TEXT — 22:1-10

1. A good name is rather to be chosen than great riches,
 And loving favor rather than silver and gold.
2. The rich and poor meet together:
 Jehovah is the maker of them all.
3. A prudent man seeth the evil, and hideth himself;
 But the simple pass on, and suffer for it.
4. The reward of humility and the fear of Jeohavh
 Is riches, and honor, and life.
5. Thorns and stars are in the way of the perverse:
 He that keepeth his soul shall be far from them.
6. Train up a child in the way he should go,
 And even when he is old he will not depart from it.
7. The rich ruleth over the poor;
 And the borrower is servant to the lender.
8. He that soweth iniquity shall reap calamity;
 And the rod of his wrath shall fail.
9. He that hath a bountiful eye shall be blessed;
 For he giveth of his bread to the poor.
10. Cast out the scoffer, and contention will go out;
 Yea, strife and ignominy will cease.

STUDY QUESTIONS OVER 22:1-10

1. Restate v. 1 in your own words.
2. What is the purpose of the statement in v. 2?
3. What does "evil" mean in v. 3?
4. What Bible characters were rewarded in keeping with v. 4:
5. What do "thorns" and "snares" stand for in v. 5?
6. What does another proverb say about a child left to help himself to grow up his own way instead of training him (v. 6)?
7. If a child does not turn out right, should we question God's promise in v. 26 or the parent's rearing?
8. Is v. 7 stating the way it is or the way it should be?
9. What is the game no one can win (v. 8)?
10. Why does v. 9 speak of one's "eye" being bountiful?
11. In Solomon's day, cast him out of what (v. 10)?

PARAPHRASE OF 22:1-10

1. If you must choose, take a good name rather than great riches; for to be held in loving esteem is better than

silver and gold.

2. The rich and the poor are alike before the Lord who made them all.
3. A prudent man forsees the difficulties ahead and prepares for them; the simpleton goes blindly on and suffers the consequences.
4. True humility and respect for the Lord lead a man to riches, honor and long life.
5. The rebel walks a thorny, treacherous road; the man who values his soul will stay away.
6. Teach a child to choose the right path, and when he is older he will remain upon it.
7. Just as the rich rules the poor, so the borrower is servant to the lender.
8. The unjust tyrant will reap disaster and his reign of terror shall end.
9. Happy is the generous man, the one who feeds the poor.
10. Throw out the mocker, and you will be rid of tension, fighting and quarrels.

COMMENTS ON 22:1-10

V. 1. Eccl. 7:1 is similar, saying a good name is better than "precious oil." Those who get rich through dishonest means choose riches rather than a good reputation. If it comes down to a choice, always choose a good name ("loving favor") to great riches ("Silver and gold"). Great possessions with no friends can be so cold and empty! There are many suicides among the rich too. An average living with many friends and the favor of God proves to be the happiest, most satisfying way to live.

V. 2. Prov. 29:13 speaks similarly concerning the two classes. Does God make them rich and poor, or is He the maker of them regardless of whether they are rich or poor? Probably the latter. In society they both help each other. "Pulpit Commentary" aptly remarks: "The labor of the poor makes the wealth of the rich; the wealth of the rich enables him to employ and aid the poor...The rich should not despise the poor (Prov. 14:31; 17:5) Job 31:15); the poor should not envy the rich (Prov. 3:31).

V. 3. This very saying is repeated in Prov. 27:12. An old saying: "Fools rush in where angels fear to tread." A discerning person can often forsee danger ahead, and his wisdom causes him to avoid it; but the simple, undiscerning person comes along, never realizing what is just ahead, and suffers the consequences. In the original, "prudent man" is singular while "the simple" is plural. "Hitzig" observes as a result: "Many simple ones are found for one prudent." And when something new (some fad) comes along that had dangerous involvements connected with it, many take up with it anyway, and you wonder if "Hitzig" isn't correct in his observation! A Cornish proverb: "He who will not be ruled by the rudder must be ruled by the rock."

V. 4. "humility" and the "fear of Jehovah" are here equated, for those who truly fear Jehovah are humble, submissive, and obedient to Him. The reward of such is threefold: riches, honor and long life. Here is the way that one can have both possessions and good reputation with life thrown in as a bonus. Abraham is a good example of all three. God "rewards" those who thus fear Him and do His will from humble hearts.

V. 5. What a contrast with v. 4! While the righteous reap riches, honor and life (v. 4), "Thorns" and "snares" await the perverse. Prov. 15:19 combines both groups: "The way of the sluggard is as a hedge of thorns; But the path of the upright is made a highway." The wicked are "perverse (perverted from what God has intended them to be). The godly are those who keep their souls; they shall avoid the thorns and snares that come upon the ungodly. Another reason (a sensible one) for being godly rather than ungodly.

V. 6. A commandment with a promise. The commandment: train up a child in the way he should go; the promise: even when he is old he will not depart from it. Such training requires many things: knowledge, wisdom, time, patience, determination and love. There are many failures in child-rearing because of lacking one or several of the above requirements. Child-training is something that is easy to neglect or try shortcuts with, but what a shame when the future of one's entire posterity is at stake! What is really more important? Eph. 6:4 commands this type of training. Timothy had been taught the Scriptures from a child (II Tim. 3:15); as a result the great faith that had dwelt in his mother and grandmother was in him also (II Tim. 1:5). No wonder that as a young man he was well reported of by his home congregation

(Lystra) and by other Christians in the area (Acts 16:1, 2). Other passages on child rearing: Prov. 1:8; 13:1; 19:18; 22:15; 23:13, 14; 29:15, 17.

V. 7. This is the way it is in life: the rich who have made financial successes are the ones who rule in governmental circles; they have power, influence and reputation that necessarily puts them at the helm. It is likely in this verse that the second statement is explanatory of the first; that is, the borrower (the poor) is servant to the lender (the rich). The borrower is limited in the amount he can borrow by the wishes of the lender; he must pay the interest-rate asked by the lender, or there will be no borrowing; he must pay it back in the time-limit set by the lender; and if he doesn't pay it back, the lender will do all he can to collect the equivalent (or more) from the borrower.

V. 8. It is a divine principle (law) that whatever a person sows in life, that he will reap in consequences (Gal. 6:7). If one sows good seeds, he will reap good (Gal. 6:8; Prov. 11:18); if he sows bad seeds, he will reap trouble (Gal. 6:8; Job 4:8; Hos. 10:13). The acts of sin may be pleasurable (Heb. 11;25), but the consequences are not (Prov. 5:8-13). Oftentimes one finds that the rod of wrath he planned for another falls upon himself instead.

V. 9. One with a "bountiful eye" is one who sees needs, who sees what he can do to alleviate the persons involved, and who generously gives of what he has. God's promise to such a liberal giver: he "shall be blessed." Similar promises: Prov. 11:25; Luke 6:38; 14:12-14; Prov. 19:17; II Cor. 9:6.

V. 10. Sometimes a circle of people is better off with one less person if that person be a scoffer, for one such person can keep a whole group in a continual state of contention, strife and ignominy (reproach). How terrible to be that warped a person!

TEST QUESTIONS OVER 22:1-10

1. One should choose a good ...... over riches (v. 1)?
2. What are we to learn from v. 2?
3. What point was made that in the Hebrew "prudent man" is singular while "simple" is plural (v. 3)?
4. What is the three-fold reward of humbly fearing God (v. 4)?
5. What two things are promised in v. 5 to the perverse?

6. What is the command in v. 6? What is the promise?
7. How do the rich rule over the poor (v. 7)?
8. Comment upon the harvest of sin (v. 8).
9. Enlarge upon the person with a "bountiful eye" (v. 9).
10. When is a group of people better off with one less person in it (v. 10)?

TEXT — 22:11-21

11. He that loveth pureness of heart,
For the grace of his lips the king will be his friend.
12. The eyes of Jehovah preserve him that hath knowledge;
But he overthroweth the words of the treacherous man.
13. The sluggard saith, There is a lion without;
I shall be slain in the streets.
14. The mouth of strange women is a deep pit;
He that is abhorred of Jehovah shall fall therein.
15. Foolishness is bound up in the heart of a child;
But the rod of correction shall drive it far from him.
16. He that oppresseth the poor to increase his gain,
And he that giveth to the rich, shall only come to want.
17. Incline thine ear, and hear the words of the wise,
And apply thy heart unto my knowledge.
18. For it is a pleasant thing if thou keep them within thee,
If they be established together upon thy lips.
19. That thy trust may be in Jehovah,
Ihave made them known to thee this day, even to thee.
20. Have not I written unto thee excellent things
Of counsels and knowledge,
21. To make thee know the certainity of the words of truth,
That thou mayest carry back words of truth to them that send thee?

STUDY QUESTIONS OVER 22:11-21

1. What New Testament verse talks of pureness of heart also (v. 11)?
2. What blasphemous Assyrian king did God overthrow (v. 12)?
3. Do you really think there was a lion in the street (v. 13)?
4. What does God think of one who is guilty of adultery (v. 14)?
5. What are some examples of childhood foolishness (v.

15)?

6. What two classes will end up in need (v. 16)?
7. What does it mean to "incline" one's ear (v. 17)?
8. What is the antecedent of "it" in v. 18?
9. True knowledge should lead one to trust in whom (v. 19)?
10. What kind of teachings had the Proverb writer set forth (v. 20)?
11. Who had "sent" this person (v. 21)?

PARAPHRASE OF 22:11-21

11. He who values grace and truth is the king's friend.
12. The Lord preserves the upright but ruins the plans of the wicked.
13. The lazy man is full of excuses. "I can't go to work!" he says. "If I go outside I might meet a lion in the street and be killed!"
14. A prostitute is a dangerous trap; those cursed of God are caught in it.
15. A youngster's heart is filled with rebellion, but punishment will drive it out of him.
16. He who gains by oppressing the poor or by bribing the rich shall end in poverty.

17-21. Listen to this wise advice; follow it closely, for it will do you good, and you can pass it on to others: Trust in the Lord. In the past, haven't I been right? Then believe what I am telling you now, and share it with others.

COMMENTS ON 22:11-21

V. 11. What a beautiful, wonderful person is portrayed by the words "loveth pureness of heart" and "the grace of his lips", meaning a person with purity abiding in his heart and who has the ability to express himself in a courteous way. Kings may not always have been virtuous people, but they admired such. Even the wicked King Herod had a high regard for John the Baptist: "Herodias set herself against him, and desired to kill him; and she could not; for Herod feared John, knowing that he was a righteous and holy man, and kept him safe. And when he heard him, he was much perplexed; and he heard him gladly" (Mark 6:19, 20). Matt 5:8 also exalts purity of heart.

V. 12. The "eyes of Jehovah" here stand for his

knowledge of the affairs upon earth and of His providential workings resulting from what He sees. He preserves those who have knowledge, who use their God-created faculties to acquire enlightment that He gives. It pleased Him that Solomon placed such a high value upon wisdom and knowledge (I Kings 3:9, 10; 4:29-34). God lamented in Hosea's day, "My people are destroyed for lack of knowledge: because thou has rejected knowledge, I will also reject thee" (Hos. 4:6). When God overthrew Sennacherib (II Kings 19:35), it was an instance of His overthrowing the words of the treacherous (II Kings 18:28-35).

V. 13. The same sluggard excuse for not going to work is in Prov. 26:13. Since wisdom would include one's physical safety, it is doubtful if there was a lion in the streets. All lazy people are full of excuses for not working, for they do not want to work. Just as where there's a will to do something, there is usually a way to do it, so where there is no will to work, there is usually a handy excuse for not doing it.

V. 14. Many times in Proverbs does the father warn the son about the wicked, immoral woman (Prov. 2:16; 5:3-23; 6:24-35; 7:5-27; 23:27, 28). Notice in the passages just cited how she uses her mouth (words and kisses) to break the young man down. Her mouth is said to be a "deep pit" into which men "fall," and usually they do not get out! That God hates this sin in a terrible way, notice the strong language: "He that is abhorred of Jehovah shall fall therein." Eccl. 7:26 says, "I find more bitter than death the woman whose heart is snares and nets and whose hands are bands: whoso pleaseth God shall escape from her; but the sinner shall be taken by her."

V. 15. A child's actions often reflect lack of good judgment and his immaturity: "When I was a child, I spake as a child, I felt as a child, I thought as a child: now that I am become a man, I have put away childish things" (I Cor. 13:11). Oh, the foolish, unwise, careless, thoughtless things that children will do! What will drive it far from him? Proper, severe punishment. Other passages teaching such punishment: Prov. 13:24; 19:18; 23:13, 14; 29:15. Many parents do not do as God commands, and that foolishness remains engrained in the natures and ways of their rebellious children.

V. 16. Proverbs shows that laziness and lack of industry can bring one to want (Prov. 6:9-11), but this verse shows that oppressing the poor to get gain and trying to bribe the rich for one's own advantage can do the same. The man described in this verse is a man to beware of.

V. 17. The "sayings" (a new saying each verse) is noticeably interrupted here for a five verse section urging the son to listen to the good instruction that he is receiving. God has given us ears with which to listen to what others say to us; they should be used when the wise are speaking. He has given us hearts or minds that can apply what we hear to our lives. The double commandment of this verse, then, is "incline thine ear" and "apply thy heart."

V. 18. To live as v. 17 says brings a "pleasant" way to live. What we hear and apply we keep within us as knowledge, and they become proverbs or sayings upon our own lips.

V. 19. True knowledge should cause us to trust in God, who is the "First" (the cause) and the "Last" (the judge). Remember, "The fear of Jehovah is the beginning of knowledge" (Prov. 1:7). That his son might come to trust in Jehovah was the purpose of the father's careful instruction.

V. 20. The father here refers to the quality of his instructions. Compare Prov. 4:1, 2; 8:6-8.

V. 21. As a young man grows up, he is going to be subjected to many ideas of people, some being diametrically opposed to others. It is easy for a youth in the state of immaturity to be "tossed to and fro" by such (Eph. 4:14). This is why it is so necessary that the truth that the father teaches be taught in such a way that his son is well grounded in that truth, for only as he knows the truth will he be able to detect the counterfeit. On the latter statement of the verse, if a son has been brought up to know truth, to respect it, and to tell it, when being sent by others on a responsible mission, he will be able to know what truth is, to evaluate the situation, and to bring back a true report.

TEST QUESTIONS OVER 22:11-21

1. What king in Bible days respected a pure man with good teaching (v. 11)?
2. What does "eyes of Jehovah" stand for in v. 12?
3. Why does a sluggard offer excuses (v. 13)?
4. What word in the second statement of v. 14 goes with "deep pit" in the first statement?
5. How does the strange woman use her "mouth" to the destruction of men (v. 14)?

6. Cite some instances of childhood foolishness (v. 15).
7. What will drive foolishness from a child (v. 15)?
8. According to v. 16 what are two ways to become poor?
9. "Incline thine ......" and "apply thy ...... (v. 17). (v. 17).
10. What does it mean for wisdom to be established upon thy "lips" (v. 18)?
11. True knowledge should lead one to ...... in Jehovah (v. 19).
12. How good should one's counsel be (v. 20)?
13. Parental teachings should be so clear that youth would not be...... to and fro (v. 21).

TEXT — 22:22-29

22. Rob not the poor, because he is poor;
Neither oppress the afflicted in the gate:
23. For Jehovah will plead their cause,
And despoil of life those that despoil them.
24. Make no friendship with a man that is given to anger;
And with a wrathful man thou shalt not go:
25. Lest thou learn his ways,
And get a snare to thy soul.
26. Be thou not one of them that strike hands,
Or of them that are sureties for debts.
27. If thou has not wherewith to pay,
Why should he take away thy bed from under thee?
28. Remove not the ancient landmark,
Which thy fathers have set.
29. Seest thou a man diligent in his business? he shall stand before kings;
He shall stand before mean men.

STUDY QUESTIONS OVER 22:22-29

1. Why would people rob the "poor" (v. 22)?
2. What other passages besides v. 23 show God's particular care for the unfortunate?
3. Why should one become a close friend to the unfortunate (v. 23)?
4. What are other verses besides v. 25 that indicate the power of evil influence?
5. What is meant in v. 26 by "strike hands"?

6. How could one lose his "bed" (v. 27)?
7. What is meant by "landmark" (v. 28)?
8. What Bible character came to stand before the king because of diligence (v. 29)?
9. Why is meant by "mean" in v. 29?

PARAPHRASE OF 22:22-29

22,23 Don't rob the poor and sick! For the Lord is their defender. If you injure them He will punish You.

24,25. Keep away from angry, short-tempered men, lest you learn to be like them and endanger your soul.

26,27. Unless you have the extra cash on hand, don't countersign a note. Why risk everything you own? They'll even take your bed!

28. Do not move the ancient boundary marks. That is stealing.

29. Do you know a hard working man? He shall be successful and stand before kings!

COMMENTS ON 22:22-29

V. 22. Both Old and New Testaments teach us to regard the unfortunate (Exo. 23:6; Jas. 1:27). Yet they are often oppressed (Zech. 7:10; Mal. 3:5;. "In the gate" was where legal matters were settled (their "courthouse"). Sometimes the poor have not gotten their proper treatment in courts because of the other side had the money to bribe those in charge.

V. 23. In the absence of human defense God has promised to take up in their behalf and take away from those who took away from them. Other passages on the same subject: Psa. 12:5; 35:10; 68:5; 140:12; Prov. 23:10,11. God saw that King Ahab was despoiled for the vineyard he took away from Naboth (I Kings 21:1-14).

V. 24. Of all the people in the world with which to make companions, what a poor companion an angry, wrathful man is! But some people are that way (quick-tempered, no judgment, etc.), and some make friends with them.

V. 25. Like all companions, the close ties leave their influence (I Cor. 15:33). Thus, one who had been blessed with a good spirit and a calm, cool disposition begins "flying off the handle" and going into a senseless rage when everything doesn't go just right. Why? Because he has been around just such a man.

V. 26. Being "co-signer" for another's debts is warned against several times in Proverbs (6:1,2; 11:15; 17:18; 20:16).

V. 27. How do you know at the time of obligating yourself whether you will be able at the time of need to put up the necessary money? You may have to get along without things that are necessary to your own life (like a "bed").

V. 28. Prov. 23:10 also contains this prohibition. The original law behind this saying is in Deut. 19:14: "Thou shalt not remove thy neighbor's landmark, which they of old time have set, in thine inheritance which thou shall inherit, in the land that Jehovah thy God giveth thee to possess it." It was one of the twelve special curses to be pronounced from Mt. Ebal: "Cursed be he that removeth his neighbor's landmark. And all the people shall say, "Amen" (Deut. 27:17). This would be like removing steel stakes or buried rocks of surveyings today. It was even worse then because the official description of a property line is recorded at the courthouse today while in Bible days the landmark was all there was.

V. 29. A person diligent in business is one who is ambitious, industrious, and aggressive. They are men of application, and they will be numbered among the great and the known. Their lifetimes will be spent in major, not minor, concerns. Jospeh tended to every business assigned to him (Gen. 39:1-6,21-23), and he stood before the Pharaoh (gen. 41:39-44). David was diligent in caring for his father's sheep. In this he deveoped both skill and bravery in protecting them against ferocious animals, and this (together with his great faith in God) had much to do with his fighting and killing Goliath (I Sam. 17:32-37). This led to his relationship with King Saul and the army (I Sam. 18:2,5). Daniel was diligent in business (Dan. 6:4,5), and he was an important man in the administration of the following kings: Nebuchadnezzar, Belshazzar, and Darius. The word "mean" in our verse means "insignificant." Paul used the same word in referring to his native city Tarsus (Acts 21:39).

TEST QUESTIONS OVER 22:22-29

1. What law has God issued concerning the unfortunate (v. 22)?
2. What does "in the gate" mean in v. 22?
3. What has God said concerning those who oppress the

unfortunate (v. 23)?
4. What will happen to a person who makes an angry man his buddy (vs. 24,25)?
5. What does Proverbs warn about being surety for another's debts (v. 26)?
6. Why was it even more serious then to remove the ancient landmarks than to remove surveyor items now (v. 28)?
7. What does "mean" mean in v. 29?
8. Cite Bible characters who were "diligent in business" and who stood before kings as a result (v. 29).

NOTICEABLE GROUPINGS IN CHAPTER 22

"*Rich*"--

"A good name is rather to be chosen than great riches, And loving favor rather than silver and gold" (v. 1).

"The reward of humility and the fear of Jehovah Is riches, and honor, and life" (v. 4).

"*Poor*"--

"The rich and the poor meet together: Jehovah is the maker of them all" (v. 2).

"The rich ruleth over the poor" (v. 7).

"He that hath a bountiful eye shall be blessed; For he giveth of his bread to the poor" (v. 9).

"He that oppresseth the poor to increase his gain...shall come only to want" (v. 16).

"Rob not the poor because he is poor" (v. 22).

"*Jehovah*"--

"Jehovah is the maker of them all" (v. 2).

"The reward of...the fear of Jehovah Is riches, and honor, and life" (v. 4).

"The eyes of Jehovah preserve him that hath knowledge; But he overthroweth the words of the treacherous man" (v. 12).

"The mouth of strange women is a deep pit; He that is abhorred of Jehovah shall fall therein" (v. 14).

"That thy trust may be in Jehovah, I have made them known to thee this day" (v. 19).

"Jehovah will plead their cause, And despoil of life those that despoil them" (v. 23).

CHAPTER 22

"*Kings*"--

"He that loveth pureness of heart, For the grace of his lips the king will be his friend" (v. 11).

"Seest thou a man diligent in his business? he shall stand before kings" (v. 29).

"*Wisdom*"--

"A prudent man seeth the evil, and hideth himself" (v. 3).

"Incline thine ear, and hear the words of the wise, And apply thy heart unto my knowledge" (v. 17).

"*Fools*"--

"The simple pass on, and suffer for it" (v. 3).

"Foolishness is bound up in the heart of a child; But the rod of correction shall drive it far from him" (v. 15).

"*Punishment*"--

"Thorns and snares are in the way of the perverse" (v. 5).

"He that soweth iniquity shall reap calamity" (v. 8).

"Jehovah...overthroweth the words of the treacherous man" (v. 12).

"He that oppresseth the poor to increase his gain, And he that giveth to the rich, shall come only to want" (v. 16).

"Jehovah will plead their cause, and Despoil of life those that despoil them" (v. 23).

"*Reward*"--

"The reward of humility and the fear of Jehovah Is riches, and honor, and life" (v. 4).

"He that hath a bountiful eye shall be blessed" (v. 9).

"He that loveth pureness of heart, For the grace of his lips the king will be his friend" (v. 11).

"The eyes of Jehovah preserve him that hath knowledge" (v. 12).

"Seest thou a man diligent in business? He shall stand before kings" (v. 29).

"*Children*"--

"Train up a child in the way he should go, And even when he is old he will not depart from it" (v. 6).

"Foolishness is bound up in the heart of a child; But the rod of correction shall drive it far from him" (v. 15).

MARRIAGE IS A GOOD STATE

There is too much levity concerning this subject of marriage. Of course, we cannot avoid some of the humorous things that happen and that are told, but the tone of things needs to be much more serious than it usually is when certain passages from the Bible on this subject are read or quoted. Here is a great passage that has experienced entirely too much humor: "Whoso findeth a wife findeth a good thing, and obtaineth favour of the Lord" (18:22). Listenting to levity-loving preaching read this to the emphasis that a wife is merely a "thing" leaves much to be desired when the author has no such thought in mind. The word "thing" is even in italics, which forbids any such meaning or emphasis. A wife is no more a "thing" than a husband is. If the woman is a "thing," a man is a bigger "thing", for she came from man. What that verse is saying is that the person who finds a wife is finding something good or is getting into a good state of life. The latter part of that passage shows that God is pleased when people marry, provided of course they do not marry contrary to His will.

As people have married, so does their marriage usually go. If they have run off to get married, it usually isn't too long until one of them is running away from the other. If they have taken the Lord into their home, they have found His blessing abiding upon their home.

Yes, marriage is good. Ask the person who is properly married. He or she would not think of becoming unmarried at all. Even those who break away from a mate are soon found trying to make another home. Marriage is not the only state in which to live, but is a mighty good one.

TEXT — 23:1-12

1. When thou sittest to eat with a ruler
Consider diligently him that is before thee;
2. And put a knife to thy throat,
If thou be a man given to appetite.
3. Be not desirous of his dainties;
Seeing they are deceitful food.
4. Weary not thyself to be rich;
Cease from thine own wisdom.
5. Wilt thou set thine eyes upon that which is not?
For riches certainly make themselves wings,
Like an eagle that flieth toward heaven.
6. Eat thou not the bread of him that hath an evil eye,
Neither desire thou his dainties:
7. For as he thinketh within himself, so is he:
Eat and drink, saith he to thee;
But his heart is not with thee.
8. The morsel which thou hast eaten shalt thou vomit up,
And lose thy sweet words.
9. Speak not in the hearing of a fool;
For he will despise the wisdom of thy words.
10. Remove not the ancient landmark;
And enter not into the fields of the fatherless;
11. For their Redeemer is strong;
He will plead their cause against thee.
12. Apply thy heart unto instruction,
And thine ears to the words of knowledge.

STUDY QUESTIONS OVER 23:1-12

1. Why "consider" the ruler (v. 1)?
2. What does "put a knife to thy throat" mean (v. 2)?
3. What makes a ruler's food "deceitful meat" (v. 3)?
4. Is getting rich really a wearisome road (v. 4)?
5. What is meant in v. 5 by "that which is not"?
6. What is meant in v. 6 by an "evil eye"?
7. Restate the first clause in v. 7 in your own words.
8. Can a person act nice to you when he really doesn't feel that way (v. 7)?
9. What might be an illustration of v. 8?
10. What statement of Jesus in Matt. 7 does v. 9 seem to parallel?

11. Is there a connection the two clauses in v. 10?
12. Who is the "Redeemer" of the fatherless (v. 11)?
13. What is the difference between learning by instruction and learning by experience (v. 12)?

PARAPHRASE OF 23:1-12

1-3. When dining with a rich man, be on your guard and don't stuff yourself, though it all tastes so good; for he is trying to bribe you, and no good is going to come of his invitation.

4-5. Don't worry yourself trying to get rich. Why waste your time? For riches can disappear as though they had the wings of a bird!

6-8. Don't become obligated to evil men; don't long for their favors and gifts. Their kindness is a trick; they want to use you as their pawn. The delicious food they serve will turn sour in your stomach and you will vomit it, and have to take back your words of appreciation for their "kindness".

9. Don't waste your breath on a rebel. He will despise the wisest advice.

10,11. Don't steal the land of defenseless orphans by moving their ancient boundary marks, for their Redeemer is strong; He Himself will accuse you.

12. Don't refuse to accept criticism; get all the help you can.

COMMENTS ON 23:1-12

V. 1. The usual one-verse "saying" of Proverbs gives way here to an eight-verse set of instructions. To be invited to dine with a ruler "would be a great honor to a man of lowly birth, or to one of the middle class, to whom the manners of courts and palaces were practically unknown" ("Pulpit Commentary"). Since the invitation was extended not out of kingly politeness but with an ulterior motive (vs. 7,8), our verses suggest that the guest should consider (look into) the one who invited him rather than just the delicious food before him.

V. 2. In the presence of such a bountiful, delicious banquet, a man of appetite would be tempted to eat much more than he should. When away from home, one should act as if he had been away from home before. The ruler's ulterior motives in inviting him might be better fulfilled if the man ate and drank beyond wisdom, for in that condition the host may be able to extract information from the guest that he would not otherwise be able to obtain (if this be his motive).

V. 3. A further warning. Dan. 1:8 also refers to the king's food as "dainties." It is "deceitful" food in that it has been insincerely set before the man, and for him to eat to excess will somehow fulfill the ruler's purpose rather than the best interests of the man eating.

V. 4. By thus associating with a ruler, the guest may have thought that this was his first step toward the life of the rich. Or, having eaten of such pleasant food, the guest may have determined that he too will someday be rich. Here he is warned of the many weary years and hardships accompanying getting and being rich. So he is told to cease from his "own wisdom" which in the long run will not prove to be truly wise at all. Other warnings against aspiring to be rich: Matt. 6:19,20; John 6:27; I Tim. 6:7-10. Other warnings against following one's own wisdom: Prov. 3:5; Rom. 12:16.

V. 5. Riches are here spoken of as "that which is not". They are "uncertain" (I Tim. 6:17). They may be "here" today but "gone" tomorrow (through economic crashes, bad investments, etc.). Kings often had to empty their treasure houses to satisfy invading kings (I Kings 18:15,16). Consider also Eccl. 5:11,15,16.

V. 6. An "evil eye" here had to do with a covetous eye. Compare Deut. 15:9 for a similar use of it. Since this is a repetition of the warning in v. 3, the ruler's ulterior motive was his own personal gain to result from the man's being his guest.

V. 7. He would be invited to eat and drink, but it was not out of sheer hospitality. This is the deceitfulness mentioned in v. 3. This saying is warning us against this type of person. Rom. 12:9 ("Let love be without hypocrisy") warns us not to be this type of person ourselves. Our verse also shows it isn't what we say or do but the heart that determines the real person.

V. 8. The dainties were sweet and tasted good, but later he would be able to see through it all, and then he would vomit them up, so to speak. In other words, it was sweeter going down than coming up. Wisdom always says to look to the end of a matter, to the outcome, before one participates, invests, etc.

V. 9. Some people show they are fools by despising words of wisdom. We are obligated to share our understanding with those who do not understand, but when we find one who will not listen, will not learn, will not appreciate, but will only laugh at and make fun of that which we say, it is time to turn away and go to someone who will listen (Acts 13:46; 18:5,6). Jesus said, "Give not that which is holy unto the dogs, neither cast your pearls before the swine" (Matt. 7:6). "Pulpit Commentary": "It is a mere casting of pearls before swine to speak to such a man of high aims, righteous motives, self-sacrifice."

V. 10. A "landmark" was usually a stone or a pillar of stones placed to mark out the boundary of one's land. This verse contains a prohibition against altering those. Deut. 19:14; 27:17; and Prov. 22:28 contain similar prohibitions. By moving (or removing) the landmark one could be claiming and using land that rightfully belonged to one's neighbor. This verse contains a special warning if the land taken belonged to the "fatherless".

V. 11. God will look out for the right of the orphaned, and He will not be easy on one who has taken land away from such. Prov. 22:23 says, "Jehovah will plead their cause, And despoil of life those that despoil thee."

V. 12. It is not merely hearing instruction but applying one's heart to what is being said that really adds learning and knowledg to one. The Bible does not favor a person going his way and finding out everything for himself; it emphasizes instruction and urges each one to learn all he can from the instruction of others.

TEST QUESTIONS OVER 23:1-12

1. Why should one not eat too much when dining with a ruler (vs. 1-3)?
2. Where else in the Bible is king's food referred to as "dainties" (v. 3)?
3. Tell of the weariness of the rich (v. 4).
4. Cite another warning from the Bible about aspiring to be rich (v. 4).
5. Why are riches spoken of as "that which is not" (v. 5)?
6. V. 6 parallels what previous verse in this chapter?
7. How does v. 7 explain an expression in v. 3?
8. What was the end of those sweet morsels (v. 8)?
9. What statement of Jesus teaches the same thing as v. 9?
10. What did a landmark often consist of (v. 10)?
11. Whom will one encounter who would take financial advantage of the orphaned (v. 11)?

12. What two things are to be applied in getting knowledge (v. 12)?

TEXT — 23:13-23

13. Withhold not correction from the child;
For if thou beat him with the rod, he will not die.
14. Thou shalt beat him with the rod,
And shalt deliver his soul from Sheol.
15. My son, if thy heart be wise,
My hear will be glad, even mine.
16. Yea, my heart will rejoice
When thy lips speak right things.
17. Let not thy heart envy sinners;
But be thou in the fear of Jehovah all the day long:
18. For surely there is a reward;
And thy hope shall not be cut off.
19. Hear thou, my son, and be wise,
And guide thy heart in the way.
20. Be not among winebibbers,
Among gluttonous eaters of flesh:
21. For the drunkard and the glutton shall come to poverty;
And drowsiness will clothe a man with rags.
22. Hearken unto thy father that begat thee,
And despise not thy mother when she is old.
25. Buy the truth, and sell it not;
Yea, wisdom, and instruction, and understanding.

STUDY QUESTIONS OVER 23:13-23

1. Does v. 13 sound like most people whip their children too hard or too easy?
2. What is meant by "Sheol" in v. 14?
3. How does Prov. 10:1 word the same truth as found in v. 15?
4. Is the opposite of v. 16 just as true (that parents' hearts weep when their children speak perverse things)?
5. Do the wicked want us to envy them (v. 17)?
6. Will a godly person in time have more than a sinner has now (v. 18)?
7. How many times in this chapter does it say, "My son" (v. 19)?
8. Why is this said so many times (v. 19)?

9. What is the wrong of winebibbing and gluttony (vs. 20,20)?
10. What is the relation of "drowsiness" to such habits (v. 21)?
11. What two crimes can one commit against parents (v. 22)?
12. What do "buy" and "sell" mean in v. 23?

PARAPHRASE OF 23:13-23

13,14. Don't fail to correct your children; discipline won't hurt them! They won't die if you use a stick on them! Punishment will keep them out of hell.

15,16. My son, how I will rejoice if you become a man of common sense. Yes, my heart will thrill to your thoughtful, wise words.

17,18. Don't envy evil men but continue to reverence the Lord all the time, for surely you have a wonderful future ahead of you. There is hope for you yet!

19,21. O my son, be wise and stay in God's paths; don't carouse with drunkards and gluttons, for they are on their way to poverty. And remember that too much sleep clothes a man with rags.

22. Listen to your father's advice and don't despise an old mother's experience.

23. Get the facts at any price, and hold on tightly to all the good sense you can.

COMMENTS ON 23:13-23

V. 13. Every child needs correction at times. He or she will not be correct in life without correction. At times this correction will have to be administered with the rod (whippings), and the language of our verse indicates that sometimes such must be administered with great severity.

V. 14. "Sheol" of the Old Testament was parallel with "Hades" of the New. When one dies, his spirit goes to "Sheol" ("Hades"). Instead of causing a child to die through physical chastisements (v. 13), such punishments will actually keep a child from a premature death through God's wrath or through a child's own foolishness or other ways.

V. 15. Other passages showing that good children bring joy to parents: Prov. 10:1; 23:24,25; 29:3. There is a play on words here: "If THY HEART be wise, MY HEART will be glad." Oh, how parents wait for and look for evidences of their children's good qualities! Surely if children thought of this, how happy they could actually make their parents!. And how we can make our heavenly Father pleased by our wisely doing His will!

V. 16. The wise "heart" of v. 15 will reflect itself in "lips" that speak right things. How much good judgment is reflected by wise words, excellent speech, etc.!

V. 17. To envy sinners is not to be fearing Jehovah properly. Other passages that warn against envying sinners: Psa. 37:1; Prov. 3:31; 24:1,19. Yet people at times do envy sinners (Psa. 73:3-7). But if one truly fears Jehovah, he will have no temptation to envy His enemies (sinners) upon whom God's wrath will ultimately fall.

V. 18. Yes, a godly person's reward is coming, and how great it will be! Such's hope will be fulfilled and not cut off: I Pet. 1:3-5; Psa. 37:37. "Pulpit Commentary": "The writer has a firm belief in the moral government of God and in a future life which shall rectify all anomalies." If the poor man of Luke 16 were tempted to envy the rich man, it would have been a mistake because he himself ended up so much better off (Luke 16:25).

V. 19. Again the father appeals for the son to be "wise". Remember, it is a "wise" son that makes a glad father (Prov. 10:1). Prov. 4:23 speaks of the necessity one keeping his heart with all diligence. We note here that one is not to let his heart wander wheresoever society, trends, fads, or friends may lead it, but one is responsible to "guide" his heart in the way it should go. Failure to do this has been a great weakness of mankind.

V. 20. The Bible sounds many warnings against taking up with wine and drunkenness: Isa. 5:22; Matt. 24:48-51; Luke 21:34; Rom. 13:13; Eph. 5:18. But gluttony is also noted here as wrong. Jesus' enemies tried to down Him by calling him a gluttonous man (Matt. 11:19). In affluent times many are guilty of both winebibbing and gluttony.

V. 21. It costs money to eat like a glutton and drink like a drunkard. Many a man has devoured and destroyed a small fortune in this way. He is also brought to poverty by not showing up for work or by not being able to hold his job. The "drowsiness" has to do with his sleeping off his drunkenness. What a perversion of life!

V. 22. We are to listen to the wisdom and instruction of our fathers (Prov. 1:8; Eph. 6:1). How many sorrows and mistakes young men can avoid by hearkening to their fathers!

Prodigals and know-it-alls don't listen; in time they will see that they should have listened. Concerning despising one's mother when she is old, "Pulpit Commentary" says, "When old age with its consequent infirmities comes upon thy mother, despise her not, but rather thank God for giving her long life, and profit by her love and long experience."

V. 23. "Truth," spoken of in this verse as "wisdom, and instruction, and understanding," is something to obtain at all costs and something not to part with regardless of what earthly or momentary gains one may get by doing so. "Pulpit Commentary": "Consider truth as a thing of the highest value, and spare no pains, cost, or sacrifice to obtain it, and, when gotten, keep it safe; do not barter it for earthly profit or the pleasures of sense; do not be reasoned out of it, or laughed out of it...do not part with it for any consideration."

TEST QUESTIONS OVER 23:13-23

1. What great message to parents is carried in v. 13?
2. How many proper whippings keep a child from "Sheol" (v. 14)?
3. What play on words is found in v. 15?
4. What is the relationship between vs. 15 and 16?
5. Why should a godly person not envy a sinner (v. 17)?
6. What is the relationship between vs. 17 and 18?
7. What is wrong with letting one's mind wander wheresoever it will go (v. 19)?
8. What two sins of the body are forbidden in v. 20?
9. Why is a drunkard and glutton brought to poverty (v. 21)?
10. How can a young man avoid both sorrows and mistakes (v. 22)?
11. Why would a person despise a mother when she is old (v. 22)?
12. How do we "buy truth"? How do we "sell" it (v. 23)?

TEXT — 23:24-35

24. The father of the righteous will greatly rejoice;
And he that begetteth a wise child will have joy of him.
25. Let thy father and thy mother be glad,

And let her that bare thee rejoice.
26. My son, give me thy heart;
And let thine eyes delight in my ways.
27. For a harlot is a deep ditch;
And a foreign woman is a narrow pit.
28. Yea, she lieth in wait as a robber,
And increaseth the treacherous among men.
29. Who hath woe? who hath sorrow? who hath contentions?
Who hath complaining? who hath wounds without cause?
Who hath redness of eyes?
30. They that tarry long at the wine;
They that go to seek out mixed wine.
31. Look not thou upon the wine when it is red,
When it sparkleth in the cup,
When it goeth down smoothly:
32. At the last it biteth like a serpent,
And stingeth like an adder.
33. Thine eyes shall behold strange things,
And thy heart shall utter perverse things.
34. Yea, thou shalt be as he that lieth down in the midst of the sea,
Or as he that lieth upon the top of the mast.
35. They have stricken me, shalt thou say, and I was not hurt;
They have beaten me, and I felt it not:
When shall I awake? I will seek it yet again.

STUDY QUESTIONS OVER 23:24-35

1. Did God feel this way concerning Jesus (v. 24)?
2. Is one's parents' happiness another motivation for doing right (v. 25)?
3. How would a son "give" his heart to his father (v. 26)?
4. Is v. 27 what the father was getting at in his previous statements?
5. What does the harlot "rob" from a person (v. 27)?
6. Show how that each of the six things in v. 29 befall a drinker?
7. Comment on tarrying "long" (v. 30).
8. Is there any significance to "red" here (v. 31)?
9. Can sinners stay the outcome of sin (v. 32)?
10. Comment upon imaginative things seen by the drunkard (v. 33).

11. What is meant by v. 34?
12. What is the pathetic truth of v. 35's last statement?

PARAPHRASE OF 23:24-35

24,25. The father of a godly man has cause for joy--what pleasure a wise son is! So give your parents joy!

26-28. O my son, trust my advice--stay away from prostitutes. For a prostitute is a deep and narrow grave. Like a robber, she waits for her victims as one after another become unfaithful to their wives.

29,30. Whose heart is filled with anguish and sorrow? Who is always fighting and quarreling? Who is the man with bloodshot eyes and many wounds? It is the one who spends long hours in the taverns, trying out new mixtures.

31. Don't let the sparkle and the smooth taste of strong wine deceive you.

32. For in the end it bites like a poisonous serpent; it stings like an adder.

33. You will see hallucinations and have delirium tremens, and you will say foolish, silly things that would embarrass you no end when sober.

34. You will stagger like a sailor tossed at sea, slinging to a swaying mast.

35. And afterwards you will say, "I didn't even know it when they beat me up...Let's go and have another drink!"

COMMENTS ON 23:24-35

V. 24. Again the subject of parental joy comes up (see v. 15; Prov. 10:1; 15:20). Jesus brought joy to His Father (Matt. 3:17; 17:5), and so have good children down through the centuries. Notice how that righteousness and wisdom bring joy and rejoicing just as unrighteousness and foolishness bring sorrow.

V. 25. V. 24 spoke of the joy of the father of a good child; this verse speaks of the joy of both the father and the mother. Much of a mother's time and life is wrapped up in her children, and she is ever ready to rejoice over every success and attainment of her children.

V. 26. Since v. 27 begins with the explanatory word "for", this verse is introducing what that and later verses develop; namely, a solemn warning against the wicked, harlot woman (a subject to which earlier sections devoted much material: 5:1-23; 6:20-35; 7:1-27). Notice, too, that the passages in chapters 5, 6, 7 are always introduced with a similar getting of the son's attention before beginning the actual material. This was to impress the son with what the father was saying.

V. 27. She is given a double description, both of which resemble: a "deep ditch" and a "narrow pit". She represents a danger to avoid. Prov. 22:14 similarly says, "The mouth of a strange woman is a deep pit; He that is abhorred of Jehovah shall fall therein." Since there is nothing to gain by falling into a deep ditch and a narrow pit, Prov. 6:32 rightfully says, "He that committeth adultery with a woman is void of understanding." Look at the dangers brought on by one's disregarding this warning: Prov. 5:11; 6:32-34; 7:22,23,26,27.

V. 28. She is out working her trade (Prov. 7:12). Like a robber she does not lose an opportunity (Prov. 7:13-21). One such person "increaseth" the sinners upon earth, here called "the treacherous among men". Men who thus become unfaithful to wives might well be described as "treacherous"! Malachi shows that men who turn from the wives of their youth deal "treacherously" with them (Mal. 2:10,14-16.

V. 29. Six questions are raised that are answered in the next verse. From the consequences of drinking, the ancients suffered the same woes and sorrows as do moderns who imbibe. The drinker has "woe" in the physical problems brought on, in his social relations, in his finances, in his slavery to his habit, and in the punishment that awaits him (I Cor. 6:9,10; Gal. 5:19-21). The drinker has "sorrow" upon "sorrow" as does his family as a result of his drinking as do others whom he injures while intoxicated. The drinker knows "contentions", for many fights take place at taverns. The drinker knows "complaining", for he often complains of the way people treat him. The drinker has "wounds without cause", for if he stayed sober, he would not get into the trouble he does. The drinker has "redness of eyes", an outward commentary on the abuse that his body is inwardly suffering. Isa. 5:11,22 also uses "woe" in warning against strong drink: "Woe unto them that rise up early in the morning, that they may follow strong drink; that tarry late into the night, till wine inflame them!...Woe unto them that are mighty to drink wine, and men of strength to mingle strong drink." So does Hab. 2:15: "Woe unto him that giveth his neighbor drink."

V. 30. The six questions raised in v. 29 are quickly and bluntly answered here: those who drink intoxicants. Time and its meaning seem to mean nothing to a drunkard, for he will spend hours drinking with others until they are drunken, and then he will sleep it off and seem not to care that he should be at his job instead of in bed. The expression "seek out" shows that drinkers go forth to get their booze; it is something they must obtain because of the habit they have developed and the appetite they have for booze.

V. 31. On "red", "Pulpit Commentary" says, "The wine of Palestine was chiefly red." Drinkers like the color; they like the sparkle in the glass; they like the taste. On going down smoothly, "Pulpit Commentary:" "The wine pleases the palate, and passes over it without roughness or harshness." This verse is a commandment to keep away from wine, to avoid even the temptation to drink, for to avoid drinking wine the verse says, "Don't even look upon it." The only way to keep out of any bad habit is to stay as far from it as one can while depending upon God to help him.

V. 32. No thinking person would ever start drinking if he considered the end of it. The booze companies don't tell him how it will end. The fellows who offer him his first drink and will laugh at him if he doesn't take it aren't thinking of drink's bitter end. But godly people are known for seeing what something produces, where it leads, and where it ends before they do it. Indeed wine "biteth like a serpent", and it "stingeth like an adder"; yet the habit is far from dying out. "Pulpit Commentary:" "Wine is like the subtle poison of a serpent, which affects the whole body, and produces the most fatal consequences." "Septuagint:" "At the last he stretches himself like one stricken by a serpent, and the venom is diffused through him as by a horned snake."

V. 33. A drunkard cannot trust his eyesight. Ever hear of a drunkard seeing two bridges before him and wondering which to drive over? And, oh, the foolish, the coarse, the vulgar, the wicked things that men say when drunk--things that embarrass polite society, that make youngsters laugh but angels weep!

V. 34. As a drunkard's whole system pitches and tosses and finally results in vomiting. His reeling, staggering, and uncertainty are referred to in Isa. 28:7,8: "These reel with wine, and stagger with strong drink...All tables are full of vomit and filthiness, so that there is no place clean." Imagine trying to sleep on top of a ship's mast! Such is comparable to a drunkard's physical feelings.

V. 35. "Pulpit Commentary": "The drunken man has been beaten...but the blows did not pain him; his condition has rendered him insensible to pain. He has some vauge idea that he has suffered certain rough treatment at the hands of his companions, but it has made no impression on him." He will not be able to remember what happened to him while he was drunk. "When shall I awake?" refers to the prolonged sleep that his drunkenness has brought on. And yet in spite of all the woes and the sorrows and other bitter consequences that such a life has brought to him, you can be sure of this: when he does wake up, he won't have any more sense than to go out and seek it again (Isa. 56:12). What a tragedy!

NOTICEABLE GROUPINGS IN CHAPTER 23

"*My son*"--

"My son, if thy heart be wise, My heart will be glad" (v. 15).

"Hear thou, my son, and be wise" (v. 19).

"My son, give me thy heart; And let thine eyes delight in my ways" (v. 26).

"*Parenthood*"--

"Withhold not correction from the child; For if thou beat him with the rod, he will not die. Thou shalt beat him with the rod, And shalt deliver his soul from Sheol" (vs. 13,14).

"Hearken unto thy father that begat thee, And despise not thy mother when she is old" (v. 22).

"The father of the righteous will greatly rejoice; And he that begetteth a wise child will have joy of him. Let thy father and thy mother be glad, And let her that bare thee rejoice" (vs. 24,25).

"*Wine*"--

"Be not among winebibbers...For the drunkard and the glutton shall come to poverty" (vs. 20,21).

"Who hath woe? who hath sorrow? who hath contentions? Who hath complaining? who hath wounds without cause? Who hath redness of eyes? They that tarry long at the wine; They that go to seek out mixed wine. Look not thou upon the wine when it is red, When it sparkleth in the cup, When it goeth down smoothly: At the last it biteth like a serpent, And stingeth like an adder. Thine eyes shall be hold strange things, And thy heart shall utter perverse things. Yea, thou shalt be as he that lieth down in the midst of the sea, Or as he that lieth upon the top of a mast. They have stricken me, shalt thou say, And I was not hurt; They have beaten me, and I felt it not: When shall I awake? I will seek it again" (vs. 29-35).

"*Eating*"--

"When thou sittest to eat with a ruler, Consider diligently him that is before thee; And put a knife to thy throat, If thou be a man given to appetite. Be not desirous of his dainties; Seeing they are deceitful food" (vs. 1-3).

"Eat thou not the bread of him that hath an evil eye, Neither desire thou his dainties: For as he thinketh within himself, so is he: Eat and drink, saith he to thee; But his heart is not with thee. The morsel which thou hast eaten shalt thou vomit up, And lose thy sweet words" (vs. 6-8).

"*Deceit*"--

"Be not desirous of his dainties; Seeing they are deceitful food" (v. 3).

"Eat and drink, saith he to thee; But his heart is not with thee" (v. 7).

"*Learning*"--

"Apply thy heart unto instruction, And thine ears to the words of knowledge" (v. 12).

"Buy the truth, and sell it not; Yea, wisdom, and instruction, and understanding" (v. 23).

CHAPTER 24

TEXT — 24:1-12

1. Be not thou envious against evil men;
Neither desire to be with them:
2. For their heart studieth oppression,
And their lips talk of mischief.
3. Through wisdom is a house builded;
And by understanding it is established;
4. And by knowledge are the chambers filled
With all precious and pleasant riches.
5. A wise man is strong;
Yes, a man of knowledge increaseth might.
6. For by wise guidance thou shalt make thy war;
And in the multitude of counsellors there is safety.
7. Wisdom is too high for a fool:
He openeth not his mouth in the gate.
8. He that deviseth to do evil,
Men shall call him a mischief-maker.
9. The thought of foolishness is sin;
And the scoffer is an abomination to men.
10. If thou faint in the day of adversity,
Thy strength is small.
11. Deliver them that are carried away unto death,
And those that are ready to be slain see that thou hold back.
12. If thou sayest, Behold, we knew not this;
Doth not he that weigheth the hearts consider it?
And he that keepeth thy soul, doth not he know it?
And shall not he render to every man according to his work?

STUDY QUESTIONS OVER 24:1-12

1. Paraphrase the two statements in v. 1.
2. What kind of "evil men" is v. 2 talking about?
3. What is meant by "house" here (v. 3)?
4. Comment upon the two adjectives in v. 4.
5. According to v. 5 wisdom is ....
6. What kind of counselors did ancient kings rely upon (v. 6)?
7. Where did a "fool" not belong (v. 7)?
8. V. 8 might remind one of people "calling a spade a ....".

9. What is meant by the "thought of foolishness" in v. 9?
10. What percentage of people "faint" when adversity comes (v. 10)?
11. What is meant by "see that thou hold back" in v. 11?
12. What is the implication of the statement in v. 12 that "we knew not this"?

PARAPHRASE OF 24:1-12

1,2. Don't envy godless men; don't even enjoy their company. For they spend their days plotting violence and cheating.

3,4. Any enterprise is built by wise planning, becomes strong through common sense, and profits wonderfully by keeping abreast of the facts.

5. A wise man is mightier than a strong man. Wisdom is mightier than strength.

6. Don't go to war without wise guidance; there is safety in many counselors.

7. Wisdom is too much for a rebel. He'll not be chosen as a counselor!

8. To plan evil is as wrong as doing it.

9. The rebel's schemes are sinful, and the mocker is the scourge of all mankind.

10. You are a poor specimen if you can't stand the pressure of adversity.

11,12. Rescue those who are unjustly sentenced to death; don't stand back and let them die. Don't try to disclaim responsibility by saying you didn't know about it. For God, who knows all hearts, knows yours, and He knows you knew! And he will reward everyone according to his deeds.

COMMENTS ON 24:1-12

V. 1. Two prohibitions: don't desire to be like evil men and don't desire to run with them. If one doesn't envy them, he won't run with them, and if one doesn't run with them, he will not become like them. Other passages about not envying such: V. 19; Psa. 37:1; 73:3; Prov. 3:31; 23:17. Another passage about not desiring to be with evil people: Prov. 1:15.

V. 2. In Proverbs the expression "evil woman" usually is

referring to an adulterous woman and a "evil man" to oppressors (as in this verse). These evil men have their "heart" involved in their sin, and they "study" how to be successful in their wickedness. II Tim. 2:15 shows that the righteous should study to show themselves approved unto God.

V. 3. After two verses on the destructive way of the wicked, it is refreshing to come to two verses on building a house through wisdom, honesty, and diligence (vs. 3,4). Notice that "wisdom" is with the builder, not the destroyer. Oppressors who take the sword will perish by the sword (Matt. 26:52), not living out half of their days (Psa. 55:23). While these will be "cut off", the righteous will live on in the earth (Psa. 37:9).

V. 4. There is really a close relationship between "wisdom", "understanding," and "knowledge". Verse 5 says the first two build and establish the house while this verse says the last mentioned fills its chambers with riches. It is obvious that these verses are dealing with the house of the wealthy. Notice the two adjectives describing riches: "precious" and "pleasant". This is godly wealth, gained in the proper way and not by oppression. This makes such wealth "precious" to the possessor and "pleasant" also.

V. 5. The thought of wisdom is continued in this verse, this time stating that its possession makes one a strong man. Grammatically the verse is Hebrew parallelism in which the second statement is a restatement of the first. Other passages on the "might" of wisdom: Prov. 21:22; Eccl. 9:16. The section in which the last mentioned verse is found tells, "There was a little city, and few men within it; and there came a great king against it, and besieged it, and built great bulwarks against it. Now there was found in it a poor wise man, and he by his wisdom delivered the city" (Eccl. 9:14,15).

V. 6. The strength referred to in v. 5 was evidently military strength as this verse shows. The first statement of this verse is found in Prov. 20:18, and its last statement is found in Prov. 11:14. Prov. 15:22 is similar to the last statement. Kings kept courts of wise men to counsel them in time of war. David (and later Absalom) had Ahithophel (II Sam. 16:23), and Ahab had his prophets (I Kings 22:6).

V. 7. A fool does not have wisdom, or he would not be a fool, for the two are considered opposites (Prov. 11:29; 14:16; 17:24; 29:11). The "gate" was the place of official and legal business where wise men presided (Prov. 31:23). Because he does not have wisdom, the fool will not be one of the elders of his city.

V. 8 The evil and wickedness that are in the world stem from the devil, but he works through human beings to bring them about; thus, there are those who devise evil. Such a one shall soon be known, and his persistence in such behavior will give him a reputation. Others may be slow in recognizing worth in an individual or in praising him, but they will not fail to notice his evil and in telling others about it. He will not fool them: "Men shall call him a mischiefmaker."

V. 9. We know that the act of foolishness is sin (IISam. 24:10); here wc are told that even the thought (whether expressed in act or not) is likewise sin. By "thoughts" adultery is committed in the heart (Matt. 5:27,28). By "Thoughts" one who hates is guilty of murder before God (I John 3:15). A "scoffer" is one who not only rejects that which he should believe but who laughs at, makes fun at, that which he should believe and at those who do believe. He is also called a "mocker", which he is: "In the last days mockers shall come...saying, Where is the promise of his coming?" (II Pet. 3:3). Such will not only lose out with God, but they have already lost out with them ("The scoffer is an abomination to men").

V. 10. Adversity (Opposition, trials, reverses) test one's strength (faith, courage, emotional composure). Some can stand more adversity than others. We should all strive to be "strong in the Lord, and in the strength of his might" (Eph. 6:10). No man should be content to remain weak, yet there are those who "faint" (lose heart, fall apart, give up) when hardships come. Such lack depth: "He hath not root in himself...when tribulation or persecution ariseth because of the word, straightway he stumbleth" (Matt. 13:21). Here is where determination and depth of character are important. One cannot be an overcomer without them. The world is divided into two classes: the "overcomers" and the "overcome".

V. 11. These are people who need delivering and who are evidently worthy. Those addressed also have the power to deliver them. Ability with opportunity represent responsibility to do so. "Hold back" those who would otherwise be slain. Sometimes people fail to save others for fear of getting themselves into troubles. But Christians will do their duty even if it involves laying down their lives (Gal. 6:2; Heb. 13:3; I John 3:16). Other passages to consult: Psa. 82:4; Isa. 58:6,7.

V. 12. People sometimes try to cover the reality of their

failures (to deliver people as in v. 11) by excusing themselves as if ignorant of the need. But this lie but adds another sin to the great sin of irresponsibility already committed. God knows the truth; He knows (weighs) the heart (Prov. 21:2). And He will someday punish a person for his neglect of duty. Other passages: Job 34:11; Psa. 62:12; Jer. 32:19; Rom. 2:6; Rev. 2:23; 22:12.

TEST QUESTIONS OVER 24:1-12

1. What two prohibitions are contained in v. 1?
2. The expression "evil men" usually refers to what kind of men in Proverbs (v. 1)?
3. What three words in vs. 3,4 are closely related to each other?
4. What two things do vs. 3,4 say will be accomplished by the informed person?
5. What quality is extolled in v. 5?
6. According to v. 6 where in is safety?
7. What about a fool and the "gate" (v. 7)?
8. What name is given to the one devising evil (v. 8)?
9. Show how "thoughts" and "sin" go together (v. 9).
10. What does the Bible say about us if we faint amid trials (v. 10)?
11. What class of people are we to help (v. 11)?
12. Suppose that helping others would endanger ourselves (v. 11).
13. Instead of saying, "I have sinned," what do more people say about their failures (v. 12)?

TEXT — 24:13-22

13. My son, eat thou honey, for it is good;
And the droppings of the honeycomb, which are sweet to thy taste:
14. So shalt thou know wisdom to be unto thy soul;
If thou hast found it, then shall there be a reward,
And thy hope shall not be cut off.
15. Lay not wait, O wicked man, against the habitation of the righteous;
Destroy not his resting-place.
16. For a righteous man falleth seven times, and riseth up again;
But the wicked are overthrown by calamity.

17. Rejoice not when thine enemy falleth,
And let not thy heart be glad when he is overthrown;
18. Lest Jehovah see it, and it displease him,
And he turn away his wrath from him.
19. Fret not thyself because of evildoers;
Neither be thou envious at the wicked:
20. For there shall be no reward to the evil man;
The lamp of the wicked shall be put out.
21. My son, fear thou Jehovah and the king;
And company not with them that are given to change:
22. For their calamity shall rise suddenly;
And the destruction from them both, who knoweth it?

STUDY QUESTIONS OVER 24:13-22

1. Why give this instruction (v. 13)?
2. Is v. 14 connected with v. 13?
3. Is the righteous aware at the first of such lying in wait for him (v. 15)?
4. Does "down" necessarily mean "out" for the righteous man (v. 16)?
5. How was David a good example of v. 17?
6. What all does God see (v. 18)?
7. What previous verse in this chapter is similar to v. 19?
8. What are the prospects for the evil man (v. 20)?
9. What two sovereigns are mentioned in v. 21?
10. What kind of "change" does v. 21 have in mind?
11. What is the meaning of the second clause in v. 22?

PARAPHRASE OF 24:13-22

13,14. My son, honey whets the appetite, and so does wisdom! When you enjoy becoming wise, there is hope for you! A bright future lies ahead!

15,1 O evil man, leave the upright man alone, and quit trying to cheat him out of his rights. Don't you know that this good man, though you trip him up seven times, will each time rise again? But one calamity is enough to lay you low.

17,18. Do not rejoice when your enemy meets trouble. Let there be no gladness when he falls--for the Lord may be displeased with you and stop punishing him!

19,20. Don't envy the wicked. Don't covet his riches. For the

evil man has no future; his light will be snuffed out.
21,22. My son, watch your step before the Lord and the king, and don't associate with radicals. For you will go down with them to sudden disaster, and who knows where it all will end?

COMMENTS ON 24:13-22

V. 13. The people of that day depended upon honey for their sweetening, and a good sweetener it was! Its properties are still highly acclaimed by health-people. Palestine was a land with an abundance of natural honey (Exo. 3:8).

V. 14. The father would urge his son to seek, find, and know wisdom with the same eagerness with which he enjoyed the sweetness of honey. The sweetness of the wisdom found in the Word of God is compared with the sweetness of honey: Psa. 19:10; 119:103. The ending of this verse is much like Prov. 23:18. It shows the great reward and the hopeful life that wisdom brings to its possessor.

V. 15. The wicked are described as lying in wait for the righteous, seeking his ruination (Psa. 37:32). Whoever does this qualifies for the title "wicked man" used here. Every persecutor of the righteous would be included in what is said here.

V. 16. The righteous will have many trials, but he will prevail through the special help of God. Notice these interesting verses: "Many are the afflictions of the righteous; But Jehovah delivereth him out of them all" (Psa. 34:19); "Though he fall, he shall not be utterly cast down; For Jehovah upholdeth him with his hand" (Psa. 37:24); "Rejoice not against me, O mine enemy: when I fall, I shall arise; when I sit in darkness, Jehovah will be a light unto me" (Mic. 7:8); "He will deliver thee in six troubles; Yea, in seven there shall no evil touch thee" (Job. 5:19). In other words, as our expressions go, "you can't keep a good man down;" he may be "down", but he isn't "out". But notice that when the wicked fall, he is not promised to come back, for he has no personal God to whom to look for restoration.

V. 17. The natural man has a tendency to rejoice over his enemy's troubles (Psa. 35:15). Oba. 12 told Edom not to rejoice over Israel's fall. David prayed that his enemies would not be given the chance to rejoice over his calamities (Psa. 35:19). Job said he had not erred in this field (Job. 31:29). And David was a good example of one who did not rejoice over his enemies' misfortunes: see him as he weeps over the death of Saul (II Sam. 1:11) and over the death of the revolting Absalom (II Sam. 18:33).

V. 18. God sees everything that takes place on the earth. He saw Adam and Eve's sin in the beginning, and He has seen every sin since. Rejoicing over an enemy's troubles or fall is displeasing to God to the point that in some way He will deal mercifully with him in the future as a result.

V. 19. Here we go again with the same instruction that must be more needful that we would realize (see v. 1 and Psa. 37:1 and Prov. 23:17). Psa. 73:3 shows the tendency toward doing this: "I was envious at the arrogant, When I saw the prosperity of the wicked."

V. 20. Really there is nothing about the prosperous wicked to envy when we consider their end (no reward and his lamp put out). Both Bildad ("Yea, the light of the wicked shall be put out, And the spark of his fire shall not shine. The light shall be dark in his tent, And his lamp above him shall be put out" Job 18:5,6) and Job ("How oft is it that the lamp of the wicked is put out?" Job 21:17) realized that God would deal with the wicked. Other passages on the light of the wicked going out: Prov. 13:9; 20:20. The Psalmist in 73:3-16 quit envying the wicked when he went into the sanctuary and considered their "latter end" (v. 17;.

V. 21. Man is to respect both God's government and that government that is over him: "Render therefore unto Caesar the things that are Caesar's and unto God the things that are God's" (Matt. 22:21). I Pet. 2:17 also says, "Fear God. Honor the king." We are to fear God because He possesses primary authority, and we are to fear the king because He possesses delegated authority from God: "Let every soul be in subjection to the higher powers...the powers that be are ordained of God. Therefore he that resisteth the power, withstandeth the ordinance of God" (Rom. 13:1,2). Those "given to change" are anarchists, revolutionists, who instead of being in subjection to the established power are found guilty of resisting it to the extent of trying to overthrow it.

V. 22. Whoever resists God, and whoever resists the government will ultimately be brought face to face with those whom they are resisting. And, oh, the severity of the ruin that will come as punishments from God and from civil authority! Who can describe it when it cannot be fully known?

TEST QUESTIONS OVER 24:13-22

1. Comment upon honey as food, both then and now (v. 13).
2. How pleasant, how desirable, was wisdom to be to the son (vs. 13,14)?
3. What is a persecutor of the righteous called in v. 15?
4. Comment upon the righteous prevailing over trials (v. 16).
5. What natural tendency toward an enemy is one not to give in to (v. 17)?
6. What might happen if one rejoices over his enemy's calamity (v. 18)?
7. V. 19 warns against envying what class?
8. Why is it foolish to envy the wicked (v. 20)?
9. We are to fear God because he possesses ...... authority and the king because he has ...... authority (v. 21).
10. What is the end of those who revolt against properly constituted authority (v. 22)?

TEXT — 24:23-34

23. These also are sayings of the wise.
To have respect of persons in judgment is not good.
24. He that saith unto the wicked, Thou art righteous,
Peoples shall curse him, nations shall abhor him;
25. But to them that rebuke him shall be delight,
And a good blessing shall come upon them.
26. He kisseth the lips
Who giveth a right answer.
27. Prepare thy work without,
And make it ready for thee in the field;
And afterwards build thy house.
28. Be not a witness against thy neighbor without cause;
And deceive not with thy lips.
29. Say not, I will do so to him as he hath done to me;
I will render to the man according to his work.
30. I went by the field of the sluggard,
And by the vineyard of the man void of understanding;
31. And, lo, it was all grown over with thorns,
The face thereof was covered with nettles,
And the stone wall thereof was broken down.
32. Then I beheld, and considered well;
I saw, and received instruction:

33. Yet a little sleep, a little slumber,
    A little folding of the hands to sleep;
34. So shall thy poverty come as a robber,
    And thy want as an armed man.

STUDY QUESTIONS OVER 24:23-34

1. Does the opening statement of v. 23 indicate some kind of change of authorship or material?
2. What did the law of Moses say concerning respect of persons (v. 23)?
3. Have people sometimes been more righteous than their leaders (v. 24)?
4. What would be the problem of their rebuking a ruler (v. 25)?
5. Kisses whose lips (v. 26)?
6. Prepare what "work" without (v. 27)?
7. In v. 28 don't deceive whom?
8. Should we do to others as they have done to us (v. 29)?
9. Does v. 30 imply that a sluggard is void of understanding?
10. What two things reflected his laziness (v. 31)?
11. V. 32 shows we can learn by the avenue of ....
12. What does a sluggard enjoy doing (v. 33)?
13. Is it a shame to be poor under these conditions (v. 34)?

PARAPHRASE OF 24:23-34

23-25. It is wrong to sentence the poor, and let the rich go free. He who says to the wicked, "You are innocent," shall be cursed by many people of many nations; but blessings shall be showered on those who rebuke sin fearlessly.

26. It is an honor to receive a frank reply.

27. Develop your business first before building your house.

28,29. Don't testify spitefully against an innocent neighbor. Why lie about him? Don't say, "Now I can pay him back for all his meanness to me!"

30-32. I walked by the field of a certain lazy fellow and saw that it was overgrown with thorns, and covered with weeds; and its walls were broken down. Then, as I looked, I learned this lesson:

33,34. "A little extra sleep, A little more slumber, A little folding of the hands to rest"--means that poverty will break in upon you suddenly like a robber, and violently like a bandit.

COMMENTS ON 24:23-34

V. 23. The opening statement indicates that the following verses form some kind of a section or collection of sayings included by Inspiration. We do not know to whom they belong as we do later groupings in Proverbs (See Prov. 25:1) 30:1; 31:1). The Bible has much to say about conducting court: "Ye shall do no unrighteousness in judgment: thou shalt not respect the person of the poor, not honor the person of the mighty; but in righteousness shalt thou judge thy neighbor" (Lev. 19:15); "Ye shall not respect persons in judgment; ye shall hear the small and the great alike" (Deut. 1:17); "Thou shalt not wrest justice: thou shalt not respect persons; neither shalt thou take a bribe" (Deut. 16:19). See Prov. 18:5; 28:21 also.

V. 24. Vs. 24-26 are also talking of court cases. Through bribes, through respect of persons, through friendships and alliances, etc., justice sometimes gets perverted, and the guilty are freed. This verse says, "Peoples shall curse him, nations shall abhor him." Isa. 5:22,23 says, "Woe unto them...that justify the wicked for a bribe, and take away the righteousness of the righteous from him!" And Prov. 17:15 says, "He that justifieth the wicked, and he that condemneth the righteous, Both of them alike are an abomination to Jehovah."

V. 25. People can usually tell when a judge is "bought off" and when he deals straightforwardly with a guilty case. They want him to rebuke the wicked, for he has it coming, and only by this means can crime be held in check in society. It is evident that the people were glad when the priest Jehoiada put down the wicked usurper Athaliah: "All the people of the land rejoiced, and the city was quiet" (II Chron. 23:21).

V. 26. A judge giving a proper sentence to the wicked is so "in stride" with the thoughts and feelings of the people as one who kisses another.

V. 27. The Scriptures show that there is preparatory work to be done before the actual construction begins: "Which of you, desiring to build a tower, doth not first sit down and count the cost, whether he have wherewith to complete it?" (Luke 14:28); "And the king commanded, and they hewed out great stones, costly stones, to lay the foundation of the house with wrought stone. And Solomon's builders and Hiram's builders and the Gebalites did fashion them, and prepared the timber and the stones to build the house" (I Kings 5:17,18).

V. 28. To do this would make one a "false witness", one who "lies". The 9th Commandment forbad this ("Thou shalt not bear false witness against thy neighbor," Exo. 20:16) as does Eph. 4:25 ("Putting away falsehood, speak ye truth each one with his neighbor"). Oh, how wicked to use one's lips purposely to deceive others, who will believe what is being said and which will result in needless grief, sorrow, and loss to the one being lied about! God did not give man the gift of speech for this purpose.

V. 29. Far too many people when wronged respond with an immediate desire to "get even"; they can think only of retaliation. But the Bible brings out that God, the Judge, will bring any retaliation that is to be brought; consequently, He commands us not to take vengeance ourselves: "Say not thou, I will recompense evil: Wait for Jehovah, and he will save thee" (Prov. 20:22); "Render to no man evil for evil...Avenge not yourselves, beloved, but give place unto the wrath of God: for it is written, Vengeance belongeth unto me; I will recompense, saith the Lord" (Rom. 12:17-19). Instead, Jesus' rule was: "All things therefore whatsoever ye would that men should do unto you, even so do ye also unto them" (Matt. 7:12).

V. 30. There has always been, and there will probably always be, a certain percentage of lazy people. They are also said to be "void of understanding"; in other words, one with good understanding will not be a sluggard. Such a person has a "field" (for wheat or some other crop) or a "vineyard" (of grapes) not because he wants to farm, not to take care of, etc. He may have come into possession of such by inheritance rather than by purchase.

V. 31. The sluggard did not plant a crop: thorns and nettles grew up and took over, and the stone wall around the vineyard to protect the vineyard was broken down here and there and had not been kept in a state of repair. Oh, the way that some people can neglect a place and let it run down! This condition existed because of a man's laziness.

V. 32. Who could keep from noticing the sad condition of both field and wall? The writer says he looked on the situation, pondered over it, and learned from it. Observation is one of wise people's greatest teachers!

V. 33. What did the onlooker learn? That a lazy person

loves to sleep too much.

V. 34. And he learned that such over-sleeping would result in a man's poverty. "Robbers" (armed men) usually had nothing, for they did not work, and what they got from robbing did not last them too long. Prov. 6:10,11 contains the same material as vs. 33,34. It is a shame to be poor because of one's refusal to work.

TEST QUESTIONS OVER 24:23-34

1. What are some other passages on showing respect of persons (v. 23)?
2. Why would anybody pronounce the wicked as righteous (v. 24)?
3. What is the people's attitude toward a judge who lets a wicked man go free (v. 25)?
4. What about his giving a right verdict (v. 26)?
5. Give a Biblical example of v. 27.
6. Cite a Bible statement about telling a lie on another person. (V. 28).
7. What does the Bible say about our taking vengeance on others (v. 29)?
8. Why might a sluggard even have a field or a vineyard (vs. 30,31)?
9. What is evidence that the sluggard had not even bothered to plant a crop (v. 31)?
10. What is evidence that we cannot keep people from noticing our failures (v. 32)?
11. What did the sluggard do instead of work (v. 33)?
12. What other passage contains the same material as vs. 33,34?

NOTICEABLE GROUPINGS IN CHAPTER 24

"*Wisdom*"--

"Through wisdom is a house builded; And by understanding it is established; And by knowledge are the chambers filled With all precious and pleasant riches" (vs. 3,4).

"A wise man is strong; Yea, a man of knowledge increaseth might" (v. 5).

"By wise guidance thou shalt make thy war" (v. 6).

"Wisdom is too high for a fool" (v. 7).

"So shalt thou know wisdom to be unto thy soul" (v. 14).

"*Mischief*"--

"Their lips talk of mischief" (v. 2).

"He that deviseth to do evil, Men shall call him a mischief-maker" (v. 8).

"*Envious*"--

"Be not thou envious against evil men" (v. 1).

"Neither be thou envious at the wicked" (v. 19).

"*Wicked*"--

"Lay not wait, O wicked man, against the habitation of the righteous" (v. 15).

"The wicked are overthrown by calamity" (V. 16).

"Neither be thou envious at the wicked" (v. 19).

"The lamp of the wicked shall be put out" (20).

"He that saith unto the wicked, "Thou art righteous, Peoples shall curse him" (v. 24).

"*Heart*"--

"Their heart studieth oppression" (v. 2).

"Doth not he that weigheth the hearts consider it?" (v. 12).

"Let not thy heart be glad when he is overthrown" (v. 17).

"*Tongue*"--

"He openeth not his mouth in the gate" (v. 7).

"The scoffer is an abomination to men" (v. 9).

"He kisseth the lips Who giveth a right answer" (v. 26).

"Be not a witness against thy neighbor without cause" (v. 28).

"Deceive not with thy lips" (v. 28).

"*Fool*"--

"Wisdom is too high for a fool" (v. 7).

"The thought of foolishness is sin" (v. 9).

"I went by the...vineyard of the man void of understanding" (v. 30).

"*Jehovah*"--

"Lest Jehovah see it, and it displease him" (v. 18).

"Fear thou Jehovah" (v. 21).

"*Abhor*"--

"The scoffer is an abomination to men" (v. 9).

"Nations shall abhor him" (v. 24).

CHAPTER 24

"*Don't*"--

"Be not thou envious against evil men" (v. 1).

"Lay not wait...against the habitation of the righteous" (v. 15).

"Rejoice not when thine enemy falleth" (v. 17).

"Fret not thyself because of evil-doers" (v. 19).

"Company not with them that are given to change" (v. 21).

"Be not a witness against thy neighbor without cause" (v. 28).

"Deceive not with thy lips" (v. 28).

"Say not, I will do so to him as he hath done to me" (v. 29).

"*Commands*"--

"Deliver them that are carried away unto death" (v. 11).

"Eat thou honey, for it is good" (v. 13).

"Fear thou Jẹhovah and the king" (v. 21).

"Prepare thy work without, And make it ready for thee in the field" (v. 27).

LAZY PEOPLE

I recall hearing the story of a man who grew lazier and lazier with the passing of time. His family could get him to do nothing. Things finally got so bad that the two grown sons finally decided to take him out and shoot him. They loaded him in the wagon and put a tarpaulin over him as they started away. As they drove down the road, they met a neighbor who asked what they had under the tarpaulin. They told him. The neighbor said he hated to see them do that and he would help get their father back on his feet. He said, "Here's a bushel of corn that I will give him." From under the cover came the voice of the father, "Is it shelled?" It wasn't. The old man said, "Drive on."

It is hard for us to imagine anyone that lazy, yet the book of Proverbs says substantially the same thing, "A slothful man hideth his hand in his bosom (Revised Version says, "burieth his hand in the dish'), and will not so much as bring it to his mouth again" (19:24).

"Sloth" (from which we get "slothful") and "slug" (from which we get "sluggard") are roots that come to us from Middle

English, both meaning "slow". That slow moving, lifeless animal in the zoo that spends his days hanging from branches upside down we call a "sloth", and that slow moving, snail-like worm we call a "slug" because they are so slow. And the book of Proverbs repeatedly speaks of certain people as "slothful" and as "sluggards" because of their lack of ambition, because they are so extremely and needlessly slow. In fact, Proverbs has much to say upon the subject.

LAZY PEOPLE'S PLACES SHOW IT

Some people are builders and improvers where ever they go. Others merely occupy while everything goes to wrack and ruin. Some build up the soil while they reap greater profits from their land while others farm the ground to death or neglect it altogether.

Solomon tells of stopping to look at the place of a slothful man. He said, "I went by the field of the slothful, and by the vineyard of the man void of understanding; and, lo, it was all grown over with thorns, and nettles had covered the face thereof, and the stone wall thereof was broken down" (24:30,31). It takes work to work a field. It takes work to tend a vineyard. The way thorns and nettles took over was a testimony to every considering passerby that such a field belonged to a lazy man. It took too much work to keep the fence up, so they had fallen apart.

Such indolence and its effect on one's place reminds one that this same Solomon said in another book (Ecclesiastes) that because of slothfulness a building rots and because of idleness a house falls in.

What a shame when people are too lazy to keep their places up, to keep things repaired and fixed, and to have things growing and green.

TEXT — 25:1-10

1. These also are proverbs of Solomon, which the men of Hezekiah king of Judah copied out.
2. It is the glory of God to conceal a thing;
But the glory of kings is to search out a matter.
3. As the heavens for height, and the earth for depth,
So the heart of kings is unsearchable.
4. Take away the dross from the silver,
And there cometh forth a vessel for the refiner:
5. Take away the wicked from before the king,
And his throne shall be established in righteousness.
6. Put not thyself forward in the presence of the king,
And stand not in the place of great men:
7. For better is it that it be said unto thee, Come up hither,
Than that thou shouldest be put lower in the presence of the prince,
Whom thine eyes have seen.
8. Go not forth hastily to strive,
Lest thou know not what to do in the end thereof,
When thy neighbor hath put thee to shame.
9. Debate thy cause with thy neighbor himself,
And disclose not the secret of another;
10. Lest he that heareth it revile thee,
And thine infamy turn not away.

STUDY QUESTIONS OVER 25:1-10

1. Why would Hezekiah take a particular interest in Solomon's proverbs (v. 1)?
2. How long after Solomon did Hezekiah live (v. 1)?
4. Why is it a glory to God to conceal a matter (v. 2)?
5. What kind of things did kings search out (v. 2)?
6. What kind of proverbs is Hezekiah interested in so far (v. 3)?
7. What is "dross" (v. 4)?
8. Is there a connection between v. 5 and v. 4?
9. Why should one not put himself forward in the presence of a king (v. 6)?
10. What teaching of Jesus is v. 7 like?
11. What does Proverbs say about one who is hasty of spirit (v. 8)?

12. What did Jesus say that is similar to v. 9?
13. Who is the "he" of v. 10?
14. What does "Infamy" mean (v. 10)?

PARAPHRASE OF 25:1-10

1. These proverbs of Solomon were discovered and copied by the aides of King Solomon of Judah:

2,3. It is God's privilege to conceal things, and the king's privilege to discover and invent. You cannot understand the height of heaven, the size of the earth or all that goes on in the king's mind!

4,5. When you remove dross from silver, you have sterling ready for the silversmith. When you remove corrupt men from the king's court, his reign will be just and fair.

6,7. Don't demand an audience with the king as though you were some powerful prince. It is better to wait for an invitation rather than to be sent back to the end of the line, publicly disgraced!

8,9,10. Don't be hot-headed and rush to court! You may start something you can't finish and go down before your neighbor in shameful defeat. So discuss the matter with him privately. Don't tell anyone else, lest he accuse you of slander and you can't withdraw what you said.

COMMENTS ON 25:1-10

V. 1. Hezekiah was one of the best kings Judah had (II Kings 18:5,6). I Kings 4:32 says that Solomon spake 3,000 proverbs. Since there are not 3,000 in the book of Proverbs, Hezekiah's scribes (under his direction and by inspiration of God—since their work is included in the Old Testament that the Jews and Jesus accepted) copied the many good sayings found in chapters 25-29. This forms one of several appendixes to this book; other appendixes: 24:23-34; 30:1-33; 31:1-31. Hezekiah lived around 270 years after the death of Solomon. The prophet Isaiah was a contemporary of Hezekiah (II Kings 19:1-2), and he may have headed the project. If so, we can see why the material would be included in the Scriptures.

V. 2. This is the first of several verses concerning "kings", a subject that held unusual fascination for King Hezekiah, especially since Solomon was looked upon as such a great king. A king busies himself searching out a matter, looking into many things, finding out what there is to find out; he is a human being and must if he is going to know, and he can because he has the men and the money of the kingdom at his disposal. But God doesn't have to search things out: He knows all about everything. While He has revealed many things to man in His Word, there is far more than He has reserved to Himself. Deut. 29:29 refers to this revealing and concealing: "The secret things belong unto Jehovah our God; but the things that are revealed belong unto us and to our children for ever."

V. 3. "Pulpit Commentary": "As you can never rise to the illimitable height of the heavens, as you can never penetrate to the immeasurable depth of the earth, so you can never fathom the heart of a king, can never find out what he really thinks." David was one who often surprised people with his pattern of thinking: II Sam. 1:1-16; 12:18-23; 16:5-12; 19:1-6; etc.

V. 4. Raw silver had to be refined to discard its alloy and impurities. When this dross was taken away, it was then ready to be made into a beautiful vessel.

V. 5. The language of this verse shows that it is the application of v. 4's illustration: the wicked men of a king's court are the "dross" that must be removed if that king's throne is to be established, "for the throne is established by righteousness" (Prov. 16:12). Oh, that our rulers today believed this and followed it! Ours would indeed be the ideal society to live in—such as they all seem to envision, talk about, and promise when they are running for office.

V. 6. A king is not one to presume upon. To force oneself upon a king is like a girl throwing herself at some boy. Just as she is out of order and becomes obnoxious to the boy whose favor she seeks, so will one defeat that which he seeks by trying to make himself too noticeable to the king, who will be smart enough to see what he is doing and who will not respect him for it.

V. 7. Once when Jesus was a guest in a Pharisee's house, He noticed how they clamored among themselves for the chief locations at the tables, and He said precisely the same thing: "When thou art bidden of any man to a marriage feast, sit not down in the chief seat; lest haply a more honorable man than thou be bidden of him, and he that bade thee and him shall come and say to thee, Give this man place; and then thou shalt begin with shame to take the lowest place. But when thou art bidden, go and sit down in the lowest place; that when he that hath bidden thee cometh, he may say to thee, Friend, go up higher" (Luke 14:8-10).

V. 8. Our saying, "Think before you speak," is here applied to our actions. The verse appears to be describing a man with more temper than judgment; that is, he triggers a situation that overcomes him instead of the other person as he had planned. Often fiery hearts lack cool heads to know what to do after the wheels of trouble have been set in motion. The time to control strife is before it begins, as Prov. 17:14 observes: "The beginning of strife is as when one letteth out water: Therefore leave off contention before there is quarrelling."

V. 9. Wisdom would dictate that if there is a serious matter to be taken up with a neighbor, you should discuss it with him alone instead of talking about it to everybody else. Two people can often settle a difference between them, but if you involve several people and he does too, the probability of getting the matter settled becomes more and more remote. Jesus taught the same thing: "If thy brother sin against thee, go, show him his fault between thee and him alone: if he hear thee, thou hast gained thy brother" (Matt. 18:15).

V. 10. If you talk over with others things that should remain secret between you and your neighbor, you will no longer be trusted by people; you have destroyed their confidence in you, and they will tell what you have done. And confidence destroyed is hard to be regained. "Thine infamy turn not away." One of the best sets of instructions in the Bible is in Jas. 1:19: "Let every man be swift to hear, slow to speak, slow to wrath."

TEST QUESTIONS OVER 25:1-10

1. What prophet was closely associated with King Hezekiah and may have headed the project of copying more of Solomon's proverbs for this book (v. 1)?
2. Altogether how many proverbs did Solomon speak (v. 1)?
3. Comment upon v. 2.
4. What king was used in the comments to illustrate v. 3?
5. Before one makes a silver vessel, what must he first do with the raw material (v. 4)?
6. What does v. 6 show the "dross" mentioned in v. 5 to represent?
7. What is wrong with forcing one's presence upon a king (v. 6)?

8. What is liable to happen if one exalts himself in the presence of a king (v. 6)?
9. What often happens to people who rush into strife (v. 8)?
10. If one has a just grievance with a neighbor, what important instruction is found in v. 9?
11. What will happen to you if you are known for revealing information that should be kept secret (vs. 9,10).

TEXT — 25:11-19

11. A word fitly spoken
Is like applies of gold in network of silver.
12. As an ear-ring of gold, and an ornament of fine gold,
So is a wise reprover upon an obedient ear.
13. As the cold of snow in the time of harvest,
So is a faithful messenger to them that send him;
For he refresheth the soul of his masters.
14. As clouds and wind without rain,
So is he that boasteth himself of his gifts falsely.
15. By long forbearing is a ruler persuaded,
And a soft tongue breaketh the bone.
16. Hast thou found honey? eat so much as is sufficient for thee,
Lest thou be filled therewith, and vomit it.
17. Let thy foot be seldom in thy neighbor's house,
Lest he be weary of thee, and hate thee.
18. A man that beareth false witness against his neighbor
Is a maul, and a sword, and a sharp arrow.
19. Confidence in an unfaithful man in time of trouble
Is like a broken tooth, and a foot out of joint.

STUDY QUESTIONS OVER 25:11-19

1. What quality do some words possess (v. 11)?
2. Is v. 12 related to v. 11?
3. How would the "cold of snow" be refreshing in harvest (v. 13)?
4. What do people think of a person who boasts (v. 14)?
5. Contrast the action mentioned in v. 15 with that of v. 8.
6. Why are there several proverbs (24:13, this verse, and 25:27) about eating or not eating honey (v. 16)?
7. Have you ever known a person to wear his/her or even their welcome out (v. 17)?

8. Comment on the 3 items mentioned in v. 18.
9. What do you get from v. 19?

PARAPHRASE OF 25:11-19

11. Timely advice is as lovely as golden apples in a silver basket.
12. It is a badge of honor to accept valid criticism.
13. A faithful employee is as refreshing as a cool day in the hot summertime.
14. One who doesn't give the gift he promised is like a cloud blowing over a desert without dropping any rain.
15. Be patient and you will finally win, for a soft tongue can break hard bones.

16. Do you like honey? Don't eat too much of it, or it will make you sick!
17. Don't visit your neighbor too often, or you will outwear your welcome!
18. Telling lies about someone is as harmful as hitting him with an axe, or wounding him with a sword, or shooting him with a sharp arrow.
19. Putting confidence in an unreliable man is like chewing with a sore tooth, or trying to run on a broken foot.

COMMENTS ON 25:11-19

V. 11. A "word fitly spoken" would be the right thing said at the right time, in the right place, to the right person, in the right way, and for the right purpose. For something to be right, everything about it must be right. Is it any wonder, then, that Jas. 3:2 says, "If any stumbleth not in word, the same is a perfect man"? Reseach on "apples of gold in network of silver" is in order. Many contend for a "silver basket" containing beautiful orange fruit. Most writers contend that "apples" from the Hebrew word "tappuach") was not our apple but possibly the orange, or more probably the apricot. Tristram (writing in "Land of Israel") says, "I have no hesitation in expresing my conviction that the apricot alone is the 'apple' of Scripture... Everywhere the apricot is common; perhaps it is, with the single exception of the fig, the most abundant fruit of the country. In highlands and lowlands alike, by the shores of the Mediterranean and on the banks of the Jordan, in the nooks of Judea, under the heights of Lebanon, in the recesses of Galiliee, and in the glades of Gilead, the apricot flourishes and yields a crop of prodigious abundance. Its characteristics meet every condition of the 'tappauch'' of Scripture.'' Then a word fitly spoken is as perfect as a beautiful, delicious group of golden apricots in a basket made of silver. See also Prov. 15:23.

V. 12. Just as they bestowed comeliness upon their faces by golden ornaments, so listening to parents' wise counsel and to wise reproofs would grace one's life (Prov. 1:9 and this verse). In the New Testament women especially are instructed to adorn and ornament their lives with spiritual beauty instead of majoring upon physical beauty (I Pet. 3:3-5; I Tim. 2:9,10).

V. 13. Not a snow storm (which would not occur at the season of harvest and which would be a calamity rather than a refreshing blessing) but likely a snow-cooled drink for the harvest workers. How would that be possible? "Clarke:" "In the East they have snow-houses—places dug under ground where they lay up snow for summer use." This snow was used to cool their summer drinks. To have a faithful messenger who could be counted upon was as refreshing to those who would send him as a cold drink in hot weather. Prov. 13:17 likens such a messenger to "health".

V. 14. "Boasteth himself of his gifts falsely" is translated by "Coverdale": "Whoso maketh great boasts, and giveth nothing," and the "Vulgate" translates: "A bragging man, who does not fulfill his promises." Such promises remind one of clouds and winds in dry weather, but no rain results. Jude 12 also refers to these clouds without water, carried along by winds" people. Some people make a big show with their words, but they do not come through with what they have promised—and sometimes they were promising to give it to God! Eccl. 5:5 says, "Better is it that thou shouldest not vow, than that thou shouldest vow and not pay." Therefore Eccl. 5:4 says, "When thou vowest a vow unto God, defer not to pay it; for he hath no pleasure in fools: pay that which thou vowest."

V. 15. One can defeat himself sometimes by being too "pushy". By being "hasty of spirit" we can sometimes "exalt folly" (Prov. 14:29) instead of success. We are commanded to "reprove, rebuke, exhort, with all longsuffering and teaching" (II Tim. 4:2). We are told in II Tim. 2:24,25 that"the Lord's servant must not strive, but be gentle towards all, apt to teach, forbearing, in meekness correcting them that oppose themselves; if peradventure God may give them repentance unto the knowledge of the truth." And we are told in Prov. 15:1 that a "soft answer turneth away wrath".

V. 16. Among the many spiritual and moral instructions we have in the Bible, there is an occasional instruction with reference to the physical or health-side of mankind. Such is this verse. Honey is good, actually great, for health (Prov. 24:13), but one should not eat so much of it that he gets turned against it permanently and thereafter wants none of it. Verse 27 warns, "It is not good to eat much honey." We should do that which is wise even in the physical realm of our being.

V. 17. Our common expressions, "Don't wear your welcome out" and "Familiarity breeds contempt", carry the same message. People have work to be done and business to be seen about. One who has nothing to do and keeps running over to the house of those who do soon makes his/her appearance an unwelcome sight. It is better to have the others say, "Come over," than to have them think, "I wish they would leave." The marginal reading is interesting: "Lest he be full of thee."

V. 18. The "paraphrase" says, "Telling lies about someone is as harmful as hitting him with an ax, or wounding him with a sword, or shooting him with a sharp arrow." Psa. 57:4 speaks of people "whose teeth are spears and arrows, and their tongue is a sharp sword". Psa. 120:3,4 speaks of the tongue as "sharp arrows of the mighty, with coals of juniper". and Prov. 12:18 speaks of the rash tongue as the "piercings of a sword".

V. 19. Putting one's trust in an unreliable person lets him down in the day of trouble. This is why some people should not be given a church class to teach, why some people should not be entrusted with important business, etc. You cannot use a broken tooth nor count on a foot out of joint. Each person should want to be reliable, responsible, and trustworthy And each of us should be wise enough not to count upon the irresponsible.

TEST QUESTIONS OVER 25:11-19

1. Comment upon the "apples of gold" of v. 11.
2. What does God say in the New Testament about ornamenting (v. 12)?
3. Comment upon "snow in the time of harvest" in v. 13.
4. Comment upon "boasteth himself of his gifts falsely" (v. 14).

5. Elaborate upon "long forebearing" and a "soft tongue" in v. 15.
6. What is different about the instruction in v. 16?
7. What does the margin give in v. 17 for "lest he be weary of thee"?
8. How is the destructive tongue compared in v. 18?
9. What lesson do you receive from v. 19?

TEXT — 25:20-28

20. As one that taketh off a garment in cold weather, and as vinegar upon soda,
So is he that singeth songs to a heavy heart.
21. If thine enemy be hungry, give him bread to eat;
And if he be thirsty, give him water to drink:
22. For thou wilt heap coals of fire upon his head,
And Jehovah will reward thee.
23. The north wind bringeth forth rain;
So doth a backbiting tongue an angry countenance.
24. It is better to dwell in the corner of the housetop,
Than with a contentious woman in a wide house.
25. As cold waters to a thirsty soul,
So is good news from a far country.
26. As a troubled fountain, and a corrupted spring,
So is a righteous man that giveth way before the wicked.
27. It is not good to eat much honey;
So for men to search out their own glory is grevious.
28. He whose spirit is without restraint
Is like a city that is broken down and without walls.

STUDY QUESTIONS OVER 25:20-28

1. Comment on the comparisons in v. 20.
2. Where in the New Testament is v. 21 quoted?
3. What is the meaning of v. 22?
4. What is a "backsliding" tongue (v. 23)?
5. What other verses in Proverbs are similar to v. 24?
6. What kind of news would they look forward to from a "far country" (v. 25)?
7. What is a "troubled fountain" (v. 26)?
8. Give an example of one searching out his own glory (v. 27)?
9. What virtue is lacking in one whose spirit is without restraint (v. 28)?

PARAPHRASE OF 25:20-28

20. Being happy-go-lucky around a person whose heart is heavy is as bad as stealing his jacket in cold weather, or rubbing salt in his wounds.

21,22. If your enemy is hungry, give him food! If he is thirsty, give him something to drink! This will make him feel ashamed of himself, and God will reward you.

23. As surely as a wind from the north brings cold, just as surely a retort causes anger!

24. It is better to live in a corner of an attic than in a beautiful home with a cranky, quarrelsome woman.

25. Good news from far away is like cold water to the thirsty.

26. If a godly man compromises with the wicked, it is like polluting a fountain or muddying a spring.

27. Just as it is harmful to eat too much honey, so also it is bad for men to think about all the honors they deserve!

28. A man without self-control is as defenseless as a city with broken-down walls.

COMMENTS ON 25:20-28

V. 20. In case of light sorrow of disappointments, we may sing with such a one to cheer him up and pep him up, but in case of extreme sorrow (such as from death) we do not say to such a one, "Come on, let's all gather around the piano and sing and have a good time." Festive singing would be as out of order under those conditions as taking away a needed garment in cold weather and would meet with emotional resistance similar to what happens when you pour vinegar upon soda, and the two boil up. "Pulpit Commentary:" "The proverb gives three instances of what is wrong, incongruous, or unwise, the first two leading up to the third, which is the pith of the maxim."

V. 21. Both Old and New Testaments teach that we should treat one who has not been good to us as we would a friend. Old Testament: "If thou meet thine enemy's ox or his ass going astray, thou shalt surely bring it back to him again" (Exo. 23:4); New Testament: "Love your enemies, and pray for them that persecute you" (Matt. 5:44). Our verse and the one following are quoted in Rom. 12:20. If you, a godly person, are seeking to win an enemy through kindness, you may get nowhere by socially inviting him over for a meal. The matter may be different "if" he is hungry (without food) or "if" he is thirsty (without drink); help offered him in dire circumstances when he might well expect you to disregard his condition or inwardly rejoice over his plight will not be refused (a drowning man will grasp a rope thrown to him regardless of who is on the other end). By such means, Rom. 12:21 shows, you may be able to overcome his evil done to you by your good done to him. How worthwhile! How both of you will rejoice!

V. 22. Counseling a woman about her difficult husband, a preacher asked her if she had tried "heaping colds of fire upon his head"; she said, "No, but I've tried boiling water, and that didn't work." The woman missed the point of this statement. "Clarke" rightfully observes: "Thou shalt heap coals of fire upon his head—not to consume, but to melt him into kindness, a metaphor taken from smelting metallic ores: 'So artists melt the sullen ore of lead By heaping coals of fire upon its head.'" God has promised to reward such actions.

V. 23. Rainfall in the north of Palestine is heavier than in the south, so a wind from that direction would bring moisture (or from the west, where the sea is, Luke 12:54) while one from the south (which is desert) would only bring parching weather (Luke 12:55). Just as surely will a tongue that "bites a person behind his back" arouse an angry countenance in the one so spoken of/against. Backbiting is serious: it is mentioned in Rom. 1:30 among the awful sins of that chapter's long list; it is mentioned in II Cor. 12:20 as a part of church-trouble; Psa. 15:1-3 shows one must be free from it to dwell in God's tabernacle on His holy hill; and Psa. 101:5 says God will destroy one guilty of it.

V. 24. The same is found, word for word, in Prov. 21:9. Prov. 21:19 agrees with the conclusion when it says, "It is better to dwell in a desert land, Than with a contentious and fretful woman." Prov. 19:31 says, "The contentions of a wife are a continual dropping." If there is anything that will "get a man" or that is obnoxious to a man, it is the nagging and continual harpings of a woman. Moral: Women, don't do it! Girls, don't develop it! Boys, don't marry it! Married men, you have a problem!

V. 25. In Bible days one received very little news from distant places (not like we do today). The welcomeness of a drink of cold water when thirsty and the refreshing relief it brings suggest that one's heart is refreshed or relieved (or both) from good news from relatives afar off, or in the case of kings good news from his army fighting afar off.

V. 26. A drinking fountain whose waters have been riled up or a spring that has had something dead or putrid fall into it to corrupt it are examples of something once good and usable now hindered and hurt and no longer good. So is a righteous man who gets corrupted by wicked people. This can happen to men who go into politics, to men who become judges, to men who go into business pursuits, to young people who go to college, to preachers who go to work with certain congregations; in fact, to almost anybody.

V. 27. Anything good to eat (like honey) can be over-indulged in. The same warning with reference to honey, a delicacy to the ancients, was mentioned in v. 16. And anything natural, like searching into one's ancestry if it was prominent or gloating over one's accomplishments, is not good but grievous. Nobody likes to see another "stuck on himself". Rom. 12:16 says, "Be not wise in your own conceits." And Prov. 27:2 says, "Let another man praise thee, and not thine own mouth; A stranger, and not thine own lips." An old saying: "Self-brag stinks."

V. 28. Another great verse on the need of self-control. A city broken down by some greater power and left without walls is weakened to the point of being defenseless against attack, and when a person has lost his sense of personal restraint or self-control, he/she is open to temptation's attack. You are responsible for saying, "Yes," to God and, "No," to Satan; God built this responsibility into you when He created you with the right of choice. Restrain yourself! We put bits in horse's mouths to restrain them; we build fences around livestock to restrain them; and God has commanded each of us to exercise self-control overselves. Paul said, "I buffet my body, and bring it into bondage: lest by any means, after that I have preached to others, I myself should be rejected" (I Cor. 9:27). James wrote, "Be subject therefore unto God; but resist the devil" (Jas. 4:7). And Prov. 16:32 praises self-control: "He that is slow to anger is better than the mighty; And he that ruleth his spirit, than he that taketh a city."

TEST QUESTIONS OVER 25:20-28

1. What does v. 20 mean, seeing that we sing songs at funerals?

2. Is the setting of v. 21 that of forcing ourselves socially upon one who does not like us, or what?
3. Give an example of heaping coals of fire upon an enemy's head (v. 22).
4. Why did a north wind bring Palestinians rain (v. 23)?
5. What does the Bible say about a "backbiting tongue" (v. 23)?
6. What terrible situation is v. 24 dealing with?
7. How did good news from family or army from afar affect the recipient (v. 25)?
8. What kind of person is v. 27 picturing?
9. How is one without self-control like a city without walls (v. 28)?

NOTICEABLE GROUPINGS IN CHAPTER 25

"*Kings*"--

"The glory of kings is to search out a matter" (v. 2).

"The heart of kings is unsearchable (v. 3).

"Take away the wicked from before the king, And his throne shall be established in righteousness" (v. 5).

"Put not thyself forward in the presence of the king, And stand not in the place of great men: For better is it that it be said unto thee, Come up hither, Than that thou shouldest be put lower in the presence of the prince" (vs. 6,7).

"By long forbearing is a ruler persuaded" (v. 15).

"*As*"--

"As the heavens for height, and the earth for depth, So the heart of kings is unsearchable" (v. 3).

"As an ear-ring of gold, and an ornament of fine gold, So is a wise reprover upon an obedient ear" (v. 12).

"As the cold of snow in the time of harvest, So is a faithful messenger to them that send him" (v. 13).

"As clouds and wind without rain, So is he that boasteth himself of his gifts falsely" (v. 14).

"As one that taketh off a garment in cold weather, and as vinegar upon soda, So is he that singeth songs to a heavy heart" (v. 20).

"As cold waters to a thirsty soul, So is good news from a far country" (v. 25).

"As a troubled fountain, and corrupted spring, So is good news from a far country" (v. 26).

"*It is*"--

"It is the glory of God to conceal a thing; But the glory of kings is to search out a matter" (v. 2).

"It is better to dwell in the corner of the housetop, Than with a contentious woman in a wide house" (v. 24).

"It is not good to eat much honey; So for men to search out their own glory is grievous" (v. 27).

"*Better*"--

"Better is it that it be said unto thee, Come up hither, Than that thou shouldest be put lower in the presence of the prince" (v. 7).

"It is better to dwell in the corner of the housetop, Than with a contentious woman in a wide house" (v. 24).

"*Commands*"--

"Debate thy cause with thy neighbor himself, And disclose not the secret of another" (v. 9).

"Hast thou found honey? eat so much as is sufficient for thee" (v. 16).

"Let thy foot be seldom in thy neighbor's house" (v. 17).

"If thine enemy be hungry, give him bread to eat; And if he be thirsty, give him water to drink" (v. 21).

"*Prohibitions*"--

"Put not thyself forward in the presence of the king" (v. 6).

"Go not forth hastily to strive" (v. 8).

"*Lest*"--

"Go not forth hastily to strive, Lest thou know not what to do in the end thereof" (v. 8).

"Debate thy cause with thy neighbor himself, And disclose not the secret of another; Lest he that heareth it revile thee, And thine infamy turn not away" (vs. 9,10).

"Hast thou found honey? eat so much as is sufficient for thee, Lest thou be filled therewith, and vomit it" (v. 16).

"Let thy foot be seldom in thy neighbor's house, Lest he be weary of thee, and hate thee" (v. 17).

"*Tongue*"--

"Debate thy cause with thy neighbor himself...disclose not the secret of another" (v. 9).

"A word fitly spoken Is like apples of gold in network of silver" (v. 11).

"As an ear-ring of gold, and an ornament of fine gold, So is

a wise reprover upon an obedient ear" (v. 12).
"As the cold of snow in the time of harvest, So is a faithful messenger to them that send him" (v. 13).
"As clouds and wind without rain, So is he that boasteth himself of his gifts falsely" (v. 14).
"A soft tongue breaketh the bone" (v. 15).
"A man that beareth false witness against his neighbor Is a maul, and a sword, and a sharp arrow" (v. 18).
"The north wind bringeth forth rain; So doth a backbiting tongue an angry countenance" (v. 23).

"*Like*"--

"Confidence in an unfaithful man in time of trouble Is like a broken tooth, and a foot out of joint" (v. 19).
"A word fitly spoken Is like apples of gold in network of silver" (v. 11).
"He whose spirit is without restraint Is like a city that is broken down and without walls" (v. 28).

"*So*" (by itself)--

"The north wind bringeth forth rain; So doth a backbiting tongue an angry countenance" (v. 23).
"It is not good to eat much honey; So for men to search out their own glory is grievous" (v. 27).

JOYS AND SORROWS OF PARENTHOOD

10:1 says, "A wise man maketh a glad father: but a foolish son is the heaviness of his mother." How true. Nothing should please a man more than his children turning out right. Even when they turn out fair, how parents do brag! Nothing brings greater heaviness to a woman than to have her children go bad.

"A foolish son is a grief to his father, and bitterness to her that bare him" (17:25). Along the same line, 17:21 says, "He that begetteth a fool doeth it to his sorrow: and the father of a fool hath no joy."

Other passages that indicate how far children can go in abuse of their parents are: "He that wasteth his father (and some sons surely do), and chaseth away his mother, is a son that causeth shame, and bringeth reproach" (19:26); "Whoso curseth his father or his mother (and some children will), his lamp shall be put out in obscure darkness" (20:20).

But, back to the more pleasant side: "My son, if thine heart be wise, my heart shall rejoice, even mine" (23:15); "The father of the righteous shall greatly rejoice: and he that begetteth a wise child shall have joy in him. Thy father and thy mother shall be glad, and she that bare thee shall rejoice" (23:24,25); "My son, be wise, and make my heart glad, that I may answer him that reproacheth me" (27:11).

CHAPTER 26

TEXT — 26:1-9

1. As snow in summer, and as rain in harvest,
So honor is not seemly for a fool.
2. As a sparrow in her wandering, as the swallow in her flying,
So the curse that is causeless alighteth not.
3. A whip for the horse, a bridle for the ass,
And a rod for the back of fools.
4. Answer not a fool according to his folly,
Lest thou also be like unto him.
5. Answer a fool according to his folly.
Lest he be wise in his own conceit.
6. He that sendeth a message by the hand of a fool
Cutteth off his own feet, and drinketh in damage.
7. The legs of the lame hang loose;
So is a parable in the mouth of fools.
8. As one that bindeth a stone in a sling,
So is he that giveth honor to a fool.
9. As a thorn that goeth up into the hand of a drunkard,
So is a parable in the mouth of fools.

STUDY QUESTIONS OVER 26:1-9

1. What does "seemly" mean (v. 1)?
2. Restate the last clause of v. 2 in your own words.
3. What does Psa. 32:9 say that fits in with v. 3?
4. What does v. 4 mean?
5. Why would God give the instruction of v. 5 after what He said in v. 4?
6. What is meant by "cutteth off his own feet" (v. 6)?
7. What can happen to a parable in the mouth of a fool (v. 7)?
8. What is the comparison in v. 8?
9. What is the comparison in v. 9?

PARAPHRASE OF 26:1-9

1. Honor doesn't go with fools any more than snow with summertime or rain with harvest time!
2. An undeserved curse has no effect. Its intended victim will be no more harmed by it than by a sparrow or swallow flitting through the sky.

3. Guide a horse with a whip, a donkey with a bridle, and a rebel with a rod to his back!

4,5. When arguing with a rebel, don't use foolish arguments as he does, or you will become as foolish as he is! Prick his conceit with silly replies!

6. To trust a rebel to convey a message is as foolish as cutting off your feet and drinking poison!

7. In the mouth of a fool a proverb becomes as useless as a paralyzed leg.

8. Honoring a rebel will backfire like a stone tied to a sling-shot!

9. A rebel will misapply an illustration so that its point will no more be felt than a thorn in the hand of a drunkard.

COMMENTS ON 26:1-9

V. 1. A fool receives no honor nor does he have a sense of honor. The two go together as poorly as snow and summer and as rain and harvest. How many times a fool shows that he is a fool with poor rearing or a poor set of values by not joining in with giving honor to those to whom honor is due. Such a one is a poor one to marry, for neither will he bestow honor on his wife as I Pet. 3:7 and Prov. 31:28,29 teach.

V. 2. The ancients feared a curse pronounced by another. The point of the verse is, Do right, and you have nothing to fear from people's curses. At times it seems that some birds are aimlessly flying, just for the sake of flying, actually going nowhere. Even so a false curse will aimlessly go nowhere. In keeping with this verse are two eastern proverbs: "The jackal howls: will my old buffalo die?" "The dog barks--still the caravan passes: will the barking of the dog reach the skies?"

V. 3. Those who have worked around animals often use a whip because animals don't always do what they want them to do by other means. So, a whip for the horse, a bridle for the ass, and a rod for the back of fools. We are told in Psa. 32:9, "Be ye not as the horse, or as the mule, which have no understanding; Whose trappings must be bit and bridle to hold them in." Prov. 10:13 says, "A rod is for the back of him that is void of understanding."

V. 4. "Pulpit Commentary": "Do not lower yourself to the fool's level by answering his silly questions or arguing with him as if he were a sensible man...Instances may be seen in Matt. 21:23-25; 22:17-21; John 21:21,22."

V. 5. Since the writer of vs. 4,5 was inspired, and since their seemingly conflicting instructions are in successive verses, there is no possible charge of contridiction as disbelievers might urge if they were found in different chapters or in different books of the Bible. Being carried together they demand that we ascertain the "why" behind the two instructions. First of all, this verse shows that sometimes you answer a fool according to his folly, and v. 4 shows that sometimes you don't. In each instance you will have to be the judge when it is appropriate and wise to do so and when it isn't. Warburton says: "The reasons given why a fool should not be answered according to his folly is 'lest he (the answerer) should be like unto him'. The reason given why the fool should be answered according to his folly is 'lest he (the fool) should be wise in his own conceit'." As an example of this verse a certain preacher was asked a silly or useless or unanswerable question (like what were the names of Jesus' sisters), and he told the man he would find the answer in the second chapter of Jude!

V. 6. Prov. 25:13 speaks of the faithful messenger: "As the cold of snow in the time of harvest, So is a faithful messenger to them that send him; For he refresheth the soul of his masters." But this verse speaks of sending a message by a "fool". Chances are something will be bersirk: maybe he will never arrive with it; maybe he will get it all mixed up; etc. He will bring "damage" to the one sending him. By so doing he will "maim" (cut off the feet of) his business, prosperity, or self in some way. Prov. 25:19 warns about putting confidence in an unfaithful man.

V. 7. A lame man's legs are not sound and may be at least in part invalid, and so is a parable or a wise saying in the mouth of a fool. He will misapply the parable or the point of the saying. He will render the parable invalid.

V. 8. Most stones shot from a sling are more or less shot at random, actually wasted, reaching no vital destination (like killing a dangerous animal). "Clarke:" "It is entirely thrown away." Is not the same true of bestowing honor upon a fool? It is wasted upon one who does not appreciate it, does not know what to do with it, and will not be the better for it. To elevate a servant to a place of rulership is to bring trouble upon the world (Prov. 30:21, 22).

TEST QUESTIONS OVER 26:1-8

1. What does a fool lack, according to v. 1?
2. How can a false curse and a flying bird be alike (v. 2)?
3. What about a horse or ass necessitates a whip at times (v. 3)?
4. Why should one not answer a fool according to his folly (v. 4)?
5. Why should one at other times answer a fool according to his folly (v. 5)?
6. What could happen by sending a message by a fool (v. 6)?
7. What about a parable in the mouths of fools (v. 7)?
8. Why should we not give honor to a fool (v. 8)?

TEXT — 26:9-19

9. As a thorn that goeth up into the hand of a drunkard,
So is a parable in the mouth of fools.
10. As an archer that woundeth all,
So is he that hireth a fool and he that hireth them that pass by.
11. As a dog that returneth to his vomit,
So is a fool that repeateth his folly.
12. Seest thou a man wise in his own conceit?
There is more hope of a fool than of him.
13. The sluggard saith, There is a lion in the way;
A lion is in the streets.
14. As the door turneth upon its hinges,
So doth the sluggard upon his bed.
15. The sluggard burieth his hand in the dish;
It wearieth him to bring it again to his mouth.
16. The sluggard is wiser in his own conceit
Than seven men that can render a reason.
17. He that passeth by, and vexeth himself with strife belonging not to him,
Is like one that taketh a dog by the ears.
18. As a madman who casteth firebrands,
Arrows, and death,
19. So is the man that deceiveth his neighbor,
And saith, Am not I in sport?

STUDY QUESTIONS OVER 26:9-19

1. What is the comparison in v. 9?
2. What do you understand from the comparison in v. 10?
3. Where is v. 11 quoted in the New Testament?
4. After many passages degrading fools, where does v. 12 place the conceited person?
5. Why was the sluggard saying what v. 13 says?
6. What does the sluggard do a lot of (v. 14)?
7. Can a person be so lazy that he is a burden even to himself (v. 15)?
8. Why would a sluggard be as v. 16 says?
9. How can the two actions of v. 17 be compared?
10. Who is a "madman" in v. 18?
11. What is meant by "in sport" (v. 19)?

PARAPHRASE OF 26:9-19

9. A rebel will misapply an illustration so that its point will no more be felt than a thorn in the hand of a drunkard.
10. The master may get better work from an untrained apprentice than from a skilled rebel!
11. As a dog returns to his vomit, so a fool repeats his folly.
12. There is one thing worse than a fool, and that is a man who is conceited.
13. The lazy man won't go out and work. "There might be a lion ouside!" he says.
14. He sticks to his bed like a door to its hinges!
15. He is too tired even to lift his food from his dish to his mouth!
16. Yet in his own opinion he is smarter than seven wise men.
17. Yanking a dog's ears is no more foolish than interfering in an argument that isn't any of your business.

18,19. A man who is caught lying to his neighbor and says, "I was just fooling," is like a madman throwing around firebrands, arrows and death!

COMMENTS ON 26:9-19

V. 9. "Pulpit Commentary:" "There is here no idea of a drunkard's hand being pierced with a thorn...but rather of his being armed with it." "Lange:" "When a drunkard carries and brandishes in his hand a sweet briar..." Would it be dangerous for a drunkard to get a branch of a thorn bush in his hand and began hitting people with it? Is a parable in the mouth of a fool not also dangerous in another way?

V. 10. "Pulpit Commentary:" "A careless, random way of doing business, taking into one's service fools, or entrusting matters of importance to any chance loiterer, is as dangerous as shooting arrows about recklessly without caring whither they flew or whom they wounded."

V. 11. The Bible here and in II Pet. 2:20 (which quotes it) calls upon one of the most obnoxious sights in nature to teach us a lesson: that of a dog who has just given up (vomited) what he had partaken of and then turning around and eating it again. This verse applies it to a fool returning to his acts of foolishness while II Pet. 2:20 applies it to a backslider returning to his former sins.

V. 12. "Pulpit Commentary:" "Nothing so shuts the door against improvement as self-conceit. 'Woe unto them,' says Isa. 5:21, 'that are wise in their own eyes, and prudent in their own sight.' Such persons, professing themselves wise, become fools (Rom. 1:22)...Touching conceit, the Oriental speaks of the fox finding his shadow very large, and of the wolf when alone thinking himself a lion." Rom. 12:3 says, "I say...to every man that is among you, not to think of himself more highly than he ought to think." Rom. 12:16: "Be not wise in your own conceits." Gal. 6:3: "If a man thinketh himself to be something when he is nothing, he deceiveth himself." This verse says there is more hope for a fool than for a conceited person; Prov. 29:20 says the same concerning a man hasty in his words.

V. 13. Prov. 22:13 says the same thing. Proverbs has much to say about laziness: 6:6-9; 10:4,5; 18:9; 19:15; 19:24; 20:4; 22:13; 24:30,31; 26:14; 26:16. That is a lot of material on the subject--more than any other Bible book gives to it.

V. 14. Just as a gate turns upon its hinges, so does the sluggard when aroused turn over (roll over onto his other side) for more sleep. Some of the other explanations given to this comparison are at least entertaining: the door turns on its hinges but goes nowhere; so does a sluggard upon his bed and goes nowhere; while the door opens to let the diligent go forth to their work, the sluggard turns upon his bed and sleeps on; the door creaks when moved, and so does the sluggard when aroused; etc.

V. 15. Prov. 19:24 says the same thing. It is hard for us to imagine people this lazy, but experience teaches one not to be too surprised at anything!

V. 16. This verse sounds like what we call "park-bench authorities" and "sidewalk superintendents"--men who are doing nothing and who have no authority over a project, but who never question their judgment: they always know how it should have been done. Many times the uneducated who are lazy are cursed with the spirit of egotism. Ever try to tell them something? Quoting from your commentator's book, "Simple, Stimulating Studies in the Proverbs:" "Those men with just enough ambition to get up town to spend the day on some benches talking, whittling, and arguing have all the answers. They can tell the President how to run this country, yet nobody ever thought enough of their insight to have them put on any political ticket. They could tell the Secretary of Agriculture (whose problems relate to the corn farmer, the cotton farmer, the fruit farmer, the wheat farmer, the nut farmer, the hay farmer, the dairy farmer, the rancher, the poultryman, the nation's surpluses, and a hundred other large fields) just how to handle his job when they themselves cannot even have a respectable garden."

V. 17. Grabbing a dog by his ears is not recommended, for he will pull loose and turn on you. Nor is getting involved with other people's strife a good thing. Ever hear of the passerby who stopped to take a woman's part against her husband who was hitting her when she turned on her helper and beaned him over the head? This does not mean that one should never try to help those who are having trouble (How else could one be a peacemaker? Matt. 5:9). But this is a warning about meddling in other people's matters (I Pet. 4:15).

V. 18. This saying is different from others in Proverbs in that the dependent clause is in one verse and the independent in the next. The "madman" may be a man gone berserk or an insane man who gets hold of dangerous weapons and begins throwing them around and endangering the lives of his fellowmen.

V. 19. Just as the law will excuse an insane person for the damage he has caused (v. 18), so some whose mischievous conduct or wicked words have brought serious damage to another try to excuse themselves by saying, "I didn't mean to, I was just joking, etc." Too many people try to joke their way through life, and then if something happens that shouldn't, they say, "I didn't mean it."

TEST QUESTIONS OVER 26:9-19

1. What verse in this chapter other than v. 9 spoke of a parable in the mouth of fools?
2. What is wrong about hiring just anybody (v. 10)?
3. How does II Pet. 2:20 apply to v. 11?
4. What does the Bible say about conceit (v. 12)?
5. Why does Proverbs have so much to say about laziness (v. 13)?
6. What are some of the ideas put forth concerning v. 14?
7. How lazy can a person get (v. 15)?
8. What kind of person do you visualize in v. 16?
9. What is like grabbing a dog by the ears (v. 17)?
10. What will a "madman" sometimes do (v. 18)?
11. How do some people try to excuse themselves from guilt in serious matters (v. 19)?

TEXT — 26:20-28

20. For lack of wood the fire goeth out;
And where there is no whisperer, contention ceaseth.
21. As coals are to hot embers, and wood to fire,
So is a contentious man to inflame strife.
22. The words of a whisperer are as dainty morsels,
And they go down into the innermost parts.
23. Fervent lips and a wicked heart
Are like an earthen vessel overlaid with silver dross.
24. He that hateth dissembleth with his lips;
But he layeth up deceit within him:
25. When he speaketh fair, believe him not;
For there are seven abominations in his heart:
26. Though his hatred cover itself with guile,
His wickedness shall be openly showed before the assembly.
27. Whoso diggeth a pit shall fall therein;
And he that rolleth a stone, it shall return upon him.
28. A lying tongue hateth those whom it hath wounded;
And a flattering mouth worketh ruin.

STUDY QUESTIONS OVER 26:20-28

1. A whisperer is to contention like ...... to a fire (v. 20).
2. Are there people who are actually given to working

trouble (v. 21)?
3. How are they like "dainty morsels" (v. 22)?
4. Explain the comparison in v. 23.
5. What does "dissembleth" mean (v. 24)?
6. Why "seven" (v. 25)?
7. Reword v. 26 into your own words.
8. Is v. 27 a new thought or a continuation of v. 26?
9. What is flattery (v. 28)?

PARAPHRASE OF 26:20-28

20. Fire goes out for lack of fuel, and tensions disappear when gossip stops.
21. A quarrelsome man starts fights as easily as a match sets fire to paper.
22. Gossip is a dainty morsel eaten with great relish.
23. Pretty words may hide a wicked heart, just as a pretty glaze covers a common clay pot.
24-26. A man with hate in his heart may sound pleasant enough, but don't believe him; for he is cursing you in his heart. Though he pretends to be so kind, his hatred will finally come to light for all to see.
27. The man who sets a trap for others will get caught in it himself. Roll a boulder down on someone, and it will roll back and crush you.
28. Flattery is a form of hatred and wounds cruelly.

COMMENTS ON 26:20-28

V. 20. For a fire to continue it must have fuel. When wood is no longer put on the fire, it will go out as soon as its present supply is consumed. Even so whispering (derogatory talking in privacy) will keep trouble brewing. Sometimes the whisperer moves away (Woe to the place where he or she moves! It too will begin experiencing trouble.), dies, may get converted, or is cornered, confronted, and quieted, and the contention ceases. The scoffer also is a cause of continual contention until he is cast out (Prov. 22:10: "Cast out the scoffer, and contention will go out").

V. 21. The "whisperer" of v. 20 is referred to here as a "contentious" man in this verse, which he is. He may say he doesn't want trouble, but he is one to make trouble. He may say he loves everybody involved and is only doing his duty in trying to get things right, but he doesn't really love (Rom. 13:10), he is not doing his duty (Rom. 14:19), and he isn't getting things right but making things wrong (Prov. 16:28). The figure of the fire is continued in this verse: note "coals", "hot embers," "wood to fire," and "inflame". Prov. 15:18 says, "A wrathful man stirreth up contention." The church needs to be stirred up all right, but not by contention!

V. 22. The same statement is found in Prov. 18:8. A "whisperer" is one who goes behind people's backs in talking about them, saying things that are not in the best interest of the ones being spoken about. The verse brings out the sad fact that people are willing to listen to such cowardly, wrong, reunous talk (they are "dainty morsels"). They are swallowed without question ("They go down into the innermost parts").

V. 23. "Pulpit Commentary:" "The next proverbs are concerned with hypocrisy...Silver dross (oxide of lead) is used to put a glaze on pottery...The comparatively worthless article (earthen vessel) is thus made to assume a finer appearance. Thus lips that seem to burn with affection and give the kiss of glowing love may mask a heart filled with envy and hatred. Judas kisses and words of friendship hide the bad feelings that lurk within."

V. 24. "Pulpit Commentary:" "The very word here used bears the meaning 'to make one's self unknown'...hence 'to make one's self unrecognizable"... The man cloaks his hatred with honeyed words...meditating all the time treachery in his heart." Adopting this as the mans allows the rest of the verse to flow and makes this verse go along with the other verses of this section.

V. 25. Yes, there are some people just this wicked; their hearts are full of abominations. Jer. 9:8 says, "Their tongue is a deadly arrow; it speaketh deceit: one speaketh peaceably to his neighbor with his mouth, but in his heart he layeth wait for him." So we are not to believe everything some people say.

V. 26. Ultimately his sin will find him out as Num. 32:23 promises concerning sin ("your sin will find you out"). Somebody with influence, leadership, and wisdom will see through the "glaze" of deceit and will bring his actions out into the open, and the result is mentioned in v. 27.

V. 27. The pit or hole that such a one had been digging for someone else becomes the fate of the whispering, contentious deceiver himself. That this is often the deserved outcome of such perverted conduct, see Psa. 7:15,16; Psa. 9:15; Psa. 10:2; Prov. 28:10; Eccl. 10:8.

V. 28. In summary this verse affirms that this whispering

tongue was actually a "lying" tongue, actually hating those it was wounding, and that such a flattering tongue is calculated to work "ruin" to its victim. What a section of the misuse of the tongue we have just studied!

TEST QUESTIONS OVER 26:20-28

1. Who is a "whisperer" (v. 20)?
2. What does a contentious man inflame (v. 21)?
3. Whose "innermost parts" (v. 22)?
4. What are "fervent lips" (v 23)?
5. Adopting what meaning unlocks the sense of v. 24?
6. Why are we not to believe everything some people say (v. 25)?
7. By what means may people's true nature get brought out into the open (v. 26)?
8. Cite two other passages that teach the same as v. 27.
9. How does v. 28 summarize the matter of the previous verses?

NOTICEABLE GROUPINGS IN CHAPTER 26

Comparisons using "as"--

"As snow in summer, and as rain in harvest, So honor is not seemly for a fool" (v. 1).

"As the sparrow in her wandering, as the swallow in her flying, So the curse that is causeless alighteth not" (v. 2).

"As one that bindeth a stone in a sling, So is he that giveth honor to a fool" (v. 8).

"As a thorn that goeth up into the hand of a drunkard, So is a parable in the mouth of fools" (v. 9).

"As an archer that woundeth all, So is he that hireth a fool and he that hireth them that pass by" (v. 10).

"As a dog that returneth to his vomit, So is a fool that repeateth his folly" (v. 11).

"As the door turneth upon its hinges, So doth the sluggard upon his bed" (v. 14).

"As a madman who casteth firebrands, Arrows, and death, So is the man that deceiveth his neighbor, And saith, Am not I in sport?" (vs. 18,19).

"As coals are to hot embers, and wood to fire, So is a contentious man to inflame strife" (v. 21).

"The words of a whisperer are as dainty morsels, And they

go down into the innermost parts" (v. 22).

"*Fools*"--

"Honor is not seemly for a fool" (v. 1).

"A rod for the back of fools" (v. 3).

"Answer not a fool according to his folly, Lest thou also be like unto him" (v. 4).

"Answer a fool according to his folly, Lest he be wise in his own conceit" (v. 5).

"He that sendeth a message by the hand of a fool Cutteth off his own feet, and drinketh in damage" (v. 6).

"The legs of the lame hang loose; So is a parable in the mouth of fools" (v. 7).

"As one that bindeth a stone in a sling, So is he that giveth honor to a fool" (v. 8).

"As a thorn that goeth up into the hand of a drunkard, So is a parable in mouth of fools" (v. 9).

"As an archer that woundeth all, So is he that hireth a fool" (v. 10).

"As a dog that returneth to his vomit, So is a fool that repeateth his folly" (v. 11).

"Seest thou a man wise in his own conceit? There is more hope of a fool than of him" (v. 12).

"*Sluggard*"--

"The sluggard saith, There is a lion in the way" (v. 13).

"As the door turneth upon its hinges, So doth the sluggard upon his bed" (v. 14).

"The sluggard burieth his hand in the dish; It wearieth him to bring it again to his mouth" (v. 15).

"The sluggard is wiser in his own conceit Than seven men that can render a reason" (v. 16).

"*Tongue*"--

"Answer not a fool according to his folly...Answer a fool according to his folly" (vs. 4,5).

"So is a parable in the mouth of fools" (vs. 7,9).

"Where there is no whisperer, contention ceaseth" (v. 20).

"The words of a whisperer are as dainty morsels, And they go down into the innermost parts" (v. 22).

"Fervent lips and a wicked heart Are like an earthen vessel overlaid with silver dross" (v. 23).

"He that hateth dissembleth with his lips; But he layeth up deceit within him: When he speaketh fair, believe him not" (vs. 24,25).

"A lying tongue hateth those whom it hath wounded" (v. 28).

"A flattering mouth worketh ruin" (v. 28).

"*Honor*"--

"Honor is not seemly for a fool" (v. 1).

"As one that bindeth a stone in a sling, So is he that giveth honor to a fool" (v. 8).

"*Conceit*"--

"Answer a fool according to his folly, Lest he be wise in his own conceit" (v. 5).

"Seest thou a man wise in his own conceit? There is more hope of a fool than of him" (v. 12).

"The sluggard is wiser in his own conceit Than seven men that can render a reason" (v. 16).

Comparisons using "like"--

"He that passeth by, and vexeth himself with strife belong not to him, Is like one that taketh a dog by the ears" (v. 17).

"Fervent lips and a wicked heart Are like an earthen vessel overlaid with silver dross" (v. 23).

"*Strife*"--

"He that passeth by, and vexeth himself with strife belonging not to him, Is like one that taketh a dog by the ears" (v. 17).

"Where there is no whisperer, contention ceaseth" (v. 20).

"So is a contentious man to inflame strife" (v. 21).

"*Deceit*"--

"So is a man that deceiveth his neighbor" (v. 19).

"He layeth up deceit within him" (v. 24).

"When he speaketh fair, believe him not; For there are seven abominations in his heart" (v. 25).

"His hatred cover itself with guile" (v. 26).

"A flattering mouth worketh ruin" (v. 28).

PONDERING THE PROVERBS

WISDOM COUCHED IN WISE SAYINGS

We are told in I Kings that Solomon spoke three thousand proverbs. Wise men of all ages have had their favorite sayings--all brief, but loaded with meaning and application. Paul in his writings talks of and coins sayings which he says are "faithful" or true and "worthy of all acceptation" or can be counted on.

Great truths are needed for everday living, and they need to be well worded that they might always be remembered and used. The first verses of Proverbs tell us the purpose of proverbs: "The proverbs of Solomon, the son of David, king of Israel: to know wisdom and instruction; to perceive the words of understanding; to receive the instruction of wisdom, justice, and judgment, and equity; to give subtilty to the simple, to the young man knowledge and discretion. A wise man will hear, and will increase learning; and a man of understanding shall attain unto wise counsels: to understand a proverb, and the interpretation; the words of the wise, and their dark sayings" (1:1-6).

TEXT — 27:1-9

1. Boast not thyself of tomorrow;
For thou knowest now what a day may bring forth.
2. Let another man praise thee, and not thine own mouth;
A stranger, and not thine own lips.
3. A stone is heavy, and the sand weighty;
But a fool's vexation is heavier than they both.
4. Wrath is cruel, and anger is overwhelming;
But who is able to stand before jealousy?
5. Better is open rebuke
Than love that is hidden.
6. Faithful are the wounds of a friend;
But the kisses of an enemy are profuse.
7. The full soul loatheth a honeycomb;
But to the hungry every bitter thing is sweet.
8. As a bird that wandereth from her nest,
So is a man that wandereth from his place.
9. Oil and perfume rejoice the heart;
So doth the sweetness of a man's friend that cometh of hearty counsel.

STUDY QUESTIONS OVER 27:1-9

1. What would boasting consist of in v. 1?
2. What New Testament passage elaborates upon v. 1?
3. Why is such instruction necessary (v. 2)?
4. Why does God not want us to praise ourselves (v. 3)?
5. Heavier than what (v. 3)?
6. Do you detect the similarities and differences in the structure of vs. 3,4?
7. Better in what sense or senses (v. 5)?
8. Faithful in what sense (v. 6)?
9. What does "profuse" mean (v. 6)?
10. What does "loatheth" mean (v. 7)?
11. What is the comparison in v. 8?
12. What does the last statement of v. 9 mean?

PARAPHRASE OF 27:1-9

1. Don't brag about your plans for tomorrow--wait and see what happens.
2. Don't praise yourself; let others do it!
3. A rebel's frustrations are heavier than sand and rocks.

4. Jealousy is more dangerous and cruel than anger.
5. Open rebuke is better than hidden love!
6. Wounds from a friend are better than kisses from an enemy!
7. Even honey seems tasteless to a man who is full; but if he is hungry, he'll eat anything!
8. A man who strays from home is like a bird that wanders from its nest.
9. Friendly suggestions are as pleasant as perfume.

COMMENTS ON 27:1-9

V. 1. Jas. 4:13-16 is an elaboration upon this verse: "Come now, ye that say, To-day or to-morrow we will go into this city, and spend a year there, and trade, and get gain: whereas ye know not what shall be on the morrow. What is your life? For ye are a vapor that appeareth for a little time, and then vanisheth away. For that ye ought to say, If the Lord will, we shall both live, and do this or that. But now ye glory in your vauntings: all such glorying is evil." The rich fool in the parable was boasting himself of "tomorrow" ("The ground of certain rich men brought forth plentifully: and he reasoned within himself, saying, What shall I do, because I have not where to bestow my fruits? And he said, This will I do: I will pull down my barns, and build greater; and there will I bestow all my grain and my goods. And I will say to my soul, Soul, thou hast much goods laid up for many years, take thine ease, eat, drink and be merry" Luke 12:16-19) when actually he had no "tomorrow" ("God said unto him, Thou foolish one, this night is thy soul required of thee"--Luke 12:20). "Pulpit Commentary:" "He boasts himself of tomorrow who counts upon it presumptuously, settles that he will do this or that, as if his life were in his own power, and he could make sure of time. This is blindness and arrogance."

V. 2. An old German proverb: "Self-brag stinks." How much better it sounded for the elders of the Jews, when entreating Jesus to come heal the centurion's servant to say, "He is worthy that thou shouldest do this for him" (Luke 7:4), than for the man himself to have said, "I am worthy that thou shouldest do this for me." There is that element of society that seems to think, "If I don't toot my own horn, it won't get tooted." We reply in the words of "Clarke" ("Self praise is no commendation"). Jesus recognized the general truthfulness of this statement when He said, "If I bear witness of myself, (that is, if I am the only one saying good things about myself), my witness is not true" (John 5:32). Remember, too, that Prov. 25:27 frowned upon men's searching out their own glory.

V. 3. Work with stone or sand very long, and your hands, your legs and your back (in fact, your whole body) soon become weary and exhausted. But to be around a fool when vexed is even more wearying and exhausting. "Pulpit Commentary:" "The ill temper and anger of a headstrong fool, which he vents on those about him, are harder to endure than any material weight is to carry." Job 6:3 speaks of his grief and trials being heavier to bear than the sand of the sea. And Jewish literature contains this statement: "Sand and salt and a mass of iron are easier to bear than a man without understanding."

V. 4. Wrath and anger may arise and subside, but not so with jealousy. "Pulpit Commentary:" "These may be violent for a time, yet they will subside when they have spent themselves." It was such non-dying jealousy that caused Joseph's brothers to sell him: "The patriarchs, moved with jealousy against Joseph, sold him into Egypt" (Acts 7:9). One who commits adultery with another man's wife will probably encounter the never-dying jealousy of her husband mentioned in Prov. 6:35,35: "Jealousy is the rage of man; And he will not spare...He will not regard any ransom; Neither will he rest content, though thou givest many gifts."

V. 5. Christ said, "As many as I love, I rebuke and chasten" (Rev. 3:19). Prov. 13:24 says, "He that spareth his rod hateth his son" (no matter how much pretension of love he may claim); "But he that loveth him chasteneth him betimes." It is in such a consideration that our verse exalts the love that rebukes over the love that does not. Thus gospel preachers and godly people who rebuke people for their sins really and truly love people more (and what they do is "better") than their pretended friends who say nothing about their sins and let them die and be lost.

V. 6. Therefore, this verse exalts the same love that administers correction over the deceitful kisses of an enemy. Judas's kiss didn't fool Jesus, but people have been fooled by the "nice" treatment of people who really didn't love them like the person who corrected them. Time will sometimes open people's eyes as to who were their true friends: "He that rebuketh a man shall afterward find more favor than he that flattereth with the tongue" (Prov. 28:23). Notice the triple contrast in this verse: "faithful" vs. "deceitful"; "wounds" vs. "kisses"; and "friend" vs. "enemy".

V. 7. Benjamin Franklin: "A hungry man never saw poor bread." People who complain about food would probably not do so if really hungry. When one is really hungry, just plain bread or dry crackers taste good, but after one has eaten a big meal at a family get-together, just to mention eating will fulfill the fact of this verse: "The full soul loatheth a honeycomb." In a sense this is why some are not hungry for the gospel: they feel no need, so they have no desire.

V. 8. Though we do not think of it as normal, there are birds who abandon their nest, their natural surroundings, and go elsewhere with sad results. In like manner do some men become wanderers and prodigals (like the Prodigal Son in the parable, Luke 15). Time has proven that strength of character is more often developed in a family and in children if they settle down to one community and make it their home than to move about from place to place. This general observation reflected itself in our forefather's maxim: "A rolling stone gathers no moss."

V. 9. They anointed their faces with olive oil and put on perfume to make themselves happy and light-hearted and carefree. Psa. 104:15 refers to this practice. What is sweeter and more burden-lifting than the good advice and counsel of a trusted friend? How much better one feels who has been burdened!

TEST QUESTIONS OVER 27:1-9

1. What man in a parable of Jesus boasted himself of "tomorrow" (v. 1)?
2. What did the German proverb say about the person who brags on himself (v. 2)?
3. How wearying can a fool be to those around him (v. 3)?
4. How do wrath and anger differ from jealousy (v. 4)?
5. What unusual fact is stated in v. 5?
6. What is the triple contrast in v. 6?
7. How can the first part of v. 7 be applied to people's appetite for the gospel?
8. Is it advisable to be a "rolling stone" in society (v. 8)?
9. How do friends help lift our burdens (v. 9)?

TEXT — 27:10-18

10. Thine own friend, and thy father's friend, forsake not;
And go not to thy brother's house in the day of thy calamity:
Better is a neighbor that is near than a brother far off.
11. My son, be wise, and make my heart glad,
That I may answer him that reproacheth me.
12. A prudent man seeth the evil, and hideth himself;
But the simple pass on, and suffer for it.
13. Take his garment that is surety for a stranger;
And hold him in pledge that is surety for a foreign woman.
14. He that blesseth his friend with a loud voice, rising early in the morning,
It shall be counted a curse to him.
15. A continual dropping in a very rainy day
And a contentious woman are alike:
16. He that would restrain her restraineth the wind;
And his right hand encountereth oil.
17. Iron sharpeneth iron;
So a man sharpeneth the countenance of a friend.
18. Whoso keepth the fig-tree shall eat the fruit thereof;
And he that regardeth his master shall be honored.
19. As in water face answereth to face,
So the heart of man to man.

STUDY QUESTIONS OVER 27:10-18

1. How does v. 10 depart from the usual form of a verse in Proverbs?
2. What does v. 10 say about our friendship-ties?
3. In what sense should one not go into his brother's house during calamity (v. 10)?
4. Why will people reproach a man because of his unfaithful children (v. 11)?
5. Illustrate v. 12 in various ways.
6. What is the meaning of v. 13?
7. What kind of person would bless his friend "with a loud voice (v. 14)?
8. Comment upon the comparison in v. 15.
9. What is meant by the last statement in v. 16?
10. Which iron sharpeneth iron (v. 17)?

11. Where does Paul state the same truth as in v. 18's first statement?

PARAPHRASE OF 27:10-18

10. Never abandon a friend--either yours or your father's. Then you won't need to go to a distant relative for help in your time of need.
11. My son, how happy I will be if you turn out to be sensible! It will be a public honor to me.
12. A sensible man watches for problems ahead and prepares to meet them. The simpleton never looks, and suffers the consequences.
13. The world's poorest credit risk is the man who agrees to pay a stranger's debts.
14. If you shout a pleasant greeting to a friend too early in the morning, he will count it as a curse!
15,16. A constant dripping on a rainy day and a cranky woman are much alike! You can no more stop her complaints than you can stop the wind or hold onto anything with oilslick hands.
17. A friendly discussion is as stimulating as the sparks that fly when iron strikes iron.
18. A workman may eat from the orchard he tends; anyone should be rewarded who protects another's interests.

COMMENTS ON 27:10-18

V. 10. This verse contains three lines instead of the customary two. This is a great verse on friendship, even stating that we should value the long-time friendships of our family as well as those of friends we have personally made. On the puzzling statement about not going into your brother's house in time of trouble, "Pulpit Commentary" observes: "The mere blood-relationship, which is the result of circumstances over which one has had no control, is inferior to the affectionate connection which arises from moral considerations and is the effect of deliberate choice. We must remember, too, that the practice of polygamy, with the separate establishments of the various wives, greatly weakened the tie of brotherhood. There was little love between David's sons; and Jonathan was far dearer to David himself than any of his numerous brothers were."

V. 11. Saying "My son," and then urging him to listen to

what the father was about to say was common in the first part of Proverbs (1:8-10; 2:1, 3:1,2; 4:1,2; 5:1,2; 6:1,2; 7:1-3), but in this verse is the only time it appears in this latter part of the book. Good children are one of a man's best recommendations. A wise son not only makes a glad father (Prov. 10:1), but fathers with good chldren "shall not be put to shame, When they speak with their enemies in the gate" (Psa. 127:5). Many leaders, even in religion, have been put to shame by the bad behavior and reputation of their sons.

V. 12. This saying is also given in Prov. 22:3. A prudent man is a man who has his eyes open and sees (in this verse he forsees the evil coming), and he acts in wisdom (he hides himself from the evil rather than walking right into it). But the simple man doesn't see the evil, doesn't pay any attention to it, and he suffers for it. Picture evil as a trap that is set; there is as much difference between men who can and cannot be caught in the trap of evil as there is between animals. Mink, foxes and a few other animals are difficult to get into a trap--it can be sometimes done by shrewd and careful means. But no ingenuity is required for getting a possum or a skunk into a trap--just put the trap in the mouth of his den and he will step on it as thoughtlessly as he would on a stick. The truth of this verse is seen in people in regard to their physical, moral, spiritual and financial life.

V. 13. This verse is very similar to Prov. 20:16. If one has become surety for a stranger or for a foreign woman, the creditor should and will hold his garment in pledge just as he would the stranger's or the foreign woman's. Exo. 22:26 shows that they took one's garment as security when loaning money.

V. 14. Haven't you seen this character who talks louder than is appropriate seemingly with the idea of drawing non-related parties' attention to what he is saying or doing? And, oh, as he talks, how he casts his eyes here and there to get other people to listen to what he is saying! Very similar to the hypocrite of Matt. 6:2 sounding a trumpet among people just before giving alms to a poor person. Jesus said not to do it (Matt. 6:1,2). and if one dies, whatever praise he might get from men will be the only reward he will get (Matt. 6:2). To rise "early" to bless a friend was as much a part of the put-on righteousness as the blessing with a "loud voice".

V. 15. "The ill-constructed roofs of Eastern houses were very subject to leakage, being flat and formed of porous material" ("Pulpit Commentary"). But even our own type of roof can spring a leak and "drip! drip! drip!" as long as there is water to drip. Such is unwelcome and wearying, and so are the contentions of a contentious woman. It is a poor way to treat a husband or anyone else. Prov. 19:13 says, "The contentions of a wife are a continual dropping."

V. 16. There was an old adage that said there are three things which cannot be hidden but always betray themselves: a woman, the wind, and ointment. This verse may have reference to this since it involves those three (all three) and nothing else. One has as much chance of stopping the wind as stopping the mouth of an angry, fretful and unreasonable woman. That's why most men married to such often say nothing back but keep on reading the paper or working at whatever they are doing. Their thought: "She'll run down in time" (like the wind). What is meant by the statement about "oil" is not so clear, some thinking it refers to the impossibility of concealing the smell of the ointment one has put on his hand and some that it refers to her slipping through his hand if he tries to do anything to her. "Clarke" confesses: "The Hebrew is very obscure and is variously translated." But we know whatever the figure, it would be attempting the impossible.

V. 17. "The proverb deals with the influence which men have upon one another" ("Pulpit Commentary"). See the harder steel file sharpen the softer steel knife edge, or watch the butcher as he sharpens his cutting knife by the use of polished steel. This is not to say that men do not use stones to sharpen knives, but the fact that they also use iron upon iron shows that things of the same material can also affect one another--just as men can affect men from sadness to gladness. And ability to cheer up a sorrowful human heart becomes a responsibility to do so. Thus, Jesus referred to our visiting the sick and those in prison (Matt. 25:36) and Heb. 12:12 to our lifting up the hands that hand down.

V. 18. One who carefully tends his fig tree will in time be rewarded for his patient effort, and one who faithfully serves his master will also find that he will be honored for it. Jesus is our Master, and to each who has faithfully served Him here on earth will hear Him say, "Well done, good and faithful servant: thou hast been faithful over a few things, I will set thee over many things; enter thou into the joy of thy lord" (Matt. 25:21).

TEST QUESTIONS OVER 27:10-18

1. Whose friend should we regard as well as a friend of our own making (v. 10)?
2. Why not go to your brother's house in a time of trouble but to a friend's (v. 10)?
3. How many times is "My son" used in the last part of Proverbs? how many times in the early part (v. 11)?
4. What is one of the best recommendations any man can have (v. 11)?
5. What does the prudent man see and do in v. 12? what about the simple?
6. What was sometimes taken as security for a debt (v. 13)?
7. While it is good to bless a friend, what is wrong in v. 14?
8. Who is compared with a leaky roof (v. 15)?
9. What about the statement about "oil" in v. 16?
10. What is impossible to do according to v. 16?
11. What is the lesson of v. 17?
12. What is our obligation to sorrowing, discouraged people about us (v. 17)?
13. V. 18 shows that righteous labor in time brings its ....

TEXT — 27:19-27

19. As in water face answereth face,
So the heart of man to man.
20. Sheol and Abaddon are never satisfied;
And the eyes of man are never satisfied.
21. The refining pot is for silver, and the furnace for gold;
And a man is tried by his praise.
22. Though thou shouldest bray a fool in mortar with a pestle along with bruised grain,
Yet will not his foolishness depart from him.
23. Be thou diligent to know the state of thy flocks,
And look well to thy herds:
24. For riches are not for ever;
And doth the crown endure unto all generations?
25. The hay is carried, and the tender grass showeth itself,
And the herbs of the mountains are gathered in.
26. The lambs are for thy clothing,
And the goats are the price of the field;

27. And there will be goats' milk enough for thy food, for the food of thy household,
And maintenance for thy maidens.

STUDY QUESTIONS OVER 27:19-27

1. Elaborate upon the comparison in v. 19.
2. What New Testament word from Greek is a parallel to "Sheol" in Hebrew (v. 20)?
3. What does "Abaddon" mean (v. 20)?
4. In what sense is the last statement of v. 21 true?
5. What do "bray", "mortar," and "pestle" in v. 22 mean?
6. Why such instruction as is found in v. 23?
7. Illustrate v. 24 by Charlemagne's offspring.
8. What is the point of v. 25?
9. What is the meaning of "the goats are the price of the field" (v. 20)?
10. Why did they not use cows' milk like we do (v. 27)?

PARAPHRASE OF 27:19-27

19. A mirror reflects a man's face, but what he is really like is shown by the kind of friends he chooses.

20. Ambition and death are alike in this: neither is ever satisfied.

21. The purity of silver and gold can be tested in a crucible, but a man is tested by his reaction to men's praise.

22. You can't separate a rebel from his foolishness though you crush him to powder.

23,24. Riches can disappear fast. And the king's crown doesn't stay in his family forever--so watch your business interests closely.

25,26,27. Know the state of your flocks and your herds; then there will be lamb's wools enough for clothing, and goat's milk enough for food for all your household after the hay is harvested, and the new crop appears, and the mountain grasses are gathered in.

COMMENTS ON 27:19-27

V. 19. See a man looking at himself in the water. It is almost as if he is talking to himself. Even so as people look at each other, it is almost as if a silent message is being sent between them.

V. 20. "Sheol" is the Hebrew word for the place of departed spirits (the same as "Hades" in Greek). "Abaddon" is the Hebrew word for destruction (the same as "Apollyon" in Greek;. Both forms of the latter are found in Rev. 9:11. "Sheol and Abaddon" are used together also in Job 26:6 and Prov. 15:11. Just as death is personified here as never satisfied but always wanting more souls, so man's eyes are never satisfied. The more he has and sees, the more he wants. This fact is also mentioned in Eccl. 1:8. Heb. 2:5 uses this same language in describing the greediness of the Chaldeans.

V. 21. "As silver and gold are tried by the art of the refiner, so is a man's heart by the praise he receives. If he feel it not, he deserves it; if he be puffed up by it, he is worthless" ("Clarke"). "Pulpit Commentary": "As the processes of metallurgy test the precious metals, so a man's public reputation shows what he is really worth...As the crucible brings all impurities to the surface, so public opinion drags for all that is bad in a man, and he who stands this test is generally esteemed."

V. 22. "Bray...mortar...pestle"--these are strange words to our modern way of living. Whenever you put something into a container and pound or mash it with something in your hand, you are "braying" it, what you are braying it with is the "pestle", and the container is the "mortar". When our mothers used to mash potatoes by hand, that was the same figure, only we didn't use those words to apply to the action and the various pieces. This verse shows that no matter how you might beat on a confirmed fool, you cannot get rid of his foolishness. Consider the drunkard in Prov. 23:35 and Judah in Isa. 1:5 and Jer. 5:3.

V. 23. From here to the end of the chapter the material has to do with shepherding and agriculture except for the illustration in v. 24 that explains this present verse. This verse presents Hebrew parallelism in which the second statement is a restatement of the first. Whatever a person's business, he must "tend to business", or he will have no business to tend. The shepherd was ever counting his sheep to be sure they were all with the flock. If any was sick, he immediately cared for it.

V. 24. Just as riches or the crown could not be taken for granted, neither could one's flock and herd. Today's ten wealthiest men in the world may not all be wealthy in a few years. Those who rule today may be overthrown tomorrow. So care and diligence must be watchwords even of a shepherd.

V. 25. One can see the diligence of the shepherd in providing food for his flock at the different seasons.

V. 26. This diligence pays off, for there is wool for the clothing, and from the sale of goats could the land be purchased for oneself.

V. 27. Additional reward for diligence: plenty of milk. They milked the goat whereas we milk the cow. On goats' milk "Geikie" says, "In most parts of Palestine goats' milk in every form makes, with eggs and bread, the main food of the people.

NOTICEABLE GROUPINGS IN CHAPTER 27

Comparisons using "as"--

"As a bird that wandereth from her nest, So is a man that wandereth from his place" (v. 8).

"As in water face answereth to face, So the heart of man to man" (v. 19).

"Friend"--

"Faithful are the wounds of a friend" (v. 6).

"Oil and perfume rejoice the heart; So doth the sweetness of a man's friend that cometh of hearty counsel" (v. 9).

"Thine own friend, and thy father's friend, forsake not" (v. 10).

"He that blesseth his friend with a loud voice, rising early in the morning, It shall be counted a curse to him" (v. 14).

"Iron sharpeneth iron; So a man sharpeneth the countenance of his friend" (v. 17).

"Praise"--

"Let another man praise thee, and not thine own mouth; A stranger, and not thine own lips" (v. 2).

"The refining pot is for silver, and the furnace for gold; And a man is tried by his praise" (v. 21).

"Fool"--

"A stone is heavy, and the sand weighty; But a fool's vexation is heavier than they both" (v. 3).

"The simple pass on, and suffer for it" (v. 12).

"Though they shouldest bray a fool in a mortar with a pestle along with bruised grain, Yet will not his foolishness depart from him" (v. 22).

"Speech"--

"Let another praise thee, and not thine own mouth" (v. 2).

CHAPTER 27

"Better is open rebuke Than love that is hidden" (v. 5).
"He that blesseth his friend with a loud voice, rising early in the morning, It shall be counted a curse to him" (v. 14).
"The refining pot is for silver, and the furnace for gold; And a man is tried by his praise" (v. 21).

HELP THE NEEDY

I like 19:17: "He that hath pity upon the poor lendeth unto the Lord; and that which he hath given will he (God) pay him again." In other words, when one GIVES to the poor, he is actually LOANING to God, and God always pays up! We can surely trust the Lord. We do not help the needy just to be helped of the Lord, but in our own limitations when it seems that we cannot do very much, it is comforting to know that if we help another, God Himself will bless us that we too might be able to make it through.

22:9 says, "He that hath a beautiful eye shall be blessed; for he giveth of his bread to the poor."

11:24,25 says, "There is that scattereth, and yet increaseth; and there is that withholdeth more than is meet, but it tendeth to poverty. The liberal soul shall be made fat: and he that watereth shall be watered also himself." It is like sowing. A farmer can take a bushel of oats, and scatter it over a portion of ground. It may look like he is throwing it away, but up comes the plants, and in a few weeks he has many bushels of oats. If the generous person shall abound, then he has not lost by being thoughtful of others. He who has watered others will himself be watered.

PONDERING THE PROVERBS

WISDOM

"Happy is the man that findeth wisdom, and the man that getteth understanding. For the merchandise of it is better than the merchandise of silver, and the gain thereof than fine gold. She is more precious than rubies: and all the things thou canst desire are not to be compared unto her. Length of days is in her right hand; and in her left hand riches and honour. Her ways are ways of pleasantness, and all her paths are peace. She is a tree of life to them that lay hold upon her: and happy is every one that retaineth her" (3:13-18).

What a great passage that is! Man thinks of material gain. Proverbs is not blind to the place of material things, but it says the merchandise and the gain of wisdom are better than that of silver, gold, rubies, and all other earthly things that one can desire. That passage pictures Wisdom's two hands full of great blessings: length of life in her right hand and riches and honor in her left. It also points out that wisdom leads the way to pleasantness and peace and is a tree of life. No wonder, then, that the passage says, "Happy is the man that findeth wisdom, and the man that getteth understanding."

"A good man obtaineth favour of the Lord: but a man of wicked devices will he condemn." If you want the favor of God, you must live right, and nobody's favor should you desire to have more than the favor of God.

To the obedient child, the father in Proverbs assures, "So shalt thou find favour and good understanding in the sight of God and man" (3:4).

TEXT — 28:1-9

1. The wicked flee when no man pursueth;
But the righteous are bold as a lion.
2. For the transgression of a land many are the princes thereof;
But by men of understanding and knowledge the state thereof shall be prolonged.
3. A needy man that oppresseth the poor
Is like a sweeping rain which leaveth no food.
4. They that forsake the law praise the wicked;
But such as keep the law contend with them.
5. Evil men understand not justice;
But they that seek Jehovah understand all things.
6. Better is the poor that walketh in his integrity,
Than he that is perverse in his ways, though he be rich.
7. Whoso keepeth the law is a wise son;
But he that is a companion of gluttons shameth his father.
8. He that augmenteth his substance by interest and increase,
Gathereth it for him that hath pity on the poor.
9. He that turneth away his ear from hearing the law,
Even his prayer is an abomination.

STUDY QUESTIONS OVER 28:1-9

1. Cite outstanding Bible examples of righteous men who were as bold as lions (v. 1).
2. What is the meaning of "for" in v. 2?
3. What is the implied contrast in v. 2?
4. Comment upon the comparison in v. 3.
5. Who praise the wicked (v. 4)?
6. What do the obedient do to the wicked (v. 4)?
7. Do evil men ever get into the field of judging (v. 5)?
8. V. 6 contrasts the honest .... with the perverse ....
9. What is the implied contrast in v. 7?
10. What was God's law to Israel about usury (v. 8)?
11. What would be a modern example of one turning away his ear from hearing God's law (v. 9)?

PARAPHRASE OF 28:1-9

1. The wicked flee when no one is chasing them! But the godly are bold as lions!
2. When there is moral rot within a nation, its government topples easily; but with honest, sensible leaders there is stability.
3. When a poor man oppresses those even poorer, he is like an unexpected flood sweeping away their last hope.
4. To complain about the law is to praise wickedness. To obey the law is to fight evil.
5. Evil men don't understand the importance of justice, but those who follow the Lord are much concerned about it.
6. Better to be poor and honest than rich and a cheater.
7. Young men who are wise obey the law; a son who is a member of a lawless gang is a shame to his father.
8. Income from exploiting the poor will end up in the hands of someone who pities them.
9. God doesn't listen to the prayers of men who flout the law.

COMMENTS ON 28:1-9

V. 1. Mischievous children and evil adults will often drop the wrong they are doing to run when they hear some sound even though it is not somebody pursuing them. House robbers seldom try to break into a home where there is a light on even though they recognize that probably nobody is there--there just might be. See Lev. 26:17 and Psa. 53:5 for fleeing when no man pursues. On the other hand (by way of contrast) the righteous have nothing to be ashamed of, and their courage causes them to stand right where they are. Noah was bold in a world of iniquity, for he was a preacher of righteousness in it (II Pet. 2:5) as well as an ark-builder (Heb. 11:7). Elijah was bold on Mt. Carmel (I Kings 18:17-40). The apostles were bold when encountered by the authorities (Acts 5:27-29).

V. 2. When a nation was wicked, God brought an unrest that produced many turnovers in leadership (nobody remained in power for long), and in time the whole government collapsed and passed out of existence. The last clause shows that the opposite was true where men of understanding and knowledge were in power. "Clarke": "Nations, as nations, cannot be judged in a future world; therefore, God judges them here."

V. 3. The needy man of this verse picks on the man who is poorer than himself, and when he takes the only thing of value that this poorer man has, there is nothing left. On a "sweeping rain": "These are frequent in the East; and sometimes carry flocks, crops, and houses, away with them" ("Clarke").

V. 4. Other passages on the disobedient praising the wicked: Psa. 10:3; Rom. 1:32. They praise the wicked because they are their kind: "If ye were of the world, the world would love its own" (John 15:19). An old saying: "Birds of a feather flock together." Elijah said to the sinning nation, "How long go ye limping between the two sides?" (I Kings 18:21). Micaiah always contended with wicked King Ahab (I Kings 22:8). Malachi contended with the sinning nation of his day (Mal. 3:5-9). John the Baptist contended with the wicked Pharisees and Sadducees (Matt. 3:7). When Paul saw the wholesale idolatry of Athens, he contended with them (Acts 17:16,17). We are told not to have fellowship with the unfruitful works of darkness but to reprove them (Eph. 5:11).

V. 5. "An evil man's moral conception is perverted; he cannot distinguish between right and wrong; the light that was in him has become darkness (Prov. 29:7" ("Pulpit Commentary"). Compare Matt. 6:23: "If therefore the light that is in thee be darkness how great is the darkness!" On the righteous knowing discernment: "If any man willeth to do his will, he shall know..." (John 7:17). While "the natural man receiveth not the things of the Spirit of God: for they are foolishness unto him; and he cannot know them, because they are spiritually judged," "the spiritual judgeth all things" (I Cor. 2:14,15). The righteous "by reason of use have their senses exercised to discern good and evil" (Heb. 5:14). Paul prayed for the Philippians to have this discernment: "And this I pray, that your love may abound yet more and more in knowledge and all discernment; so that ye may approve the things that are excellent" (Phil. 1:9,10). That God's enlightened people possess discernment, John affirmed, "Ye have an anointing from the Holy One, and ye know all things" (I John 2:20).

V. 6. The comparison is between a poor man who is honest and a rich man who is perverting his way. Prov. 16:8 affirms the same: "Better is a little, with righteousness, Than great revenues with injustice." In other words righteousness and justice are more important in the sight of God than riches, even great riches. We are to seek righteousness first and foremost (Matt. 6:33). Prov. 19:1 also speaks of the poor who walk in their integrity (and praises them for it) and of those who pervert their ways. So does Prov. 28:18.

V. 7. This verse reflects that which is seen so often throughout the Bible; namely, that though all people live in the same world and are more or less exposed to the same things, some live right, and some don't. This is even true of one's offspring: a son may be a "wise" son, or he may be a "companion of gluttons". This same contrast is seen in Prov. 29:3: "Whoso loveth wisdom rejoiceth his father; But he that keepeth company with harlots wasteth his substance" (like the Prodigal Son).

V. 8. Of the wicked oppressing the poor to increase their own substance, "Clarke" exclaims, "Oh, that the names of all those unfeeling, hard-hearted, consummate villains in the nation, who thus take advantage of their neighbour's necessities to enrich themselves, were published at every market cross; and then the deliquents all sent to their brother savages in New Zealand!" Other passages bearing out that such ill-gotten gain will in time get back where it belongs: "Though he heap up silver as the dust, And prepare raiment as the clay; He may prepare it, but the just shall put it on, And the innocent shall divide the silver" (Job 27:16,17); "The wealth of the sinner is laid up for the righteous" (Prov. 13:22); "To the man that pleaseth him God giveth wisdom, and knowledge, and joy; but to the sinner he giveth travail, to gather and to heap up, that he may give to him that pleaseth God" (Eccl. 2:26).

V. 9. Of those who turn away their ears from hearing God's Word, Zech. 7:11 says, "They refused to hearken, and pulled away the shoulder, and stopped their ears, that they might not hear." God refused to hear the prayers of many in Isaiah's day because of their disobedience: "When ye spread forth your hands, I will hide mine eyes from you; yea, when ye make many prayers, I will not hear: your hands are full of blood" (Isa. 1:15). The curse of God is upon all who turn their ears from His Word: "Whosoever shall not receive you, nor hear your words...it shall be more tolerable for the land of Sodom and Gomorrah in the day of judgment, than for that city" (Matt. 10:14,15). All religious acts by the disobedient are obnoxious to God: "The sacrifice of the wicked is an abomination to Jehovah" (Prov. 15:8).

TEST QUESTIONS OVER 28:1-9

1. Give Bible examples of righteous people who were bold (v. 1).
2. Why does God judge nations here (v. 2)?
3. Comment upon "sweeping rain" from their weather pattern (v. 3).
4. Why do those who forsake the law "praise the wicked" (v. 4)?
5. Give Bible examples of the obedient contending with the wicked (v. 4).
6. Comment upon those who seek Jehovah understanding all things (v. 5).
7. The comparison in v. 6 is between what two classes?
8. Show from v. 7 that all people do not react the same.
9. Where does the wealth of the rich sometimes come from (v. 8)?
10. Comment upon turning away one's ears from God's law (v. 9).

TEXT — 28:10-18

10. Whoso causeth the upright to go astray in an evil way,
He shall fall himself into his own pit;
But the perfect shall inherit good.
11. The rich man is wise in his own conceit;
But the poor that hath understanding searcheth him out.
12. When the righteous triumph, there is great glory;
But when the wicked rise, men hide themselves.
13. He that covereth his transgressions shall not prosper;
But whoso confesseth and forsaketh them shall obtain mercy.
14. Happy is the man that feareth alway;
But he that hardeneth his heart shall fall into mischief.
15. As a roaring lion, and a ranging bear,
So is a wicked ruler over a poor people.
16. The prince that lacketh understanding is also a great oppressor;
But he that hateth covetousness shall prolong his days.
17. A man that is laden with the blood of any person
Shall flee unto the pit; let no man stay him.
18. Whoso walketh uprightly shall be delivered;
But he that is perverse in his ways shall fall at once.

STUDY QUESTIONS OVER 28:10-18

1. Who might cause the righteous to go astray (v. 10)?
2. Are all poor men ignorant men (v. 11)?
3. Is v. 12 referring primarily to rulers?
4. Cite a Bible example of one who tried to cover his transgression but did not prosper (v. 13).
5. Cite a Bible example of one who confessed and forsook sin and obtained mercy (v. 13).
6. In what sense is "fear" used in v. 14?
7. What would a wicked ruler do to his people (v. 15)?
8. Whom does his covetousness oppress (v. 16)?
9. Is v. 17 a "capital punishment" verse?
10. Is v. 18 another contrasting verse?

PARAPHRASE OF 28:10-18

10. A curse on those who lead astray the godly. But men who encourage the upright to do good shall be given a worthwhile reward.
11. Rich men are conceited, but their real poverty is evident to the poor.
12. When the godly are successful, everyone is glad. When the wicked succeed, everyone is sad.
13. A man who refuses to admit his mistakes can never be successful. But if he confesses and forsakes them, he gets another chance.
14. Blessed is the man who reveres God, but the man who doesn't care is headed for serious trouble.
15. A wicked ruler is as dangerous to the poor as a lion or bear attacking them.
16. Only a stupid prince will oppress his people, but a king will have a long reign if he hates dishonesty and bribes.
17. A murderer's conscience will drive him into hell. Don't stop him!
18. Good men will be rescued from harm, but cheaters will be destroyed.

COMMENTS ON 28:10-18

V. 10. "Clarke": "He who strives to pervert one really converted to God in order that he may pour contempt on religion shall fall into that hell to which he has endeavored to lead the other." Satan is out to cause the upright to go astray (I

Pet. 2:8; II Cor. 2:11). It is no wonder that those who are all-out for Satan cause many to stumble if they can: "They think it strange that ye run not with them into the same excess of riot, speaking evil of you" (I Pet. 4:4). About falling into one's own pit see Prov. 26:27. While the plotter falls into his own pit, the perfect (whose downfall he sought) will inherit good. David could say, "Thou preparest a table before me in the presence of mine enemies: Thou hast anointed my head with oil; My cup runneth over" (Psa. 23:5). Did you notice that our verse has three lines instead of the customary two?

V. 11. Because wealth and great earthly possessions often bring conceit to the rich, I Tim. 6:17 warns, "Charge them that are rich in this present world, that they be not highminded." because he is out to get more money, he may be plotting new schemes and moves to increase his wealth, but in so doing he may not fool some of the poor people. Some poor man of understanding may face him with what he is up to, to the rich man's embarrassment. Not all poor people are ignorant people.

V. 12. Judah knew what it was to have both good and bad kings. When men like Hezekiah and Josiah were on the throne, it was a glorious time for the nation. Prov. 11:10 says, "When it goeth well with the righteous, the city rejoiceth." Prov. 11:11: "By the blessing of the upright the city is exalted." But when wicked rulers like Ahaz and Manasseh came to power, there was fear. V. 28 also says, "When the wicked rise, men hide themselves," and "when the wicked perish there is shouting" (Prov. 11:11), and "the righteous increase" (Prov. 28:28). Because Archelaus was ruling in Judea, Joseph was afraid to settle there with his family. (Matt. 2:22,23).

V. 13. When one has done wrong, he can go one of two ways: either seek to cover or conceal his transgress (like Achan--Josh. 7:1,16-26) or confess the transgression and forsake it (like I John 1:9 teaches us to do: "If we confess our sins, he is faithful and righteous to forgive us our sins"). The Prodigal Son is a good example of the latter (Luke 15:21-24). When one tries to conceal sin when he should confess and forsake it, things are not going to go right. It is like keeping a thorn in one's hand that ought to be removed, like keeping a bad tooth in one's mouth that ought to be extracted, like driving a car that is badly out of time, etc. Not until one removes the bad and gets things fixed will things be like they ought to be. Nathan did King David a great favor when he dealt with him about his sin (II Sam. 12:1-13). After David 's sin was all over, after God had uncovered it, and after God had forgiven it, he could write, "Blessed is he whose transgression is forgiven, Whose sin is covered. Blessed is the man unto whom Jehovah imputeth not iniquity, And in whose spirit there is no guile"--no dishonesty in attempting to cover it up (Psa. 32:1,2). And then as he looked back at his own covering up attempt, he said, "When I kept silence, my bones wasted away through my groaning all the day long. For day and night thy hand was heavy upon me: My moisture was changed as with the drought of summer" (Psa. 32:3,4). Then Nathan came, and now David could say, "I acknowledged my sin unto thee, And mine iniquity did I not hide: I said, I will confess my transgressions unto Jehovah; And thou forgavest the iniquity of my sin" (Psa. 32:5).

V. 14. One's attitude toward God is under consideration. He will either fear God (the reverence and godly fear mentioned in Heb. 12:28 and Eccl. 12:13) and depart from evil (Prov. 16:6), or he will harden his heart so he won't fear, and he will continue in his sins. Rom. 2:5 speaks of this "hardness" and "impenitent heart," and they do go together. Prov. 23:13 says we should not envy sinners (that leads to sinning) but to be in the fear of Jehovah all day long.

V. 15. The next two verses have to do with "kings" as do a number of verses in Proverbs. The Hebrews' own history contained a classic example of a "wicked ruler" (Pharaoh) over a "poor people" (when he had them in Egyptian bondage). First the Egyptians "made their lives bitter with hard service, in mortar and in brick, and in all manner of service in the field, all their service, wherein they made them serve with rigor" (Exo. 1:14). But that wasn't enough, so Pharaoh said to the Egyptian midwives, "When ye do the office of a midwife to the Hebrew women, and see them upon the birth-stool; if it be a son, then ye shall kill him" (Exo. 1:16). And when he saw that that wasn't working, he issued this order to the Hebrew people themselves: "Every son that is born ye shall cast into the river" (Exo. 1:22). Wicked King Herod, who killed at will throughout his reign, was like a roaring lion and a ranging bear when he "sent forth, and slew all the male children that were in Bethlehem, and in all the borders thereof, from two years old and under" (Matt. 2:16).

V. 16. Greedy tyrants (like Hitler) want more and more territory, and they become great oppressors (such as he did of

Poland, France, England, Russia, and others). This verse says such a ruler lacks understanding: he does not have the welfare of his people at heart as many of them fall in his battles, and he finally bites off more than he can handle and is finally defeated (as Hitler was). "Bloodthirsty and deceitful men shall not live out half their days" (Psa. 55:23). In contrast the ruler who is not greedy ("hateth covetousness") shall prolong his days. The contrast of this verse is reflected in Psa. 37: "Evildoers shall be cut off; But those that wait for Jehovah, they shall inherit the land. For yet a little while, and the wicked shall not be: Yea, thou shalt diligently consider his place, and he shall not be. But the meek shall inherit the land, And shall delight themselves in the abundance of peace...The wicked have drawn out the sword, and have bent their bow, To cast down the poor and needy, To slay such as are upright in the way. Their sword shall enter into their own heart, And their bows shall be broken...I have seen the wicked in great power, And spreading himself like a green tree in its native soil. But one passed by, and, lo, he was not" (vs. 9-36).

V. 17. "Clarke": "He who...slays the innocent...may flee to hide himself: but let none given him protection. The law demands his life, because he is a murderer; and let none deprive justice of its claim. Murder is the most horrid crime." What law did "Clarke" have in mind? "Whoso sheddeth man's blood, by man shall his blood be shed" (Gen. 9:6); "He that smiteth a man, so that he dieth, shall surely be put to death" (Exo. 21:14); "Whoso killeth any person, the murderer shall be slain...Moreover ye shall take no ransom for the life of a murderer, that is guilty of death; but he shall surely be put to death...Blood, it polluteth the land; and no expiation can be made for the land for the blood that is shed therein, but by the blood of him that shed it" (Num. 35:30-33).

V. 18. A double contrast: "whoso walketh uprightly" vs. "he that is perverse in his ways" and "shall be delivered" vs. "shall fall at once". Prov. 10:9 is similar: "He that walketh uprightly walketh surely; But he that perverteth his ways shall be known." The right way to live proves to be the best way to live!

TEST QUESTIONS OVER 28:10-18

1. Comment upon the wicked causing the righteous to go astray (v. 10).
2. Describe a situation as you visualize one from v. 11.

3. Who were some of the good kings and then some of the bad ones of Judah's history (v. 12)?
4. What will happen if one tries to cover his transgression (v. 13)?
5. What will happen if he confesses and forsakes his transgression (v. 13)?
6. Comment upon the difference between fearing and hardening one's heart (v. 16).
7. Connect Pharaoh and Israel with the truth of v. 15.
8. How did Hitler exemplify v. 16?
9. What verse or verses of the Bible command capital punishment (v. 17)?
10. What is the double contrast in v. 18?

TEXT — 28:19-28

19. He that tilleth his land shall have plenty of bread;
But he that followeth after vain persons shall have poverty enough.
20. A faithful man shall abound with blessings;
But he that maketh haste to be rich shall not be unpunished.
21. To have respect of persons is not good;
Neither that a man should transgress for a piece of bread.
22. He that hath an evil eye hasteth after riches,
And knoweth not that want shall come upon him.
23. He that rebuketh a man shall afterward find more favor
Than he that flattereth with the tongue.
24. Whoso robbeth his father or his mother, and saith, It is no transgression,
The same is the companion of a destroyer.
25. He that is of a greedy spirit stirreth up strife;
But he that putteth his trust in Jehovah shall be made fat.
26. He that trusteth in his own heart is a fool;
But whoso walketh wisely, he shall be delivered.
27. He that giveth unto the poor shall not lack;
But he that hideth his eyes shall have many a curse.
28. When the wicked rise, men hide themselves;
But when they perish, the righteous increase.

STUDY QUESTIONS OVER 28:19-28

1. Describe one who is following vain persons (v. 19).
2. Why will the man seeking to be rich hastily suffer punishment (v. 20)?
3. What does a "piece of bread" in v. 21 imply?
4. Connect "evil eye" of v. 22 with "lust of the eye" of I John 2:16.
5. Who believes and who does not believe the statement in v. 23?
6. How perverse is one described in v. 24?
7. Why would the greedy stir up strife (v. 25)?
8. Cite a contrast between statements in vs. 25,26.
9. What wonderful promise does v. 27 contain?
10. Rise where (v. 28)?

PARAPHRASE OF 28:19-28

19. Hard work brings prosperity; playing around brings poverty.
20. The man who wants to do right will get a rich reward. But the man who wants to get rich quick will quickly fail.
21. Giving preferred treatment to rich people is a clear case of selling one's soul for a piece of bread.
22. Trying to get rich quick is evil and leads to poverty.
23. In the end, people appreciate frankness more than flattery.
24. A man who robs his parents and says, "What's wrong with that?" is no better than a murderer.
25. Greed causes fighting; trusting God leads to prosperity.
26. A man is a fool to trust himself! But those who use God's wisdom are safe.
27. If you give to the poor, your needs will be supplied! But a curse upon those who close their eyes to poverty.
28. When the wicked prosper, good men go away; when the wicked meet disaster, good men return.

COMMENTS ON 28:19-28

V. 19. Prov. 12:11 is very similar: "He that tilleth his land shall have plenty of bread; But he that followeth after vain persons is void of understanding." A double contrast: "he that tilleth his land" vs. "he that followeth after vain persons" and "shall have plenty of bread" vs. "shall have poverty enough". The normal and expected reward of honest labor is to be supplied from it ("bread"). Thus, Prov. 14:23 says, "In all labor there is profit." Getting in with the non-working bunch, with the play-around group, with the no-good element is a good way to have "poverty enough" instead of "plenty of bread". One's companionships will often affect his working-outlook.

V. 20. This is one of several verses dealing with getting-rich-quick: see v. 22; v. 25. Another double contrast: "a faithful man" vs. "he that maketh haste to be rich" and "shall abound with blessings" vs. "shall not be unpunished". Notice in Deut. 28:1-14 the promises that God made to Israel if they were faithful. "Abound" is related to "abundant". God will punish--not bless--one who hastens to be rich, for he has the wrong goal in mind, and he will likely sin in pursuing his goal: "They that are minded to be rich fall into a temptation and a snare and many foolish and hurtful lusts, such as drown men in destruction and perdition. For the love of money is a root of all kinds of evil: which some reaching after have been led astray from the faith, and have pierced themselves through with many sorrows" (I Tim. 6:9,10).

V. 21. The first statement is found in Prov. 18:5 also. We should not have respect of persons when it comes to right and wrong, truth and error. Wrong is wrong even if our best friend does it, and right is right even if somebody does it who doesn't like us personally. God will not save those who have not obeyed the gospel even if they are our relatives or friends. He has no respect of men's persons (Rom. 2:11). The second statement of our verse is probably mentioning another thing that should not be done; namely, transgressing for a paltry gain. Of course, the two statements might be related as when a judge would show respect for persons for a small bribe.

V. 22. Hastening after riches is also mentioned in v. 20. "Lust of the eyes" in I John 2:16 is desiring something that we should not have: it might be to desire one who is not our mate or to desire earthly gain at the expense of one's spirituality. This is an "evil eye" for it leads one into sin. Jesus mentions "evil eye" in Mark 7:22 and says it is one of the things that proceed from within man. We know that the eye feeds the heart, and the wicked heart prompts the eye to be evil—a vicious circle! Our verse is warning against getting-rich-quick, saying that such a one will in time lose it ("want shall come upon him").

V. 23. Prov. 27:5,6 praises "open rebuke" as "better" than "love that is hidden". Such "wounds of a friend" are said to be "faithful". Our verse says that one that rebukes a man will later find more favor than those who flattered the man when they should have been rebuking him. If a preacher believes this, he will be more faithful to God's Word and will not let the people be lost without saying something about their sins. The "smooth talkers" who never say anything about the sins of the people will really do the people no good. In time to come (sometimes years later) people will look back and have more respect for the honest, outspoken, plain-spoken man than for the coward who was full of good words and fair speeches.

V. 24. Why would somebody rob his father and mother? First of all, it would be easy to do as compared to robbing anybody else, for he would know where everything was, he would be present in the house at times when they weren't, etc. Or, he might think they would be more lenient upon him than upon somebody else, if what he did was ever found out. Or, he might salve his conscience by saying, "It's all going to belong to us children in time anyway." This last thought could account for his saying to himself, "It is no transgression." But as long as one's parents live, it is still theirs, and to take from them is robbing, and the "whoso" of our verse shows that it doesn't matter who does it, it is still robbing. How perverse to rob the very ones who gave him life, provisions, and rearing.!
He is a "companion of a destroyer" because he is destroying their financial holdings. A similar expression ("brother to him that is a destroyer") is said of a lazy person (Prov. 18:9).

V. 25. "He that is of a greedy spirit" is put over against "he that putteth his trust in Jehovah". Most people who have lived on the earth could have used more than they had, especially at times. Some have been able to content themselves with the bare necessities ("having food and covering we shall be therewith content"--I Tim. 6:8), trusting the Lord to take care of them through the situation. But others of a greedy spirit will not thus content themselves. They fret under their situation and will do anything to get their hands on more, and their greediness usually results in trouble ("stirreth up strife"), for in order for him to get more, it usually means that somebody else has less. He usually outwits somebody else, and hard feelings result. But in the long run, who ends up better? The one who trusts in Jehovah "shall be made fat" (be prosperous).

V. 26. This may or may not be connected with v. 25. If it is, it talks of the greedy one trusting in his own schemes rather than in God, and the one who walks wisely is the one who trusts in God. Likely, though, it is not connected but is another saying all by itself. If so, what does it mean? Always should one trust God and what He says. When one's heart says to do something but God says not to, we should do what He says. This is walking wisely, and he will end up blessed ("he shall be delivered"). But oh, how many will go "their" way instead of "God's"! That is why God said, "My thoughts are not your thoughts, neither are your ways my ways" (Isa. 55:8). He calls upon those thus living to "forsake his way, and...his thoughts; and...return to Jehovah" (Isa. 55:7). Jeremiah knew the human heart when he said, "O Jehovah, I know that the way of man is not in himself; it is not in man that walketh to direct his steps" (Jer. 10:23); and, "The heart is deceitful above all things, and it is exceedingly corrupt: who can know it?" (Jer. 17:9).

V. 27. Jesus said there will always be some poor among us (Mark 14:7), and He went on to say, "Whensoever ye will ye can do them good" (same verse). As we have opportunity, therefore, to give to the poor and needy, we are to do so (Gal. 6:10; I John 3:17). Deut. 15:7 says, "If there be with thee a poor man, one of thy brethren, within any of thy gates in thy land which Jehovah thy God giveth thee, thou shalt not harden thy heart, not shut thy hand from thy poor brother." Prov. 22:9 also says a man shall be blessed who "giveth of his bread to the poor". God will repay all that we give to the poor (Prov. 19:17). Our verse talks about hiding one's eyes from the poor. This is what many do as they merrily go on their own way or busily pursue their business interests. Listen to Prov. 29:7: "The righteous taketh knowledge of the cause of the poor; The wicked hath not understanding to know it." So Jesus made a helpful Samaritan the hero of His parable and the heartless Jewish priest and Levite the goats (Luke 10:30-37). The ultimate blessing and curse to come upon us for our dealings with the poor will be at the Judgment (Matt. 25:34-46).

V. 28. "Rise to power" is the thought. How tragic that in the world's history there have been so many wicked as rulers! This may be partly due to the humility of the godly, causing them to be meek among men, not seeking places of eminence even though they be places of service to mankind. But the wicked are often graspy, covetousness, and proud, and they by nature seek such places of prominence. The first statement of our verse is also found in v. 12. Prov. 29: 2 says, "When a wicked man beareth rule, the people sigh." Israel probably liked the first years of Solomon's reign, when he was seeking to do God's will, better than his latter years, when he was idolatrous. They demanded a more civil rule from his son Rehoboam (I Kings 12:4). Our verse shows that when the wicked leadership passes, righteousness increases to the true exaltation of the nation (Prov. 14:34). "Pulpit Commentary": "The overthrow of the ungodly adds to the prosperity of the righteous...promotes their advancement in influence and numbers."

TEST QUESTIONS OVER 28:19-28

1. What word or thought is emphatic in v. 19?
2. What about getting in with the non-working, play-around group (v. 19)?
3. According to the contrast in v. 20, one hastening to be rich is probably not a .... man.
4. What New Testament passage shows the dangers of desiring to be rich (v. 20)?
5. Should we put "persons" before "principle" (v. 21)?
6. What vicious circle was discussed under v. 22?
7. What are the "wounds of a friend" (v. 23)?
8. In what sense is "companion" used in v. 24?
9. Comment upon v. 25.
10. Does v. 26 show that our thoughts are sometimes wrong?
11. What is the double contrast in v. 27?
12. Why have so many rulers been wicked men (v. 28)?

NOTICEABLE GROUPINGS IN CHAPTER 28

"Wicked"--

"The wicked flee when no man pursueth" (v. 1).
"They that forsake the law praise the wicked" (v. 4).
"Evil men understand not justice" (v. 5).
"Better is the poor that walketh in his integrity, Than he that is perverse in his ways, though he be rich" (v. 6).
"When the wicked rise, men hide themselves" (vs. 12,28).
"He that is perverse in his ways shall fall at once" (v. 18).

"Poor"--

"A needy man that oppresseth the poor Is like a sweeping

rain which leaveth no food" (v. 3).

"Better is the poor that walketh in his integrity, Than he that is perverse in his ways, though he be rich" (v. 6).

"He that augmenteth his substance by interest and increase, Gathereth it for him that hath pity on the poor" (v. 8).

"The poor that hath understanding searcheth him out" (v. 11).

"As a roaring lion, and a ranging bear, So is a wicked ruler over a poor people" (v. 15).

"He that giveth unto the poor shall not lack; But he that hideth his eyes shall have many a curse" (v. 27).

"Obedient"--

"Such as keep the law contend with them" (v. 4).

"Whoso keepeth the law is a wise son" (v. 7).

"The perfect shall inherit good" (v. 10).

"Ruler"--

"For the transgression of a land many are the princes thereof" (v. 2).

"As a roaring lion, and a ranging bear, So is a wicked ruler over a poor people" (v. 15).

"The prince that lacketh understanding is also a great oppressor; But he that hateth covetousness shall prolong his days" (v. 16).

"Pit"--

"Whoso causeth the upright to go astray in an evil way, He shall fall himself into his own pit" (v. 10).

"A man that is laden with the blood of any person Shall flee unto the pit" (v. 17).

"Bad associates"--

"He that is a companion of gluttons shameth his father" (v. 7).

"He that followeth vain persons shall have poverty enough" (v. 19).

"Riches"--

"Better is the poor that walketh in his integrity, Than he that is perverse in his ways though he be rich" (v. 6).

"He that augmenteth his substance by interest and increase, Gathereth it for him that hath pity on the poor" (v. 8).

"The rich man is wise in his own conceit" (v. 11).
"He that maketh haste to be rich shall not be unpunished" (v. 20).
"He that hath an evil eye hasteth after riches, And knoweth not that want shall come upon him" (v. 22).
"He that is of a greedy spirit stirreth up strife" (v. 25).

"Righteous--

"The righteous are bold as a lion" (v. 1).
"When the righteous triumph, there is great glory" (v. 12).

"Children"--

"Whoso keepeth the law is a wise son; But he that is a companion of gluttons shameth his father" (v. 7).
"Whoso robbeth his father or his mother, and saith, It is no transgression, The same is the companion of a destroyer" (v. 24).

"Understanding"--

"By men of understanding and knowledge the state thereof shall be prolonged" (v. 2).
"Evil men understand not justice; But they that seek Jehovah understand all things" (v. 5).
"The poor that hath understanding searcheth him out" (v. 11).
"The prince that lacketh understanding is also a great oppressor" (v. 16).

"Oppression"--

"A needy man that oppresseth the poor Is like a sweeping rain which leaveth no food" (v. 3).
"The prince that lacketh understanding is also a great oppressor" (v. 16).
"A man that is laden with the blood of any person Shall flee unto the pit" (v. 17).

Transgress"--

"For the transgression of a land many are the princes thereof" (v. 2).
"He that covereth his transgressions shall not prosper" (v. 13).
"Whoso robbeth his father or his mother, and saith, It is no transgression, The same is the companion of a destroyer" (v. 24).

"Hide"--

"When the wicked rise, men hide themselves" (vs. 12,28).

"He that covereth his transgressions shall not prosper" (v. 13).

"He that hideth his eyes shall have many a curse" (v. 27).

"Law"--

"They that forsake the law praise the wicked; But such as keep the law contend with them" (v. 4).

"Whoso keepeth the law is a wise son" (v. 7).

"He that turneth away his ear from hearing the law, Even his prayer is an abomination" (v. 9).

FOOLS THINK IT IS SMART TO SIN

"It is as sport to a fool to do mischief" (10:23). They think it is smart to cuss somebody out. Some think it is smart to smoke more cigarettes or drink more beers than others. One fool will brag to another fool about how many women he has had. Proverbs has well pin-pointed such people when it calls them fools.

We can surely see the truth of 14:9, "Fools make a mock at sin."

You try to get a fool to repent of his sinful ways, and he will make fun of you and laugh about sin. He is not about to give up his crowd and his fun. Nothing would be more miserable to him to settle down and live the Christian life. To him, nothing would be more miserable; therefore, to him, nothing is more unthinkable. 13:19 says, "It is abomination to fools to depart from evil." He doesn't think any evil is going to come upon him because of the way he is living. 14:16 puts it like this, "A wise man feareth and departeth from evil: but the fool rageth, and is confident."

TEXT – 29:1-9

1. He that being often reproved hardeneth his neck
   Shall suddenly be destroyed, and that without remedy.
2. When the righteous are increased, the people rejoice;
   But when a wicked man beareth rule, the people sigh.
3. Whoso loveth wisdom rejoiceth his father;
   But he that keepeth company with harlots wasteth his substance.
4. The king by justice establisheth the land;
   But he that exacteth gifts overthroweth it.
5. A man that flattereth his neighbor
   Spreadeth a net for his steps.
6. In the transgression of an evil man there is a snare;
   But the righteous doth sing and rejoice.
7. The righteous taketh knowledge of the cause of the poor;
   The wicked hath not understanding to know it.
8. Scoffers set a city in a flame;
   But wise men turn away wrath.
9. If a wise man hath a controversy with a foolish man,
   Whether he be angry or laugh, there will be no rest.

STUDY QUESTIONS OVER 29:1-9

1. What strong warning does v. 1 contain?
2. What verses in Proverbs besides v. 2 state similar truth?
3. What character in a parable of Jesus fulfilled the last statement of v. 3?
4. Reword the last statement of v. 4.
5. A previous verse on flattery said, "A flattering tongue ...."
6. A "snare" to whom (v. 6)?
7. Does v. 7 indicate that the righteous themselves are not always poor?
8. How would scoffers set a city aflame (v. 8)?
9. Does "whether he be angry or laugh" go with "wise man" or "foolish man" (v. 9)?

PARAPHRASE OF 29:1-9

1. The man who is often reproved but refuses to accept criticism will suddenly be broken and never have

another chance.

2. With good men in authority, the people rejoice; but with the wicked in power, they groan.
3. A wise son makes his father happy, but a lad who hangs around with prostitutes disgraces him.
4. A just king gives stability to his nation, but one who demands bribes destroys it.

5,6. Flattery is a trap; evil men are caught in it, but good men stay away and sing for joy.

7. The good man knows the poor man's rights; the godless don't care.
8. Fools start fights everywhere while wise men try to keep peace.
9. There's no use arguing with a fool. He only rages and scoffs, and tempers flare.

COMMENTS ON 29:1-9

V. 1. Jehovah had tried to get Judah to do right, but they would not listen; therefore, He destroyed them without remedy: "Jehovah...sent to them by his messengers, rising up early and sending...but they mocked the messengers of God, and despised his words, and scoffed at his prophets, until the wrath of Jehovah arose against his people, until there was no remedy" (II Chron. 36:15,17). When wisdom is thus despised, this is the result: "Ye have set at naught all my counsel, and would none of my reproof...when your fear cometh as a storm, and your calamity cometh on as a whirlwind; when distress and anguish come upon you, then will they call upon me, but I will not answer" (Prov. 1:25-28).

V. 2. The contrast is between a righteous and a wicked ruler and between the people's rejoicing under the righteous ruler and their sighing under the wicked. Previous contrasts involving the same in Proverbs: "When it goeth well with the righteous, the city rejoiceth; And when the wicked perish, there is shouting" (11:10); "When the righteous triumph, there is great glory; But when the wicked rise, men hide themselves" (28:12); "When the wicked rise, men hide themselves; But when they perish, the righteous increase" (28:28).

V. 3. This verse talks of two altogether different kinds of sons and the consequences. Other passages showing a son's conduct's effect upon his parents: "A wise son maketh a glad father; But a foolish son is the heaviness of his mother" (Prov.

10:1); "A wise son maketh a glad father, But a foolish man despiseth his mother" (Prov. 15:20); "My son, be wise, and make my heart glad" (Prov. 27:11). Yes, men have been made poor though their evil lusts: "Lest strangers be filled with thy strength" (Prov. 5:10)--margin says "wealth" instead of "strength"; "On account of a harlot a man is brought to a piece of bread" (Prov. 6:26). The Prodigal Son "wasted his substance with riotous living" (Luke 15:13). According to his elder brother, he spent it on "harlots" (Luke 15:30).

V. 4. A double contrast: "by justice" vs. "exacteth gifts" and "establisheth the land" vs. "overthroweth it". When a king rules according to the laws of justice, things go well with both him and the land, for God blesses, and the people are happy. The bribe-taking king ("he that exacteth gifts") overthrows it because such is not right, God is not pleased, and the people do not approve it.

V. 5. Flattery is insincere compliments. This verse shows it is "buttering" a person in order to "eat" him. "A flattering tongue worketh ruin" (Prov. 26:28). When some people speak "fair", they should not be believed; their hearts may be filled with abominations (Prov. 26:25). The flatteries of our verse are nothing more than something that will draw one's attentions away from the net that is being spread in one's way. Such operate on the idea expressed in Prov. 1:17: "In vain is the net spread in the sight of any bird."

V. 6. The contrast within the verse shows that the "snare" ensnares the transgressor himself. This very language is used in several other passages, all relating to one's transgression: "A fool's mouth is his destruction, And his lips are the snare of his soul" (Prov. 18:7); "It is a snare to a man rashly to say, It is holy and vows to make inquiry" (Prov. 20:25); "Lest thou learn his ways, and get a snare to thy soul" (Prov. 22:25). But righteousness does not ensnare one; it leads to singing and rejoicing.

V. 7. The righteous give to the poor because they first of all take knowledge of their situation and then care. Because the wicked do not care, they do not bother themselves to take knowledge of their condition, and if they know about it, they dismiss it from their thoughts. Job is an example of one who investigated need: "I was a father to the needy: And the cause of him that I knew not I searched out" (Job 29:16). Psa. 41:1 says, "Blessed is he that considereth the poor." This would not be the priest and the Levite of Jesus' parable (Luke 10:31,33).

V. 8. The setting of this verse is an attacked or besieged city. Men may scoff at the enemy that is able to overthrow the city. Conquerors often spared a city destruction if it surrendered, but if it resisted, it was conquered and then destroyed. Thus, "it is overthrown by the mouth of the wicked" (Prov. 11:11). The wise men who turn away wrath would be those who, seeing that they were hopelessly outnumbered and defeated, asked for terms or conditions of peace.

V. 9. When a foolish men is encountered in a controversy, he may get angry (realizing he is getting the worst end of it), or he may laugh (not sensing that he is being defeated). Such a controversy never comes to a suitable, satisfying point of conclusion as it should. "Pulpit Commentary": "After all has been said, the fool only falls into a passion or laughs at the matter, argument is wasted upon him, and the controversy is never settled." "Wordsworth": "The irreligious fool is won neither by the austere preaching of John the Baptist nor by the mild teaching of Christ, but rejects both (Matt. 11:16-19)."

TEST QUESTIONS OVER 29:1-9

1. What was cited as an example of v. 1?
2. Comment upon v. 2.
3. Tie v. 3 in with Prov. 6:32.
4. Comment upon the truthfulness of v. 4.
5. Why does one seeking another's destruction employ flattery at times (v. 5)?
6. Where else is "snare" used in this sense (v. 6)?
7. Why do the righteous take knowledge of the poor (v. 7)? Why don't the wicked?
8. What is the setting of v. 8?
9. Comment upon v. 9.

TEXT — 29:10-18

10. The bloodthirsty hate him that is perfect:
And as for the upright, they seek his life.
11. A fool uttereth all his anger;
But a wise man keepeth it back and stilleth it.
12. If a ruler hearkeneth to falsehood, all his servants are wicked.
13. The poor man and the oppressor met together;

Jehovah lighteneth the eyes of them both.
14. The king that faithfully judgeth the poor,
His throne shall be established for ever.
15. The rod and reproof give wisdom;
But a child left to himself causeth shame to his mother.
16. When the wicked are increased, transgression increaseth;
But the righteous shall look upon their fall.
17. Correct thy son, and he will give thee rest;
Yea, he will give delight unto thy soul.
18. Where there is no vision, the people cast off restraint;
But he that keepeth the law, happy is he.

STUDY QUESTIONS OVER 29:10-18

1. What two things does v. 10 say the bloodthirsty do?
2. What does v. 11 say about losing one's temper?
3. Why would this be the case (v. 12)?
4. Why does v. 13 say, "Jehovah lighteneth the eyes of them both"?
5. What promise does v. 14 contain?
6. Differentiate between "rod" and "reproof" (v. 15)?
7. Describe a child "left to himself" (v. 15).
8. What increases trangression (v. 16)?
9. Comment upon the truthfulness of the first statement in v. 17.
10. What two things will a properly trained child bring to his parents (v. 17)?
11. What is meant by "vision" in v. 18?

PARAPHRASE OF 29:10-18

10. The godly pray for those who long to kill them.
11. A rebel shouts his anger; a wise man holds his temper in and cools it.
12. A wicked ruler will have wicked aides on his staff.
13. Rich and poor are alike in this: each depends on God for light.
14. A king who is fair to the poor shall have a long reign.
15. Scolding and spanking a child helps him to learn. Left to himself, he brings shame to his mother.
16. When rulers are wicked, their people are too; but good men will live to see the tyrant's downfall.

17. Discipline your son and he will give you happiness and peace of mind.
18. Where there is ignorance of God, the people run wild; but what a wonderful thing it is for a nation to know and keep His laws!

COMMENTS ON 29:10-18

V. 10. One must pause to analyze this verse. It is Hebrew parallelism in which the latter statement is a restatement of the first. Let us rerun the verse in our own understanding of it: "The bloodthirsty hate him that is perfect; they (the bloodthirsty) seek the life of the upright." Why do they do this? Some out of envy (like Cain--I John 3:12). Some because they are rebuked by the upright (like Ahab--I Kings 22:7,8). Some because the upright are an abomination to them (see v. 27 of this chapter). Some because they fear the upright (like King Saul--I Sam. 18:5-9; 24:17-20; 26:1,2). Some because they can more easily get what the perfect have than they can what others have (see Prov. 1:11-13). Three times does Psa. 37 refer to the wicked seeking to devour the righteous: "The wicked plotteth against the just, And gnasheth upon him with his teeth" (v. 12); "The wicked have drawn out the sword, and have bent their bow, To cast down the poor and needy, to slay such as are upright in the way" (v. 14); "The wicked watcheth the righteous, and seeketh to slay him" (v. 32).

V. 11. A fool does not exercise self-control, for self-control is based upon wisdom which he does not have. Therefore, a wise person quiets his spirit when it could erupt, but a fool doesn't. Compare Prov. 14:33: "Wisdom resteth in the heart of him that hath understanding; but that which is in the inward part of fools is made known."

V. 12. This verse pictures a wicked ruler of which there have been many. Both their advisers are wicked (he hearkens to their "falsehood"), and his servants are "wicked". A wicked ruler, wicked counselors, and wicked servants can only add up to a wicked reign.

V. 13. Prov. 22:2 is similar. Whether a man is poor or an oppressor, God has made him (Prov. 22:2), he lives in God's world, and he is a recipient of God's good whether he makes good use or it or not: "He maketh his sun to rise on the evil and the good, and sendeth rain on the just and the unjust" (Matt.

5:45). This does not say that God is pleased with both (or with either).

V. 14. There will be the poor in every king's realm, and the law of God is to care for them: "The poor will never cease out of the land: therefore I command thee, saying, 'thou shalt surely open thy hand unto thy brother, to thy needy, and to thy poor, in thy land" (Deut. 15:11). This verse makes a special promise to the king who obeys God's will in the matter as does Psa. 72:2,3: "'He will judge thy people with righteousness, And thy poor with justice. The mountains shall bring peace to the people, And the hills, in righteousness." Other factors establishing one's throne: "Kindness and truth" (Prov. 20:28); "Righteousness" (Prov. 25:5).

V. 15. When children misbehave, they need correction ("Correct thy son, and he will give thee rest"--Prov. 29:17). If you don't, if you let him keep on in his ways, he will bring "shame to his mother" and other heartaches to both parents: "A foolish son is the heaviness of his mother" (Prov. 10:1); "He that begetteth a fool doeth it to his sorrow; And the father of a fool hath no joy" (Prov. 17:21); "A foolish son is a grief to his father, And bitterness to her that bare him" (Prov. 17:25). In correcting, some merely "talk" to their children, and others merely "whip" them. But this verse points out the necessity of doing both properly, for it speaks of the "rod" (whipping) and of "reproof" (talking) giving wisdom. Don't you want your child to be wise? Then wisely reprove him and wisely whip him. This is Bible: Prov. 19:18; 22:15; 23:13,14; Eph. 6:4; Heb. 12:9. A child "left to himself" is one who is neglected, whose parents have not taught him, have not overseen him, have not been with him, have not loved him, and have not corrected him. "Pulpit Commentary": "The verb translated 'left' is used in Job 39:5 of the wild ass left to wander free where it wills." No child is capable of self-rearing. Such neglected offspring "causeth shame". His parents who neglected him will be ashamed of him, and his desire to get away from home will probably be matched by their relief to see him go!

V. 16. The more wicked those people are, the more sin there will be. Sin spreads like a mighty contagion: "Because iniquity shall be multiplied, the love of the many will wax cold" (Matt. 24;12). John tells us that there has been a big "take-over" of this world by sin: "The whole world lieth in the evil one" (I John 5:19). Paul speaks of "this present evil world"

(Gal. 1:4). If you "follow the crowd," you will be lost, for Jesus said, "Wide is the gate, and broad is the way, that leadeth to destruction, and many are they that enter in thereby" (Matt. 7:14). Knowing the tendency of mankind to do whatever the crowd does, Exo. 23:2 says, "Thou shalt not follow a multitude to do evil; neither shalt thou speak in a cause to turn aside after a multitude to wrest justice". Thank God, there will always be some who will not give in to the ways of the world. They are "the righteous". There will always be a "Noah" or a "Jeremiah" or an "Elijah" or a "Daniel" or a "Caleb and Joshua" to uphold what is right and who will be spared when the wicked fall: "He that dwelleth in the secret place of the Most High shall surely abide under the shadow of the Almighty...A thousand shall fall at thy side, And ten thousand at thy right hand; But it shall not come nigh thee. Only with thine eyes shalt thou behold, And see the reward of the wicked" (Psa. 91:1-8).

V. 17. Any godly parent is grieved at the wrongdoing of a child. And an undisciplined child will go from bad to worse until his parents' nerves can take no more. "Correct" him, and he will give you "rest"; yes, and more: he will actually grow out into something good to bring "Delight" to your heart. Your author observes in his book, "Simple, Stimulating Studies in the Proverbs": "Some parents have no rest because of the misdeeds of their children. They are always into something, always tearing something up, always breaking something, always doing something the parents don't want them to do; in short, they weary the parents going from one thing to another. The right kind of correction...will not only give you rest concerning your child, but the child will actually be a delight to your soul. What a difference!"

V. 18. The word "vision" here implies the inspired message of God (often by a living representative of it). When there was not prophet to reveal God's will to the people or no preacher to hinder their going into sin, people get into sin with nothing to restrain them. "We note the license of Eli's time, when there was no open vision (I Sam.3:1); in Asa's day, when Israel had long been without a teaching priest (II Chron. 15:3); and when the impious Ahaz 'made Judah naked' (II Chron. 28:19); or when the people were destroyed by reason of lack of knowledge of Divine things (Hos. 4:6)" ("Pulpit Commentary"). Yet, even in those days there would still be some who would keep the law, and those who did would be blessed of God:

"Blessed are they that hear the word of God, and keep it" (Luke 11:28); "If you know these things, blessed are ye if ye do them" (John 13:17); "He that looketh into the perfect law...and so continueth, being not a hearer that forgetteth but a doer that worketh, this man shall be blessed in his doing" (Jas. 1:25).

TEST QUESTIONS OVER 29:10-18

1. Why do the wicked seek the life of the upright (v. 10)?
2. Self-control is based upon what which a fool lacks (v. 11)?
3. Locate three wicked persons or groups in v. 12.
4. Where did Jesus show that God makes earthly benefits available to both just and unjust (v. 13)?
5. What is God's promise for the king who properly regards the poor in his realm (v. 14)?
6. According to v. 15, where do some parents fail?
7. Who have been some of the righteous when sin has flourished (v. 16)?
8. Correction of a child can change a parent's disgust to ....(v. 17).
9. Comment upon the first statement in v. 18.
10. What are some Bible promises to the obedient (v. 18)?

TEXT — 29:19-27

19. A servant will not be corrected by words;
For though he understand, he will not give heed.
20. Seest thou a man that is hasty in words?
There is more hope of a fool than of him.
21. He that delicately bringeth up his servant from a child
Shall have him become a son at last.
22. An angry man stirreth up strife,
And a wrathful man aboundeth in transgression.
23. A man's pride shall bring him low;
But he that is of a lowly spirit shall obtain honor.
24. Whoso is partner with a thief hateth his own soul;
He heareth the adjuration and uttereth nothing.
25. The fear of man bringeth a snare;
But whoso putteth his trust in Jehovah shall be safe.
26. Many seek the ruler's favor;
But a man's judgment cometh from Jehovah.
27. An unjust man is an abomination to the righteous;

And he that is upright in the way is an abomination to the wicked.

STUDY QUESTIONS OVER 29:19-27

1. What kind of person do you envision in v. 19?
2. Our saying, "Think before you ....," is similar to v. 20.
3. Why would v. 21 be so?
4. Find other passages in the Bible on anger to go along with v. 22.
5. Cite some New Testament passages that say the same as v. 23.
6. What does "adjuration" mean (v. 24)?
7. Illustrate the first statement of v. 25.
8. What do you understand by v. 26?
9. Is v. 27 why people usually change crowds when they become Christians?

PARAPHRASE OF 29:19-27

19. Sometimes mere words are not enough--discipline is needed. For the words may not be heeded.
20. There is more hope for a fool than for a man of quick temper.
21. Pamper a servant from childhood, and he will expect you to treat him as a son!
22. A hot-tempered man starts fights and gets into all kinds of trouble.
23. Pride ends in a fall, while humility brings honor.
24. A man who assists a thief must really hate himself! For he knows the consequence but does it anyway.
25. Fear of man is a dangerous trap, but to trust in God means safety.
26. Do you want justice? Don't fawn on the judge, but ask the Lord for it.
27. The good hate the badness of the wicked. The wicked hate the goodness of the good.

COMMENTS ON 29:19-27

V. 19. Servants were an uneducated group of persons. Personal gain and advancement held no motivation for them. There were likely times when they would sulk. When they got into this mood, it took more than words to get them going again. Bodily punishment was the only "language" that would get through to them ("A whip for the horse, a bridle for the ass, And a rod for the back of fools"--Prov. 26:3), and sometimes not even that worked ("A rebuke entereth deeper into one that hath understanding than a hundred stripes into a fool"--Prov. 17:10). Such sullen, unresponding stubbornness might result in his death or his sale. An observation: Such stubbornness is not limited to slaves of long-ago. There are people who will not respond to words of wisdom, for even though they understand, they prefer the preservation of their ego than giving heed to the wisdom of another.

V. 20. Yes, there are some who are hasty of speech. They may be nervous, fidgety people to whom a moment of silence is killing and who speak from the top of their heads instead of the bottom their hearts. Such will have many an apology to make throughout life or suffer the loss of friends. Or some are hasty of speech because of not being aware of the problems that can be caused by such utterances. We have a saying, "Think before you speak." Some say, "think twice before you speak." A quick-tongued person suffers from this verse's comparison ("There is more hope of a fool than of him") as does a conceited man in Prov. 26:12.

V. 21. "Delicately bringeth up" means to pamper, to spoil, to give one privileges and favors without expecting corresponding responsibilities and obligations. On "son", the marginal note reads: "The meaning of the word is doubtful," accounting for various translations: "ungrateful" (Ewald); "as a son" ("American Bible Union"); "his continuator" ("Young's Literal"). "Clarke" observes that "such persons are generally forgetful of their obligations, assume the rights and privileges of children, and are seldom good for anything." Isn't that true of most people who are "delicately brought up", pampered, spoiled? Such boys grow up to be men in name only, and such girls grow up to be poor wives.

V. 22. Hebrew parallelism again: "angry man" and "wrathful man"; "stirreth up" and "aboundeth"; and "strife" and "transgression". Prov. 15:8 says, "A wrathful man stirreth up contention;" and Prov. 28:25 says, "He that is of a greedy spirit stirreth up strife." One who is angry is stirred up, and this causes him to say things and to do things that stirs up strife in others. This "strife" is not usually a passing thing, but it causes transgression to abound. Because of this Eph. 4:26

says, "be ye angry, and sin not." In other words, when angry, take care that you do not sin by what you do and say. How can one keep from sinning further when angry? By taking care of oneself instead of the other fellow: "Let not the sun go down upon your wrath" (Eph. 4:26)--get yourself under control immediately. Let us remember Jas. 1:20: "The wrath of man worketh not the righteousness of God."

V. 23. Each individual will have likes and dislikes, spirit, and desires, but just as v. 22 shows that such can get out of control by way of anger, this verse shows that such can get out of control by way of pride. Man's pride is when he is puffed up, but such actually leads down instead of up. Humility (being of a lowly spirit) actually leads up instead. Others sense a person's pride and deplore it. So does God. Both are against promoting such. For teaching and instances of this subject, see Prov. 15:33; 16:18; 18:12; Isa. 66:2; Dan. 4:30,31; Matt. 23:12; Luke 14:11; Luke 18:14; Acts 12:23; Jas. 4:6,10; I. Pet. 5:6.

V. 24. This is a court scene. The thief is brought in, and the one wronged. The judge has pronounced a curse upon the thief and upon anyone who knows the crime but refuses to divulge the information. He "hateth his own soul" in that he is bringing a curse upon himself by his action.

V. 25. What "snare"? "The snare of the devil" (II Tim. 2:26). Fearing men caused Abraham to deny that Sarah was his wife (Gen. 12:11-13; 20:2), some of the Jewish rulers who believed on Jesus not to say openly (John 12:42), Peter to deny Jesus (Matt. 26:69-74) and to withdraw himself from some Gentiles (Ga. 2:12), leaders to compromise the truth (I Sam. 15:24), weak Christians to recant under persecution (Matt. 13:20,21), etc. This is one of the greatest causes of preachers failing to preach the Word of God as they should.

V. 26. The last statement of the verse indicates that people try to buy off the king from condemning them in court. They will do everything they can (legitimate and illegitimate) to secure his favorable verdict, but even if they succeed in doing this, they still have God to deal with. Men may have let Jonah on board, but God still prevailed in his case. Ahab may have gotton Naboth's vineyard, but God didn't let him enjoy it (I Kings 21:17-19).

V. 27. The just and the unjust live in the same world, both eat to sustain physical life, live in houses, etc., but there the comparison ends, for they have adopted altogether different ways of living. The righteous deplore the ways of the wicked (stealing, lying, cheating, drinking, fighting, hating, immorality, etc.). Jesus commended the church at Ephesus: "Thou canst not bear evil men" (Rev. 2:2). But the wicked deplore the upright just as much, for their ways are a rebuke to them. The wicked have often persecuted the righteous.

TEST QUESTIONS OVER 29:19-27

1. V. 19 reflects what attitude sometimes encountered even today?
2. What kind of person is often "hasty in his words" (v. 20)?
3. What often happens when people are pampered in childhood (v. 21)?
4. What does the New Testament say about man's wrath (v. 22)?
5. Cite other passages of Scripture on pride besides v. 23.
6. V. 24 pictures what kind of scene?
7. Cite Bible instances of v. 25.
8. Whose favor in v. 26 should one be seeking?
9. What is mutual, according to v. 27?

NOTICEABLE GROUPINGS IN CHAPTER 29

"*Ruler*"--

"When a wicked man beareth rule, the people sigh" (v. 2).
"The king by justice established the land; But he that exacteth gifts overthroweth it" (v. 4).
"If a ruler hearkeneth to falsehood, all his servants are wicked" (v. 12).
"The king that faithfully judgeth the poor, His throne shall be established for ever" (v. 14).
"Many seek the ruler's favor" (v. 26).

"*Righteous*"--

"When the righteous are increased, the people rejoice" (v. 2).
"The righteous doth sing and rejoice" (v. 6).
"The righteous take knowledge of the cause of the poor" (v. 7).
"The righteous shall look upon their fall" (v. 16).
"An unjust man is an abomination to the righteous" (v. 27).
"He that is upright in the way is an abomination to the wicked" (v. 27).

"*Trap*"--

"A man that flattereth his neighbor Spreadeth a net for his steps" (v. 5).

"In the transgression of an evil man there is a snare" (v. 6).

"*Wise*"--

"Whoso loveth wisdom rejoiceth his father" (v. 3).

"Wise men turn away wrath" (v. 8).

"If a wise man hath a controversy with a foolish man, Whether he be angry or laugh, there will be no rest" (v. 9).

"A wise man keepeth it back and stilleth it" (v. 11).

"The rod and reproof give wisdom" (v. 15).

"*Parenthood*"--

"Whoso loveth wisdom rejoiceth his father; But he that keepeth company with harlots wasteth his substance" (v. 3).

"The rod and reproof give wisdom; But a child left to himself causeth shame to his mother" (v. 15).

"Correct thy son, and he will give thee rest; Yea, he will give delight unto thy soul" (v. 17).

"He that delicately bringeth up his servant from a child Shall have him become a son at the last" (v. 21).

"*Destruction*"--

"He that being often reproved hardeneth his neck shall suddenly be destroyed, and that without remedy" (v. 1).

"He that exacteth gifts overthroweth it" (v. 4).

"A man that flattereth his neighbor spreadeth a net for his steps" (v. 5).

"Scoffers set a city in a flame" (v. 8).

"The righteous look upon their fall" (v. 16).

"*Wicked*"--

"In the transgression of an evil man there is a snare" (v. 6).

"The wicked hath not understanding to know it" (v. 7).

"The bloodthirsty hate him that is perfect; And as for the upright, they seek his life" (v. 10).

"If a ruler hearkeneth to falsehood, all his servants are wicked" (v. 12).

"When the wicked are increased, transgression increaseth" (v. 16).

"*Abomination*"--

"The bloodthirsty hate him that is perfect" (v. 10).

"An unjust man is an abomination to the righteous; And he

that is upright in the way is an abomination to the wicked" (v. 27).

"*Poor*"--

"The righteous taketh knowledge of the cause of the poor; The wicked hath not understanding to know it" (v. 7).

"The poor and the oppressor meet together; Jehovah lighteneth the eyes of them both" (v. 13).

"The king that faithfully judgeth the poor; His throne shall be established for ever" (v. 14).

"*Fool*"--

"If a wise man hath a controversy with a foolish man; Whether he be angry or laugh, there will be no rest" (v. 9).

"A fool uttereth all his anger" (v. 11).

"Seest thou a man that is hasty in his words: There is more hope of a fool than of him" (v. 20).

"*Speech*"--

"A man that flattereth his neighbor spreadeth a net for his steps" (v. 5).

"Scoffers set a city in a flame" (v. 5).

"The rod and reproof give wisdom" (v. 15).

"A servant will not be corrected by words" (v. 19).

"Seest thou a man that is hasty in his words? there is more hope of a fool than of him" (v. 20).

"*Bad company*"--

"He that keepeth company with harlots wasteth his substance" (v. 3).

"Whoso is partner with a thief hateth his own soul" (v. 24).

"*Anger*"--

"Wise men turneth away wrath" (v. 8).

"If a wise man hath a controversy with a foolish man, Whether he be angry or laugh, there will be no rest" (v. 9).

"A fool uttereth all his anger; But a wise man keepeth it back and stilleth it" (v. 11).

"*Established*"--

"The king by justice establisheth the land" (v. 4).

"The king that faithfully judgeth the poor, His throne shall be estblished for ever" (v. 14).

"*Jehovah*"--

"The poor man and the oppressor meet together; Jehovah lighteneth the eyes of them both" (v. 13).

"Whoso putteth his trust in Jehovah shall be safe" (v. 25).

"A man's judgment cometh from Jehovah" (v. 26).

"*Rejoice*"--

"When the righteous are increased, the people rejoice" (v. 2).

"Whoso loveth wisdom rejoiceth his father" (v. 3).

"The righteous doth sing and rejoice" (v. 6).

"Correct thy son, and he will give thee rest; Yea, he will give delight unto thy soul" (v. 17).

"He that keepeth the law, happy is he" (v. 18).

THOUGHTS OF THE WICKED

"The thoughts of the wicked are an abomination to the Lord: but the words of the pure are pleasant words" (15:26).

The wicked have thoughts. They are usually expressing them too. You talk to them about Jesus, and you will see that they have thoughts. But, they are not the kind of thoughts that God would have. They are thoughts that do not agree with God's thoughts. They are thoughts that lead away from God rather than to Him. They are thoughts that degrade instead of inspire. They are thoughts that oppose God rather than submit to Him.

Because of the way that wicked people think, it is hard to help them, it is hard to deal with them for God. God knows this. The just deplore the way of the wicked, and the feeling is mutual--the wicked deplore the way of the righteous (29:27). God deplores the way of the wicked and would have them turn from it immediately.

TEXT — 30:1-10

1. The words of Agur the son of Jakeh; the oracle.
The man saith unto Ithiel, unto Ithiel and Ucal:
2. Surely I am more brutish than any man,
And have not the understanding of a man;
3. And I have not learned wisdom,
Neither have I the knowledge of the Holy One.
4. Who hath ascended up into heaven and descended?
Who hath gathered the wind in his fists?
Who hath bound the waters in his garment?
Who hath established all the ends of the earth?
What is his name, and what is his son's name, if thou knowest?
5. Every word of God is tried:
He is a shield unto them that take refuge in him.
6. Add thou not unto his words,
Lest he reprove thee, and thou be found a liar.
7. Two things I have asked of thee;
Deny me them not before I die:
8. Remove far from me falsehood and lies;
Give me neither poverty nor riches; Feed me with the food that is needful for me:
9. Lest I be full, and deny thee, and say, Who is Jehovah?
Or lest I be poor, and steal,
And use profanely the name of my God.
10. Slander not a servant unto his master,
Lest he curse thee, and thou be held guilty.

STUDY QUESTIONS OVER 30-1-10

1. Who was "Agur" (v. 1)?
2. What does "oracle" mean (v. 1)?
3. Who were "Ithiel" and "Ucal" (v. 1)?
4. Does "brutish" in v. mean what we usually understand by this word?
5. What is meant by the statements in v. 3?
6. What is the author getting at in v. 4?
7. "Tried" in what sense (v. 5)?
8. Where else in the Bible is the same instruction given (v. 6)?
9. What are these "two things" (v. 7)?
10. Was this his own "falsehood" or somebody else's (v. 8)?

11. What is the danger of having too much (v. 9)?
12. What is a danger of having too little (v. 9)?
13. What is "slander" (v. 10)?

PHARAPHRASE OF 30:1-10

1. These are the messages of Agur, son of Jakeh, from Massa, addressed to Ithiel and Ucal:

2-4. I am tired out, O God, and ready to die. I am too stupid even to call myself a human being! I cannot understand man, let alone God. Who else but God goes back and forth to heaven? Who else holds the wind in his fists, and wraps up the oceans in His cloak? Who but God has created the world? If there is any other, what is name--and his son's name--if you know it?

5-6. Every word of God proves true. He defends all who come to Him for protection. Do not add to His words, lest He rebuke you, and you be found a liar.

7-10. O, God, I beg two favors from you before I die: First, help me never to tell a lie. Second, give me neither poverty nor riches! Give me just enough to satisfy my needs! For if I grow rich, I may become content without God. And if I am too poor, I may steal, and thus insult God's holy name. Never falsely accuse a man to his employer, lest he curse you for your sin.

COMMENTS ON 30:1-10

V. 1. Four names are here introduced to us, unknown to us but probably well known in those days: "Agur" (the author), "Jakeh" (his father); and "Ithiel" and "Ucal" (the ones being addressed). Ithiel is more important of the two in that he is not only mentioned first but twice. These last two chapters contain material that is not compiled by Solomon (this chapter by "Agur" and chapter 31 by "King Lemuel"). Both chapters depart from the one-verse "sayings" to sections of material. The word "Oracle" shows that what follows is inspired even if not written by Solomon.

V. 2. Whoever Agur was, he here reveals the fact that it was not through natural endowment that he was about to write. Psa. 73:22 also uses the word "brutish", and it carries the idea of a low level of understanding.

V. 3. And this verse shows that it was not through

education received from others that he was about to write. "It is very probable that he was a rustic, without education, and without any human help, as was the prophet Amos; and that all that he knew now was by the inspiration of the Almighty, independent of which he was rustic and uneducated" ("Clarke").

V. 4. Here are five questions dealing with the sublime and divine. Concerning the ascending and descending, Rom. 10:6,7 asks two questions: "Who shall ascend into heaven?...and Who shall descend into the abyss?" What would be the purpose of such ascending and descending? Deut. 30:11-13 is that from which Rom. 10 is quoting, and it shows that such going up and going down (or out) was for the purpose of gaining divine knowledge and bringing it back to mankind: "This commandment...is not in heaven, that thou shouldest say, Who shall go up for us to heaven, and bring it to us, and make us hear it, that we may do it? Neither is it beyond the sea, that thou shouldest say, Who shall go over the sea for us, and bring it to us?" The answer to the first four questions in this verse is, "No man!" Creation and Providence are the works of God--Job 38- Psa. 104; Isa. 40:12-14 (questions 2-4), and so is the Revelation--I Cor. 2:9-11 (question 1). If somebody insisted that some man has done these things which we attribute to God, Agur wanted to know his name and his son's name.

V. 5. "As the light of nature and metaphysical speculation are of no avail in obtaining the perfect knowledge of God which the seeker craves, he must be all the more thankful for the revealed Word of God, which teaches him as much as he is capable of learning" ("Pulpit Commentary"). The message that Agur is bringing is the "Word of God", and every word of it is true for it is "tried": "The words of Jehovah are pure words; As silver tried in a furnace of the earth, Purified seven times" (Psa. 12:6); "Thy word is very pure" (Psa. 119:140). Psa. 19:8 again states its purity and what it does for mankind: "The precepts of Jehovah are right, rejoicing the heart: The commandment of Jehovah is pure, enlightening the eyes." God and His Word are spokes of as a shield to those who take refuge in Him: "The word of Jehovah is tried; He is a shield unto all them that take refuge in him" Psa. 18:30); "Jehovah God is a sun and a shield" (Psa. 84:11); "O Israel, trust thou in Jehovah: He is their help and their shield. O house of Aaron, trust ye in Jehovah: He is their help and their shield. Ye that fear Jehovah, trust in Jehovah: He is their help and their shield"

(Psa. 115:9-11)

V. 6. Since God's Word is pure (just like He wants it), true, and right, He does not want man tampering with it. Twice in Deut. did God sound the same warning: "Ye shall not add unto the word which I command you, neither shall ye diminish from it" (4:2); "What thing soever I command you, that shall ye observe to do: thou shalt not add thereto, nor diminish from it" (12:32). And the last warning in the Bible says, "If any man shall add unto them, God shall add unto him the plagues which are written in this book: and if any man shall take away from the words of the book of this prophecy, God shall take away his part from the tree of life, and out of the holy city, which are written in this book" (Rev. 22:18,19). Anyone wrestling (twisting) the Scripture does so to his own destruction (II Pet. 3:16). If we deny God's Word, He will "reprove" us (prove us wrong, deal with us), and we will be found to be nothing less in His sight than a "liar" (absolutely wrong). Examples: II Kings 6:24-31; 7:1-17; Jer. 27:2,6,8; 28:1-4, 10-17.

V. 7. This chapter contains several groupings (vs. 7-9, vs. 11-14, vs. 15,16, vs. 18,19, vs. 21-23, vs. 24-28, vs. 29-31), and this verse introduces the first group or set. "Two things" were urgently desired or were asked of God, and which he did not want to be denied. "Before I die" means "while I am in the flesh" or "while I live."

V. 8. No. 1: "Remove far from me falsehood and lies"; No. 2: "Give me neither poverty nor riches". "Feed me with the food that is needful for me" goes with No. 2 as a restatement of it. And v. 9 is an explanation of request No. 2. As we look as these two requests, the first is what he wished God to remove from him, and the second is what he wished God to give him. Now knowing Agur (the compiler), we do not know whether he was personally plagued with "falsehood and lies" and wanted to be delivered from them or whether he saw so much unfaithfulness in humanity that he personally wanted to be completely free from it himself (let us hope it was the latter). And we too need to be free from such unfaithfulness: "Wherefore, putting away falsehood, speak ye truth each one with his neighbor" (Eph. 4:25). Agur also wished that in God's providential dealings with him, he would spare him from the extremes of both poverty and wealth, for he saw dangers in both (see comments on v. 9). His wish was that he might merely have the provisions that were suitable for him. And observation shows that people are more righteous, happier, and more satisfied when they are found in the great middle class that has to work for what they have, and that appreciate what they get.

V. 9. What was the danger of "riches"? "Lest I be full, and deny thee, and say, Who is Jehovah?" Over and over in the Bible shows this tendency: "Lest, when thou hast eaten and art full, and hast built goodly houses, and dwelt therein; and when thy herds and thy flocks multiply, and thy silver and thy gold is multiplied; then thy heart be lifted up, and thou forget Jehovah thy God...and lest thou say in thy heart, My power and the might of my hand hath gotten me this wealth" (Deut. 8:12-17); "Thou are waxed fat, thou art grown thick, thou art become sleek; Then he forsook God" (Deut. 32:15). Also see Deut. 31:20; Neh. 9:25,26; Job 31:24,25,28; Hos. 13:6. What was the danger of "poverty"? "Lest I be poor, and steal, And use profanely the name of my God." Stealing is wrong whether one is stealing out of want or otherwise, "Situation Ethics" notwithstanding. But one cannot deny the tendency of the poverty-stricken to steal from others. Under those circumstances one might "use profanely" the name of God by cursing Him for his circumstances, or he might affirm his innocence by an oath in which he used God's name (likely the former: "When they shall be hungry, they shall fret themselves, and curse by their king and by their God"--Isa. 8:21).

V. 10. "Slander" is not good: Rom. 3:8; Psa. 101:5; Psa. 50:19,20; I. Tim. 3:11. "Lest he curse thee"--who is the "he"? More likely the "servant" than the "master"--the one slandered rather than the one who hears the slander. Since the slanderer would be "guilty", the "curse" would be effective.

TEST QUESTIONS OVER 30:1-10

1. What four persons are mentioned in v. 1, and what do we know of each?
2. What word in v. 1 shows the contents of the chapter to be inspired?
3. From what two sources did the author of this chapter not get the material he was about to present (vs. 2,3)?
4. Discuss the ascending and descending of v. 4.
5. How "pure" is the Word of God said to be (v. 5)?
6. Where else besides v. 6 does God warn about tampering with His Word?
7. Why did Agur want falsehood and lies removed from

him (v. 8)?

8. What is meant by "Food that is needful for me" (v. 8)?
9. Where else besides v. 9 does the Bible warn about the danger of riches?
10. How might a poverty-stricken person use the name of God "profanely" (v. 9)?
11. Who is the "he" of v. 10?

TEXT — 30:11-20

11. There is a generation that curse their father,
And bless not their mother.
12. There is a generation that are pure in their own eyes,
And yet are not washed from their filthiness.
13. There is a generation, of how lofty are their eyes!
And their eyelids are lifted up.
14. There is a generation whose teeth are as swords, and their jaw teeth as knives,
To devour the poor from off the earth, and the needy from among men.
15. The horseleach hath two daughters, crying, Give, give.
There are three things that are never satisfied, Yea, four that say not, Enough:
16. Sheol; and the barren womb;
The earth that is not satisfied with water;
And the fire that saith not, Enough.
17. The eye that mocketh at his father,
And despiseth to obey his mother,
The ravens of the valley shall pick it out,
And the young eagles shall eat it.
18. There are three things which are too wonderful for me,
Yea, four which I know not:
19. The way of an eagle in the air;
The way of a serpent upon a rock;
The way of a ship in the midst of the sea;
And the way of a man with a maiden.
20. So is the way of an adulterous woman;
She eateth, and wipeth her mouth,
And saith, I have done no wickedness.

STUDY QUESTIONS OVER 30:11-20

1. Is "generation" used in v. 11 as we use it?

2. Is the generation in v. 12 the same as in v. 11 or some other generation?
3. What is wrong with the generation mentioned in v. 13?
4. To what extent will greedy peole go in order to get gain (v. 14)?
5. Comment on "horseleach" (v. 15).
6. Can you name these four things without looking (v. 16)?
7. What is meant by the birds picking out such a one's eyes (v. 17)?
8. "Too wonderful" in what sense (v. 18)?
9. Comment upon each thing mentioned in v. 19.
10. What does sin do to a person (v. 20)?

PARAPHRASE OF 30:11-20

11-14. There are those who curse their father and mother, and feel themselves faultless despite their many sins. They are proud beyond description, arrogant, disdainful. They devour the poor with teeth as sharp as knives!

15,16. There are two things never satisfied, like a leech forever craving more: no, three things! no, four! Hell, the barren womb, a barren desert, fire.

17. A man who mocks his father and despises his mother shall have his eye plucked out by ravens and eaten by vultures.

18,19. There are three things too wonderful for me to understand--no four! How an eagle glides through the sky, how a serpent crawls upon a rock, how a ship finds its way across the heaving ocean, the growth of love between a man and a girl.

20. There is another thing too: how a prostitute can sin and and then say, "What's wrong with that?"

COMMENTS ON 30:11-20

V. 11. The next four verses all begin with, "There is a generation." Is this a prophecy of a coming wicked generation? He doesn't say, "There shall be a generation." Was it his own generation? He didn't say, "This generation." Or was it four different generations being described in the four different statements? Likely what he says has fit various generations from time to time. For sure the four statements seem to fit our own generation, and others who have lived before us have felt that they fit theirs also. Our verse is picturing a generation openly violating the Fifth Commandment ("Honor thy father and thy mother"--Exo. 20:12). A child who does not honor and respect his parents is off to a bad start in life: the basis of good character is lacking. Imagine a whole generation of such and the society that would result! This verse and "disobedient to parents" in II Tim. 3:2 aptly find their fulfillment in the "juvenile delinquency" of our times.

V. 12. It is natural for any people to have a concern over human guilt before God, not that everbody comes to God for cleansing and forgiveness. But our verse pictures a time when men will feel no need for such cleansing: they will feel all right as they are. Gospel preaching, evangelistic appeals, and surrender to Christ are indeed foreign, unnecessary, and indeed foolish to such a people. Nor does our present generation miss being this generation by much!

V. 13. This verse describes a proud, conceited age. This was the sin of King Nebuchadnezzar. Remember his pride when one day as he was walking in his palace, he proudly said to himself, "Is this not great Babylon, which I have built for the royal dwelling-place, by the might of my power and for the glory of my majesty" (Dan. 4:30)? This spirit is not far from the present attitude: "See what we have done! Look at what man has accomplished!" The more that man is puffed up with his own knowledge, own attainments, and own importance, the less he bows before God, seeks His will, and walks by faith. This is a dangerous spirit to get into.

V. 14. This verse tells of a greedy age, when the "big" eat up the "little," when the "rich" devour the "poor". Have we not come to this time when everytihng big drives everything small out of business. The small farmer with no capital can no longer farm. The man with his small store on the corner can no longer compete. The greed mentioned in this verse has characterized many generations Amos 8:4 uses the same language: "Hear this, O ye that would swallow up the needy, and cause the poor of the land to fail."

V. 15. This verse and the one following will deal with things that seemingly cannot get enough, are never satisfied. To begin with, he compares them with the blood-sucking horseleach whose two daughters can never get enough blood ("Give, give," they cry). But the number of things he has in mind are not two, so he raises it to three; and finally he says there are "Four that say not, Enough."

V. 16. Wat are those four? (1) "Sheol"--the abode of men's departed spirits. Sheol is never satisfied: it keeps claiming new victims and never says, "Enough." Prov. 27:20 and Hab. 2:5 also states that Sheol is never satisfied. (2) The barren womb--the married woman who has not been able to bear children. It keeps crying out for conception. Recall that the barren Rachel said to her husband Jacob, "Give me children, or else I die" (Gen. 30:1). Elkannah's words to his barren wife Hannah ("Am I not better off to thee than ten sons?"--I Sam. 1:8) did not satisfy her longing for offspring (read I Sam. 1:4-11). (3) The earth--oh, how quickly it dries out after a heavy rain and is ready for more! (4) Fire--instead of being extinguished from fuel put upon it, fire leaps higher and roars louder as if to say, "More, more." Acutally, what is the moral of such a verse? We conjecture a guess: not so much for the sake of the earth and fire not being satisfied but to remind man of the coming of death and that the barren womb of woman can be a problem.

V. 17. Mixed in with the groupings of this chapter are occasional single-proverbs (such as this verse and v. 10). This verse returns to the subject of v. 11. Other passages on showing disrespect to one's parents: Gen. 9:22; Lev. 20:9, Prov. 20:20. On this verse: "Such an undutiful son shall die a violent death; his corpse shall lie unburied, and the birds of prey shall feed upon him...Ravens, vultures, and other birds that live on carrion first attack the eyes of their prey" ("Pulpit Commentary").

V. 18. Agur begins another series--this time four things he can but wonder at but not comprehend. Job 42:3 speaks of "Things too wonderful for me, which I knew not."

V. 19. What are these four things that excited Agur's wonderment? (1) The way of an eagle in the air--how marvelous his flight! (2) The way of a serpent on a rock--how man likes to conceal himself and study such! (3) The way of a ship in the midst of the sea--to see a large vessel take to the deep waters and to go with no land in sight was another marvel. (4) The way of a man with a maiden--it remains a marvel the way that love develops between two people and grows into the ultimate relation of husband and wife. We personally think the "Paraphrase" gets to the correct idea better than the commentaries. The "Paraphrase" reads: "There are three things too wonderful for me to understand--no four! How an eagle glides through the sky. How a serpent crawls upon a rock. How a ship finds its way across the heaving ocean. The growth of love between a man and a girl."

V. 20. And here is another thing to marvel at: how an adulterous woman can sin, knowing she has sinned, and say, "I have done no wickedness." She would fit the "Generation" spoken in v. 12 ("pure in their own eyes, and yet are not washed from their filthiness").

TEST QUESTIONS OVER 30:11-20

1. Comment upon "generation" as used in vs. 11-14.
2. Which commandment of the Ten would be violated by those in v. 11?
3. What is the picture of those in v. 12?
4. What evidence can you think of that might relate our generation with what is said in v. 13?
5. Has v. 14 characterized many generations or an occasional one?
6. V. 15 introduces four things that seemingly are never ....
7. What are those four (v. 16)?
8. Comment upon v. 17.
9. What type of things does v. 18 introduce?
10. What are those four things (v. 19)?
11. What additional thing to marvel at was mentioned in v. 20?

TEXT — 30:21-33

21. For three things the earth doth tremble,
And for four, which it cannot bear:
22. For a servant when he is king;
And a fool when he is filled with food;
23. For an odious woman when she is married;
And a handmaid that is heir to her mistress.
24. There are four things which are little upon the earth,
But they are exceeding wise:
25. The ants are a people not strong,
Yet they provide their food in the summer;
26. The conies are but a feeble folk,
Yet make they their houses in the rocks;
27. The locusts have no king,

Yet go they forth all of them by bands;
28. The lizard taketh hold with her hands,
Yet is she in kings' palaces.
29. There are three things which are stately in their march,
Yea, four which are stately in going:
30. The lion, which is the mightiest among beasts,
And turneth not away for any;
31. The greyhound; the he-goat also;
And the king against whom there is no rising up.
32. If thou hast done foolishly in lifting up thyself,
Or if thou hast thought evil,
Lay thy hand upon thy mouth.
33. For the churning of milk bringeth forth butter,
And the wringing of the nose bringeth forth blood;
So the forcing of wrath bringeth forth strife.

STUDY QUESTIONS OVER 30:21-33

1. Why should the things mentioned in vs. 21,22 cause the earth to "tremble"?
2. Comment upon the two things mentioned in v. 22.
3. What does "odious" mean (v. 23)?
4. By contrast, what are some things that are large but not wise (v. 24)?
5. Comment on the ant as used in v. 25.
6. What are conies (v. 26)?
7. Comment on the locust as used in v. 27.
8. Comment on the lizard as used in v. 28.
9. What does "stately" mean (v. 29)?
10. In what passage are the righteous compared to a lion (v. 30)?
11. Comment on each thing mentioned in v. 31.
12. When did ancients lay their hands upon their mouths (v. 32)?
13. Comment upon v. 33.

PARAPHRASE OF 30:21-33

21-23. There are three things that make the earth tremble--no, four it cannot stand: A slave who becomes a king. A rebel who prospers. A bitter woman when she finally marries. A servant girl who marries her mistress' husband.

24-28. There are four things that are small but continually wise: Ants: they aren't strong, but they store up food for the winter. Cliff badgers: delicate little animals who protect themselves by living among the rocks. The locusts: though they have no leader, they stay together in swarms. The spiders: they are easy to catch and kill, yet are found even in king's palaces!

29-31. There are three stately monarchs in the earth--no, four: The lion, king of the animals. He won't turn aside for anyone. The peacock. The he-goat. A king as he leads his army.

32. If you have been a fool by being proud or plotting evil, don't brag about it--cover your mouth with your hand in shame.

33. As the churning of cream yields butter, and a blow to the nose causes bleeding, so anger causes quarrels.

COMMENTS ON 30:21-33

V. 21. This verse begins another group, a group of four, four things that bring sorrow, trouble and anguish. "Earth" here concerns those who live upon it.

V. 22,23. What four things? (1) A servant when he is king--sometimes a servant is elevated to a ruling status, and sometimes he "grabbed the reins of power". Prov. 19:10 speaks of a servant having rule over princes, and Eccl. 10:7 speaks of servants upon horses instead of their usual place (walking). Former servants now ruling or being in charge can become "drunk" with their newly found position of authority--each will show everybody who is boss! (2) A fool when he is filled with food--another case of "promotion" that doesn't work anymore, so in allows much evil to result. (3) An odious woman when she is married--a hateful woman, a woman with a bad disposition, who finally gets married. Watch out! She will cause her husband trouble, his people trouble, etc. "She is a woman who has passed much of her life without love, having nothing about her attractive either in looks, attainments, or manner, and is consequently soured and ill-tempered. If such a one does at last win a husband, she uses her new position to vex those who formerly depreciated her, and to make them as miserable as she can" ("Pulpit Commentary"). One person like that in a previously quiet set of people can be like a "bombshell". (4) A handmaid that is heir to her mistress--another "elevation" that backfires. It was agreeable to Abraham and Sarah for him to father a child by the handmaid Hagar (Gen. 16:1,2). The result: "When she [Hagar] saw that she was conceived, her mistress wad despised in her eyes" (Gen. 16:4).

V. 24. With this verse Agur begins another series of things, this time four things that are little but exceedingly wise. "Pulpit Commentary": "In contrast with the intolerable pretensions of the last group."

V. 25-28. What four? (1) Ants. An ant may not be strong, but an ant is wise enough to prepare his food in the summertime for the winter when it would be hard to find. Ever notice how busy ants are as they work? "In countries where ants do not hibernate, they do make granaries for themselves in the summer, and use these supplies as food in the winter months" ("Pulpit Commentary"). (2) Conies--the "rock-badger" (Hart in "Animals of the Bible"). "Geike": "The coney abounds in the gorge of the Kedron and along the foot of the mountains west of the Dead Sea." Because they are small (about the size of a rabbit) they live in the rocks. ("The rocks are a refuge for the conies"--(Psa. 104:18). Their wisdom is displayed in their other protective measures: "It is very hard to capture one...They have sentries regularly placed on the lookout while the rest are feeding; a squeak from the watchman sufficing to send the flock scudding to their holes" ("Pulpit Commentary"). (3) The locusts. They have no leader, yet they all seem to know what to do. Joel 2:7,8 says of them, "They run like mighty men; they climb the wall like men of war; and they march every one on his ways, and they break not their ranks. Neither doth one thrust another; they march every one in his path; and they burst through their weapons, and break not off their course." (4) The lizard--the small kind with special suction-cup toes that enable it to run up walls and cling to ceilings. This would be the "taketh hold with her hands". "Small as it is, and easy to catch and crush, it is agile and clever enough to make its way into the very palace of the king, and to dwell there" ("Pulpit Commentary"). The unstated conclusion of this list would be that we should be wise, and we will succeed in spite of various limitations.

V. 29. This verse introduces another set of four, this time things that are "stately in their going" or whose movements are remarkable.

V. 30,31. What four? (1) The lion who fearlessly walks

wherever he chooses and is fearlessly unafraid. (2) The greyhound who can run like the wind. (3) The he-goat. "Clarke" says this is referring to "How he walks, and what state he assumes, in the presence of his part of the flock". (4) A king who has things under control so that there is no danger of rebelling against him. This is the way every king wishes it to be.

V. 32,33. Butter results from churning, nosebleed results from twisting the nose, and strife results from stirring up wrath. What will stir up this wrath? Foolishly lifting oneself up (like James and John were doing in their request for the chief seats in Christ's then-coming kingdom: "When the ten heard it, they were moved with indignation concerning the two brethren"--Matt. 20:24) or sometimes even just thinking evil about another (like Eccl. 10:20 pictures: "Revile not the king, no, not in thy thought; and revile not the rich in thy bedchamber: for a bird of the heavens shall carry the voice, and that which hath wings shall tell the matter"). Putting the hand over the mouth is also mentioned in Job 21:5, Job 40:4; Mic. 7:16. This was done when one recognized he had said the wrong thing or to keep from saying more.

NOTE: "Noticeable Groupings" within a chapter are found only in those chapters made up of 1-verse sayings (chapters 10-29).

TEST QUESTIONS OVER 30:21-33

1. What does "earth" mean in v. 21?
2. What 2 ways might a "servant" rise to power (v. 22)?
3. Name 3 other "promotions" in vs. 22,23 that don't usually succeed.
4. How did "Pulpit Commentary" contrast the group-of-four things in vs. 24,25 with those in vs. 22,23?
5. What are ants known for (v. 25)?
6. How large is a "conie" (v. 26)?
7. What other Old Testament book described the ways of the locust (v. 27)?
8. What is meant by the lizard taking "hold with her hands" (v. 28)?
9. What is the unstated conclusion of vs. 27, 28?
10. What is the group-of-four set forth in vs. 29-31 known for?
11. What would you say was the purpose of vs. 29-31?
12. What is the lesson of vs. 32,33?

CHAPTER 31

TEXT – 31:1-9

1. The words of king Lemuel:
The oracle which his mother taught him.
2. Why, my son? and what, O son of my womb?
And what, O son of my vows?
3. Give not thy strength unto women,
Nor thy ways to that which destroyeth kings.
4. It is not for kings, O Lemuel, it is not for kings to drink wine;
Nor for princes to say, Where is strong drink?
5. Lest they drink, and forget the law,
And pervert the justice due to any that is afflicted.
6. Give strong drink unto him that is ready to perish,
And wine unto the bitter in soul:
Let him drink, and forget his poverty,
And remember his misery no more.
8. Open thy mouth for the dumb,
In the cause of all such as are left desolate.
9. Open thy mouth, judge righteously,
And minister justice to the poor and needy.

STUDY QUESTIONS OVER 31:1-9

1. Who was Lemuel (v. 1)?
2. What three things did Lemuel's mother call him in v. 2?
3. How did kings behave (v. 3)?
4. What city in the U.S.A. is said to consume the most liquor per capita (v. 4)?
5. Why should rulers especially leave strong drink alone (v. 5)?
6. How did ancients use alcohol besides as a beverage (v. 6)?
7. Is strong drink really for well people to drink to forget their sorrow (v. 7)?
8. What does "open thy mouth" mean in v. 8?
9. Why have the poor and needy often suffered in court (v. 9)?

PARAPHRASE OF 31:1-9

1. These are the wise sayings of King Lemuel of Massa, taught to him at his mother's knee:

2,3. O my son, whom I have dedicated to the Lord, do not spend your time with women--the royal pathway to destruction.

4-7. And it is not for kings, O Lemuel, to drink wine and whiskey. For if they drink they may forget their duties and be unable to give justice to those who are oppressed. Hard liquor is for sick men at the brink of death, and wine for those in deep depression. Let them drink to forget their poverty and misery.

8,9. You should defend those who cannot help themselves. Yes, speak up for the poor and needy and see that they get justice.

COMMENTS ON 31:1-9

V. 1. This chapter is another supplement (just like Chapter 30). History has not preserved, nor has archaeology uncovered, information that would help us identify "king Lemuel". If his father was a king with a harem of wives, the rearing and teaching of his sons became the work of his own mother. "Oracle" indicates a divine message. We are glad for this suplement that closes out the book of Proverbs, especially the material about the virtuous woman (vs. 10-31).

V. 2. "The thrice repeated...'what', which Luther appropriately rendered by 'Ach!', is plainly an impassioned exclamation expressing the inward emotion of the mother's heart at the thought that the son might possible fall into an evil way" ("Lange"). The preciousness of this son to his mother is evident from her three expressions concerning him: (1) "my son"--her very own son, one of the dearest possessions that any woman can have; (2) "son of my womb"--not adopted by her but born by her, the fruit of her own body as blessed and enabling by God; (3) "son of my vows"--she, like Hannah (I Sam. 1:2,8,10,11), may have been barren, earnestly prayed for a child, and vowed that if God granted her a child she would rear the same to His honor and glory. Her teaching these important things to Lemuel were likely part of her fulfilling those vows.

V. 3. Her first plea was for him not to sacrifice his strength (Hebrew: "vigor") to women (kings kept harems). Her second plea concerning "that which destroyeth kings" was likely referring to "strong drink", which she goes on to discuss in succeeding verses. She was warning him against "wine" and "women".

V. 4. Solomon rightfully prayed for wisdom that he might be capable of ruling Israel (I Kings 3:9), but strong drink can affect man's reasoning powers. A king needs all of his mentality (and then some!) all the time, so his mother correctly said, "It is not for kings, O Lemuel." Ben-hadad and the thirty-two kings with him were drinking themselves drunk, and the Israelites defeated them that day (I KIngs 20:16-21). Belshazzar was having a drunken feast when the handwriting appeared on the wall, telling him that that very night his kingdom would be given to the Medes and Persians (Dan. 5:1-5,25-28). Eccl. 10:17 observes, "Happy art thou, O land, when thy king is the son of nobles, and thy princes eat in due season, for strength, and not for drunkenness!". It is too bad that our own capital city (Washington D.C.) has been consuming more alcoholic beverages per capita than other city in the U.S.A.

V. 5. A drinking monarch will not be a good king: he will "forget the law" and "pervert...justice". Matters that need attention will be neglected because of drinking. As was observed, boozing affects one's mental powers, judgment-ability and general direction. Hos. 4:11 says, "Whoredome and wine and new wine take away the understanding."

Vs. 6,7. Another case of Hebrew parallelism in which the latter statement is but a restatement of the first. In other words, the "bitter in soul" is the same as "him that is ready to perish". We do utilize drugs and alcoholic-based medicines to relieve the afflicted in their final sufferings. If one overlooks the Hebrew parallelism here, he would end up having God advising the sorrowful to turn to booze. But life has proven that people who do that don't "drown their sorrows"; it is more as Archie Word observes: "They only give them swimming lessons."

V. 8. "The 'dumb' is any one who for any reason whatever is unable to plead his own cause; he may be of tender age, or of lowly station, or ignorant, timid, and boorish; and the prince is enjoined to plead for him" ('Pulpit Commentary"). The next verse continues the subject.

V. 9. The command to "judge righteously" is found elsewhere in the Bible also: "Ye shall do no unrighteousness in judgment: thou shalt not respect the person of the poor, nor honor the person of the mighty; but in righteousness shalt thou judge thy neighbor" (Lev. 19:15); "I charged your judges at that time, saying, Hear the causes between your brethren, and judge righteously between a man and his brother, and the sojourner that is with him. Ye shall not respect persons in judgment; ye shall hear the small and the great alike" (Deut. 1:16,17); "Judge not according to appearance, but judge righteous judgment" (John 7:24). But often the poor and afflicted had no one to see that they received justice. The Bible speaks elsewhere on that also: "Judge the fatherless, plead for the widow" (Isa. 1:17); "He judged the cause of the poor and needy; then it was well" (Jer. 22:16); "I delivered the poor that cried, The fatherless also, that had none to help" (Job 29:12).

TEST QUESTIONS OVER 31:1-9

1. Why is Lemuel's mother teaching him instead of his father (v. 1)?
2. Comment on each of the ways Lemuel's mother spoke of him in v. 2.
3. Lemuel was not to dissipate his strength upon ...... (v. 3).
4. What else was Lemuel warned about in v. 3?
5. What instruction is given again in v. 4?
6. Suppose Lemuel drank as a king (v. 6).
7. What use for wine is mentioned in v. 7?
8. Who all would be included under "dumb" in v. 8?
9. What does the Bible say about judging rightesouly (v. 9)?

TEXT — 31:10-21

10. A worthy woman who can find?
For her price is far above rubies.
11. The heart of her husband trusteth in her,
And he shall have no lack of gain.
12. She doeth him good and not evil.
All the days of her life.
13. She seeketh wool and flax,
And worketh willingly with her hands.
14. She is like the merchant-ships;
She bringeth her bread from afar.
15. She riseth also while it is yet night,
And giveth food to her household.
16. She considereth a field, and buyeth it;
With the fruit of her hands she planteth a vineyard.
17. She girdeth her loins with strength,

And maketh strong her arms.
18. She perceiveth that her merchandise is profitable;
Her lamp goeth not out by night.
19. She layeth her hands to the distaff,
And her hands hold the spindle.
20. She stretcheth out her hand to the poor;
Yea, she reacheth forth her hands to the needy.
21. She is not afraid of the snow for her household;
For all her household are clothed with scarlet.

STUDY QUESTIONS OVER 31:10-21

1. Would such a woman be put into the slave market (v. 10)?
2. "Trust" in her in what sense (v. 11)?
3. "Good and not evil" in what ways (v. 12)?
4. What was flax used for (v. 13)?
5. How far (v. 14)?
6. What about her and late-morning sleeping (v. 15)?
7. Was she acting independent of her husband or for her husband (v. 16)?
8. How does v. 17 contrast her with many women?
9. Why "goeth not out" (v. 18)?
10. What are the "distaff" and "spindle" (v. 19)?
11. Did this busy woman think only of her family (v. 20)?
12. What is the connection between the two statements in v. 21?

PARAPHRASE OF 31:10-21

10-21. If you can find a truly good wife, she is worth more than precious gems! Her husband can trust her, and she will richly satisfy his needs. She will not hinder him, but help him all her life. She finds wool and flax and busily spins it. She buys imported foods, brought by ship from distant ports. She gets up before dawn to prepare breakfast for her household, and plans the day's work for her servant girls. She goes out to inspect a field, and buys it; with her own hands she plants a vineyard. She is energetic, a hard worker, and watches for bargains. She works far into the night! She sews for the poor, and generously gives to the needy. She has no fear of winter for her household, for she has made warm clothes for all of them.

COMMENT ON 31:10-21

V. 10 From here to the end of the chapter sets forth the beautiful description of a virtuous woman, wife and mother. It is the Bible's longest and best description of her. It has been a favorite of many Christian women, and every Christian girl should know it well. Each of the verses of this detailed description begins with the different letters of the Hebrew alpahbet. To describe it in English, V. 10 begins with A, v. 11 with B, v. 12 with C, etc. to the end. Other passages on the virtuous woman: "A worthy woman is the crown of her husband" (Prov. 12:4); "A prudent wife is from Jehovah" (Prov. 18:22); "Whose adorning let it not be the outward adorning...but let it be the hidden man of the heart, in the incorruptible apparel of a meek and quiet spirit, which is in the sight of God of great price. For after this manner aforetime the holy women also, who hoped in God, adorned themselves" (I Pet. 3:3-5).

V. 11. The first part of this description relates her to her husband, and the first thing it says is that he can trust her. "The husband of such a wife goes forth to his daily occupations, having full confidence in her whom he leaves at home that she will act discreetly and promote his interests while he is absent" ("Pulpit Commentary"). See the contrast in Prov. 7:18,19. "The man is not at home; He is gone on a long journey...Come, let us take our fill of love until morning." His confidence in her integrity and her attention to the family's interests shows up in "he shall have no lack of gain". V. 13 onward shows the important part she plays in the sound financial condition of the home. Contrast her relationship to this with the spendthrift wives who fairly wreck their husbands financially.

V. 12. She is altogether an asset to him and in no sense a liability. Again, she brings him joy and not sorrow by her behaviour and by her contributions. "Her good is unmixed: she will do him good and not evil...Her good is...constant and permanent...all the days of her life" ("Clarke"). "All the days of her life" shows that she will still be his wife in years to come; she will be faithful to the marriage vow: "Until death do us part." She will not only do good to him while he is strong and able but also when he is older and infirm.

V. 13. Wool and flax (from whence comes linen) were made into yarn or thread, the yarn or thread into cloth, and the cloth into garments. This made it a big job to make clothes for the family, but she did it "willingly" and cheerfully. She was neither lazy nor complaining.

V. 14. Even as she sought wool and flax (v. 13), evidently wanting good materials to work with, even so she provides her family with good food, some of which came from distant places. Their markets contained items made possible by merchant-ships. She had planned meals--not just thrown-together ones or krick-krack eating.

V. 15. We notice three things: (1) she gets up early--is no late-sleeper who is only concerned about herself instead of her family; (2) she cooks a good breakfast for the family--a good breakfast is a good foundation for the family's day's activities: they do not leave the house with empty stomachs; (3) she gets the family's maidens busy with their work for the day. By that time some of our society-loving women finally get out of bed, she has a half-day's work already done. She is filling her God-indended role in the home.

V. 16. In this she is probably not acting independent of her husband, but since he is one of the elders of the land (v. 23), she acts as his agent to investigate the worth of a particular field, to purchase it, and to plant it with vines for a vineyard.

V. 17. All of this activity and working with her own hands elevated her out of being a weak, sickly woman. She was strong and healthy and able to uphold her part of the family's work and projects. And she didn't think she needed to be "liberated"!

V. 18. She is a busy woman. She not only gives tasks to the maidens (v. 15), but she herself works. She not only works outdoors, planting vineyards, etc. (v. 16), but she makes garments and sells them (v. 24). No wonder "her lamp goeth not out by night"! Yet she is not just a slave who works but has no responsibility to see that the business is profitable: she so manages things that her merchandise is "profitable".

V. 19. In v. 13 we saw that "she seeketh wool and flax" (the raw materials). In this verse she is using the "distaff" and the "spindle" to make the thread or yarn. V. 24 tells of her going on to make the actual garments and delivering them to the merchant to sell to the public. The distaff-and-spindle system of making thread preceded the spinning wheel: "The spindle and distaff are the most ancient of all the instruments used for spinning, or making thread. The spinning wheel superseded them" ("Clarke"). The distaff held the wool to be made into thread or yarn, and the spindle was what the finished thread or yarn was collected on. Before the spinning wheel, which mounted both of these on its solid framework, they were two independent pieces that had to be held and handled by the hands, under the arm, on the lap, etc. during the operation.

V. 20. More Hebrew parallelism: "stretcheth out her hand" is the same as "reacheth forth her hands"; "to the poor" is the same as "to the needy". She works for her family (v. 20), but she does not forget others who are needy. Again, she is interested in business (personal, legitimate gain), but in so doing she is not unmindful of those who are having financial difficulties. We are taught to remember the unfortunate also: Matt. 25:34-36; Acts 11:29; I Cor. 16:1,2; Eph. 4:28; I John 3:17.

V. 21. They did not have the severe winters that we do; on the other hand, they didn't have the weather-tight houses and furnaces that we have. So they had to have warm clothing to cope with their times of colder weather. Her children were well and comfortably clothed--they were not neglected waifs of the street. The scarlet color would be warmer than plain white garments and dressier too. Every good mother wants her family to look nice.

TEST QUESTIONS OVER 30:10-21

1. What subject is discussed in these verses (v. 10(
2. How does each verse from v. 10 to the end of the chapter begin (v. 10)?
3. What is the first thing affirmed of the virtuous woman (v. 11)?
4. What does v. 12 say of her goodness to her husband?
5. What caused making clothing to be such a big job in those times (v. 13)?
6. What is said of her spirit in v. 13?
7. How concerned was she that her family was well fed (v. 14)?
8. What three things are affirmed of her in v. 15?
9. Why is she doing all this work instead of her husband (v. 16)?
10. Why is she a strong, healthy woman (v. 17)?
11. Comment upon the busy life that she leads (v. 18).
12. What was made with the distaff and spindle (v. 19)&
13. What does v. 20 tell us about this busy woman?
14. What about her family's clothing (v. 21)?

TEXT — 31:22-31

22. She maketh for herself carpets of tapestry;
Her clothing is fine linen and purple.
23. Her husband is known in the gates,
When he sitteth among the elders of the land.
24. She maketh linen garments and selleth them,
And delivereth girdles to the merchant.
25. Strength and dignity are her clothing;
And she laugheth at the time to come.
26. She openeth her mouth with wisdom;
And the law of kindness is on her tongue.
27. She looketh well to the ways of her household,
And eateth not the bread of idleness.
28. Her children rise up, and call her blessed;
Her husband also, and he praiseth her saying:
29. Many daughters have done worthily,
But thou excellest them all.
30. Grace is deceitful, and beauty is vain;
But a woman that feareth Jehovah, she shall be praised.
31. Give her of the fruit of her hands;
And let her works praise her in the gates.

STUDY QUESTIONS OVER 31:22-31

1. What kind of man did the virtuous woman marry (v. 22)?
2. Why would she work (making and selling things) when her husband was one of the leaders of the city (v. 24)?
3. Why does she "laugh at the time to come" (v. 25)?
4. Why give special attention to her speech in v. 26?
5. What is meant by the "ways of her husband" (v. 27)?
6. How long has it been since you praised your wife (or been praised by your husband if you are a woman) (v. 28)?
7. She has excelled whom (v. 29)?
8. What is "grace" in v. 30?
9. Why is beauty "vain" (v. 30)?
10. What is meant by "in the gates" in v. 31?

PARAPHRASE OF 31:22-31

22-24. She also upholsters with finest tapestry; her own clothing is beautifully made--a purple gown of pure linen. Her husband is well known, for he sits in the council chamber with the other civic leaders. She makes belted linen garments to sell to the merchants.

25-29. She is a woman of strength and dignity, and has no fear of old age. When she speaks, her words are wise, and kindness is the rule for everything she says. She watches carefully all that goes on throughout her household, and is never lazy. Her children stand and bless her; so does her husband. He praises her with these words: "There are many fine women in the world, but you are the best of them all!"

30,31. Charm can be deceptive and beauty doesn't last, but a woman who fears and reverences God shall be greatly praised. Praise her for the many fine things she does. These good deeds of hers shall bring her honor and recognition from even the leaders of the nation.

COMMENTS ON 31:22-31

V. 22. The virtuous woman continues to be described in her relationship to different aspects of life. This verse shows that she likes nice things ("Carpets of tapestry") and is gifted at making them. She not only likes outdoor work ("she planteth a vineyard"--v. 16) but indoor work (needlework) as well. But she doesn't go overboard on making nice things--she doesn't neglect her family making them. Our verse also shows that this healthy, hardworking woman also likes to look nice ("her clothing is fine linen and purple"). Her wearing purple and fine linen shows that the family was not poor (compare Luke 16:19).

V. 23. And what about her husband? Is he a lazy, no-good type of man? No, she was married to a prominent man, a successful man, one of the rulers of the land. Instead of a courthouse where legal transactions were recorded, their legal business was transacted in the city gates in the presence of the elders: Ruth 4:11; Deut. 25:5-10. He was one of them.

V. 24. Reference has already been made to her business enterprises: see vs. 16,18,19.

V. 25. Clothes, we are told, express the person. In this sense this woman is expressed by two qualities: "strength" and "dignity". These two qualities are evident in all that has been said of her. "This 'laughing at the future' is of course not to be understood as expressive of a presumptuous self-confidence, but only of a consciousness of having all appropriate and possible preparation and competence for the future" ("Lange").

V. 26. Special mention is here made of her speech habits. An idle woman will often get herself into tongue-trouble: "Withal they learn also to be idle, going about from house to house; and not only idle, but tattlers also and busybodies, speaking things which they ought not" (I Tim. 5:13). The busy, useful life lived by Proverbs' "virtuous woman" would help keep her from the above. Tit. 2:3 instructs womanhood to be "not slanderers". This will be foreign to the virtuous woman, for she is both wise and kind in her speech. When she speaks, it is wisdom that comes forth, and the "law of kindness" governs her lips also.

V. 27. Her thorough care of her household is again emphasized (we might say in contrast with those women who are neglectful of their households, not seeing that they have proper meals, not seeing that their clothing is in good order, not keeping up the house, etc.). And her busyness in their behalf is again emphasized (we might say in contrast with those women who are lazy, sleeping in far beyond the proper time to get up, and then not working with diligence after they get up).

V. 28. And her household notices her care of them and her work in their behalf, and she is greatly appreciated. Her husband does not overlook her good life and work, but "he praiseth her" (to herself, privately, to others upon appropriate occasion, and to God who gave her to him). And he teaches the children to appreciate her many efforts too, and the longer they live and the older they get, the more they rise up and call her "blessed", making "Mother" one of the sweetest and dearest words in all the world to them. "Mother and goodness" and "Mother and love" go together in their minds. You men have good wives, tell them so, and you children who have good mothers, tell them so.

V. 29. "Many daughters" means "many women" (or "many daughters of men"). Yes, the husband admits that there are many women who have done worthily, but to him his own is the very best of all! And isn't this the way it should be? Thinking of her in this way, he will be happy and satisfied with her. He will not be thinking of other women nor leaving her for them.

V. 30. He realizes that others may have "grace", and others may display "beauty", but it is better to be married to a woman who "feareth Jehovah". Such a woman as he has will be praised, but to fall for the grace of the other woman will be found to be "deceitful", and he will see how empty ("vain") her beauty can be when she lacks the important qualities of womanhood. Oh, that all women realized how deceitful grace can be and how vain mere physical beauty is! Concerning "elegance of shape, symmetry of features, dignity of mien, and beauty of countenance," "Clarke" says, "Sickness impairs them, suffering deranges them, and death destroys them."

V. 31. Psa. 128:1,2 speaks of the righteous person getting to eat the product of one's hands: "Blessed is every one that feareth Jehovah, That walketh in his ways. For thou shalt eat the labor of thy hands." God's final message concerning her to us is that we should give her what she deserves, what she has rightfully earned, especially priase and public recognition ("in the gates"). Let us listen to "Clarke" in his rather eloquent close: "Let what she has done be spoken of for a memorial to her; let her bright example be held forth in the most public places. Let it be set before the eyes of every female, particularly of every wife, and especially of every mother; and let them learn from this exemplar what men have a right to expect in their wives, the mistresses of their families and the mothers of their children."

TEST QUESTIONS OVER 31:22-31

1. What new thoughts concerning the virtuous woman are found in v. 22?
2. Tell of her husband (v. 23).
3. What items did she make to sell (v. 24)?
4. What two qualities stand out in her (v. 25)?
5. How is her speech described (v. 26)?
6. What does v. 27 re-emphasize concerning this good woman?
7. Besides the satisfaction that she receives from a job well done, what does v. 28 tell us of her reward?
8. How does her husband express his feelings concerning her great worth (v. 29)?
9. V. 30 says, "...... is deceitful, and ...... is vain."
10. What is God's final message concerning her to us (v. 31)?

NOTE: "Noticeable Groupings" within a chapter are found only in those chapters made up of 1-verse sayings (chapters 10-29).

OUTLINE OF THE VIRTUOUS WOMAN

I. She is married to a good man (v. 23).
II. Her husband has no fears of her unfaithfulness to him (vs. 11,12).
III. She gets up early, cooks breakfast for the family, and gets the day underway (v. 15).
IV. She lives a busy, industrious, useful life:
  A. She clothes her family in a commendable way (vs. 13,19,21).
  B. She raises some of their food (v. 16), but she buys those things that she cannot raise (v. 14).
  C. She looks after every need of her household (v. 27).
  D. She is strong and healthy as a result of her work (v. 17).
  E. She likes nice things and makes them (v. 22).
  F. She makes extras and sells them (v. 24).
  G. She puts in a long day (v. 26).
V. She is known for her kind speech (v. 26).
VI. She looks nice (v. 22), but she steers away from feminine vanities (v. 30).
VII. She is not afraid of the passing of years but will grow old gracefully (v. 25).
VIII. She should and shall be praised (vs. 28-31).

PONDERING THE PROVERBS

GOD BELIEVES IN CORRECTION

God is not with the modern trend to let evil go unrebuked. He Himself is a corrector: "My son, despise not the chastening of the Lord; neither be weary of his correction: for whom the Lord loveth he correcteth; even as a father the son in whom he delighteth" (3:11,12).

He says to fathers, "Withhold not correction from the child: for if thou beatest him with the rod, he shall not die. Thou shalt beat him with the rod, and shalt deliver his soul from hell" (23:13, 14). He says, "Correct thy son, and he shall give thee rest; yea, he shall give delight unto thy soul" (29:17).

God says that people who believe in keeping His law believe in contending with the wicked, that those who pat the wicked on the back are the ones who depart from the law themselves: "They that forsake the law praise the wicked: but such as keep the law contend with them" (28:4).

These verses present but a sample of the many things said in the book of Proverbs on the subject of correction.

TOPICAL INDEX OF THE PROVERBS

ABHOR (See "Hate")
ABOMINATION (See "Hate")
ANGER, WRATH

"Riches profit not in the day of wrath" (11:4).
"The expectation of the wicked is wrath" (11:23).
"A fool's vexation is presently known" (12:16).
"He that is slow to anger is of great understanding" (14:29).
"The king's...wrath will be against him that causeth shame" (14:35).
"A soft answer turneth away wrath (15:1).
"Grievous words stirreth up anger" (15:1).
"A wrathful man stirreth up contention" (15:18).
"He that is slow to anger appeaseth strife" (15:18).
"The wrath of a king is as messengers of death; But a wise man will pacify it" (16:14).
"He that is slow to anger is better than the mighty" (16:32).
"The discretion of a man maketh him slow to anger" (19:11).
"The king's wrath is as the roaring of a lion" (19:12).
"A man of great wrath shall bear the penalty; For if thou deliver him, thou must do it yet again" (19:19).
"The terror of a king is as the roaring of a lion: He that provoketh him to anger sinneth against his own life" (20:2).
"A gift in secret pacifieth anger; And a present in the bosom, strong wrath" (21:14).
"He that soweth iniquity...the rod of his wrath shall fail" (22:8).
"A stone is heavy, and the sand weighty; But a fool's vexation is heavier than they both" (27:3).
"Wrath is cruel, and anger is overwhelming" (27:4).
"Wise men turn away wrath" (29:8).
"If a wise man hath a controversy with a foolish man, Whether he be angry or laugh, there will be no rest" (29:9).
"The forcing of wrath bringeth forth strife" (30:33).

BRIBES, GIFTS

"He that hateth bribes shall live" (15:27).
"A bribe is a precious stone in the eyes of him that hath it; Whithersoever it turneth, it prospereth" (17:8).
"A wicked man receiveth a bribe out of the bosom, To pervert

the ways of justice" (17:23).
"He that exacteth gifts overthroweth it" (29:4).

CHEERFUL (See "Joy")
CHILDREN (See "Parent-Child")
COMMANDMENTS IN "PROVERBS"

"Hear the instruction of thy father" (1:8).
"Refrain thy foot from their path" (1:15).
"Turn you at my reproof" (1:23).
"Let thy heart keep my commandments" (3:1).
"Bind them about thy neck; Write them upon the tablet of thy heart" (3:3).
"Trust in Jehovah with all they heart" (3:5).
"In all thy ways acknowledge him" (3:6).
"Fear Jehovah, and depart from evil" (3:7).
"Honor Jehovah with thy substance, And with the first-fruits of all thine increase" (3:9).
"Keep sound wisdom and discretion" (3:21).
"Hear, my sons, the instruction of a father" (4:1).
"Attend to know understanding" (4:1).
"Let thy heart retain my words; Keep my commandments" (4:4).
"Get wisdom, get understanding" (4:5).
"Love her" (4:6).
"Exalt her" (4:8).
"Hear, O my son, and receive my sayings" (4:10).
"Take fast hold of instruction...Keep her" (4:13).
"Avoid it...Turn from it, and pass on" (4:15).
"My son, attend to my words; Incline thine ear unto my sayings...Keep them in the midst of thy heart" (4:20,21).
"Keep thy heart with all diligence" (4:23).
"Put away from thee a wayward mouth, And perverse lips put far from thee" (4:24).
"Let thine eyes look right on, And let thine eyelids look straight before thee" (4:25).
"Remove thy foot from evil" (4:27).
"My son, attend unto my wisdom; Incline thine ear to my understanding" (5:1).
"My sons, hearken unto me" (5:7).
"Remove thy way far from her" (5:8).
"Drink waters out of thine own cistern, And running waters out

of thine own well" (5:15).

"Let them be for thyself alone" (5:17).

"Let thy fountain be blessed; And rejoice in the wife of thy youth" (5:18).

"Let her breasts satisfy thee at all times" (5:19).

"Deliver thyself...as a roe from the hand of the hunter" (6:3,5).

"Go to the ant, thou sluggard; Consider her ways, and be wise" (6:6).

"Keep the commandment of thy father...Bind them continually upon thy heart; Tie them about thy neck" (6:20,21).

"My son, keep my words, And lay up my commandments with thee. Keep my commandments" (7:1,2).

"Say unto wisdom, Thou art my sister" (7:4).

"Call understanding thy kinswoman" (7:4).

"My sons, hearken unto me, And attend to the words of my mouth" (7:24).

"Understand prudence...be of an understanding heart" (8:5).

"Receive my instruction...And knowledge rather than choice gold" (8:10).

"My sons, hearken unto me...Hear instruction, and be wise" (8:32,33).

"Leave off, ye simple ones...Walk in the way of understanding" (9:6).

"Reprove a wise man" (9:8).

"Give instruction to a wise man...Teach a righteous man" (9:9).

"Walk with wise men" (13:20).

"Commit thy works unto Jehovah" (16:3).

"Leave off contention, before there is quarrelling" (17:14).

"Chasten thy son" (19:18).

"Hear counsel, and receive instruction" (19:20).

"Smite a scoffer, and the simple will learn prudence; And reprove one that hath understanding, and he will understand knowledge" (19:25).

"Cease, my son, to hear instruction Only to err from words of knowledge" (19:27).

"Open thine eyes" (20:13).

"Take his garment that is surety for a stranger; And hold him in pledge that is surety for foreigners" (20:16).

"By wise guidance make thou war" (20:18).

"Train up a child in the way he should go" (22:6).

"Cast out the scoffer" (22:10).

"Incline thine ear, and hear the words of the wise, And apply thy heart unto my knowledge" (20:17).

"When thou sittest to eat with a ruler, Consider diligently him that is before thee; And put a knife to thy throat, If thou be a man given to appetite" (23:1,2).

"Cease from thine own wisdom" (23:4).

"Apply thy heart unto instruction, And thine ears to the words of knowledge" (23:12).

"Hear thou, my son, and be wise, And guide thy heart in the way" (23:19).

"Hearken unto thy father that begat thee" (23:22).

"Buy the truth" (23:23).

"Let thy father and thy mother be glad, And let her that bare thee rejoice" (23:25).

"My son, give me thy heart; And let thine eyes delight in my ways" (23:26).

"Deliver them that are carried away unto death, And those that are ready to be slain see that thou hold back" (24:11).

"Eat thou honey...And the droppings of the honeycomb" (24:13).

"Fear Jehovah and the king" (24:21).

"Prepare thy work without, And make it ready for thee in the field; And afterwards build thy house" (24:27).

"Take away the dross from the silver...Take away the wicked from before the king" (25:4,5).

"Debate thy cause with thy neighbor himself" (25:9).

"Let thy foot be seldom in thy neighbor's house" (25:17).

"If thine enemy be hungry, give him bread to eat; And if he be thirsty, give him water to drink" (25:21).

"Answer a fool according to his folly" (26:5).

"Let another praise thee" (27:2).

"My son, be wise, and make my heart glad" (27:11).

"Take his garment that is surety for a stranger; And hold him in pledge that is surety for a foreign woman" (27:13).

"Be thou diligent to know the state of thy flocks, And look well to thy herds" (27:23).

"Correct thy son" (29:17).

"If thou hast done foolishly in lifting up thyself, Or if thou hast thought evil, Lay thy hand upon thy mouth" (30:32).

"Give strong drink unto him that is ready to perish, And wine unto the bitter of soul" (31:6).

"Open thy mouth for the dumb...judge righteously" (31:8,9).

"Give her of the fruit of her hands; And let her works praise her in the gates" (31:31).

TOPICAL INDEX OF THE PROVERBS

COMPANIONSHIP

"If sinners entice thee, Consent thou not. If they say, Come with us, Let us lay wait for blood...walk not thou in the way with them; Refrain thy foot from their path" (1:10,11,15).
"Walk with wise men, and thou shalt be wise: But the companion of fools shall smart for it" (13:20).
"Make no friendship with a man that is given to anger; And with a wrathful man thou shalt not go: Lest thou learn his ways" (22:24,25).
"Company not with them that are given to change" (24:21).
"He that is a companion of gluttons shameth his father" (28:7).
"He that followeth after vain persons shall have poverty enough" (28:19).
"He that keepeth company with harlots wasteth his substance" (29:3).
"Whoso is partner with a thief hateth his own soul" (29:24).

CONCEAL, COVER, HIDE

"Love covereth all transgressions" (10:12).
"He that hideth hatred is of lying lips" (10:18).
"He that goeth about as a talebearer revealeth secrets; But he that is of a faithful spirit concealeth a matter" (11:13).
"A prudent man concealeth shame" (12:16).
"A prudent man concealeth knowledge" (12:23).
"He that covereth a transgression seeketh love" (17:9).
"A prudent man seeth the evil, and hideth himself" (22:3).
"It is the glory of God to conceal a thing" (25:2).
"Though his hatred cover itself with guile, His wickedness shall be openly showed before the assembly" (26:26).
"A prudent man seeth the evil, and hideth himself" (27:12).
"When the wicked rise, men hide themselves" (28:12).
"He that covereth his transgressions shall not prosper" (28:13).
"He that giveth unto the poor shall not lack; But he that hideth his eyes shall have many a curse" (28:27).
"When the wicked rise, men hide themselves" (28:28).

CONCEIT (See "Pride")

CORRECTION, REBUKE, REPROVE

"Turn you at my reproof" (1:23).
"Ye...would none of my reproof" (1:25).
"They despised all my reproof" (1:30).

"Despise not the chastening of Jehovah; Neither be weary of his reproof" (3:11).
"My heart despised reproof" (5:12).
"Reproofs of instruction are the way of life" (6:23).
"...as one in fetters to the correction of the fool" (7:22).
"He that correcteth a scoffer getteth to himself reviling" (9:7).
"He that reproveth a wicked man getteth himself a blot" (9:7).
"Reprove not a scoffer, lest he hate thee" (9:8).
"Reprove a wise man, and he will love thee" (9:8).
"He is in the way of life that heedeth correction" (10:17).
"He that forsaketh reproof erreth" (10:17).
"Whoso loveth correction loveth knowledge" (12:1).
"He that hateth reproof is brutish" (12:1).
"A scoffer heareth not rebuke" (13:1).
"Poverty and shame shall be to him that refuseth correction" (13:18).
"He that regardeth reproof shall be honored" (13:18).
"A fool despiseth his father's correction" (15:5).
"He that regardeth reproof getteth prudence" (15:5).
"There is grievous correction for him that forsaketh the way" (15:10).
"He that hateth reproof shall die" (15:10).
"A scoffer loveth not to be reproved" (15:12).
"The ear that hearkeneth to the reproof of life shall abide among the wise" (15:31).
"He that refuseth correction despiseth his own soul" (15:32).
"He that hearkeneth to reproof getteth understanding" (15:32).
"A rebuke entereth deeper into one that hath understanding than a hundred stripes into a fool" (17:10).
"Reprove one that hath understanding, and he will understand knowledge" (19:25).
"Foolishness is bound up in the heart of a child; But the rod of correction shall drive it far from him" (22:15).
"Withhold not correction from the child" (23:13).
"To them that rebuke him shall be delight, And a good blessing shall come upon them" (24:25).
"As an ear-ring of gold, and an ornament of fine gold, So is a wise reprover upon an obedient ear" (25:12).
"Better is open rebuke Than love that is hidden" (27:5).
"He that rebuketh a man shall afterward find more favor Than he that flattereth with the tongue" (28:23).
"The rod and reproof give wisdom" (29:15).

"Add thou not unto his words, Lest he reprove thee, and thou be found a liar" (30:6).

COUNSEL

"That the man of understanding may attain unto sound counsels" (1:5).
"Ye have set at nought all my counsel" (1:25).
"They would none of my counsel" (1:30).
"Counsel is mine" (8:14).
"In the multitude of counsellors there is safety" (11:14).
"The counsels of the wicked are deceit" (12:5).
"He hearkeneth unto counsel" (12:15).
"To the counsellors of peace is joy" (12:20).
"Where there is no counsel, purposes are disappointed" (15:22).
"In the multitude of counsellors they are established" (15:22).
"Hear counsel...That thou mayest be wise in thy latter end" (19:20).
"The counsel of Jehovah, that shall stand" (19:21).
"Counsel in the heart of man is like deep water; But a man of understanding will draw it out" (20:5).
"Every purpose is established by counsel" (20:18).
"There is no...counsel against Jehovah" (21:30).
"Have not I written unto thee excellent things of counsels?" (22:20).
"In the multitude of counsellors there is safety" (24:6).
"Oil and perfume rejoice the heart; So doth the sweetness of a man's friend that cometh of hearty counsel" (27:9).

COVER (See "conceal")

DECEIT

"The counsels of the wicked are deceit" (12:5).
"He that uttereth truth showeth forth righteousness; But a false witness, deceit" (12:17).
"Be not desirious of his dainties; Seeing they are deceitful food" (23:3).
"Eat and drink, saith he to thee; But his heart is not with thee" (23:7).
"So is the man that deceiveth his neighbor, And saith, Am not I in sport?" (26:19).
"He layeth up deceit within him" (26:24).
"When he speaketh fair, believe him not; For there are seven

abominations in his heart" (26:25).
"Though his hatred cover itself with guile, His wickedness shall be openly showed before the assembly" (26:26).
"A lying tongue hateth those whom it hath wounded" (26:28).
"A flattering mouth worketh ruin" (26:28).

DELIGHT, FAVOR, PLEASE

"How long...will...scoffers delight them in scoffing?" (1:22).
"Who rejoice to do evil, And delight in the perverseness of evil" (2:14).
"Whom Jehovah loveth he reproveth, Even as a father the son in whom he delighteth" (3:12).
"I was daily his delight" (8:30).
"A just weight is his delight" (11:1).
"Such as are perfect in their way are his delight" (11:20).
"He that diligently seeketh good seeketh favor" (11:27).
"A good man shall obtain favor of Jehovah" (12:2).
"A man shall be commended according to his wisdom" (12:8).
"They that deal truly are his delight" (12:22).
"Good understanding giveth favor" (13:15).
"Among the upright there is good will" (14:9).
"The king's favor is toward a servant that dealeth wisely" (14:35).
"The prayer of the upright is his delight" (15:8).
"Righteous lips are the delight of kings; And they love him that speaketh right" (16:13).
"His favor is as a cloud of the latter rain" (16:15).
"A fool hath no delight in understanding" (18:2).
"Whoso findeth a wife...obtaineth favor of Jehovah" (18:22).
"Many will entreat the favor of the liberal man" (19:6).
"His favor is as dew upon the grass" (19:12).
"His neighbor findeth no favor in his eyes" (21:10).
"A good name is rather to be chosen than great riches, And loving favor rather than silver and gold" (22:1).
"To them that rebuke him shall be delight" (24:25).
"Correct thy son, and...he will give delight unto thy soul" (29:17).
"Many seek the ruler's favor" (29:26).
"Grace is deceitful" (31:30).

DELIVER

"To deliver thee from the way of evil, From the men that speak

perverse things" (2:12).
"To deliver thee from the strange women" (2:16).
"Deliver thyself, Seeing thou art come into the hand of thy neighbor" (6:3).
"Deliver thyself as a roe from the hand of the hunter" (6:5).
"Righteousness delivereth from death" (10:2).
"Righteousness delivereth from death" (11:4).
"The righteousness of the upright shall deliver them" (11:6).
"The righteous is delivered out of trouble" (11:8).
"Through knowledge shall the righteous be delivered" (11:9).
"The seed of the righteous shall be delivered" (11:21).
"The mouth of the upright shall deliver them" (12:6).
"A true witness delivereth souls" (14:25).
"A man of great wrath shall bear the penalty; For if thou deliver him, thou must do it yet again" (19:19).
"Thou shalt beat him with the rod, And shalt deliver his soul from Sheol" (23:14).
"Deliver them that are carried away unto death" (24:11).
"Whoso walketh wisely, he shall be delivered" (28:26).

DILIGENCE, DILIGENT

"Keep thy heart with all diligence" (4:23).
"Therefore came I forth to meet thee, Diligently to seek thy face, and I have found thee" (7:15).
"The hand of the diligent maketh rich" (10:4).
"He that gathereth in summer is a wise son" (10:5).
"The labor of the righteous tendeth to life" (10:16).
"He that diligently seeketh good seeketh favor" (11:27).
"The hand of the diligent shall bear rule" (12:24).
"The precious substance of men is to the diligent" (12:27).
"The soul of the diligent shall be made fat" (13:4).
"The thoughts of the diligent tend only to plenteousness" (21:5).
"Seest thou a man diligent in his business? he shall stand before kings; He shall not stand before mean men" (22:29).
"When thou sittest to eat with a ruler, Consider diligently him that is before thee" (23:1).
"Be thou diligent to know the state of thy flocks, And look well to thy herds" (27:23).

DIRECT QUOTATIONS

Because some of these are lengthy, the references are given

where they may be found rather than their statements: 1:10; 1:11; 1:12-14; 1:22-33; 2:28; 4:4; 4:5; 5:12-14; 6:10; 7:14-20; 8:4-10; 8:14-36; 9:4-6; 9:16; 9:17; 20:9; 20:14; 22:13; 26:13; 26:18,19; 28:24; 30:2-4; 30:7-9; 30:18,19; 30:20; 31:2-7.

DISHONESTY IN BUSINESS

"A false balance is an abomination to Jehovah" (11:1).
"Diverse weights, and diverse measures, Both of them alike are an abomination to Jehovah" (20:10).
"It is bad, it is bad, saith the buyer; But when he is gone his way, then he boasteth" (20:14).
"Diverse weights are an abomination to Jehovah; And a false balance is not good" (20:23).

EATING (See "Gluttony")
ENVY, ENVIOUS

"Envy thou not the man of violence" (3:31).
"Envy is the rottenness of the bones" (14:30).
"Let not thy heart envy sinners" (23:17).
"Be not thou envious against evil men" (24:1).
"Neither be thou envious at the wicked" (24:19).

EVIL (See "Wicked")
FATHERS (See "Parent-Child")
FAVOR (See "Delight")
FEAR

"The fear of Jehovah is the beginning of knowledge" (1:7).
"I will mock when your fear cometh; When your fear cometh as a storm" (1:26,27).
"They...did not choose the fear of Jehovah" (1:29).
"Whoso hearkeneth unto me...shall be quiet without fear of evil" (1:33).
"Then shalt thou understand the fear of Jehovah" (2:5).
"Fear Jehovah, and depart from evil" (3:7).
"Be not afraid of sudden fear" (3:25).
"The fear of Jehovah is to hate to evil" (8:13).
"The fear of Jehovah is the beginning of wisdom" (9:10).
"The fear of the wicked, it shall come upon him" (10:24).
"The fear of Jehovah prolongeth days" (10:27).
"He that feareth the commandment shall be rewarded" (13:13).
"He that walketh in his uprightness feareth Jehovah" (14:2).

"In the fear of Jehovah is strong confidence" (14:26).
"The fear of Jehovah is a fountain of life, That one may depart from the snares of death" (14:27).
"Better is a little, with the fear of Jehovah, Than great treasure and trouble therewith" (15:16).
"The fear of Jehovah is the instruction of wisdom" (15:33).
"By the fear of Jehovah men depart from evil" (16:6).
"The fear of Jehovah tendeth to life; And he that hath it shall abide satisfied; He shall not be visited with evil" (19:23).
"The terror of a king is as the roaring of a lion" (20:2).
"The reward of humility and the fear of Jehovah is riches, and honor, and life" (22:4).
"Be thou in the fear of Jehovah all the day long" (23:17).
"Fear thou Jehovah and the king" (24:21).
"Happy is the man that feareth alway" (28:14).
The fear of man bringeth a snare" (29:25).
"A woman that feareth Jehovah, she shall be praised" (31:30).

FOOLS, FOOLISH, FOOLISHNESS, FOLLY

"The foolish despise wisdom and instruction" (1:7).
"How long, ye simple ones, will ye love simplicity...And fools hate knowledge?" (1:22).
"The careless ease of fools shall destroy them" (1:32).
"Shame shall be the promotion of fools" (3:35).
"...as one in fetters to the correction of the fool" (7:22).
"O...ye fools, be of an understanding heart" (8:5).
"The foolish woman is clamorous" (9:13).
"A foolish son is the heaviness of his mother" (10:1).
"A prating fool shall fall" (10:8).
'A prating fool shall fall" (10:10).
"The mouth of the foolish is a present destruction" (10:14).
"He that uttereth a slander is a fool" (10:18).
"The foolish die for lack of understanding" (10:21).
"It is as sport to a fool to do wickedness" (10:23).
"The foolish shall be servant to the wise of heart" (11:29).
"The way of a fool is right in his own eyes" (12:15).
"A fool's vexation is presently known" (12:16).
"The heart of fools proclaimeth foolishness" (12:23).
"A fool flaunteth his folly" (13:16).
"It is an abomination to fools to depart from evil" (13:19).
"The companion of fools shall smart for it" (13:20).

"The foolish plucketth it down with her own hands" (14:1).
"In the mouth of the foolish is a rod for his pride" (14:3).
"Go into the presence of an foolish man, And thou shalt not perceive in him the lips of knowledge" (14:7).
"The folly of fools is deceit" (14:8).
"A trespass-offering mocketh fools" (14:9).
"The fool beareth himself insolently, and is confident" (14:16).
"He that is soon angry will deal foolishly" (14:17).
"The folly of fools is only folly" (14:24).
"He that is hasty of spirit exalteth folly" (14:29).
"That which is in the inward part of fools is made known" (14:33).
"The mouth of fools poureth out folly" (15:2).
"A fool despiseth his father's correction" (15:5).
"The lips of the wise disperse knowledge; But the heart of the foolish doeth not so" (15:7).
"The mouth of fools feedeth on folly" (15:14).
"A foolish man despiseth his mother" (15:20).
"Folly is joy to him that is void of wisdom" (15:21).
"The correction of fools is their folly" (16:22).
"Excellent speech becometh not a fool" (17:7).
"Rebuke entereth deeper into one that hath understanding Than a hundred stripes into a fool" (17:10).
"Let a bear robbed of her whelps meet a man, Rather than a fool in his folly" (17:12).
"Wherefore is there a price in the hand of a fool to buy wisdom, Seeing he hath no understanding?" (17:16).
"He that begetteth a fool doeth it to his sorrow" (17:21).
"The father of a fool hath no joy" (17:21).
"The eyes of a fool are in the ends of the earth" (17:24).
"A foolish son is a grief to his father, And bitterness to her that bare him" (17:25).
"Even a fool, when he holdeth his peace, is counted wise; When he shutteth his lips, he is esteemed as prudent" (17:28).
"A fool hath no delight in understanding, But only that his heart may reveal itself" (18:2).
"A fool's lips enter into contention, And his mouth calleth for stripes" (18:6).
"A fool's mouth is his destruction, And his lips are the snare of his soul" (18:7).
"He that giveth answer before he heareth, It is folly and shame unto him" (18:13).

"Better is the poor that walketh in his integrity Than he that is perverse in his lips and is a fool" (19:1).
"The foolishness of man subverteth his way" (19:3).
"Delicate living is not seemly for a fool" (19:10).
"A foolish son is the calamity of his father" (19:13).
"Judgments are prepared for scoffers, And stripes for the back of fools" (19:29).
"Every fool will be quarrelling" (20:3).
"There is precious treasure and oil in the dwelling of the wise; But a foolish man swalloweth it up" (21:20).
"Foolishness is bound up in the heart of a child; But the rod of correction shall drive it far from him" (22:15).
"Speak not in the hearing of a fool; For he will despise the wisdom of thy words" (23:9).
"Wisdom is too high for a fool: He openeth not his mouth in the gate" (24:7).
"The thought of foolishness is sin" (24:9).
"Honor is not seemly for a fool" (26:1).
"A whip for the horse, a bridle for the ass, And a rod for the back of fools" (26:3).
"Answer not a fool according to his folly, Lest thou also be like unto him. Answer a fool according to his folly, Lest he be wise in his own conceit" (26:4,5).
"The legs of the lame hang loose; So is a parable in the mouth of fools" (26:7).
"As a thorn that goeth up into the hand of a drunkard, So is a parable in the mouth of fools" (26:9).
"As one that bindeth a stone in a sling, So is he that giveth honor to a fool" (26:8).
"As an archer that woundeth all, So is he that hireth a fool" (26:10).
"As a dog that returneth to his vomit, So is a fool that repeateth his folly" (26:11).
"Seest thou a man wise in his own conceit? There is more hope of a fool than of him" (26:12).
"A stone is heavy, and the sand weighty; But a fool's vexation is heavier than they both" (27:3).
"Though thou shouldest bray a fool in a mortar with a pestle along with bruised grain, Yet will not his foolishness depart from him" (27:22).
"He that trusteth in his own heart is a fool" (28:26).
"If a wise man hath a controversy with a foolish man, Whether

he be angry or laugh, there will be no rest" (29:9).
"A fool uttereth all his anger" (29:11).
"Seest thou a man that is hasty in his words? There is more hope of a fool than of him" (29:20).
"The earth doth tremble...for...a fool when he is filled with food" (30:21,22).
"If thou hast done foolishly in lifting up thyself...Lay thy hand upon thy mouth" (30:32).

FRIENDSHIP

"The rich hath many friends" ')14:20).
"A whisperer separateth chief friends" (16:28).
"He that harpeth on a matter separateth chief friends" (17;9).
"A friend loveth at all times" (17:17).
"He that maketh many friends doeth it to his own destruction" (18:24).
"Wealth addeth many friends; But the poor is separated from his friend" (19:4).
"Every man is a friend to him that giveth gifts" (19:6).
"All the brethren of the poor do hate him: How much more do his friends go far from him!" (19:7).
"He that loveth pureness of heart, For the grace of his lips the king will be his friend" (22:11).
"Make no friendship with a man that is given to anger" (22:24).
"Faithful are the wounds of a friend" (27:6).
"Oil and perfume rejoice the heart; So doth the sweetness of man's friend that cometh of hearty counsel" (27:9).
"Thine own friend, and thy father's friend, forsake not" (27:10).
"He that blesseth his friend with a loud voice, rising early in the morning, It shall be counted a curse to him" (27:14).
"Iron sharpeneth iron; So a man sharpeneth the countenance of his friend" (27:17).

GIFTS (See "Bribes")
GLUTTONY, EATING

"When thou sittest to eat with a ruler, Consider diligently him that is before thee; And put a knife to thy throat, If thou be a man given to appetite. Be not desirous of his dainties; Seeing they are deceitful food" (23:1-3).
"Eat thou not the bread of him that hath an evil eye, Neither desire thou his dainties: For as he thinketh within himself, so is

he: Eat and drink, saith he to thee; But his heart is not with thee. The morsel which thou hast eaten shalt thou vomit up, And lose thy sweet words" (23:6-8).

"My son, eat thou honey, for it is good; And the droppings of the honeycomb, which are sweet to thy taste" (24:13).

"Hast thou found honey? eat so much as is sufficient for thee, Lest thou be filled therewith, and vomit it" (25:16).

"If thine enemy be hungry, give him bread to eat; And if he be thirsty, give him water to drink" (25:21).

"It is not good to eat much honey" (25:27).

"Whoso keepeth the fig-tree shall eat the fruit thereof" (27:18).

HAPPY (See "Joy")

HATE, ABHOR, ABOMINATION

"The foolish despise wisdom and instruction" (1:7).

"How long...will...fools hate knowledge?" (1:22).

"They hated knowledge" (1:29).

"They despised all my reproof" (1:30).

"Despise not thou the chastening of Jehovah" (3:11).

"The perverse is an abomination to Jehovah" (3:32).

"How have I hated instruction, And my heart despised reproof" (5:12).

"There are six things which Jehovah hateth; Yea, seven which are an abomination unto him: Haughty eyes, a lying tongue, And hands that shed innocent blood; A heart that deviseth wicked purposes, Feet that are swift in running to mischief, A false witness that uttereth lies, And he that soweth discord among brethren" (6:16-19).

"Men do not despise a thief, if he steal To satisfy himself when he is hungry" (6:30).

"Wickedness is an abomination to my lips" (8:7).

"The fear of Jehovah is to hate evil" (8:13).

"Pride, and arrogancy, and the evil way, And the perverse mouth, do I hate" (8:13).

"All they that hate me love death" (8:36).

"Reprove not a scoffer, lest he hate thee" (9:8).

"A false balance is an abomination to Jehovah" (11:1).

"He that despiseth his neighbor is void of wisdom" (11:12).

"He that hateth suretyship is secure" (11:15).

"They that are perverse in heart are an abomination to Jehovah" (11:20).

"He that hateth reproof is brutish" (12:1).
"He that is of a perverse heart shall be despised" (12:8).
"Better is he that is lightly esteemed, and hath a servant, Than he that honoreth himself, and lacketh bread" (12:9).
"Lying lips are an abomination to Jehovah" (12:22).
"A righteous man hateth lying" (13:5).
"A wicked man is loathsome, and cometh to shame" (13:5).
"It is an abomination to fools to depart from evil" (13:19).
"He that spareth his rod hateth his son" (13:24).
"He that is perverse in his ways despiseth him" (14:2).
"A man of wicked devices is hated" (14:17).
"The poor is hated even of his own neighbor" (14:20).
"He that despiseth his neighbor sinneth" (14:21).
"A fool despiseth his father's correction" (15:5).
"The sacrifice of the wicked is an abomination to Jehovah" (15:8).
"The way of the wicked ia an abomination to Jehovah" (15:9).
"He that hateth reproof shall die" (15:10).
"A foolish man despiseth his mother" (15:20).
"Evil devices are an abomination to Jehovah" (15:26).
"He that hateth bribes shall live" (15:27).
"He that refuseth correction despiseth his own soul" (15:32).
"Every one that is proud in heart is an abomination to Jehovah" (16:5).
"It is an abomination to kings to commit wickedness" (16:12).
"All the brethren of the poor do hate him: How much more do his friends go far from him!" (19:7).
"Diverse weights, and diverse measures, Both of them alike are an abomination to Jehovah" (20:10).
"Diverse weights are an abomination to Jehovah" (20:23).
"The sacrifice of the wicked is an abomination; How much more, when he bringeth it with a wicked mind!" (21:27).
"He that is abhorred of Jehovah shall fall therein" (22:14).
"A fool...will despise the wisdom of thy words" (23:9).
"Despise not thy mother when she is old" (23:22).
"The scoffer is an abomination to men" (24:9).
"He that saith unto the wicked, Thou art righteous, Peoples shall curse him, nations shall abhor him" (24:24).
"Let thy foot be seldom in thy neighbor's house, Lest he be weary of thee, and hate thee" (25:17).
"He that hateth dissembleth with his lips" (26:24).
"When he speaketh fair, believe him not; For there are seven

abominations in his heart" (26:25).
"A lying tongue hateth those whom it hath wounded" (26:28).
"He that turneth away his ear from hearing the law, Even his prayer is an abomination" (28:9).
"The bloodthirsty hate him that is perfect" (29:10).
"Whoso is partner with a thief hateth his own soul" (29:24).
"An unjust man is an abomination to the righteous" (29:27).
"He that is upright in the way is an abomination to the wicked" (29:27).
"The eye that...despiseth to obey his mother, The ravens of the valley shall pick it out" (30:17).

HEART

"Apply thy heart to understanding" (2:2).
"Wisdom shall enter into thy heart, And knowledge shall be pleasant unto thy soul" (2:10).
"Let thy heart keep my commandments" (3:1).
"Write them upon the tablet of thy heart" (3:3).
"Trust in Jehovah with all thy heart" (3:5).
"Let thy heart retain my words" (4:4).
"Keep them in the midst of thy heart" (4:21).
"Keep thy heart with all diligence; For out of it are the issues of life" (4:23).
"How have I hated instruction, And my heart despised reproof" (5:12).
"In whose heart is perverseness" (6:14).
"A heart that deviseth wicked purposes" (6:18).
"Bind them continually upon thy heart" (6:21).
"Lust not after her beauty in thy heart" (6:25).
"Write them upon the tablet of thy heart" (7:3).
"Wily of heart" (7:10).
"Let not thy heart decline to her ways" (7:25).
"Ye fools, be of an understanding heart" (8:5).
"The wise in heart will receive commandments" (10:8).
"The heart of the wicked is little worth" (10:20).
"They that are perverse in heart are an abomination to Jehovah" (11:20).
"The foolish shall be servant to the wise of heart" (11:39).
"He that is of a perverse heart shall be despised" (12:8).
"Deceit is in the heart of them that devise evil" (12:20).
"The heart of fools proclaimeth foolishness" (12:23).

"Heaviness in the heart of a man maketh it stoop" (12:25).
"Hope deferred maketh the heart sick" (13:12).
"The heart knoweth its own bitterness; And a stranger doth not intermeddle with its joy" (14:10).
"Even in laughter the heart is sorrowful" (14:13).
"A tranquil heart is the life of the flesh" (14:30).
"Wisdom resteth in the heart of him that hath understanding" (14:33).
"The heart of the foolish doeth not so" (15:7).
"Sheol and Abaddon are before Jehovah; How much more then the hearts of the children of men!" (15:11).
"A glad heart maketh a cheerful countenance; But by sorrow of heart the spirit is broken" (15:13).
"The heart of him that hath understanding seeketh knowledge" (15:14).
"He that is of a cheerful heart hath a continual feast" (15:15).
"The heart of the righteous studieth to answer" (15:28).
"The light of the eyes rejoiceth the heart" (15:30).
"The plans of the heart belong to man" (16:1).
"Every one that is proud in heart is an abomination to Jehovah" (16:5).
"A man's heart deviseth his way" (16:9).
"The wise in heart shall be called prudent" (16:21).
"The heart of the wise instructeth his mouth, And addeth learning to his lips" (16:23).
"Jehovah trieth the hearts" (17:3).
"He that hath a wayward heart findeth no good" (17:20).
"A cheerful heart is a good medicine; But a broken spirit drieth up the bones" (17:22).
"A fool hath no delight in understanding, But only that his heart may reveal itself" (18:2).
"Before destruction the heart of man is haughty" (18:12).
"The heart of the prudent getteth knowledge" (18:15).
"His heart fretteth against Jehovah" (19:3).
"There are many devices in a man's heart" (19:21).
"Counsel in the heart of man is like deep water" (20:5).
"Who can say, I have made my heart clean, I am pure from my sin?" (20:9).
"The king's heart is in the hand of Jehovah as the watercourses: He turneth it whithersoever he will" (21:1).
"Jehovah weigheth the heart" (21:2).
"A proud heart...is sin" (21:4).

"How much more, when he bringeth it with a wicked mind!" (21:27).
"He that loveth pureness of heart, For the grace of his lips the king will be his friend" (22:11).
"Foolishness is bound up in the heart of a child" (22:15).
"Apply thy heart unto my knowledge" (22:17).
"As he thinketh within himself, so is he" (23:7).
"Apply thy heart unto instruction" (23:12).
"My son, if thy heart be wise, My heart will be glad...My heart will rejoice" (23:15,16).
"Let not thy heart envy sinners" (23:17).
"Guide thy heart in the way" (23:19).
"My son, give me thy heart" (23:26).
"Thy heart shall utter perverse things" (23:33).
"Their heart studieth oppression" (24:2).
"Doth not he that weigheth the hearts consider it?" (24:12).
"Let not thy heart be glad when he is overthrown" (24:17).
"The heart of kings is unsearchable" (25:3).
"So is he that singeth songs to a heavy heart" (25:20).
"Fervent lips and a wicked heart Are like an earthen vessel overlaid with silver dross" (26:23).
"There are seven abominations in his heart" (26:25).
"Oil and perfume rejoice the heart" (27:9).
"My son, be wise, and make my heart glad" (27:11).
"As in water face answereth to face, So the heart of man to man" (27:19).
"He that hardeneth his heart shall fall into mischief" (28:14).
"He that trusteth in his own heart is a fool" (28:26).
"The heart of her husband trusteth in her" (31:11).

HIDE (See "Conceal")

HONOR

"Honor Jehovah with thy substance, And with the first-fruits of all thine increase" (3:9).
"In her left hand are riches and honor" (3:16).
"She will bring thee to honor, when thou dost embrace her" (4:8).
"Lest thou give thine honor unto others" (5:9).
"Riches and honor are with me" (8:18).
"The memory of the righteous is blessed" (10:7).
"A gracious woman obtaineth honor" (11:16).

"In the multitude of people is the king's glory" (14:28).
"Before honor goeth humility" (15:33).
"Before honor goeth humility" (18:12).
"It is an honor for a man to keep aloof from strife (20:3).
"He that followeth after righteousness and kindness findeth... honor" (21:21).
"A good name is rather to be chosen than great riches, and Loving favor rather than silver and gold" (22:1).
"The reward of humility and the fear of Jehovah Is...honor" (22:4).
"It is the glory of God to conceal a thing; But the glory of kings is to search out a matter" (25:2).
"Honor is not seemly for a fool" (26:1).
"As one that bindeth a stone in a sling, So is he that giveth honor to a fool" (26:8).
"He that is of a lowly spirit shall obtain honor" (29:23).
"Strength and dignity are her clothing" (31:25).

JEHOVAH

The following passages use "Jehovah": 1:7; 1:29; 2:6-8; 3:5-7; 3:9; 3:11,12; 3:19,20; 3:26; 3:32; 3:33,34; 5:21; 6:16-19; 8:13; 8:22; 8:35; 9:10; 10:3; 10:27; 10:29; 11:1; 11:20; 12:?2; 12:22; 14:26,27; 15:3; 15:9; 15:11; 15:16; 15:25; 15:26; 15:29; 15:33; 16:1; 16:2; 16:3; 16:4; 16:5; 16:6; 16:7; 16:9; 16:11; 16:20; 16:33; 17:3; 17:15; 18:10; 18:22; 19:17; 19:21; 19:23; 20:10; 20:12; 20:22; 20:23; 20:24; 20:27; 21:1; 21:2; 21:3; 21:30; 22:2; 22:12; 22:14; 22:19; 22:22,23; 23:17; 24:17,18; 24:21; 25:21,22; 28:5; 28:25; 29:13; 29:25; 30:8,9; 31:30.

JOY, HAPPY, REJOICE, CHEERFUL

"Who rejoice to do evil" (2:14).
"Happy is every one that retaineth her" (3:18).
"Rejoice in the wife of thy youth" (5:18).
"I was daily his delight, Rejoicing always before him, Rejoicing in his habitable earth" (8:30,31).
"When it goeth well with the righteous, the city rejoiceth" (11:10).
"To the counsellors of peace is joy" (12:20).
"The light of the righteous rejoiceth" (13:9).
"A stranger doth not intermeddle with its joy" (14:10).
"He that hath pity on the poor, happy is he" (14:21).

"A glad heart maketh a cheerful countenance" (15:13).
"Folly is joy to him that is void of wisdom" (15:21).
"A man hath joy in the answer of his mouth" (15:23).
"The light of the eyes rejoiceth the heart" (15:30).
"Whoso trusteth in Jehovah, Happy is he" (16:20).
"The father of a fool hath no joy" (17:21).
"It is joy to the righteous to do justice" (21:15).
"My son, if thy heart be wise, My heart will be glad, even mine: Yea, my heart will rejoice, When thy lips speak right things" (23:15,16).
"Thy father of the righteous will greatly rejoice" (23:24).
"Let thy father and thy mother be glad" (23:25).
"Rejoice not when thine enemy falleth, And let not thy heart be glad when he is overthrown" (24:17).
"Oil and perfume rejoice the heart" (27:9).
"Happy is the man that feareth alway" (28:14).
"When the righteous are increased, the people rejoice" (29:2).
"Whoso loveth wisdom rejoiceth his father" (29:3).
"The righteous doth sing and rejoice" (29:6).
"He that keepeth the law, happy is he" (29:18).
"She laugheth at the time to come" (31:25).

KINDNESS

"That which maketh a man to be desired is his kindness" (19:22).
"Most men will proclaim every one his own kindness" (20:6).
"Kindness and truth preserve the king; And his throne is upholden by kindness" (20:28).
"The law of kindness is on her tongue" (31:26).

KING, RULER

"The proverbs of Solomon...king of Israel" (1:1).
"By me kings reign, And princes decree justice. By me princes rule, And nobles, even all the judges of the earth" (8:15,16).
"A divine sentence is in the lips of the king; His mouth shall not transgress in judgment" (16:10).
"It is an abomination to kings to commit wickedness; For the throne is established by righteousness" (16:12).
"Righteous lips are the delight of kings; And they love him that speaketh right" (16:13).
"The wrath of a king is as messengers of death; But a wise man

will pacify it" (16:14).
"In the light of the king's countenance is life; And his favor is as a cloud of the latter rain" (16:15).
"The terror of a king is as the roaring of a lion: He that provoketh him to anger sinneth against his own life" (20:2).
"A king that sitteth on the throne of judgment Scattereth away all evil with his eyes" (20:8)
"A wise king winnoweth the wicked, And bringeth the threshing-wheel over them" (26).
"Kindness and truth perserve the king; And his throne is upholden by kindness" (20:28)
"He that loveth pureness of heart, For the grace of his lips the king will be his friend" (22:11).
"Seest thou a man diligent in his business? He shall stand before kings; He shall not stand before mean men" (22:29).
"Fear thou Jehovah and the king" (24:21).
"These also are proverbs of Solomon, which the men of Hezekiah king of Judah copied out" (25:1).
"The glory of kings is to search out a matter" (25:2).
"As the heavens for height, and the earth for depth, So the heart of kings is unsearchable" (25:3).
"Take away the wicked from before the king, And his throne shall be established in righteousness" (25:5).
"Put not thyself forward in the presence of the king...For better is it that it be said unto thee, Come up hither, Than that thou shouldest be put lower in the presence of the prince" (25:6,7).
"By long forbearing is a ruler persuaded" (25:15).
"For the transgression of a land many are the princes thereof" (28:2).
"As a roaring lion, and a raging bear, So is a wicked ruler over a poor people" (28:15).
"The prince that lacketh understanding is a great oppressor" (28:16).
"When a wicked man beareth rule, the people sigh" (29:2).
"The king by justice establisheth the land" (29:4).
"If a ruler hearkeneth to falsehood, All his servants are wicked" (29:12).
"The king that faithfully judgeth the poor, His throne shall be established for ever" (29:14).
"Many seek the ruler's favor" (29:26).
"The locusts have no king" (30:27).
"The lizard taketh hold with her hands, Yet is she in kings'

palaces" (30:28).

"There are three things which are stately in their march...and the king against whom there is no rising up" (30:31).

"The words of king Lemuel" (31:1).

"Give not thy strength unto women, Nor thy ways to that which destroyeth kings" (31:3).

"It is not for kings to drink wine" (31:4).

KNOWLEDGE, UNDERSTANDING

"To discern the words of understanding" (1:2).

"To give...to the young man knowledge and discretion" (1:4).

"...that the man of understanding may attain unto wise counsels" (1:5).

"To understand a proverb, and a figure" (1:6).

"The fear of Jehovah is the beginning of knowledge" (1:7).

"So as to...apply thy heart to understanding" (2:2).

"If thou...lift up thy voice for understanding; If thou seek her as silver, And search for her as for his treasures: Then shalt thou understand the fear of Jehovah, And find the knowledge of God" (2:3-5).

"Out of this mouth cometh knowledge and understanding" (2:6).

"Then shalt thou understand righteousness and justice" (2:9).

"So shalt thou find favor and good understanding In the sight of God and man" (3:4).

"Lean not unto thine own understanding" (3:5).

"Happy is...the man that getteth understanding" (3:13).

"Attend to know understanding" (4:1).

"Walk in the way of understanding" (9:6).

"So is wisdom to a man of understanding" (10:23).

"Through knowledge shall the righteous be delivered" (11:9).

"A man of understanding holdeth his peace" (11:12).

"Whoso loveth correction loveth knowledge" (21:1

"Good understanding giveth favor" (13:15).

"Knowledge is easy unto him that hath understanding" (14:6).

"He that is slow to anger is of great understanding" (14:29).

"The heart of him that hath understanding seeketh knowledge" (15:14).

"A man of understanding maketh straight his going" (15:21).

"Wisdom is before the face of him that hath understanding" (17:24).

"He that is of a cool spirit is a man of understanding" (17:27).

"That the soul be without knowledge is not good" (19:2).
"He that keepeth understanding shall find good" (19:8).
"Reprove one that hath understanding, and he will understand knowledge" (19:25).
"A man of understanding will draw it out" (20:5).
"The lips of knowledge are a precious jewel" (20:15).
"Apply...thine ears to the words of knowledge" (23:12).
"Through wisdom is a house builded; And by understanding it is established; And by knowledge are the chambers filled With all precious and pleasant riches" (24:3,4).
"By men of understanding and knowledge the state thereof shall be prolonged" (28:2).
"Evil men understand not justice" (28:5).
"They that seek Jehovah understand all things" (28:5).
"The poor that hath understanding searcheth him out" (28:11).
"The prince that lacketh understanding is also a great oppressor" (28:16).

LAW, COMMANDMENT

"Forsake not the law of thy mother" (1:8).
"Let thy heart keep my commandments" (3:1).
"Forsake ye not my law" (4:2).
"Keep the commandment of thy father" (6:20).
"Forsake not the law of thy mother" (6:20).
"The commandment is a lamp; and the law is light" (6:23).
"Lay up my commandments with thee" (7:1).
"Keep my commandments...And my law as the apple of thine eye" (7:2).
"When he gave to the sea its bound, That the waters should not transgress his commandment..." (8:29).
"The wise in heart will receive commandments" (10:8).
"He that feareth the commandment shall be rewarded" (13:13).
"The law of the wise is a fountain of life" (13:14).
"He that keepeth the commandment keepeth his soul" (19:16).
"They that forsake the law praise the wicked; But such as keep the law contend with them" (28:4).
"Whoso keepeth the law is a wise son" (28:7).
"He that turneth away his ear from hearing the law, Even his prayer is an abomination" (28:9).
"He that keepeth the law, happy is he" (29:18).
"Lest they drink, and forget the law" (31:5).
"The law of kindness is on her tongue" (31:26).

TOPICAL INDEX OF THE PROVERBS

LAZINESS, SLOTHFULNESS, SLUGGARD

"Go to the ant, thou sluggard; Consider her ways, and be wise: Which having no chief, Overseer, or ruler, provideth her bread in the summer, And gathereth her food in the harvest. How long wilt thou sleep, O sluggard? When wilt thou arise out of thy sleep?" (6:6-9).

"The slothful shall be put under taskwork" (12:24).

"The slothful man roasteth not that which he took in hunting" (12:27).

"The soul of the sluggard desireth, and hath nothing" (13:4).

"The way of the sluggard is as a hedge of thorns" (15:19).

"He also that is slack in his work Is brother to him that is a destroyer" (18:9).

"Love not sleep, lest thou come to poverty" (20:13).

"The desire of the sluggard killeth him; For his hands refuse to labor" (21:25).

"The sluggard saith, There is a lion without; I shall be slain in the streets" (22:13).

"The sluggard saith, There is a lion in the way; A lion is in the streets" (26:13).

"As the door turneth upon its hinges, So doth the sluggard upon his bed" (26:14).

"The sluggard burieth his hand in the dish; It wearieth him to his mouth" (26:15).

"The sluggard is wiser in his own conceit Than seven men that can render a reason" (26:16).

MOTHERS (See "Parent-Child")

NEIGHBOR

"Say not unto thy neighbor, Go, and come again, And to-morrow I will give thee" (3:28).

"Devise not evil against thy neighbor, Seeing he dwelleth securely by thee" (3:29).

"So is he that goeth in to his neighbor's wife; Whosoever toucheth her shall not be unpunished" (6:29).

"With his mouth the godless man destroyeth his neighbor" (11:9).

"He that despiseth his neighbor is void of wisdom" (11:12).

"The righteous is a guide to his neighbor; But the way of the wicked causeth them to err" (12:26).

"The poor is hated even of his own neighbor" (14:20).

"He that despiseth his neighbor sinneth" (14:21).
"A man of violence enticeth his neighbor, And leadeth him in a way that is not good" (16:29).
"He that pleadeth his cause first seemeth just; But his neighbor cometh and searcheth him out" (18:17).
"The soul of the wicked desireth evil: His neighbor findeth no favor in his eyes" (21:10).
"Be not a witness against thy neighbor without cause" (24:28).
"Go not forth hastily to strive, Lest thou know not what to do in the end thereof, When thy neighbor hath put thee to shame. Debate thy cause with thy neighbor himself, And disclose not the secret of another" (25:8,9).
"Let thy foot be seldom in thy neighbor's house, Lest he be weary of thee, and hate thee" (25:17).
"A man that beareth false witness against his neighbor Is a maul, and a sword, and a sharp arrow" (25:18).
"As a madman who casteth firebrands, Arrows, and death, So is the man that deceiveth his neighbor, And saith, Am not I in sport?" (26:18,19).
"Better is a neighbor that is near than a brother far off" (27:10).
"A man that flattereth his neighbor Spreadeth a net for his steps" (29:5).

NET (See "Snares")

OBEDIENCE

"Keep my commandments, and live" (4:4).
"Keep the commandment of thy father, And forsake not the law of thy mother" (6:20).
"Keep my words, And lay up my commandments with thee. Keep my commandments...And my law as the apple of thine eye" (7:1,2).
"Blessed are they that keep my ways" (8:32).
"Hearken unto thy father" (23:22).
"As an ear-ring of gold, and an ornament of fine gold, So is a wise reprover upon an obedient ear" (25:12).
"They that forsake the law praise the wicked, But such as keep the law contend with them" (28:4).
"Whoso keepeth the law is a wise son" (28:7).
"He that keepeth the law, happy is he" (29:18).

OPPRESS, OPPRESSION, STEAL, THIEF

"If they say, Come with us, Let us lay wait for blood; Let us lurk privily for the innocent without cause; Let us swallow them up alive as Sheol, And whole, as those that go down into the pit; We shall find all precious substance; We shall fill our houses with spoil; Thou shalt cast thy lot among us; We will all have one purse: My son, walk not thou in the way with them; Refrain thy foot from their path: For their feet run to evil, And they make haste to shed blood" (1:11-16).

"Envy thou not the man of violence, And choose none of his ways" (3:31).

"Men do not despise a thief, if he steal To satisfy himself when he is hungry" (6:30).

"He that oppresseth the poor reproacheth his Maker" (14:31).

"He that oppresseth the poor to increase his gain...shall come only to want" (22:16).

"Rob not the poor, because he is poor; Neither oppress the afflicted in the gate: For Jehovah will plead their cause, and despoil of life those that despoil them" (22:22).

"A needy man that oppresseth the poor Is like a sweeping rain which leaveth no food" (28:3).

"The prince that lacketh understanding is also a great oppressor" (28:16).

"Whoso robbeth his father or his mother, and saith, It is no transgression, The same is the companion of a destroyer" (28:24).

"...lest I be poor, and steal" (30:9).

PARENT-CHILD, SON, CHILDREN, FATHERS, MOTHERS

"The proverbs of Solomon the son of David" (1:1).

"My son, hear the instruction of thy father, And forsake not the law of thy mother" (1:8).

"My son, if sinners entice thee, Consent thou not" (1:10).

"My son, walk not thou in the way with them; Refrain thy foot from their path" (1:15).

"My son, if thou wilt receive my words, And lay up my commandments with thee...Then shalt thou understand the fear of Jehovah, And find the knowledge of God" (2:1-5).

"My son, forget not my law; But let thy heart keep my commandments" (3:1).

"My son, despise not the chastening of Jehovah; Neither be weary of his reproof" (3:11).

"Whom Jehovah loveth he reproveth, Even as a father the son

in whom he delighteth" (3:12).
"My son, let them not depart from thine eyes; Keep sound wisdom and discretion" (3:21).
"Hear, my sons, the instruction of a father, And attend to know understanding" (4:1).
"I was a son unto my father, Tender and only beloved in the sight of my mother. And he taught me, and said unto me: Let thy heart retain my words; Keep my commandments, and live..." (4:3-9).
"Hear, O my son, and receive my sayings; And the years of thy life shall be many" (4:10).
"My son, attend to my words; Incline thine ear unto my sayings. Let them not depart from thine eyes; Keep them in the midst of thy heart" (4:20,21).
"My son, attend unto my wisdom; Incline thine ear to my understanding" (5:1).
"My sons, hearken unto me, And depart not from the words of my mouth" (5:7).
"Why shouldest thou, my son, be ravished with a strange woman, And embrace the bosom of a foreigner?" (5:20).
"My son, if thou art become surety for thy neighbor, If thou hast stricken thy hands for a stranger; Thou art snared with the words of thy mouth...Do this now, my son, and deliver thyself, Seeing thou art come into the hand of thy neighbor: Go humble thyself and importune thy neighbor" (6:1-3).
"My son, keep the commandment of thy father, And forsake not the law of thy mother: Bind them continually upon thy heart; Tie them about thy neck" (6:20,21).
"My son, keep my words, And lay up my commandments with thee. Keep my commandments and live; And my law as the apple of thine eye. Bind them upon thy fingers; Write them upon the tablet of thy heart" (7:1-3).
"My sons, hearken unto me, And attend to the words of my mouth" (7:24).
"A wise son maketh a glad father; But a foolish son is the heaviness of his mother" (10:1).
"He that gathereth in summer is a wise son; But he that sleepeth in harvest is a son that causeth shame" (10:5).
"A wise son heareth his father's instruction" (13:1).
"A good man leaveth an inheritance to his children's children" (13:22).
"He that spareth his rod hateth his son; But he that loveth him

chasteneth him betimes" (13:24).

"A wise son maketh a glad father; But a foolish man despiseth his mother" (15:20).

"A servant that dealeth wisely shall have rule over a son that causeth shame" (17:2).

"Children's children are the crown of old men; And the glory of children are their fathers" (17:6).

"He that begetteth a fool doeth it to his sorrow; And the father of a fool hath no joy" (17:21).

"A foolish son is a grief to his father, And bitterness to her that bare him" (17:25).

"A foolish son is the calamity of his father" (19:13).

"House and riches are an inheritance from fathers" (19:14).

"Chasten thy son, seeing there is hope; And set not thy heart on his destruction" (19:18).

"He that doeth violence to his father, and chaseth away his mother, Is a son that causeth shame and bringeth reproach" (19:26).

"Cease, my son, to hear instruction Only to err from the words of knowledge" (19:27).

"Even a child maketh himself known by his doings, Whether his work be pure, and whether it be right" (20:11).

"Who curseth his father or his mother, His lamp shall be put out in blackness of darkness" (20:20).

"Train up a child in the way he should go, And even when he is old he will not depart from it" (22:6).

"Foolishness is bound up in the heart of a child; But the rod of correction shall drive it far from him" (22:15).

"Remove not the ancient landmark which thy fathers have set" (22:28).

"Withhold not correction from the child; For if thou beat him with the rod, he will not die. Thou shalt beat him with the rod, And shalt deliver his soul from Sheol" (23:13,14).

"My son, if thy heart be wise, My heart will be glad, even mine: Yea, my heart will rejoice, When thy lips speak right things" (23:15,16).

"Hear thou, my son, and be wise, And guide thy heart in the way" (23:19).

"Hearken unto thy father that beget thee, And despise not thy mother when she is old" (23:22).

"The father of the righteous will greatly rejoice; And he that begetteth a wise child will have joy of him. Let thy father and

thy mother be glad, And let her that bare thee rejoice" (23:24,25).
"My son, give me thy heart; And let thine eyes delight in my ways" (23:26).
"My son, eat thou honey, for it is good; And the droppings of the honeycomb, which are sweet to thy taste" (24:13).
"My son, be wise, and Make my heart glad, That I may answer him that reproacheth me" (27:11).
"Whoso keepeth the law is a wise son; But he that is a companion of gluttons shameth his father" (28:7).
"Whoso robbeth his father or his mother, and saith, It is no transgression, The same is the companion of a destroyer" (28:24).
"Whoso loveth wisdom rejoiceth his father" (29:3).
"The rod and reproof give wisdom; But a child left to himself causeth shame to his mother" (29:15).
"Correct thy son, and he will give thee rest; Yea, he will give delight unto thy soul" (29:17).
"He that delicately bringeth up his servant from a child Shall have him become a son at the last" (29:21).
"The words of Agur the son of Jakeh" (30:1).
"There is a generation that curse their father, And bless not their mother" (30:11).
"The eye that mocketh at his father, And despiseth to obey his mother, The ravens of the valley shall pick it out, And the young eagles shall eat it" (30:17).
"The words of King Lemuel; the oracle which his mother taught him" (31:1).
"What, my son? and what, O son of my womb? And what, O son of my vows?" (31:2).
"She is not afraid of the snow for her household; For all her household are clothed with scarlet" (31:21).
"She looketh well to the ways of her household" (31:27).
"Her children rise up, and call her blessed" (31:28).

PLEASE (See "Delight")

POOR

"He becometh poor that worketh with a slack hand" (10:4).
"The destruction of the poor is their poverty" (10:15).
"There is that maketh himself poor, yet hath great wealth" (13:7).

"The poor heareth no threatening" (13:8).
"Much food is in the tillage of the poor" (13:23).
"The poor is hated even of his own neighbor" (14:20).
"He that hath pity on the poor, happy is he" (14:21).
"He that oppresseth the poor reproacheth his Maker; But he that hath mercy on the needy honoreth him" (14:31).
"Whoso mocketh the poor reproacheth his Maker" (17:5).
"The poor useth entreaties" (18:23).
"Better is the poor that walketh in his integrity Than he that is perverse in his lips and is a fool" (19:1).
"The poor is separated from his friend" (19:4).
"All the brethren of the poor do hate him: How much more do his friends go far from him!" (19:7).
"He that hath pity upon the poor lendeth unto Jehovah, And his good deed will he pay him again" (19:17).
"A poor man is better than a liar" (19:22).
"Every one that is hasty hasteth only to want" (21:5).
"Whoso stoppeth his ears at the cry of the poor, He also shall cry, but shall not be heard" (21:13).
"He that loveth pleasure shall be a poor man" (21:17).
"The rich and the poor meet together: Jehovah is the maker of them all" (22:2).
"The rich ruleth over the poor" (22:7).
"He that hath a bountiful eye shall be blessed; For he giveth of his bread to the poor" (22:9).
"He that oppresseth the poor to increase his gain...shall come only to want" (22:16).
"Rob not the poor, because he is poor" (22:22).
"A needy man that oppresseth the poor Is like a sweeping rain which leaveth no food" (28:3).
"Better is the poor that walketh in his integrity, Than he that is perverse in his ways, though he be rich" (28:6).
"He that augmenteth his substance by interest and increase, Gathereth it for him that hath pity on the poor" (28:8).
"The rich man is wise in his own conceit; But the poor that hath understanding searcheth him out" (28:11).
"As a roaring lion, and a ranging bear, So is a wicked ruler over a poor people" (28:15).
"He that giveth unto the poor shall not lack; But he that hideth his eyes shall have many a curse" (28:27).
"The righteous taketh knowledge of the cause of the poor; The wicked hath not understanding to know it" (29:7).

"The poor man and the oppressor meet together; Jehovah lighteneth the eyes of them both" (29:13).
"The king that faithfully judgeth the poor, His throne shall be established for ever" (29:14).
"...lest I be poor, and steal" (30:9).
"There is a generation whose teeth are as swords, and their jaw teeth as knives, To devour the poor from off the earth, and the needy from among men" (30:14).
"Open thy mouth, judge righteously, And minister justice to the poor and needy" (31:9).
"She stretcheth out her hand to the poor; Yea, she reacheth forth her hands to the needy" (31:20).

PRAISE

"Let another man praise thee, and not thine own mouth; A stranger, and not thine own lips" (27:2).
"The refining pot is for silver, and the furnace for gold; And a man is tried by his praise" (27:21).
"They that forsake the law praise the wicked" (28:4).
"Her children rise up, and call her blessed; Her husband also, and he praiseth her" (31:28).
"A woman that feareth Jehovah, she shall be praised" (31:30).
"Let her works praise her in the gates" (31:31).

PRIDE (See "Conceit")

PROHIBITIONS (All the prohibitions in Proverbs)

"Forsake not the law of thy mother" (1:8).
"If sinners entice thee, Consent thou not" (1:10).
"Walk not thou in the way with them" (1:15).
"My son, forget not my law" (3:1).
"Let not kindness and truth forsake thee" (3:3).
"Lean not upon thine own understanding" (3:5).
"Be not wise in thine own eyes" (3:7).
"Despise not the chastening of Jehovah; Neither be weary of his reproof" (3:11).
"My son, let them not depart from thine eyes" (3:21).
"Be not afraid of sudden fear, Neither of the desolation of the wicked, when it cometh" (3:25).
"Withhold not good from them to whom it is due, When it is in the power of thy hand to do it. Say not unto thy neighbor, Go, and come again, And to-morrow I will give; When thou hast it

he mouth of the foolish is a present destruction" (10:14).
/hen the whirlwind passeth, the wicked is no more" (10:25).
he years of the wicked shall be shortened" (10:27).
he way of Jehovah...is a destruction to the workers of
uity" (10:29).
e wicked shall not dwell in the land" (10:30).
e perverse tongue shall be cut off" (10:31).
en pride cometh, then cometh shame" (11:2).
perverseness of the treacherous shall destroy them"
).
hes profit not in the day of wrath" (11:4).
wicked shall fall by his own wickedness" (11:5).
treacherous shall be taken in their own iniquity" (11:6).
hat is cruel troubleth his own flesh" (11:17).
hat pursueth evil doeth it to his own death" (11:19).
hat searcheth after evil, it shall come unto him" (11:27).
hat trusteth in his riches shall fall" (11:28).
righteous shall be recompensed in the earth; How much
the wicked and the sinner!" (11:31).
n of wicked devices will he condemn" (12:2).
vicked are overthrown, and are not" (12:7).
at openeth wide his lips shall have destruction" (13:3).
dness overthroweth the sinner" (13:6).
despiseth the word bringeth destruction on himself"

ay of the transgressor is hard" (13:15).
mpanion of fools shall smart for it" (13:20).
lly of the wicked shall want" (13:25).
use of the wicked shall be overthrown" (14:11).
s a way which seemeth right unto a man; But the end
re the ways of death" (14:12).
ked is thrust down in his evil-doing" (14:32).
will root up the house of the proud" (15:25).
is far from the wicked" (15:29).
eth before destruction, And a haughty spirit before a
8).
a way which seemeth right unto a man, But the end
e the ways of death" (16:25).
s glad at calamity shall not be unpunished" (17:5).
aiseth high his gate seeketh desctuction" (17:19).
nouth is his destruction, And his lips are the snare of
8:7).

by thee" (3:27,28).
"Devise not evil against thy neighbor" (3:29).
"Strive not with a man without cause, If he have done thee no harm" (3:30).
"Envy thou not the man of violence, And choose none of his ways" (3:31).
"Forsake ye not my law" (4:2).
"Forget not, neither decline from the words of my mouth" (4:5).
"Forsake her not" (4:6).
"Enter not into the path of the wicked, And walk not in the way of evil man...Pass not by it" (4:14,15).
"Let them not depart from thine eyes" (4:21).
"Turn not to the right hand nor to the left" (4:27).
"Depart not from the words of my mouth" (5:7).
"Come not nigh the door of her house" (5:8).
"Let them be for thyself alone, And not for strangers with thee" (5:17).
"Give not sleep to thine eyes; Nor slumber to thine eyelids" (6:4).
"Forsake not the law of thy mother" (6:20).
"Lust not after her beauty in thy heart; Neither let her take thee with her eyelids" (6:25).
"Let not thy heart decline to her ways; Go not astray in her paths" (7:25).
"Refuse it not" (8:33).
"Reprove not a scoffer" (9:8).
"Love not sleep" (20:13).
"Company not with him that openeth wide his lips" (20:19).
"Say not thou, I will recompense evil" (20:22).
"Rob not the poor, because he is poor; Neither oppress the afflicted in the gate" (22:22).
"Make no friendship with a man that is given to anger; And with a wrathful man thou shalt not go" (22:24).
"Be thou not one of them that strike hands, Or of them that are sureties for debts" (22:26).
"Remove not the ancient landmark, Which thy fathers have set" (22:28).
"Be not desirous of his dainties" (23:3).
"Weary not thyself to be rich" (23:4).
"Eat thou not the bread of him that hath an evil eye, Neither desire thou his dainties" (23:6).
"Speak not in the hearing of a fool" (23:9).

"Remove not the ancient landmark; And enter not into the fields of the fatherless" (23:10).
"Withhold not correction from the child" (23:13).
"Let not thy heart envy sinners" (23:17).
"Be not among winebibbers, Among gluttonous eaters of flesh" (23:20).
"Despise not thy mother when she is old" (23:22).
"Buy the truth, and sell it not" (23:23).
"Look not thou upon the wine when it is red, When it sparkleth in the cup, When it goeth down smoothly" (23:31).
"Be not thou envious against evil men; Neither desire to be with them" (24:1).
"Lay not wait, O wicked man, against the habitation of the righteous; Destroy not his resting-place" (24:15).
"Rejoice not when thine enemy falleth, And let not thy heart be glad when he is overthrown" (24:17).
"Fret not thyself because of evil-doers; Neither be thou envious at the wicked" (24:19).
"Company not with them that are given to change" (24:21).
"Be not a witness aginst thy neighbor without cause; And deceive not with thy lips" (24:28).
"Say not, I will do so to him as he hath done to me; I will render to the man according to his work" (24:29).
"Put not thyself forward in the presence of the king, And stand not in the place of great men" (25:6).
"Go not forth hastily to strive, Lest thou know not what to do in the end thereof, When thy neighbor hath put thee to shame" (25:8).
"Disclose not the secret of another" (25:9).
"Answer not a fool according to his folly" (26:4).
"When he speaketh fair, believe him not; For there are seven abominations in his heart" (26:25).
"Boast not thyself of tomorrow" (27:1).
"Thine own friend, and thy father's friend, forsake not" (27:10).
"Go not to thy brother's house in the day of thy calamity: Better is a neighbor that is near than a brother far off" (27:10).
"Add thou not unto his words" (30:6).
"Slander not a servant unto his master" (30:10).
"Give not thy strength unto women, Nor thy ways to that which destroyeth kings" (31:3).

PUNISHMENT

"Because I have called, and ye have refused; I
out my hand, and no man regarded; But ye hav
all my counsel, And would none of my reproof:
in the day of your calamity; I will mock when y
When your fear cometh as a storm, And your
on as a whirlwind; When distress and anguish
Then will they call upon me, but I will not a
seek me diligently, but they shall not find me
"Her house inclineth unto death, And her pat
None that go unto her return again, Neither
the paths of life" (2:18,19).
"The wicked shall be cut off from the land, A
shall be rooted out of it" (2:22).
"The curse of Jehovah is in the house of th
"Shame shall be the promotion of fools" (3:
"The way of the wicked is as darkness; Th
they stumble" (4:19).
"In the end she is bitter as wormwood,
sword" (5:4).
"Remove thy way far from her, And com
her house; Lest thou give thine honor
years unto the cruel; Lest strangers be
And thy labors be in the house of an al
thy latter end, When thy flesh and t
(5:8-11).
"He shall die for lack of instruction" (
"Therefore shall his calamity come su
he be broken, and that without reme
"On account of a harlot a man is br
(6:26).
"He that committeth adultery...wo
Wounds and dishonor shall he get; A
wiped away" (6:32,33).
"Her house is the way to Sheol, Go
death" (7:27).
"He that sinneth against me wro
that hate me love death" (8:36).
"He thrusteth away the desire of
"A prating fool shall fall" (10:8).
"A prating fool shall fall" (10:10

by thee" (3:27,28).
"Devise not evil against thy neighbor" (3:29).
"Strive not with a man without cause, If he have done thee no harm" (3:30).
"Envy thou not the man of violence, And choose none of his ways" (3:31).
"Forsake ye not my law" (4:2).
"Forget not, neither decline from the words of my mouth" (4:5).
"Forsake her not" (4:6).
"Enter not into the path of the wicked, And walk not in the way of evil man...Pass not by it" (4:14,15).
"Let them not depart from thine eyes" (4:21).
"Turn not to the right hand nor to the left" (4:27).
"Depart not from the words of my mouth" (5:7).
"Come not nigh the door of her house" (5:8).
"Let them be for thyself alone, And not for strangers with thee" (5:17).
"Give not sleep to thine eyes; Nor slumber to thine eyelids" (6:4).
"Forsake not the law of thy mother" (6:20).
"Lust not after her beauty in thy heart; Neither let her take thee with her eyelids" (6:25).
"Let not thy heart decline to her ways; Go not astray in her paths" (7:25).
"Refuse it not" (8:33).
"Reprove not a scoffer" (9:8).
"Love not sleep" (20:13).
"Company not with him that openeth wide his lips" (20:19).
"Say not thou, I will recompense evil" (20:22).
"Rob not the poor, because he is poor; Neither oppress the afflicted in the gate" (22:22).
"Make no friendship with a man that is given to anger; And with a wrathful man thou shalt not go" (22:24).
"Be thou not one of them that strike hands, Or of them that are sureties for debts" (22:26).
"Remove not the ancient landmark, Which thy fathers have set" (22:28).
"Be not desirous of his dainties" (23:3).
"Weary not thyself to be rich" (23:4).
"Eat thou not the bread of him that hath an evil eye, Neither desire thou his dainties" (23:6).
"Speak not in the hearing of a fool" (23:9).

"Remove not the ancient landmark; And enter not into the fields of the fatherless" (23:10).
"Withhold not correction from the child" (23:13).
"Let not thy heart envy sinners" (23:17).

"Be not among winebibbers, Among gluttonous eaters of flesh" (23:20).
"Despise not thy mother when she is old" (23:22).
"Buy the truth, and sell it not" (23:23).
"Look not thou upon the wine when it is red, When it sparkleth in the cup, When it goeth down smoothly" (23:31).
"Be not thou envious against evil men; Neither desire to be with them" (24:1).

"Lay not wait, O wicked man, against the habitation of the righteous; Destroy not his resting-place" (24:15).
"Rejoice not when thine enemy falleth, And let not thy heart be glad when he is overthrown" (24:17).
"Fret not thyself because of evil-doers; Neither be thou envious at the wicked" (24:19).

"Company not with them that are given to change" (24:21).
"Be not a witness aginst thy neighbor without cause; And deceive not with thy lips" (24:28).
"Say not, I will do so to him as he hath done to me; I will render to the man according to his work" (24:29).
"Put not thyself forward in the presence of the king, And stand not in the place of great men" (25:6).
"Go not forth hastily to strive, Lest thou know not what to do in the end thereof, When thy neighbor hath put thee to shame" (25:8).

"Disclose not the secret of another" (25:9).
"Answer not a fool according to his folly" (26:4).
"When he speaketh fair, believe him not; For there are seven abominations in his heart" (26:25).
"Boast not thyself of tomorrow" (27:1).

"Thine own friend, and thy father's friend, forsake not" (27:10).
"Go not to thy brother's house in the day of thy calamity: Better is a neighbor that is near than a brother far off" (27:10).
"Add thou not unto his words" (30:6).
"Slander not a servant unto his master" (30:10).
"Give not thy strength unto women, Nor thy ways to that which destroyeth kings" (31:3).

PUNISHMENT

"Because I have called, and ye have refused; I have stretched out my hand, and no man regarded; But ye have set at nought all my counsel, And would none of my reproof: I also will laugh in the day of your calamity; I will mock when your fear cometh; When your fear cometh as a storm, And your calamity cometh on as a whirlwind; When distress and anguish come upon you. Then will they call upon me, but I will not answer; They will seek me diligently, but they shall not find me" (1:24-28).

"Her house inclineth unto death, And her paths unto the dead; None that go unto her return again, Neither do they attain unto the paths of life" (2:18,19).

"The wicked shall be cut off from the land, And the treacherous shall be rooted out of it" (2:22).

"The curse of Jehovah is in the house of the wicked" (3:33).

"Shame shall be the promotion of fools" (3:35).

"The way of the wicked is as darkness; They know not at what they stumble" (4:19).

"In the end she is bitter as wormwood, Sharp as a two-edged sword" (5:4).

"Remove thy way far from her, And come not nigh the door of her house; Lest thou give thine honor unto others, And thy years unto the cruel; Lest strangers be filled with thy strength, And thy labors be in the house of an alien, And thou mourn at thy latter end, When thy flesh and thy body are consumed" (5:8-11).

"He shall die for lack of instruction" (5:23).

"Therefore shall his calamity come suddenly; On a sudden shall he be broken, and that without remedy" (6:15).

"On account of a harlot a man is brought to a piece of bread" (6:26).

"He that committeth adultery...would destroy his own soul. Wounds and dishonor shall he get; And his reproach shall not be wiped away" (6:32,33).

"Her house is the way to Sheol, Going down to the chambers of death" (7:27).

"He that sinneth against me wrongeth his own soul: All they that hate me love death" (8:36).

"He thrusteth away the desire of the wicked" (10:3).

"A prating fool shall fall" (10:8).

"A prating fool shall fall" (10:10).

"The mouth of the foolish is a present destruction" (10:14).
"When the whirlwind passeth, the wicked is no more" (10:25).
"The years of the wicked shall be shortened" (10:27).
"The way of Jehovah...is a destruction to the workers of iniquity" (10:29).
"The wicked shall not dwell in the land" (10:30).
"The perverse tongue shall be cut off" (10:31).
"When pride cometh, then cometh shame" (11:2).
"The perverseness of the treacherous shall destroy them" (11:3).
"Riches profit not in the day of wrath" (11:4).
"The wicked shall fall by his own wickedness" (11:5).
"The treacherous shall be taken in their own iniquity" (11:6).
"He that is cruel troubleth his own flesh" (11:17).
"He that pursueth evil doeth it to his own death" (11:19).
"He that searcheth after evil, it shall come unto him" (11:27).
"He that trusteth in his riches shall fall" (11:28).
"The righteous shall be recompensed in the earth; How much more the wicked and the sinner!" (11:31).
"A man of wicked devices will he condemn" (12:2).
"The wicked are overthrown, and are not" (12:7).
"He that openeth wide his lips shall have destruction" (13:3).
"Wickedness overthroweth the sinner" (13:6).
"Whoso despiseth the word bringeth destruction on himself" (13:13).
"The way of the transgressor is hard" (13:15).
"The companion of fools shall smart for it" (13:20).
"The belly of the wicked shall want" (13:25).
"The house of the wicked shall be overthrown" (14:11).
"There is a way which seemeth right unto a man; But the end thereof are the ways of death" (14:12).
"The wicked is thrust down in his evil-doing" (14:32).
"Jehovah will root up the house of the proud" (15:25).
"Jehovah is far from the wicked" (15:29).
"Pride goeth before destruction, And a haughty spirit before a fall" (16:18).
"There is a way which seemeth right unto a man, But the end thereof are the ways of death" (16:25).
"He that is glad at calamity shall not be unpunished" (17:5).
"He that raiseth high his gate seeketh desctuction" (17:19).
"A fool's mouth is his destruction, And his lips are the snare of his soul" (18:7).

"Before destruction the heart of man is haughty" (18:12).
"He that maketh many friends doeth it to his own destruction" (18:24).
"A false witness shall not be unpunished; And he that uttereth lies shall perish" (19:9).
"He that provoketh him to anger sinneth against his own life" (20:2).
"He shall beg in harvest, and have nothing" (20:4).
"Afterwards his mouth shall be filled with gravel" (20:17).
"Whoso curseth his father or his mother, His lamp shall be put out in blackness of darkness" (20:20).
"An inheritance may be gotten hastily at the beginning; But the end thereof shall not be blessed" (20:21).
"The getting of treasures by a lying tongue Is a vapor driven to and fro by them that seek death" (21:6).
"The violence of the wicked shall sweep them away" (21:7).
"The righteous man considereth the house of the wicked, How the wicked are overthrown to their ruin" (21:12).
"To do justice...is a destruction to the workers of iniquity" (21:15).
"The man that wandereth out of the way of understanding Shall rest in the assembly of the dead" (21:16).
"A false witness shall perish" (21:28).
"Thorns and snares are in the way of the perverse" (22:5).
"He that soweth iniquity shall reap calamity" (22:8).
"He overthroweth the words of the treacherous man" (22:12).
"Foolishness is bound up in the heart of a child; But the rod of correction shall drive it far from him" (22:15).
"He that oppresseth the poor to increase his gain, And he that giveth to the rich, shall come only to want" (22:16).
"Jehovah will...despoil of life those that despoil them" (22:23).
"Who hath woe? who hath sorrow? who hath contentions? Who hath complaining? who hath wounds without cause? Who hath redness of eyes? They that tarry long at the wine" (23:29,30).
"There shall be no reward to the evil man: The lamp of the wicked shall be put out" (24:20).
"Whoso diggeth a pit shall fall therein" (26:27).
"Whoso causeth the upright to go astray in an evil way, He shall fall himself into his own pit" (28:10).
"He that covereth his transgressions shall not prosper" (28:13).
"He that hardeneth his heart shall fall into mischief" (28:14).
"A man that is laden with the blood of any person Shall flee

unto the pit" (28:17).
"He that is perverse in his ways shall fall at once" (28:18).
"He that hideth his eyes shall have many a curse" (28:27).
"He that being often reproved hardeneth his neck Shall suddenly be destroyed, and that without remedy" (29:1).
"He that exacteth gifts overthroweth it" (29:4).
"Scoffers set a city in a flame" (29:8).
"The righteous shall look upon their fall" (29:16).

QUESTIONS

"How long, ye simple ones, will ye love simplicity? And scoffers delight them in scoffing, And fools hate knowledge?" (1:22).
"Should thy springs be dispersed abroad, And streams of water in the streets?" (5:16).
"Why shouldest thou...be ravished with a strange woman, And embrace the bosom of a foreigner?" (5:20).
"How long wilt thou sleep, O sluggard? When wilt thou arise out of thy sleep?" (6:9).
"Can a man take fire in his bosom, And his clothes not be burned? Or can one walk upon hot coals, And his feet not be scorched?" (6:27,28).
"Doth not wisdom cry, And understanding put forth her voice?" (8:1).
"Do they not err that devise evil?" (14:22).
"Wherefore is there a price in the hand of a fool to buy wisdom, Seeing he hath no understanding?" (17:16).
"A broken spirit who can bear?" (18:14).
"A faithful man who can find?" (20:6).
"Who can say, I have made my heart clean, I am pure from my sin?" (20:9).
"How then can man understand his way?" (20:24).
"Have not I written unto thee excellent things...?" (22:20,21).
"If thou hast not wherewith to pay, Why should he take away thy bed from under thee?" (22:27).
"Seest thou a man diligent in his business? he shall stand before kings" (22:29).
"Wilt thou set thine eyes upon that which is not? For riches certainly make themselves wings" (23:5).
"Who hath woe? who hath sorrow? who hath contentions? Who hath complaining? who hath wounds without cause? Who hath redness of eyes? They that tarry long at the wine" (23:29,30).
"When shall I awake? I will seek it yet again" (23:35).

"If thou sayest, Behold, we knew not this; Doth not he that weigheth the hearts consider it? And he that keepeth thy soul, doth not he know it? And shall not he render to every man according to his work?" (24:12).
"Their calamity shall rise suddenly; And the destruction from them both, who knoweth it?" (24:22).
"Hast thou found honey? eat so much as is sufficient for thee" (25:16).
"Seest thou a man wise in his own conceit? There is more hope of a fool than of him" (26:12).
"So is the man that deceiveth his neighbor, And saith, Am not I in sport?" (26:19).
"Who is able to stand before jealousy?" (27:4).
"Doth the crown endure unto all generations?" (27:24).
"Seest thou a man that is hasty in his words? There is more hope of a fool than of him" (29:20).
"Who hath ascended up into heaven, and descended? Who hath gathered the wind in his fists? Who hath bound the waters in his garment? Who hath established all the ends of the earth? What is his name, and what is his son's name, if thou knowest?" (30:4).
"What, my son? and what, O son of my womb? And what, O son of my vows?"(31:2).
"It is not for kings...Nor for princes to say, Where is strong drink?" (31:4).
"A worthy woman who can find?" (31:10).

QUOTATIONS (See "Direct Quotations")
REBUKE (See "Correction")
REJOICING (See "Joy")
REPROVE (See "Correction")
REWARD

"My son, hear the instruction of thy father, And forsake not the law of thy mother: For they shall be a chaplet of grace unto thy head, And chains about thy neck" (1:8,9).
"Whoso hearkeneth unto me shall dwell securely, And shall be quiet without fear of evil" (1:33).
"My son, if thou wilt receive my words, And lay up my commandments with thee; So as to incline thine ear unto wisdom, And apply thy heart to understanding; Yea, if thou cry after discernment, And lift up thy voice for understanding; If thou seek her as silver, And search for her as for hid treasures:

Then shalt thou understand the fear of Jehovah, And find the knowledge of God...Then shalt thou understand righteousness and justice, And equity, yea, every good path (2:1-9).
"The upright shall dwell in the land. And the perfect shall remain in it" (2:21).
"My son, forget not my law; But let thy heart keep my commandments: For length of days, and years of life, And peace, will they add to thee" (3:1,2).
"Let not kindness and truth forsake thee: Bind them about thy neck; Write them upon the tablet of thy heart: So shalt thou find favor and good understanding In the sight of God and man" (3:3,4).
"In all thy ways acknowledge him, And he will direct thy paths" (3:6).
"Be not wise in thine own eyes; Fear Jehovah, and depart from evil: It will be health to thy navel, And marrow to thy bones" (3:7,8).
"Honor Jehovah with thy substance, And with the first-fruits of all thine increase: So shall thy barns be filled with plenty, And thy vats shall overflow with new wine" (3:9,10).
"My son, let them not depart from thine eyes; Keep sound wisdom and discretion: So shall they be life unto thy soul, And grace to thy neck. Then shalt thou walk in thy way securely, And thy foot shall not stumble. When thou liest down, thou shalt not be afraid: Yea, thou shalt lie down, and thy sleep shall be sweet. Be not afraid of sudden fear, Neither of the desolation of the wicked, when it cometh: For Jehovah will be thy confidence, And will keep thy foot from being taken" (3:21-26).
"He blesseth the habitation of the righteous" (33:33).
"The wise shall inherit glory" (3:33).
"Forsake her not, and she will preserve thee; Love her, and she will keep thee" (4:6).
"Exalt her, and she will promote thee; She will bring thee to honor, when thou dost embrace her. She will give to thy head a chaplet of grace; A crown of beauty will she deliver to thee" (4:8,9).
"Hear, O my son, and receive my sayings; And the years of thy life shall be many" (4:10).
"The path of the righteous is as the dawning light, That shineth more and more unto the perfect day" (4?18).
"My son, attend to my words; Incline thine ear unto my sayings. Let them not depart from thine eyes; Keep them in the

midst of thy heart. For they are life unto those that find them, And health to all their flesh" (4:20-22).
"My son, keep the commandment of thy father, And forsake not the law of thy mother: Bind them continually upon thy heart; Tie them about thy neck. When thou walkest, it shall lead thee; When thou sleepest, it shall watch over thee; And when thou awakest, it shall talk with thee. For the commandment is a lamp; and the law is light; And reproofs of instruction are the way of life: To keep thee from the evil woman" (6:20-24).
"I love them that love me; And those that seek me diligently shall find me. Riches and honor are with me; Yea, durable wealth and righteousness. My fruit is better than gold, yea, than fine gold; And my revenue than choice silver. I walk in the way of righteousness, In the midst of the paths of justice; That I may cause those that love me to inherit substance, And that I may fill their treasuries" (8:17-21).
"My sons, hearken unto me; For blessed are they that keep my ways" (8:32).
"Hear instruction, and be wise" (8:33).
"Blessed is the man that heareth me...For whoso findeth me findeth life, And shall obtain favor of Jehovah" (8:34,35).
"By me thy days shall be multiplied, And the years of thy life shall be increased" (9:11).
"Righteousness delivereth from death" (10:2).
"Jehovah will not suffer the soul of the righteous to famish" (10:3).
"Blessings are upon the head of the righteous" (10:6).
"He is in the way of life that heedeth correction" (10:17).
"The desire of the righteous shall be granted" (10:24).
"The hope of the righteous shall be gladness" (10:28).
"The way of Jehovah is a stronghold to the upright" (10:29).
"The righteous shall never be removed" (10:30).
"Righteousness delivereth from death" (11:4).
"The righteousness of the perfect shall direct his way" (11:5).
"The righteousness of the upright shall deliver them" (11:6).
"The righteous is delivered out of trouble" (11:8).
"He that soweth righteousness hath a sure reward" (11:18).
"The seed of the righteous shall be delivered" (11:21).
"The liberal soul shall be made fat; And he that watereth shall be watered also himself" (11:25).
"The righteous shall flourish as the green leaf" (11:28).
"The righteous shall be recompensed in the earth" (11:31).

"A good man shall obtain favor of Jehovah" (12:2).
"The root of the righteous shall not be moved" (12:3).
"The house of the righteous shall stand" (12:7).
"The root of the righteous yieldeth fruit" (12:12).
"The righteous shall come out of trouble" (12:13).
"He that feareth the commandment shall be rewarded" (13:13).
"The tent of the upright shall flourish" (14:11).
"The righteous hath a refuge in his death" (14:32).
"Righteousness exalteth a nation" (14:34).
"Jehovah...heareth the prayer of the righteous" (15:29).
"Hear counsel, and receive instruction, That thou mayest be wise in thy latter end" (19:20).
"He that followeth after righteousness and kindness Findeth life, righteousness, and honor" (21:21).
"Train up a child in the way he should go, And even when he is old he will not depart from it" (22:6).
"If thine enemy be hungry, give him bread to eat; And if he be thirsty, give him water to drink: For thou wilt heap coals of fire upon his head, And Jehovah will reward thee" (25:21,33).
"Whoso keepeth the fig-tree shall eat the fruit thereof" (27:18).
"He that regardeth his master shall be honored" (27:18).
"The perfect shall inherit good" (28:10).
"Whoso confesseth and forsaketh them shall obtain mercy" (28:13).
"Whoso walketh uprightly shall be delivered" (28:18).
"A faithful man shall abound with blessings" (28:20).
"Whoso walketh wisely, he shall be delivered" (28:26).
"He that giveth unto the poor shall not lack" (28:27).
"The king that faithfully judgeth the poor, His throne shall be established for ever" (29:14).
"Whoso putteth his trust in Jehovah shall be safe" (29:25).

RICH, RICHES

"In her left hand are riches and honor" (3:16).
"Riches and honor are with me; Yea, durable wealth and righteousness" (8:18).
"The hand of the diligent maketh rich" (10:4).
"The rich man's wealth is his strong city" (10:15).
"The blessing of Jehovah, it maketh rich" (10:22).
"Riches profit not in the day of wrath" (11:4).
"Violent men obtain riches" (11:16).
"He that trusteth in his riches shall fall" (11:28).

"There is that maketh himself rich, yet hath nothing" (13:7).
"The ransom of a man's life is his riches" (13:8).
"The rich hath many friends" (14:20).
"The crown of the wise is their riches" (14:24).
"The rich man's wealth is his strong city, And as a high wall in his own imagination" (18:11).
"The rich answereth roughly" (18:23).
"Wealth added many friends" (19:4).
"Houses and riches are an inheritance from fathers" (19:14).
"The thoughts of the diligent tend only to plenteousness" (21:5).
"The getting of treasures by a lying tongue Is a vapor driven to and fro by them that seek death" (21:6).
"He that loveth wine and oil shall not be rich" (21:17).
"There is precious treasure and oil in the dwelling of the wise" (21:20).
"A good name is rather to be chosen than great riches, And loving favor rather than silver and gold" (22:1).
"The rich and the poor meet together: Jehovah is the maker of them all" (22:2).
"The reward of humility and the fear of Jehovah Is riches, and honor, and life" (22:4).
"The rich ruleth over the poor" (22:7).
"He that oppresseth the poor to increase his gain, And he that giveth to the rich, shall come only to want" (22:16).
"Weary not thyself to be rich" (23:4).
"Wilt thou set thine eyes upon that which is not? For riches certainly make themselves wings, Like an eagle that flieth toward heaven" (23:5).
"By knowledge are the chambers filled With all precious and pleasant riches" (24:4).
"Riches are not for ever" (27:24).
"Better is the poor that walketh in his integrity, Than he that is perverse in his ways, though he be rich" (28:6).
"He that augmenteth his substance by interest and increase, Gathereth it for him that hath pity on the poor" (28:8).
"The rich man is wise in his own conceit; But the poor that hath understanding searcheth him out" (28:11).
"He that maketh haste to be rich shall not be unpunished" (28:20).
"He that hath an evil eye hasteth after riches, And knoweth not that want shall come upon him" (28:22).
"He that is of a greedy spirit stirreth up strife" (28:25).

"Give me neither poverty nor riches; Feed me with the food that is needful for me: Lest I be full, and deny thee, and say, Who is Jehovah?" (30:8,9).

RIGHTEOUS, RIGHTEOUSNESS

"He layeth up sound wisdom for the upright; He is a shield to them that walk in integrity; That he may guard the paths of justice, And preserve the way of his saints" (2:7,8).
"Then shalt thou understand righteousness and justice, And equity, yea, every good path" (2:9).

"That thou mayest walk in the way of good men, And keep the paths of the righteous" (2:20).
"His friendship is with the upright" (3:32).
"I have led thee in paths of uprightness" (4:11).
"Let thine eyes look right on, And let thine eyelids look straight before thee" (4:25).
"Hear, for I will speak excellent things; And the opening of my lips shall be right things" (8:6).
"All the words of my mouth are in righteousness" (8:8).
"They are all plain to him that understandeth, And right to them that find knowledge" (8:9).
"I walk in the way of righteousness" (8:20).

"Righteousness delivereth from death" (10:2).
"Jehovah will not suffer the soul of the righteous to famish" (10:3).
"The memory of the righteous is blessed" (10:7).
"The mouth of the righteous is a fountain of life" (10;11).
"The labor of the righteous tendeth to life" (10:16).
"The tongue of the righteous is as choice silver" (10:20).
"The lips of the righteous feed many" (10:21).
"The desire of the righteous shall be granted" (10;24).
"The righteous is an everlasting foundation" :10:25).
"The hope of the righteous shall be gladness" (10:28).
"The righteous shall never be removed" (10:30).
"The mouth of the righteous bringeth forth wisdom" (10:31).
"The lips of the righteous know what is acceptable" (10:32).
"The integrity of the upright shall guide them" (11:3).
"Righteousness delivereth from death" (11:4).
"The righteousness of the perfect shall direct his way" (11:5).
"The righteousness of the upright shall deliver them" (11:6).
"The righteous is delivered out of trouble" (11:8).

"Through knowledge shall the righteous be delivered" (11:9).
"When it goeth well with the righteous, the city rejoiceth" (11:10).
"By the blessing of the upright the city is exalted" (11(11).
"He that soweth righteousness hath a sure reward" (11:18).
"He that is stedfast in righteousness shall attain unto life" (11:19).
"The seed of the righteous shall be delivered" (11:21).
"The desire of the righteous is only good" (11:23).
"He that diligently seeketh good seeketh favor" (11:27).
"The righteous shall flourish as the green leaf" (11:28).
"The fruit of the righteous is a tree of life" (11:30).
"The righteous shall be recompensed in the earth" (11:31).
"A good man shall obtain favor of Jehovah" (12:2).
"The root of the righteous shall not be moved" (12:3).
"The thoughts of the righteous are just" (12:5).
"The mouth of the upright shall deliver them" (12:6).
"The house of the righteous shall stand" (12:7).
"A righteous man regardeth the life of his beast" (12:10).
"The root of the righteous yieldeth fruit" (12:12).
"The righteous shall come out of trouble" (12:13).
"He that uttereth truth showeth forth righteousness" (12:17).
"There shall no mischief happen to the righteous" (12:21).
"The righteous is a guide to his neighbor" (12:26).
"In the way of righteousness is life, And in the pathway thereof there is no death" (12:28).
"A righteous man hateth lying" (13:5).
"Righteousness guardeth him that is upright in the way" (13:6).
"The light of the righteous rejoiceth" (13:9).
"The righteous shall be recompensed with good" (13:21).
"A good man leaveth an inheritance to his children's children" (13:22).
"The righteous eateth to the satisfying of his soul" (13:25).
"He that walketh in his uprightness feareth Jehovah" (14:2).
"Among the upright there is good will" (14:9).
"The tent of the upright shall flourish" (14:11).
"There is a way that seemeth right unto a man; But the end thereof are the ways of death" (14:12).
"A good man shall be satisfied from himself" (14:14).
"The evil bow down before the good; And the wicked, at the gates of the righteous" (14:19).
"Mercy and truth shall be to them that devise good" (14:22).

"The righteous hath a refuge in his death" (14:32).
"Righteousness exalteth a nation" (14:34).
"In the house of the righteous is much treasure" (15:6).
"The prayer of the upright is his delight" (15:8).
"He loveth him that followeth after righteousness" (15:9).
"The path of the upright is made a highway" (15:19).
"The heart of the righteous studieth to answer" (15:28).
"He heareth the prayer of the righteous" (15:29).
"Better is a little, with righteousness, Than great revenues with injustice" (16:8).
"The throne is established by righteousness" (16:12).
"Righteous lips are the delight of kings; And they love him that speaketh right" (16:13).
"The hoary head is a crown of glory; It shall be found in the way of righteousness" (16:31).
"To respect the person of the wicked is not good, Nor to turn aside the righteous in judgment" (18:5.
"The name of Jehovah is a strong tower; The righteous runneth into it, and is safe" (18:10).
"Even a child maketh himself known by his doings, Whether his work be pure, and whether it be right" (20:11).
"Every way of a man is right in his own eyes" (21:2).
"To do righteousness and justice Is more acceptable to Jehovah than sacrifice" (21:3).
"As for the pure, his work is right" (21:8).
"The righteous man considereth the house of the wicked, How the wicked are overthrown to their ruin" (21:12).
"It is joy to the righteous to do justice" (21:15).
"The wicked is a ransom for the righteous" (21:18).
"He that followeth after righteousness and kindness Findeth life, righteousness, and honor" (21:21).
"The righteous giveth and withholdeth not" (21:26).
"As for the upright, he establisheth his ways" (21:29).
"The father of the righteous will greatly rejoice; And he that begetteth a wise child will have joy of him" (23:24).
"Lay not wait, O wicked man, against the habitation of the righteous" (24:15).
"He kisseth the lips Who giveth a right answer" (24:26).
"Take away the wicked from before the king, And his throne shall be established in righteousness" (25:5).
"As a troubled fountain, and a corrupted spring, So is a righteous man that giveth way before the wicked" (25:26).

"The righteous are bold as a lion" (28:1).
"Whoso causeth the upright to go astray in an evil way, He shall fall himself into his own pit" (28:10).
"The perfect shall inherit good" (28:10).
"When the righteous triumph, there is great glory" (28:12).
"When they perish, the righteous increase" (28:28).
"When the righteous are increased, the people rejoice" (29:2).
"The righteous doth sing and rejoice" (29:6).
"The righteous taketh knowledge of the cause of the poor" (29:7).
"The righteous shall look upon their fall" (29:16).
"An unjust man is an abomination to the righteous; And he that is upright in the way is an abomination to the wicked" (29:27).
"Open thy mouth, judge righteously" (31:9).

RULER (See "King")

SACRIFICE

"The sacrifice of the wicked is an abomination to Jehovah" (15:8).
"To do righteousness and justice Is more acceptable to Jehovah than sacrifice" (21:3).
"The sacrifice of a wicked is an abomination; How much more, when he bringeth it with a wicked mind!" (21:27).

SCORNER

"How long...will...scoffers delight them in scoffing?" (1:22).
"He that correcteth a scoffer getteth to himself reviling" (9:7).
"Reprove not a scoffer, lest he hate thee" (9:8).
"If thou scoffest, thou alone shalt bear it" (9:12).
"A scoffer heareth not rebuke" (13:1).
"A scoffer seeketh wisdom, and findeth it not" (14:6).
"A scoffer loveth not to be reproved; He will not go unto the wise" (15:12).
"Smite a scoffer, and the simple will learn prudence" (19:25).
"A worthless witness mocketh at justice" (19:28).
"Judgments are prepared for scoffers" (19:29).
"When the scoffer is punished, the simple is made wise" (21:11).
"The proud and haughty man, scoffer is his name; He worketh in the arrogance of pride" (21:24).
"Cast out the scoffer, and contention will go out; Yea, strife and ignominy will cease" (22:10).
"The scoffer is an abomination to men" (24:9).

"Scoffers set a city in a flame" (29:8).

SIMPLE

"To give prudence to the simple" (1-4).
"How long, ye simple ones, will ye love simplicity?" (1:22).
"The backsliding of the simple shall slay them" (1:32).
"I beheld among the simple ones, I discerned among the youths, A young man void of understanding, Passing through the street near her corner; And he went the way to her house" (7:7,8).
"O ye simple, understand prudence" (8:5).
"Whoso is simple, let him turn in hither" (9:4).
"She is simple, and knoweth nothing" (9:13).
"Whoso is simple, let him turn in hither" (9:16).
"The simple believeth every word" (14:15).
"The simple inherit folly" (14:18).
"Smite a scoffer, and the simple will learn prudence" (19:25).
"When the scoffer is punished, the simple is made wise" (21:11).
"The simple pass on, and suffer for it" (22:3).
"The simple pass on, and suffer for it" (27:12).

SLOTHFULNESS (See "Laziness")
SLUGGARD (See "Laziness")
SNARE, NET

"In vain is the net spread In the sight of any bird" (1:17).
"Thou art snared with the words of thy mouth, Thou art taken with the words of thy mouth" (6:2).
"Till an arrow strike through his liver; As a bird hasteth to the snare, And knoweth not that it is for his life" (7:23).
"The wicked desireth the net of evil men" (12:12).
"In the transgression of the lips is a snare to the evil man" (12:13).
"A fool's...lips are the snare of his soul" (18:7).
"It is a snare to a man rashly to say, It is holy, And after vows to make inquiry" (20:25).
"Thorns and snares are in the way of the perverse" (22:5).
"Lest thou learn his ways, And get a snare to thy soul" (22:25).
"A man that flattereth his neighbor Spreadeth a net for his steps" (29:5).
"In the transgression of an evil man there is a snare" (29:6).
"The fear of man bringeth a snare" :29:25).

SONS (See "Parent-Child")

SPEECH (Bad Speech)

"Violence covereth the mouth of the wicked" (10:6).
"Violence covereth the mouth of the wicked" (10:11).
"The mouth of the foolish is a present destruction" (10:14).
"He that hideth hatred is of lying lips" (10:18).
"He that uttereth a slander is a fool" (10:18).
"In the multitude of words there wanteth not transgression" (10:19).
"The perverse tongue shall be cut off" (10:31).
"The mouth of the wicked speaketh perverseness" (10:32).
"The words of the wicked are of lying in wait for blood" (12:6).
"In the transgression of the lips is a snare to the evil man" (12:13).
"A false witness, deceit" (12:17).
"There is that speaketh rashly like the piercings of a sword" (12:18).
"A lying tongue is but for a moment" (12:19).
"Lying lips are an abomination to Jehovah" :12:22).
"The heart of fools proclaimeth foolishness" (12:23).
"He that openeth wide his lips shall have destruction" (13:3).
"A righteous man hateth lying" (13:5).
"In the mouth of the foolish is a rod for his pride" (14:3).
"A grievous word stirreth up anger" (15:1).
"The mouth of fools poureth out folly" (15:2).
"Perverseness therein is a breaking of the spirit" (15:4).
"The mouth of fools feedeth on folly" (15:14).
"The mouth of the wicked poureth out evil things" (15:28).
"A worthless man deviseth mischief; And in his lips there is as a scorching fire" (16:27).
"A whisperer separateth chief friends" (16:28).
"He that compresseth his lips bringeth evil to pass" (16:30).
"An evil-doer giveth heed to wicked lips" (17:4).
"A liar giveth ear to a mischievous tongue" (17:4).
"Excellent speech becometh not a fool: Much less do lying lips a prince" (17:7).
"He that harpeth on a matter separateth chief friends" (17:9).
"He that hath a perverse tongue falleth into mischief" (17:20).
"A fool's lips enter into contention, And his mouth calleth for stripes" (18:6).
"A fool's mouth is his destruction, And his lips are the snare of his soul" (18:7).

"The words of a whisperer are as dainty morsels. And they go down into the innermost parts" (18:8).
"He that giveth answer before he heareth, It is folly and shame unto him" (18:13).
"A man's belly shall be filled with the fruit of his mouth" (18:20).
"Death and life are in the power of the tongue" (18:21).
"The rich answereth roughly" (18:23).
"Better is the poor that walketh in his integrity Than he that is perverse in his lips and is a fool" (19:1).
"A false witness shall not be unpunished; And he that uttereth lies shall not escape" (19:5).
"A false witness shall not be unpunished; And he that uttereth lies shall perish" (19:9).
"The contentions of a wife are a continual dropping" (19:13).
"A poor man is better than a liar" (19:22).
"A worthless witness mocketh at justice" (19:28).
"The mouth of the wicked swalloweth iniquity" (19:28).
"Most men will proclaim every one his own kindness; But a faithful man who can find?" (20:6).
"He that goeth about as a talebearer revealeth secrets" (20:19).
"Company not with him that openeth wide his lips" (20:19).
"Whoso curseth his father or his mother, His lamp shall be put out in blackness of darkness" (20:20).
"It is a snare to a man rashly to say, It is holy, And after vows to make inquiry" (20:25).
"The getting of treasures by a lying tongue Is a vapor driven to and fro by them that seek death" (21:6).
"A false witness shall perish" (21:28).
"The scoffer is an abomination to men" (24:9).
"Be not a witness against thy neighbor without cause" (24:28).
"Deceive not with thy lips" (24:28).
"As clouds and wind without rain, So is he that boasteth himself of his gifts falsely" (25:14).
"A man that beareth false witness against his neighbor Is a maul, and a sword, and sharp arrow" (25(18).
"The north wind bringeth forth rain; So doth a backbiting tongue an angry countenance" (25:23).
"The legs of the lame hang loose; So is a parable in the mouth of fools" (26:7).
"As a thorn that goeth up into the hand of a drunkard, So is a parable in the mouth of fools" (26:9).

"Where there is no whisperer, contention ceaseth" (26:20).
"The words of a whisperer are as dainty morsels, And they go down into the innermost parts" (26:22).
"Fervent lips and a wicked heart Are like an earthen vessel overlaid with silver dross" (26:23).
"He that hateth dissembleth with his lips; But he layeth up deceit within him: When he speaketh fair, believe him not; For there are seven abominations in his heart: Though his hatred cover itself with guile, His wickedness shall be openly showed before the assembly" (26:24-26).
"A lying tongue hateth those whom it hath wounded; And a flattering mouth worketh ruin" (26:28).
"Let another man praise thee, and not thine own mouth; A stranger, and not thine own lips" (27:2).
"A man is tried by his praise" (27:21).
"A man that flattereth his neighbor Spreadeth a net for his steps" (29:5).
"Seest thou a man that is hasty in his words? There is more hope of a fool than of him" (29:20).

SPEECH (Good Speech)

"In the lips of him that hath discernment wisdom is found" (10:13).
"He that refraineth his lips doeth wisely" (10:19).
"The tongue of the righteous is as choice silver" (10:20).
"The lips of the righteous feed many" (10:21).
"The mouth of the righteous bringeth forth wisdom" (10:31).
"The lips of the righteous know what is acceptable" (10:32).
"The mouth of the righteous shall deliver them" (12:6).
"A man shall be satisfied with good by the fruit of his mouth" (12:14).
"He that uttereth truth showeth forth righteousness" (12:17).
"The tongue of the wise is health" (12:18).
"The lip of truth shall be established for ever" (12:19).
"Heaviness in the heart of a man maketh it stoop; But a good word maketh it glad" (12:25).
"A man shall eat good by the fruit of his mouth" (13:2).
"He that guardeth his mouth keepeth his life" (13:3).
"The lips of the wise shall preserve them" (14:3).
"A soft answer turneth away wrath" (15:1).
"The tongue of the wise uttereth knowledge aright" (15:2).
"A gentle tongue is a tree of life" (15:4).

"The lips of the wise disperse knowledge" (15:7).
"A man hath joy in the answer of his mouth" (15:23).
"A word in due season, how good is it! (15:23).
"Pleasant words are pure" (15:26).
"The heart of the righteous studieth to answer" (15:28).
"The answer of the tongue is from Jehovah" (16:1).
"A divine sentence is in the lips of the king; His mouth shall not transgress in judgment" (16:10).
"Righteous lips are the delight of kings; And they love him that speaketh right" (16:13).
"The sweetness of the lips increaseth learning" (16:21).
"The heart of the wise instructeth his mouth, And addeth learning to his lips" (16:23).
"Pleasant words are as a honeycomb, Sweet to the soul, and health to the bones" (16:24).
"The words of a man's mouth are as deep waters; The wellspring of wisdom is as a flowing brook" (18:4).
"With the increase of his lips shall he be satisfied" (18:20).
"Death and life are in the power of the tongue; And they that love it shall eat the fruit thereof" (18:21).
"The poor useth entreaties" (18:23).
"The lips of knowledge are a precious jewel" (20:15).
"Whoso keepeth his mouth and his tongue Keepeth his soul from troubles" (21:23).
"The man that heareth shall speak so as to endure" (21:28).
"He kisseth the lips Who giveth a right answer" (24:26).
"Debate thy cause with thy neighbor himself" (25:9).
"A word fitly spoken Is like apples of gold in network of silver" (25:11).
"As an ear-ring of gold, and an ornament of fine gold, So is a wise reprover upon an obedient ear" (25:12).
"As the cold of snow in the time of harvest, So is a faithful messenger to them that send him; For he refresheth the soul of his masters" (25:13).
"A soft tongue breaketh the bone" (25:15).
"Answer a fool according to his folly, Lest he be wise in his own conceit" (26:5).
"The rod and reproof give wisdom" (29:15).

STEAL (See "Oppress")

STRIFE

"Hatred stirreth up strifes" (10:12

"A wrathful man stirreth up contention; But he that is slow to anger appeaseth strife" (15:18).

"Better is a dry morsel, and quietness therewith, Than a house full of feasting with strife" (17:1).

"The beginning of strife is as when one letteth out water: Therefore leave off contention, before there is quarrelling" (17:14).

"He loveth transgression that loveth strife" (17:19).

"He that passeth by, and vexeth himself with strife belonging not to him, Is like one that taketh a dog by the ears" (26:17).

"Where there is no whisperer, contention ceaseth" (26:20).

"As coals are to hot embers, and wood to fire, So is a contentious man to inflame strife" (26:21).

"He that is of a greedy spirit stirreth up strife" (28:25).

"An angry man stirreth up strife, And a wrathful man aboundeth in transgression" (29:22).

"The churning of milk bringeth forth butter, And the wringing of the nose bringeth forth blood; So the forcing of wrath bringeth forth strife" (30:33).

STRONG DRINK (See "Wine")

THIEF (See "Oppress")

TRANSGRESS, TRANSGRESSION, TRANSGRESSOR

"In the transgression of the lips is a snare to the evil man" (12:13).

"The way of the transgressor is hard" (13:15).

"A divine sentence is in the lips of the king; His mouth shall not transgress in judgment" (16:10).

"He that covereth a transgression seeketh love" (17:9).

"He loveth transgression that loveth strife" (17:19).

"The discretion of a man maketh him slow to anger; And it is his glory to pass over a transgression" (19:11).

"For the transgression of a land many are the princes thereof" (28:2).

"To have respect of persons is not good; Neither that a man should transgress for a piece of bread" (28:21).

"Whoso robbeth his father or his mother, and saith, It is no transgression, The same is the companion of a destroyer" (28:24).

"In the transgression of an evil man there is a snare" (29:6).

"When the wicked are increased, transgression increaseth"

(29:16).
"A wrathful man aboundeth in transgression" (29:22).

UNDERSTANDING (See "Knowledge")
WICKED, EVIL

"Their feet run to evil" (1:16).
"To deliver thee from the way of evil" (2:12).
"Who rejoice to do evil, And delight in the perverseness of evil" (2:14).
"The wicked shall be cut off from the land" (2:22).
"Fear Jehovah, and depart from evil" (3:7).
"Be not afraid of sudden fear, Neither of the desolation of the wicked, when it cometh" (3:25).
"Devise not evil against thy neighbor" (3:29).
"The curse of Jehovah is in the house of the wicked" (3:33).
"Enter not into the path of the wicked, And walk not in the way of evil man. Avoid it, pass not by it; Turn from it, and pass on. For they sleep not, except they do evil; And their sleep is taken away, unless they cause some to fall. For they eat the bread of wickedness, And drink the wine of violence" (4:14-17).
"The way of the wicked is as darkness" (4:19).
"Remove thy foot from evil" (4:27).
"His own iniquities shall take the wicked, And he shall be holden with the cords of his sin" (5:22).
"A worthless person, a man of iniquity, Is he that walketh with a perverse mouth" (6:12(.
"A heart that deviseth wicked purposes, Feet that are swift in running to mischief" (6:18).
"To keep thee from the evil woman" (6:24).
"Wickedness is an abomination to my lips" (8:7).
"The fear of Jehovah is to hate evil: Pride, and arrogancy, and the evil way, And the perverse mouth, do I hate" (8:13).
"He that reproveth a wicked man getteth himself a blot" (9:7).
"Treasures of wickedness profit nothing" (10:2).
"He thrusteth away the desire of the wicked" (10:3).
"Violence covereth the mouth of the wicked" (10:6).
"The name of the wicked shall rot" (10:7).
"Violence covereth the mouth of the wicked" (10:11).
"The increase of the wicked, to sin" (10:16).
"The heart of the wicked is little worth" (10:20).
"The fear of the wicked, it shall come upon him" (10:24).
"When the whirlwind passeth, the wicked is no more" (10:25).

"The years of the wicked shall be shortened" (10:27).
"The expectation of the wicked shall perish" (10:28).
"The wicked shall not dwell in the land" (10:30).
"The mouth of the wicked speaketh perverseness" (10:32).
"The wicked shall fall by his own wickedness" (11:5).
"When a wicked man dieth, his expectation shall perish; And the hope of iniquity perisheth" (11:7).
"The wicked cometh in his stead" (11:8).
"When the wicked perish, there is shouting" (11:10).
"The city...is overthrown by the mouth of the wicked" (11:11).
"The wicked earneth deceitful wages" (11:18).
"He that pursueth evil doeth it to his own death" (11:19).
"Though hand join in hand, the evil man shall not be unpunished" (11:21).
"The expectation of the wicked is wrath" (11:23).
"The righteous shall be recompensed in the earth; How much more the wicked and the sinner!" (22:31).
"A man of wicked devices will be condemn" (12:2).
"A man shall not be established by wickedness" (12:3).
"The counsels of the wicked are deceit" (12:5).
"The words of the wicked are of lying in wait for blood" (12:6).
"The wicked are overthrown, and are not" (12:7).
"The tender mercies of the wicked are cruel" (12:10).
"The wicked desireth the net of evil men" (12:12).
"In the transgression of the lips is a snare to the evil man" (12:13).
"Deceit is in the heart of them that devise evil" (12:20).
"The wicked shall be filled with evil" (12:21).
"The way of the wicked causeth them to err" (12:26).
"A wicked man is loathsome, and cometh to shame" (13:5).
"Wickedness overthroweth the sinner" (13:6).
"The light of the wicked shall be put out" (13:9).
"A wicked messenger falleth into evil" (13:17).
"It is abomination to fools to depart from evil" (13:19).
"Evil pursueth sinners" (13:21).
"The belly of the wicked shall want" (13:25).
"The house of the wicked shall be overthrown" (14:11).
"A wise man feareth, and departeth from evil" (14:16).
"A man of wicked devices is hated" (14:17).
"The evil bow down before the good; And the wicked, at the gates of the righteous" (14:19).
"Do they not err that devise evil?" (14:22).

"The wicked is thrust down in his evil-doing" (14:32).
"The eyes of Jehovah are in every place, Keeping watch upon the evil and the good" (15:3).
"In the revenues of the wicked is trouble" (15:6).
"The sacrifice of the wicked is an abomination to Jehovah" (15:8).
"The way of the wicked is an abomination to Jehovah" (15:9).
"Evil devices are an abomination to Jehovah" (15:26).
"The mouth of the wicked poureth out evil things" (15:28).
"Jehovah is far from the wicked" (15:29).
"Jehovah hath made everything for its own end; Yea, even the wicked for the day of evil" (16:4).
"By the fear of Jehovah men depart from evil" (16:6).
"It is an abomination to kings to commit wickedness" (16:12).
"The highway of the upright is to depart from evil" (16:17).
"A worthless man deviseth mischief" (16:27).
"He that compresseth his lips bringeth evil to pass" (16:30).
"An evil-doer giveth heed to wicked lips" (17:4).
"An evil man seeketh only rebellion" (17:11).
"Whoso rewardeth evil for good, Evil shall not depart from his house" (17:13).
"He that justifieth the wicked...an abomination to Jehovah" (17:15).
"A wicked man receiveth a bribe out of the bosom, To pervert the ways of justice" (17:23).
"When the wicked cometh, there cometh also contempt" (18:3).
"To respect the person of the wicked is not good" (18:5).
"The mouth of the wicked swalloweth iniquity" (19:28).
"A king that sitteth on the throne of judgment Scattereth away all evil with his eyes" (20:8).
"Say not thou, I will recompense evil" (20:22).
"A wise king winnoweth the wicked, And bringeth the threshing-wheel over them" (20:26).
"Stripes that wound cleanse away evil" (20:30).
"The lamp of the wicked, is sin" (21:4).
"The violence of the wicked shall sweep them away" (21:7).
"The soul of the wicked desireth evil: His neighbor findeth no favor in his eyes" (21:10).
"The righteous man considereth the house of the wicked, How the wicked are overthrown to their ruin" (21:12).
"The wicked is a ransom for the righteous" (21:18).
"The sacrifice of the wicked is abomination, How much more,

when he bringeth it with a wicked mind!" (21:27).
"A wicked man hardeneth his face" (21:29).
"Eat not the bread of him that hath an evil eye" (23:6).
"Be not thou envious against evil men; Neither desire to be with them" (24:1).
"He that deviseth to do evil, Men shall call him a mischief-maker" (24:8).
"Lay not wait, O wicked man, against the habitation of the righteous" (24:15).
"The wicked are overthrown by calamity" (24:16).
"Fret not thyself because of evil-doers; Neither be thou envious at the wicked" (24:19).
"There shall be no reward to the evil man; The lamp of the wicked shall be put out" (24:20).
"He that saith unto the wicked, Thou art righteous, Peoples shall curse him" (24:24).
"Take away the wicked from before the king, And his throne shall be established in righteousness" (25:5).
"As a troubled fountain, and a corrupted spring, So is a righteous man that giveth way before the wicked" (25:26).
"Fervent lips and a wicked heart Are like an earthen vessel overlaid with silver dross" (26:23).
"Though his hatred cover itself with guile, His wickedness shall be openly showed before the assembly" (26:26).
"The wicked flee when no man pursueth" (28:1).
"They that forsake the law praise the wicked" (28:4).
"Evil men understand not justice" (28:5).
"Whoso causeth the upright to go astray in an evil way, He shall fall himself into his own pit" (28:10).
"When the wicked rise, men hide themselves" (28:12).
"As a roaring lion, and a ranging bear, So is a wicked ruler over a poor people" (28:15).
"When the wicked rise, men hide themselves; But when they perish, the righteous increase" (28:28).
"When a wicked man beareth rule, the people sigh" (29:2).
"In the transgression of an evil man there is a snare" (29:6).
"The wicked hath not understanding to know it" (29:7).
"If a ruler hearkeneth to falsehood, All his servants are wicked" (29:12).
"When the wicked are increased, transgression increaseth" (29:16).
"An unjust man is an abomination to the righteous" (29:27).

"He that is upright in the way is an abomination to the wicked" (29:27).
"An adulterous woman...wipeth her mouth, And saith, I have done no wickedness" (30:20).
"If thou hast thought evil, Lay thy hand upon thy mouth" (30:32).
"She doeth him good and not evil All the days of her life" (31:12).

WIFE, WOMAN, WOMEN

"To deliver thee from the strange woman" (2:16).
"Rejoice in the wife of thy youth" (5:18).
"To keep thee from the evil woman" (6:24).
"On account of a harlot a man is brought to a piece of bread" (6:26).
"So is he that goeth into his neighbor's wife; Whosoever toucheth her shall not be unpunished" (6:29).
"He that committeth adultery with a woman is void of understanding" (6:32).
"That they may keep thee from the strange woman" (7:5).
"There met him a woman With the attire of a harlot, and wily of heart" (7:10).
"The foolish woman is clamorous; She is simple, and knoweth nothing" (9:13).
"A gracious woman obtaineth honor" (11:16).
"As a ring of gold in a swine's snout, So is a fair woman that is without discretion" (11:22).
"A worthy woman is the crown of her husband; But she that maketh ashamed is as rottenness in his bones" (12:4).
"The foolish plucketh it down with her own hands" (14:1).
"Whoso findeth a wife findeth a good thing, And obtaineth favor of Jehovah" (18:22).
"The contentions of a wife are a continual dropping" (18:13).
"A prudent wife is from Jehovah" (19:14).
"It is better to dwell in the corner of the housetop, Than with a contentious woman in a wide house" (21:9).
"It is better to dwell in a desert land, Than with a contentious and fretful woman" (21:19).
"A harlot is a deep ditch; And a foreign woman is a narrow pit" (23:27).
"It is better to dwell in the corner of the housetop, Then with a contentious woman in a wide house" (25:24).

"Take his garment that is surety for a stranger; And hold him in pledge that is surety for a foreign woman" (27:13).

"A continual dropping in a very rainy day And a contentious woman are alike" (27:15).

"So is the way of an adulterous woman; She eateth, and wipeth her mouth, And saith, I have done no wickedness" (30:20).

"For three things the earth doth tremble...an odious woman when she is married" (30:21-23).

The greatest section in the Bible on womanhood is in 31:10-31 (which see). It begins with the words, "A worthy woman who can find? For her price is far above rubies."

WINE, STRONG DRINK, WINEBIBBER

"Thy vats shall overflow with new wine" (3:10).

"They...drink the wine of violence" (4:17).

"She hath mingled her wine" (9:2).

"Come...drink of the wine which I have mingled" (9:5).

"Wine is a mocker, strong drink a brawler; And whosoever erreth thereby is not wise" (20:1).

"He that loveth wine and oil shall not be rich" (21:17).

"Be not among winebibbers, Among gluttonous eaters of flesh: For the drunkard and the glutton shall come to poverty; And drowsiness will clothe a man with rags" (23:20,21).

"Who hath woe? who hath sorrow? who hath contentions? Who hath complaining? who hath wounds without cause? Who hath redness of eyes? They that tarry long at the wine; They that go to seek out mixed wine. Look not thou upon the wine when it is red, When it sparkleth in the cup, When it goeth down smoothly: At the last it biteth like a serpent, And stingeth like an adder. Thine eyes shall behold strange things, And thy heart shall utter perverse things. Yea, thou shalt be as he that lieth down in the midst of the sea, Or as he that lieth upon the top of the mast. They have stricken me, shalt thou say, and I was not hurt; They have beaten me, and I felt it not: When shall I awake? I will seek it yet again" (23:29-35).

"It is not for kings, O Lemuel, it is not for kings to drink wine; Nor for princes to say, Where is strong drink? Lest they drink, and forget the law, And pervert the justice due to any that is afflicted" (31:4,5).

"Give strong drink unto him that is ready to perish, And wine unto the bitter in soul: Let him drink, and forget his poverty, And remember his misery no more" (31:6,7).

WISDOM, WISE

Because of the length of some of the sections, some have merely been introduced (see 1:20-33 below).

"To know wisdom" (1:2).

"To receive instruction in wise dealing" (1:3).

"That the wise man may hear, and increase in learning" (1:5).

"To understand...the words of the wise, and their dark sayings" (1:6).

"The foolish despise wisdom and instruction" (1:7).

"Wisdom crieth aloud in the street..." (1:20-33).

"Incline thine ear unto wisdom" (2:2).

"Jehovah giveth wisdom" (2:6).

"He layeth up sound wisdom for the upright" (2:7).

"Wisdom shall enter into thy heart...To deliver thee from the way of evil...To deliver thee from the strange woman (2:10-16).

"Be not wise in thine own eyes" (3:7).

"Happy is the man that findeth wisdom..." (3:13-18).

"Jehovah by wisdom founded the earth..." (3:19,20).

"Keep sound wisdom and discretion" (3:21).

"The wise shall inherit glory" (3:35).

"Get wisdom...Wisdom is the principal thing; therefore get wisdom...Exalt her, and she will promote thee..." (4:5-9).

"I have taught thee in the way of wisdom" (4:11).

"My son, attend unto my wisdom..." (5:1,2).

"Say unto wisdom, Thou art my sister" (7:4).

"Doth not wisdom cry, And understanding put forth her voice?..." (8:1-12).

"Wisdom hath builded her house..." (9:1-5).

"Give instruction to a wise man, and he will be yet wiser" (9:9).

"The fear of Jehovah is the beginning of wisdom" (9:10).

"If thou art wise, thou art wise for thyself" (9:12).

"A wise man maketh a glad father" (10:1).

"The wise in heart will receive commandments" (10:8).

"In the lips of him that hath discernment wisdom is found" (10:13).

"Wise men lay up knowledge" (10:14).

"The mouth of the righteous bringeth forth wisdom" (10:31).

"He that is wise winneth souls" (11:30).

"A man shall be commended according to his wisdom" (12:8).

"He that is wise hearkeneth unto counsel" (12:15).

"The tongue of the wise is health" (12:18).

"A wise son heareth his father's instruction" (13:1).

"With the well-advised is wisdom" (13:10).
"The law of the wise is a fountain of life, That one may depart from the snares of death" (13:14).
"Walk with wise men, and thou shalt be wise" (13:20).
"Every wise woman buildeth her house" (14:1).
"The lips of the wise shall preserve them" (14:3).
"The wisdom of the prudent is to understand his way" (14:8).
"A wise man feareth, and departeth from evil" (14:16).
"The crown of the wise is their riches" (14:24).
"Wisdom resteth in the heart of him that hath understanding" (14:33).
"The king's favor is toward a servant that dealeth wisely" (14:35).
"The tongue of the wise uttereth knowledge aright" (15:2).
"The lips of the wise disperse knowledge" (15:7).
"A wise son maketh a glad father" (15:20).
"To the wise the way of life goeth upward, That he may depart from Sheol beneath" (15:24).
"The ear that hearkeneth to the reproof of life Shall abide among the wise" (15:31).
"A servant that dealeth wisely shall have rule over a son that causeth shame, And shall have part in the inheritance among the brethren" (17:2).
"Wisdom is before the face of him that hath understanding" (17:24).
"The wellspring of wisdom is as a flowing brook" (18:4).
"He that getteth wisdom loveth his own soul" (19:8).
"Hear counsel, and receive instruction, That thou mayest be wise in thy latter end" (19:20).
"When the scoffer is punished, the simple is made wise" (21:11).
"When the wise is instructed, he receiveth knowledge" (21:11).
"There is precious treasure and oil in the dwelling of the wise" (21:20).

"A wise man scaleth the city of the mighty, And bringeth down the strength of the confidence thereof" (21:22).
"Incline thine ear, and hear the words of the wise" (22:17).
"Buy the truth, and sell it not; Yea, wisdom, and instruction, and understanding" (23:23).
"Through wisdom is a house builded" (24:3).
"A wise man is strong" (24:5).
"By wise guidance thou shalt make thy war" (24:6).
"Wisdom is too high for a fool: He openeth not his mouth in the

gate" (24:7
"So shalt thou know wisdom to be unto thy soul; If thou hast found it, then shall there be a reward, And thy hope shall not be cut off" (24:14).
"Whoso loveth wisdom rejoiceth his father" (29:3).
"Scoffers set a city in a flame; But wise men turn away wrath" (29:8).
"If a wise man hath a controversy with a foolish man, Whether he be angry or laugh, there will be no rest" (29:9).
"A fool uttereth all his anger; But a wise man keepeth it back and stilleth it" (29:11).
"The rod and reproof give wisdom" (29:15).

WOMAN (See "Wife")
WRATH (See "Anger")

SPECIAL INDEX TO THE COMPARISONS AND CONTRASTS IN PROVERBS

Many of the Proverbs involve either a comparison or a contrast. Therefore, we include this special index concerning them.

COMPARISONS USING "AS":

"The tongue of the righteous is as choice silver" (10:20).

"As vinegar to the teeth, and as smoke to the eyes, So is the sluggard to them that send him" (10:26).

"As a ring of gold in a swine's snout, So is a fair woman that is without discretion" (11:22).

"The king's...favor is as a cloud of the latter rain" (16:15).

"Pleasant words are as a honeycomb, Sweet to the soul, and health to the bones" (16:24).

"A bribe is as a precious stone in the eyes of him that hath it" (17:8).

"The beginning of strife is as when one letteth out water: Therefore leave off contention, before there is quarrelling" (17:14).

"The words of a man's mouth are as deep waters" (18:4).

"The wellspring of wisdom is as a flowing brook" (18:4).

"The words of the whisperer are as dainty morsels, And they go down into the innermost parts" (18:8).

"The king's wrath is as the roaring of a lion" (19:12).

"The king's...favor is a dew upon the grass" (19:12).

"The terror of a king is as the roaring of a lion: He that provoketh him to anger sinneth against his own life" (20:2).

"The king's heart is in the hand of Jehovah as the water-courses: He turneth it withsoever he will" (21:1).

"As an ear-ring of gold, and an ornament of fine gold, So is a wise reprover upon an obedient ear" (25:12).

"As the cold of snow in the time of harvest, So is a faithful messenger to them that send him; For he refresheth the soul of his masters" (25:13).

"As one that taketh off a garment in cold weather, and as vinegar upon soda, So is he that singeth songs to a heavy heart" (25:20).

"As cold waters to a thirsty soul, So is good news from a far country" (25:25).

"As a troubled fountain, and corrupted spring, So is a righteous man that giveth way before the wicked" (25:26).

"As snow in the summer, and as rain in harvest, So honor is not seemly for fool" (26:1).

"As the sparrow in her wandering, as the swallow in her flying, So the curse that is causeless alighteth not" (26:2).

"As one that bindeth a stone in a sling, So is he that giveth honor to a fool" (26:8).

"As a thorn that goeth up into the hand of a drunkard, So is a parable in the mouth of fools" (26:9).

"As an archer that woundeth all, So is he that hireth a fool and he that hireth them that pass by" (26:10).

"As a dog that returneth to his vomit, So is a fool that repeateth his folly" (26:11).

"As the door turneth upon its hinges, So doth the sluggard upon his bed" (26:14).

"As a madman who casteth firebrands, Arrows, and death, So is the man that deceiveth his neighbor, And saith, Am not I in sport?" (26:18,19).

"As coals are to hot embers, and wood to fire, So is a contentious man to inflame strife" (26:21).

"The words of a whisperer are as dainty morsels, And they go down into the innermost parts" (26:22).

"As a bird that wandereth from her nest, So is a man that wandereth from his place (27:8).

"As in water face answereth to face, So the heart of man to man" (27:19).

"As a roaring lion, and raging bear, So is a wicked ruler over a poor people" (28:15).

COMPARISONS USING "SO" (not introduced by as)

"The north wind bringeth forth rain; So doth a backbiting tongue an angry countenance" (25:23).

"It is not good to eat much honey; So for men to search out their own glory is grievous" (25:27).

"The legs of the lame hang loose; So is a parable in the mouth of fools" (26:7).

"Oil and perfume rejoice the heart; So doth the sweetness of a man's friend that cometh of hearty counsel" (27:9).

"Iron sharpeneth iron; So a man sharpeneth the countenance of his friend" (27(17).

"The churning of milk bringeth forth butter, And the wringing of the nose bringeth forth blood; So the forcing of wrath bringeth forth strife" (30:33).

SPECIAL INDEX TO THE COMPARISONS AND CONTRASTS IN PROVERBS

COMPARISONS USING "IS":

"The mouth of the righteous is a fountain of life" (10:11).
"The righteous is an everlasting foundation" (10:25).
"He also that is slack in his work Is brother to him that is a destroyer" (18:9).
"The name of Jehovah is a strong tower; The righteous runneth into it, and is safe" (18:10).
"A man that beareth false witness against his neighbor Is a maul, and a sword, and a sharp arrow" (25:18).

COMPARISONS USING "LIKE":

"Counsel in the heart of a man is like deep water; But a man of understanding will draw it out" (20:5).
"A word fitly spoken Is like apples of gold in network of silver" (25:11).
"Confidence is an unfaithful man in time of trouble Is like a broken tooth and a foot out of joint" (25:19).
"He whose spirit is without restraint Is like a city that is broken down and without walls" (25:28).
"He that passeth by, and vexeth himself with strife belonging not to him, Is like one that taketh a dog by the ears" (26:17).
"Fervent lips and a wicked heart Are like an earthen vessel overlaid with silver dross" (26:23).
"A needy man that oppresseth the poor Is like a sweeping rain which leaveth no food" (28:3).

COMPARISONS USING "BETTER":

"Happy is the man that findeth wisdom, And the man that getteth understanding. For the gaining of it is better than the gaining of silver, And the profit thereof than fine gold" (3:13,14).
"Wisdom is better than rubies; And all the things that may be desired are not to be compared unto it" (8:11).
"My fruit is better than gold, yea, than fine gold; And my revenue than choice silver" (8:19).
"Better is he that is lightly esteemed, and hath a servant, Than he that honoreth himself, and lacketh bread" (12:9).
"Better is little, with the fear of Jehovah, Than great treasure and trouble therewith" (15:16).
"Better is a dinner of herbs, where love is, Than a stalled ox and hatred therewith" (15:17).

"Better is a little, with righteousness, Than great revenues with injustice" (16:8).
"How much better is it to get wisdom than gold!" (16:16).
"Better is it to be of lowly spirit with the poor, Than to divide the spoil with the proud" (16:19).
"He that is slow to anger is better than the mighty; And he that ruleth his spirit, than he that taketh a city" (16:32).
"Better is a dry morsel, and quietness therewith, Than a house full of feasting with strife" (17:1).
"Better is the poor that walketh in his integrity Than he that is perverse in his lips and is a fool" (19:1).
"A poor man is better than a liar" (19:22).
"It is better to dwell in the corner of the housetop, Than with a contentious woman in a wide house" (21:9).
"It is better to dwell in a desert land, Than with a contentious and fretful woman" (21:19).
"Better is it that it be said unto thee, Come up hither, Than that thou shouldest be put lower in the presence of the prince" (25:7).
"It is better to dwell in the corner of the housetop, Than with a contentious woman in a wide house" (25:24).
"Better is open rebuke Than love that is hidden" (27:5).
"Better is a neighbor that is near than a brother far off" (27:10).
"Better is the poor that walketh in his integrity, Than he that is perverse in his ways, though he be rich" (28:6).

COMPARISONS USING "MORE THAN" OR "THAN":

"Wisdom...is more precious than rubies; And none of the things thou canst desire are to be compared unto her" (3:13-15).
"To get understanding is rather to be chosen than silver" (16:16).
"A rebuke entereth deeper into one that hath understanding Than a hundred stripes into a fool" (17:10).
"A good name is rather to be chosen than great riches, And loving favor rather than silver and gold" (22:1).
"The sluggard is wiser in his own conceit Than seven men that can render a reason" (26:16).
"A stone is heavy, and the sand weighty; But a fool's vexation is heavier than they both" (27:3).

SPECIAL INDEX TO THE COMPARISONS AND CONTRASTS IN PROVERBS

COMPARISONS USING "MUCH MORE":

"The righteous shall be recompensed in the earth; How much more the wicked and the sinner" (11:31).

"Sheol and Abaddon are before Jehovah; How much more then the hearts of the children of men!" (15:11).

"All the brethren of the poor do hate him: How much more do his friends go far from him!" (19:7).

"The sacrifice of the wicked is an abomination; How much more, when he bringeth it with a wicked mind" (21:27).

COMPARISONS USING "MUCH LESS":

"Excellent speech becometh not a fool; Much less do lying lips a prince" (17:7).

"Delicate living is not seemly for a fool; Much less for a servant to have rule over princes" (19:10).

CONTRASTS

Because there are so many contrasts in Proverbs, we only cite their references. Most of the contrasts are double contrasts (like 3:33: (1) "curse" vs. "blessing" and (2) "wicked" vs. "righteous"), but there are some single contrasts and some triple.

SINGLE CONTRASTS:

12:18, 20:17

DOUBLE CONTRASTS:

3:33; 3:34; 10:2; 10:3; 10:4; 10:5; 10:12; 10:13; 10:17; 10:21; 10:27; 10:28; 10:29; 10:30; 10:31; 10:32; 11:1; 11:4; 11:13; 11:14; 11:18; 11:19; 11:23; 11:26; 11:27; 11:28; 12:2; 12:3; 12:4; 12:6; 12:7; 12:8; 12:10; 12:13; 12:16; 12:17; 12:19; 12:20; 12:21; 12:22; 12:24; 12:25; 12:27; 13:2; 13:3; 13:4; 13:5; 13:9; 13:11; 13:12; 13:16; 13:17; 13:19; 13:20; 13:24; 13:25; 14:1; 14:2; 14:3; 14:4; 14:5; 14:6; 14:11; 14:15; 14:18; 14:20; 14:22; 14:23; 14:25; 14:28; 14:29; 14:30; 14:32; 14:33; 14:34; 15:1; 15:2; 15:13; 15:19; 15:21; 15:22; 15:27; 15:29; 16:9; 16:22

17:22; 17:24; 18:14; 20:21; 21:5; 21:8; 21:12; 21:29; 27:12; 28:1; 28:4; 28:5; 28:7; 28:10; 28:11; 28:13; 28:14; 28:18; 28:19; 28:20; 28:26; 28:27; 28:28; 29:2; 29:4; 29:6; 29:7; 29:8; 29:10; 29:11; 29:15; 29:18; 29:23; 29:25

TRIPLE CONTRASTS:

10:1; 10:6; 10:7; 10:8; 10:15; 10:16; 10:19; 11:3; 11:17; 11:20; 12:5; 12:33; 13:1; 13:6; 13:18; 14:8; 14:16; 14:21; 14:24; 14:35; 15:5; 15:6; 15:7; 15:8; 15:14; 15:21; 15:25; 15:26; 15:28; 15:32; 19:4; 27:6; 27:27

52 MEMORY VERSES SELECTED BY THE AUTHOR

MEMORIZE 1 EACH WEEK

1. 1:10
2. 3:5
3. 3:9
4. 4:7
5. 4:14
6. 4:23
7. 10:1
8. 11:13
9. 11:30
10. 11:31
11. 12:4
12. 12:15
13. 12:19
14. 12:22
15. 13:4
16. 13:19
17. 13:20
18. 14:12
19. 14:12
20. 14:14
21. 14:23
22. 14:29
23. 14:34
24. 15:1
25. 15:3
26. 15:9
27. 15:29
28. 16:8
29. 16:18
30. 16:32
31. 17:5
32. 17:9
33. 17:15
34. 20:1
35. 20:14
36. 20:29
37. 21:2
38. 21:13
39. 21:23
40. 22:1
41. 22:6
42. 22:29
43. 23:23
44. 28:17
45. 27:1
46. 27:2
47. 28:1
48. 28:4
49. 28:9
50. 28:13
51. 28:23
52. 29:27